Great Adventures
and Explorations

WORKS OF
VILHJALMUR STEFANSSON

My Life with the Eskimo, 1913
Anthropological Papers
 (American Museum of Natural History), 1914
The Friendly Arctic, 1921
Hunters of the Great North, 1922
The Northward Course of Empire, 1922
The Adventure of Wrangel Island, 1925
My Life with the Eskimo (abridged), 1927
The Standardization of Error, 1927
Adventures in Error, 1936
The Three Voyages of Martin Frobisher, 1938
 (With collaboration of Eloise McCaskill)
Unsolved Mysteries of the Arctic, 1938
Iceland: The First American Republic, 1939
The Problem of Meighen Island, 1939
Ultima Thule, 1940
Greenland, 1942
The Friendly Arctic (new edition), 1943
Arctic Manual, 1944
Compass of the World, 1944
 (With Hans Weigert)
Not by Bread Alone, 1946

BOOKS FOR YOUNGER READERS
(In collaboration with Violet Irwin)

Kak, the Copper Eskimo, 1924
The Shaman's Revenge, 1925
The Mountain of Jade, 1926
Northward Ho!, 1925
 (In collaboration with Julia Schwartz)

Great Adventures and Explorations

From the Earliest Times to the Present,
as told by the Explorers Themselves

Edited with an introduction and comments by

Vilhjalmur Stefansson

With the collaboration of OLIVE RATHBUN WILCOX

Maps designed by RICHARD EDES HARRISON

LONDON
ROBERT HALE LIMITED
18 BEDFORD SQUARE W.C.1
MCMXLVII

Printed in the United States of America by The Haddon Craftsmen

Table of Contents

Introduction   ix
1   The Mediterranean Discovers the Arctic   1
2   The Europeans Cross the Atlantic   27
3   The Polynesians Cross the Pacific   87
4   China Discovers North America   107
5   Northern Europe Discovers North America   117
6   The Portuguese Find a Way to the Indies   157
7   The Latins Discover Latin America   189
8   Balboa Discovers the Pacific   223
9   Europe Proves That the World Is Round   234
10   The Discovery of the Amazon and the First Crossing
     of South America   267
11   The First Crossing of North America   321
12   Discovery of the Northeast Passage   385
13   Discovery of the Northwest Passage   473
14   North to the Indies   545
15   The Attainment of the North Pole   565
16   Discovery of Australia   623
17   The Great Southland   691
18   The Attainment of the South Pole   757
Acknowledgments   780
Index   783

Note on the Maps

The maps illustrating this volume were designed primarily to place the various explorations in their proper world perspective. This was deemed more important to the reader than complete detail, some of which is necessarily sacrificed in the larger view. Accordingly most of the maps are on the orthographic projection. This shows exactly a hemisphere and gives a good visual impression of the globe. Exceptions were made in several chapters where either a hemisphere could not show the complete route, or the area traveled was so small that a full hemisphere could not be justified. Thus in Chapter 16 (Discovery of Australia) an azimuthal equidistant projection centered near New Zealand was used. This shows well over half the world. In Chapter 2 (The Europeans Cross the Atlantic) and in Chapter 13 (Discovery of the Northwest Passage) the maps are enlarged portions of orthographic projections, permitting larger scale. In Chapters 15 (The Attainment of the North Pole) and 18 (The Attainment of the South Pole) azimuthal equidistant projections were used, and in Chapters 8 (Balboa Discovers the Pacific), 10 (The Discovery of the Amazon and the First Crossing of South America) and 11 (The First Crossing of North America) oblique conic projections.

The maps were designed by Richard Edes Harrison and for the most part executed by Harold Faye.

LIST OF ILLUSTRATIONS

DISCOVERY OF ARCTIC AND
FIRST CROSSING OF THE AT-
LANTIC   1
    Pytheas (330 B.C.)
    Ottar (890 A.D.)

EARLY ATLANTIC CROSSINGS   27
    Brendan (*circa* 500)
    Erik *the* Red (982)
    Frobisher (1578)
    Davis (1585)

FIRST PACIFIC CROSSING   87

CHINA DISCOVERS NORTH
AMERICA   107
    Hoei Sin (499)

NORTHERN EUROPE DISCOVERS
NORTH AMERICA   117
    Leif Eriksson (1000)
    Karlsefni (*circa* 1004-7)
    Cabot (1497)
    Cortereal (1500-1)

PASSAGE TO THE INDIES   157
    Vasco da Gama (1497-9)

DISCOVERY OF LATIN AMERICA   189
    Columbus (1475-1502)

SPAIN DISCOVERS THE PACIFIC   223
    Balboa (1513)

THE WORLD IS ROUND   234
    Magellan (1519-22)

FIRST CROSSING OF SOUTH
AMERICA   267
    Orellana (1541-2)

FIRST CROSSING OF NORTH
AMERICA   321
    Mackenzie (1779-93)

THE NORTHEAST PASSAGE   385
    Chancellor (1553)
    Barents (1596-7)
    Nordenskiöld (1878-9)

THE NORTHWEST PASSAGE   473
    Baffin (1616)
    Parry (1820)
    Amundsen (1903-6)
    Larsen (1944)

NORTH TO THE INDIES   545
    Hudson (1607)

THE NORTH POLE   555
    Parry (1827)
    Peary (1909)

DISCOVERY OF AUSTRALIA   623
    Janszoon (1605-6)
    Torres (1605-7)
    Pelsart (1629)
    Tasman (1642)
    Cook (1769-70)

THE GREAT SOUTH LAND   691
    Cook (1772-5)
    Palmer (1820-1)

THE SOUTH POLE   757
    Shackleton (1908-9)
    Amundsen (1910-2)
    Scott (1910-3)

Concerning the Use of Symbols
in this Book

Wherever lengthy passages of quoted material appear in this book, I have felt it advisable, in the interests of easier reading, to eliminate quotation marks and to use instead the symbol ⧫ at the beginning and at the end of these passages.

While the wording and style of those narratives which were published by the Hakluyt Society have not been altered in any way, the spelling has been modernized to conform with current usage, the punctuation has occasionally been changed, chiefly for the purpose of breaking up long sentences into shorter ones, and of making several paragraphs where the original had one of extreme length.

Similar changes in spelling and punctuation have been made in the selections from other sources, particularly those from the collections of Churchill, Hakluyt, Pinkerton and Purchas, so as to bring them into conformity with modern American practice.

V. S.

INTRODUCTION

THIS BOOK contains the great stories of explorations and tells them in the words of the discoverers themselves, their companions, or their contemporaries. We know of others no less great which cannot be included because the books that told them have been lost.

In a sense, however, the very greatest stories of geographic discovery were never written.

The supreme discovery of new land upon this earth is the finding of a continent. Africa and Asia could never be discovered by man, for he originated in one or the other of them, if not both. These men, Asiatic or African, discovered Europe at least a million years ago and thus so long before the invention of writing that no chisel, stylus, or pen was available for the making of a record until long after the tradition of the discovery had died away. Indeed there was never properly such a tradition; for the unveiling must have been so gradual that no one realized it was taking place.

The Indonesians discovered Australia before the bow and arrow were invented, thus in the remote past. The discovery of North America from Asia must have been at least ten thousand years before the development of any proper writing anywhere in the world, for Sandia man of New Mexico is dated between 15,000 and 30,000 years ago. Even South America must have been discovered by the North Americans many thousands of years before the first pyramids were built in Egypt or Yucatan.

The one continent whose true human discoverers are known is Antarctica. This only historical first-rate discovery was committed to writing at the time it happened and we are able to tell that story in the words of the discoverer and his associates in this book.

With that one exception, the great tales which we are able to present are those of rediscovery. We can tell how the Greeks, discovered the British Isles with the British already in them; how North Europeans discovered North America with the Indians there to meet them; how the Spaniards discovered the Pacific Ocean when the Chinese had already maintained on its shores a great empire through long ages; how modern navigators discovered islands a thousand miles from the nearest inhabited land to find living there the descendants of Stone Age navigators who had been the real discoverers. Our very best stories are lucky when they are no worse than second-best.

Nor are the great tales always noble. We know nothing to the discredit of the earliest giant figure among the historical explorers, the philosopher Pytheas who discovered Britain and was the first known European to cross the Atlantic to the New World, where he visited Iceland and sailed beyond it. But the "hardy" Norsemen who colonized Iceland a thousand years later had Irish and German slaves to wait on them and were, so far as we know, the pioneers in bringing chattel slavery from the European side of the Atlantic to the American. The most impressive figure among Latin explorers, Prince Henry the Navigator, helped to build up the African slave trade; that other famous Latin, Columbus, became the authentic founder of Europe's modern practice of slavery in the Western Hemisphere.

The self-confessed greed for riches, lust for conquest, bigotry in religion, which appear through the firsthand narratives of our book, show themselves to have been powerful factors in European man's spread throughout the world. But there have been many exceptions.

We do not suggest the canonization of Erik the Red; but there is immeasurably more cause for pride than shame in the record of the sturdy man of vision who planned and carried out the exploration and colonization of Greenland, who was a leader in founding a republic in that vast island, and who gave his relatively mediocre son, Leif, the opportunity to discover the mainland of North America and to fetch the missionaries who converted the Greenlanders, to lay in the year 1000 the foundation of what was throughout four centuries the most westerly bishopric of the Church of Rome. Nor are there many records in the history of England cleaner than that of the Yorkshire farmer, James Cook, a side excursion of one of whose voyages gave Britain a reasonable and successfully enforced claim to Australia, the Sixth Continent.

There appears to be no rule about the great discoverers as to whether, by this year's standards, they are good men or bad, noble or despicable. Nor are the chief figures necessarily great men in the sense of genius, vision, skill, even mere competence. No name is written larger in the history of British participation in Arctic discovery than that of a sturdy gentleman of the early Victorian period, Sir John Franklin, by the canons of that age noble, generous, just and brave; by any standards, however, about the least professionally competent man who ever won a secure place in history. Against this, some of the explorers had competence that measured up to or above their notable reputations, among them Baffin, Davis, Hudson.

In our book you find some of history's big success stories, with merit finally and justly awarded, as in the case of the indomitable twenty-three-year struggle of Peary which led to his demonstrating that Greenland is an island, instead of being larger than Australia and thus a continent as many had expected; a struggle which finally led to showing that it was possible for a white man and a Negro as well as three Eskimos to walk safely about 900 miles, round trip, over the drifting ice floes of the polar sea to the spot in the northern hemisphere that is farthest from the equator.

Peary's is the world's greatest success story of men against the elements; Scott's is the noblest. Those are fortunate who can remember the newspapers in the year 1913 and the mood of heartbreak and exaltation that swept every land. Neither a Shakespearean nor a Greek tragedy has ever been so played as to cast a spell upon its audience like that which held mankind in thrall while the Scott tragedy was being unfolded.

This book, as the story of how man came to know his world, has endeavored to secure historical continuity by leading from one major narrative to the next through summaries of less important ones that belong in between, and by occasional passages of interpretation which seek to give the reader a needed perspective.

In a way, the book is an outline history of the world, told by its chief discoverers from Pytheas to Peary.

V. S.

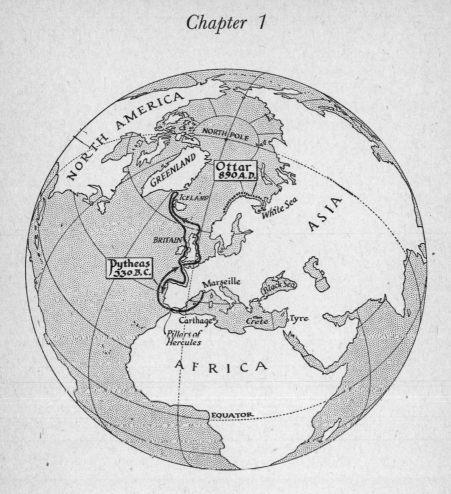

The Mediterranean Discovers the Arctic

THE MEDITERRANEAN
DISCOVERS THE ARCTIC

CHAPTER 1

THE ANNALS of geographic discovery must start with how the subtropics found the Arctic, for speculation is futile as to which of the Old World continents—Europe, Asia, Africa—discovered the others. Indeed it is probable that at least those parts of the three continents which border on the Mediterranean were known to each other from the time of the earliest navigators, thus from 30,000 or perhaps 40,000 B.C.

Although not without disadvantages, the tideless Mediterranean had many advantages for the primitive mariner. Among the advantages were the numerous mid-sea islands that were steppingstones from place to place, and the still more numerous headlands and inshore islands that provided shelter in bad weather to the early explorers. With some of the peoples, among them perhaps the Egyptians, the knowledge of the ocean beyond the Red and Mediterranean seas was no doubt largely hearsay. Among others, notably the Cretans and Phoenicians, it was based upon experience.

The evidence is variously interpreted to show that intercourse between the eastern and western ends of the Mediterranean can be traced back to anything from 4000 to 10,000 B.C. It is held reasonably certain that for long parts of the same periods there was land-sea communication and exchange of commodities between Crete and the peoples of the East, with goods coming by ancient trade routes not only from Mesopotamia but even from distant China.

Beyond mere likelihood, there are various kinds of evidence to show that the Arctic first became known to the Mediterranean peoples through overland trade that followed the north-flowing

3

and the south-flowing rivers, which in some cases head near each other, thus giving early man a thoroughfare across Europe. This may have been some twenty thousand years ago, perhaps thirty or forty thousand.

As for the knowledge that came by sea, Mediterranean familiarity with the Atlantic was in itself a step toward the Arctic. That step seems to have been made by Crete, for long before the rise of Hellenic power, and even before the heyday of the Phoenicians, the Cretans dominated the whole Mediterranean, which would include its entrance at the Pillars of Hercules (Strait of Gibraltar).

While the importance of the Phoenicians, formerly regarded as the true pioneers in this region, has been reduced by the comparatively recent discovery of the role played by Crete, still the Phoenician exploits are considerable. By 1100 B.C. they had founded the colony of Utica on the African coast, at the western extremity of the Mediterranean basin near where Carthage was established about three hundred years later. Before this they had passed the Pillars of Hercules and reached the western ocean, had established and fortified Gades (Cádiz) and had become familiar with the neighboring region of southern Spain (Tarshish, Tartessus).

From Gades expeditions were sent north to Britain and south along the west coast of Africa. It is through these that we may assign precedence to the Phoenicians as discoverers and explorers in the modern sense.

Precedent-making also was their policy of suppression of geographical knowledge. At any rate, it is from the Phoenicians that we have what may be the earliest evidence of that secrecy (for purposes of military security or trade advantage) concerning maritime discovery which, practiced in all parts of the world by most of their successors, has almost ever since required that a place be "discovered" over and over again by different nations. This has in many instances made it impossible to determine who the original discoverer was.

The policy of the Phoenicians apparently consisted in part of the suppression of facts and in part of the spreading of misleading and frightening tales. So it was that by the time of the Greeks almost the whole of that real knowledge which came from the Phoenicians had been lost, though some of the horror stories circulated by them were still current at the time of Herodotus (484-25 B.C.).

Most of the Phoenician tales related by Herodotus may be classified as tall tales; but one, that of the circumnavigation of Africa as a joint venture of Egyptians and Phoenicians, has the earmarks of truth, no doubt because it came to the Greeks from an Egyptian source. If the Phoenicians had been left to tell it, they probably would have reported failure due to one or more of the stock explanations—that the sea was muddy, that it was full of rocks and whirlpools, that the water was full of serpents and the air full of dragons, that the sun did not shine.

We do not possess from the Greeks, or from any other source, anything like a connected narrative of Phoenician sailing north along western Europe in the direction of the Arctic till we come to Himilco, around 470 B.C.

Since Himilco is believed to have been the son of the great Hamilcar, who as leader of the Carthaginians invaded Sicily about 480 B.C. with 3,000 ships and 300,000 men, there seems no doubt that his expedition was on a scale not much inferior to that of the better-known contemporary voyage of his brother Hanno, to which it was complementary in the sense that both first sailed westerly from Carthage, turning in opposite directions after they had passed through the Strait of Gibraltar. Hanno coasted Africa southward with a fleet of 60 ships carrying (if we may believe it!) 500 persons each; Himilco coasted Europe northward with presumably a similar fleet.

This grandeur of scale is of course a mere assumption, for we have not the fortune of a preserved narrative as in the case of Hanno, and must depend for Himilco on a confused metrical statement in the poem *Ora Maritima,* written by Rufius Festus Avienus sometime around A.D. 400.

If there had been nothing but the Avienus tale, the chance is that historians would have taken it to be fiction. Luckily there is confirmatory evidence; for Pliny, who wrote some four centuries earlier and who is usually respected by the authorities, tells us that Himilco was sent north at the same time that Hanno was ordered south. Moreover, long before Avienus.

there were in wide circulation many of the reports to which he makes reference.

It is a usual conclusion of historians that Avienus is to be understood as telling us—what we know to be correct in any case—that around 500 B.C. the people of Spain and France were in touch not only with Great Britain but also with Ireland through commercial sea voyages. Indeed, the Bronze Age archaeologists, among them Professor H. O'Neill Hencken of Harvard, are inclined to feel that these voyages were not coastal but what we would now call great-circle. One of the routes is thought to have been direct to Ireland from Cape Finisterre, at the northwest corner of the Iberian Peninsula, probably without sighting any part of France or Britain—thus a voyage comparable to those which we know Stone Age man used to make in the Pacific.

The Avienus narrative of the Himilco voyage, or rather the jumbled description of western Europe which he associates in part with Himilco, runs in a free translation, with some omission of roundabout figures of speech and some interpretative straightening out of kinks:

🖅 Next [in Brittany?] rises a projecting ridge, called by the ancients Oestrimnis, the high mass of which turns mostly toward the south. Beneath this promontory the Oestrimnian Bay opens, in the middle of which lie the scattered Oestrimnides Islands, which have an abundance of such metals as tin and lead. Here live many enterprising people that occupy themselves with commerce and who navigate the monster-filled ocean far and wide in small ships. They do not understand how to build wooden ships in the usual way. Believe it or not, they make their boats by sewing hides together and carry out deep-sea voyages in them.[1]

A two-day voyage farther north lies the great island formerly called Holy Island, where the Hierne people [Irish] live, and near it lies Albion [Britain].

[1] This would seem to refer to such deep-sea voyages as the Irish are known to have made in skin boats (curraghs), particularly before A.D. 700, though the confidence of the Irish in the superiority of skin boats over wooden boats in seafaring persisted long thereafter. Indeed the Arran Islanders of the Irish coast still use a pygmy version of the old curraghs in their fishing.

Tartessus [in Spain] traded in those days [Himilco's] with the Oestrimnides, both being colonists from Carthage. Sailors who pass the Pillars of Hercules frequent these regions. The Carthaginian Himilco tells that these sea distances are so great that ships can hardly make them in four months, as he learned by personal experience on his voyage; but that is (in part) because winds are lacking for driving a ship ahead in this sluggish, becalmed sea. He tells, moreover, that the water [along the west coast of Europe] is so filled with seaweed that it keeps vessels back somewhat as brush delays a man in walking. He reports this sea to be so shoal that the muddy bottom is scarcely covered with water.

The monsters of this sea are everywhere, and keep swimming around the slow-moving ships.

If one has the courage to sail from the Oestrimnides to where the weather is cold at the axis of the Great Bear [that is, in the direction of the North Pole], he will reach the Ligurian country, which is uninhabited because of a war with the Celts. The fugitive Ligurians were driven to a land where there is very little except brush. The stones there are sharp, the rocks cold, and the fearsome mountains rise into the heavens. The fugitives did not at first dare to come down to the coast, for fear of the old danger [from the Celts]. Later, peace encouraged them to leave their mountain hideouts, and now there are places where they come down to the sea. 🖌

In the opinion of Dr. Fridtjof Nansen, the Oestrimnides of Himilco may be the later-famous Cassiterides, the tin islands, with which the Carthaginians are known to have traded in the fourth century B.C. The Ligurians were perhaps the Ligyans of whom Hesiod wrote in the eighth century B.C. as being in western Europe, west of the Scythians, who were seemingly around and east of the Don.

The monsters that swam around the Himilco ships may have been the whales that were formerly numerous in the Bay of Biscay and indeed along most coasts of western Europe. Much of the darkness, fog, seaweed, and mud described by Avienus is doubtless derived from the terror campaign of the Phoenicians by which they tried to frighten the Greeks out of becoming trade competitors along the Atlantic shores, whether south along Africa or north along Europe.

Nansen concludes that Himilco's voyage, when the Avienus account is studied in relation to other knowledge that we have, probably extended to Britain, but not likely beyond. At any rate, it is the Greeks who are usually considered to have made the historical, as distinguished from the prehistoric, discovery of Britain.

In nearly uniform agreement the scholars believe that the Phoenicians had two chief methods to frighten the Greeks from the Atlantic voyaging—they guarded the Strait of Gibraltar with ships of war, and they circulated the mentioned terror stories about the Atlantic.

Through lethargy or preoccupation in wars, there were periods when the Phoenicians were not able to guard the strait with their armed ships. One of these periods is usually called upon to explain how it happened that Pytheas, whose story is told below, was able to pass the Pillars of Hercules both going and coming about 330 B.C.

Pytheas, although practically unknown when the middle-aged of our time went to college, has been emerging in the last few decades as a towering figure both in exploration and in that early science which the Greeks called philosophy, so that he is now looked upon as one of the greatest figures in all human history. Among other things, it was he who discovered that the tides are controlled by the moon and who first found out how to apply astronomy to geography so as to locate a place on the earth, which is the basis of accurate map-making.

This man, already great, made one of the greatest voyages of all time. Having eluded the guardians of the strait and doubled Gibraltar, Pytheas was free to go where he wished. And go he did, for without known hitch he sailed from his home city of Massilia (now Marseille) to Britain and to the northern end of Scotland, thence to Iceland and beyond it for a distance of about 100 miles, where further progress was stopped by the slushy edge of the drifting pack ice. Not only was the return to Marseille also accomplished without difficulty, but Pytheas somehow found opportunity as well, on either the outward or the homeward voyage, to turn east to investigate the Baltic Sea.

The Ocean, the book which Pytheas certainly wrote, is lost, nor do we find more than a bare trace of another book he may have written, *The Periplus*—which, from its reported name, must have been what we now call "sailing directions," a "coast pilot."

Furthermore there have been preserved no works of any writers who are known to have read *The Ocean.* What we possess is nothing better than authority thrice removed, the books of men who comment on and quote the books of earlier men who had read *The Ocean.* Worst of all, the fragments of quotation and paraphrase which have been saved to us were mostly chosen from a point of view that tends to neutralize their value—they are, in many cases, quoted with disbelief and for purpose of ridicule.

It would seem that when Pytheas returned from his journey to the Arctic and published his book, his report was at first taken in good faith. This was especially so, no doubt, along the south shore of what is now France, for the Greek colonists there were in touch with at least the North Sea and the Baltic by overland commerce and by tribe-to-tribe hearsay. So the Pytheas reports fitted in with what they knew from other sources.

In the rest of the Greek world the book was at first given a reception clearly in the main favorable, for Pytheas is treated with respect by the earliest of the writers who quote or paraphrase him. For instance, about 200 B.C. the great mathematician Eratosthenes took the narrative at face value, thus more than a century after the publication of *The Ocean.*

All this had been reversed by the time of Strabo's *Geography,* in the third decade after Christ, for meantime the doctrine of the Five Zones had triumphed. That concept was born, presumably, in the sixth century B.C., but its influence over Greek geographic thinking developed slowly and did not become a tyranny until some two centuries after Pytheas. Thenceforth, in spite of a few skeptics, it was generally considered to be known that there were on the earth five zones, three of them uninhabitable—the equatorial because of the heat and the two polar zones because of the cold.

The zone that aroused Strabo's skepticism regarding Pytheas

was the Arctic, the southern edge of which was thought by Strabo to lie just north of Scotland, where, in his belief, no living thing could exist, plant or animal. Yet Pytheas maintained that he had sailed six days north beyond Scotland (which to Strabo would be like 600 miles to us) and that there he had found an island of reasonable climate, then called Thule and now called Iceland, even beyond which he had sailed 100 miles.

Now to Strabo the ocean a little beyond Scotland would cease being liquid, so that no one could sail through it, and the weather would be so cold that no one could live in it. Necessarily, then, Pytheas was a liar. This is what Strabo called him, and so he remained in the minds of scholarly Europe until modern times. Indeed, his full rehabilitation, his change from the greatest known liar of antiquity to one of the greatest discoverers of all time, dates from less than fifty years ago.

Fridtjof Nansen, himself one of the foremost of explorers and a learned historian of exploration, concludes that Pytheas is the first great explorer whose name is known to us and one of the greatest that history reveals. He specifies that the Greek navigator "pushed back the limit of the learned world's knowledge from the south coast of Britain to the Arctic Circle, or about 16 degrees [1100 miles] farther north." Indeed, Pytheas would appear to have gone a day's sail, about 100 miles, beyond the Arctic Circle.

Strabo did not have the same reasons for being skeptical about the first section of the Pytheas voyage, from Marseille to Britain, as he had for disbelief concerning the Scotland-Iceland section. Instead he had positive reasons for acceptance, since what the Greek explorer told for the stretch from Spain to Cornwall fitted in with the usual Mediterranean view.

There has been difficulty, however, in piecing the story together from the scattered bits of thirdhand and fourthhand quotations. The best reconstruction job known to me was done by Sir Clements Markham, a naval officer and polar explorer who was through a long term of years president of the Royal Geographical Society of London.

In his "Pytheas, the Discoverer of Britain," *Geographical Journal*, June 1893, Markham traces from about 1060 B.C. the history of the Ionian Greeks, who appeared then at the eastern edge of the Mediterranean and who gradually developed in maritime skill and power until they possessed colonies well scattered throughout that inland sea. Their settlement which chiefly concerns us is Massilia, or Massalia, on what is now the French south coast, founded near 600 B.C.

After sketching the pre-eminent contributions of the Ionians, and especially the Phocaeans, Markham continues:

Voyage of Pytheas, 330 B.C.

Any discovery beyond the Pillars of Hercules by the Phocaeans of Massalia must have been achieved by their own unaided efforts, without guidance from the experience of Himilco or any other foreign navigator. Fortunately, the colony possessed a man eminently fitted to conduct an exploring expedition in the person of Pytheas, the mathematician and astronomer.

It is alleged by Polybius that Pytheas was in poor circumstances, and we may therefore conclude that the enterprise was a government expedition of which Pytheas was placed in command. The nearest approximation we can get to its date is the time of Alexander the Great and Aristotle, about 330 B.C., and we may well suppose that the object was the discovery of the countries whence came those rare and valuable products which reached the Massalians by a long overland route and a descent of the Rhone.

Pytheas prepared for his perilous undertaking by carefully fixing the latitude of Massalia as a point of departure. His pre-eminence in his own day will be obvious when we recollect that he lived before the principal Greek astronomers, Eratosthenes and Hipparchus, and that none of his predecessors had demonstrated the methods which he adopted.

The earliest way of calculating the distance of a place from the equator was by observing the length of the longest and shortest days. The ancient geographers divided the earth into parallel zones, within which the longest day had a certain length, generally an hour: one zone from twelve to thirteen hours, the next from thirteen to fourteen, and so on. The zones were called "climates," from the Greek word *klima*, "slope" or "inclination." They were unequal in width, the zone in which the longest day was from fourteen to fifteen hours being 600 miles in width, while the zone in which the longest day was from nineteen to twenty hours had a width of only 125 miles.

Pytheas used this system during his voyage; but in fixing the latitude of Massalia he adopted a more accurate method.

The Phocaean astronomer erected a large gnomon at Massalia, divided into one hundred and twenty parts. He observed its shadow at noon on the day of the solstice, and found that its length was forty-two of the parts on the gnomon, less one-fifth— that is, forty-one and four-fifths to one hundred and twenty, or two hundred and nine to six hundred. This proportion gave 70 degrees 47 minutes 50 seconds for the altitude of the sun. The length of the longest day was fifteen hours fifteen minutes.

Eratosthenes and Hipparchus [later] found the obliquity of the ecliptic to be 23 degrees 51 minutes 15 seconds, which they deducted from the altitude. The complement of the result was the latitude of the place less the semidiameter of the sun, namely, 43 degrees 3 minutes 25 seconds. With the semidiameter added, the result is almost exactly the latitude of the Marseille observatory.

Another important point was to fix upon the nearest star to the pole as a guide for steering the ship. Pytheas found that there was no star on the pole, but that there were three very close to it. These would have been Beta Ursae Minoris and Alpha Draconis in those days; and Pytheas used one of these as his polestar.[2]

It is probable that there was no other man, in the days of Alexander the Great, who could have prepared for a voyage of discovery by fixing the exact latitude of his point of departure, and by selecting correctly the star by which he should shape his course.

For the rest, his countrymen were well able to furnish him with a serviceable vessel. A large Massalian ship was a good sea boat, and well able to make a voyage into the northern

[2] Other authorities say Pytheas was even more precise than this—that he determined the pole at a place in the heavens where there was no star and used this imaginary point as the pole.

ocean. She would be from 150 to 170 feet long—the beam of a merchant ship being a quarter and of a warship one-eighth the length—a depth of hold of 25 or 26 feet, and a draught of 10 to 12. Her tonnage would be 400 to 500, so that the ship of Pytheas was larger and more seaworthy than the crazy little *Santa Maria* with which, eighteen hundred years afterward, Columbus discovered the New World. . . .

In the days of Alexander, a voyage of discovery beyond the Pillars of Hercules was as bold and daring a conception as was a voyage in search of the Indies by the western route in the days of Ferdinand and Isabella.

We have seen that Pytheas, the first of the great explorers, like the illustrious Genoese of later times, prepared himself for his difficult task by long and patient study of the astronomical bearings of the question. Thus well provided with all the knowledge of his time, he raised his anchor, and commenced his coasting voyage toward the Sacred Promontory [Cape St. Vincent], the western limit of the known world. The Grecian ships were supposed to make an average of about 500 stadia, or 50 miles, in a day's sail, the stadium being the unit of measurement for all geographical distances.

Coasting along near the shore, the ship of Pytheas would first have come to the Massalian settlement at the mouth of the Rhone, and then to Rhoda and Emporium (the modern Ampurias) in the beautiful bay of Rosas, at the base of the Pyrenees. Next the temple of Artemis, crowning the lofty promontory now dedicated to Saint Martin, came in sight, where the Massalians had their *hemeroskopion* or lookout station. There was a settlement called Artemisia (the modern Denia) at the foot of the heights, where the explorers could anchor and find rest. The last friendly haven would be at Maenaca, the modern Malaga.

Sailing through the Straits of Calpe [Strait of Gibraltar], the Greek mariners would scarcely venture to stop at Carthaginian Gadeira [Cádiz], although in times gone by the native ruler of the country had been on such cordial terms with Phocaea. But the cruel Semites since established at Gadeira were enemies of western civilization, and Pytheas sailed slowly on to the Sacred Promontory, the end of the known world—very slowly, for the 48 leagues from Cádiz to Cape St. Vincent took him five sailing days.

Pytheas continued his coasting voyage to the north as far as Cape Finisterre, the probable furthest point of Himilco, then eastward along the north coast of Iberia, and round the Bay of Biscay. His narrative is lost, but we gather that he described the coasts of Iberia, made valuable observations respecting the tides, and furnished information touching the best way of passing from Iberia to Celtica, or Gaul. "He had acquired a practical acquaintance of the navigation along the north coast of Spain." His first recorded observation on the voyage had for its result that the longest day was fifteen hours, which would be in latitude 40 degrees 59 minutes off Oporto.

Pytheas found that the northwestern part of Gaul formed a long promontory called Calbion, the country of a tribe called the Ostimii, which stretched far to the westward. He even thought that it extended for 2000 stadia to the west of Cape Finisterre of Spain. But great allowances must be made for errors in longitude at a time when no means were known of estimating it, beyond guesswork.

He mentions an island off the coast called Uxisama, evidently intended for Ushant. A second observation is given of sixteen hours for the length of the longest day, equal to 49 degrees north, which is within 30 miles of the latitude of Ushant.

The explorer left the north coast of Gaul, and shaped a direct course for a part of Britain which he called Cantion, the Cantium of Caesar. This must have been the route, because he reported that the coast of Gaul where he left it was some days' sail from Cantion.

The Cantion of Pytheas was doubtless the modern Kent, although it may be intended to include additional territory to the north. Here he stopped, and we are told that he not only landed, but traveled over a part of Britain on foot. He probably went westward to collect information respecting the tin trade, which in those days would have entailed a very difficult and perilous journey.

Britain in the third century before Christ was almost in a state of nature. The valleys were covered with primeval forests, their lower parts were occupied by vast swamps, and it was only on the downs and hill ranges that there were *gwents*, or open clearings.

Still the Keltic tribes had been in possession for several centuries, and had made some advances in civilization. They brought domestic animals with them, raised wheat and other cereals, and had iron tools and arms, wooden chariots with iron fittings, and ornaments of bronze and gold. Pytheas saw and made note of the farming operations and way of living among the natives of Cantion.

Between this southeastern district and the *gwent* now comprising the downs of Wiltshire and South Hampshire there was the great forest of Anderida, extending from Hampshire to the Medway. Pytheas would have to pass this forest on his way to the western part of Britain (the present Cornwall), which was called Belerion. Here he found the country of the tin, which was dug out of the ground in mines with shafts and galleries.

The people were very hospitable, their commerce with foreign merchants having civilized them and softened their manners. The metal was carried by them in six days' journey to an island called Ictis (St. Michael's Mount), whence the traders from Gaul conveyed it across the Channel, and down the Rhone to Massalia. "This island is described as surrounded by the sea at high water, but connected with the mainland by a tract of sand left bare at low water, so as to render it a peninsula to which the tin was carried in wagons."

Pytheas no doubt gave a stimulus to this trade, and was probably the first to introduce coined money into Britain. After the discovery of the gold mines of Crenides [Philippi] in 356 B.C., Philip of Macedon produced £250,000 worth of gold coin a year. The beautiful stater of Philip was everywhere diffused. It soon reached Massalia, whence it was circulated inland, and it was seized on by the Gauls as an object of imitation in about 300 B.C.

Pytheas may well have brought the first staters of Philip to Britain, thus introducing the use of money. They were afterward roughly imitated by the natives; but no British coin has an earlier date than 200 B.C.

Several pieces of information respecting the natives of Britain related by Pytheas have been preserved.

In consequence of the rain and absence of sun, the former did not use [open] threshing floors, but threshed their corn in large barns. They stored the ears of corn in pits underground, and the part that had been longest in store was brought out daily and prepared for food.

They made a fermented liquor from barley, which they used instead of wine; it was called *curmi*. As Columbus was the discoverer of tobacco, so his great predecessor, Pytheas, discovered beer. Pytheas also says that the Britons made another drink from honey.

Their houses were of wood and thatch, and he mentions the war chariots, but adds that the chiefs were generally at peace with each other. He believed the people to have been *autochthones*, or aborigines.

When Pytheas returned to his ship, in some haven of Kent, he proceeded northward along the coast of Britain; and his next observation gave seventeen hours as the length of the longest day. This would be in latitude 54 degrees 2 minutes north, somewhere in the neighborhood of Flamborough Head.

Still coasting to the north in his great voyage of discovery, he reached a point at the northern end of Britain where the length of the longest day was eighteen hours. The corresponding latitude is 57 degrees 58 minutes 41 seconds north, which is that of Tarbett Ness, in Ross-shire [now Northeastern Scotland.]

As he advanced to the pole he found that the cultivated grains and fruits, and almost all domesticated animals, gradually disappeared. The people in the far north were reduced to live on millet, herbs, and roots.

The intrepid explorer still pushed onward to discover the northernmost point of the British Isles. Coasting along the shores of Caithness and the Orkney Islands, he finally arrived at a land where the length of the longest day was nineteen hours. This was in latitude 60 degrees 51 minutes 54 seconds north, in Burra Fjord [Firth], on Unst Island, the northernmost of the Shetlands. Pytheas gives the name of Orcas to this extreme point of the British Isles—a name which in later times was transferred to the Orcades, or Orkney Islands. It was doubtless a native name.

It was at Orcas that Pytheas received information of an Arctic land called Thule, at a distance of six days' sail, and near the frozen ocean. . . .

It may therefore be accepted as an established historical fact that Pytheas of Massalia obtained the first information [for the Greeks] respecting the Arctic regions, and that he was the discoverer of the British Isles. 🖋

In a book which I published in 1940, *Ultima Thule* (Macmillan) I have gone into the long and stubborn debate on what land was Thule, whether it was Norway, the Orkneys, the Shetlands, or Iceland. In the present volume the belief will be accepted that Thule was Iceland, a belief which has been held by the majority of learned men from the time when Iceland, as Thule, first became well known throughout Europe.

There is ambiguity about the quotations from *The Ocean* which tell about what it was that Pytheas learned at the north of Britain. But when everything he is said to have said about Thule is weighed, it becomes reasonably clear that he learned about Thule in Britain, that he went to Thule, that he reported what he saw there, and that he proceeded a day's sail farther north.

True, some historians maintain that the British knew not Thule at the time and that Pytheas first of all human beings was the discoverer of this New World island. But this rests on the gratuitous assumption that the British of 330 B.C. were less competent than the Greeks for making deep-sea voyages, which belief is a mere inheritance from the school days of those who were educated while it was still fashionable to teach that the Phoenicians were the originators of deep-sea navigation.

It is possible to argue that the British told Pytheas about Thule and that he never went there. But, as Nansen has it, "in order to do this almost all the statements that have been preserved on this part of Pytheas' voyage must be arbitrarily distorted; and to alter or to explain away one's authorities so as to make them fit a preconceived opinion is an unfortunate proceeding."

No writer of antiquity, no scholar of modern times, has attempted to make a connected narrative of how Pytheas sailed from Britain to Thule. Here this will not be tried either. Instead, under subject headings the relevant quotations are grouped.

1. How far was Thule from northern Scotland, and in what direction did it lie?

"Pytheas says that Thule is, by ship, six days away from Britain toward the North." (Strabo)

"As Pytheas of Massilia writes occurs on the island of Thule, six days' distant sailing north from Britain . . ." (Pliny)

"The last of all the islands which have been mentioned, Thule . . ." (Pliny)

"Seeking Thule from the promontory of Caledonia . . . The sailing from the Orkneys to Thule is all of five days and nights." (G. Julius Solinus)

"Thule is an island of the ocean northwest of Britain, next after the Orkneys and Ireland." (Servius)

It is our practice nowadays to speak of one place being north of another if it lies in the quadrant between northeast and northwest, in which sense Iceland is north of Scotland. Actually it is closer to northwest, and that may be what Pytheas himself reported, as is indicated by one of our authorities, Servius. The distance, too, is right for Iceland, since "a day's sail" meant "an average day's sail," and this the authorities usually agree was about the equivalent of 100 of our miles. That makes Thule 600 miles from Scotland, which is about the right distance for Iceland.

2. Then we have astronomical references. Some of the ancient commentators on Pytheas give the location of Thule in terms of the movements of the sun, the equivalent of our latitude determinations. Under this head the writers describe a situation for Thule that fits Iceland.

"In reference to the island called Thule, where rumors say that the philosopher Pytheas of Massilia went, it is said that the entire circle described by the sun at the summer solstice is above the horizon, so that it coincides in these places with the Arctic Circle. In these regions, when the sun is in Cancer the day lasts one month, if at least all the parts of that sign are visible." (Cleomedes)

"Accordingly, Pytheas of Massilia says that the regions of

Thule, the northernmost of the British Isles, are the last [habitable regions], and that because of this the tropic circle of summer is the same as the Arctic Circle." (Strabo)

(This passage, true for the north coast of Iceland, must not be taken to show that Strabo was accepting the word of Pytheas. Strabo thought Pytheas had invented this description, for he thought Pytheas had invented Thule.)

"Thule . . . on that island . . . the nights in summer are light, because at [throughout] that time of the year the sun, mounting higher without being itself visible, nevertheless illuminates with its neighboring splendor the places which are nearest to it. But during the solstice there are no nights, because then the sun shows not only its radiance but also the greater part of itself." (Mela)

"Thule, where we have shown there are no nights in the summer solstice, when the sun crosses the sign of Cancer, and where, conversely, there are no days in the winter solstice . . ." (Pliny)

"Cutting forward through the waves of the ocean by a long way you will reach the isle of Thule on a good ship; Thule where, from the sun that has approached the Arctic pole an ever-shining fire spreads out through days and nights." (Dionysius Periegetes)

"There are many other islands around Britain, of which Thule is the farthest, on which there is no night during the summer solstice when the sun is crossing the sign of Cancer; likewise, during the winter solstice, no day." (Solinus)

On the south coast of Iceland at midsummer, you will find that although the sun is invisible for two or three hours, the twilight with a clear sky is so bright that you can read ordinary print at midnight. In that sense there is, even on the south coast, a continuous June-July day of several weeks.

Along the north coast of Iceland at midsummer, the upper edge of the sun will be barely seen straight north at midnight if you are near the head of one of the south-penetrating fjords; but if you are on the most northern promontory, the lower limb of the midnight sun will be well clear of the horizon and with favoring skies the whole sun will be visible for several days continuously before its lower edge begins to dip into the sea at midnight. If it is daylight when you can read print out of doors the twenty-four hours through, then there are some two months of perpetual day on the north coast of Iceland.

To sum up: All the quoted Pytheas references fit Iceland, some the south coast and some the north coast. It seems clear, then, that the common information upon which all of them were based must have come from a narrative source which described a circumnavigation of the island. At any rate, familiarity is shown with the whole of the island.

3. We are told how Thule looked when viewed from the sea.

"From here if anyone should speed along the vast seas in a swift boat and to the north should impel his vessel, he would come upon Thule rising with immense summit." (Avienus)

Of this passage it is necessary to remark only that, with the exception of Greenland and Jan Mayen, Iceland is spectacular beyond any Atlantic shore.

4. The commentators tell us how far it was from Thule to the ice-filled sea. The ancient writers, depending on Pytheas, place the island not merely with reference to Scotland and to the midnight sun but also with reference to the ice-carrying ocean.

"Thule, which Pytheas says lies six days' sail north of Britain, and is near to the congealed sea . . ." (Strabo)

"Beyond Thule we meet with the sluggish and congealed sea." (Solinus)

"After one day's sail from Thule the frozen sea is reached, called by some 'Cronium.'" (Pliny)

According to this, Pytheas reached the ice-infested sea about 100 miles north from Thule, which fits Iceland if he sailed north from its northwestern corner. For the Greeks were there in midsummer, at which season the first drifting sea ice might easily be met with in the East Greenland Current, about 100 miles north of northwestern Iceland.

5. The writers describe the appearance of the edge of the frozen sea beyond Thule. Strabo, after saying that Pytheas claimed to have explored all of Britain, continues:

"He had also undertaken investigations concerning Thule
and those regions in which there was no longer any distinction
of land or sea or air, but a mixture of the three like sea lung,
in which he says that land and sea and everything floats, and
this [that is, the mixture] binds all together, and can be traversed neither on foot nor by boat. The substance resembling
lung he had seen himself, as he says; the rest he relates according to what he has heard. This is Pytheas' tale." (Strabo)

During that long period of skepticism with regard to the
Pytheas narrative which began a century or two before Christ
and continued to our nineteenth century, it was the fashion to
poke fun at this passage, particularly the "sea lung"; but now
that we are in an era of Pytheas-worship the efforts to explain
away the sea lung are correspondingly frequent and ingenious.
It has been suggested, for instance, that some counterpart of
a jellyfish which is called in the Mediterranean "sea lung" may
have been found by the Greeks to the north of Iceland.

More promising than any ingenuity is it to adopt for this
problem the principle favored by scientists, that among several
explanations the likeliest to be right is the simplest one. This
critical principle is supported by the further consideration that
men who have sailed around Iceland, and on the Greenland
coast, have a certain advantage over armchair students when
dealing with the marginal phenomena which are frequent
where warm waters such as those of the Iceland branch of the
Gulf Stream rub against such cold waters as those of the East
Greenland Current. So Nansen, experienced with northern
conditions and frequenter of the waters around Iceland and
Greenland, is quoted:

"This much-disputed description of the sea beyond Thule
has first passed through Polybius, who did not believe in
Pytheas and tried to throw ridicule upon him. Whether Polybius
obtained it directly, or at second hand through some older
writer, we do not know. From him it came down to Strabo, who
had as little belief in it, and was, moreover, liable to misunder-
stand and to be hasty in his quotations. The passage is evidently
torn from its context and has been much abbreviated in order
to accentuate its improbability."

Nansen then goes on to say: "What Pytheas himself saw may have been the ice sludge in the sea which is formed over a great extent along the edge of the drift ice when this has been ground to a pulp by the action of waves. The expression 'can be traversed neither on foot nor by boat' is exactly applicable to this ice sludge. If we add to this the thick fog which is often found near drift ice, then the description that the air is also involved in the mixture, and that land and sea and everything is merged in it, will appear very graphic."

Throughout his voluminous comments on Pytheas, Strabo gives a variety of reasons for his skepticism about the Thule stories. That the main reason was, as has been said, Strabo's view that the Arctic Zone was uninhabitable, is shown by one of his summaries:

"True, Pytheas of Massilia claims that the farthest country north of the British islands is Thule, where he says the summer tropic and the Arctic Circle are one. Other writers, however, tell us nothing on this subject, nor even that there is an island named Thule, nor that lands continue to be habitable up there where the tropical circle of summer is the same as the Arctic Circle.

"I think, for my part, that the northern boundaries of the habitable earth are much farther south. Modern writers tell us of nothing beyond Ireland, which lies just north of Britain, where people entirely savage live miserably because of the intense cold. Here, in my opinion, is where the bounds of the habitable earth should be fixed."

The next move in our consideration of how the Arctic was discovered is to remind ourselves that Norway extends north far beyond the Arctic Circle and that just as the British found Britain long before the Greeks did, so the Norwegians discovered Norway long before the British did. At any rate, they discovered and colonized it long before the time of that English king from whom we have the first preserved narrative of a voyage that reached farther north than that of Pytheas.

There are rock carvings in Norway to indicate that Norwegians were sailing the seas, and doubtless visiting Britain, contemporaneously with the New Stone Age sailors of Crete, who have been considered here as of from 4000 to 10,000 B.C. The same navigators were, in that case, visiting the Arctic in the same period—those of them, that is, who were not living within the Arctic Circle and visiting the Temperate Zone instead. Likewise the same British who told Pytheas how to find Iceland were no doubt in the habit of coasting the western shores of Norway to and beyond the Arctic Circle, perhaps visiting the Murmansk region and the White Sea.

However that be, a voyage around the north of the Scandinavian Peninsula and to the eastward seems to have been news to King Alfred of England in the ninth century when he inserted into his edition of the Latin writer Orosius an account of what a Norwegian visitor told him concerning an Arctic voyage. The King wrote the visitor's name as Othere or Octher, but his own countrymen probably called him Ottar. The story was broadcast by Richard Hakluyt in his *The Principall Navigations, Voiages, Traffiques and Discoveries of the English Nation,* the first edition of which appeared in 1589. The following is from Hakluyt, "The Voyage of Octher made to the Northeast parts beyond Norway, reported by himself unto Alfred the famous king of England about the year 890."

The Voyage of Ottar

Octher said that the country wherein he dwelt was called Helgoland [Helgeland, a district in northern Norway]. Octher told his lord King Alfred that he dwelt furthest north of any other Norman. He said that he dwelt toward the north part of the land toward the west coast; and affirmed that the land, notwithstanding it stretcheth marvelous far toward the north, yet it is all desert and not inhabited, unless it be very few places, here and there, where certain Fynnes [Lapps] dwell upon the coast, who live by hunting all the winter and by fishing in summer.

He said that upon a certain time he fell into a fantasy and desire to prove and know how far that land stretched northward, and whether there were any habitation of men north beyond the desert. Whereupon he took his voyage directly north along the coast, having upon his starboard always the desert land, and upon the larboard the main ocean, and continued his course for the space of three days. In which space he was come as far toward the north as commonly the whale-hunters use to travel.

Whence he proceeded in his course still toward the north so far as he was able to sail in other three days. At the end whereof he perceived that the coast turned toward the east, or else the sea opened with a main gulf into the land, he knew not how far. Well he wist and remembered that he was fain to stay till he had a western wind, and somewhat northerly. And thence he sailed plain east along the coast still so far as he was able in the space of four days. At the end of which time he was compelled again to stay till he had a full northerly wind, forsomuch as the coast bowed thence directly toward the south, or at leastwise the sea opened into the land, he could not tell how far. So that he sailed thence along the coast continually full south so far as he could travel in five days, and at the fifth day's end he discovered a mighty river [the Dvina] which opened very far into the land.

At the entry of which river he stayed his course, and in conclusion turned back again, for he durst not enter thereinto for fear of the inhabitants of the land, perceiving that on the other side of the river the country was thoroughly inhabited. Which was the first peopled land that he had found since his departure from his own dwelling, whereas continually throughout all his voyage he had evermore on his starboard a wilderness and desert country—except that in some places he saw a few fishers, fowlers, and hunters, which were all Fynnes—and all the way upon his larboard was the main ocean.

The Biarmes [as the Norse called the people of northern Russia] had inhabited and tilled their country indifferently well. Notwithstanding, he was afraid to go upon shore. But the country of the Terfynnes lay all waste, and not inhabited, except it were, as we have said, whereas dwelled certain hunters, fowlers, and fishers. The Biarmes told him a number of stories both of their own country and of the countries adjoining. Howbeit, he knew not nor could affirm anything for certain truth, forsomuch as he was not upon land, nor saw any himself. This only he judged, that the Fynnes and Biarmes speak but one language.

The principal purpose of his travel this way was to increase the knowledge and discovery of these coasts and countries, for the more commodity of fishing of horse whales [whale horses, walrus; also called sea horses], which have in their teeth bones of great price and excellency, whereof he brought some at his return unto the King. Their skins are also very good to make cables for ships, and so used. This kind of whale is much less in quantity than other kinds, having not in length above 7 ells.

And as for the common kind of whales, the place of most and best hunting of them is in his own country. Whereof some be 48 ells of length, and some 50, of which sort he affirmed that he himself was one of the six which in the space of three days killed threescore. He was a man of exceeding wealth in such riches, wherein the wealth of that country doth consist.

At the same time that he came to the King, he had of his own breed 600 tame deer of that kind which they call reindeer, of the which number 6 were stall reindeer, a beast of great value and marvelously esteemed among the Fynnes for that with them they catch the wild reindeer. He was among the chief men of his country one, and yet he had but 20 kine and 20 swine, and that little which he tilled, he tilled it all with horses.

Their principal wealth consisteth in the tribute which the Fynnes pay them, which is all in skins of wild beasts, feathers of birds, whalebones, and cables and tacklings for ships made of whales' or seals' skins. Every man payeth according to his ability. The richest pay ordinarily fifteen cases of martens, five reindeer skins and one bear, ten bushels of feathers, a coat of a bear's skin, two cables threescore ells long apiece, the one made of whale's skin, the other of seal's.

He said that the country of Norway was very long and small. So much of it as either beareth any good pasture or may be tilled lieth upon the seacoast, which notwithstanding in some places is very rocky and stony. And all eastward, all along against the inhabited land, lie wild and huge hills and mountains, which are in some places inhabited by the Fynnes.

The inhabited land is broadest toward the south, and the further it stretcheth toward the north, it groweth evermore smaller and smaller. Toward the south it is peradventure threescore miles in breadth, or broader in some places; about the middest, 30 miles or above; and toward the north, where it is smallest, he affirmeth that it proveth not 3 miles from the sea to the mountains.

The mountains be in breadth of such quantity as a man is able to travel over in a fortnight, and in some places no more than may be traveled in six days. Right over against this land, on the other side of the mountains somewhat toward the South, lieth Swethland [Sweden], and against the same toward the north lieth Queenland. The Queens [Finns] sometimes, passing the mountains, invade and spoil the Normans; and on the contrary part, the Normans likewise sometimes spoil their country.

Among the mountains be many and great lakes in sundry places of fresh water, into which the Queens use to carry their boats upon their backs overland, and thereby invade and spoil the country of the Normans. These boats of theirs be very little and very light. ▨

For more than six hundred years British knowledge of the Arctic northeastward, to and past the White Sea, did not progress much beyond what Alfred copied down from Ottar. Meantime, however, John Cabot, an Italian in British service, had tried in 1497 to reach China by going around that inconvenient land mass (since called North America) which prevented Europe from sailing direct westerly to those Indies which are rich, though not so fabulously golden as Europe then supposed. In the course of this attempt Cabot may have gone well north along the west side of Greenland. The easterly waters of Greenland, and doubtless parts of the east coast, had long been known to northwestern Europe, particularly to the English, who sailed customarily by way of Iceland, disappearing to the northwest beyond the horizon of Icelanders, who watched them and wrote about it in their annals.

So the Arctic, as such, was becoming known to the Western Europe of modern times well before the expedition which is usually considered as the first northeastward extension of British knowledge beyond what Ottar told Alfred. This was the voyage of Hugh Willoughby and Richard Chancellor in 1553. Since they went in search of a northeastern seaway around Asia, and not otherwise for northerly penetration, that narrative is left for the section on the Northeast Passage.

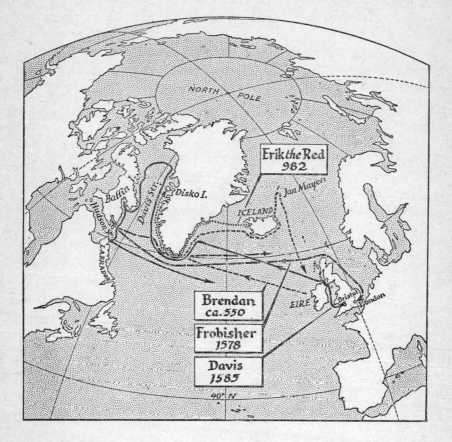

The Europeans Cross the Atlantic

THE EUROPEANS CROSS
THE ATLANTIC

CHAPTER 2

THE proof that prehistoric man reached all islands of considerable size in the Pacific, Indian, and Atlantic oceans is that they were all inhabited when first reached by historical Europeans. The presumption that men of the New Stone and Bronze ages carried on navigation between the continents lies in the fact that the big land masses are not farther from each other, or from inhabited islands, than some of these islands are from each other, and that the various continents show in their archaeology and culture the likelihood, if not the proof, that each borrowed from one or more of the others.

As was said in the last chapter, around 330 B.C. the people of northern Scotland were able to tell Pytheas about Iceland. Pytheas followed their directions, reached Iceland, and sailed one day beyond it, a distance of about 100 miles, to where he got into ice such that men could not walk upon it and boats could not make their way through it, and where the fog was so thick that there was no way of telling sea from sky.

The alternative to these interpretations of the narrative of Pytheas is that perhaps he did not make any voyage beyond Scotland. In that case the Scots told him about Iceland, about the ice and fog a day's sail beyond, and he reported their information through his book *The Ocean.*

Which of the interpretations we prefer does not matter. Here it is important to show merely that Europeans, whether Greeks or Britons, knew about Iceland and about the ice in the East Greenland Current at least as early as the fourth century before our era.

If Europeans had crossed from Britain, Ireland, or Norway

to Iceland before Pytheas got there, they doubtless used as steppingstones the islands that lie scattered on the map between Europe and the New World. Of these there are within paddling distance from Scotland and from each other the islets of the first two groups, the Orkneys and the Shetlands. Far beyond visual range from these, and in a particularly stormy sea, lie the Faeroes, so located that they are equally a natural way station whether you come from Scotland or from Norway.

Since the Faeroes are, in round numbers, 180 miles from the Shetlands and 370 miles from Norway, it is not certain that they were actually steppingstones to Iceland in the first discovery, although they were so used by some of the navigators in historical time. Or the discovery of Iceland may have been made direct from Ireland by a sea route that gives the Faeroes a wide berth.

Once having reached Iceland, by whatever route, Europeans had crossed the main channel of the Atlantic; for Iceland is 600 miles distant from Scotland and from Norway and a little farther than that from Ireland, while Greenland is only 180 miles beyond Iceland.

Having reached Greenland, the Europeans could walk the rest of the way to the mainland of North America, as the Eskimos must have done in reverse when they arrived from Canada to settle Greenland, and as sledge parties of modern explorers have done in both directions.

It is thus clear that whoever discovered Iceland discovered the New World.

After the publication of the travel narrative of Pytheas, about 325 B.C., we find no clear reference in European literature to crossings of any part of the Atlantic until we come to the traditions and writings of the Irish in the sixth century of our era.

At the time of the first preserved Irish mention of Iceland, their favorite craft for long sea voyages was the skin boat or curragh. On the stormy North Atlantic these boats, by Irish tradition, carried sixty persons; on the even stormier North Pacific, around the Aleutian Islands, the early Russian explorers found similar boats carrying up to seventy persons.

The traditions and writings of Ireland do not always specify whether the voyages referred to were in curraghs, but that is the presumption, for there is a deal of support from many sources for the opinion that skin boats, those of Bering Sea as well as the Irish curragh, are among the most seaworthy craft ever invented by man. One of the most striking tributes to their seaworthiness is an Irish dirge from the sixteenth century. A party had been lost by drowning on their way to church. The poet laments that unfortunately they tried to make the passage in a wooden boat; if only they had been in a skin boat, they would have been safe!

As has been said, the discovery of Iceland was the discovery of the New World, for under exceptional conditions of visibility the high mountains of Greenland are visible from the high mountains of northwestern Iceland. Nor can Iceland be circumnavigated many times without some vessel making too much leeway in a storm, or getting out of course in a fog, enough to bring it within sight of Greenland.

However, the records appear to show that the first historical discovery of Greenland was not made in a circumnavigation of Iceland but was made from Ireland on a voyage that reached Iceland only after it had first coasted Greenland. Such appears to be the factual basis for one of the Brendan voyage narratives.

Brendan, an Irish priest, is considered to have lived from 484 to 578. There is no contemporary written account of his exploits, but there gradually grew up in Ireland a body of myth known as the Brendan legends, in which, however, there is enough proof of a factual basis, be it ever so embroidered with fancy and folklore, for us to say that a partial authenticity for the Brendan story is established. One such piece of evidence is that Brendan is said to have used a skin boat, a type of boat which we know from other sources was considered in the early historical period of Ireland as an ideal craft for deep-sea voyages and which, from our modern experience, we know to be suitable for navigation among the ice that drifts south along the east coast of Greenland.

The Brendan story is one of the most widespread in the literature of the early Middle Ages. It is found not merely in the folk literature of the Irish, but also in that of many other northwestern European countries, and is available also in Latin transcript.

We must not think, of course, that all the voyages now credited to Brendan were necessarily made by him, even if they were real voyages. For adventure and miracle tales gather around a hero like Brendan just as funny stories gather around recognized humorists like Abraham Lincoln. It is not sure, therefore, that the voyage to Greenland, Iceland, and Jan Mayen was made by Brendan, nor even that it was made during his lifetime. It should, nevertheless, be dated about in his period, so that the probable time of the Greenland-Iceland voyage is the middle of the sixth century. The voyage was doubtless made in a cowhide curragh, with a personnel of anything from a dozen to threescore.

We follow the Reverend Denis O'Donoughue's *Brendaniana* as published at Dublin, in 1893, that part of the account being used first which is believed to relate to Greenland:

Brendan's Voyage to Greenland, Iceland, and Jan Mayen

One day they saw a column in the sea, which seemed not far off, yet they could not reach it for three days. When they drew near, Saint Brendan looked toward its summit, but could not see it because of its great height, which seemed to pierce the skies. It was covered over with a rare canopy, the material of which they knew not; but it had the color of silver, and was hard as marble, while the column itself was of the clearest crystal.

Saint Brendan ordered the brethren to take in their oars and to lower the sails and mast, and directed some of them to hold on by the fringes of the canopy, which extended about a mile from the column, and about the same depth into the sea.

When this had been done, Saint Brendan said: "Run in the boat now through an opening, that we may get a closer view of the wonderful works of God." And when they had passed through the opening and looked around them, the sea seemed to them transparent like glass, so that they could plainly see everything beneath them, even the base of the column and the skirts or fringes of the canopy, lying on the ground, for the sun shone as brightly within as without.

Saint Brendan then measured an opening between four pavilions, which he found to be 4 cubits on every side. While they sailed along for a day by one side of the column, they could always feel the shade as well as the heat of the sun beyond the ninth hour; and after thus sailing about the column for four days, they found the measurement of each side to be 400 cubits.

Some of the points about the description that should be noted are:

The original narrative may have said the pillar was *as clear as crystal*, from which, in medieval times, it was only a natural step to say that it was a crystal pillar. The pillar is usually identified by students as an iceberg adrift off the Greenland coast. This could well be right, for towering bergs miles in length have been reported from the Greenland vicinity and are common in the Antarctic. More probably the Irish are here describing a glacier front, which, as it were, is the iceberg before it breaks off from its parent glacier.

There has been spoofing about the pillar's being so tall that its upper reaches were hidden by cloud. But a cloud is only a fog that is drifting above. On Fifth Avenue in New York, it is a common sight on overcast days to see the lower several hundred feet of the Empire State Building clearly visible, then a few hazy stories, and above that all is hidden. Go up in one of the elevators and look out of an eightieth-story window. You will on many days find the cloud so dense outside that neither can you see down to the street nor are the buildings roundabout visible. Such things happen constantly with icebergs and are still more common with the glacier fronts, which are likely to be higher.

Lastly, a glacier front is prone to be undercut by the waves and, particularly if you are in a skin boat, you might well paddle beneath an overhang and even through caverns—your life insurance company would hate to have you do it, but the Irish, miracles apart, would not have known the danger, at least if this was their first encounter with a berg or with a glacier fronting the sea. Moreover, navigating a few hundred yards away, parallel to the ice cliff, would be practically as dangerous, for waves are huge when a glacier calves; they endanger great ships and swamp small boats.

In reading the section of the Brendan account which has been identified as dealing with Iceland, remember that this is one of the most volcanic countries in the world, and that its capital was named Smoky Bay (Reykjavik) by the early settlers because of the pillars of smoke (steam) rising from the hot springs near the coast. Some of the lava flows reach the sea, whereupon there is a great bubbling and hissing.

Fragments of hot rock would have been seen and heard dropping into the water if the Irish voyagers happened along at the time of a violent eruption from one of the coastal volcanoes. A stench would be mentioned logically in an account of a passage to leeward, for then the Irish would have smelled sulphurous fumes.

When those [eight] days had passed, they came within view of an island which was very rugged and rocky, covered over with slag, without trees or herbage, but full of smith's forges . . . they heard the noise of bellows blowing like thunder, and the beating of sledges on the anvils and iron. . . . Soon after, one of the inhabitants came forth to do some work. He was all hairy and hideous, begrimed with fire and smoke. When he saw the servants of Christ near the island, he withdrew into his forge, crying aloud: "Woe! Woe! Woe!"

Saint Brendan again armed himself with the sign of the cross, and said to the brethren: "Put on more sail, and ply your oars more briskly, that we may get away from this island." Hearing this, the savage man . . . rushed down to the shore bearing in his hand a tongs with a burning mass of the slag, of great size and intense heat, which he flung at once after the servants of Christ. . . . It passed them at a furlong's distance, and where it fell into the sea it fumed up like a heap of burning coals, and a great smoke arose as if from a fiery furnace.

When they had passed on about a mile beyond the spot where this burning mass had fallen, all the dwellers on the island crowded down to the shore, bearing, each one of them, a large mass of burning slag, which they flung, every one in turn, after the servants of God. And then they returned to their forges, which they blew up into mighty flames, so that the whole island seemed one globe of fire, and the sea on every side boiled up and foamed, like a caldron set on a fire well supplied with fuel.

All the day the brethren, even when they were no longer within view of the island, heard a loud wailing from the inhabitants thereof, and a noisome stench was perceptible at a great distance. 🖾

The next country visited by the sixth-century Irish explorers has been identified as the island of Jan Mayen, which like Iceland is volcanic, though at present not so active. It lies some 300 miles a little east of north from Iceland, and fronts the sea in a manner even more spectacular. To the approaching navigator it is far more striking than anything that can be seen on a coast of Europe, for its Beerenberg peak rises to more than 7000 feet within a few miles from the beach, thus 2000 feet higher than the highest mountains of Iceland, which in any case are farther from the shore.

The account of the Brendan voyage from the second to the third of the lands visited runs:

🖾 On another day there came into view a large and high mountain in the ocean, not far off toward the north, with misty clouds about it and a great smoke issuing from its summit, when suddenly the wind drove the boat rapidly toward the island until it almost touched the shore. The cliffs were so high they could scarce see the top, were black as coal, and upright like a wall. . . .

Afterward a favorable breeze caught the boat and drove them southward. And as they looked back, they saw the peak of the mountain unclouded, and shooting up flames into the sky, which it drew back again to itself so that the mountain seemed a burning pyre. After this dreadful sight, they sailed for seven days toward the south. 🖾

While the Brendan legends were growing up in Ireland, a parallel body of myth was forming in Britain. Both have the character of verbal folk creation where a factual scaffolding gets covered with more and more garlands of fiction. In Ireland these were the Brendan legends, in Britain they were the Arthurian cycle.

Brendan was no doubt a real priest. Arthur, though apparently never a king, was a real general. He is believed to have been born late in the fifth century, and as a relatively young man to have taken part in the battle of Mount Badon (516). Arthur's growth into a fabulous king was slow, the eleventh and twelfth centuries perhaps being the most active period. What the legends tell of his having done centuries before King Alfred's reign may therefore derive from centuries after that distinguished man of letters became ruler of England.

The quotation here is from *The Principall Navigations, Voiages* . . . of Richard Hakluyt, being extracts from "Certain testimonies concerning K. Arthur and his conquests of the North regions, taken out of the historie of the Kings of Britaine, written by Galfridus Monumetensis [Geoffrey of Monmouth, 1100-1154], and newly printed at Heidelberge, Anno 1587."

The Conquest of Arthur

In the year of Christ 517, King Arthur in the second year of his reign, having subdued all parts of Ireland, sailed with his fleet into Iceland, and brought it and the people thereof under his subjection. . . .

Arthur, which was sometime the most renowned King of the Britains, was a mighty and valiant man, and a famous warrior. This kingdom was too little for him, and his mind was not contented with it. He therefore valiantly subdued all Scantia, which is now called Norway, and all the Islands beyond Norway; to wit, Iceland and Greenland, which are appertaining unto Norway, Sweveland, Ireland, Gotland, Denmark, Semeland, Windland, Curland, Roe, Femeland, Wireland, Flanders, Cherilland, Lapland, and all the other lands and islands of the east sea, even unto Russia (in which Lapland he placed the easterly bounds of his British Empire) and many other islands beyond Norway, even under the North Pole, which are appendances of Scantia, now called Norway.

These people were wild and savage, and had not in them

the love of God nor of their neighbors, because all evil commeth from the North, yet there were among them certain Christians living in secret. 📭

While 'the traditions and legends of Britain and Ireland were developing, references to Iceland and Greenland began to appear in the writings of learned men.

The first book that deals at some length with Iceland is *De Mensura Orbis Terrae*, which was completed by the Irish monk Dicuil on the continent in 825, seemingly at the court of Louis the Pious of the Frankish kingdom.

As implied by the title, *On the Measurement of the Earth*, the author of the *De Mensura* is more concerned with mathematical and philosophical than with historical matters. The work is based largely, Dicuil says, on the surveys made upon order of the Emperor Theodosius. Apart from this source, the *De Mensura* uses several of the usual classic writers, and then Dicuil has a few things which he inserts on the basis of his own knowledge or that of persons with whom he has conversed.

That journeys to and from Iceland were in Dicuil's time considered of no especial note is confirmed by the casual manner in which he tells of a round trip from Ireland to Iceland that began in February and ended in August.

Dicuil's information about Iceland falls in the category of firsthand hearsay, which is fortunate; he actually conversed with men who had been there. It is not so fortunate that in this section of his book Dicuil is engaged in an argument with those who have theorized about how conditions would be on and near the Arctic Circle, with particular reference to the movements of the sun and the amount of daylight at various times of year. So from the historical point of view we learn little beyond the inference that Iceland had been well known for so long to the Irish that they took the place for granted and were no longer interested in details of voyages to it or in descriptions of it.

The extract from Dicuil's *De Mensura Orbis Terrae* used here is in the translation of Eloise McCaskill, as collated from two Latin editions [the version here used is from *Greenland*, by Vilhjalmur Stefansson, Doubleday, 1942]:

Dicuil Tells of Thule

🐌 We do not read of any islands being in the sea west or north of Spain. Around our own island of Hibernia [Ireland] there are islands, but some are small and others are infinitesimal. Near the island of Britain there are many islands, some large, some small, and some middle-sized. Some are in the sea to the south and others to the west, but islands are found more abundantly in the region of the Arctic Circle and the North. Upon some of these I have dwelt, others I have landed upon, others I have just seen, and others read about.

Pliny the Younger in his Book IV informs us that Pytheas of Marseille relates that Thule is six days' sailing distant from Britain. In Book XIV he speaks of it as always deserted. Isidore in his *Etymologiae* writes as follows: "Thule, the remotest island of the ocean between the northern and western zones beyond Britain, taking its name from the sun because the sun makes there its summer solstice."

Priscian in his *Periegesis* speaks of it more clearly than Isidore:

"He skims with his ships the open plain of ocean.
Coming to Thule, which gleams both day and night
With Titan's rays, he ascends with his car to the poles
Of heaven, kindling the boreal realms with his torch."

Julius Solinus, in that portion of his selections dealing with Britain, writes more clearly and fully than Priscian about this same island, thus: "Thule, the remotest isle, where during the summer solstice when the sun crosses the constellation of Cancer, there is no night, during the winter no day."

It is now the thirtieth year since some monks who dwelt upon that island from the calends of February [February 1] to the calends of August [August 1] told me that not only during the summer solstice, but also during the days near that time, toward evening the setting sun hides itself as if behind a small hill, so that there is no darkness for even a very short time; but a man may do whatever he wishes, actually pick the lice from his shirt just as if it were by the light of the sun; and if they [the monks] had been on top of the mountains, the sun probably never would have been hidden from their eyes. In the middle of that short period of time it is midnight in the middle of the earth, and so I believe that on the other hand, during the winter solstice and during a few days around that time dawn occurs for only a brief time in Thule; that is to say, when it is midday in the middle of the earth.

Therefore [it is evident that] those are lying who have written that the sea around Thule is frozen and that there is continuous day without night from the vernal to the autumnal equinox; and that, vice versa, from the autumnal to the vernal equinox there is perpetual night, when those monks who sailed there during a time of year when naturally it would be at the coldest, and landed on this island and dwelt there, always had alternate day and night after the solstice, but they found that one day's sail from it toward the north sea was frozen.

This description of the night light of midsummer on the south coast of Iceland has the eyewitness touch. A modern tourist would say that looking north he saw the mountains silhouetted against the twilight behind them, and would clarify by remarking that he could read fine print outdoors at midnight. Dicuil was using the familiar speech of his day when he said the equivalent by telling that there was twilight so bright that a man could pick lice from his shirt.

From the writings of the European scholars let us turn to the records that have been preserved in Iceland through the historical sagas.

Those sagas that deal with the finding of Iceland by the Norsemen have the arrogance of the superior nation; for the Norse were in that time what the British became after Queen Elizabeth. It is a part of this mentality that although they had conquered northern Ireland, and must have learned about Thule from the kinsmen of Dicuil, yet they speak in the sagas as if they themselves had discovered beyond the Atlantic a wholly new country. Their sagas mention the Irish as having been in Iceland when the Norse arrived, yet in almost the same breath they imply that it was the Norse who discovered Iceland. An exception to this attitude is found in a passage in the

Landnamabók (*Book of the Colonizers*) of Sturla Thordarson, which tells:

"Before Iceland was settled from Norway, there were here people whom the Norse called Papar. They were Christians . . . there have been found as remains of them Irish books, bells, croziers, and other articles which show that they were Westmen (Irish). These were found to the east in Papey and in Papili. Moreover it is stated in English books that at this time there were sailings between the two countries."

Thus Sturla is explicit about what many of the sagas rather gloss over, that there were Irish people living in Iceland before the Norwegians got there. Other Icelandic authorities specify that these people were clergy, from which it has been assumed that no women were involved. But the institution of celibacy is not so old as that in Ireland. In the time of Dicuil Roman priests were as free to marry as are the Methodist and Episcopalian clergy of today. Besides, parties commanded by priests might well have included families of laymen.

It is implied in the sagas that the Irish in Iceland were at this time, at least mainly, a floating population. There is no evidence that the island was inhabited before the Irish came there.

Knut Gjerset emphasizes in his *History of Iceland* [Macmillan, 1924] that there were no doubt voyages in the immediate pre-Norse period of which the Norse settlers have preserved us no record. He comments:

"When Iceland was first discovered by the Norsemen, and by whom the discovery was made, is not definitely known. Traditions which have been preserved by old Icelandic writers credit the Norseman [Norwegian] Naddod [Naddodd] and the Swede Gardar with the discovery, but the accounts do not agree, and *cannot well be regarded as anything but reminiscences of early voyages to the island.*" (Italics ours.)

The best account of the voyages of the first accredited Norwegian and the similarly remembered Swede is found in the already quoted *Landnamabók* from which I have here made my own translation. This saga tells of the first Swede:

Gardar's and Naddodd's Travels

A man was named Gardarr [Gardar] the son of Svavar the Swede. He owned land in Sealand, but had been born in Sweden. He went to the Hebrides to collect his wife's inheritance from her father. When he sailed through the Pentland Firth he got into bad weather and his ship was driven out into the western sea. He struck land east of Horn [in Iceland], where there was a harbor.

Gardar sailed around the country and determined that it was an island. He entered a fjord which he named Skjalfandi [The Trembler, or Quiverer]. They put out a boat manned by Nattfari and by a slave that belonged to him. The rope [by which they were being towed] broke and the boat went ashore in Nattfaravik beyond Skuggabjorg.

Gardar landed on the other side of the fjord and spent the winter. That is why he called the place Husavik [Bay of Houses]. Nattfari stayed behind with a man slave and a woman slave; this is why the place is called Nattfaravik. Gardar sailed back east and praised the land greatly, naming it Gardarsholm [Gardar's Island]."

The same authority's account of the first Norwegian reads:

A man was named Naddodd, the brother of Oxna-Thorir, brother-in-law of Olvir Barnakarl. He was a great Viking. He settled in the Faeroe Islands, for elsewhere he was unwelcome.

He sailed from Norway toward those islands, but went astray at sea, struck Gardarsholm, reaching Reydarfjord in the Austfjord district. They climbed the highest mountains to see if they could discern any dwellings of people or smokes, but they saw none.

As they were sailing away from the country, a heavy snow fell on the land; therefore they named it Snowland.

By this *Landnamabók* version the "discoverer" of Iceland is the Swede Gardar Svavarson; other versions of the saga, while preserving the rest of the narrative little changed, give the precedence to the Norwegian. There is little to quarrel

about, for these voyages, made just after A.D. 860, are no
doubt merely ones that happened to be remembered from
among many.

The first recorded attempt by Scandinavians to colonize was
probably around 865 and was made by Raven-Floki, a Norwegian, who brought with him livestock. Using the Shetlands
and the Faeroes as way stations, he reached southeastern
Iceland.

The party sailed west along the south coast. When they got
beyond Reykjanes, a fjord opened to them so they could see
Snaefellsnes, whereupon Faxi remarked: "What we have found
must be a great land, for the rivers are big." The place has
since been called Faxaos; that is, Bay at the Mouth of Faxi's
River.

Floki and his men sailed westward across Breidafjord. The
fishing there was so good that they neglected to make hay, and
the next winter their cattle all died.

The spring proved cold. Floki climbed a mountain to the
north and saw a fjord that was full of (drifting sea) ice. So
they named the country Iceland, as it has been called ever
since.

This appears to be the first reference in the literature to
ocean ice being seen by Norwegians. At home in Norway they
were familiar with ice on high mountains; there was snow
on the land and their rivers and lakes froze in winter. But you
might camp a dozen years on top of the highest hill in northernmost Norway and sea ice would never come within your
horizon. This may have been, therefore, the first knowledge
Norwegians ever had that there could be ice floating around
in the sea, what we call pack ice.

So the marveling Norsemen gave to Iceland a name which
to this day makes people shiver throughout the world, no
matter that the Icelanders themselves seldom use fur coats,
because their winters are more rainy than frosty. With a capital
city of about the same average January temperature as Milan,
with no midwinter extreme as low as those of upstate New
York, this island protégé of the Gulf Stream has suffered
through the ages from the inexperience with sea ice of colonists
who were in any case disgruntled because they could not

both have their cake and eat it—could not both fish through the haying season and also carry their livestock safe through the winter.

There were three chief men on this forlorn colonizing venture, Floki and his two henchmen, Herjolf and Thorolf. When after two winters in Iceland the party returned to Europe, they told each his own story. The saga comments that according to Floki the land had no merits, according to Herjolf there were good and bad points, according to Thorolf there was scarcely a drawback.

It was a sort of poetic justice that when Iceland later became fashionable, when everybody who could was moving there from Norway to an eventual total of 30,000 or 40,000 emigrants, Floki succumbed to the spell too, but got there so late that he, who once could have had the finest homestead in the country, was of necessity resigned to taking what others did not want.

The year of the first successful colonization was probably 870 or 871, according to Professor Halldór Hermannsson of Cornell University, but sometime ago the Government of Iceland officially declared 874 as the year of the landing of the first permanent settlers. The Althing, the oldest functioning parliament in the world today, was established in the summer of 930 at Thingvellir (The Plains of Assembly) and thereby Iceland became the first American republic.

Nothing is more important with relation to how knowledge of the lands west of the Atlantic spread through Europe than to keep in mind their relation to the Church. Therefore, this volume does not turn at once to the documents that tell of journeys west from Iceland, but pauses for a sketch of the religious situation.

A considerable number of the chieftains who colonized Iceland came by way of Ireland, where the families of some of them had been for two or three generations in the role of conquerors. Now among the institutions of that time in northwestern Europe were slavery and polygamy or concubinage. The chieftains who led the colonizing groups brought in their entourage their wives, some of whom were Irish, and their concubines and slaves, most of whom were Irish.

But Ireland was in this period the most Christian as well as the most learned of the nations in this part of the world. Therefore among the cultural elements which the Norse brought with them from Ireland were not merely native Irish lore and literature, but also Christianity, with its attendant Roman affiliations and Latin scholarship. This included the Latin method of writing, to replace the Scandinavian runic, which was well enough for carving inscriptions on monuments and tablets but not suited for the flowing transcription of laws and literature.

Being the religion of a militarily overawed people, Christianity was at first not socially the thing in Iceland. Being the religion of the Irish wife or, concubine of the heathen chief, it was considered effeminate. But the man child as well as the girl baby learned the faith at their mother's knee, so the influence of the Nazarene spread.

Just before the turn of the millennium the stigma of effeminacy of the new religion disappeared of a sudden, for a king had come to power in Norway, Olaf Tryggvason, who while both a supreme athlete and an aggressive soldier was also a devout Christian. It has been said of him, perhaps in oversimplification, that he would preach the Gospel one year to a heathen section of his kingdom and that next year he would baptize any recalcitrants at the point of the spear.

When this report reached Iceland, it had not merely the effect of bringing Christianity into fashion. A still more powerful influence was political, if any force can be stronger than fashion.

The petty kings, earls, and lesser nobility who colonized Iceland had mainly done so because they preferred exile from Norway to paying taxes and yielding allegiance there to an over-all King. Their dislike for this chief King and their jealousy of each other were the main forces which had made and kept Iceland a republic. Now they saw a chance that if they did not accept the Christian religion promptly, the King of Norway might under the guise of a baptizing mission conquer Iceland and make it a part of Norway.

So when missionaries arrived from Olaf in the spring of the year 1000, the parliament, the Althing, promptly voted to accept Christianity. Similar action was taken by the national assembly of the Greenland republic.

It was a joke on these first two republics of the New World that meantime, without their knowing it, King Olaf had been defeated in a great battle and killed. Had the western democracies been aware of this, the formal adoption of Christianity as a religion might have been delayed years, if not decades. But the adoption would have come, for nothing succeeds like success, and Christianity was succeeding throughout every part of that world which was known to the Icelanders and Greenlanders.

As to the progress of discovery westward from Iceland, we find that the first Norseman chronicled as possibly sighting Greenland was one Gunnbjörn, in about the year 900 (the date may have been as early as 877). Although the sagas carry many references to his discovery, there is no real account of it. Perhaps the nearest to a combined narrative and explanation is found in an annal which is a rewrite from the saga reference in combination with the views of the annalist, Björn Jonsson. The following is translated from the Icelandic.

"*On the Gunnbjörn Islands and others in the Iceland Sea.* The origin and cause of Erik the Red's voyage to Greenland [982] was merely that old men still remembered that Gunnbjörn, son of Ulf the Crow, claimed that he had seen a snow-capped mountain to the west at the same time as he saw (to the east) Mount Snaefell in Iceland, which was when he was driven westward by gales after he had found the Gunnbjörn Islands.

"At that time Iceland was as yet uncolonized and newly found by Gardar, who had sailed around it close inshore, from promontory to promontory, naming the country Gardar's Island. Next after him (as a circumnavigator) came this Gunnbjörn. He sailed around the land farther offshore, so far that he could barely see the coast. Therefore he spoke of the islands as skerries; but in many (written) accounts since then they are spoken of as islands, in some of the accounts they are called large islands."

This reference to the Gunnbjörn islands, like many others, places them to the west of southwestern Iceland. But some references place them to the northwest of northwestern Iceland, which fits in with the explanation that Gardar failed to see these islands because he kept inshore, but Gunnbjörn found them because he stood so far offshore that Iceland was barely visible—which is exactly the condition under which, with perhaps a slight benefit of mirage, the Blosseville Coast of Greenland can be seen while Iceland is still in view.

If the "skerries" were seen west of Snaefell, they were probably icebergs, which even modern explorers, with all their experience and caution, every now and then misidentify as land. Gunnbjörn had probably never in his life seen a berg, perhaps had never even heard of one, and would not be on his guard.

When Erik the Red planned his Greenland exploration in 981, the voyage of Gunnbjörn barely lived in the memory of the older generation, but thereafter, as we shall see, knowledge of this western island-continent spread rapidly, not only in Iceland but throughout all Europe.

Rated by critical historians of geographic discovery as one of the greatest explorers of whom we have knowledge, Erik demands some biographical notice.

Around 950 a man was living in the Jaeder district of Norway, Thorvald Asvaldsson. He was quick-tempered, got into a fight, killed a prominent man, and was exiled. Most Norwegian exiles in those days went to Iceland, and so did Thorvald, taking with him in his family a small son, Erik, probably five or ten years of age, who must have had red hair in view of his later nickname.

The best parts of Iceland had been homesteaded by then and Thorvald was forced to be content with rocky land in the northwest. There his son grew up, became quarrelsome in his turn, killed a man, was outlawed in the summer of 981, and that winter prepared a ship for the decreed three-year exile. In the spring of 982 Erik sailed to explore the land seen by Gunnbjörn.

It has been said that what made this one of the great ventures of history was that the exploration of Greenland led inevitably to the discovery of the North American mainland. However, as has been noted, the really decisive thing in this connection had already happened—the discovery of Iceland, which led inevitably to the discovery of Greenland. For to reach Iceland the navigators must go several days without seeing land while crossing the main stream of the Atlantic, but after that they can see from land to land until the mainland is reached.

Destined to lead directly to the white man's first historically known discovery of any continent, the expedition for the discovery of the world's largest island, Greenland, was simple in plan and homely in execution. The ship was practically an open boat, perhaps 80 or 90 feet long, with a single mast and a square sail. The crew were Erik's family, with servants or slaves and a neighbor family or two—perhaps thirty or forty people all together. They had with them the common Icelandic domestic animals, including cattle, sheep, and horses, with hay to feed the livestock on the voyage.

By piecing together evidence from the sagas with what we know of conditions at sea as they are now and must have been then, it appears that Erik was barred from direct approach to Greenland by the drift of pack ice and bergs in the turgid south-flowing current along the east coast, and by that fog over the ice which Pytheas had described as resembling a sea lung and which sailors nowadays describe as so dense it can be cut in chunks and piled up on the deck. So Erik coasted southwesterly, rounded Cape Farewell, and moved up along the west shore where they were able to land, the ice doubtless thinning out then as it does now.

Unlike Floki in Iceland, who did not make hay because the fishing was so good, the Greenland explorers evidently built barns and made hay, for we read nothing of difficulties, the inference being that they lived in the new land as they had done on the farms from which they came. During the next three years the party explored the west coast of Greenland, perhaps as far north as Disko Island.

With this introduction, let us turn to the brief summary found in Ari Thorgilsson's *Book of the Icelanders*, in the translation of Professor Hermannsson (Cornell University Library, 1930). The sixth chapter bears the title "Of the Settlement of Greenland" and reads: "The country which is called Greenland was discovered and settled from Iceland.

"Erik the Red was the name of a man from Breidafjord who went from here thither and took possession of land at the place which since has been called Eriksfjord. He gave a name to the country and called it Greenland, and said that people would desire to go thither if the country had a good name.

"Both east and west in the country they found human habitations, fragments of skin boats, and stone implements from which it was evident that the same kind of people had been there as inhabited Wineland and whom the Greenlanders called Skrellings [Skraelings].

"He began colonizing the country fourteen or fifteen winters before Christianity came to Iceland, according to what a man who himself had gone thither with Erik the Red told Thorkel Gellisson in Greenland."

So successfully did Erik publicize Greenland upon his return to Iceland that in 986 twenty-five shiploads of colonists started southwest with him for the new land. Some vessels were lost and some turned back, but fourteen won through, landing about 500 settlers.

The colony prospered, so that at its height the Greenland republic is considered to have had a population of about 10,000 settled on at least 290 farms. These were in two colonies, the so-called Eastern Settlement (we would call it the Southern Settlement) and the Western Settlement (to us the Northern Settlement), both on the west coast. The densest population was in the southern colony, around what is now Julianehaab; the northern colony was centered around the present Godthaab.

The story of how Christianity came to Greenland is a logical continuation of the Greenland story, but that must be reserved for the chapter on how the mainland of North America was discovered, for the events are blended together.

With Greenland formally Christian after the year 1000, what had been chiefly a woman's religion now welled up to all the people and they became, it would seem, more devout than the Icelanders. At any rate, they built larger and more substantial churches, the ruins of which, with the graveyards containing runic memorials, give us today a further check on the Icelandic literary sources that tell the story of Greenland.

While the first missionaries arrived in Greenland in the year 1000, the first regularly constituted local priest who lived and died in the country did not get there before 1056. In 1126 the country became a separate bishopric, first under the Archbishop of Hamburg, Germany, with the authority transferred later to Nidaros (Trondheim), Norway. There were eventually sixteen churches, a monastery, and a nunnery under the local bishopric, which had its seat at Gardar in the present Julianehaab district.

The Greenlanders were at first mainly pastoral, as we know from the Icelandic sources, from the tax-collection records of the Church, and from recent excavation of barn ruins, the largest so far examined having contained stalls for more than a hundred head of cattle. There were sheep barns of corresponding size.

As Nansen, among others, has well shown, this pastoralism is not an indication that the climate was materially different from what it is now. The stock farming shows merely that the settlers were by tradition pastoral. Indeed a modern sheep industry, re-established in Greenland a few years ago, is now doing well.

Greenland is not by nature one of the good pastoral regions, but it is one of the finest hunting and fishing countries. The sea is rich in fish and there is an abundance of sea game—whales, walrus, seals, and polar bears. So we find in the records, and in the refuse heaps near the ruins of the houses, signs of a steadily increasing dependence on hunting through the eleventh, twelfth, and thirteenth centuries.

In Greenland the colonists discovered what is now well understood, that the northern-ocean mammals, particularly the seals, are better hunted from ice than from land, and that the ice brings the game with it—that an icy summer is a prosperous one through the food and fur that come with the drifting pack.

The furs were not to be sneezed at by the colonists, for traders came from Iceland and from Europe who wanted them, and so did the Church, for tithes. Then there was the export of Greenlandic rawhide thongs of walrus and white whale that became famous throughout Europe because of their unequaled merit and the wide distribution they got from the tax collectors and from the middlemen with whom the Church dealt.

For publicity value, two of Greenland's exports were special, the white bears and the white or whitish falcons. Neither of these was commercial in the ordinary way, for they were used chiefly as gifts, in effect as bribes. When the Greenlanders wanted something from a potentate or a magnate, they gave him a bear cub or a falcon. In Europe these became royal gifts. For instance, a King of Norway-Denmark sent a number of Greenland falcons as a gift to the King of Portugal, and received in return the gift of a cargo of wine.[1]

Although of concern to sportsmen as a source of falcons, and to the Church as a source of taxes (and for other reasons), Greenland was faring badly during the thirteenth and fourteenth centuries, at least from the point of view of European contacts. For this the rulers of Norway and Denmark were largely to blame.

In the Middle Ages people took seriously the slogan that kings ruled "by the grace of God." A king was the Lord's anointed, fittingly ruler on earth somewhat as God was ruler in heaven. In the thirteenth century it was practically impious not to have a king. Besides, fashions are strong, and there were at the time no republics in northwestern Europe, only monarchies. So the Greenlanders, as well as the Icelanders, let themselves be talked into applying for admission to the kingdom of Norway. Both were admitted in 1261-62.

A big talking point for joining up with Norway had been that the King promised better shipping connections with Europe. The Greenlanders had no timber of their own to build ships, and the craft they owned grew smaller and smaller, no doubt chiefly built from wood which they fetched from Labrador. Excepting timber from North America, most of the Greenland trade came from Norway by way of Iceland.

But instead of growing more numerous after the union with Norway, the trading ships became fewer and fewer. Instead of

---

[1] For extensive discussion of Greenlandic bears and falcons in the royal and other relations of Europe during the Middle Ages see the index of Stefansson's *Greenland*, Doubleday, Doran, 1942.

one or two a year there was now one every year or two. Presently there was only one every five or six years. The Crown had a legal monopoly, which was sold to a firm of Bergen merchants who knew they could get everything the Greenlanders had for however little they might bring them in the way of goods.

So far as is definitely known, there were no sailings from Norway to Greenland after 1412, but some think there was a Norwegian voyage in 1448.

It was formerly considered that the decrease of foreign trade brought on a decrease of the Greenland population through famine and malnutrition. It is now becoming fairly clear that there is no evidence for this, but that there is evidence of another sort—that, irrespective of whether the people were tending toward extinction, the European culture was gradually becoming extinct. The Europeans were adopting Eskimo ways of life, because these were better suited to the country, and they were intermarrying with the Eskimos.

The fate of the Christian Church was similar to that of the European political and social institutions. However, the Church did not abolish the Bishopric of Greenland until it lapsed in 1537 with Norway and Denmark going Lutheran and the last Bishop of Greenland dying in Denmark, a prisoner of the Reformers. The bishops, however, had not been resident in Greenland since 1385, but had held their dignities and drawn their pay in Norway or elsewhere in Europe.

Some of the more interesting side lights on the history of Greenland in this period are thrown by letters that were written by the Popes and preserved at the Vatican. The series of papal documents so far published begins with a letter of February 13, 1206, written by Innocent III, referring to the decree of Nicholas II (1058-61) by which Greenland had been transferred from the jurisdiction of the Archbishopric of Hamburg to that of Nidaros.

Then come letters from later Popes, telling of the difficulty of maintaining contact and of collecting tithes from so remote a country. Finally the series closes with two documents that are among the most striking: In 1448, Pope Nicholas wrote of the deplorable conditions of the Church in Greenland, telling of the invasion of that country by "pagans" who had destroyed all but nine parochial churches. In 1492 Alexander VI wrote along the same line, mentioning his own interest in Greenland from the time when he was in minor orders, which must have been around 1455.

Now Alexander VI, a member of the notorious Spanish family of Borgia, is recognized as having had two chief loyalties —to his family and to the kingdom of Spain. His letter about Greenland was written in the year of his accession, before he as yet realized that a voyage in which Columbus was then engaged was going to have a material bearing on the fortunes of Spain. So far as I have been able to learn, all publicity from the Vatican about the Bishopric of Greenland, or about any knowledge the Vatican had of lands beyond the Atlantic, ceased with the announcement of the discovery of San Salvador and other neighboring islands by Columbus, and was not revived (at least not formally) until four hundred years later, when the above-mentioned series of papal letters was published in connection with the Chicago World's Fair (Columbian Exposition) of 1893.

The activities of English navigators in Iceland-Greenland waters during this period received little publicity, but there are many proofs that as the frequency of Norwegian sailings decreased, the cultivation of these seas by the English grew apace, particularly through Bristol shipping. The most striking of the documents in evidence is a treaty signed in 1432 between Henry VI, King of England, and Eric of Pomerania, King of Denmark, Norway, and Sweden, by which Henry promised to forbid his subjects to trade with Greenland.

That this treaty was honored chiefly in the breach we know from many sources, among them Icelandic annals which record English ships sailing northwest from Iceland toward the Blosseville Coast of Greenland; these voyages would have been for trading with Eskimos or for seal and walrus "fishing." Further evidence of contact with Europe is furnished by Greenland cemeteries, where have been found corpses clad in garments of European fashion as it was after 1450.

In this period, no doubt partly because of the treaty with the Scandinavian King, there was such secrecy about England's trade to the northwest that there has not as yet been found written evidence that adequately corresponds with the archaeological proof discovered in Greenland of a commerce with Europe in the second half of the fifteenth century. It is thought the traders must have been from the British Isles, because of the evidence procurable in Iceland, but a few of them may have been from some other nation.

The openly recorded contact between England and Greenland starts in 1578 with the visit of Martin Frobisher.

Sir Martin was commissioned by Queen Elizabeth to seek a near way to the Far East by sailing around the north of America, thus continuing the search for the Northwest Passage begun by John Cabot in 1497. He discovered on his first voyage, 1576, what he thought was a strait cutting through North America to the Pacific, but was induced not to attempt following this to the South Sea on his second voyage, 1577, by the discovery of what he thought was gold in vast quantity. We know now that his supposed strait was really a bay in the shore of Baffin Island and that what he thought ordinary gold was fool's gold—iron pyrites.

It was on the third voyage, the second of those that were to fetch gold, that Frobisher in 1578 visited southwestern Greenland. The following quotation is from George Best's narrative as published by the Argonaut Press, 1936, in the volume of documents and comments which was edited by me and published as *The Three Voyages of Martin Frobisher*. Best's original narrative (he accompanied the expedition) was published at London in 1578, and is referred to as the *True Discourse*.

The quotation begins where the Frobisher expedition has rounded Cape Farewell and is about to reach the southern part of the west coast of Greenland, the locality of the Gardabishopric Christians. Best did not know that this was Greenland but called it instead; West England; his Meta Incognita is Baffin Island, where the expedition had been mining fool's gold the previous two summers.

Frobisher in the North

◢ The twentieth of June, at two of the clock in the morning, the General descried land, and found it to be West Freeseland now named West England. Here the General and other gentlemen went ashore, being the first known Christians that we have true notice of that ever set foot upon that ground; and therefore the General took possession thereof to the use of our sovereign lady the Queen's Majesty, and discovered here a goodly harbor for the ships, where there were also certain little boats of that country. And being there landed, they espied certain tents and people of that country, which were (as they judge) in all sorts very like those of Meta Incognita [Baffin Island], as by their apparel, and other things which we found in their tents, appeared.

The savage and simple people, so soon as they perceived our men coming toward them (supposing there had been no other world but theirs) fled fearfully away, as men much amazed at so strange a sight, and creatures of human shape so far in apparel, complexion, and other things different from themselves. They left in their tents all their furniture for haste behind them, where amongst other things were found a box of small nails, and certain red herrings, boards of fir tree well cut, with divers other things artificially wrought, whereby it appeareth that they have trade with some civil people, or else are indeed themselves artificial workmen.

Our men brought away with them only two of their dogs, leaving in recompense bells, looking-glasses, and divers of our country toys behind them.

This country no doubt promiseth good hope of great commodity and riches, if it may be well discovered . . .

Some are of opinion that this West England is firm land with the northeast parts of Meta Incognita, or else with Greenland. And their reason is because the people, apparel, boats, and other things are so like to theirs. And another reason is the multitude of islands of ice which lie between it and Meta Incognita doth argue that on the north side there is a bay, which cannot be but by conjoining of these two lands together.

And having a fair and large wind, we departed from thence toward Frobishers straits the three and twentieth of June. 🦋

Since this is a book that deals chiefly with how Europeans discovered various countries, and since the vanishing of the

10,000 Christians of the Greenland bishopric is one of the tantalizing mysteries, the story of the first recorded modern landing in Greenland is given over again from the point of view of a second chronicler, another of Frobisher's companions, Edward Sellman:

The twentieth of June, 1578, early in the morning, the General caused a small pinnace to be hoisted out of the *Ayde*, and with her he passed aboard the *Gabriel*, and did bear in with the land, sailing along it until he found a sound to enter in upon the south side of the land. Which sound after he was entered, called it Luke's Sound, by reason of one Luke Ward that went with him a-land; in which sound they found people and tents, but the people fled from them, and they entered their tents, finding thereby by all things therein that they are a people like the people of Meta Incognita with like boats of all sorts. But the General doth take them to be a more delicate people in lodging and feeding than the others.

They found of their seals which they had taken sundry, and other victual which they could not tell what flesh or fish it was. At their said tent they found also forty young whelps, whereof two they brought away with them. They are also like the dogs of the place aforenamed.

Some of our men that were with the General a-land did see in their tent nails like scupper nails, and a trivet of iron, but the General took order with the company that none should bring any of their things away.

The Sellman reference to the people of Greenland as more "delicate" than the Eskimos of Baffin Island and the Best reference to them as more "civil" are both of them indications of European contact. The iron trivet is proof of this contact.

Next of record as voyaging to Greenland is John Davis, for whom Davis Strait is named. He had a better opportunity than Frobisher to see the people and describe them. He did not know what an Eskimo should look like; nor did he realize when he went ashore near where now is the Danish trading station and administrative center of Godthaab, that he was in

a neighborhood where there had been in the Middle Ages
European colonists the complexions and features of whom he
might possibly discern as a result of those intermarriages with
the heathen (Eskimos) which we infer to have been frequent
because the Church inveighed so against them.

But in our eyes, the very unawareness of men like Frobisher
and Davis that such problems might exist gives added value to
whatever they say that has a bearing. The narrative which follows is from the Hakluyt Society's *The Voyages and Works of
John Davis the Navigator*, edited by Albert Hastings Markham, London, 1880. The quotation begins where Davis is
about to go ashore for the first time in southern West Greenland
on his first expedition in search of the Northwest Passage, 1585:

Narrative of John Davis

The twenty-ninth of July we discovered land in 64 degrees
15 minutes of latitude, bearing northeast from us. The wind
being contrary to go to the northwestward, we bore in with
this land to take some view of it, being utterly void of the
pester of ice, and very temperate. Coming near the coast, we
found many fair sounds and good roads for shipping, and many
great inlets into the land, whereby we judged this land to be
a great number of islands standing together. Here, having
moored our bark in good order, we went on shore upon a
small island to seek for water and wood.

Upon this island we did perceive that there had been
people, for we found a small shoe and pieces of leather sewed
with sinews, and a piece of fur, and wool like to beaver. Then
we went upon another island on the other side of our ships.
And the Captain, the master, and I being got up to the top
of a high rock, the people of the country, having espied us,
made a lamentable noise, as we thought, with great outcries
and screechings. We, hearing them, thought it had been the
howling of wolves.

At last I hallooed again, and they likewise cried. Then we,
perceiving where they stood, some on the shore, and one
rowing in a canoe about a small island fast by them, we made
a great noise, partly to allure them to us and partly to warn
our company of them. Whereupon M. Bruton, and the master

of his ship, with others of their company, made great haste toward us, and brought our musicians with them from our ship, purposing either by force to rescue us, if need should so require, or with courtesy to allure the people. When they came unto us, we caused our musicians to play, ourselves dancing and making many signs of friendship.

At length there came ten canoes from the other islands, and two of them came so near the shore where we were that they talked with us, the others being in their boats a pretty way off. Their pronunciation was very hollow through the throat, and their speech such as we could not understand; only we allured them by friendly embracings and signs of courtesy.

At length one of them, pointing up to the sun with his hands, would presently strike his breast so hard that we might hear the blow. This he did many times before he would any way trust us. Then John Ellis, the master of the *Moonshine*, was appointed to use his best policy to gain their friendship; who struck his breast and pointed to the sun after their order; which when he had diverse times done, they began to trust him, and one of them came on shore, to whom we threw our caps, stockings, and gloves, and such other things as then we had about us, playing with our music and making signs of joy and dancing.

So, the night coming, we bade them farewell and went aboard our barks.

The next morning, being the thirtieth of July, there came thirty-seven canoes rowing by our ships, calling to us to come on shore. We not making any great haste unto them, one of them went up to the top of the rock and leapt and danced as they had done the day before, showing us a seal's skin, and another thing made like a timbrel, which he did beat upon with a stick, making a noise like a small drum. Whereupon we manned our boats and came to them, they all staying in their canoes. We came to the waterside where they were; and after we had sworn by the sun after their fashion, they did trust us. So I shook hands with one of them, and he kissed my hand, and we were very familiar with them.[2]

---

[2] If it be correct that the local people kissed the hands of the Europeans, in anything other than mere imitation of the Davis party, it is a sign that they themselves had this custom from Europe, either through having pre-

We were in so great credit with them upon this single acquaintaince that we could have anything they had. We bought five canoes of them. We bought their clothes from their backs, which were all made of sealskins and bird skins; their buskins, their hose, their gloves, all being commonly sewed and well dressed, so that we were fully persuaded that they have divers artificers among them. We had a pair of buskins of them full of fine wool like beaver. Their apparel for heat was made of birds' skins with their feathers on them. We saw among them leather dressed like glover's leather, and thick thongs like white leather of a good length.

We had of their darts and oars, and found in them that they would by no means displease us, but would give us whatsoever we gave them. They took great care one of another; for when we had bought their boats, then two others would come and carry him [the former owner] away between them that had sold us his. They are a very tractable people, void of craft or double dealing, and easy to be brought to any civility or good order. But we judge them to be idolaters and to worship the sun.

During the time of our abode among these islands, we found reasonable quantity of wood, both fir, spruce, and juniper; which, whether it grew in some great islands near the same place by us not yet discovered, we know not. But we judge that it groweth there further into the land than we were, because the people had great store of darts and oars, which they made none account of, but gave them to us for small trifles, as points and pieces of paper.

We saw about this coast marvelous great abundance of seals schooling together like schools of small fish. We found no fresh water among these islands, but only snow water, whereof we found great pools. The cliffs were all of such ore as M. Frobisher brought from Meta Incognita. We had diverse shows of study or Muscovy glass [mica] shining not altogether unlike to crystal.

---

served it as inheritance from the white element in their ancestry, the medieval Christians, or having learned it from recent visitors, possibly Bristol merchants or whalers from some other European country. For kissing is not an Eskimo custom, whether of lips or hands—nor is rubbing of noses except between mother and child, or more especially grandmother and grandchild.

We found an herb growing upon the rocks whose fruit was sweet, full of red juice, and the ripe ones were like currants. We found also birch and willow growing like shrubs low to the ground.

[The Davis expedition now stood toward Baffin Island, and then turned south toward Labrador. The account passes to the following summer, 1586, when they were again on the southern west coast of Greenland, in the neighborhood of the old European settlements.]

The ships being within the sounds [the present Godthaab Fjord, which Davis called Gilbert Sound], we sent our boats to search for shoal water where we might anchor, which in this place is very hard to find. And as the boat went sounding and searching, the people of the country, having espied them, came in their canoes toward them with many shouts and cries. But after they had espied in the boat some of our company that were the year before here with us, they presently rowed to the boat and took hold on the oar, and hung about the boat with such comfortable joy as would require a long discourse to be uttered. They came with the boats to our ships, making signs that they knew all those that the year before had been with them.

After I perceived their joy and small fear of us, myself with the merchants and others of the company went ashore, bearing with me twenty knives. I had no sooner landed but they leapt out of their canoes and came running to me and the rest, and embraced us with many signs of hearty welcome. At this present there were eighteen of them, and to each of them I gave a knife. They offered skins to me for reward, but I made signs that it was not sold, but given them of courtesy, and so dismissed them for that time, with signs that they should return again after certain hours.

The next day, with all possible speed, the pinnace was landed upon an isle, there to be finished, to serve our purpose for the discovery, which isle was so convenient for that purpose as that we were very well able to defend ourselves against many enemies. During the time that the pinnace was there setting up, the people came continually unto us, sometime a hundred canoes at a time, sometime forty, fifty, more or less as occasion served. They brought with them sealskins, stag skins, white hares, seal fish, salmon peal, small cod, dry capelin, with other fish and birds such as the country did yield.

Myself, still desirous to have a farther search of this place, sent one of the ship boats to one part of the land, and myself went to another part, to search for the habitation of this people, with strait commandment that there should be no injury offered to any of the people, neither any gun shot.

The boats that went from me found the tents of the people made with sealskins set up upon timber, wherein they found great store of dried capelin, being a little fish no bigger than a pilchard. They found bags of train oil, many little images cut in wood, sealskins in tan tubs, with many other such trifles, whereof they diminished nothing.

They also found, 10 miles within the snowy mountains, a plain champaign country, with earth and grass, such as our moory and waste grounds of England are. They went up into a river (which in the narrowest place is 2 leagues broad) about 10 leagues, finding it still to continue they knew not how far. But I, with my company, took another river,[3] which although at the first it offered a large inlet, yet it proved but a deep bay, the end whereof in four hours I attained, and there leaving the boat well manned, went with the rest of my company 3 or 4 miles into the country, but found nothing, nor saw anything, save only gripes [falcons], ravens, and small birds, as lark and linnet.

The third of July I manned my boat and went, with fifty canoes attending upon me, up into another sound, where the people by signs willed me to go, hoping to find their habitation. At length they made signs that I should go into a warm place to sleep, at which place I went ashore and ascended the top of a high hill to see into the country. But perceiving my labor vain, I returned again to my boat, the people still following me and my company, very diligent to attend us and to help us up the rocks, and likewise down.

At length I was desirous to have our men leap with them, which was done, but our men did overleap them. From leaping

---

[3] Evidently these "rivers" were narrow fjords.

they went to wrestling; we found them strong and nimble, and to have skill in wrestling, for they cast some of our men that were good wrestlers.

The fourth of July we launched our pinnace, and had forty of the people to help us, which they did very willingly. At this time our men again wrestled with them, and found them as before, strong and skillful.

This fourth of July the master of the *Mermaid* went to certain islands to store himself with wood, where he found a grave with divers buried in it, only covered with sealskins having a cross laid over them.[4]

The people are of good stature, well in body proportioned, with small slender hands and feet, with broad visages, and small eyes, wide mouths, the most part unbearded, great lips, and close-toothed. Their custom is as often as they go from us, still at their return to make a new truce; in this sort, holding his hand up to the sun, with a loud voice crieth *Ylyaoute*, and striketh his breast. With like signs being promised safety, he giveth credit. These people are much given to bleed, and therefore stop their noses with deer hair, or the hair of an elan [caribou].

They are idolaters, and have images great store, which they wear about them and in their boats, which we suppose they worship. They are witches, and have many kinds of enchantments, which they often used, but to small purpose, thanks be to God.

Being among them at shore the fourth of July, one of them, making a long oration, began to kindle a fire in this manner:

---

[4] Of the grave with a cross upon it, Admiral A. H. Markham, himself a famous polar explorer, says in his introduction to the Davis volume: "It is possible that this spot was the last resting place of some of the old Norman colonists of South Greenland, those settlers in the East and West Bygd, whose fate, to this day, is involved in mystery."

The alternative to Markham's suggestion that the people here were (mixed-blood) descendants of the Christian Norsemen of the medieval republic is that there might have been recent European visitors from whom the custom of using the cross at a grave could have been derived. It does, truly, seem probable that there were European whalers and traders in these waters occasionally, both before and after Frobisher; but it does not seem as probable that the burial customs of the people were affected by these visitors as that the use of the cross had been inherited from European ancestors.

He took a piece of a board wherein was a hole half-through. Into that hole he puts the end of a round stick like unto a bed-staff, wetting the end thereof in train [oil], and in fashion of a turner, with a piece of leather, by his violent motion doth very speedily produce fire. Which done, with turfs he made a fire, into which, with many words and strange gestures, he put divers things, which we supposed to be a sacrifice.

Myself and divers of my company standing by, they were desirous to have me go into the smoke. I willed them likewise to stand in the smoke, which they by no means would do. I then took one of them and thrust him into the smoke, and willed one of my company to tread out the fire and to spurn it into the sea, which was done to show them that we did contemn their sorcery.

These people are very simple in all their conversation, but marvelous thievish, especially for iron, which they have in great account. They began through our lenity to show their vile nature. They began to cut our cables; they cut away the *Moon-light's* boat from her stern; they cut our cloth where it lay to air, though we did carefully look unto it; they stole our oars, a caliver [small hand gun], a boar spear, a sword, with divers other things. Whereat the company and masters, being grieved, for our better security desired me to dissolve this new friendship, and to leave the company of these thievish miscreants. Whereupon there was a caliver shot among them, and immediately upon the same a falcon [small cannon], which strange noise did sore amaze them, so that with speed they departed.

Nothwithstanding, their simplicity is such that within ten hours after they came again to us to entreat peace; which being promised, we again fell into a great league. They brought us sealskins, and salmon peal, but seeing iron, they could in no wise forbear stealing. Which when I perceived it, it did but minister unto me an occasion of laughter, to see their simplicity, and willed that in no case they should be any more vigilant to keep their things, supposing it to be very hard in so short time to make them know their evils.

They eat all their meat raw, they live most upon fish, they drink salt water, and eat grass and ice with delight. They are never out of the water, but live in the nature of fishes, but only when dead sleep taketh them, and then under a warm rock, laying his boat upon the land, he lieth down to sleep.

Their weapons are all darts, but some of them have bow and arrows and slings.

They make nets to take their fish, of the fin of a whale. They do all their things very artificially. And it should seem that these simple thievish islanders have war with those of the main, for many of them are sore wounded, which wounds they received upon the mainland, as by signs they gave us to understand. We had among them copper ore, black copper and red copper. They pronounce their language very hollow, and deep in the throat. ⚑

In the last few paragraphs Davis attributes three things to the Greenlanders of the Godthaab region which, if correctly reported, are signs of European influence.

1. The narrative says that the people drank salt water. But Eskimos, wherever they have been carefully observed while as yet uninfluenced by whites, are particular to avoid all taste of salt in food or drink, while the use of salt with food (and with some drinks, such as beer) is a common practice in Europe, Africa, and large parts of Asia. When first visited by white men, most of the Forest Indians of Canada avoided salt, as well as the Canadian Eskimos. It is a habit to which they take readily, however, when they see Europeans salting their food.

2. These Greenlanders were found to be using nets, which is a non-Eskimo trait. Along the north coast of Alaska, for instance, nets came in so recently, from the West, that the grandparents of men still living in 1906 remembered when first a net was used at the Mackenzie River delta. Fish nets, in pre-white-man times, never got more than some 300 miles east beyond the Mackenzie.

3. The alleged eating of "grass" is a strange trait if given for real Eskimos, who normally eat vegetable food only in time of famine. The eating of vegetables is, however, a common European practice, which is known to have been brought by the Norwegians and Irish to Iceland in colonial times and

which would have been taken by the Icelandic settlers to Greenland, thus giving the custom a chance to survive among their descendants.

John Davis, who prints the first reasonably good description of the people of Greenland that has been preserved in modern literature, does not mention further traits that might reasonably connect the men he saw with the lost Europeans. But the people he saw were mainly on the promontories and islands of the Godthaab neighborhood, so there were perhaps considerable numbers of other Greenlanders not far away whom he did not see. We infer this from the difference between his description of the physical appearance of the natives and that of a visitor of seventy years later, Nicolas Tunes.

The Tunes account is the most remarkable of early modern descriptions of the Greenland people, one of the most particular and (I judge) accurate descriptions that have come to us deriving from the early exploration of the North American Arctic. It is also one of the least-known of descriptions, and for a good and curious reason, since it is concealed in a *Natural and Moral History of the West Indies!*

The book was little known, if at all, to northern scholarship until there was, in 1912, a newspaper furor about whether there were "blond Eskimos" in the Canadian Arctic. One of the frequent assertions was that if such existed they would have been reported by earlier travelers, whereupon people started writing in to call attention to earlier reports—by Franklin in the 1820's, by Simpson in the 1830's, and so on.

One of the letters on the "blond-Eskimo" problems came from a distinguished Scottish anthropologist who had been working in a library on tropical matters, who had also been reading the newspaper assertions that no one had ever reported "blond" people from the American Arctic, and who now informed the London scientific journal *Nature* that he had come upon one such report, from 1656, an account of two kinds of people living in the same district, one kind described as if they might be Eskimos and the other as if they might be to a considerable extent of European blood.

The document to which David MacRitchie called attention is of such curious interest, of such possible historical and anthropological importance, that the full text of the relevant section, is printed here.

The *Histoire naturelle et morale des Iles Antilles de l'Amérique* was printed anonymously. It was almost certainly written by Charles de Rochefort, but claims for the authorship have been made on behalf of César de Rochefort and also on behalf of Louis de Poincy. It first appeared in Rotterdam, 1658. There is a second edition, Rotterdam, 1665, and we have in English a paraphrase, or free translation, by John Davies, London, 1666, *The History of the Caribby-Islands*, now rare. We have made our own translation from the Rotterdam edition of 1658, pp. 188-204. Says De Rochefort:

The Account of Nicolas Tunes

As we were about to publish this work a ship from Flushing commanded by Nicolas Tunes—in which M. the Burgomaster Lampson, who is now Deputy of his province in the Assembly of the States-General, M. Biens, M. Sandra, and other merchants of the same city were interested—having safely returned from Davis Strait, brought thence among other rarities several excellent trophies of those narwhals of the north sea of which we have just spoken.

Since the account sent us from this voyage can throw considerable light on the subject with which we are dealing, we believe that the curious reader will think it proper that we give him this novelty as a digression, and we shall do so, giving him the news as accurately as we received it.

The captain from whom we received this account left Zealand late in the spring of 1656, planning to open new commerce with northern lands, and arrived toward the end of June in Davis Strait. He called first at a fjord in 64 degrees and ten minutes north, and then sailed to the 72d degree, to the land we are going to describe.

The inhabitants of the country, who were fishing when they saw the vessel, came out to examine it in their little skiffs [kayaks], which carry only one person. The first who came were followed by so many others that in a short time they formed an escort of seventy of these little vessels, which did not

leave the strange ship until it had anchored in the best roadstead. There they demonstrated by exclamations, and by all
signs of friendliness that one could expect from a people so
little civilized, their extraordinary joy in this safe arrival. These
little vessels are so admirable, whether one considers their
material, the marvelous ingenuity by which they are fashioned,
or the incomparable dexterity by which they are managed,
that they well deserve to hold first place in the descriptions
that this pleasant digression affords us.

They are made of small, slender strips of wood, most of which
are split like hoops. These slats are fastened together by strong
cords of fish gut [probably seal rawhide thongs] which keep
them in place and give them the proper shape for their intended use. They are covered on the outside with sealskins,
which are so neatly sewn together and the seams so carefully
coated with gum [gummy seal oil; seal tar] that no water
can penetrate them.

These little boats are ordinarily 15 to 16 feet long; in the
center, where they are widest, they may have a circumference
of about 5 feet. From here they begin to narrow, so that they
end in points tipped with white bones or tusks of the narwhal
of which we have spoken. The upper part is flat and covered
with skin like the rest; the underpart has the shape of the belly
of a great fish, so that they are well adapted to glide over
the water. They have only one opening, which is directly in the
middle of the craft. This opening has a raised edge of whalebone all around, and it is made in proportion to and of the
size of a man's body.

When the savages who invented this type of little vessel
desire to use them, whether for going fishing or for amusing
themselves on the sea, they thrust their legs and thighs into
this opening and, having seated themselves, they fasten the
cassock which covers them so tightly to the edge of this opening that they seem to be grafted on the skiff and to be a
part of it.

So much for the shape and material of these little vessels;
let us now consider the dress of the men who use them. When
they intend to go to sea, they cover their other clothes over
with a cassock, which is designed for no other use. This sea

garment is made of several skins, with the hair removed, which are so well prepared and joined together that you would think it to be made of a single piece. It covers them from the top of the head to below the navel. It is coated all over with a blackish gum [seal tar], which does not dissolve in water and which prevents it from leaking.

The hood which covers the head fits so tightly under the neck and on the forehead that it leaves nothing but the face uncovered. The sleeves are tied at the wrist, and the bottom of this cassock is also fastened to the edge of the vessel's opening with so much care and with such skill that the body thus covered is always dry in the midst of the waves, which, with all their efforts, can wet only the face and hands.

Although they have neither sails, mast, rudder, compass, anchor, nor any piece of all that paraphernalia which is required to render our ships capable of going to sea, they nevertheless undertake long voyages with these little skiffs, into which they seem to be sewn. They have a thorough knowledge of the stars, and they have need of no other guide during the night.

The oars they use broaden at each end to form a paddle, and that they may more easily cut the waves and may last longer, they tip them with a white bone; they also adorn the edges of the paddles with bone, attached with pegs of horn, which serve them in place of nails. The middle of these oars is embellished with bone or with precious horn, as are the ends, and it is there that they hold them so they may not slip out of their hands.

And they handle these double oars with so much dexterity and speed that their little vessels easily outdistance ships under full sail that have favorable wind and tide.

They are so bold in their skiffs, and so adroit in directing them, that they do a thousand caracoles for the entertainment of those who are watching. They also sometimes try their skill against the waves with so much force and agility that they make them foam as if they had been agitated by a violent tempest, at which times one might rather take them for sea-battling monsters than for men.

To show they are without fear, and that they are masters

of this element which nourishes and caresses them, they twirl, plunge, and roll in the sea, making as many as three consecutive [sidewise] somersaults, so that they might pass for true amphibians.

When they intend to make voyages longer than ordinary, or when they fear being carried out into the open sea by a gale, they carry in the empty space of their vessel a bladder of fresh water to quench their thirst and some sun-dried or frost-preserved fish to eat instead of fresh meat.

But it rarely happens that they are compelled to resort to these provisions, for they have arrows that are like small spears which are fastened to their boats and which they hurl so deftly at fish [sea mammals] they meet with that they seldom lack fresh food. They do not need fire to cook their meat, for both at sea and on land they are accustomed to eating their food raw. They carry the teeth of certain great fish [that is, narwhal or walrus tusks] or pieces of sharpened bone, which serve them in place of knives to dress and cut up the fish they have taken.

There can be no altercation in these vessels, since one and the same man is master, sailor, purser, and pilot. He can stop his craft when he pleases or let it go before wind and tide while he secures the rest necessary to restore his strength. In the latter case he fastens his paddle by some deerskin straps which are designed for that purpose and which are attached by bands to the upper part of the boat; or else he ties the paddle to a ring which hangs at the front of his cassock.

Women do not use these little skiffs at all; but so that they may amuse themselves on the sea occasionally, their husbands, who have a great deal of gentleness and affection for them, take them out in other vessels [umiaks] about the size of our longboats and capable of carrying fifty persons. These are made of long slats tied together and are covered with sealskins, like the other [boats] we have described. When the weather is calm they are propelled by oars; when there is wind they hoist leather sails on their masts. . . .

As to the country in which these skilled navigators live, the latitude we have mentioned is witness enough that the climate is frigid. It is true that during the months of June and July, which make up the summer of this country and which are lightened by perpetual day (just as December and January are only a single night), the air is pleasantly warm and serene; but during the rest of the year the days, which first lengthen and then shorten, are accompanied by dense fogs, snow, or sleet, so the weather is cold and unpleasant.

The land near the sea is barren and bristling with naked rocks, which are as frightful as possible; and when the snow melts it is largely inundated by many dreadful torrents which pour their troubled waters into the vast bosom of the sea. But when one has negotiated a short league of very bad going, one comes to beautiful country, which is carpeted during the summer with an agreeable verdure. There are also mountain slopes covered with small trees which marvelously refresh the eye, and which support a great multitude of land birds and water-fowl. One traverses valleys that are watered by many clear and pleasant streams that reach the sea.

The commander of this ship from Flushing, from whose late voyage we have this account, examined the land carefully with a party of his men and found among other things worthy of notice a vein of a certain brown earth, studded with glittering and silvery spangles, with which he filled a cask so that it might be tested; but when it was placed in a crucible it was found to be suitable only for encrusting the tops of boxes and such other small wooden things, to which it gives a beautiful luster. Nevertheless this substance gives some hope that silver mines might be found if one went further inland.

Although the land is cold, there are many large and beautiful birds of a black-and-white plumage, and of various other colors, which the inhabitants dress so as to eat the flesh and to clothe themselves with the skins. One finds there also deer, elk, bears, foxes, hares, rabbits, and an abundance of other four-footed beasts, almost all with white or grayish fur, very thick, long, soft, and very suitable for making good hats or beautiful and valuable commercial furs.

As for the people who inhabit this country, our travelers saw two sorts, who live together in good accord and perfect amity. One kind are of tall stature, well built physically, rather fair of complexion, and very fleet of foot. The others are very much smaller, olive-complexioned, fairly well-proportioned save that their legs are short and thick. The first delight in hunting, to which they are inclined by their agility and their great natural aptness; the others pursue fishing.[5] Both kinds have very white and close set teeth, black hair, bright eyes, and such regular features that no striking deformity could be seen. They are also all so vigorous and of such a strong constitution that many were seen who, having passed their hundredth year, still were very alert and robust.

In their ordinary relations they seem cheerful, hardy, and courageous. They like the strangers who visit them, because they bring them needles, fishhooks, knives, bill hooks, hatchets, and all the other iron tools which are useful to them, and which they value so highly that they purchase them at the price of their own clothes and of all that they hold most precious. But they are such foes of innovation when their clothes and food are concerned that it would be very difficult to make them accept any change in either. Although they are one of the poorest and most barbarous nations under the sun, they believe themselves to be very happy and the best-favored people in the world. And they have such a good opinion of their manner of life that the civilities of all other peoples appear to them as unseemly, savage, and most ridiculous.

This high esteem of their present condition contributes not a little to that satisfaction and to that contentment of spirit which one reads in their faces. They do not interest themselves in the vanity of many schemes which might disturb their tranquility. They know nothing of all those gnawing cares and besetting sorrows which torment most other peoples in their inordinate desire for riches. The luxury of fine and sumptuous buildings, worldly glory, the delights of banquets, the knowl-

---

[5] By the dictionary, the contrast is between hunting and fishing. Evidently, however, the contrast in the writer's mind is between that hunting which is done afoot and the kind done from a boat. In this connection it is well to remember that during the seventeenth century the "Greenland fishery" of Spitsbergen and the "Davis Strait fishery" of West Greenland (in which latter Nicolas Tunes was engaged) had nothing to do with fishing as we understand it; it was wholly concerned with the capture of sea mammals, the whales and seals. In the Elizabethan period, you might have made a successful fishing voyage without ever catching a fish.

edge of beautiful things, and all we consider to be pleasant
and restful in life, has not reached them, and they are thus
not worried by any thought of possessing them, which would
interrupt the smooth tranquility which they enjoy. All their
efforts are directed toward acquiring, without too much trouble,
what is absolutely necessary in the way of clothing and food.

The usual occupations are fishing and hunting. Although they
have neither firearms nor fish nets, necessity has developed
other suitable methods by which they can prosper. They eat
all their food without cooking it, and with no other sauce than
that supplied by their keen appetites. They laugh at those
who cook fish or venison, for they hold that fire destroys the
natural flavor and everything that makes them most palatable.

Although they have no need of fire for cooking their food,
they nevertheless command its wide use, and their caves
are never unprovided with it during winter,[6] as much to
illumine and mitigate by its light the darkness and terror of
the long night which prevails in their country as to temper by
its agreeable warmth the chill that besieges them on all sides.
But when they take their rest, or when they are forced to go
out of their grottoes, they put on a certain fur which by an excellent disposal of Divine Providence has the virtue of protecting them from all the injuries of the cold, even when they lie
in the midst of the snow.

The clothing of the men consists of a shirt, a pair of breeches,
a cassock, and half-boots. The shirt comes only a little below
the waist. It has a hood which covers the head and neck. It is
made of the bladders of great fishes [no doubt slit intestines

---

6 Two things seem to go together throughout the Eskimo world; that travelers
of slight acquaintance with Eskimos report them living in caves or dugouts,
and that no Eskimos have ever been found on careful investigation to live in
either—unless it be that the cousins of the Eskimos, the Aleuts of the North
Pacific, did use caves. Seemingly, the impression that the houses were underground resulted from the common Eskimo custom of having a partially underground passage (roofed trench) leading into the house. These passages are
sometimes 40 or 50 feet long, and are likely to be dark in summer when the
people are living near by in tents, although practically certain to be lighted
in winter when the dwellings are occupied. A stranger going from 30 to 50
feet through a dark, covered passage, and then coming up into a surface-level
dwelling through the floor, may well have the impression that he is underground.

of sea mammals], which are cut into strips of equal width and most neatly sewn together. It has no opening at the breast as ours have, but that it may not tear when putting it on, the ends of the sleeves, the headpiece, and the bottom have a narrow border of black leather. . . .

Their other clothes, and even their half-boots, are also of pieces joined together in the same manner as their shirts, but they are of a much stronger material, deerskins or sealskins perfectly prepared and with the hair on.

The clothes of the savage whose portrait, drawn from life, we place here [omitted] was of skin of two colors, the strips being cut of equal width and arranged in such fine order that one white band was sewn between two dark ones, making a pleasing combination. The hair, which was on the outside, was as smooth and as soft as velvet, and it was so uniformly stretched and the various pieces so perfectly joined together that one would have judged from the outside that the whole garment had been cut from a single skin. . . .

The savages who inhabit this strait never go inland without having across their shoulders a quiver filled with arrows, and a bow or a spear in their hands. Their arrows are of several kinds. Some are for killing hares, foxes, birds, and all sorts of small game; others are designed for killing deer, elk, bears, and other large animals. The former are only 2 or 3 feet long; in place of iron they are tipped with a slender bone, edged and very sharp, which has one side armed with three or four hooks, so that they cannot be pulled away from the place which they have pierced without enlarging the wound.

The latter kind, which are at least 4 or 5 feet long, are armed at the end with a pointed bone, which also has hooks made like the teeth of a saw. They throw these latter with the hand; but to give them greater force and to make them go farther, they attach to their right arm a piece of wood 1½ feet long, with a deep groove in one side into which they put the large end of this javelin, which, being hurled in this manner, has a greater driving force and has a much more powerful effect.

They also sometimes carry in the hand a kind of spear, of a strong and heavy wood, which is tipped at the small end with a round bone whose point has been sharpened on a stone, or else it is provided with those horns or fish teeth which we have already described. These lances are 7 or 8 feet in length, and are embellished at the large end with two pinions of wood, or of whalebone, which give them a little more grace than they would have otherwise.

In addition to many kinds of hooks which they use for catching the small fish that frequent their coasts, they have several kinds of javelins which they know how to throw with unequaled dexterity at the large and monstrous fish [whales, walrus] which they seek in the open sea.

To prevent those wounded with this kind of dart from sinking to the bottom and frustrating their hopes, they fasten to the large end a deer thong 25 or 30 fathoms long, and attach to the end of this strap or thong of leather an inflated bladder which, floating always on top of the water, indicates the place where the fish is. By this they draw their quarry to them, or quietly drag it to land after it has spent itself in struggling.

The young women wear a garment which does not differ much from that of the men, but the old ones are often clad in the skins of certain large birds which have a black-and-white plumage and which are very common in that country. The women know how to flay them so neatly that the feathers remain attached to the skin. These garments reach only to the calf of the leg. They are belted with a leather strap, to which instead of keys there are attached many little bones that are pointed like bodkins, and of about the same length.

They wear neither bracelets nor necklaces nor earrings; as their only ornament they make a gash in each cheek, filling the scar with a certain black color, which in their opinion makes them appear far more attractive.

While the men enjoy themselves hunting or fishing, the women are occupied with sewing clothes and at making tents, baskets, and all the little things necessary for the household. They also take excellent care of the small children, and if they are obliged to move their residence or to accompany their husbands on some journey, they carry or lead the children wherever they go.

To amuse the children on the way, and to quiet them when they cry, they have little drums covered with fish bladders on which they can make such good harmony that the drums of the Basques are not sweeter or more pleasant. They sound the drums also to frighten away the bears and other wild animals which often come prowling near the caves where these savages spend the winter with their families, or around the tents in which they live during the summer.

These poor barbarians do not have much government, but they do have petty kings and captains who govern them, and who preside at all their assemblies. They exalt to these positions those who are the most perfect physically, the best hunters, and the most valiant. These wear better skins and more precious furs than their subjects, and as a token of their importance they wear an insigne in the form of an embroidered rose (*ils portent une enseigne en forme de roze de broderie*), which is stitched to the front of their cassock. When they travel they are always escorted by several young men armed with bows and arrows, who faithfully execute all their commands.[7]

They have not the ingenuity to build houses, but during summer they live in the country in skin tents, which they carry with them to be pitched in any place where they find it convenient to camp; and during winter they live in caves, either natural ones in the mountains or ones which they have contrived to hollow out.

---

[7] If Tunes here describes a folk of pure Eskimo culture, then he is so far from the mark that he must be drawing chiefly upon his imagination. For it is fundamental in Eskimo culture that they are communistic anarchists, where no man has authority over another and where no one could wear insignia of rank or a better dress due to rank. If an Eskimo's clothes are particularly good, it is for one or both of two reasons: that he is a good hunter and/or that his wife or mother is a good seamstress.

But if Tunes is describing not plain Eskimos but a people of mixed Eskimo and Norse Greenlandic culture, then what he says fits the probabilities. For after describing much that is pure Eskimo he outlines just about the social organization and customs that are known to us from the Norse in Greenland through such documents as the *Saga of Erik the Red*, the *Saga of Einar Sokkason*, and the Greenlandic *Lay of Atilla*.

Tunes has said a little earlier that near 72 degrees north latitude were living two kinds of people, one tall and blond, the other dark and short. (No doubt there were transition types.) His cultural description just fits that situation when he describes boats, clothes, and food typically Eskimo (for the short dark people), but social customs typically Norse Greenlandic (for the tall blond ones).

They neither sow nor reap any grain of the earth for the maintenance of their lives. Nor do they have any trees or plants bearing fruits which are fit to eat, with the exception of a few strawberries and a species of raspberry; but they subsist, as we have already intimated, only by their hunting and fishing. Pure water is their ordinary drink, and for their most delicious treat they drink the blood of seals and of deer and other land animals which they have killed or which have fallen into the traps which they prepare with marvelous ingenuity [the typical Eskimo blood soup].

The winter being so long and rigorous in this country, it is impossible for them to avoid much suffering from scarcity during this gloomy season of the year, especially during that dreadful night which envelops them for two whole months.

But they endure hunger easily in case of necessity, and have besides enough foresight so that in summer they dry the surplus of their hunting and fishing and keep it in reserve, with all the fat and tallow which they have been able to collect, as provision for that unpleasant and tiresome season. It is even said that they are so clever at hunting by moonlight that during the thickest gloom which covers them they are rarely unprovided with fresh meats.

They have no curiosity to see any other country than that of their birth; and if it happens that a rough storm or some other chance casts them in a strange country, they everlastingly sigh for their beloved native land, and give themselves no rest until they are restored to it. [8] If that favor is denied them, or too long deferred, they will attempt, at the risk of their lives, to return in their little vessels, in which they are exposed to all the perils of the sea, with no other guide than the stars, of which they have sufficient knowledge to determine the navigation of their course.

Their language has nothing in common with that of any other people of the world. We have a small vocabulary of it; but for fear of lengthening this digression a little too much, we keep it in reserve until the second voyage which is being planned to this strait shall have enlightened us further.

---

[8] There are reports of Eskimos who got lost at sea and landed in Scotland and on the other coasts of Europe.

It has not yet been observed what sort of religion is in use among these poor barbarians; but because they often look at the sun and point it out with admiration, raising their hands aloft, it is inferred that they consider it their god.

The ship which gave us this account returned from Davis Strait laden with much good wares, of which we shall here give a list in order to show that the cold which reigns in that country is not so rigorous that its frost has prevented all manner of commerce.

1. Nine hundred sealskins, most of them from 7 to 8 feet long, spotted and waved with black, russet, yellow, tawny, and several other colors, which enhance their price beyond what is common in Holland.

2. Many valuable skins of deer, elk, bears, foxes, hares, and rabbits, most of which were perfectly white.

3. A great number of precious furs of various four-footed animals which are all peculiar to that region and for which we do not yet have any name.

4. Several packs of whalebone of extraordinary length.

5. Some complete costumes of the inhabitants of the country, some of which were of [animal] skins and others of bird skins, of the fashion that we have described.

6. Several of their shirts made of fish bladders, very neatly sewn; of their caps, gloves, and half-boots; of their quivers, arrows, bows, and other arms which they use, as also several of their tents, bags, baskets, and other little articles of household stuff.

7. A great number of those little sea vessels which are made to carry only one man. A large boat, 45 feet long, which could conveniently carry fifty persons.

8. But the most rare and most precious was a very considerable quantity of the teeth or horns of those fish which are called narwhals [*licornes de mer*—sea unicorns], which are considered to be the largest, the finest, and the best-proportioned of any that have yet been seen.

Some of these were sent to Paris and some to other parts of Europe, where they were well received; but there is great likelihood that they will be even more prized when their admirable medicinal qualities become known. Their beauty and their

rarity must give them first place among the most precious
riches of any cabinet of curiosities, and many celebrated doctors and apothecaries of Denmark and Germany who have
tested them on various occasions consistently testify that they
drive out poison and that they have all the same properties
that are commonly attributed to the horn of the land unicorn
[*licorne de terre*].

This is enough, and perhaps too much for the liking of some,
for a mere digression.

As we read the Tunes account, retailed by De Rochefort,
we marvel at the scrupulous accuracy with which he describes
some things and the lightheartedness with which he in other
places states airy conjecture as if it were staid fact. We know
he is right about such things as the construction, maneuver-
ability and speed of the one-man skin canoe, the kayak, and
about the boatcraft of the Eskimos where they roll over as
much as three times in quick succession, man and boat turning
upside down, the paddler coming up on the other side after
passing under the boat. But where does our author, whether
De Rochefort or Tunes, get his information that some of the
people he saw in excellent health were centenarians? The
difficulty there is not merely linguistic, that Tunes could
scarcely have had any fluent conversations with the local
people. More serious is it, if these were Eskimos, that they
never keep track of such things as birthdays or age.

So far as can be judged at this distance and from a
knowledge of Greenland and of Eskimo culture, it appears that
what Tunes was able to see with his physical eyes he reported
correctly, but that his social interpretations are more revealing
of the European thought of the day than of Greenlandic institutions. However, what is most interesting in his report is a
matter of eyesight—the complexion and stature of the two
kinds of people whom he saw.

Of the "two sorts" he says that "one kind are of tall stature,
well built physically, rather fair of complexion," and this fits
such a mixture of Scandinavian-Irish as moved from Iceland
to become the medieval Greenlanders. It fits, too, a mixed-
blood group of their descendants, if in them the white blood

still predominated. The other sort, who were smaller, are said to have been "olive-complexioned, fairly well-proportioned save that their legs are short and thick," which is a fairly good description of Eskimos, particularly if seen dressed in furs that make their legs appear thick.

Today we are so used to thinking of Scandinavians as great fishermen that we are not prepared thereby for accepting readily that the European Greenlanders (if such they were) would be the land hunters; but it is well known to scholars that the Icelanders have been great fishermen only within the last century or two, depending formerly on animal husbandry. So far as we know the Greenland story, that was also at first the way of the colonists. The Eskimo of the kayak and the umiak is the great seaman—has always been so, particularly in western Greenland, since first we knew of him.

There is not anywhere in the Tunes account, or elsewhere in the De Rochefort book, any indication that either of them knew that European Christians had disappeared in Greenland from the eyes of Europe. That there is no suggestion that the tall and fair people might be European makes it seem the more probable that Tunes did describe correctly what he saw.

In 1722, sixty-six years after Tunes, when the Norwegian Hans Egede planted in western Greenland the first mission of the Lutheran Church—acting on behalf of the Danish Government, which then claimed rule over both Norway and Greenland—he was in definite search for the lost Europeans. What he looked for was Norse-speaking Roman Catholics whom he was prepared to convert to Lutheranism. He had no idea what a "pure-blood" Eskimo ought to look like, so he accepted as a true Eskimo type whatever he saw. But he did describe the people in such a way that to those who know that the "true" Eskimo should look approximately Chinese, there are signs that Egede really did observe mixed-bloods, though apparently few that had more than perhaps a half-white appearance.

A Norwegian sociologist, Eilert Sundt, has summed up the case for Greenland in his book on the first Greenland missionary in *Egedes Dagbok I Udtag* (Extracts from Egede's Diary), Christiania, 1860, from which I translate.

◤ It is by no means settled that the Norwegian population was completely destroyed by the Eskimos. . . . When the connection with the mother country stopped so that the Norsemen [in Greenland] had to get along without such things as iron for tools and clergymen for the maintenance of divine service, it will be understood that the Norse culture and way of living was no longer possible. But it was possible to live in the Eskimo manner.

Then it could have happened—although it is very embarrassing for us to think about it—that one and another of the Norse families had to make friends with the Eskimos, take up their manner of living, and begin to travel with them along the coast, where there is most food. With this way of life all better things would soon be forgotten, and now it might happen that a Norse girl preferred an Eskimo kayak-paddler as a suitor and master to a less successful family-supporter of Norse descent. . . .

While the genuine Eskimos were easy [for Egede] to recognize from their black, stiff hair, a rather dark complexion, low stature, and an inclination to fatness, Rink found so much European appearance among the Greenlanders that he assumes there has been a considerable mixing with Norse blood from the time of the old settlement. . . .

We are not accustomed to think that a population of higher education, Christian and relatively civilized, would fall so low, and disappear in mixing with a crude race. But that a population like the Norse in Greenland, which had been living there four hundred years, should disappear completely is just as rare an occurrence. . . . And when we, in our own time and in our own country, learn that the Norwegians in small out-of-the-way districts in Finmark mix with the Laplanders in marriage and associate with them so that the Laplanders' language and way of life becomes prevalent among the children, or at least the grandchildren, of the mixed families, then you can understand that this may also have been the case with our former countrymen [Norwegians] in the desperate circumstances of Greenland. . . .

Egede had probably expected to find recognizable countrymen of his own; but the indefatigable way in which he took care of the "savages" that he found there will please us still more when there is reason to think that the remains of the Norse population really had assimilated with the Eskimos, so that he—though without understanding what he saw—had on his journey south a glimpse of his countrymen's fair hair and blue eyes. 📖

Not recognizing what they saw, and believing they knew in any case that the Western Settlement had been destroyed by Eskimos centuries before, the missionaries no doubt passed along to the Eskimos a combination of the theories they evolved and the beliefs they held. At any rate, there soon appeared among the Eskimos a cycle of stories purporting to relate how the Eskimos had exterminated the Europeans.

But, as Nansen has shown in his two-volume *In Northern Mists* (Stokes, 1911) and as I have supported him in showing through my *Greenland*, there is no sound reason to believe anything else than that the view sketched above by Eilert Sundt is the correct one. In a hunting country a small colony of farmers, when once cut off in the main from European support, commercial and moral, found themselves locally an inferior people, less successful in making a living. So, rather than die, they tacitly acknowledged the superiority of the Eskimos by learning their methods of hunting and other ways of life, at the same time adopting the Eskimo tongue.

Apparently one of the last things to which the Greenlanders clung from their European ways and Christian days was the symbolism of the cross. For Davis, who recognized no other European trait, was able to report from latitude 64 degrees, in the present Godthaab district, that the people were still in the habit of laying crosses upon the graves of their dead. (True, Frobisher, eight years before, had noticed in the same locality that the people were more civilized than the Eskimos of Baffin Island.)

That Tunes saw a more European-like people 500 miles farther north, at latitude 72 degrees in the Svartenhuk region, is consonant with our expectations. For the last Icelandic records show that in the fourteenth century the Greenlanders were depending increasingly on hunting, and conditions for

hunting are well known to improve along the west coast of
Greenland as you go north. Indeed, runic inscriptions of
Christian tenor have been found along this coast as far north
as 100 miles beyond the Tunes latitude, some 20 miles north
of Upernivik.

Most significant of the northward spread of European culture in the late Middle Ages are the camp-site excavations
made just before World War II along the Inglefield Coast, latitude 79 degrees, about 450 miles north of where Tunes had
been. Reports in the Danish press, confirmed by a personal
letter from Dr. Erik Holtved, the archaeologist who did the
excavating, are to the effect that here lived at one time people
who were either Eskimos strongly influenced by European
culture or Europeans who had partly adopted an Eskimo way
of life.

The Egede missionaries were, following 1722, the first
modern Europeans who ever could talk freely with the local
people. By that time the Greenlanders had forgotten what they
probably would have been able to tell Davis a hundred and
forty years before, about why they laid a cross upon the graves
of their dead. Some believe that in the same period Europe
had forgotten correspondingly about Greenland. Two documents have a bearing on this question. The first is *The King's
Mirror*, a book published around the middle of the thirteenth
century which shows what it was that Europe then knew about
Greenland; the second is a compendium of sailing directions
written about a hundred years later by a Norwegian just returned from Greenland, which was preserved in such form that
Henry Hudson was able to use it in his work during the first
decade of the seventeenth century.

Medieval Europe's knowledge of Greenland was not, of
course, uniform throughout all countries. The sportsmen of
most or all lands knew a deal more than the average person,
through their interest in the land from which some of the best
falcons came. These sportsmen were both the temporal and the
spiritual nobility of the day—they were kings, earls and barons,
cardinals, bishops and deans, with their hangers-on. The clergy
knew about the Greenland bishopric of Gardar through the
collection of tithes there and through such letters of the

Popes as those already mentioned. But the knowledge was most uniform in the Scandinavian countries, for they were nearest to Greenland, jurisdictionally, commercially, and in ties of blood.

The Icelanders were best informed of all, as we can tell from their sagas and annals. That Norway came next is shown by many things, but by nothing so clearly as by the writing and publication there of the *Speculum Regale*, known more widely by its Old Norse title *Konungs Skuggsja*, (*The King's Mirror*), a book which has been spoken of by Dr. George Sarton in his recent and great *Introduction to the History of Science* (2 vols., Williams & Wilkins, 1927-31) as "the most important geographical work of Christendom in the first half of the thirteenth century."

From the *Mirror* we see that while the Norwegians of the thirteenth century still believed in fabulous creatures of the Greenland sea, such as mermen and mermaids, they also had of the land and its surroundings a knowledge which, when separated from the then conventional mythology, indicates a more realistic grip on things up there than was shown by North American and European school geographies until within our time. For instance, our kindergartens and primary schools are still singing "For in Greenland there is nothing green to grow," while the well-instructed Norwegian prince of the Middle Ages, who used *The King's Mirror* as a textbook, learned that dairying was one of the chief industries of Greenland.

Available in Latin as well as in Norwegian and Old Norse (Icelandic), the *Mirror*, composed between 1220 and 1260, must have made a considerable impression on Europe, though one that faded with distance away from the Scandinavian lands.[9]

The second document bearing on the question contains the sailing directions carried by Henry Hudson when he searched for the Northwest Passage. The directions are of importance because they show that much factual information about Greenland survived in Europe from the time of the Norse colonization to the period during which Virginia, Massachusetts, and

[9] For extensive quotations from *The King's Mirror*, see my *Greenland*.

New York were colonized from England and the Netherlands.

Purchas was first to print the manuscript, which is described by Hudson himself as, in his spelling:

"A Treatise of Iver Boty [Ivar Bardarson] a Gronlander, translated out of the Norsh language into High Dutch, in the yeere 1560. And after out of High Dutch, into Low Dutch, by William Barentson of Amsterdam, who was chiefe pilot aforesaid. The same copie in High Dutch is in the hands of Iodocus Hondius, which I have seene. And this was translated out of Low Dutch by Master William Stere, Marchent, in the yeere 1608, for the use of me Henrie Hudson. William Barentsons Booke is in the hands of Master Peter Plantius, who lent the same to me."

Bardarson's treatise, written about the middle of the fourteenth century, gives directions for sailing from Norway to eastern Iceland and thence to southwestern Greenland. Continuing along the west coast of Greenland, there are descriptions of the principal fjords and of the churches and settlements of the Norse colonists. While having a high degree of accuracy in many respects, the document shows too that during the more than two centuries that intervened between Bardarson and Hudson the facts which constitute the larger part of the manuscript got mixed with some misinformation.

The sailing directions carried by Hudson contain some passages that do not derive from the original work of Bardarson. Among these is the statement:

"This sea card was found in the isles of Ferro or Farre [Faeroe] lying between Shot-lant and Island [Shetland and Iceland], in an old reckoning book, written above one hundred years ago [i.e., around 1500, thus at the time of Columbus], out of which this was all taken.

"Item Punnus [Pining] and Potharse [Pothorst] have inhabited Island [Iceland] certain years, and sometimes have gone to sea, and have had their trade in Groneland [Greenland]. Also Punnus did give the Islanders their laws, and caused them to be written, which laws do continue to this day in Island, and are called by name Punnus Lawes."

The origin of this information is unknown, so far as concerns Hudson's source, and many scholars, unfamiliar with

Icelandic history, were long at a loss to account for "Pun-nus and Potharse." Now the passage has been confirmed from other sources, both Icelandic and Danish.

In Iceland, Pining's laws are well known, for he was a sort of governor there on behalf of the Danes around 1476, when he visited Greenland, as the Hudson document says and as most authorities now agree.

Evidence of the Pining and Pothorst voyage does not come primarily from Iceland, but from Denmark, where a letter of March 3, 1551, from Carsten Grip, Burgomaster of Kiel, was discovered in 1909, which says in part:

"The two sceppere [commodores, admirals] Pyningk and Poidthorsth who were sent out by your Majesty's royal grand-father, King Christiern [Christian] the First, at the request of His Majesty of Portugal, with certain ships to explore new countries and islands in the north, have raised on the rock Wydthszerck, lying off Greenland and toward Sniefeldskiekel in Iceland on the sea, a great seamark on account of the Green-land pirates, who with many small ships without keels [the dory-shaped umiaks] fall in large numbers upon other ships."

Two governments, then, were concerned in Pining's voyage to Greenland. With its known policy of secrecy, Portugal may have been moderately successful in preventing news of this particular journey from spreading in southern Europe. But in northern Europe, in spite of anything Denmark may have tried to do, the tidings naturally spread. It is therefore not strange that the same hands which passed on to Hudson the Bardarson sailing directions of the middle of the fourteenth century would also let him have a report on Pining's journey of about 1476.

The documents tell us, then, that no more than twenty-one years elapsed between the Pining voyage and the John Cabot voyage of 1497. Meantime, as we know from the records of both Iceland and England, ships from Bristol were constantly around Iceland, while the Icelandic annals tell that English ships were seen from Iceland sailing northwest toward Green-land. And, be it remembered, an important part of the service of the Bristol merchants was to act as middlemen between Portugal and Iceland in the fish business.

Summing up two thousand years, we find that the records first give us an intermittent history of Europe's relation with Greenland for twelve hundred years, from the visit of Pytheas to the edge of the Greenland Current near 330 B.C. to the first visit of Erik the Red in A.D. 982. Thereafter the story is continuous, from Icelandic, Vatican, and other sources, unbroken from the time of Erik to the time of Cabot, thus to our time. The story is in reality more definitely continuous than has been shown here, for there has been space to quote only a few of the main documents, barely referring to an additional small number of them.

The first proper map of Greenland that has come down to us may have derived from the Bardarson sailing directions. It was drawn in Italy between 1424 and 1427 by a Dane living there, Claudius Clavus. It is not known how widely this draft was circulated in the 1430-80 period of Italo-Portuguese geographical ferment, for it was not printed in the early Ptolemys and was rediscovered, in the Nancy Codex, only in 1835.

But another map of the northern Atlantic showing Greenland was drawn by Clavus in 1430 and did have wide distribution, for it was printed in the Ulm edition of Ptolemy in 1482 —thus six years after the Columbus voyage to Iceland and the Pining one to Greenland, and ten years *before* the 1492 West Indies voyage of Columbus.

A superficially strange thing about the Clavus map is that it not merely shows Greenland in its approximate position with regard to the British Isles, Norway, and Iceland, but actually shows this transatlantic country more correctly than it does some of Europe. The probable explanation of this is that with regard to Europe, Clavus copied older maps, with their standardized errors; but that he drew Greenland either from such a reliable firsthand description as Bardarson's, or else, as some think, from a journey made by himself or by some friend of his.

The story of Greenland in the early days is bound up with the story of the northeastern part of the continent of North America, which is dealt with in a later chapter.

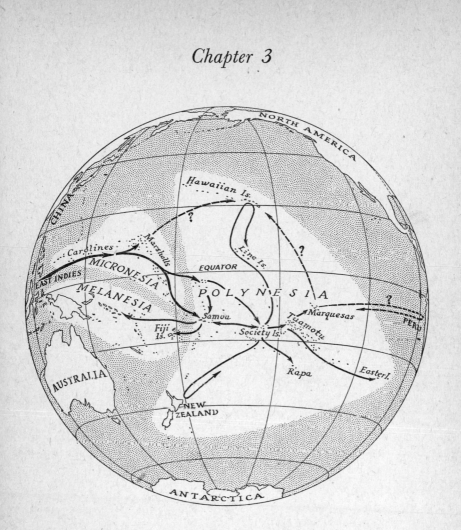

The Polynesians Cross the Pacific

THE POLYNESIANS
CROSS THE PACIFIC

CHAPTER 3

Easter island has been called the most romantic place in the world. To the historian of geographic discovery it is at once mysterious and a key to mysteries. It answers difficult and fascinating questions; it poses many that have not as yet found a solution. One question it does answer is: How good a navigator was Stone Age man?

There have been those who thought that Stone Age man was not much of a sailor, so they have wanted to postulate, for instance, that Bering Strait must have had a bridge across it, either of land or of ice, when the first American came over. The traditional historian finds it hard to believe that even a passage so narrow that you can see across it was crossable in boats so long ago. These historians similarly balk at the claim that the Scots of 330 B.C. were able to tell Pytheas about Iceland, for it goes against the grain with them to concede that the British or the Norwegians may have been able at that time to cross 600 miles of Gulf Stream water to discover an island that is bigger than Ireland, with towering mountains that are seen from afar. To all such it is an eye-opener to learn that tiny Easter Island, 13 miles long and with a highest mountain of only 1730 feet, was inhabited by Stone Age men when Europeans first saw it; for of necessity these people must have come from some inhabited island, the nearest of which would have had to be more than 1000 miles away.

Easter Island lies alone in the ocean 2000 miles west of South America, which is farther than Ireland is from Newfoundland. It is some 1100 miles from Pitcairn, the nearest inhabited island, and is the most easterly outpost of the Polynesians.

89

In the opinion of Dr. Peter H. Buck, Director of the Bishop Museum, Honolulu, Easter Island was probably colonized not by any one large group, but by a series of small parties, during the great period of Polynesian colonizing activity that extended from the twelfth to the fourteenth centuries. The settlers appear to have come from the Marquesas, some of them stopping at Mangareva, and others continuing on to Easter Island, 1500 miles farther east.

It is estimated that when the first Europeans landed there were about 3000 people living on the 50 or 55 square miles of Easter Island. By about 1871 the population had been reduced to 111 by the depredations of slavers and through being killed off by measles, smallpox, and other diseases introduced by white men. The population now is about 450.

There seems to have been as much crisscross movement of peoples through the Pacific at A.D. 400 as at 1400. It is considered, for example, that the Hawaiian Islands, nearly as far from other inhabited islands as even Easter, were settled before A.D. 500. In any case it is well known that around 1100 and 1300 there were frequent canoe voyages between islands 2000 and more miles apart, as from Hawaii to Samoa and Tahiti. In fact, it is thought that Hawaii was originally colonized from the Society Islands, "the hub of the Polynesian universe."

There is not space to detail here the navigation methods that made possible the 1000- and 2000-mile deep-sea voyages of prehistoric man in the Pacific, but we may try to get some light on the general problem from our knowledge of corresponding navigation in the Atlantic.

Through seemingly reliable tradition we do have some information on what the Polynesians of a thousand years ago knew of seafaring and on how they felt about it. But studying the same facts and views for the same period is easier with the Norsemen, for they wrote books which we still have, the narratives called sagas, which range from being as factual as Bradford's account of Plymouth Colony to being as fictional as *Robinson Crusoe*. Whether fact, fancy, or halfway between, the local color in an Icelandic saga is likely to be as authentic as in a good modern history or novel.

The Norsemen roamed the North Atlantic freely in open boats a thousand years ago, colonizing Iceland, rediscovering Greenland, discovering the North American mainland. In a similar way the Polynesians roamed the tropical Pacific in open boats, discovering every habitable island in this vast expanse and colonizing most of them, discovering also New Zealand, and probably South America.

The large double canoes of the "Vikings of the Sunrise," as Peter Buck calls the Polynesian seafarers, carried parties of men, women, and children, dogs, chickens, and pigs, as well as provisions for several weeks. The stories of these voyages are so well preserved in the tales and songs of the people of today that the families of each island can trace their genealogies back to the original colonists. In New Zealand, for instance, which was settled about A.D. 1350, every Maori can name the vessel in which his forebears arrived from central Polynesia.

Both Norsemen and Polynesians operated on seas visited by terrific gales; both sets of navigators had their problems, such as holding a course, finding the place they were looking for, provisioning themselves with food and water or securing those by the way. Neither had compass or any other modern help to navigation; both managed with what they had, using that common sense which today is spread with near-uniformity throughout the world, and which seems to go back with similar uniformity to the farthest time of which we have any knowledge.

The Norsemen and the Polynesians alike knew how to steer by sun and star. They memorized and passed on by tradition the facts of tide and current, of calm and storm, of deep and shoal water. They knew how to catch fish over the side and how to gather and preserve the water that fell in rain.

As discoverers, the Pacific navigators had only one marked advantage over those in the Atlantic—that usually "weather comes from the west." The Europeans found themselves living on the eastern shore of the Atlantic and had to work their way westward against prevailing winds; but the Asiatics were on the western shore of the Pacific and, more often than not, could sail or drift easterly before the wind. This, however, applies chiefly to the North Pacific. In the South Pacific, where the great Polynesian migrations are known to have taken place, there are more easterly than westerly winds, but still enough westerlies so that good navigators could take advantage of them, making their eastward journeys at one season, the return voyages at another.

A thousand years ago there were, however, navigators on both oceans who worked freely in any direction. The Icelanders sailed east to Norway and the Baltic, south to Africa and Constantinople, west to Greenland, north to Jan Mayen and perhaps Spitsbergen. The Greenlanders sailed east to Norway and west to Labrador. At that same time the Hawaiians were making still longer voyages, to Samoa and Tahiti.

On long or short voyages, the Norse attitude was to take danger for granted, to ignore it as we do the annihilating power of lightning. Like our present fishermen of New England and Nova Scotia, whose vessels come to port at midwinter sheathed in ice, the medieval Norsemen came back from their seafaring with few tales of hardship. For instance, the sagas that describe the first years of the Greenland colony have much to say of banquets, table manners, protocol in seating arrangements, jokes that were told; but seldom is there a mention of scarcity of food, and then without detail, merely saying that this year there was a famine or that a certain household ran out of beer. There is reference now and then to an unfavorable season, but rarely if ever the mention of a cold day or the description of a blizzard. The navigators of old did not have our concept of hardship; there were no intrepid explorers in those days, merely competent sailors who went about their job of crossing the ocean much as does today the engine-room stoker or the dining-room steward.

We must remember things like these when we try to understand the Icelandic sagas that tell of deep-sea voyages lasting several months, and Polynesian traditions to the same effect. Native to their element, the Polynesians in the tropics and subtropics, the Norsemen in the Temperate Zone and the Arctic, made use of wind and current instead of fighting them.

To the Polynesians as to the Norsemen, the dangers involved seem to have accentuated the challenge of the Unknown and the thrill of adventure, as is shown by the following extracts from a

Maori poem, published by Peter H. Buck in his *Vikings of the Sunrise*. These lines are from a longer Maori deep-sea chantey composed for the Aotea canoe which sailed from the Society Islands to New Zealand in about 1350 A.D. The Aotea had two steering paddles, Te Roku-o-whiti and Kautu-ki-te-rangi, and each is mentioned in the poem.[*]

Aotea is the canoe,
Turi is the chief,
Te Roku-o-whiti is the paddle.

Behold my paddle!
It is laid by the canoe side,
Held close to the canoe side.
Now it is raised on high—the paddle!
Poised for the plunge—the paddle,
Now we leap forward.

Behold my paddle, Te Roku-o-whiti!
See how it flies and flashes,
It quivers like a bird's wing,
This paddle of mine.

Ah, the outward lift and the dashing,
The quick thrust in and the backward sweep,
The swishing, the swirling eddies,
The foaming white wake, and the spray
That flies from my paddle. . . .

The handle of my steering paddle thrills to action,
My paddle named Kautu-ki-te-rangi.
It guides to the horizon but dimly discerned.
To the horizon that lifts before us,
To the horizon that ever recedes,
To the horizon that ever draws near,
To the horizon that causes doubt,
To the horizon that instills dread,
The horizon with unknown power,
The horizon not hitherto pierced.

[*] From *Vikings of the Sunrise*, by Peter H. Buck, copyright, 1938, J. B. Lippincott Company.

The lowering skies above,
The raging seas below,
Oppose the untraced path
Our ship must go.

Such a poem might well have been composed to commemorate the Polynesian voyage to Easter Island, the most isolated
and remote of islands known to have been discovered by Stone
Age man. Centuries later it may have been Easter that was
sighted in 1687 by the *Bachelor's Delight*, one of the ships of
of the famous buccaneer William Dampier. The *Delight's* skipper, Edward Davis, reported the discovery to Dampier, who
has a paragraph about it in his *New Voyage round the World*.
A more circumstantial account was given by Lionel Wafer,
surgeon's mate of the *Delight*.

"We steered south and by east half-easterly, until we came
to the latitude of 27 degrees 20 minutes south, when about
two hours before day we fell in with a small, low sandy island,
and heard a great roaring noise, like that of the sea beating
upon its shore, right ahead of the ship. Whereupon the sailors,
fearing to fall foul upon the shore before day, desired the captain to put the ship about, and to stand off till day appeared,
to which the captain gave his consent.

"So we plied off till day and then stood in again with the
land, which proved to be a small flat island, without the guard
of any rocks. We stood in within a quarter of a mile of the
shore, and could see it plainly, for 'twas a clear morning, not
foggy nor hazy.

"To the westward, about 12 leagues by judgment, we saw a
range of high land, which we took to be islands, for there were
several partitions in the prospect. This land seemed to reach
about 14 or 16 leagues in a range, and there came thence great
flocks of fowls.

"I, and many more of our men, would have made this land,
and have gone ashore on it, but the captain would not permit us."

In the early eighteenth century the West India Company of
the Netherlands decided, as it proved unwisely, to put itself
in competition with the East India Company of the same na-

tion. It was surely the account given by Davis and Wafer that was responsible for the secret instructions given Mynheer Jacob Roggeveen to search for land in this vicinity.

It was not an island Roggeveen was seeking, but the hypothetical Southern Continent, Terra Australis, which was at this time supposed to occupy most of the space south of Africa, South America, and Java. The mountains seen in the distance, as reported by the *Delight*, furnished the wishful thinkers of the period with what evidence they needed for making it seem likely that the elusive continent had at last been detected.

Indeed it was pretty clearly the chief object of the Roggeveen expedition to discover the land seen by Davis, known also as Tierra de David.

Roggeveen's expedition had three ships, one of which was lost sometime after the discovery of Easter Island. The other two reached Batavia, where they were confiscated. The officers and crews were arrested and sent home to Holland, for the East India Company considered that their monopoly had been infringed by this expedition of the West India Company. One result was that the official records were suppressed. It was not until 1836, when a careful search was instituted for them among the records of the two companies, that Roggeveen's official journal and other papers relating to the expedition were unearthed.

However, an anonymous—and largely fictitious—account of the Roggeveen voyage was published in 1728, with second and third editions in 1758 and 1774. A better account, written in German, was published in 1737 by Carl Friedrich Behrens, who had been on one of the ships.

Roggeveen's official journal in the original Dutch was published in Middleburg in 1838. An extract, consisting of the part relating to the discovery of Easter Island, was translated into English by Bolton Glanville Corney and published by the Hakluyt Society in 1908. This is an account of the search for the island, the landing upon it, and what the Europeans saw there.

The Dutch Discover Easter Island

✠ [April 5, 1722] About the tenth glass in the afternoon watch *The African Galley*, which was sailing ahead of us, lay to wait for us, making the signal of land in sight. When we came up with her, after four glasses had run out, for the breeze was light, we asked what they had seen. On this we were answered that they had all very distinctly seen a low and flattish island lying away to starboard, about 5½ miles off, to the nor'ard and west'ard.

Hereupon it was deemed well to stand on under easy sail to the end of the first watch, and then to lie to and await the dawn. This being decided, the necessary information was given to Captain Bouman, who was astern, and to the land the name of Paåsch Eyland, because it was discovered by us on Easter Day.

There was great rejoicing among the people, and everyone hoped that this low land might prove to be a foretoken of the coast line of the unknown Southern Continent.

[April 6] Had a light breeze out of the southeast, and east-southeast, Paåsch Eyland lying west by north 8 to 9 miles from us. Laid our course between west by south and northwest, in order to run under the lee of the island and so avoid the dangers of a lee shore. At noon the corrected course was west, distance 10 miles, latitude by reckoning 27 degrees 4 minutes south, and longitude 265 degrees 42 minutes.

In the ninth glass of the afternoon we saw smoke rising in several places, from which we concluded that there were people dwelling on the same. We therefore thought it would be well to consider with the captains of the other ships whether it were not needful to undertake an expedition ashore, to the end that we might gain a fitting knowledge of the interior of the country.

On this, it was decided that both the shallops of the ships *Arend* and *Thienhoven*, well manned and armed, should proceed inshore, and find out a convenient place for landing a party from the boats, and also to take soundings. This decision being come to, we stood off and on for the night with our ships.

[April 7] The weather was very variable, with thunder, sheet lightning, and showers. The wind unsteady from the northwest, and occasional calms, so that our shore expedition could not be undertaken with any prospect of success.

During the forenoon Captain Bouman brought an Easter

Islander on board, together with his craft, in which he had come off close to the ship from the land. He was quite nude, without the slightest covering for that which modesty shrinks from revealing.

This hapless creature seemed to be very glad to behold us, and showed the greatest wonder at the build of our ship. He took special notice of the tautness of our spars, the stoutness of our rigging and running gear, the sails, the guns—which he felt all over with minute attention—and everything else that he saw; especially when the image of his own features was displayed before him in a mirror, seeing the which, he started suddenly back and then looked toward the back of the glass, apparently in the expectation of discovering there the cause of the apparition.

After we had sufficiently beguiled ourselves with him, and he with us, we started him off again in his canoe toward the shore, having presented him with two strings of blue beads round his neck, a small mirror, a pair of scissors, and other like trifles which seemed to have a special attraction for him.

But when we had approached within a short distance of the land, we saw distinctly that the account of the sandy and low island (so described by Captain William Dampier, in accordance with the statement and testimony of Captain Davis, and of the narrator Lionel Wafer, whose log of this and other discoveries the aforesaid Dampier had made known through the press, and inserted as a prominent feature in his book, which comprises all his own travels and voyages) was not in the least in conformity with our find, and that neither could it be the land which the aforementioned discoverers declare to be visible 14 to 16 miles beyond it and stretching away out of sight, being a range of high land which the said Dampier conjectured might be the extremity of the unknown Southland.

That this Easter Island cannot be the sandy island is clear, from the fact that the sandy one is small, and low, whereas Easter Island, on the contrary, extends some 15 or 16 [Dutch] miles in circuit, and has at its eastern and western points— which lie about 5 miles from each other—two high hills sloping gradually down, with three or four other smaller hills about their bases which rise above the plain, so that this land is of moderate elevation, and raised above the force of the sea.

The reason why at first, when at a farther distance off, we had regarded the said Easter Island as being of a sandy nature is that we mistook the parched-up grass and hay, or other scorched and charred brushwood, for a soil of that arid nature, because from its outward appearance it suggested no other idea than that of an extraordinarily sparse and meager vegetation, and the discoverers had consequently bestowed upon it the term "sandy."

It may therefore be concluded, in the light of the foregoing explanation, that this Easter Island now discovered will turn out to be some other land lying farther to the eastward than that which is one of the objectives of our expedition. Or else the discoverers must stand convicted of a whole bundle of lies in their reports, told by word of mouth as well as in writing.

[April 8] We had the wind south, south by east, and sou'-sou'-west, with a reefed topsail breeze, unsteady. After breakfast had been served, our shallop was well manned and armed, and likewise the shallop of the ship *Thienhoven*, now close in with the land. And having received their orders, they reported that the inhabitants there were very finely clad in some stuffs of all kinds of colors, and that they made many signs that we should come on shore, but as our orders were not to do so if the Indians should be present in large numbers, that was not permitted. Furthermore, some thought they had seen the natives to have plates of silver in their ears and mother-of-pearl shell ornaments about their necks.

By sundown, having come into the roadstead between the ships *Thienhoven* and *The African Galley*, which had already brought to in readiness for us, we let go our anchor in 22 fathoms, coral bottom, at the distance of a quarter of a mile from the beach, the eastern point of the island bearing east by south, and the west point west-nor'-west from us.

[April 9] A great many canoes came off to the ships. These people showed us at that time their great cupidity for everything they saw, and were so daring that they took the seamen's hats and caps from off their heads and sprang overboard with the spoil; for they are surpassingly good swimmers, as would seem from the great numbers of them who came swimming off from the shore to the ships.

There was also an Easter Islander who climbed in through the cabin window of *The African Galley* from his canoe, and seeing on the table a cloth with which it was covered, and deeming it to be a good prize, he made his escape with it there and then; so that one must take special heed to keep close watch over everything. Furthermore, a shore party of 134 men was organized to make investigations for the purpose of reporting upon our mission.

[April 10] In the morning we proceeded with three boats and two shallops, manned by 134 persons, all armed with musket, pistols, and cutlass. On reaching the shore, the boats and shallops kept close together in order to lay down their grapnels, leaving 20 men in them, armed as above, to take care of them. *The African Galley's* boat was mounted besides with two carronades in the bows.

Having seen to all these arrangements, we proceeded in open order, but keeping well together, and clambered over the rocks, which are very numerous on the sea margin, as far as the level land or flat, making signs with the hand that the natives, who pressed round us in great numbers, should stand out of our way and make room for us.

Having got so far, a *corps de bataille* was formed up of all the seamen of the three ships, the Commodore, Captains Koster, Bouman, and Rosendaal leading, each at the head of his own crew. This column, three ranks in width, occupying a position to the rear of the others, was covered by one half the soldiers under the command of Lieutenant Nicolaas Thonnar, constituting the right wing; and the left, made up of the other half of the military, was led by Mr. Martinus Keerens, Ensign. After thus disposing our forces we marched forward a little, to make room for some of our people who were behind, that they might fall in with the ranks, who were accordingly halted to allow the hindmost to come up, when, quite unexpectedly and to our great astonishment, four or five shots were heard in our rear, together with a vigorous shout of "It's time, it's time! Fire!"

On this, as in a moment, more than thirty shots were fired, and the Indians, being thereby amazed and scared, took to flight, leaving 10 or 12 dead, besides the wounded. The leaders of the party, standing in front, prevented those in advance from firing on the fugitives, demanding, moreover, who had given the order to shoot, and what had induced him to do so.

After a little while the assistant pilot of the ship *Thienhoven* came up to me saying that he, with six other men, was the hindmost of the party; that on one of the natives laying hold of the muzzle of his piece to snatch it from him, he struck him a blow. And further, that another Indian had attempted to strip the jacket off one of the seamen, and that some of the natives, seeing our men resist, picked up stones, using threatening gestures as if to pelt us with them. Whereby, from all appearance, the firing on the part of my small troop was brought about, although he declared that until then he had given no orders of the least kind. This was, however, no time for hearing other versions of the affair, and that much had to be deferred till a better opportunity.

After the astonishment and terror of the natives were somewhat allayed on their seeing that our hostilities were not persisted in, they were given to know by signs that the victims had threatened to make an assault upon us by stone-throwing, and the inhabitants, who had been just in front of us all the time, approached our leaders again—in particular one who seemed to be in authority over the other headmen, for, giving a general direction that everything they had should be fetched and laid before us, including fruit, root crops, and poultry, the order was promptly obeyed with reverence and bowing by those roundabout, as the event proved. For in a little while they brought a great abundance of sugar cane, fowls, yams, and bananas. But we gave them to understand through signs that we desired nothing excepting only the fowls, which were about sixty in number, and thirty bunches of bananas, for which we paid them ample value in striped linen, with which they appeared to be well pleased and satisfied.

By the time we had fully investigated things, and especially their cloth stuffs and the dyes of them, and also the supposed silver plates and mother-of-pearl, it was found that they were made up of pieces patched together; that is, that the wraps worn on their bodies were composed of some field product, sewn three-ply or four-ply in thickness, yet neat and trim, which material (as called in the West Indies) is a sort of *piet*. Further, that the soil of the country (as we saw in several places) was red and yellowish, into the which when mixed with water they dip their garments and afterward let them dry. Which shows that their dye is not fast, for when felt about and handled one finds the color come off on one's fingers, not only after touching new articles but also from old and worn ones.

The plates imagined to be of silver were made out of the root of some vegetable—as one might say in Holland, of good stout parsnips or carrots. This ear ornament is roundish or oval, having a diameter of about 2 inches measured through the widest section, and 1½ inches across the lesser, being 3 inches, at a guess, in length.

To understand how these supposed silver plates are fixed in the ears as ornaments one must know that the lobes of these people's ears are stretched from their youth up; and their center is slit open in such wise that the lesser rim of the plug, being stuck through the opening in the lobe, is then pushed on toward the thicker end, which accordingly faces toward the front, and completely stuffs the opening.[1] Furthermore, the mother-of-pearl which was seen as a neck pendant is a flat shell of the same tint as the inner lip of our oysters.

When these Indians go about any job which might set their earplugs waggling, and bid fair to do them any hurt, they take them out and hitch the rim of the lobe up over the top of the ear, which gives them a quaint and laughable appearance.

These people have well-proportioned limbs, with large and strong muscles. They are big in stature, and their natural hue is not black, but pale yellow or sallowish, as we saw in the case of many of the lads, either because they had not painted their bodies with dark blue or because they were of superior rank and had consequently no need to labor in the field.

These people have also snow-white teeth, with which they

---

[1] Behren says: "Their ears were so long that they hung down as far as to the shoulders. Some wore white ornaments in the lobes as a special embellishment."

are exceptionally well provided, even the old and hoary, as was evidenced by the cracking of a large and hard nut, whose shell was thicker and more resisting than our peach stones.

The hair of their heads, and the beards of most of them, were short, although others wore it long and hanging down the back, or plaited and coiled on the top of the head in a tress, like the Chinese at Batavia, which is there termed *condé*.

What the form of worship of these people comprises we were not able to gather any full knowledge of, owing to the shortness of our stay among them. We noticed only that they kindle fire in front of certain remarkably tall stone figures they set up, and thereafter squatting on their heels with their heads bowed down, they bring the palms of their hands together and alternately raise and lower them.

At first, these stone figures caused us to be filled with wonder, for we could not understand how it was possible that people who are destitute of heavy or thick timber, and also of stout cordage, out of which to construct gear had been able to erect them; nevertheless some of these statues were a good 30 feet in height and broad in proportion. This perplexity ceased, however, with the discovery, on removing a piece of the stone, that they were formed out of clay or some kind of rich earth, and that small smooth flints had been stuck over afterward, which are fitted very closely and neatly to each other, so as to make up the semblance of a human figure.[2] Moreover, one saw reaching downward from the shoulders a slight elevation or prominence which represented the arms, for all the statues seem to convey the idea that they were hung about with a long robe from the neck right down to the soles of the feet. They have on the head a basket heaped up with flints painted white deposited in it.[3]

It was incomprehensible to us how these people cook their food, for no one was able to perceive or find that they had

---

[2] Roggeveen was in error here. The figures really are of soft volcanic stone, which is easily worked, and was carved by the islanders with stone tools.

[3] Roggeveen's description of the statues seems to show that he never got close to one of them, but saw them only from a distance of some hundreds of yards. His "basket" was doubtless one of the coronoid cylinders of tufaceous rock by which most of the figures were surmounted.

any earthen pots, pans, or vessels. The only thing which appeared to us was that they scrape holes in the ground with their hands, and lay large and small flint pebbles in them (for we saw no other kinds of stone). Then, having got dried litter from the fields and laid over the pebbles, they set fire to it, and in a little time brought us a boiled fowl to eat, very neatly wrapped round in a kind of rush, clean and hot.

Though they were thanked by means of signs, we had quite enough business in hand to look after our people so as to keep order among them and prevent any affront being offered, and also that in the event of any struggle occurring they should not allow themselves to be taken by surprise. For although these people showed us every sign of friendship, yet the experience of others has taught us that one may not put too much trust in any Indians, as recounted in the journal of the Nassau Fleet, which lost 17 men on one occasion through the willingness of the natives of Terra de Feu [Tierra del Fuego] to help being mistaken for a proof that they were well disposed.

We then, being balked from making any sufficiently detailed inquiry, concluded that they must have large hollow flint stones under the soil, which hold water when they set about boiling anything, and that afterward they arch it over with stones on which to light the fire, and thus boil their food, by means of the heat thrown downward, until tender.

It is also very remarkable that we saw no more than two or three old women. Those were wearing a garment reaching from the waist down to below their knees and another slung on the shoulders, yet so that the skin covering their pendent breasts was bare. But young women and lasses did not come forward among the crowd, so that one must believe the jealousy of the men had moved them to hide them away in some distant place in the island.[4]

Their houses or huts are without any ornamentation, and have a length of 50 feet and a width of 15, the height being 9 feet, as it appeared by guess. The construction of their

---

[4] "They either have but few females among them, or many were restrained from making their appearance, during our stay," says James Cook, "for though we saw nothing to induce us to believe the men were of a jealous disposition, or the women afraid to appear in public, something of this kind was probably the case."

walls, as we saw in the framework of a new building, is begun with stakes which are stuck into the ground and secured straight upright, across which other long strips of wood which I may call laths are lashed, to the height of four or five, thus completing the framework of the building. Then the interstices, which are all of oblong shape, are closed up and covered over with a sort of rush or long grass, which they put on very thickly, layer upon layer, and fasten on the inner side with lashings (the which they know how to make from a certain field product called *piet*, very neatly and skillfully, and is in no way inferior to our own thin cord); so that they are always as well shut in against wind and rain as those who live beneath thatched roofs in Holland.

These dwellings have no more than one entrance way, which is so low that they pass in creeping on their knees, being round above, as a vault or archway. The roof is also of the same form.

All the chattels we saw before us (for these long huts admit no daylight except through the one entrance way, and are destitute of windows and closely shut in all around) were mats spread on the floor, and a large flint stone which many of them use for a pillow. Furthermore, they had round about their dwellings certain big blocks of hewn stone, 3 or 4 feet in breadth, and fitted together in a singularly neat and even manner. And according to our judgment these serve for a stoop on which to sit and chat during the cool of the evening.

It only remains to say, in concluding the subject of these dwelling huts, that we did not see more than six or seven of them at the place where we landed, from which it may be clearly inferred that all the Indians make use of their possessions in common, for the large size and small number of their dwellings give one to know that many live together and sleep in a single building. But if one should therefore conclude that the women are held in common among them, one must naturally expect depravity and bickering to ensue.

Finally, as to their seagoing craft, they are of poor and flimsy construction; for their canoes are fitted together of a number of small boards and light frames, which they skillfully lace together with very fine-laid twine made from the above-mentioned vegetable product *piet*. But as they lack the knowledge, and especially the material, for calking the great number of seams of their canoes and making them tight, they consequently leak a great deal, on account of which they are necessitated to spend half their time in bailing.

Their canoes are about 10 feet long, not counting the high and pointed stem and stern pieces. Their width is such that with their legs packed close together they can just sit in them so as to paddle ahead.

It was now deemed advisable to go to the other side of the island, whereto the king or head chief invited us, as being the principal place of their plantations and fruit trees—for all the things they brought to us of that kind were fetched from that quarter—inasmuch as the northerly wind which began to blow made our anchorage a lee shore, the more so because we had not many people on board the ships who could get help from us if necessary in the event of the wind waxing strong. Moreover, the boats and shallops being filled to the utmost with men, these would in such a case not have been able to get back on board, either by reason of the heavy sea on the beach or of its becoming impossible for them to row. Therefore it was deemed well to pull off at once in good order, the which was presently put into practice.

Having arrived on board, we resolved to sail another hundred miles farther to the westward so that by thus doing we should punctually follow our instructions and the resolution adopted in reference to them, in all details; although, before doing so, we should make a short cruise away down eastward, to see whether we could discover the low and sandy island; for in the event of our finding it, the first portion of our cruise in the South Sea would necessarily terminate, as having accomplished its purpose. ✄

The ships sailed eastward till Easter Island was no longer visible from the masthead, but there was no sign of the low and sandy island. Then they turned and sailed far enough west beyond Easter so that Roggeveen was sure no land of any size lay in that quarter. Nothing remained of the range of bold mountains seen by the Dampier expedition beyond a triangular island with a longest reach of 13 miles, small consolation to wishful thinkers who had conjured up a mountain range fronting a shore of a mighty Southern Continent.

But Easter Island has proved a great consolation to scientists who were looking for unquestionable proof that Stone Age man swarmed the biggest ocean, even to the discovery and colonization of its most isolated island. For with this key have been unlocked at least some of the antechambers of mystery in the problem of how man spread over the earth and of why we find so many similarities of culture in places far from each other, so much otherwise inexplicable blending of races.

As to Dampier, Davis, and Wafer, the Roggeveen expedition concluded: "Nothing more remains to be said than that these three, who were Englishmen, must have been rovers from the truth as well as rovers after the goods of the Spaniards."

China Discovers North America

CHINA DISCOVERS
NORTH AMERICA

CHAPTER 4

CHINA, favorably situated for reaching North America by way of the Aleutian Islands, was not, three thousand years ago in a mood for discovering new continents. On this the scholars agree, the ones at least whom I have consulted through their books.

One of these books is named *Fusang* and was published in 1875 by the American Charles G. Leland. He considers that in view of the self-satisfied and self-centered attitude of the Chinese people they "would undertake no voyage of discovery. Not a single instance occurs during the entire four thousand years of the history of Eastern Asia of an individual who had traveled in foreign lands for the purpose of adding to his own information or that of others." In this connection Leland says of one journey later claimed, represented as having been made by Lao-tse, that it was "a tale deliberately invented for the purpose of connecting his doctrine with that of Buddhism."

Leland characterizes this Chinese position of spiritual isolationism on the first page of his book:

"'To retain laws and customs according to the traditionary manner, and to extend these laws and customs to other lands,' was the precept of the founders of the Celestial Empire, as well as of other civilized nations. 'But this extension,' they added, 'is not to be effected by the oratorical powers of single messengers, nor through the force of armed hordes. This renovation, as in every other sound organic growth which forces itself from within, can only take place when the Outer Barbarians, irresistibly compelled by the virtue and majesty

109

of the Son of Heaven, blush for their barbarism, voluntarily obey the image of the Heavenly Father, and become men.'

"It will be readily understood that a race holding such opinions would undertake no voyage of discovery, and attempt no conquests."

On this contemptuous if not oblivious position which China held toward foreign countries we find British agreement in Sir Charles Raymond Beazley's monumental three-volume *The Dawn of Modern Geography* (Oxford University Press, 1897-1906). He says, in effect, that the Chinese of the time made journeys rather to teach than to learn, except that pilgrimages were made to the shrines of Buddhism. There were some commercial travels, no doubt, and others pretendedly commercial that were really for spying out the lands and resources of potential invaders—for even in those remote times the Chinese thought more in terms of defense than in those of attack.

In the main China has been typified through the millenniums by its Great Wall—an exclusive nation trying to exclude both foreign people and foreign ideas.

But although the travels of devout Buddhists were chiefly toward the shrines of that religion, to the west and south of China, there were some missionary journeys in other directions. Of these the most famous abroad, also the most doubted and debated, was alleged to have been made to the northeast. Those who take the record seriously maintain that here we have the discovery of Alaska and British Columbia, and possibly the discovery of California and Mexico, with some claiming that Peru may have been reached.

A notice of the discovery of Fusang by the monk Hoei-sin was entered in the annals of China as of A.D. 499. This section of the annals was brought to the attention of Europe by the distinguished French scholar Joseph de Guignes at a date not exactly known, but clearly before 1752, for in that year a letter was written from Peking by another Frenchman to the effect that De Guignes was wrong to take the yarn seriously. A number of other German and French scholars wrote skeptically, including the great Humboldt. The dissent of the learned was general till 1844, when distinguished scholars of both France and Germany began coming to favorable conclusions, which was true also of the American Leland.

In 1885 appeared a nearly exhaustive book on this controversy by Edward P. Vining of Chicago, *An Inglorious Columbus*. (D. Appleton & Co.). In 800 pages it reviews most previously issued writings on Fusang, reprints much of the evidence, and concludes that we can trace through Hoei-sin, and others who followed him during the next few years, an Asiatic discovery of western America at least as far south as Mexico.

Beazley, who may be looked upon as having the typical conservatism of the Oxford scholar, finds it inherently probable that the Fusang journey was actually made, though not beyond Alaska or its vicinity, and that there were other voyages, perhaps going farther. He says that "it seems unreasonable to reject entirely the Chinese tradition of a Far Eastern land answering to some part of Western North America . . . it is impossible to doubt that in the past, as in the present, men could pass from one continent to the other by the stepping-stones of the Aleutian Islands, or the narrow passage of Behring's Straits."

Beazley summarizes: "The Chinese record, if it be treated fairly, must not be minimized any more than it must be exaggerated; and if its words and measurements forbid us to identify Fusang with Mexico or Panama, they also surely require something more extensive than a journey to Japan . . . which is distinctly named in our present narrative as a starting point for the Land of Marked Bodies."

In the Fusang and related narratives "marked bodies" clearly means tattooed bodies. That looks confirmatory, for all travelers who have seen Alaska Eskimos that were still in their primitive condition have been impressed with their extensive tattooing, particularly that of the women, which covered forehead, cheeks, chin, breasts, arms, and torso. The body tattooing was particularly impressive to travelers because of the universal Eskimo custom of sitting withindoors either completely naked or stripped to the waist.

Leland's *Fusang*, from which the translation of the Hoei-sin narrative is to be quoted, is put forward by him as an elaboration of a work by the famous Karl Friedrich Neumann, professor in Munich, with whom Leland had studied during his two years of German university residence. Leland says of Neumann that "having distinguished himself as a sinologist, he went in 1829 to China, where he remained nearly two years, occupied in collecting Chinese books. . . . In 1838 he received an appointment as professor of the Chinese and Armenian languages at the University of Munich."

That a journey into a far and previously unknown country was possible even from China, though only to Buddhist missionaries, Leland explains: "In the first century of our reckoning, the pride and vanity induced by the Chinese social system were partly broken by the gradual progress of Buddhism over all Eastern Asia. He who believed in the divine mission [of Buddha] . . . must strive . . . to extend the joyful mission of salvation to all nations of the earth." The devout Buddhist would then have two powerful and opposed desires—to visit sacred India that he might learn, and to visit heathen lands that he might teach.

According to Neumann and Leland, as well as several other writers since their time, the Chinese before A.D. 450 were familiar by hearsay with the tattooed people of the Aleutians and with reports that 5000 Chinese miles (1000 to 2000 English miles) beyond them was a country which they called Tahan, or Great China. They probably named it Great China from having heard of the continent which extends eastward from the Aleutians. Tahan would thus have been somewhere in Alaska or the British Columbia region; Fusang, which lay beyond Tahan, as seen from China, has been thought by some to be in the region of our Pacific Coast states, but there are those who think it was in Mexico, if not in Peru.

There seems little doubt that the Chinese accounts of Fusang, and the interpretation of them by scholars, were among the reasons which induced Peter the Great to send the Bering expedition in search of land east from Kamchatka. The first landfalls of each ship, Bering's own and the one commanded by his aide Chirikov, were on the south coast of Alaska and in the Panhandle near Mount St. Elias, thus far to the east of the Aleutians and actually in the region where Fusang has been supposed by many to lie.

In the introduction to his translation, Leland says of Hoei-sin's report of his journey to Fusang that it was "regularly entered in the yearbooks or annals of the Chinese Empire" in the year the monk returned from the journey, and that from the annals "It passed not only to the pages of historians, but also to those of poets and writers of romances, by whom it was so confused with absurd inventions and marvelous tales that even at the present day discredit is thrown by a certain class of critics on the entire narrative."

It is usual for students of Irish lore to consider that the Saint Brendan and related legends are based on fact, though crusted with myth and miracle so thickly that the original truth can be found only by patient and reasonable study. Leland, and the school of Fusang students to which he belongs, take the same position.

The following is the story as given by Leland from Neumann:

During the reign of the dynasty of Tsi, in the first year of the year-naming, "Everlasting Origin" [A.D. 499], came a Buddhist priest from this kingdom, who bore the cloister name of Hoei-sin—that is, Universal Compassion—to the present district of Hukuang, and those surrounding it, who narrated that Fusang is about 20,000 Chinese miles in an easterly direction from Tahan, and east of the Middle Kingdom.

Many Fusang trees grow there, whose leaves resemble the *Dryanda cordifolia*; the sprouts, on the contrary, resemble those of the bamboo tree, and are eaten by the inhabitants of the land. The fruit is like a pear in form, but is red.

From the bark they prepare a sort of linen which they use for clothing, and also a sort of ornamented stuff. The houses are built of wooden beams. Fortified and walled places are there unknown.

They have written characters in this land, and prepare paper from the bark of the Fusang. The people have no weapons, and make no wars, but in the arrangements for the kingdom they have a northern and a southern prison. Trifling offenders were lodged in the southern prison, but those confined for greater offenses in the northern, so that those who were about to receive grace could be placed in the southern prison, and those who were not, in the northern.

Those men and women who were imprisoned for life were allowed to marry. The boys resulting from these marriages were, at the age of eight years, sold as slaves, the girls not until their ninth year. If a man of any note was found guilty of crimes, an assembly was held; it must be in an excavated place. There they strewed ashes over him, and bade him farewell.

If the offender was one of a lower class, he alone was punished, but when of rank, the degradation was extended to his children and grandchildren. With those of the highest rank it attained to the seventh generation.

The name of the king is pronounced Ichi. The nobles of the first class are termed Tuilu; of the second, Little Tuilu; and of the third, Na-to-scha. When the prince goes forth, he is accompanied by horns and trumpets. The color of his clothes changes with the different years. In the two first of the ten-year cyclus they are blue; in the two next, red; in the two following, yellow; in the two next, red; and in the last two, black.

The horns of the oxen are so large that they hold ten bushels. They use them to contain all manner of things. Horses, oxen, and stags are harnessed to their wagons. Stags are used here as cattle are used in the Middle Kingdom, and from the milk of the hind they make butter. The red pears of the Fusang tree keep good throughout the year. Moreover, they have apples and reeds. From the latter they prepare mats. No iron is found in this land, but copper, gold, and silver are not prized, and do not serve as a medium of exchange in the market.

Marriage is determined upon in the following manner: The suitor builds himself a hut before the door of the house where the one longed-for dwells, and waters and cleans the ground every morning and evening. When a year has passed by, if the maiden is not inclined to marry him, he departs; should she be willing, it is completed.

When the parents die, they fast seven days. For the death of the paternal or maternal grandfather they lament five days, at the death of elder or younger sisters or brothers, uncles or aunts, three days. They then sit from morning to evening before an image of the ghost absorbed in prayer, but wear no mourning clothes. When the king dies, the son who succeeds him does not busy himself for three years with state affairs.

In earlier times these people lived not according to the laws of Buddha. But it happened that in the second year-naming, "Great Light," of Song [A.D. 458], five beggar monks from the kingdom of Kipin went to this land, extended over it the religion of Buddha, and with it his holy writings and images. They instructed the people in the principles of monastic life, and so changed their manners.

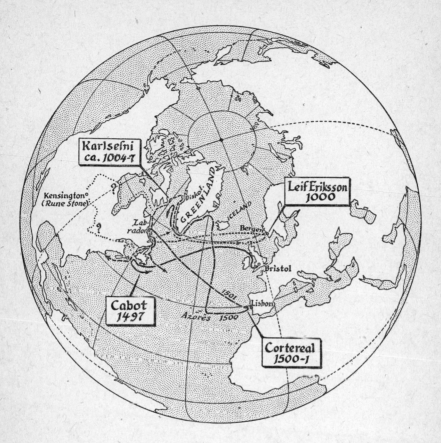

Northern Europe Discovers North America

NORTHERN EUROPE DISCOVERS
NORTH AMERICA

CHAPTER 5

With the Atlantic crossed, with Iceland and Greenland discovered and colonized, a sector of the New World had been unveiled and brought into a permanent relation with the Old World. But the mainland of North America was as yet unrevealed to the eyes of Europe. That revelation came in the year 1000, and through an accident.

In 999 Leif, one of Erik's two sons, crossed from Greenland to Norway by way of the Scottish islands and, as was usual with chieftains, was invited to spend the winter at the court of the King, that dauntless proselytizer Olaf Tryggvason. Before spring the monarch had convinced the young Greenlander that he had better get baptized, so he did. Then the King asked him to take missionaries back home with him. Leif agreed to carry two priests.

It seems that with the clergymen aboard Leif was anxious to get back early in the season, perhaps so as to be in time for the Greenland Thing. At any rate, he did what seems to have been rare in those days—indeed, he may have been the first to attempt it—sailing direct from Norway for the south tip of Greenland instead of going by way of Iceland. Evidently he steered too far to the left, for he missed Cape Farewell, and the first land he struck was Labrador (possibly Nova Scotia or Newfoundland). Realizing he must have overshot his mark, Leif turned northeast and reached Greenland. The country he found was christened Vinland (Wineland), for reasons which will come out when the detailed narrative, the *Saga of Erik the Red*, is cited.

It has been mentioned in a different connection that in the eleventh century the Scandinavian countries were ecclesiastically a part of the Archbishopric of Hamburg. The famous *History of the Church of Hamburg*, finished around 1070, was the first medieval book to tell Europe about the mainland of North America under its Norse name, Wineland. Its author, Adam of Bremen, had been up in Denmark some years before, at the court of King Svein Estridsson, who, Adam found, "knew the history of the barbarians by heart, as if it had been in writing." At the court, and especially from the King, Adam heard much concerning Iceland and Greenland. He heard of Vinland, too:

"Moreover he [the King of Denmark] mentioned yet another island, which had been discovered by many in that ocean, and which is called 'Winland,' because vines grow there of themselves and give the noblest wine. And that there is abundance of unsown corn we have obtained certain knowledge, not by fabulous supposition, but from trustworthy information of the Danes."

Thus was North America introduced to the literature of Europe. It had to be an island, for according to the geographic concepts of Adam as revealed in his book, there were only three continents: Europe, Asia, and Africa. It did not occur to him that Vinland could be a part of one of these.

Numerous Icelandic sagas mention or describe the discovery of Vinland. As information passed by father to son they date from before 1070, but they were not written down until a half-century later than Adam's book, some of them a hundred or more years later. During that interval a good deal of embroidery had had time to develop—which, as the critical historians usually think, did not so much replace or alter facts as confuse them.

One of the developments was a certain jealousy between Greenland and Iceland, or perhaps rather the growth of a tendency in Iceland to give more credit to Icelanders than to Greenlanders—this partly because these traditions were most likely to be preserved by the descendants of men who had taken part in the Vinland adventures, each scribe as he copied having a tendency to magnify somewhat the role played by his ancestor, it may be occasionally transferring credit from one character to another.

It was perhaps in this way that there appeared in Iceland a variant of the story to the effect that it had not really been the Greenlander Leif, the son of Erik the Red, who found Wineland, the Good, but an Icelander named Bjarni; and that other men had later sailed in search of the land seen by Bjarni, somewhat as Erik had sailed a generation before in search of the land seen by Gunnbjörn. However that be, we follow the orthodox critics and take Leif to have been ahead of Bjarni, if indeed this Bjarni ever sailed.

So we revert to the version of the Erik saga which was used in describing the colonization of Greenland. We learn through it the finding of Helluland, which is southeastern Baffin Island; of Markland, which is the forested middle and southern part of Labrador; and of Vinland, which is the Gulf of St. Lawrence region and may have included other parts as far south as New England. Indeed, a few enthusiasts carry the Greenlandic and Icelandic voyagers as far south as Georgia.

The opening chapters of the saga, besides giving lengthy genealogies, tell the story of Greenland and of home life there. The account of the discovery of the North American mainland, and the events leading up to it, begins with the fifth chapter. The translation which follows is from that version of the saga which was published at Reykjavik in 1935 by Hid Islenzka Fornritafelag. (The text is the same as in my *Greenland*, Doubleday, Doran, 1942.)

Saga of Erik the Red

The wife of Erik was Thjodhild, and they had two sons, Thorstein and Leif. They were both promising young men. Thorstein remained at home with his father, and it was considered that not in all of Greenland was there a man of his quality.

Leif sailed to Norway [by way of the Hebrides] . . . arriving there in the autumn. He went to the court of Olaf Tryggvason. The King showed him much consideration and evidently thought him a man of ability.

At one time the King said to Leif: "Are you returning to Greenland next summer?" "That is my plan," said Leif, "if it meets with your approval." The King replied: "I do approve, and you shall be my messenger to spread the faith of Christianity."

Leif said that of course he would follow the King's direction, but this kind of mission to Greenland he thought would be difficult. The King replied he knew of no one better suited for the undertaking, "and I feel sure your fortune will carry you to success." "That will happen," said Leif, "only if I have your support."

Leif set out upon his voyage. They were a long time at sea, and finally struck a land they had not expected. It had fields of self-sown wheat, and wine berries. Among the trees were maples. Of all these things they took aboard specimens, including beams so long that they were suitable for house-building.

[On his way back to Greenland] Leif found men on a stranded ship and took them home with him. In the rescue he showed those personal qualities which distinguished him in many other things, like those which made him instrumental in Christianizing the country. He was ever after called Leif the Lucky.

Leif struck the coast of Greenland at Eriksfjord and went home to Brattahlid. Everybody was delighted to see him. He began preaching Christianity through the land immediately. When proclaiming the faith he showed people the tokens he had from Olaf Tryggvason, explaining how excellent and how glorious was the new religion.

His father, Erik, was not inclined to be much impressed with the new ideas, but his mother, Thjodhild, accepted them readily and had a church built near the farm. This building was thereafter called the Church of Thjodhild. Here she worshiped, and so did the rest of those who accepted Christianity. She would not associate with Erik after she was converted, which annoyed him.

Now there was great talk that people ought to seek out the land which had been discovered by Leif. The leader in this was the accomplished and popular Thorstein, Erik's son. People wanted Erik to come along, for they had the greatest confidence in his foresight and his good luck. He was reluctant, but he finally refrained from saying no when his friends beseeched him.

The ship which Thorbjörn had brought with him [from Iceland] was now made ready. Twenty men were chosen for the voyage, which was to carry little trade goods, only weapons and provisions.

The morning Erik left the house he took a box which contained gold and silver and hid it. Riding along toward the ship, he fell off his horse, breaking some ribs and injuring his shoulder. This led him to tell his wife, Thjodhild, that she might have the treasure; he considered the accident a visitation, the result of having secreted the valuables.

Amidst great rejoicing the ship stood out from Eriksfjord; everybody was much pleased with how things were going. But they encountered difficulties at sea, were much delayed, and did not attain to where they wanted to go. At one time they had a view of Iceland, at another they saw birds from Ireland. Their ship kept being driven back and forth across the sea. Toward autumn they returned to Greenland, discouraged and tired. Winter was already beginning when they reached Eriksfjord.

Now Erik said: "There was more jollity when we sailed out of the fjord last summer than there is now, but still we are not so badly off." Thorstein replied: "It is our responsibility as leaders to make some provision for all these men, who are now without resources. We must find them a home for the winter." Erik remarked: "There is much truth in the saying that no one knows the reply to his question till he gets the answer, and that is how things are now. I shall do as you suggest." Everyone who had no other home went with Erik and his son. They proceeded to Brattahlid and spent the winter.

Now we have to tell that Thorstein Eriksson sought the hand of Gudrid, which was well received by both her and her father. The arrangements were made and they were married at Brattahlid in the autumn. The wedding was seemly and was well attended.

Thorstein had a farm in the Western Settlement, the name of

which was Lysufjord. Another man owned half of that farm, whose name was also Thorstein; his wife was Sigrid.

When Thorstein Eriksson and his wife arrived at Lysufjord in the fall they were well received and they spent there the winter.

An epidemic was sweeping the district and reached their farm early in the winter. Gardar, the superintendent of the farm, an unpopular man, was the first taken ill, and he died. Thereafter it was not far between one death and the next.

Among those who became ill were Thorstein Eriksson and Sigrid, the wife of the other Thorstein.

One evening Sigrid was going out of doors, and Gudrid with her. They had just gone out beyond the front door when Sigrid screamed. Gudrid said: "We are being careless in going out. You must not get chilled. Let us go right back into the house." Sigrid replied: "We can't do that, for all the dead men are standing lined up in front of the door, barring it, and Thorstein, your husband, is among them. I can also see myself among them, and that I don't like." After a moment, however, the vision departed and she said: "Let us go back in, Gudrid. Now I cannot see the dead men barring our way."

[Here follows a long and circumstantial account of ghosts and marvels—dead men coming to life and falling back dead again, visions and prodigies. The last part of the chapter tells that Thorstein Eriksson had been dead for some time when he sat up and spoke to his wife Gudrid.]

"It is not proper, as has been the case here in Greenland since we became Christian, that men should be buried in ground not consecrated and with scant singing of the mass. I desire that I be carried to a proper church, and so with the others who have died here. However, the body of Gardar should be burned in a great fire as soon as possible, for he is responsible for all the supernatural things which have been happening this winter." He also told her about her future, that her career would be remarkable, and begged her to refrain from being married to a Greenlander. He asked her to see to it that their money went as a gift to the Church, but that some of it should go to the poor. Having spoken, he fell down dead a second time.

It had been the custom in Greenland since Christianity that men were buried near the farms where they had died, and in unconsecrated ground. The practice was to set a rod upright upon the breast of the corpse. Later, when a priest came, the rod was pulled up and holy water poured down through the hole, and then there were masses said, although it might be long after the burial.

The bodies of Thorstein and the rest who had died were brought to the church at Eriksfjord and were there properly buried, with masses sung by the correct religious functionaries. Erik received Gudrid into his home as if he had been her father. . . .

A man named Thord dwelt at Höfdi in Hofdaströnd [in Iceland]. [Here follows a genealogy tracing the ancestry of his wife to one of the kings of Ireland.] A son of Thord was named Thorfinn Karlsefni. He was customarily on merchant voyages and was considered a good navigator.

One summer Karlsefni prepared his ship for a voyage to Greenland. With him went Snorri Thorbrandsson from Alptafjord, and there were 40 men on that ship.

Another man was named Bjarni Grimolfsson from Breidafjord, still another was Thorhall Gamlason from the eastern fjords. That same summer they also were getting a ship ready for Greenland, which likewise had a crew of 40.

The two ships set out together. It is not reported how long they were at sea, but only that both reached Eriksfjord by autumn.

Erik the Red and a number of other Greenlanders rode down to meet the ships, and there was brisk trading. The captains of the two vessels offered Erik whatever goods he wanted from their cargoes. To show equal generosity, he invited the entire crews of both to be his guests for the winter. The merchants accepted gratefully. Hereupon their goods were transported to Brattahlid, where there were ample vacant storehouses for accommodation. Erik's guests found that his home was well provided, and they spent a pleasant winter.

But when it drew toward Christmas, Erik began to seem depressed, much more gloomy than was his nature. So one day

Karlsefni asked him what the trouble was: "Why are you sad, Erik? Everybody seems to feel that you are more depressed than is your nature. You have been generous to us, and it is our duty to reciprocate as best we can. Do tell us what is the trouble."

Erik replied: "Your whole attitude is proper and is to your credit. I am much concerned that you shall not get the worst of our exchanges. Besides, I cannot be happy to think that when you go elsewhere it shall become known that you have nowhere had a worse Yule than this which is now approaching, when Erik the Red was your host at Brattahlid in Greenland."

"That will never be the case, my dear sir," said Karlsefni. "We have in our cargoes both malt and corn [for making beer], and you shall have of these as much as you like to use in as rich a banquet as you care to arrange."

The offer was accepted by Erik, and a Yule feast prepared such that those who were there could not imagine anything more sumptuous in a land of so few resources.

After the feast Karlsefni sought the hand of Gudrid, for he had reason to believe he would be successful. Erik received his proposal favorably and said that she would have to yield to her fate [that is, fulfill the behest of Erik's dead son, Thorstein, not to marry a Greenlander]. Besides, he said, he had heard nothing but good of Karlsefni. The outcome was that Thorfinn and Gudrid were married, whereupon the Yule festivities were prolonged into a wedding feast. They dwelt at Brattahlid the rest of the winter.

At Brattahlid was great talk that there ought to be a search for Wineland the Good, for it was said that the conditions there were favorable in soil and climate. The upshot was that Karlsefni and Snorri prepared their ship for a voyage which was to search for that country in the spring.

Bjarni and Thorhall decided to join the expedition with their ship and the crew which had accompanied them. A man named Thorvard, whose wife was a natural daughter of Erik the Red, went with the expedition, and so did Thorvald, the son of Erik, and Thorhall, who was called the Hunter. He had been with Erik a long time as a hunter during the summer and as a steward in winter. He was a large man, strong and uncouth, usually silent but ill-spoken when he was not silent. He ever tried to persuade Erik to the less desirable of two courses. He had not become a real Christian. His knowledge of the wilderness was extensive. He was on the ship of Thorvard and Thorvald, which was the vessel that Thorbjörn had brought [from Iceland]. Altogether the expedition had 160 people.

They sailed first to the Western Settlement and then to Bear Island (Disko). Thence they sailed two days southwestward, when they discovered land. They manned a boat and explored it, finding large flat stones, some of them 12 ells [18 feet]. Foxes were numerous. They gave the land a name and called it Helluland (Land of Flat Stones; Flagstoneland). [According to the direction sailed and the distance, this would be Baffin Island, just north of Cumberland Sound.]

Thence they sailed a day and a night, turning from southwest to south, and discovered a forested country with abundant game. An island lay to the south. There they killed a bear, and so they named it Bjarney (Bear Island). But the land they called Markland (Land of Forest).[1]

Thence they stood southwest along the coast for a long time and came to a ness. Here the land was on the starboard. The beaches were long, and there were sands. They rowed ashore and found on the ness the keel of a ship, wherefore they named it Kjalarnes (Keelness). Also they gave to the coast the name Furdustrandir (Wonder Strands), for it took so long to sail past them.

Now the coast began to be deeply cut up with bays. They steered the ships into one of the bays.

King Olaf Tryggvason had assigned to Leif two Scots: the man was named Haki and the woman Hekja. They could run faster than reindeer. They were on Karlsefni's ship. When the expedition passed Wonder Strands, they put the Scots ashore and asked them to run southwest into the country to find out

---

[1] It is generally agreed that Markland was Labrador, although some think it was Nova Scotia. Many books and innumerable shorter dissertations have been published disputing on where Wineland lay. The Gulf of St. Lawrence has recently been favored by many. There have been contenders for Maine, Massachusetts, and indeed all the way to Georgia. The explorers themselves were a bit hazy on the location, as will be seen on p. 129, *post* of the saga.

the quality of the land. They were to be gone two days and the intervening night. They had a garment named a *kjafal* [Irish *cabhal*]. It was so designed that it had a hood and was slit at the sides, without sleeves, and was fastened together between their legs with a button and a loop. Apart from this both of them were unclad.

The .expedition waited. When the messengers returned, one of them carried a twig with wine berries, the other carried an ear of self-sown wheat. They went aboard ship and the expedition proceeded.

They stood into a fjord. Outside its mouth was an island around which were strong currents. Therefore they named it Straumey (Island of the Violent Currents). The eider ducks were so numerous on this island that one could hardly step without breaking an egg. They named the bay Straumfjord (Fjord of the Strong Currents).

Here they unloaded their ships and made preparations for residence. They had with them every kind of domestic animal. It was a fair country, and they paid attention to nothing much but exploring [that is, they neglected haying, and so on]. They wintered there, although they had not made suitable preparation during the summer. The hunting became poor, and food started running short.

Now Thorhall the Hunter disappeared. Up to this time they had been praying to God [the Christian God] for food, but the response to their prayers had not been as prompt as they would have liked. They searched for Thorhall for three days and found him at last high up on a cliff. There he lay with his face toward the sky, mouth and nostrils wide, mumbling. They asked why he was there, which he said was none of their business. Then they asked him to come home with them, and he did.

A little hereafter they secured a whale, which they cut up, not being able to recognize, however, what kind of whale it was. The cooks boiled the meat, but when they ate of it everyone became ill. Then said Thorhall: "Redbeard [the Norse god Thor] turned out to be a better provider than your Christ. This [whale] is what I got for composing a poem to Thor, the most dependable of gods. He has seldom failed me."

When the people heard this, they turned the whale adrift upon the sea, and put their trust in the Lord. Then the weather improved so that they were able to row out [for fish or sea game]. There was no longer a scarcity, with hunting on the land, eggs upon the island, and fish in the sea.

Thorhall the Hunter wanted to go north beyond Wonder Strands and Keelness in search of Vinland, but Karlsefni wanted to go south. Thorhall made his preparations in the shelter of the island, and there were only nine that accompanied him. All the rest went with Karlsefni. As Thorhall was watering his ship he composed a stanza. [We give it in the Arthur Middleton Reeves translation:]

> When I came, these brave men told me,
> Here the best of drink I'd get,
> Now with water pail behold me—
> Wine and I are strangers yet.
> Stooping at the spring, I've tested
> All the wine this land affords;
> Of its vaunted charms divested,
> Poor indeed are its rewards.

When the ship was fully prepared, they hoisted sail. Thorhall composed a stanza:

> Comrades, let us now be faring
> Homeward to our own again!
> Let us try the sea steed's daring,
> Give the chafing courser rein.
> Those who will may bide in quiet,
> Let them praise their chosen land,
> Feasting on a whale-steak diet,
> In their home by Wonder Strand.

Then they sailed beyond Wonder Strands and Keelness and desired to head west, but there came against them a west wind and they were driven to Ireland, where they were beaten and enslaved. Thorhall lost his life there, according to the report of merchants.[2]

[2] These would be Irish merchants who came to Iceland. Many Irish trading ships did in this period.

The story about Karlsefni is that he stood southwest along the coast, as well as Snorri and Bjarni, with their companions. They sailed a long time, even till they came to a river that flowed from the land into a lake and thence into the sea. There were extensive gravel bars, so that it was not possible for the ships to enter the river except at the highest tide.

Karlsefni and his men sailed into the mouth of the river, which they called Hop.[3] In this country they discovered fields of self-sown wheat wherever the land was low, but wine wood [possibly grapevines] wherever there were hills. Their brook was full of fish. They dug pits where the land met the most frequent high-tide currents; when the tide fell, these pits contained halibut. There were great numbers of wild animals of every kind in the forest.

The party remained a half-month, enjoyed themselves well, and saw no signs of natives. They had their domestic animals with them.

Early one morning as they looked around they saw a great number of skin boats. Pieces of wood were waved from the boats as if grain were beaten with flails, and the motion was sunwise.[4]

Then spoke Karlsefni: "What would be the meaning of that sign?" Snorri Thorbrandsson answered: "It may be that this is a peace signal. Let us take a white shield and carry it toward them." They did so.

The visitors came rowing toward them and marveled at them as they scrambled ashore. They were dark and villainous-looking, with coarse hair on their heads. Their eyes were conspicuous, and they were broad across the cheeks. They stayed awhile marveling, and then rowed away south beyond the ness.

The Karlsefni party had built their dwellings on a slope by the lake and some of the buildings were near the water, others

---

[3] The word is pronounced like our "hope." It is the Icelandic word for a small, landlocked bay that is salt with the high tide but fresh with low tide. Cf. English place names like Stanhope, Easthope.

[4] This describes the windmill effect you see when canoes are propelled with double-ended paddles such as the Eskimos use for their kayaks.

farther away. They spent the winter. There was no snow, and the domestic animals fared out all winter.

That spring they saw early one morning that a multitude of skin boats came rowing past the ness, as many as if charcoal had been scattered over the whole estuary. As before, staves were waving from every boat. Karlsefni's party raised their shields aloft. When the two parties met they started trading.

What these people most desired was red cloth. They had for exchange peltries and skins that were uniformly gray. They also wanted to buy swords and spears, but the sale of these was forbidden by Karlsefni and Snorri. The natives, whom the Norsemen called Skraelings, took a span's breadth of red cloth in exchange for a good pelt, and they bound the pieces of cloth around their heads. That is how the trading went for some time.

When the cloth which the Karlsefni party had with them became scarce, they began to cut it into smaller pieces, so that finally some of them were no more than a finger's breadth, but the natives paid as much for these as they had paid for the larger pieces, and even more.

It happened that a bull which belonged to the Karlsefni party came running down from the woods, bellowing loudly. This frightened the natives. They ran to their boats and rowed southward around the cape.

Now there was no sign of the natives for three weeks together. Thereupon, however, Karlsefni's people saw a multitude of boats coming from the south, moving forward as in a steady stream. This time all the staves were being waved countersunwise and everybody was screaming at the top of their voices. In reply Karlsefni's people raised a red shield and carried it toward them. The natives jumped from their boats and the two parties met in battle. There came a shower of missiles, for the natives used war slings (catapults).

Karlsefni's people saw that the natives were raising a large sphere on a pole. This was about as big as the [inflated] stomach of a sheep, seemed bluish in color, and was thrown from the pole up on the land above the heads of Karlsefni's people. There was a terrifying sound when it struck the earth.

This frightened Karlsefni's men so that they had no desire but to flee and to retreat upstream along the river. It seemed to them that the natives were approaching from all sides, so they did not stop retreating until they came to some cliffs, where they made a resolute stand.

The woman Freydis now came out from her house and saw that Karlsefni and his men were retreating. "Why do you flee from these wretches? Such stout fellows as you are, it seems to me you could just butcher them as if they were domestic animals. It looks to me that if I only had weapons I could make a better fight than any of you." They paid no attention to her.

Freydis tried to follow them, but was slow, for she was with child. Still, she reached the forest, with the natives attacking her. She came upon a dead man. He was Thorbrand Snorrason, and there was a flat stone sticking in his head. His unsheathed sword lay beside him. She took this up and prepared to defend herself. When the natives approached her, she exposed her bare breast and whetted the sword on it. This proceeding frightened the natives. They went to their boats and rowed away.

Karlsefni and his companions went up to her and praised her stratagem. Two of their men had been killed, and many of the natives. The Karlsefni party had been greatly outnumbered.

They returned to their houses, dressed their wounds, and considered what the multitude could have been which came toward them from inland. Finally they concluded that the only people actually in the fight had been those who came from the boats, and and that those who appeared to be coming from inland were figures of their imagination.

The [retreating] natives found a dead man, and there lay an ax beside him. One of them took the ax and chopped with it into a tree, and so did one after another. Evidently they thought it was a marvel of sharpness. Then one of them tried to chop a stone with it and the [edge of the] ax broke. Apparently they decided it was worthless when it could not stand being used chopping rocks, and they threw it away.

Karlsefni and his men decided that although the land was fertile, there would always be fear of the natives, and strife with them. So they prepared to leave, intending to sail for home, and stood northeast along the coast, where they found five natives sleeping under fur robes near the sea. They had with them boxes containing deer marrow mixed with blood. Karlsefni's party thought it probable that these men were outlaws. They killed them.

Now the party came to a ness on which there were many animals. The whole ness was one cake of manure, for the deer had spent the nights there.

The Karlsefni party arrived at Straumfjord, where they found awaiting them an abundance of everything they needed.

It is one variant of the story that Bjarni and Gudrid had remained behind there with 100 people, not having gone farther, and that it was only Karlsefni and Snorri who went farther south, accompanied by 40 men, that they did not stay at Hop more than a scant two months, and that they returned [to where Bjarni and Gudrid were] the same summer.

Now Karlsefni took a single vessel to go in search of Thorhall the Hunter, the rest staying behind. They went northeast beyond Keelness and advanced to the northwest, with the land on their port side. Here they found nothing but uninhabited forests so far as they could see, with never a clearing. When they had traveled a long way, they found a river which entered the sea coming from the southeast and flowing northwest. They went into the mouth of this river and placed their ship along the southwestern bank.

One morning Karlsefni and his men saw on the other side of a clearing something that glittered, and they gave a shout. It moved, and turned out to be a uniped, which scuttled down the riverbank where the ship lay. Thorvald, the son of Erik the Red, sat at the helm. The uniped shot an arrow into his abdomen. Thorvald pulled out the arrow and said: "There is a lot of fat around my guts. We have certainly discovered a good country, but do not seem likely to have long use of it." He died of the wound sometime later. The uniped ran off north.

Karlsefni and his party gave chase and caught sight of the uniped now and then. The last they saw was that he disappeared into a ravine. Thereupon they turned back. . . .

Now they stood toward the northeast and thought they could see the land of the unipeds. They decided not to risk the lives of their company further. In their opinion those were the same mountains which they saw here and which were at Hop, and they concluded that the distance either way from Straumfjord was about the same.

They spent the third winter at Straumfjord. The party became divided into cliques, and the women were responsible for it. Those who were unmarried wanted to get them away from those who were married, which caused the greatest disorder.

It had been during the first winter that Snorri was born, the son of Karlsefni. He was three years of age when they took their departure.

When they sailed from Vinland they got a southerly wind. They reached Markland, where they met with five natives, one of whom was bearded. There were two women and two children. The Karlsefni party captured the two boys but the rest escaped, disappeared into the ground. They took the boys along with them, taught them to speak [Icelandic], and they were baptized.

They called their mother Vethildi, their father Ovaegi. They said that two kings governed the natives, one of them named Avaldamon, the other Avaldidida. They explained there were no proper houses; people dwelt in caves or in holes in the ground. They said that across the water opposite to their country was a land with people dressed in white clothes who carried long staves to which cloths were fastened [that is, flags], and that they made great outcries. It is considered that this must have been the Land of the White Men, or Ireland the Great.

They reached Greenland and spent the winter with Erik the Red.

The second summer thereafter Karlsefni went to Iceland, to his home in Reynines, and with him Gudrid. His mother felt he had married beneath him and so refused to live with him the first winter. But experience showed her that Gudrid was an able woman, so she returned home. They got along well thereafter.

The daughter of Snorri, the son of Karlsefni, was Hallfrid, the mother of Bishop Thorlak Runolfsson. They had a son named Thorbjörn, whose daughter Thorun was the mother of Bishop Bjarni.

The son of Snorri was Thorgeir, the father of Yngvild, who was the mother of Bishop Brand the First.

Here ends this saga. ▨

The usual date given for the return of the colonists from the mainland to Greenland is 1006. It could not well be later than 1010.

The record of contacts between the North American mainland and the American islands of Greenland and Iceland, as well as between them and Europe, is fragmentary after the return of Karlsefni, for a number of reasons.

The Church, while it sent at least one party of missionaries to Vinland, never established a separate bishopric there, and thus preserved no such record of tax collections as it did from Iceland and Greenland.

The Icelanders maintained their own continuous records for the land in which they lived, and less continuously for Greenland. They were not so careful about places which the Greenlanders merely visited now and then, as when they went to Markland (southern Labrador, or Nova Scotia) for timber.

The main difficulty with colonizing the mainland was that the natives offered stout opposition and that the Europeans of the eleventh century did not as yet have firearms with which to overawe and drive away the possessors of the land. This difficulty in fact continued down to and even after Columbus, as we shall see by the way the natives of the Philippines slew Magellan, in spite of his armor, with arrows of reeds which did not even have stone or metal points.

After the discovery voyages and the colonizing attempt, the first known voyage to Wineland the Good was in 1121, thus more than a century after Karlsefni. The record, from the annals of Iceland, is simply that in this year "Bishop Erik Gnupsson of Greenland went to Vinland." Nothing is said as to whether he returned. That the annals mentioned the journey at all was likely because trips to Vinland (the St. Lawrence-Newfoundland-New England region) were less common, and thus more noteworthy, than visits to that nearer mainland section which we call Labrador, their Markland.

The next specific references to contact with the mainland of North America are in the Icelandic annals for 1347 and 1348. This wide gap of two hundred and twenty-six years needs comment.

There was in the European Norse countries, especially in Norway, a considerable vernacular literature. Nearly all of this has disappeared, except for the share that was preserved in Iceland.

Since nearly the exclusive preserver was Iceland, we must keep in mind that after 1262 legal commerce with Greenland was from Norway only, chiefly from Bergen. Icelanders were forbidden to sail to Greenland and Greenlanders to Iceland. Therefore most records of the external relations of Greenland would have to be preserved in Greenland itself, or in Norway. With the disappearance of European culture from Greenland in the sixteenth century, every record and memory there would be lost. Norway succeeded in preserving little.

In parts of the story which there has not been time to cover are accounts of the legal difficulties that ships got into when, even through stress of weather, Greenlandic vessels landed in Iceland. It had to be proved on such occasions that these were not camouflaged trading ventures. Apparently Norway did not take the same attitude toward contacts between Greenland and Markland-Vinland, so there was less chance to get such voyages recorded through litigation.

But one Greenland ship that had been to the Labrador-Newfoundland section did get itself into legal troubles through becoming lost and turning up in Iceland. The Icelandic annals have it, for 1347:

"There arrived a ship from Greenland which was smaller than the smallest type of Icelandic mercantile craft. It came into outer Straumfjord and was without anchor. There were seventeen aboard. The ship had been to Markland. It was later driven here [to Iceland] by a gale."

One of the annals has it that the next year the crew were taken from Iceland to Bergen, Norway. There would be two reasons for this: first, that they were under suspicion of infringing the Bergen monopoly by attempting to trade with Iceland, so there might be need for punishing them, and second, that the said monopoly arrangement prevented sailings from Iceland direct to Greenland—to be legal the return voyage had to be from Iceland to Norway and thence to Greenland.

From this we see that because of the •monopoly there was now a much closer contact with Greenland from Norway than from Iceland. So if there was any novelty to Norwegians of this period about voyages to the North American mainland, there must have been excitement when the seventeen Greenlanders reached Bergen.

There was a certain timeliness and poetic fitness about this visit of the seventeen. In 1000 a King of Norway enthusiastic about missionary work, Olaf Tryggvason, had placed clergy-men aboard the ship that was to discover the North American mainland. Now, three hundred and forty-eight years later, these Greenlanders who had been to Markland found themselves in a city, Bergen, which contained the court of another devout soldier of the Church, Magnus Eriksson, ruler of Sweden as well as Norway, who was just then engaged upon a series of campaigns intended to force Russia to shift from the Greek to the Roman side of the ecclesiastical boundary. After preliminary success, these plans were defeated, in part by Russian soldiers and in part by the Black Death.

The holy war failing him to the east, King Magnus faced west and sent an expedition to Greenland. We know from other sources that just in this period the Greenlanders were turning away in considerable numbers from the practices of the Church of Rome, which the seventeen no doubt reported to the King, who decided to do something about it.

The documents in this case are neither consecutive nor complete, nor are they all contemporary. For instance, one of the more important was written in Iceland during the seventeenth century in Latin as a summary of Icelandic annals which had been destroyed by fire just then and which Bishop Gisli Oddson, who had been thoroughly familiar with them, was attempting to replace from memory. For the year 1342 the Bishop's paraphrase reads in translation:

"The people of Greenland voluntarily abandoned the true faith and the Christian religion. They abandoned all good customs and true virtues and turned to the people of America (*ad Americae populos se converterunt*). It is said that Greenland lies very near the western lands of the world."

There has been much dispute over whether "*ad Americae populos se converterunt*" meant that the Christians of the Gardar diocese had adopted the heathen customs of the Greenland Eskimos (whom the sagas throughout specifically recognize as the same kind of people that lived in Markland and Vinland). Others have thought, first, that the Bishop was translating the Icelandic Markland (and/or Vinland) into the current name, America, and second, that he meant to say that the Christian Greenlanders had left their home country to settle in the heathen districts of the American mainland. If the first is what the Bishop meant, the document we are about to give will apply chiefly, if not solely, to Greenland. But if the second was the intended meaning, then the Norwegian King's Greenland expedition, which is described below, was intended for visiting Markland to save from apostasy those Greenlanders who had moved to Labrador to join the heathen Americans.

After the failure of a second expedition against Russia, King Magnus, as has been said, gave up hope that he could forcibly Romanize the lands to the east of Sweden. So he carried on by issuing a directive in 1354 for an enterprise to support the Church in the West. The commander of the expedition was Powell (Paul) Knutsson, one of the foremost men of Norway, and to him the directive is addressed. The translation is from the third volume of *Grönlands Historiske Mindesmaerker*, Copenhagen, 1845:

¶Letters of authorization for sailing to Greenland from King Magnus to Powell Knutsson:

Magnus, by grace of God King of Norway, Sweden, and Skone, sends to all those who see or hear this letter, greetings:

We desire you to know that you [Knutsson] are to take as ship's company for the *Knör* [the regular merchant ship that sailed from Bergen to Greenland] any men, whether named or unnamed, from Our bodyguard or from the retainers of other men whom you may wish to use on the voyage, and that Powell Knutsson, who is to be commander on the *Knör*, shall have full authority to choose for the *Knör* such men as appear to him most suitable, whether as officers or privates.

We ask that you accept these Our orders in the warmest goodwill toward the cause, for We do this for the glory of God and for the good of Our soul as well as for the sake of our ancestors, who established Christianity in Greenland and supprted it till now, so that We are determined it shall not be destroyed in Our day.

Know all men for truth that whoever disregards this command shall be under Our displeasure, and upon him shall be visited such punishment as fits those who disobey Our written orders.

Done at Bergen on the Monday following the day of Simon and Judah [October 28] in the thirty-sixth year of Our rule [1354]. By Our Regent Orm Eisteinsson, with seal affixed.

The expedition sailed the year following the date of the order, 1355. The only thing known of it from Norwegian sources thereafter is that it returned to Norway in 1363 or 1364.

Apart from the desire of Magnus to spread the Roman form of Christianity, two special reasons for the expedition having been sent at just this time are given in the books—that the *Knör* had returned from Greenland in 1346 with a specially rich cargo of trade, and that the seventeen voyagers to Labrador had visited the court city of Bergen in 1348.

The long delay between 1348 and 1355 is explained by the King's preoccupation with the war on Russia and later by the enervation caused throughout Europe by the Black Death.

Hjalmar R. Holand, cited below, is one of those who has suggested that, apart from the King's general desire to support the Church, the immediate reason for the expedition was probably the visit to Bergen of the seventeen who had been in Markland and who would have told Magnus not merely that the Europeans in Greenland were falling away from the true faith, but also that there were heathen on the mainland of North America, in Markland and Vinland, who needed conversion.

The possible connection with the mainland of North America is in that from the period of the Knutsson expedition comes a runic inscription carved on stone and found near Kensington, Minnesota. About this Holand published in 1932 the book *Kensington Rune Stone* (privately printed, Ephraim, Wisconsin) followed in 1940 by the larger and better considered *Westward from Vinland* (Duell, Sloan and Pearce), a work that should be read by those interested in the problem discussed here.

Holand's view is, in essence, that the Knutsson group, who came from Norway by way of Greenland, finally penetrated as far west as Minnesota and left there a memorial such as Norsemen customarily did leave at the farthest points of their expeditions, a message cut in runes upon a stone. The ship mentioned in the inscription, which is quoted below, might well have been built locally, as many explorers of that and later periods were in the habit of doing. If the "sea" spoken of was Hudson Bay, then the route used was the same as employed later by the Hudson's Bay Company. If the "sea" was Lake Superior, the route would have been from the St. Lawrence Vinland section, and the method that of ascending by the river and the various lakes, building new ships above each waterfall. The ships of that time, be it remembered, were more like our idea of an open boat.

As deciphered, the Kensington inscription runs:

[We are] 8 Goths (Swedes) and 22 Norwegians on an exploratory journey from Vinland through the West. We had camped by [a lake with] 2 skerries one day's journey north from this stone. We were [out] and fished one day. After [when] we came home [we] found 10 [of our] men red with blood and dead. Ave Maria, save [us] from evil.

That is the inscription on the face of the stone. On one edge are the lines:

[We] have 10 of [our party] by the sea to look after our ship fourteen days' journey from this island [in the] year 1362.

It seems agreed that the Kensington stone was discovered in 1898, enmeshed in the roots of a tree of considerable age—discovered when the stump was pulled. Many years later it was first noticed, when the stone was being used as a threshold, that there were inscriptions on it. When these were identified as runes, and deciphered, skepticism about Norsemen having been in Minnesota during the fourteenth century was nearly universal.

The arguments marshaled against the authenticity of the stone seemed at first to be conclusive. But several of them have been weakened or destroyed by later research, so that now it seems close to the mark to say that of all persons more or less entitled to an opinion through competence and study, 60 per cent are still against authenticity of the inscription, and about 40 per cent have been won over. In caliber and integrity the two groups seem to average about the same.

A sample objection is that the reference in the inscription to "this island" is absurd, since the stone was not found on an island. But it was suggested in rebuttal, on grounds of mere logic, that a faker would not have made a nearly incredible story even harder to believe through referring to a hill as an island. Then along came geologists who concluded that the slight rise on which the stone was discovered might well have been an island in a lake during the fourteenth century.

The skeptics have found it absurd that a small party could penetrate so far inland so long ago without being stopped by Indians. But if Norsemen in those days were in the habit of treating the Indians as sympathetically as the French did in the period following Cartier, then a party of fourteenth-century missionaries could have made long journeys as easily as did the later French. (The sagas demonstrate that Norsemen did act the superman on the exploring expeditions and in the colonizing ventures of the eleventh century. By their own account, they got along badly with the Indians. But intermarriages with natives were common in Greenland by the time of Knutsson, and the former Germanic arrogance of the Norse may already have been replaced by a Frenchlike adaptability.)

The big argument against the Kensington stone is linguistic, that there are upon it verbal forms which were unknown in the time of the Knutsson expedition. But this argument has collapsed, at least partly; for later research has demonstrated that the word forms alleged by the linguists to have been non-existent in the Norway-Sweden of Knutsson's time have since been found carved in runes on monuments in the Scandinavian countries which are beyond doubt from the Knutsson period or older. So if a charlatan faked the Kensington stone, he must have been a deeper student of the history of language than any known scholar of the nineteenth century.

These things, and others like them, have enabled the Stoneites to formulate an argument which has gained them much support: "You have more and harder things to explain away if you claim the stone is a fake."

It has been objected that if the stone is genuine, it is strange that it is the only known relic from the period of Norse visits. But the defenders claim to have discovered, either in records or as now bodily present, many ruins and other remains of medieval Norsemen in the United States and Canada. We mention only one, the Newport Tower.

The poet Longfellow was among those who believed that Norsemen of a pre-Columbian time settled in Rhode Island. In accord with this view, his poem "The Skeleton in Armor" tells us in the words of a departed Viking:

> "There for my lady's bower
> Built I the lofty tower,
> Which, to this very hour,
> Stands looking seaward."

The belief in the thirteenth- or fourteenth-century dating of the Newport Tower, strong in Longfellow's time, was later superseded by a rival theory—that the building was a mill constructed by Governor Benedict Arnold, the grandfather of General Benedict Arnold, thus dating merely from the early New England colonial period. So the "Tower" became the "Old Stone Mill."

But in 1942 Philip Ainsworth Means showed in his book *Newport Tower* (Henry Holt) that Governor Arnold was not the builder, that the building was older than the Arnoldist theory would have it, and that in architecture the tower was

similar to thirteenth-century churches found from Spain to
Scandinavia. In short, the Means presentation made it seem
likely that Longellow was right about the Norse and pre-Columbian origin of the tower, though wrong about the "lady's bower"
part of the speech which he attributes to the ghost.

After the decline of Norse seafaring, the first substantially
documented voyages to the North American mainland are
Portuguese and English, in the late 1400's.

. The 1476 voyage of Pining when the King of Denmark, at
the suggestion of the King of Portugal, sent the governor of
Iceland westward across the sea, has been mentioned. It has
been conjectured that Pining sailed far enough north along
the west coast of Greenland, and far enough offshore, to see
land beyond the narrow waters—Labrador or Baffin Island.
Some evidence has been brought forward to bolster the probabilities. At any rate, the Portuguese followed up the 1476
voyage by repeated voyages to the Labrador region that were
commanded by different members of the family Cortereal.

As interpreted by H. P. Biggar in his *Voyages of the Cabots
and Corte-Reals* (Paris, 1903), the first expedition, commanded
by Gaspar Cortereal, left Lisbon the summer of 1500 and went
to the east coast of Greenland by way of the Azores and Iceland,
proceeding north into Denmark Strait, but getting turned
back there, to the west or northwest of Iceland, by the south-
moving ice of the Greenland current. They then turned southwesterly along the coast, rounded Cape Farewell, and
penetrated north beyond latitude 63, in the present Godthaab
district, which in location corresponds to the more northerly of
the two medieval European colonies. There they met, according to contemporary sources, people who were "very wild
and barbarous, almost to the extent of the natives of Brazil,
except that these are white." The obvious suggestion has been
made that these white people were European Greenlanders
who had not yet intermarried with Eskimos sufficiently to become darker than were the Portuguese observers themselves.

Apparently Cortereal turned south when he reached
Sukkertoppen, hard by the Arctic Circle. Without touching the
mainland on this voyage, he reached Lisbon the autumn of
1500. He described the west coast of Greenland as having nu-

merous mountains which were snow-clad. Some of the descriptions of localities are so specific that a number of places can be identified.

The Cortereals thought they had been on the coast of northeastern Asia, and wanted to follow up with a second expedition to locate the spice countries. Accordingly, three ships, still commanded by Gaspar, sailed to the northwest in 1501, and after many vicissitudes struck the shores of Labrador just north of what the Greenlanders and Icelanders had been calling Markland, in the present Okkak region, near 58 degrees north latitude. The coast was nearly as rugged and chilly to the Southland Portuguese as Greenland had been the previous summer.

Following the coast southeasterly, they had their first chance to turn west when they reached Hamilton Inlet, which they entered and penetrated to the Narrows, about 35 miles up. They saw a lot of caribou, and named the inlet Bay of Does.

In another inlet, just north of the Strait of Belle Isle, perhaps St. Lewis Bay, they found trees so large they were too big for the masts of even the largest ships—they were now in the Markland-Labrador lumbering regions of the old Greenlanders. In the same vicinity they met with a band of natives, who were probably Eskimos but may have been Naskapi Indians. Of these they kidnapped fifty and crowded them below hatches for sale as slaves when they should return to Portugal.

They passed Belle Isle Strait without entering it, thinking it would not be deeper than the other inlets they had been exploring. Soon after this the expedition divided, two of the three vessels heading straight for Portugal, no doubt to get the slaves there in as marketable a condition as possible and perhaps also because feeding them was hard on the commissariat. The diet must have been uncongenial to the slaves, if not unwholesome, for the records mention that the captives had been accustomed to living in their own country exclusively on flesh food, which, indeed, conforms with the rest of our information on this region in the sixteenth century.

The records have it that Gaspar Cortereal did not wish to return to Portugal without first going far enough south to determine the relation of the coasts they were following to the islands near the equator that had been discovered by Columbus. So he headed southwest with one ship while the other two struck southeast for Portugal, where they arrived on the ninth and eleventh of October. The King was pleased with many features of their report, but especially with the prospect of a new man-hunting ground. Biggar summarizes that "the natives would make excellent slaves. These would prove the more valuable as the African Negro had now become so wary that his capture was a matter of some difficulty."

By the New Year Portugal was worried because Gaspar had not returned, and his brother Miguel received authority on January 15, 1502, to go in search of him and also to make independent discoveries. In June this third Cortereal expedition was in Newfoundland; on the twenty-fourth of that month they entered what is now the harbor of St. John's, which they named St. John's River. The three ships searched northward to the Belle Isle neighborhood, south along the east coast, and west along the south coast. They were to rendezvous at St. John's late in August, and two of them did. The third, under Miguel Cortereal, did not keep the tryst and was never definitely heard from again.

An elder brother, Vasqueanes, desired permission from King Manoel (Emanuel) to search for Gaspar and Miguel, but permission was refused. Two ships were sent, however, but the brothers were not found, nor any clear trace of them, then or afterward.

Several long letters have been preserved that tell of the return of the second Gaspar Cortereal expedition, the one that followed the Labrador coast south and took the fifty or so slaves. These agree so remarkably that there is little reason to quote more than one, unless to prove how consonant they are. Here is the letter of Alberto Cantino, Minister at Lisbon for the Duke of Ferrara, written October 17, 1501, to the Duke. The translation is that of H. P. Biggar as published in his *The Precursors of Jacques Cartier* (Ottawa, 1911).

The Cortereal Voyage of 1501

🖋 Nine months have now passed since this most serene monarch [King Manoel I] sent to the northern parts two well-equipped ships, for the sole purpose of finding out if it were possible to discover in that region any lands or islands. Now on the eleventh of the present month one of them has arrived safe and with some booty, and has brought people and news which it appeared to me ought not to pass without your Excellency's hearing thereof; and thus I have set down here below clearly and exactly all that in my presence was told the King by the captain.

First of all, they relate that after setting sail as they did from the port of Lisbon, they made their way for four months continuously, always in the same direction and toward the same pole, and never in all that time did they see anything at all. Nevertheless, in the fifth month, still wishing to push on, they say that they met huge masses of solid snow floating upon the sea and moving under the influence of the waves, from the summit of which by the force of the sun's rays a clear stream of sweet water was melted and, once dissolved, ran down in little channels made by itself, eating its way splashingly to the base. Since the ships now lacked fresh water, the boats approached and took as much as was then needed.

Fearing to remain in that region by reason of this present danger, they wished to turn back, but yet, spurred by hope, decided to go forward as best they could for a few days more, and having got under way, on the second day they again discovered the sea to be frozen, and were forced to give up the undertaking. They then began to turn toward the northwest and the west, in which direction they made their way for three more months, always with favorable weather.

And on the first day of the fourth month they caught sight between these two courses of a very large country, which they approached with very great delight. And since throughout this region numerous large rivers flowed into the sea, by one of these they made their way about a league inland, where on landing they found abundance of most luscious and varied fruits, and trees and pines of such measureless height and girth that they would be too big as a mast for the largest ship that sails the sea.

No corn of any sort grows there, but the men of that country say they live altogether by fishing and hunting animals, in which the land abounds, such as very large deer covered with extremely long hair, the skins of which they use for garments and also make houses and boats thereof, and again wolves, foxes, tigers [lynx], and sables. They [the explorers] affirm that there are—what appears to me wonderful—as many falcons as there are sparrows in our country, and I have seen some of them and they are extremely pretty.

They forcibly kidnapped about fifty men and women of this country and have brought them to the King. I have seen, touched, and examined these people, and beginning with their stature, declare that they are somewhat taller than our average, with members corresponding and well formed. The hair of the men is long, just as we wear ours, and they wear it in curls, and have their faces marked with great signs, and these signs are like those of the Indians. Their eyes are greenish, and when they look at one, this gives an air of great boldness to their whole countenance. Their speech is unintelligible, but nevertheless is not harsh, but rather human. Their manners and gestures are most gentle; they laugh considerably and manifest the greatest pleasure.

So much for the men. The women have small breasts and most beautiful bodies, and rather pleasant faces. The color of these women may be said to be more white than otherwise, but the men are considerably darker.

In fine, except for the terribly harsh look of the men, they appear to me to be in all else of the same form and image as ourselves. They go quite naked except for their privy parts, which they cover with a skin of the above-mentioned deer. They have no arms nor iron, but whatever they work or fashion they cut with very hard sharp stones, with which they split in two the very hardest substances.

This vessel came home thence in one month, and they say the distance is 2800 miles. The other consort decided to make her way far enough along that coast to be able to learn whether it is an island or yet mainland. And thus the

King awaits with great eagerness both that one and others, and when they have arrived, should they bring anything worthy of your Excellency's consideration, I shall immediately send you word of the same.

My respects to your Excellency.

Your most Illustrious and most Excellent
Grace's servant,
ALBERT CANTINO

Lisbon, 17 October, 1501 🖎

We have noticed out of their chronological order the three voyages connected with the name of Cortereal; for they are in logical connection with the 1476 Columbus voyage to Iceland that was made aboard a ship engaged in the Bristol-Portugal trade, and with the 1476 Pining voyage that was carried out by the Danes on behalf of the Portuguese. These voyages form a group not merely in that they all had a Portuguese connection, but also in that they in effect took the same routes, for the Cortereals did their work in the sequence Iceland, Greenland, Labrador, Newfoundland.

We have thus overshot by three years the earlier venture of John Cabot, who—apparently since about 1486—had been trying to stir up English concern for northwest discovery.

The Italian Giovanni Caboto (Zuam Gabota) first appears over the rim of history in 1461 when he applied for Venetian citizenship because the opportunities in foreign trade were better than in his native Genoa. Before this he had been given to understand when he was at Mecca that spices and other precious things which he saw there had come ultimately from northeastern Asia. Knowing the world to be spherical, he figured that northeastern Asia would be close to northwestern Europe. For that and other reasons he moved to London about 1484, becoming part of a considerable body of Italian merchants and seafarers then resident in England. Later he moved to Bristol, which was specially conscious of lands beyond the Atlantic because of its flourishing business with Iceland, where Bristol acted partly as intermediary in the fish trade between the Iberian Peninsula and Iceland.

Bristol was interested, too, in the Isle of Brazil that was

supposed to lie in the sea to the west of Ireland. This was perhaps a folk memory of the land southwest of Greenland called Vinland, from which, as we have seen by the *Saga of Erik the Red*, at least one ship had come direct to be wrecked on the coast of Ireland. Or perhaps the Brazil report was of more recent origin, built upon a fourteenth-century knowledge of Markland, which also is southerly from Greenland, though not so far south as Vinland.

The view that Markland was Brazil has been supported by one of half a dozen or so contending etymologies, where it has been claimed that Brazil means "Wooded" and is a translation of Markland, which means "Forest Land." Markland is west from Ireland, for Labrador is west from the British Isles, the southern part of it a little farther south than southernmost Ireland.

There had already been at least one English expedition in search of Brazil, in 1480, and thus some years before Cabot got there. It was initiated by John Jay, a merchant intermediary between Iceland and Bristol. The commander, John Lloyd, was one of the ablest seamen of his day.

We know that in 1481 there was further westward search for land from Bristol, and it is probable that the search was nearly continuous. A Spanish ambassador to England wrote in 1498 that each year of the preceding seven a vessel from Bristol had been upon this western adventure. It seems that in 1491 and 1492 Cabot was influential in this, for when the news came that Columbus had succeeded in a like quest, it was Cabot who was commissioned by Henry VII to open up what would be, on a spherical earth, a shorter route than the Spanish one to Asia.

Although commissioned in 1496, Cabot did not get started until May 2, 1497, on which date he sailed from Bristol in the tiny *Matthew*, with a complement of 18. He went north between Britain and Ireland and then steered northerly toward Iceland, which course he may have taken so as to remain as long as possible in waters familiar to Bristol seamen. We know, however, that he understood the principles of spherical sailing, and he may have been governed simply by the desire to save miles through using a great-circle course. At any rate, he evidently followed near the great circle, for he turned west, and later enough south so that his first landfall is a good deal farther south than Bristol, for Cape Breton Island is abreast of southern France.

The 1497 ship's journal of Cabot, like most records of him and his work, is lost, so that it is hard to pin him down to places and dates. His landfall may have been in Newfoundland, and Nova Scotia is second choice. Cape Breton seems most likely. All we know for certain is that Cabot followed the land till he was satisfied it was continental, not an island. Perhaps his thinking was that he had merely confirmed the Vinland-Markland reports of the Icelanders. J. A. Williamson says in *The Ocean in English History* (Oxford University Press, 1941) that while Cabot had brought with him to England the Italian view that Asia could be reached rather easily by sailing west, he had been able to supplement that doctrine with practical knowledge gained in England. Williamson continues:

"They [the merchants of Bristol] on their side had something to tell [Cabot], namely, the Icelandic knowledge that a main continent existed at no impossible distance across the Atlantic."

When his western land had been proved not to be a small island, Cabot turned for home, no doubt to procure larger and more numerous ships with which to follow up his exploration of what he thought to be Asia, which he considered himself to have reached, as he had promised to do, by a shorter route than that of Columbus. Besides, he did not have with him such goods as he believed, from his reading of Marco Polo, would be needed for trading with the Grand Khan of Tartary.

On the way back (to quote Williamson again) Cabot's "Bristol mariners caught cod in such profusion (on the Newfoundland Banks) that they declared it to be a better fishing ground than the coast of Iceland."

From Bristol itself, from the records of the English Government, and from letters written home by discovery-conscious representatives of the countries of southern Europe, we have a few—deplorably and surprisingly few—documents that bear on the first Cabot voyage.

Maurice Toby completed in or about 1565 a *Chronicle* which spanned the activities of Bristol from 1217 to 1565. H. P. Biggar's *The Precursors of Cartier* quotes from this for 1496:

"This year on St. John the Baptist's day, the land of America was found by the merchants of Bristowe in a ship of Bristowe called the *Mathew*, the which said ship departed from the port of Bristowe the second day of May and came home again the sixth of August next following."

Implied confirmation of the return date, August 6, is that the English Treasury paid on August 10, 1496, a reward of £10 sterling to "him that found the new isle." Orders were given for a pension of £20 on December 13, 1497, and again on February 22, 1498, this to be "granted yearly during Our pleasure."

December 18, 1497, Raimondo de Raimondi de Soncino, who represented the Duke of Milan in London, wrote from there to his master:

My most Illustrious and most Excellent Lord:

Perhaps amidst so many occupations of your Excellency it will not be unwelcome to learn how His Majesty here has acquired a portion of Asia without a stroke of his sword.

In this kingdom there is a lower-class Venetian named Master Zoanne Caboto, of a fine mind, very expert in navigation, who, seeing that the most serene Kings, first of Portugal then of Spain, have occupied unknown islands, meditated the achievement of a similar acquisition for His Majesty aforesaid, and having obtained royal grants securing to himself the profitable control of whatever he should discover, since the sovereignty was reserved to the Crown, with a small ship and 18 persons he committed himself to fortune and set out from Bristol, a western port of this kingdom, and having passed Ireland, which is still farther to the west, and then shaped a northerly course, he began to navigate to the eastern parts, leaving (during several days) the North Star to the right. And having wandered about considerably, at length he fell in with terra firma, where he set up the royal standard, and having taken possession for this King and collected several tokens, he came back again.

The said Master Zoanne, being a foreigner and a poor man, would not be believed if the crew, who are nearly all English and from Bristol, did not testify that what he says is true.

This Master Zoanne has a drawing of the world on a map and also on a solid globe, which he has made, and shows the point he reached; and going toward the east, he has passed considerably the country of the Tanais [Asia].

And they say that the land is excellent and [the air] temperate, and they think that Brazil wood and silks grow there. And they affirm that the sea is covered with fish which are caught not merely with nets but with baskets, a stone being attached to make the basket sink in the water, and this I heard the said Master Zoanne relate. And said Englishmen, his companions, say that they will fetch so many fish that this kingdom will have no more need of Iceland, from which country there comes a very great store of fish which are called stockfish.

But Master Zoanne has set his mind on something greater; for he expects to go from that place already occupied, constantly hugging the shore, farther toward the east until he is opposite an island called by him Cipango [Japan], situated in the equinoctial region, where he thinks grow all the spices of the world and also the precious stones. And he says that once upon a time he was at Mecca, whither the spices are brought by caravan from distant countries, and those who brought them, on being asked where the said spices grow, answered that they did not know, but that other caravans come with this merchandise to their homes from distant countries, who again say that they are brought to them from other remote regions.

And he argues thus: that if the Orientals affirm to the southerners that these things come from a distance, and so from hand to hand, presupposing the rotundity of the earth, it must be that the last people gets them in the north toward the west. And he speaks of it in such a way that not costing me more than it does, I too believe him. And what is more, His Majesty here, who is wise and not lavish, likewise puts some faith in him, for since his return he makes him a very fair allowance, as this Master Zoanne himself tells me.

And it is said that in the spring His Majesty aforesaid will fit out some ships, and besides will give him all the malefactors, and they will proceed to that country to form a colony, by means of which they hope to establish a greater depot for spices in London than there is at Alexandria. And the chief men in the enterprise belong to Bristol, great sailors, who now that they know where to go say that it is not more than a fifteen days' voyage thither, nor do they ever have storms after they leave Ireland.

I have also talked with a Burgundian, a companion of Master Zoanne's, who confirms everything, and wishes to return there because the Admiral (for thus Master Zoanne now styles himself) has given him an island. And he has given another to a barber of his from Genoese Castiglione, and both of them consider themselves counts, nor does my lord the Admiral esteem himself less than a prince.

I think that on this voyage will also go some poor Italian monks, who all have promises of bishoprics. And having become a friend of the Admiral's, if I wish to go I should have an archbishopric, but I have thought the benefices which your Excellency has reserved for me a safer thing, and I beg indeed that should any become vacant in my absence, your Excellency will see that possession is given to me, making the necessary arrangements in the meanwhile that they be not taken from me by others who, being on the spot, are able to be much more diligent than I, who am reduced in this country to eating at every meal ten or twelve courses and to remaining three hours at table each time, twice a day, for love of Your Excellency, to whom I humbly recommend myself.

Your Excellency's most humble servant,

RAIMUNDUS ✠

Various other letters and documents have been preserved that bear on the first Cabot voyage. Although they contain a few additional points, the total gives less detailed information than we have from the Cortereal voyages. But as in the Portuguese case, the agreement between the sources leaves us feeling that while the information is limited, it is reliable as far as it goes.

In 1498 Cabot sailed again, this time with a large vessel provided by the merchants of London, and four Bristol ships.

With this, John Cabot so nearly disappears from history that until recently we have been restricted to inference about his disappearance, for there was no known contemporary statement even to the effect that he had never returned. But such a statement has now been found and was published in May, 1939, by Denys Hay in the *English Historical Review*. The reference was discovered in the manuscript of the contemporary historian Polydore Vergil, and is to the effect that Cabot and his ship disappeared with all hands. The reference is more tantalizing than conclusive, for the wording is "ship" and Cabot is thought to have had five ships. Possibly it was with him as with the Cortereals, that the commander's vessel was lost while the rest of the fleet got back.

Williamson, upon whom I continue to rely, is the author of several well-considered books dealing with this period, including a work devoted to Cabot. The best solution he can offer for the absence of records of the second voyage, and the scarcity of records on the first, is that both were failures from the commercial point of view and thus seemed, to men of that day, best soon forgotten.

Neither was there political concern. For it had not yet occurred to the Government of England to lay claim to a continent on the strength of the 1497 *Matthew* discovery. There must have been held one of two views, neither of which at that stage would lead to the making of such a claim. To begin with, the men of Bristol likely thought of the Cabot voyages as just two English visits to the lands frequented by the Greenlanders, of which they had learned in Iceland if not in Greenland. Those swayed by such theories about a spherical earth as were held by Cabot himself would think that he had been skirting northerly shores of Asia, which he had found spiceless and worthless.

In a nutshell, the true explanation is, no doubt, that of Williamson: "The [Columbus-Cabot] discovery of America made but a small impression upon English consciousness until half a century after it had taken place." The announcement that Cabot had discovered Newfoundland made hardly more of an impression in 1498 than had been made by Adam of Bremen's announcement in 1070 that the Scandinavians had discovered Vinland.

So it is deplorably true that a man who, from what we know of him in the period 1461-92, seems quite the intellectual match for Columbus is practically unknown as relates to the years of his greatest physical achievements, those of his two voyages.

In addition to the prime reason, just stated through the Williamson quotation, the main secondary reason for this scarcity of information on Cabot, as compared with his fellow Genoese, is that Columbus was fortunate in having a learned and loyal son, Ferdinand, who devoted himself to the preservation of his father's memory, while John Cabot was unfortunate in having a learned but self-centered son, Sebastian, who not merely failed to give his father due credit but who actually did his best to make people believe, though chiefly through implications and silences rather than through outright lying, that he himself and not his father was the great voyager.

Sebastian was, true enough, a great promoter of voyages, for it would appear that he had a good deal to do with starting the search for the Northeast Passage. He made a notable attempt himself to find a Northwest Passage, in 1509.

The voyages of the elder Cabot were hardly in search of a passage around North America, even if it be correct to suppose that his second attempt led him up into Davis Strait. For John believed that Nova Scotia was in Asia, and there would have been no sense in trying to round Asia by a northern route that would lead home to England by way of the North Cape of Norway and the North Sea—no sense which could have been discernible to the men with whom he was associated, who saw nothing in anything unless there was money in it.

But from what we know of the Cortereal voyages it does seem that the Portuguese may have had in mind, even that early, at least a tentative Northwest Passage program, based on a doubt that Labrador was in Asia. By 1509 Sebastian Cabot was definitely trying to circumvent a country that blocked the desired path to the riches of the Orient.

After the voyages of John Cabot and the Cortereals the

further unveiling of the North American continent was steady, if not routine.

British interest, and that of northern Europe, was slow in developing, and centered at first on fisheries, later on fur trading. To the south the Spanish were actually finding gold, though not as much as they expected. Slavery was profitable in Central and South America, or at least they expected it to be, which encouraged exploration and exploitation.

As to Europe's general concern about North America, this came chiefly from its nuisance value—it barred the route to China and so had to be detoured or crossed. As Lawrence J. Burpee has shown in his *The Search for the Western Sea* (New York, 1908), it was this nuisance relation of our continent to Europe and to the Indies which led to the discovery of most of our Atlantic coast line and many of our great lakes, rivers, and other natural features.

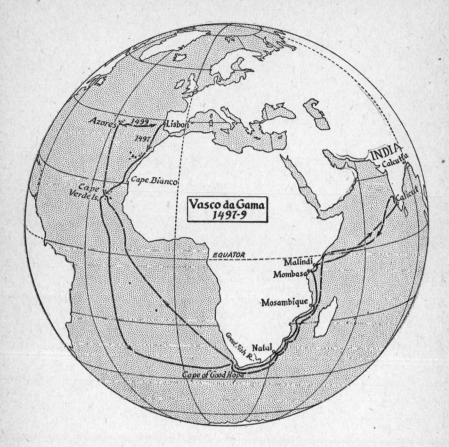

The Portuguese Find a Way to the Indies

THE PORTUGUESE FIND A WAY
TO THE INDIES

CHAPTER 6

Among the many schools of historians are included the opposing groups of those who contend that leaders shape their age and those who maintain that the trend of the age is beyond the control of individuals. Members of the former school often select Henry of Portugal as one of the great molders of destiny; both schools would agree that the age of Prince Henry is probably the most remarkable in the entire history of geographic discovery. For in his time, if not under his chief inspiration, the Portuguese did in exploration what fifteen centuries had "known" no man could ever do.

As we have seen, the Mediterranean philosophers built up gradually, between the fifth and second centuries B.C., the doctrine of the five zones, five belts around a spherical earth only two of which were habitable, the Temperate Zones. The uninhabitable middle belt, the Burning or Torrid Zone, was so near the sun, so directly beneath it, that life was impossible because of the heat, nor could any man ever make a successful dash across it. By a like reasoning the uninhabitable polar belts or areas of the sphere were so far from the sun, and its rays so slanting and weak there, that life was impossible because of the cold; nor could any man ever cross them.

By this doctrine the southern edge of the Northern Frigid Zone could be reached from the North Temperate Zone, but it could never be deeply penetrated and certainly could never be crossed. The South Temperate and South Frigid zones could not even be approached, for the uncrossable Torrid Zone barred the way, and so those two zones would never be known to dwellers in the northern livable zone otherwise than by theory. Whether there were animals and plants south of the Burning Zone would always remain a matter of speculation.

The rebuttal to this theorizing was to point out that ancient writers, among them Herodotus, told in their books of men who had crossed the tropics, which thus were not burning, unlivable, or uncrossable. There appear to have been in most centuries a few scholars who agreed with this, but the overwhelming weight of opinion was behind those who "knew" that tales like those of Herodotus were folklore. You were not sound, not orthodox, unless you believed that the Torrid Zone was literally burning, or at a minimum blistering and steaming, unlivably hot.

This type of cosmography still held sway in Europe during the early fifteenth century when there came upon the stage Prince Henry of Portugal (1394-1460), third surviving son of King John (João) I.

At this distance, and because the records are deficient through calculated secrecy or inadvertence, we cannot decide whether Henry's remarkable program was shaped by events or whether it was consciously invented and doggedly carried out by a single man of genius or by a small group. But whatever the reason, and whoever the moving spirit, there developed a program under the patronage of Henry through which a series of expeditions went southward along the coast of Africa, westward to and perhaps beyond the Azores, and in other directions. Besides rediscovery of the Azores there was now a revived interest in the Canaries, and finally the definite beginning of inroads into the fearsome tropics. Cape Bojador, on the very edge of the tropics, was passed in 1434. The next year Cape Blanco was nearly attained, and it lies almost 200 miles within the tropics.

Then came a gap of several years without progress, because of war and politics. But the leavening idea had been introduced—the tropics might be crossable.

For a variety of reasons, physical progress was slow. The Portuguese had not reached within nearer than about 600 miles from the equator when Henry died. Still the Navigator had seen the real conquest of the burning tropics, for since 1441 ships had been passing south beyond Cape Blanco, which meant they had the sun vertically above the mast if they were there in summer. Now the dogma had been that the killing heat would start being effective where the sun became vertical, or only a little south of there. But on trial the heat produced no casualties, nor even great discomfort.

As ships went farther and farther south they did not observe that steady increase of heat which had been postulated. It was no hotter at sea within the tropics than it may be at times on shore in Portugal. With the imagined terrors once banished, the real difficulties were of minor concern.

Henry had not accompanied his ships. He sent them out, with one commander after another, each to go farther than the last. Most of them came back safe. By 1460 there was a feeling that doggedness would do the rest. For this reason, among others, Henry's death did not greatly inhibit the progress of southward discovery.

Still it was not until nearly a half-century had gone by that in 1487 the Portuguese, under Bartholomeu Diaz, finally reached the South Temperate Zone on the west coast of Africa.

After crossing the tropics, Diaz headed straight south, with no land in sight for thirteen days. Then he turned about and, searching to the east and north, finally struck land where the coast of Africa was trending north of east. That was on February 3, 1488. He followed the shore till it was definitely running northeastward, yielding the presumption that the southern tip of the continent had been rounded. So he turned back, and discovered the Cape of Good Hope on his way home.

Through the program of southward discovery the equatorial region had now been crossed, the burning tropics had been shown to be imaginary, and mankind had been relieved at last from an incubus of the spirit—the feeling that, like rats in a cage, they were prisoners of the North Temperate Zone, restrained by a wall of fire to the south and one of ice to the north. For, by implication, the frozen Arctic of hypothesis would prove no more uncrossable than the burning tropics.

But Diaz, the man who brought to supreme triumph the program of Henry the Navigator, the first man to cross the tropics, Europe's discoverer of the South Temperate Zone, received no great honor or other reward. Instead, promotion, wealth, and glory were heaped upon Vasco da Gama a few years later when he capitalized on the discovery that the tropics were crossable and Africa circumnavigable.

Columbus had sailed west from Spain in 1492 to try to reach an Asia which could not be reached by that course. Da Gama headed south in 1497 to seek a monarch who did not exist, the fabled Prester John, who was supposed to rule over a kingdom in the interior of Africa. Or at least the search for the Presbyter was a main concern with King John II when he started planning an expedition which did not come off until after his death, thus under his successor King Emanuel (Manoel, Manuel) I.

By Emanuel's time the news had been circulated that the Spaniards had found a westward seaway to Asia. But by that time also, as has been remarked in connection with the expeditions of the Cortereals, the Portuguese at least, if not the Spaniards, were feeling sure that Columbus had mis-identified the lands he had reached. So it was the discovery of a commercially practical route to the Indies that the Portuguese now desired, in addition to finding Prester John.

After touching at the Cape Verde Islands, Da Gama steered south through the Atlantic on a course which, as we now believe, took him past the bulge of Brazil at a distance of from 600 to 800 miles. Approaching the latitude 30 degrees south, he turned easterly in a curve and struck Africa just south of 30 degrees. From that point the story is told here according to the Hakluyt Society edition of *A Journal of the First Voyage of Vasco da Gama, 1497-1499*, as published in 1898 under the editorship of E. G. Ravenstein.

Ravenstein considers "it is certain that Vasco da Gama furnished official reports of his proceedings which were still available when João de Barros wrote his *Decades*, but are so no longer." The main contemporary source on the voyage that we now possess, the *Roteiro*, has not survived in the hand of its author but in a contemporary copy made by an unknown scribe. This author too is unknown, but it is agreed that he was a member of the Da Gama expedition. The translation into English is by Ravenstein.

Voyage of Vasco da Gama

⚓ In the name of God. Amen!

In the year 1497 King Dom Manuel, the first of that name in Portugal, dispatched four vessels to make discoveries and go in search of spices. Vasco da Gama was the captain major of these vessels. Paulo da Gama, his brother, commanded one of them, and Nicolau Coelho another.

[The account is omitted of the voyage from Lisbon to the Cape Verde Islands, where the expedition stayed from July 27 to August 3, and of the crossing of the South Atlantic. The narrative is resumed as the vessels are approaching the west coast of the southern tip of Africa.]

On Saturday, the fourth of the same month [November 1497], a couple of hours before break of day, we had soundings in 110 fathoms, and at nine o'clock we sighted the land. We then drew near to each other, and having put on our gala clothes, we saluted the Captain Major by firing our bombards, and dressed the ships with flags and standards. In the course of the day we tacked so as to come close to the land, but as we failed to identify it, we again stood out to sea.

THE BAY OF ST. HELENA

On Tuesday [November 7], we returned to the land, which we found to be low, with a broad bay opening into it. The Captain Major sent Pero d'Alenquer in a boat to take soundings and to search for good anchoring ground. The bay was found to be very clean, and to afford shelter against all winds except those from the northwest. It extended east and west, and we named it Santa Helena.

On Wednesday [November 8], we cast anchor in this bay, and we remained there eight days, cleaning the ships, mending the sails, and taking in wood.

The river Samtiagua [São Thiago] enters the bay 4 leagues to the southeast of the anchorage. It comes from the interior (sertao), is about a stone's throw across at the mouth, and from 2 to 3 fathoms in depth at all states of the tide.

The inhabitants of this country are tawny-colored. Their

food is confined to the flesh of seals, whales, and gazelles and
the roots of herbs. They are dressed in skins, and wear sheaths
over their virile members. They are armed with poles of olive
wood to which a horn, browned in the fire, is attached. Their
numerous dogs resemble those of Portugal, and bark like them.
The birds of the country, likewise, are the same as in Portugal,
and include cormorants, gulls, turtledoves, crested larks, and
many others. The climate is healthy and temperate, and
produces good herbage.

On the day after we had cast anchor, that is to say, on
Thursday [November 9], we landed with the Captain Major,
and made captive one of the natives, who was small of
stature, like Sancho Mexia. This man had been gathering honey
in the sandy waste, for in this country the bees deposit their
honey at the foot of the mounds around the bushes. He was
taken on board the Captain Major's ship, and being placed at
table, he ate of all we ate. On the following day the Captain
Major had him well dressed and sent ashore.

On the following day [November 10], fourteen or fifteen
natives came to where our ships lay. The Captain Major landed
and showed them a variety of merchandise, with the view of
finding out whether such things were to be found in their
country. This merchandise included cinnamon, cloves, seed
pearls, gold, and many other things, but it was evident that
they had no knowledge whatever of such articles, and they
were consequently given round bells and tin rings. This happened on Friday, and the like took place on Saturday.

On Sunday [November 12], about forty or fifty natives made
their appearance, and having dined, we landed, and in exchange for the *seitils* [copper coins], with which we came provided, we obtained shells, which they wore as ornaments in
their ears and which looked as if they had been plated, and
fox tails attached to a handle, with which they fanned their
faces. I also acquired for one *seitil* one of the sheaths which
they wore over their members, and this seemed to show that
they valued copper very highly. Indeed, they wore small
beads of that metal in their ears.

On that day Fernão Velloso, who was with the Captain
Major, expressed a great desire to be permitted to accompany
the natives to their houses, so that he might find out how they

lived and what they ate. The Captain Major yielded to his importunities and allowed him to accompany them, and when we returned to the Captain Major's vessel to sup, he went away with the Negroes. Soon after they had left us they caught a seal, and when they came to the foot of a hill in a barren place they roasted it, and gave some of it to Fernão Velloso, as also some of the roots which they eat. After this meal they expressed a desire that he should not accompany them any farther, but return to the vessels. When Fernão Velloso came abreast of the vessels he began to shout, the Negroes keeping in the bush.

We were still at supper, but when his shouts were heard the Captain Major rose at once, and so did we others, and we entered a sailing boat. The Negroes then began running along the beach, and they came as quickly up with Fernão Velloso as we did, and when we endeavored to get him into the boat, they threw their assegais and wounded the Captain Major and three or four others. All this happened because we looked upon these people as men of little spirit, quite incapable of violence, and had therefore landed without first arming ourselves. We then returned to the ships.

ROUNDING THE CAPE

At daybreak of Thursday, the sixteenth of November, having careened our ships and taken in wood, we set sail. At that time we did not know how far we might be abaft the Cape of Good Hope. Pero d' Alenquer thought the distance about 30 leagues, but he was not certain, for on his return voyage [when with Diaz] he had left the cape in the morning and had gone past this bay with the wind astern, while on the outward voyage he had kept at sea, and was therefore unable to identify the locality where we now were. We therefore stood out toward the south-southwest, and late on Saturday [November 18] we beheld the cape.

On that same day we again stood out to sea, returning to the land in the course of the night. On Sunday morning, November 19, we once more made for the cape, but were again unable to round it, for the wind blew from the south-southwest, while the cape juts out toward the southwest. We then again stood out to sea, returning to the land on Monday night. At last, on Wednesday [November 22] at noon, having the wind astern, we succeeded in doubling the cape, and then ran along the coast.

To the south of this Cape of Good Hope, and close to it, a vast bay, 6 leagues broad at its mouth, enters about 6 leagues into the land.

THE BAY OF SÃO BRAZ

Late on Saturday, November 25, the day of Saint Catherine, we entered the bay (*angra*) of Sam Bras, where we remained for thirteen days, for there we broke up our store ship and transferred her contents to the other vessels.

On Friday [December 1], while still in the Bay of Sam Bras, about ninety men resembling those we had met at St. Helena Bay made their appearance. Some of them walked along the beach, while others remained upon the hills. All, or most, of us were at the time in the Captain Major's vessel. As soon as we saw them we launched and armed the boats, and started for the land.

When close to the shore, the Captain Major threw them little round bells, which they picked up. They even ventured to approach us, and took some of these bells from the Captain Major's hand. This surprised us greatly, for when Bartholomeu Diaz was here, the natives fled without taking any of the objects which he offered them. Nay, on one occasion, when Diaz was taking in water close to the beach, they sought to prevent him, and when they pelted him with stones from a hill, he killed one of them with the arrow of a crossbow.

It appeared to us that they did not fly on this occasion because they had heard from the people at the Bay of St. Helena (only 60 leagues distant by sea) that there was no harm in us, and that we even gave away things which were ours.

The Captain Major did not land at this spot, because there was much bush, but proceeded to an open part of the beach, when he made signs to the Negroes to approach. This they did. The Captain Major and the other captains then landed, being attended by armed men, some of whom carried crossbows. He then made the Negroes understand by signs that they were to disperse, and to approach him only singly or in couples.

To those who approached he gave small bells and red caps, in return for which they presented him with ivory bracelets such as they wore on their arms, for it appears that elephants are plentiful in this country. We actually found some of their droppings near the watering place where they had gone to drink.

On Saturday [December 2], about two hundred Negroes came, both young and old. They brought with them about a dozen oxen and cows and four or five sheep. As soon as we saw them we went ashore. They forthwith began to play on four or five flutes, some producing high notes and others low ones, thus making a pretty harmony for Negroes, who are not expected to be musicians; and they danced in the style of Negroes. The Captain Major then ordered the trumpets to be sounded, and we in the boats danced, and the Captain Major did so likewise when he rejoined us. This festivity ended, we landed where we had landed before, and bought a black ox for three bracelets. This ox we dined off on Sunday. We found him very fat, and his meat as toothsome as the beef of Portugal.

On Sunday [December 3], many visitors came, and brought with them their women and little boys, the women remaining on the top of a hill near the sea. They had with them many oxen and cows. Having collected in two spots on the beach, they played and danced as they had done on Saturday.

It is the custom of this people for the young men to remain in the bush with their weapons. The [older] men came to converse with us. They carried a short stick in the hand, attached to which was a fox's tail, with which they fan the face. While conversing with them by signs we observed the young men crouching in the bush, holding their weapons in their hands. The Captain Major then ordered Martin Affonso, who had formerly been in Manicongo [Congo], to advance and to buy an ox, for which purpose he was supplied with bracelets. The natives, having accepted the bracelets, took him by the hand and, pointing to the watering place, asked him why we took away their water, and simultaneously drove their cattle into the bush.

When the Captain Major observed this, he ordered us to gather together, and called upon Martin Affonso to retreat, for he suspected some treachery. Having drawn together, we proceeded [in our boats] to the place where we had been at first. The Negroes followed us. The Captain Major then ordered us to land, armed with lances, assegais, and strung crossbows and wearing our breastplates, for he wanted to show that we had the means of doing them an injury, although we had no desire to employ them. When they observed this they ran away.

The Captain Major, anxious that none should be killed by mischance, ordered the boats to draw together; but to prove that we were able, although unwilling, to hurt them, he ordered two bombards to be fired from the poop of the longboat. They were by that time all seated close to the bush not far from the beach, but the first discharge caused them to retreat so precipitately that in their flight they dropped the skins with which they were covered, and their weapons. When they were in the bush, two of them turned back to pick up the articles which had been dropped. They then continued their flight to the top of a hill, driving their cattle before them.

The oxen of this country are as large as those of Alemtejo, wonderfully fat and very tame. They are geldings, and hornless. Upon the fattest among them the Negroes place a pack saddle made of reeds, as is done in Castile, and upon this saddle they place a kind of litter made of sticks, upon which they ride. If they wish to sell an ox, they pass a stick through his nostrils, and thus lead him.

There is an island in this bay, three bowshots from the land, where there are many seals. Some of these are as big as bears, very formidable, with large tusks. These attack man, and no spear, whatever the force with which it is thrown, can wound them. There are others much smaller and others quite small. And while the big ones roar like lions, the little ones cry like goats.

One day when we approached this island for our amusement, we counted, among large and small ones, three thousand, and we fired among them with our bombards from the sea. On the same island there are birds as big as ducks [Cape penguins], but they cannot fly, because they have no feathers on their wings. These birds, of whom we killed as many as we chose, are called *fotylicayos*, and they bray like asses.

While taking in water in this Bay of Sam Bras on a Wednesday, we erected a cross and a pillar. The cross was made out of a mizzenmast, and very high. On the following Thursday [December 7], when about to set sail, we saw about ten or twelve Negroes, who demolished both the cross and the pillar before we had left.

SÃO BRAZ TO NATAL

Having taken on board all we stood in need of, we took our departure, but as the wind failed us, we anchored the same day, having proceeded only 2 leagues.

On Friday morning, the day of the Immaculate Conception [December 8], we again set sail. On Tuesday [December 12], the eve of Santa Lucia, we encountered a great storm and ran before a stern wind with the foresail much lowered. On that day we lost sight of Nicolau Coelho, but at sunset we saw him from the top 4 or 5 leagues astern, and it seemed as if he saw us too. We exhibited signal lights and lay to. By the end of the first watch he had come up with us, not because he had seen us during the day, but because, the wind being scant, he could not help coming in our waters.

On the morning of Friday [December 15], we saw the land near the Ilheos Chãos (Flat Islands). These are 5 leagues beyond the Ilheo da Cruz (Cross Island). From the Bay of Sam Bras to Cross Island is a distance of 60 leagues, and as much from the Cape of Good Hope to the Bay of Sam Bras. From the Flat Islands to the last pillar erected by Bartholomeu Diaz is 5 leagues, and from this pillar to the Rio do Infante is 15 leagues.

On Saturday [December 16], we passed the last pillar, and as we ran along the coast we observed two men running along the beach in a direction contrary to that which we followed. The country about here is very charming and well wooded. We saw much cattle, and the farther we advanced, the more did the character of the country improve, and the trees increase in size.

During the following night we lay to. We were then already

beyónd the last discovery made by Bartholomeu Diaz [Great Fish River]. On the next day [December 17], till vespers we sailed along the coast before a stern wind, when, the wind springing round to the east, we stood out to sea. And thus we kept making tacks until sunset on Tuesday [December 19], when the wind again veered to the west. We then lay to during the night, in order that we might on the following day examine the coast and find out where we were.

In the morning [December 20] we made straight for the land, and at ten o'clock found ourselves once more at the Ilheo da Cruz (Cross Island); that is, 60 leagues abaft our dead reckoning! This was due to the currents, which are very strong here.

That very day we again went forward by the route we had already attempted, and being favored during three or four days by a strong stern wind, we were able to overcome the currents, which we had feared might frustrate our plans. Henceforth it pleased God in His mercy to allow us to make headway! We were not again driven back. May it please Him that it be thus alway!

NATAL

By Christmas Day, the twenty-fifth of December, we had discovered 70 leagues of coast [beyond Diaz' furthest]. On that day after dinner, when setting a studding sail, we discovered that the mast had sprung a couple of yards below the top, and that the crack opened and shut. We patched it up with backstays, hoping to be able to repair it thoroughly as soon as we should reach a sheltered port.

On Thursday [December 28], we anchored near the coast, and took much fish. At sunset we again set sail and pursued our route. At that place the mooring rope snapped and we lost an anchor.

We now went so far out to sea, without touching any port, that drinking water began to fail us and our food had to be cooked with salt water. Our daily ration of water was reduced to a quartilho [about 1½ pints]. It thus became necessary to seek a port.

TERRA DA BOA GENTE AND RIO DO COBRE

On Thursday, January 11 [1498], we discovered a small river, and anchored near the coast. On the following day we went close inshore in our boats, and saw a crowd of Negroes, both men and women. They were tall people, and a chief (*senhor*) was among them. The Captain Major ordered Martin Affonso, who had been a long time in Manicongo, and another man, to land.

They were received hospitably. The Captain Major in consequence sent the chief a jacket, a pair of red pantaloons, a Moorish cap, and a bracelet. The chief said that we were welcome to anything in his country of which we stood in need— at least this is how Martin Affonso understood him.

That night, Martin Affonso and his companion accompanied the chief to his village, while we returned to the ships. On the road the chief donned the garments which had been presented to him, and to those who came forth to meet him he said with much apparent satisfaction, "Look what has been given to me!" The people upon this clapped hands as a sign of courtesy, and this they did three or four times until he arrived at the village.

Having paraded the whole of the place thus dressed up, the chief retired to his house, and ordered his two guests to be lodged in a compound, where they were given porridge of millet, which abounds in that country, and a fowl just like those of Portugal. All the night through, numbers of men and women came to have a look at them.

In the morning the chief visited them, and asked them to go back to the ships. He ordered two men to accompany them, and gave them fowls as a present for the Captain Major, telling them at the same time that he would show the things that had been given him to a great chief, who appears to be the king of that country. When our men reached the landing place where our boats awaited them, they were attended by quite two hundred men, who had come to see them.

This country seemed to us to be densely peopled. There are many chiefs, and the number of women seems to be greater than that of the men, for among those who came to see us there were forty women to every twenty men. The houses are built of straw.

The arms of the people include long bows and arrows and spears with iron blades. Copper seems to be plentiful, for the people wore [ornaments] of it on their legs and arms and in their twisted hair. Tin likewise is found in the country, for it is to be seen on the hilts of their daggers, the sheaths of which are made of ivory. Linen cloth is highly prized by the people, who were always willing to give large quantities of copper in exchange for shirts. They have large calabashes in which they carry sea water inland, where they pour it into pits, to obtain the salt [by evaporation].

We stayed five days at this place taking in water, which our visitors conveyed to our boats. Our stay was not, however, sufficiently prolonged to enable us to take in as much water as we really needed, for the wind favored a prosecution of our voyage.

We were at anchor here near the coast, exposed to the swell of the sea. We called the country Terra da Boa Gente (Land of Good People), and the river Rio do Cobre (Copper River).

RIO DOS BONS SIGNAES

On Monday [January 22], we discovered a low coast thickly wooded with tall trees. Continuing our course, we perceived the broad mouth of a river. As it was necessary to find out where we were, we cast anchor. On Thursday [January 25], at night, we entered. The *Berrio* was already there, having entered the night before—that is, eight days before the end of January [January 24].

The country is low and marshy, and covered with tall trees yielding an abundance of various fruits, which the inhabitants eat.

These people are black and well made. They go naked, merely wearing a piece of cotton stuff around their loins, that worn by the women being larger than that worn by the men. The young women are good-looking. Their lips are pierced in three places, and they wear in them bits of twisted tin. These people took much delight in us. They brought us in their almadias [bark canoes] what they had, while we went into their village to procure water.

When we had been two or three days at this place, two gentlemen (*senhores*) of the country came to see us. They were very haughty, and valued nothing which we gave them. One of them wore a *touca*, with a fringe embroidered in silk, and the other a cap of green satin. A young man in their company —so we understood from their signs—had come from a distant country, and had already seen big ships like ours.

These tokens (*signaes*) gladdened our hearts, for it appeared as if we were really approaching the bourne of our desires. These gentlemen had some huts built on the riverbank close to the ships, in which they stayed seven days, sending daily to the ships, offering to barter cloths which bore a mark of red ocher. And when they were tired of being there, they left in their almadias for the upper river.

As to ourselves, we spent thirty-two days in the river taking in water, careening the ships, and repairing the mast of the *Raphael*. Many of our men fell ill here [with scurvy], their feet and hands swelling, and their gums growing over their teeth, so that they could not eat.

We erected here a pillar which we called the Pillar of Saint Raphael, because it had been brought in the ship bearing that name. The river we called Rio dos Bons Signaes (River of Good Signs or Tokens).

TO MOZAMBIQUE

On Saturday [February 24], we left this place and gained the open sea. During the night we stood northeast, so as to keep away from the land, which was very pleasing to look upon. On Sunday [February 25], we still stood northeast, and at vesper time discovered three small islands out in the open, of which two were covered with tall trees while the third and smallest was barren. The distance from one island to the other was 4 leagues.

On the following day we pursued our route, and did so during six days, lying to at night.

On Thursday, the first of March, we sighted islands and the mainland, but as it was late we again stood out to sea, and lay to till morning. We then approached the land, of which I shall speak in what follows.

MOZAMBIQUE

On Friday morning [March 2], Nicolau Coelho, when attempting to enter the bay, mistook the channel and came upon a bank. When putting about ship toward the other ships which followed in his wake, Coelho perceived some sailing boats approaching from a village on this island, in order to welcome the Captain Major and his brother. As for ourselves, we continued in the direction of our proposed anchorage, these boats following us all the while and making signs for us to stop.

When we had cast anchor in the roadstead of the island from which these boats had come, there approached seven or eight of them, including almadias, the people in them playing upon *anafils* [trumpets]. They invited us to proceed farther into the bay, offering to take us into port if we desired it. Those among them who boarded our ships ate and drank what we did, and went their way when they were satisfied.

The Captain thought that we should enter this bay in order that we might find out what sort of people we had to deal with; that Nicolau Coelho should go first in his vessel, to take soundings at the entrance; and that, if found practicable, we should follow him. As Coelho prepared to enter he struck the point of the island and broke his helm, but he immediately disengaged himself and regained deep water. I was with him at the time. When we were again in deep water, we struck our sails and cast anchor at a distance of two bowshots from the village.

The people of this country are of a ruddy complexion and well made. They are Mohammedans, and their language is the same as that of the Moors [Arabic]. Their dresses are of fine linen or cotton stuffs, with variously colored stripes, and of rich and elaborate workmanship. They all wear *toucas* with borders of silk embroidered in gold. They are merchants, and have transactions with white Moors, four of whose vessels were at the time in port, laden with gold, silver, cloves, pepper, ginger, and silver rings, as also with quantities of pearls, jewels, and rubies, all of which articles are used by the people of this country.

We understood them to say that all these things, with the exception of the gold, were brought thither by these Moors; that farther on, where we were going to, they abounded, and that precious stones, pearls, and spices were so plentiful that there was no need to purchase them, as they could be collected in baskets. All this we learned through a sailor the Captain Major had with him and who, having formerly been a prisoner among the Moors, understood their language.

These Moors, moreover, told us that along the route which we were about to follow we should meet with numerous shoals; that there were many cities along the coast, and also an island one half the population of which consisted of Moors and the other half of Christians, who were at war with each other. This island was said to be very wealthy.

We were told, moreover, that Prester John resided not far from this place, that he held many cities along the coast, and that the inhabitants of those cities were great merchants and owned big ships. The residence of Prester John was said to be far in the interior, and could be reached only on the back of camels. These Moors had also brought hither two Christian captives from India. This information, and many other things which we heard, rendered us so happy that we cried with joy, and prayed God to grant us health, so that we might behold what we so much desired.

In this place and island of Moncobiquy [Mozambique] there resided a chief [senhor] who had the title of Sultan, and was like a viceroy. He often came aboard our ships attended by some of his people. The Captain Major gave him many good things to eat, and made him a present of hats, marlotas [Persian-type dresses], corals, and many other articles. He was, however, so proud that he treated all we gave him with contempt, and asked for scarlet cloth, of which we had none. We gave him, however, of all the things we had.

One day the Captain Major invited him to a repast, when there was an abundance of figs and comfits, and begged him for two pilots to go with us. He at once granted this request, subject to our coming to terms with them. The Captain Major gave each of them 30 mitkals [coins reckoned at about $3] in gold and two *marlotas*, on condition that from the day on which they received this payment one of them should always remain on board if the other desired to go on land. With these terms they were well satisfied.

On Saturday, March 10, we set sail and anchored one league out at sea close to an island, where mass was said on Sunday, when those who wished to do so confessed and joined in the communion.

One of our pilots lived on the island, and when we had anchored we armed two boats to go in search of him. The Captain Major went in one boat and Nicolau Coelho in the other. They were met by five or six boats (*barcas*) coming from the island, and crowded with people armed with bows and long arrows and bucklers, who gave them to understand by signs that they were to return to the town. When the Captain saw this he secured the pilot, whom he had taken with him, and ordered the bombards to fire upon the boats.

Paulo da Gama, who had remained with the ships so as to be prepared to render succor in case of need, no sooner heard the reports of the bombards than he started in the *Berrio*. The Moors, who were already flying, fled still faster, and gained the land before the *Berrio* was able to come up with them. We then returned to our anchorage.

The vessels of this country are of good size and decked. There are no nails, and the planks are held together by cords, as are also those of their boats (*barcos*). The sails are made of palm matting. Their mariners have Genoese needles, by which they steer, quadrants, and navigating charts.

The palms of this country yield a fruit as large as a melon, of which the kernel is eaten [coconut]. It has a nutty flavor. There also grow in abundance melons and cucumbers, which were brought to us for barter.

On the day in which Nicolau Coelho entered the port, the lord of the place came on board with a numerous suite. He was received well, and Coelho presented him with a red hood, in return for which the lord handed him a black rosary which he made use of when saying his prayers, to be held as a pledge. He then begged Nicolau Coelho for the use of his boat to take him ashore. This was granted. And after he had landed he invited those who had accompanied him to his house, where he gave them to eat. He then dismissed them, giving them a jar of bruised dates made into a preserve with cloves and cumin, as a present for Nicolau Coelho. Subsequeutly he sent many things to the Captain Major.

All this happened at the time when he took us for Turks or for Moors from some foreign land, for in case we came from Turkey he begged to be shown the bows of our country and our books of the Law. But when they learned that we were Christians, they arranged to seize and kill us by treachery. The pilot, whom we took with us, subsequently revealed to us all they intended to do, if they were able.

FALSE START AND RETURŃ TO MOZAMBIQUE

On Sunday [March 11], we celebrated mass beneath a tall tree on the island [of São Jorge]. We returned on board and at once set sail, taking with us many fowls, goats, and pigeons, which had been given us in exchange for small glass beads.

On Tuesday [March 13], we saw high mountains rising on the other side of a cape. The coast near the cape was sparsely covered with trees resembling elms. We were at that time over 20 leagues from our starting place, and there we remained becalmed during Tuesday and Wednesday. During the following night we stood offshore with a light easterly wind, and in the morning [March 15] found ourselves 4 leagues abaft Mozambique. But we went again forward on that day until the evening, when we anchored once more close to the island [of São Jorge] on which mass had been celebrated the preceding Sunday, and there we remained eight days waiting for a favorable wind.

During our stay here the King of Mozambique sent word that he wanted to make peace with us and to be our friend. His ambassador was a white Moor and a sherif—that is, priest— and at the same time a great drunkard.

While at this place, a Moor with his little son came on board one of our ships, and asked to be allowed to accompany us, as he was from near Mecca and had come to Mozambique as pilot of a vessel from that country.

As the weather did not favor us, it became necessary once more to enter the port of Mozambique in order to procure the water of which we stood in need, for the watering place is on the mainland. This water is drunk by the inhabitants of the island, for all the water they have there is brackish.

On Thursday [March 22], we entered the port, and when it grew dark we lowered our boats. At midnight the Captain Major and Nicolau Coelho, accompanied by some of us, started in search of water. We took with us the Moorish pilot, whose object appeared to be to make his escape rather than to guide us to a watering place. As a matter of fact, he either would not or could not find a watering place, although we continued our search until morning. We then withdrew to our ships.

In the evening [March 23], we returned to the mainland, attended by the same pilot. On approaching the watering place we saw about twenty men on the beach. They were armed with assegais, and forbade our approach. The Captain Major upon this ordered three bombards to be fired upon them, so that we might land. We having effected our landing, these men fled into the bush, and we took as much water as we wanted. When the sun was about to set, we discovered that a Negro belonging to João de Coimbra had effected his escape.

On Sunday morning, the twenty-fourth of March, being the eve of Lady Day, a Moor came abreast our ships, and [sneeringly] told us that if we wanted water we might go in search of it, giving us to understand that we should meet with something which would make us turn back. The Captain Major no sooner heard this [threat] than he resolved to go, in order to show that we were able to do them harm if we desired it. We forthwith armed our boats, placing bombards in their poops, and started for the village [town].

The Moors had constructed palisades by lashing planks together, so that those behind them could not be seen. They were at the time walking along the beach, armed with assegais, swords, bows, and slings, with which they hurled stones at us. But our bombards soon made it so hot for them that they fled behind their palisades. But this turned out to their injury rather than their profit.

During the three hours that we were occupied in this manner [bombarding the town] we saw two men killed, one on the beach and the other behind the palisades. When we were weary of this work, we retired to our ships to dine. They at once began to fly, carrying their chattels in almadias to a village on the mainland.

After dinner we started in our boats, in the hope of being able to make a few prisoners, whom we might exchange for the two Indian Christians whom they held captive and the Negro who had deserted. With this object in view we chased an almadia which belonged to the sherif and was laden with his chattels, and another in which were four Negroes. The latter was captured by Paulo da Gama, while the one laden with chattels was abandoned by the crew as soon as they reached the land. We took still another almadia, which had likewise been abandoned. The Negroes we took on board our ships.

In the almadias we found fine cotton stuffs, baskets made of palm fronds, a glazed jar containing butter, glass phials with scented water, books of the Law, a box containing skeins of cotton, a cotton net, and many small baskets filled with millet. All these things, with the exception of the books, which were kept back to be shown to the King, were given by the Captain Major to the sailors who were with him and with the other captains.

On Sunday [March 25], we took in water, and on Monday we proceeded in our armed boats to the village, when the inhabitants spoke to us from their houses, they daring no longer to venture on the beach. Having discharged a few bombards at them, we rejoined our ships.

On Tuesday [March 27], we left the town and anchored close to the islets of São Jorge, where we remained for three days, in the hope that God would grant us a favorable wind.

MOZAMBIQUE TO MOMBASA

On Thursday, the twenty-ninth of March, we left these islets of São Jorge, and as the wind was light, we covered only 28 leagues up to the morning of Saturday, the thirty-first of the month.

In the morning of that day we were once more abreast of the

land of the Moors, from which powerful currents had previously carried us.

On Sunday, April 1, we came to some islands close to the mainland. The first of these we called Ilha do Asoutado (Island of the Flogged One), because of the flogging inflicted upon our Moorish pilot, who had lied to the captain on Saturday night by stating that these islands were the mainland. Native craft take their course between these islands and the mainland, where the water is 4 fathoms deep, but we kept outside of them. These islands are numerous, and we were unable to distinguish one from the other. They are inhabited.

On Monday [April 2], we sighted other islands 5 leagues off the shore.

On Wednesday, the fourth of April, we made sail to the northwest, and before noon we sighted an extensive country, and two islands close to it, surrounded with shoals. And when we were near enough for the pilots to recognize these islands, they told us that we had left 3 leagues behind us an island [Quiloa or Kilwa] inhabited by Christians. We maneuvered all day in the hope of fetching this island, but in vain, for the wind was too strong for us. After this we thought it best to bear away for a city called Mombasa, reported to be four days ahead of us.

The above island was one of those which we had come to discover, for our pilots said that it was inhabited by Christians.

When we bore away for the north it was already late, and the wind was high. At nightfall we perceived a large island, which remained to the north of us [Mafia]. Our pilot told us that there were two towns on this island, one of Christians and the other of Moors.

That night we stood out to sea, and in the morning [April 5] we no longer saw the land. We then steered to the northwest, and in the evening we again beheld the land. During the following night we bore away to the north by west, and during the morning watch we changed our course to the north-northwest. Sailing thus before a favorable wind, the *São Raphael*, two hours before break of day [April 6], ran aground on a shoal, about 2 leagues from the land.

Immediately the *Raphael* touched bottom, the vessels following her were warned by shouts, and these were no sooner heard than they cast anchor about the distance of a gunshot from the stranded vessel, and lowered their boats. When the tide fell, the *Raphael* lay high and dry. With the help of the boats many anchors were laid out, and when the tide rose again in the course of the day, the vessel floated, and there was much rejoicing.

On the mainland, facing these shoals, there rises a lofty range of mountains, beautiful of aspect. These mountains we called Serras de São Raphael, and we gave the same name to the shoals.

While the vessel was high and dry, two almadias approached us. One was laden with fine oranges, better than those of Portugal. Two of the Moors remained on board, and accompanied us next day to Mombasa.

On Saturday morning, the seventh of the month, and eve of Palm Sunday, we ran along the coast and saw some islands [really one island, Pemba] at a distance of 15 leagues from the mainland, and about 6 leagues in extent. They supply the vessels of the country with masts. All are inhabited by Moors.

MOMBASA

On Saturday [April 7], we cast anchor off Mombasa, but did not enter the port. No sooner had we been perceived than a *zavra* [small open vessel] manned by Moors came out to us. In front of the city there lay numerous vessels all dressed in flags. And we, anxious not to be outdone, also dressed our ships, and we actually surpassed their show, for we wanted in nothing but men, even the few whom we had being very ill [with scurvy]. We anchored here with much pleasure, for we confidently hoped that on the following day we might go on land and hear mass jointly with the Christians reported to live there under their own alcaide in a quarter separate from that of the Moors.

The pilots who had come with us told us there resided both Moors and Christians in this city; that these latter lived apart under their own lords; and that on our arrival they would receive us with much honor and take us to their houses. But they said this for a purpose of their own, for it was not true.

At midnight there approached us a *zavra* with about a hundred men, all armed with cutlasses (*tarsados*) and bucklers. When they came to the vessel of the Captain Major, they attempted to board her, armed as they were, but this was not permitted, only four or five of the most distinguished men among them being allowed on board. They remained about a couple of hours, and it seemed to us that they paid us this visit merely to find out whether they might not capture one or the other of our vessels.

On Palm Sunday [April 8], the King of Mombasa sent the Captain Major a sheep and large quantities of oranges, lemons, and sugar cane, together with a ring as a pledge of safety, letting him know that in case of his entering the port he would be supplied with all he stood in need of. This present was conveyed to us by two men, almost white, who said they were Christians, which appeared to be the fact.

The Captain Major sent the King a string of coral beads as a return present, and let him know that he purposed entering the port on the following day. On the same day the Captain Major's vessel was visited by four Moors of distinction.

Two men were sent by the Captain Major to the King, still further to confirm these peaceful assurances. When these landed, they were followed by a crowd as far as the gates of the palace. Before reaching the King they passed through four doors, each guarded by a doorkeeper with a drawn cutlass.

The King received them hospitably, and ordered that they should be shown over the city. They stopped on their way at the house of two Christian merchants, who showed them a paper (*carta*), an object of their adoration, on which was a sketch of the Holy Ghost. When they had seen all, the King sent them back with samples of cloves, pepper, and corn, with which articles he would allow us to load our ships.

On Tuesday [April 10], when weighing anchor to enter the port, the Captain Major's vessel would not pay off, and struck the vessel which followed astern. We therefore again cast anchor. When the Moors who were in our ship saw that we did not go on, they scrambled into a *zavra* attached to our stern, while the two pilots whom we had brought from Mozambique jumped into the water and were picked up by the men in the *zavra*.

At night the Captain Major questioned two Moors [from Mozambique] whom we had on board, by dropping boiling oil upon their skin, so that they might confess any treachery intended against us. They said that orders had been given to capture us as soon as we entered the port, and thus to avenge what we had done at Mozambique. And when this torture was being applied a second time, one of the Moors, although his hands were tied, threw himself into the sea, while the other did so during the morning watch.

About midnight two almadias with many men in them approached. The almadias stood off while the men entered the water, some swimming in the direction of the *Berrio*, others in that of the *Raphael*. Those who swam to the *Berrio* began to cut the cable. The men on watch thought at first that they were tunny fish, but when they perceived their mistake, they shouted to the other vessels. The other swimmers had already got hold of the rigging of the mizzenmast. Seeing themselves discovered, they silently slipped down and fled. These and other wicked tricks were practiced upon us by these dogs, but Our Lord did not allow them to succeed, because they were unbelievers.

Mombasa is a large city seated upon an eminence washed by the sea. Its port is entered daily by numerous vessels. At its entrance stands a pillar, and by the sea a low-lying fortress. Those who had gone onshore told us that in the town they had seen many men in irons, and it seemed to us that these must be Christians, as the Christians in that country are at war with the Moors.

The Christian merchants in the town are only temporary residents, and are held in much subjection, they not being allowed to do anything except by the order of the Moorish King.

It pleased God in His mercy that on arriving at this city all our sick recovered their health, for the climate (air) of this place is very good.

After the malice and treachery planned by these dogs had been discovered, we still remained on Wednesday and Thursday [April 11 and 12].

MOMBASA TO MALINDI

We left in the morning [April 13], the wind being light, and anchored about 8 leagues from Mombasa, close to the shore. At break of day [April 14] we saw two boats (*barcas*) about 3 leagues to the leeward in the open sea, and at once gave chase with the intention of capturing them, for we wanted to secure a pilot who would guide us to where we wanted to go. At vesper time we came up with one of them and captured it, the other escaping toward the land. In the one we took we found seventeen men, besides gold, silver, and an abundance of maize [no doubt millet] and other provisions; as also a young woman, who was the wife of an old Moor of distinction who was a passenger. When we came up with the boat, they all threw themselves into the water, but we picked them up from our boats.

That same day [April 14] at sunset, we cast anchor off a place called Milinde (Malindi), which is 30 leagues from Mombasa. The following places are between Mombasa and Malindi; viz., Benapa, Tosa, and Nuguoquioniete.

MALINDI

On Easter Sunday [April 15], the Moors whom we had taken in the boats told us that there were at this city of Malindi four vessels belonging to Christians from India, and that if it pleased us to take them there, they would provide us, instead of them, Christian pilots and all we stood in need of, including water, wood, and other things. The Captain Major much desired to have pilots from the country, and having discussed the matter with his Moorish prisoners, he cast anchor off the town at a distance of about half a league from the mainland. The inhabitants of the town did not venture to come aboard our ships, for they had already learned that we had captured a vessel and made her occupants prisoners.

On Monday morning [April 16], the Captain Major had the old Moor taken to a sandbank in front of the town, where he was picked up by an almadia. The Moor explained to the King the wishes of the Captain Major, and how much he desired to make peace with him. After dinner the Moor came back in a *zavra*, accompanied by one of the King's cavaliers and a sherif. He also brought three sheep.

These messengers told the Captain General that the King would rejoice to make peace with him, and to enter into friendly relations; that he would willingly grant to the Captain Major all his country afforded, whether pilots or anything else. The Captain Major upon this sent word that he proposed to enter the port on the following day, and forwarded by the King's messengers a present consisting of a *balandrau* [surtout], two strings of coral, three wash-hand basins, a hat, little bells, and two pieces of *lambel* [cotton cloth].

Consequently on Tuesday [April 17] we approached nearer to the town. The King sent the Captain Major six sheep, besides quantities of cloves, cumin, ginger, nutmeg, and pepper, as also a message telling him that if he desired to have an interview with him he (the King) would come out in his *zavra*, when the Captain Major could meet him in a boat.

On Wednesday [April 18] after dinner, when the King came up close to the ships in a *zavra*, the Captain Major at once entered one of his boats, which had been well furnished, and many friendly words were exchanged when they lay side by side. The King having invited the Captain Major to come to his house to rest, after which he (the King) would visit him on board his ship, the Captain Major said that he was not permitted by his master to go on land, and if he were to do so a bad report would be given of him. The King wanted to know what would be said of himself by his people if he were to visit the ships, and what account could he render them? He then asked for the name of our King, which was written down for him, and said that on our return he would send an ambassador with us, or a letter.

When both had said all they desired, the Captain Major sent for the Moors whom he had taken prisoner, and surrendered them all. This gave much satisfaction to the King, who said that he valued this act more highly than if he had been presented with a town. And the King, much pleased, made the circuit of our ships, the bombards of which fired a salute.

About three hours were spent in this way. When the King went away, he left in the ship one of his sons and a sherif, and took two of us away with him, to whom he desired to show his palace. He moreover told the Captain that as he would not go ashore, he would himself return on the following day to the beach, and would order his horsemen to go through some exercises.

The King wore a robe (royal cloak) of damask trimmed with green satin, and a rich *touca*. He was seated on two cushioned chairs of bronze, beneath a round sunshade of crimson satin attached to a pole. An old man who attended him as page carried a short sword in a silver sheath. There were many players on *anafils*, and two trumpets of ivory, richly carved and of the size of a man, which were blown from a hole in the side, and made sweet harmony with the *anafils*.

On Thursday [April 19], the Captain Major and Nicolau Coelho rowed along the front of the town, bombards having been placed in the poops of their longboats. Many people were along the shore, and among them two horsemen, who appeared to take much delight in a sham fight.

The King was carried in a palanquin from the stone steps of his palace to the side of the Captain Major's boats. He again begged the Captain to come ashore, as he had a helpless father who wanted to see him, and he and his sons would go on board the ships as hostages. The Captain, however, excused himself.

We found here four vessels belonging to Indian Christians. When they came for the first time on board Paulo da Gama's ship, the Captain Major being there at the time, they were shown an altarpiece representing Our Lady at the foot of the cross, with Jesus Christ in her arms and the Apostles around her. When the Indians saw this picture they prostrated themselves, and as long as we were there they came to say their prayers in front of it, bringing offerings of cloves, pepper, and other things.

These Indians are tawny men. They wear but little clothing, and have long beards and long hair, which they braid. They told us that they ate no beef. Their language differs from that of the Arabs, but some of them know a little of it, as they hold much intercourse with them.

On the day on which the Captain Major went up to the town

in the boats, these Christian Indians fired off many bombards from their vessels, and when they saw him pass they raised their hands and shouted lustily *Christ! Christ!*

That same night they asked the King's permission to give us a night fete. And when night came they fired off many bombards, sent up rockets, and raised loud shouts.

These Indians warned the Captain Major against going on shore, and told him not to trust to their fanfares, as they came neither from their hearts nor from their good will.

On the following Sunday, the twenty-second of April, the King's *zavra* brought on board one of his confidential servants, and as two days had passed without any visitors, the Captain Major had this man seized, and sent word to the King that he required the pilots whom he had promised. The King, when he received this message, sent a Christian pilot, and the Captain Major allowed the gentleman whom he had retained in his vessel to go away.

We were much pleased with the Christian pilot whom the King had sent us. We learned from him that the island of which we heard at Mozambique as being inhabited by Christians was in reality an island subject to this same King of Mozambique; that half of it belonged to the Moors and the other half to the Christians; that many pearls were to be found there; and that it was called Quyluee [Kilwa]. This is the island the Moorish pilots wanted to take us to, and we also wished to go there, for we believed that what they said was true.

The town of Malindi lies in a bay and extends along the shore. It may be likened to Alcouchette. Its houses are lofty and well whitewashed, and have many windows. On the land side are palm groves, and all around it maize and vegetables are being cultivated.

We remained in front of this town during nine days, and all this time we had fetes, sham fights, and musical performances (fanfares).

ACROSS THE GULF—THE ARABIAN SEA

We left Malindi on Tuesday, the twenty-fourth of the month [of April], for a city called Qualecut [Calicut], with the pilot whom the King had given us. The coast there runs north and south, and the land encloses a huge bay with a strait. In this bay, we were told, were to be found many large cities of Christians and Moors, including one called Quambay [Cambay], as also six hundred known islands, and within it the Red Sea and the "house" [Kaabah] of Mecca.

On the following Sunday [April 29], we once more saw the North Star, which we had not seen for a long time.

On Friday, the eighteenth of May, after having seen no land for twenty-three days, we sighted lofty mountains, and having all this time sailed before the wind, we could not have made less than 600 leagues. The land when first sighted was at a distance of 8 leagues, and our lead reached bottom at 45 fathoms. That same night we took a course to the south-south-west, so as to get away from the coast. On the following day [May 19], we again approached the land, but owing to the heavy rain and a thunderstorm which prevailed while we were sailing along the coast, our pilot was unable to identify the exact locality. On Sunday [May 20], we found ourselves close to some mountains, and when we were near enough for the pilot to recognize them, he told us that they were above Calicut, and that this was the country we desired to go to.

CALICUT

[Arrival] That night [May 20] we anchored 2 leagues from the city of Calicut. 🏴

In Calicut, on the western or Malabar coast of India (and not to be confused with Calcutta), Da Gama found Arab merchants well entrenched with the Hindu rulers, and was not successful in establishing a Portuguese trading post. Nevertheless, when he got home in September, 1499, he was received with honor and substantial rewards.

Portugal had succeeded where Spain had failed. It had reached the Indies, and by a commercially feasible sea route.

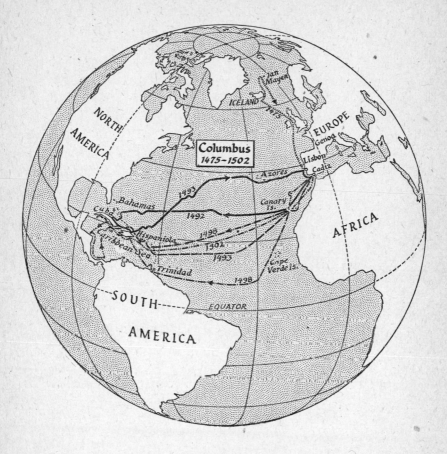

The Latins Discover Latin America

THE LATINS DISCOVER
LATIN AMERICA

CHAPTER 7

IT WAS doubly natural that northern Europe should discover northern America before southern Europe discovered southern America, for the distance across the Atlantic is least in the north, and the greatest navigators of the Middle Ages were the Norsemen. It was, however, inevitable that southern Europe should know about these northern matters, for the Church of Rome had its headquarters by the Mediterranean and was so organized that its machinery for administration, which included the gathering of both facts and taxes, reached not merely all over Europe but also beyond the Atlantic to Iceland and Greenland.

That there were lands beyond the Atlantic westward from northern Europe was, then, common knowledge throughout southern Europe in the Middle Ages. But there is no indication that anyone anywhere in Europe was much interested. At that time no country, north or south, felt an urge for colonization; nor did there seem to be chances for wealth through trade. The goods obtainable from the New World, so far as the Old World then realized, were chiefly furs and "fish" oil, for neither of which there was any great demand. The oil was, true enough, a necessity for the lamps of Europe, but the tendency was to seek it northward rather than westward—beyond Iceland to the north rather than beyond it to the west.

But the prehistoric and historically ancient overland trade to the eastward from southeastern Europe was attracting more and more attention. A fillip had been given this by the narrative of Marco Polo, which reinforced the impression that the wealthiest section of the whole world lay to the east.

On a spherical earth, as then conceived by the learned, the countries that were east of Europe were also west of it. The arts of seamanship were developing, and with them a preference for sea commerce as against the use of overland routes. Besides, hostile powers made the overland journey additionally difficult and at certain times impossible. It was a natural development to think increasingly of reaching the Far East by sailing west.

The whole trend of the discovery literature which has been reviewed earlier in this book—of the report concerning North America by Adam of Bremen, of the papal documents thereafter, and most emphatically that of the Icelandic sagas—is to the effect that the land discovered to the west of northern Europe was new country, not any part of the old and long-ago reported vast domains of Asia.

Then gradually it began to dawn on Europe that the lands to the west might be Asia, a group of countries worth reaching, cultivating, conquering if that proved feasible. The great figure in the resulting agitation was Christopher Columbus.

Most things about Columbus are debated. There is, for instance, no uniform agreement with the conclusion of the Spanish historian Salvador de Madariaga, in his *Christopher Columbus* (Macmillan, 1940), that Columbus was a Jew, born in Italy of Spanish ancestry, who found the West Indies while in the service of Spain. In fact, three of these four statements have been controverted frequently and violently—that Columbus was a Jew, that he was of Spanish ancestry, and that he was born in Italy. Against even the fourth assertion, that Columbus was in the service of Spain when he first reached countries westward from southern Europe, the Chilean historian Luis de Ulloa claims to have discovered evidence to the effect that before sailing on his 1492 voyage he informed his patrons in Spain that he had already found land to the west and that it was to revisit this, and to claim it for Spain, that he then wanted support.

Ferdinand Columbus says in his life of his father that in 1476 (or 1477) the Admiral had been in Iceland and had sailed 100 Spanish leagues beyond it in February without finding any ice in the sea, upon which experience he based the view that those were equally wrong who thought uninhabitable the tropics because of the heat and the polar regions because of the cold.

Since it is universally agreed that the Icelanders were well informed on Greenland and on the countries beyond it—the Baffin-Labrador-New England section—there has been hot debate as to whether Columbus could have received information in Iceland which initiated or strengthened his belief in lands west of the Atlantic. Both sides to the dispute have gone amusingly far.

On the one hand, it has been related circumstantially, although without discernible support from any Icelandic source, that Columbus learned in Iceland practically everything that the Icelanders knew about the seas and countries to the west. On the other hand, that he could not have learned anything pertinent from the Icelanders has been maintained with perhaps even greater vehemence, and with novel arguments. There are those, for instance, who allow that Columbus probably did visit Iceland, and then proceed to say that even so he could not have learned anything from the Icelanders, because he did not know any Icelandic. This is, of course, ignoring that Latin and not Icelandic was the language of international relations in the Middle Ages, and that the Icelanders, then as more recently, were well up on Latin scholarship.

It is debated whether Columbus knew Latin in 1476, although by agreement he was moderately good in it later. But Latin apart, if he was in Iceland he was there aboard an English ship from Bristol, and Bristol was in constant trade relations, as well as fishing relations, with the Icelanders. Surely two countries like England and Iceland cannot carry on intimate commerce for centuries without the development of at least a small class of interpreters. Columbus would have known a little English; or there would have been aboard the ship, at the minimum, an interpreter for the Icelanders who could also interpret for the Portuguese—since the Bristol merchants, in dealing with Iceland, were in large part intermediaries for Portugal. Columbus got along sufficiently well with the Portuguese later on, so we may suppose he was not wholly unfamiliar with that language in 1476.

However, Columbus would not have been able to stir up

interest in Spain or elsewhere concerning lands to the west if he had maintained that these were the same lands that had been mentioned in the book of Adam of Bremen and in the papal documents. So his talk was all to the effect that westward lay Japan, China, and the rest of the Indies, the region of the Great Khan, about which Marco Polo had told.

He did not have to convince anyone that the earth is spherical, for this was the common learned assumption in his day, as it had been through many centuries preceding. What he needed to do was to dangle a sufficiently attractive bait, and this could not be the furs and fish oil of the Northwest. It had to be gold and jewels, perfumes, spices, and fine cloths. So that was the line of his salesmanship, which finally led to the well-known departure from Spain of the three ships *Santa Maria, Nina,* and *Pinta* on August 3, 1492.

Columbus is known to have kept two journals of the voyage, one open and for the encouragement of his men, the other secret and for his own use. Both have been lost, though the story they told is known in outline. It is to the effect that there were no serious troubles with the elements, but that there was on more than one occasion danger of mutiny, the sailors wanting to turn back. That the Admiral won through by cajoleries is well known, and we have his explanation of them. The need for persuasion ended with the sighting of the first island of the West Indies on October 12, 1492.

Since the account of the voyage has not been preserved in the original of Columbus, no one of the résumés made up by others is printed here, but instead there is used the first of those voyage documents that have been preserved in what appears to be substantially the correct text as written by the Admiral. This is the "First Letter" [1] in which Columbus describes what it was he found. From this we can read his own views of 1493 as to the meaning of the discoveries, gathering at a minimum what it was he wanted his sovereigns and contemporaries to believe concerning them.

---

[1] The letter is included in *Select Documents Illustrating The Four Voyages of Columbus,* ed. by Cecil Jane, 2 vols., Hakluyt Society, London, 1930.

First Voyage of Christopher Columbus

🖎 Sir, As I know that you will be pleased at the great victory
with which Our Lord has crowned my voyage, I write this to
you, from which you will learn how in thirty-three days I
passed from the Canary Islands to the Indies with the fleet
which the most illustrious King and Queen, our sovereigns,
gave to me. And there I found very many islands filled with
people innumerable, and of them all I have taken possession
for Their Highnesses, by proclamation made and with the
royal standard unfurled, and no opposition was offered to me.

To the first island which I found I gave the name San
Salvador [Watling Island], in remembrance of the Divine
Majesty, Who has marvelously bestowed all this; the Indians
call it "Guanahani." To the second I gave the name Isla de
Santa Maria de Concepción [Rum Cay]; to the third, Fer-
nandina [Long Island]; to the fourth, Isabella [Crooked Island];
to the fifth, Isla Juana [Cuba]; and so to each one I gave a
new name.

When I reached Juana, I followed its coast to the westward,
and I found it to be so extensive that I thought that it must
be the mainland, the province of Catayo [Cathay, China]. And
since there were neither towns nor villages on the seashore,
but only small hamlets, with the people of which I could
not have speech, because they all fled immediately, I went
forward on the same course, thinking that I should not fail
to find great cities and towns.

And at the end of many leagues, seeing that there was no
change and that the coast was bearing me northward—which
I wished to avoid, since winter was already beginning and I
proposed to make from it to the south—and as moreover the
wind was carrying me forward, I determined not to wait for a
change in the weather and retraced my path as far as a certain
harbor known to me. And from that point I sent two men
inland to learn if there were a king or great cities. They
traveled three days' journey and found an infinity of small
hamlets and people without number, but nothing of importance. For this reason, they returned.

I understood sufficiently from other Indians whom I had

already taken that this land was nothing but an island. And therefore I followed its coast eastward for 107 leagues to the point where it ended. And from that cape I saw another island, distant 18 leagues from the former, to the east, to which I at once gave the name Española [Hispaniola].

And I went there and followed its northern coast, as I had in the case of Juana, to the eastward for 188 great leagues in a straight line.

This island and all the others are very fertile to a limitless degree, and this island is extremely so. In it there are many harbors on the coast of the sea, beyond comparison with others which I know in Christendom, and many rivers, good and large, which is marvelous. Its lands are high, and there are in it very many sierras and very lofty mountains, beyond comparison with the island of Teneriffe. All are most beautiful, of a thousand shapes, and all are accessible, and filled with trees of a thousand kinds and tall, and they seem to touch the sky. And I am told that they never lose their foliage, as I can understand, for I saw them as green and as lovely as they are in Spain in May, and some of them were flowering, some bearing fruit, and some in another stage, according to their nature. And the nightingale was singing, and other birds of a thousand kinds, in the month of November there where I went.

There are six or eight kinds of palm, which are a wonder to behold on account of their beautiful variety, but so are the other trees and fruits and plants. In it are marvelous pine groves, and there are very large tracts of cultivatable lands, and there is honey, and there are birds of many kinds and fruits in great diversity. In the interior are mines of metals, and the population is without number. Española is a marvel.

The sierras and mountains, the plains and arable lands and pastures, are so lovely and rich for planting and sowing, for breeding cattle of every kind, for building towns and villages. The harbors of the sea here are such as cannot be believed to exist unless they have been seen, and so with the rivers, many and great, and good waters, the majority of which contain gold. In the trees and fruits and plants, there is a great difference from those of Juana. In this island there are many spices, and great mines of gold and of other metals.

The people of this island, and of all the other islands which I have found and of which I have information, all go naked, men and women, as their mothers bore them, although some women cover a single place with the leaf of a plant or with a net of cotton which they make for the purpose. They have no iron or steel or weapons, nor are they fitted to use them, not because they are not well-built men and of handsome stature, but because they are very marvelously timorous. They have no other arms than weapons made of canes, cut in seeding time, to the ends of which they fix a small sharpened stick.

And they do not dare to make use of these, for many times it has happened that I have sent ashore two or three men to some town to have speech, and countless people have come out to them, and as soon as they have seen my men approaching they have fled, even a father not waiting for his son. And this not because ill has been done to anyone; on the contrary, at every point where I have been and have been able to have speech, I have given to them of all that I had, such as cloth and many other things, without receiving anything for it. But so they are, incurably timid.

It is true that after they have been reassured and have lost their fear, they are so guileless and so generous with all they possess that no one would believe it who has not seen it. They never refuse anything which they possess, if it be asked of them. On the contrary, they invite anyone to share it, and display as much love as if they would give their hearts, and whether the thing be of value or whether it be of small price, at once with whatever trifle of whatever kind it may be that is given to them, with that they are content.

I forbade that they should be given things so worthless as fragments of broken crockery and scraps of broken glass and ends of straps, although when they were able to get them, they fancied that they possessed the best jewel in the world. So it was found that a sailor for a strap received gold to the weight of two and a half castellanos [gold coins], and others much more for other things which were worth much less. As for new blancas [silver coins], for them they would give everything which they had, although it might be two or three castellanos' weight of gold or an arroba [about 25 lbs] or two of spun cotton. . . .

They took even the pieces of the broken hoops of the wine barrels and, like savages, gave what they had, so that it seemed to me to be wrong, and I forbade it. And I gave a thousand handsome good things which I had brought, in order that they might conceive affection, and more than that, might become Christians and be inclined to the love and service of Their Highnesses and of the whole Castilian nation, and strive to aid us and to give us of the things which they have in abundance and which are necessary to us. And they do not know any creed and are not idolaters; only they all believe that power and good are in the heavens, and they are very firmly convinced that I, with these ships and men, came from the heavens, and in this belief they everywhere received me, after they had overcome their fear.

And this does not come because they are ignorant. On the contrary, they are of a very acute intelligence and are men who navigate all those seas, so that it is amazing how good an account they give of everything, but it is because they have never seen people clothed or ships of such a kind.

And as soon as I arrived in the Indies, in the first island which I found I took by force some of them,[2] in order that they might learn and give me information of that which there is in those parts. And so it was that they soon understood us, and we them, either by speech or signs, and they have been very serviceable. I still take them with me, and they are always assured that I come from Heaven, for all the intercourse which they have had with me. And they were the first to announce this wherever I went, and the others went running from house to house and to the neighboring towns, with loud cries of, "Come! Come to see the people from Heaven!"

So all, men and women alike, when their minds were set at rest concerning us, came, so that not one, great or small, remained behind, and all brought something to eat and drink, which they gave with extraordinary affection.

[2] Bartolomé de Las Casas, great though largely unsuccessful defender of American human rights against the master-race traits of the Spanish conquerors, argued that the forcible taking of these natives was wholly unjustifiable, and found in it the beginning of the maltreatment of the Indians.

In all the islands they have very many canoes, like rowing *fustas*,[3] some larger, some smaller, and some are larger than a *fusta* of eighteen benches. They are not so broad, because they are made of a single log of wood, but a *fusta* would not keep up with them in rowing, since their speed is a thing incredible. And in these they navigate among all those islands, which are innumerable, and carry their goods. One of these canoes I have seen with seventy and eighty men in her, and each one with his oar.

In all these islands, I saw no great diversity in the appearance of the people or in their manners and language. On the contrary, they all understand one another, which is a very curious thing, on account of which I hope that Their Highnesses will determine upon their conversion to our holy faith, toward which they are very inclined.[4]

I have already said how I have gone 107 leagues in a straight line from west to east along the seashore of the island Juana, and as a result of that voyage, I can say that this island is larger than England and Scotland together, for, beyond these 107 leagues, there remain to the westward two provinces to which I have not gone. One of these provinces they call Avan, and there the people are born with tails; and these provinces cannot have a length of less than 50 or 60 leagues, as I could understand from those Indians whom I have and who know all the islands.

The other, Española, has a circumference greater than all Spain, from Colibre, by the seacoast, to Fuenterabia in Vizcaya, since I voyaged along one side 188 great leagues in a straight line from west to east. It is a land to be desired, and seen, it is never to be left.

And in it, although of all I have taken possession for Their Highnesses and all are more richly endowed than I know how, or am able, to say, and I hold them all for Their Highnesses, so that they may dispose of them as, and as absolutely as, of the kingdoms of Castile—in this Española, in the situation most convenient and in the best position for the mines of gold and

---

[3] A *fusta* was a light-oared vessel. Some had one or two masts, lateen-rigged. The Spaniards occasionally fixed masts to the native canoes.

[4] Columbus later understood that there was great diversity of languages.

for all intercourse as well with the mainland here as with that there, belonging to the Grand Khan, where will be great trade and gain, I have taken possession of a large town, to which I gave the name Villa de Navidád. And in it I have made fortifications and a fort, which now will by this time be entirely finished, and I have left in it sufficient men for such a purpose with arms and artillery and provisions for more than a year, and a *fusta*, and one, a master of all seacraft, to build others, and great friendship with the king of that land, so much so that he was proud to call me, and to treat me as, a brother.

And even if he were to change his attitude to one of hostility toward these men, he and his do not know what arms are, and they go naked, as I have already said, and are the most timorous people that there are in the world. So that the men whom I have left there alone would suffice to destroy all that land, and the island is without danger for their persons, if they know how to govern themselves.

In all these islands, it seems to me that all men are content with one woman, and to their chief or king they give as many as twenty. It appears to me that the women work more than the men. And I have not been able to learn if they hold private property; what seemed to me to appear was that in that which one had, all took a share, especially of eatable things.

In these islands I have so far found no human monstrosities, as many expected, but on the contrary the whole population is very well formed, nor are they Negroes as in Guinea, but their hair is flowing, and they are not born where there is intense force in the rays of the sun. It is true that the sun has there great power, although it is distant from the equinoctial line 26 degrees. In these islands, where there are high mountains the cold was severe this winter, but they endure it, being used to it and with the help of meats which they eat with many and extremely hot spices.

As I have found no monsters, so I have had no report of any, except in an island, Quaris, the second at the coming into the Indies, which is inhabited by a people who are regarded in all the islands as very fierce and who eat human flesh. They have many canoes with which they range through all the islands of India and pillage and take as much as they can. They are no more malformed than the others, except that they have the custom of wearing their hair long like women, and they use bows and arrows of the same cane stems, with a small piece of wood at the end, owing to lack of iron, which they do not possess.

They are ferocious among these other people, who are cowardly to an excessive degree, but I make no more account of them than of the rest. These are those who have intercourse with the women of Matinino, which is the first island met on the way from Spain to the Indies, in which there is not a man. These women engage in no feminine occupation, but use bows and arrows of cane like those already mentioned, and they arm and protect themselves with plates of copper, of which they have much.

In another island, which they assure me is larger than Española, the people have no hair. In it there is gold incalculable, and from it and from the other islands I bring with me Indians as evidence.

In conclusion, to speak only of that which has been accomplished on this voyage, which was so hasty, Their Highnesses can see that I will give them as much gold as they may need, if Their Highnesses will render me very slight assistance; moreover, spice and cotton, as much as they shall order to be shipped and which, up to now, has been found only in Greece, in the island of Chios, and the Seignory sells it for what it pleases; and aloe wood, as much as they shall order to be shipped; and slaves, as many as they shall order to be shipped and who will be from the idolaters.

And I believe that I have found rhubarb and cinnamon, and I shall find a thousand other things of value, which the people whom I have left there will have discovered. For I have not delayed at any point, so far as the wind allowed me to sail, except in the town of Navidád in order to leave it secured and well established, and in truth I should have done much more if the ships had served me, as reason demanded.

This is enough [Here occurs a blank space in the original] and the eternal God, Our Lord, Who gives to all those who walk in His way triumph over things which appear to be impossible, and this was notably one. For although men have talked or have written of these lands, all was conjectural, without suggestion of ocular evidence, but amounted only to this, that those who heard for the most part listened and judged it to be rather a fable than as having any vestige of truth.

So that, since Our Redeemer has given this victory to our most illustrious King and Queen and to their renowned kingdoms in so great a matter, for this all Christendom ought to feel delight and make great feasts and give solemn thanks to the Holy Trinity, with many solemn prayers for the great exaltation which they shall have in the turning of so many peoples to our holy faith, and afterward for temporal benefits; for not only Spain but all Christians will have hence refreshment and gain.

This, in accordance with that which has been accomplished thus briefly.

Done in the caravel, off the Canary Islands, on the fifteenth of February, in the year one thousand four hundred and ninety-three.

At your orders.

El Almirante

After having written this, and being in the sea of Castile, there came on me so great a south-southwest wind that I was obliged to lighten ship. But I ran here today into this port of Lisbon, which was the greatest marvel in the world, whence I decided to write to Their Highnesses.

In all the Indies, I have always found weather like May; where I went in thirty-three days, and I had returned in twenty-eight save for these storms which have detained me for fourteen days, beating about in this sea. Here all the sailors say that never has there been so bad a winter nor so many ships lost.

Done on the fourth day of March.

The second voyage of Columbus, 1493-96, was devoted to further exploration of what are now the West Indies and to the consolidation of the power of Spain in those islands. On his own behalf he made constant attempts to strengthen his position as Governor of the new lands and Admiral of the Ocean Sea. As against the 88 men and three ships of the first voyage, he now had 1500 men on three large and fourteen small ships.

The Spanish Government instructed Columbus to treat the natives "well and lovingly." This the Admiral, and many of his contemporaries, found not inconsistent with enslaving them for the commercial exploitation of their own islands, a process that went hand in hand with Christianizing them. There was, as well, the development of export slavery.

Bartolomé de Las Casas, contemporary historian and eloquent but unsuccessful defender of human rights on behalf of the Indians, felt that Columbus initiated the slave trade during his first voyage when he seized captives for exhibition to his sovereigns. C. R. Beazley, British historian of geographic discovery, differs as to the time. He says of Columbus that during the second voyage, "on February 2, 1494, he sent home, by Antonio de Torres, that dispatch to Their Catholic Highnesses by which he may be said to have founded the West Indian slave trade."

It was not till June 24, 1495, that the first large shipment of kidnapped people started for Spain, when, according to Beazley, "five shiploads of Indians were sent off to Seville to be sold as slaves." This was one of the ways the Spanish took for keeping abreast of their great maritime rivals, the Portuguese, who secured their slaves in Africa. However, the conduct of the Admiral and his deputies did not find universal favor in Spain, Queen Isabella being among those who deplored the shipment of Indian slaves to Europe.

Before Columbus, at least from the fifteenth century B.C. to the fifteenth A.D., geographic discoveries were usually looked upon as trade secrets. New territories might prove sources of revenue, roads to them highways to riches. So why should the discovering trader or nation reveal the discovery? Usually they did not, hiding it as well and as long as they could.

As has been dwelt on already, the Phoenicians were in ancient times the nation that carried out this principle more elaborately and with more success than any other known maritime power. In the late Middle Ages the Phoenician type of secrecy was applied by no country more consistently or more successfully than by the Portuguese—so successfully, indeed, that today, when they would like to have the credit for as many as possible of their great discoveries, they have trouble in finding the evidence. For the things that needed to be hidden from all the rest of the world in the fourteenth and fifteenth centuries were of necessity hidden from most Portuguese as well.

It is common for historians of geographic discovery, therefore, to feel it as something between a possibility and a probability that the continent of South America was known to the Portuguese before it was first visited by the Spaniards, under Columbus. The Portuguese were, in such case, keeping Brazil a trade secret.

But since a mere probability is no proof, it is historical etiquette to assume that the true European discoverer of South America was Columbus, on his third voyage in 1498. The assumption is, however, without prejudice to the doctrine, discussed in an earlier section, that there was a golden age of navigation between 3000 and 1500 B.C., during which Stone Age and Bronze Age man swarmed the Atlantic, somewhat as Stone Age man is known to have swarmed the Pacific in the period between A.D. 500 and 1500.

One of the reasons why many think the Portuguese knew of South America before Columbus reached it is that the King of Portugal, Dom João II (John II), believed there was such a continent. According to Samuel Eliot Morison's *Admiral of the Ocean Sea* (1942), Columbus was impressed with this view of the Portuguese sovereign and "the Admiral's primary purpose on this [the third] voyage was to test the truth of this royal surmise."

Columbus sailed in the spring of 1498 in a company of six ships, while two others had been sent ahead. The story is told here by extracting the narrative from a long document Columbus sent back from Hispaniola on October 18, 1498, to the "most serene and high and most powerful princes, the King and Queen, our sovereigns." There is in this account a great deal of religious interpretation and philosophical speculation, most of which is eliminated.

Third Voyage of Christopher Columbus

I departed, in the name of the Most Holy Trinity, on Wednesday, 30 May, from the town of San Lucar, very wearied from my journey, for I had hoped for rest there when I left these Indies, and my pain had been doubled. And I navigated to the island of Madeira by an unaccustomed route, to avoid trouble which I might have had with a fleet from France, which waited for me at Cape St. Vincent. And from there I navigated to the Canary Islands, whence I departed with one ship and two caravels, and I sent the other ships on the direct course to the Indies to the island of Española. And I sailed southward, with the intention of reaching the equinoctial line and from there following it westward so that the island of Española would be left to the north of me.

And having reached the islands of Cape Verde—a false name, since they are so barren that I saw no green thing in them and all the people were infirm, so that I did not dare to remain in them—I sailed to the southwestward, 480 miles, which is 120 leagues, where, when it grew dark, I found the North Star to be in the fifth degree.

There the wind failed me and I came into so great heat and so intense that I believed that the ships and people would be burned, so that all suddenly fell into such confusion that there was no one who dared to go below deck to attend to the water cask and provisions. This heat lasted for eight days. On the first day it was fine, and on the seven days following it rained and was cloudy, and yet we found no relief. I believe certainly that if it had been sunny as it was on the first day, it would have been in no wise possible to escape.

[The paragraph just quoted refers to that doctrine of the burning and impassable equatorial zone of the earth to which several references have been made in the explanatory parts of this anthology. As has been said, the uncrossability of this middle zone of the earth had been a dogma from 200 or 300 B.C. to the fifteenth century A.D., when the "burning tropics" were crossed by the Portuguese. Commenting on the passage, Cecil

Jane says in his 1930 Hakluyt Society edition of *The Voyages of Columbus*:

"This was within the traditional 'burning zone' (although constantly passed and repassed by the Portuguese), and Columbus paints an exaggerated picture of the sufferings of himself and his crew in order to enhance the supposed advantages of the hemisphere that lay beyond the Pope's Line"—meaning that Columbus was pretending that while the ancient doctrine of torrid heat in the middle zone applied east of the line assigned by Pope Alexander as the western boundary of the discovery sphere of Portugal, it nevertheless did not apply west of that line, in the discovery province of Spain—as indeed Columbus himself explains in the next paragraph.]

I recalled that in navigating to the Indies, whenever I passed to the westward of the islands of the Azores 100 leagues, there I found the temperature change, and that everywhere from north to south.

And I determined that if it pleased Our Lord to give me a wind and fair weather so that I could get away from where I was, I would cease to go more to the south and would not go back either, but navigate westward, following that course in the hope of finding the same temperature as I had found when I navigated in the parallel of the Canaries. And then, if it were so, I should still be able to proceed more to the south.

And it pleased Our Lord at the end of these eight days to give me a favorable east wind, and I steered westward, but I did not dare to go lower down to the south, because I found a very great change in the sky and in the stars, but I did not find change in the temperature. So I decided to proceed farther always directly westward, in a straight line from Sierra Leone, with the intention of not changing my course up to the point where I had thought that land would be found, and there to repair the vessels and, if possible, to renew our supplies and to take in the water which was needed.

And at the end of seventeen days, during which Our Lord gave me a favoring wind, on Tuesday, 31 July, at midday, land appeared to us, and I had expected to sight it on the previous Monday and held to this course up to then.

But as the strength of the sun grew, and on account of deficiency of water, of which we were short, I determined to go to the islands of the Caribs, and took that route. And as the Divine Majesty has always shown mercy toward me, a sailor went up to the maintop to look out and to the westward saw three mountains near one another. We repeated the *Salve Regina* and other prayers, and we all gave many thanks to Our Lord.

And after this I abandoned the northerly course and made for the land, and I arrived there at the hour of compline at a cape which I called La Galea, having already named the island Trinidad. There is there a very good harbor if bottom could be reached, and there were houses and very fair lands, as lovely and as green as the orchards of Valencia in March. It weighed upon me that I could not enter the harbor, and I ran along the coast of this land to the westward, and having gone 5 leagues, I found a very good bottom and anchored.

And the next day I set sail on this course, seeking a harbor in order to repair the ships and take in water, and to add to the corn and the only provisions which I had brought. There I took in a pipe of water, and then went on so until we arrived at the cape. There I found shelter from the east wind and a good bottom, and so I commanded to anchor and to repair the water cask and to take in water and wood.

And I ordered the people to land to rest themselves on account of having suffered fatigue for so long a time during which they were voyaging. To this point I gave the name Del Arenal [now Point Ycacos]. And there all the ground was trodden by some animals which had footprints like those of a goat, and although, as it appeared, there were many there, I saw none except one that was dead.

On the following day there came from toward the east a large canoe with twenty-four men, all in the prime of life and very well provided with arms—bows and arrows and wooden shields—and they, as I have said, were all in the prime of life, well proportioned and not Negroes, but whiter than the others who have been seen in the Indies, and very graceful and with handsome bodies, and hair long and smooth, cut in the manner of Castile. They had their heads wrapped in scarves of cotton, worked elaborately and in colors, which I believed were *almaizares* [Moorish gauze veils]. They wore another of these scarves round the body and covered themselves with them in place of drawers.

When this canoe arrived, it hailed us from a great distance, and neither I nor anyone else could understand them. However, I ordered signs to be made to them that they should approach, and in this way more than two hours passed, and if they came a little nearer, they at once sheered off again. I caused pans and other things which shone to be shown to them in order to attract them to come, and after a good while they came nearer than they had hitherto done. And I greatly desired to have speech with them, and it seemed to me that I had nothing that could be shown to them now which would induce them to come nearer.

But I caused to be brought up to the castle of the poop a tambourine, that they might play it, and some young men to dance, believing that they would draw near to see the festivity. And as soon as they observed the playing and dancing, they all dropped their oars and laid hand on their bows and strung them, and each one of them took up his shield, and they began to shoot arrows. I immediately stopped the playing and dancing, and then ordered some crossbows to be discharged.

They left me and went quickly to another caravel and in haste got under its stern. And the pilot accosted them, and gave a coat and a hat to a man who seemed to be one of the chief among them, and it was arranged that he should go to speak with them there on the shore, where they went at once in the canoe to wait for him. And he would not go without my permission, and when they saw him come to my ship in the boat, they entered their canoe again and went away, and I never saw any more of them or of the other inhabitants of this island.

When I reached this Punta del Arenal, I found that the island of Trinidad formed with the land of Gracia [the mainland of South America] a strait 2 leagues broad from west to east, and that it was necessary to enter it in order to pass to the north. There were some signs of currents which crossed that strait and which made a very great roaring, and I believed that there must be a reef with shallows and rocks, owing to which it would not be possible to enter it. And behind this current there was another and another, which all made a great roaring like that of the sea when it breaks and dashes against rocks. I anchored there at the said Punta del Arenal, outside the said strait, and I found that the water came from the east toward the west with as much fury as that of the Guadalquivir when it is in flood. This was continuous, night and day, so that I believed that it would not be possible to go against the current, or to go forward owing to the shallows.[5]

And in the night, when it was already very late, being on the deck of the ship, I heard a very terrible roaring which came from the direction of the south toward the ship. And I stayed to watch, and I saw the sea from west to east rising like a hill as high as the ship, and still it came toward me little by little. And above it there came a wave which advanced roaring with a very great noise with the same fury of roaring as that of the other currents, which I have said appeared to me as the waves of the sea breaking on rocks. To this very day I remember the fear that I had lest the wave should overwhelm the ship when it came upon her, and it passed by and reached the strait, where it continued for a great while.

And the next day following I sent the boats to take soundings and I found that in the shallowest part of the strait there were 6 or 7 fathoms of water, and there were constantly those currents flowing, some into and others out of the strait. And it pleased Our Lord to give me a fair wind, and I passed into this strait and soon found calm water. And by chance I drew some water from the sea and I found it to be fresh.

I navigated northward as far as a very lofty mountain range, 26 leagues or so from this Punta del Arenal, and there were there two headlands of very high ground, one on the eastern side, which belonged to the same island of Trinidad, and the other on the west, belonging to the land which I called Gracia. And there a strait was formed, much narrower than that by Punta del Arenal, and there were there the same currents and that great roaring of the water as there was at Punta del Arenal, and there also the sea was fresh water.

[5] This proved to be due to the vast inflowing volume of Orinoco River water.

Up to then I had not had speech with any people of these lands, and I greatly desired to do so. For this reason, I navigated along the coast of this land toward the west, and the farther I went, the fresher and more wholesome I found the water of the sea. Having gone a great distance, I arrived at a place where the land appeared to me to be cultivated. I anchored and sent the boats ashore. They found that there had recently been people there, and they found the whole mountain covered with monkeys. They returned and, as the country here was mountainous, it appeared to me that farther to the west there would be flatter land, and that for that reason it would be inhabited.

I ordered the anchors to be weighed and I ran along this coast to the end of this mountainous part, and there I anchored in a river. And immediately many people came, and they told me that they called this land Paria, and that farther westward from there it was more populated. I took four of them, and afterward I navigated to the west, and having gone 8 leagues farther westward, beyond a point which I named Punta del Aguja [now Punta del Alcatraz] I found there some lands, the most lovely in the world and very populous. I arrived there one morning at the hour of tierce, and on seeing this verdure and this beauty, I decided to anchor and to see these people.

Of them, some came at once in canoes to the ship to ask me, on behalf of their king, that I should land. And when they saw that I was not concerned at them, they came in infinite numbers to the ship in canoes, and many wore pieces of gold on their breasts, and some had some pearls round their arms. I rejoiced greatly when I saw these things, and made great efforts to know where they procured them, and they told me in that place and to the northward of that land.

I could have wished to remain there, but these supplies which I was carrying, corn and wine and flesh for these people who are here, were on the verge of being lost, when I had brought them so far with such great labor. And accordingly I sought to do nothing else than to go on to be able to place them in security, and not to wait for anything.

I endeavored to obtain some of those pearls, and I sent the boats ashore. These people are very numerous, and all are of very good appearance, of the same color as the others before, and very tractable. Our people who went ashore found them very well disposed, and they received them very courteously.

They say that as soon as the boats reached land, two principal persons came with all the people; they believe that one was the father and the other his son. And they led them to a very large house, built with two *aguas* and not round like field tents, as are the others. They had there many seats on which they caused them to sit, and others on which they seated themselves. They caused bread to be brought and fruit of many kinds and wine of many kinds, white and red, but not made from grapes. The wine must be made from fruits of different kinds, some from one fruit and some from another, and also some of it may be made from maize, which is a plant bearing an ear like an ear of wheat, some of which I brought home, and there is now much in Castile. It seems that the best is regarded as most excellent and has great value.

All these men were together at one end of the house, and all the women at the other. Both parties were grieved that they did not understand one another, they in order to ask the others of our country, and our men in order to learn about their land. And after they had been given a meal there in the house of the elder, the younger took them to his own house, and made them another equal meal, and after that they got into the boats and came back to the ship.

And at once I weighed anchor, for I went in great haste to save the supplies, which were being ruined and which I had brought with so great toil, and also to restore my own health. For as a result of lack of sleep I was suffering in my eyes, and although on that voyage, when I went to discover Tierra Firme, I was thirty-three days without tasting sleep and was for so great a time blind, my eyes were not so injured, nor did they run with blood and cause so much pain, as now.

These people, as I have already said, are all of very fine stature, tall and very graceful in their movements. Their hair is very long and smooth, and they have their heads bound with certain worked scarves, as I have said, handsome, which from a distance appear to be of silk, and *almaizares*. They wear another scarf, very large, girded round them, with which they cover themselves in place of drawers, as well men as women. The color of these people is whiter than that of any other race that has been seen in the Indies. They all wear something on the breast and on the arms, as is the custom in these lands, and many wear pieces of gold hanging below the breast. Their canoes are very large and better built than are those of the others, and lighter, and in the middle of each they have a separate division, like a room, in which I saw that the chief men went with their women. I called this place there *jardines*, for it corresponded to that name.

I made great endeavors to know where they collected that gold, and they all indicated to me a land bordering on them to the west, which was very lofty but not at a distance. But all told me that I should not go there, for there they ate men, and I understood then that they said that there were cannibals there, and that they were like the other cannibals. And since I have thought that it may be that they said this because there are there wild animals.

Also I asked them where they gathered the pearls, and they also indicated that it was to the westward and to the north, beyond this land, where they were. I omitted to prove this, on account of the supplies and of the bad state of my eyes, and because a large ship which I had was not suited for such an undertaking. And as the time was short, it was all spent in questioning, and they returned to the ships, which was at the hour of vespers, as I have said.

And at once I weighed anchor and navigated to the westward, and so on the following day, in the belief that this was certainly an island and that I should be able to come out to the northward, until I found that there were hardly 3 fathoms of water. Having seen this, I sent a light caravel in advance to see if there was a way out or if it was closed. And so it went a great distance as far as a very large gulf, where it appeared that there were four other gulfs of moderate size and into one a very great river flowed [Rio Guarapiche?]. They always found 5 fathoms depth and the water very fresh, in very great quantity, and such that I never drank its like.

I was very discomforted at that, when I saw that it was not possible to come out to the north and that it was already im-

possible to go to the south or to the west because I was shut
in by the land on all sides. So I weighed anchor and turned
back to go out to the northward by the passage which I have
mentioned above, and I was not able to go by the village where
I had been, on account of the currents which bore me away
from it. And always, at every cape, I found the water fresh and
clear, and that it carried me very swiftly to the eastward
toward the two straits which I have mentioned above.

Then I surmised concerning the streaks of current and the
rolling waves, which went out of and entered into these straits
with that great and violent roaring, that there was a battle between the fresh water and the salt. The fresh struggled with
the other to prevent its entrance, and the salt with the other
that it might not come out. And I conjectured that there where
are these two straits there may at one time have been continuous
land between the island of Trinidad and the land of Gracia,
as Your Highnesses will be able to see from the drawing of it
which I send to you with this.

I went out by this strait to the north and I found that the
fresh water was always victorious, and when I passed through,
which was by the force of the wind, being on one of these
waves, I found in those waves on the inner side fresh water,
and on the outer side salt.

When I navigated from Spain to the Indies, I found that
immediately after passing 100 leagues to the west of the Azores
[that is, after passing the Pope's Line], there was a very great
change in the sky and in the stars and in the temperature of
the air and in the waters of the sea. I have used much care in
verifying this. I found that from north to south, passing there
the said 100 leagues from the said islands, immediately the
needle of the compass, which up to then had turned to the
northeast, turned a full quarter of the wind to the northwest.
And on reaching that line there it is as if a hill had been carried there.

And also I found all the sea full of vegetation [Sargasso Sea]
of a kind which resembles pine branches and very full of fruit
like that of the mastic tree. And it is so dense that on the first
voyage I thought that it was a shallow and that the ships
would run aground, and until this line was reached not a single

branch was found. I found also on arriving there the sea very gentle and smooth, and that though the wind was strong, it never became rough.

Also I found within this line, toward the west, the temperature of the sky very mild, and that there was no change in its character whether it was winter or whether it was summer. When I was there, I found that the North Star described a circle which was 5 degrees in diameter, and when the guards are in the right arm, the star is at its lowest point, and it continues to rise until they are in the left arm, and then it is 5 degrees, and from that point it sinks until they reach again the right arm.

On this occasion I went from Spain to the island of Madeira, and thence to the Canaries, and thence to the Cape Verde Islands. From that point I steered a course to navigate southward to below the equinoctial line, as I have already said. Arriving at a point directly on the parallel which passed through Sierra Leone in Guinea, I found so great heat, and the rays of the sun were so intense, that I thought that I should be burned, and although it rained and the sky was very overcast, I was always in that state of exhaustion until Our Lord gave me a fair wind and put into my heart the wish to navigate to the west, with the encouragement that on reaching the line of which I have already spoken, I should find there a change in temperature.

As soon as I came to be directly on this line, immediately I found the temperature very mild, and as I went farther forward, so it became more mild, but I did not find the stars corresponding with this. I found there that when night came on the pole star was 5 degrees high, and then the guards were overhead, and afterward at midnight the star had risen to 10 degrees, and at daybreak to 15, when the guards were below. I found the same smoothness of the sea, but not the same vegetation.

In the matter of the pole star, I felt great wonder, and accordingly with great care I spent many nights in examining it carefully with the quadrant, and always I found that the lead and line fell to the same point. I regard this as something new, and it may be that it will be held that the sky undergoes a great change in a brief space.

I have always read that the world, land and water, was spherical, and authoritative accounts on the experiments which Ptolemy and all the others have recorded concerning this matter so describe it and hold it to be, by the eclipses of the moon and by other demonstrations made from east to west, as well as from the elevation of the pole star from north to south.

Now, as I have already said, I have seen so great irregularity that as a result, I have been led to hold this concerning the world, and I find that it is not round as they describe it, but that it is the shape of a pear which is everywhere very round except where the stalk is, for there it is very prominent. Or that it is like a very round ball, and on one part of it is placed something like a woman's nipple, and that this part where this protuberance is found is the highest and nearest to the sky, and it is beneath the equinoctial line and in this Ocean Sea at the end of the East. I call that "the end of the East" where end all the land and islands.

[Here several pages of Ptolemaic, Aristotelian, and Biblical speculation are omitted.]

Holy Scripture testifies that Our Lord made the earthly paradise and in it placed the tree of life, and from it issues a fountain from which flow four of the chief rivers of this world, the Ganges in India, the Tigris and Euphrates in . . . [blank space in original] which cut through a mountain range and form Mesopotamia and flow into Persia, and the Nile, which rises in Ethiopia and enters the sea at Alexandria.

I do not find and I have never found any writing of the Romans or of the Greeks which gives definitely the position in the world of the earthly paradise, nor have I seen it in any world map placed with authority based upon proof. Some placed it there where are the sources of the Nile in Ethiopia, but others traversed all these lands and found no similarity to it in the climate or in elevation toward the sky, to make it comprehensible that it was there, nor that the rising waters of the Deluge had reached that place, and Saint Isidore and Bede and Strabo and the Master of Scholastic History and Saint Ambrose and Scotus and all the learned theologians agree that the earthly paradise is in the East, &c.

I have already said that which I hold concerning this

hemisphere and its shape, and I believe that if I were to pass beneath the equinoctial line, then, arriving there at the highest point, I should find an even more temperate climate and difference in the stars and waters. Not that I believe that to the summit of the extreme point is navigable, or water, or that it is possible to ascend there, for I believe that the earthly paradise is there and to it, save by the will of God, no man can come.

And I believe that this land which your Highnesses have now sent to discover is very extensive, and that there are many other lands in the south, of which there has never been any report.

I do not hold that the earthly paradise is in the form of a rugged mountain, as its description declares to us, but that it is at the summit, there where I have said that the shape of the stalk of the pear is, and that going toward it from a distance, there is a gradual ascent to it. And I believe that no one could reach the summit, as I have said, and I believe that this water may originate from there, though it be far away and may come to collect there where I came, and may form this lake.

These are great indications of the earthly paradise, for the situation agrees with the opinion of those holy and wise theologians, and also the signs are very much in accord with this idea, for I have never read or heard of so great a quantity of fresh water so coming into and near the salt. And the very mild climate also supports this view, and if it does not come from there, from paradise, it seems to be a still greater marvel, for I do not believe that there is known in the world a river so great and so deep.

After that I had issued forth from La Boca del Drago, which is the one of the two straits which is toward the north and to which I so gave a name, on the following day, which was the day of Our Lady in August, I found that the sea ran so strongly to the westward that from the hour of mass, when I began the voyage, to the hour of compline, I traveled 65 leagues of 4 miles each. And the wind was not violent, but very gentle, and this confirmed the view that going thence to the south, there is a continuous ascent, and going thence to the north, as we then did, there is a continuous descent.

I hold it to be very certain that the waters of the sea take their course from east to west with the heavens, and that there in this region, when they pass they go more rapidly, and accordingly have eaten away so great a part of the land, for which cause there are here so many islands. And the very islands themselves supply evidence of this, for on the one hand all those which lie west and east, or a little more obliquely northwest and southeast, are broad, and those lying north and south, and northeast and southwest, are narrow, for they are opposed to the said winds.

And here, in all the islands, precious things are produced, owing to the mild climate, which comes to them from Heaven as they lie toward the loftiest part of the world. It is true that in some parts the waters do not appear to take this course, but this is only so in some particular places, where there is some land which meets them, and causes it to seem that they flow in different directions. . . .

I turn to my subject, the land of Gracia and the river and lake which I found there, the latter so great that it is possible to call it a sea rather than a lake, since a "lake" is a small expanse of water, and if the expanse be great it is called a "sea," as we talk of the Sea of Galilee and the Dead Sea. And I say that if it be not from the earthly paradise that this river comes, it originates from a vast land lying to the south, of which hitherto no knowledge has been obtained.

But I am much more convinced in my own mind that there where I have said is the earthly paradise, and I rely upon the arguments and authorities given above. May it please Our Lord to grant long life and health and leisure to Your Highnesses, that you may be able to persevere in this most noble undertaking, from which in my opinion Our Lord will receive much service and Spain greatly increase her grandeur and all Christians receive much consolation and pleasure, since there will be spread abroad the name of Our Lord.

And in all the lands to which the ships of Your Highnesses go, and on every cape, I command a lofty cross to be set up, and I inform all the people whom I find of the estate of Your Highnesses and how your seat is in Spain, and I tell them of our holy faith, as far as I am able, and of the creed of Holy

Mother Church, which has her members in all the world, and I speak to them of the civilization and nobility of all Christians, and of the faith which they have in the Holy Trinity.

May it please Our Lord to forgive the persons who have calumniated and who do calumniate so excellent an undertaking, and who have opposed and do oppose it so that it may not go forward, without considering how much honor and glory it is for your royal estate throughout the world. They do not know what to urge in order to malign it, save that there is in it expense and that there have not been immediately sent back ships laden with gold, without regarding the brevity of the time and the many difficulties which there have been here.

And they do not consider that in Castile, in the household of Your Highnesses, there are every year persons who by their merit earn, each one of them, more there than it is necessary should be expended on this undertaking. Nor do they consider that no princes of Spain ever won lands beyond their own borders, except now that Your Highnesses have here another world, where our holy faith may be so greatly increased, and whence so great benefits can be derived. For although ships laden with gold have not been sent back, sufficient evidence of it and of other things of value has been sent back, whence it is possible to judge that in a little while much profit may be gained.

And they do not regard the great courage of the princes of Portugal who have for so much time prosecuted the enterprise of Guinea, and who prosecute that of Africa, where they have expended half the population of their realm, and today the King is more determined on the undertaking than ever. Our Lord provide in this matter, as I have said, and lead them to consider all this which I have written, which is not the thousandth part of that which I might write of the deeds of princes who have occupied themselves in gaining knowledge and with conquests and their maintenance.

All this I have said, and not because I believe that Your Highnesses have any wish save to persevere in this as long as you live, and I regard as very sure that which Your Highnesses once answered me concerning this by word of mouth, and not because I have seen any change in Your Highnesses, but from fear of that which I have heard of those whom I have mentioned, for so a drop of water falling on a stone will make a hole.

And Your Highnesses answered me with that magnanimity which you are known throughout the world to possess, and told me to feel no concern at all this, since it was your will to prosecute this undertaking and to support it, although there should be from it nothing but stones and sand; and that you took no account of the expense which was incurred in it, since on other affairs, not so great, you were spending much more; and that you held that which had been expended in the past, and that which might be expended in the future, as having been very well spent, since you believed that our holy faith would be increased and your royal dignity enhanced; and that they were not friends of your royal estate who spoke evil of this enterprise.

And now, while you receive information concerning the matter of these lands which I have newly discovered, in which I am assured in my heart that the earthly paradise is, the adelantado will go with three ships, well equipped, to that place to examine it further, and they will discover all that they can in those parts.

Meanwhile, I will send to Your Highnesses this writing and the drawing of the land, and you will determine that which is to be done in the matter and will send to me your orders, and with the help of the Holy Trinity it shall be fulfilled with all diligence, so that Your Highnesses be served and have pleasure.

Thanks be to God.

While Columbus was on his third voyage, accusations of many kinds were made in Spain against him and his lieutenants, some of them true. He was sent home in irons; but by the time he arrived the tide of popular and royal favor had turned and he rode the crest of the wave again.

By now Columbus was realizing, at least subconsciously, that he had not yet found Asia, or at any rate not the rich territories that the Portuguese were able to reach by circumnavigating Africa. So even he began to develop that resentment against the new lands, as blocking the road to the desired old lands, which later became nearly universal throughout Europe and which remained strong for centuries. Beazley has it that Columbus now "determined to find a strait through which he might penetrate westward into Portuguese Asia." This led to the fourth voyage, which began the spring of 1502 with four ships and 150 men.

Between July and December of 1502 the Admiral cruised the shores of what are now Honduras, Nicaragua, Costa Rica, and Panama. He nearly or quite reached that section of the east coast of Panama which is opposite the Gulf of San Miguel, where Balboa a few years later crossed the isthmus to become the European discoverer of the Pacific. Columbus found no strait and had to give up the search.

Under pathetic circumstances of discontent among his men, and discouraging miscarriages of several kinds, the Admiral returned to Spain in the autumn of 1504. As the next two years dragged on there was upon his shoulders an increasing burden of disappointment. His search for a passage through the new land had been of itself a confession that he had previously been wrong in thinking he had found Asia (neglecting here the dispute over whether he himself "always" knew he had not found it, his Asia claims in that case being fraudulent, devised to create interest). His authority as Governor and Admiral, pledged him by the Crown, was not being maintained; his financial rewards were inadequate; he was being criticized for having started a slave trade which was not even very successful, since the Indians died too easily when subjected to the restraints of their bondage.

The Admiral may not have been born earlier than 1451, but it was an old man, spiritually bowed if not broken, who died on May 20, 1506.

Even before Columbus died, the knowledge that Asia had not been reached was common throughout Europe. Indeed, as has been said, John Cabot probably understood this in 1498 if not in 1497. The Cortereals certainly understood it before their work ceased in 1503.

Various writers, notably J. A. Williamson in his *The Ocean in English History*, have made it clear that after a brief awakening, which did not even last the decade that followed the 1492

Columbus announcement, northwestern Europe slumped back
into the feeling that the "New Found Lands" of the West, in
the latitude of Britain and France, were nothing but the old
lands which they had known about, and which offered no rewards for enterprise beyond fish and fur. This explains, says
Williamson, how it came about that all records of the second
Cabot voyage to North America were lost, and nearly all those
of the first voyage. Nobody cared, nobody was interested.

Needless to say, Britain at this stage did not consider seriously
claiming North America through right of discovery. Still less
was there thought of colonization.

After some nearly perfunctory ventures before 1510 that are
connected with the name of Sebastian Cabot, there was no determined effort for more than half a century even to circumvent
North America by way of the north to discover a short route
to the Indies. Not before 1576 was there an attempt to reach
the Indies by the Northwest, the voyage of Frobisher, the narrative of which is quoted in our section on the Northwest
Passage. Moderately serious attempts to colonize from Britain
the territory that is now the United States were not started
until nine years later, Raleigh's venture at Roanoke Island
in 1585.

Interest in the Americas for their own sake developed more
quickly and continued more steadily in and through the Latin
countries, chiefly Spain and Portugal. The Latins were finding
profit in slaves, both for commercial export from America and
to work mines and plantations in the new country. Considerable
gold and some jewels were discovered, and secured through
violence and fraud, with profit or at least the hope of profit.
A campaign for the spread of Christianity was dovetailed with
military invasions and plundering expeditions.

By the time that the colonization of what are now the United
States and Canada got well started, the Latins had established
themselves in the southern United States, in nearly all the
country south of there from the Rio Grande to the Straits of
Magellan, and in most of the American islands. The story of
this development is merely touched here, through print-
ing the narratives of Balboa's crossing of the Isthmus of Panama
and Orellana's descent of the Amazon, which was also the first
crossing of South America.

Balboa Discovers the Pacific

BALBOA DISCOVERS THE PACIFIC

CHAPTER 8

LIKE many young Spaniards of his day, Vasco Núñez de Balboa (c. 1475-1517), the discoverer of the Pacific, was infected by that fever of adventure and conquest which, among the Latins, followed the voyages of Columbus.

Balboa's first chance to reach the new lands came in 1501, when he sailed as a member of an expedition fitted out by Rodrigo de Bastidas, a wealthy merchant. The cargo of gaudy cloth and beads was profitably exchanged for gold and pearls; more important, historically, was the reconnoitering of the Darien region, in what is now the Republic of Panama.

On the return voyage through the Caribbean, the ships began to leak and had to be beached on the island of Hispaniola. The most valuable things were saved from the wrecks, but only to be taken away later by the governor of the island. Bastidas returned to Spain; Balboa, penniless, remained in Hispaniola. For some years he appears to have engaged in farming, evidently without much success, for he continued in debt.

In 1509 an expedition to plant a colony in South America started from Santo Domingo under command of Alonso de Ojeda, the plan being that Martín Fernández de Enciso, a lawyer, should follow in ten months with two ships bringing reinforcements and supplies.

This was Balboa's chance, and he seized it. Stratagem was necessary, for a close watch was kept on all outgoing vessels to prevent the escape of debtors, armed boats going far out to sea in order to search the ships and bring back any stowaways. Balboa, anxious to get away from his creditors and to indulge

225

his taste for adventure, is said to have hidden himself in a cask of "victuals for the voyage," which was taken from his farm to the ship. When the escort had made a fruitless search and had headed back for Hispaniola, Balboa revealed himself, and eventually succeeded in gaining the confidence of Enciso.

While searching for Ojeda's settlement of San Sebastian, the expedition met one of Ojeda's vessels as they were entering the bay where now stands Cartagena. From Francisco Pizarro, who commanded the ship, it was learned that, through starvation and attacks from the hostile natives, the expedition party had been reduced from 300 to 60. Ojeda had set out for Hispaniola to try to get help, leaving Pizarro in command, with permission to use his own judgment as to where to go if Ojeda had not returned within fifty days.

The fifty-day period had expired, and Pizzaro was on his way to Hispaniola when he met Enciso, who ordered him to turn back and accompany him to San Sebastian. Here, in the Gulf of Urabá which forms the head of the Gulf of Darien, they found the settlement in ruins.

Prevented by the Indians from securing food, Enciso was undecided which way to turn when Balboa suggested that they should try the Darien district, where there were large grain-fields and much gold. He carried his point and a new settlement, Santa Maria de la Antigua del Darien, was founded at the mouth of the small Darien River, northwest of the mouth of the Atrato.

Trouble developed among the adventurers, resulting in Enciso's being deposed, imprisoned, and finally sent back to Spain, while Balboa assumed command.

Balboa now set about conquering the surrounding country, and "by his bravery, courtesy, kindness of heart, and just dealing" gained the confidence and friendship of several native chieftains. From one of these, the Cacique Comogre, he learned of the ocean on the other side of the mountains, and of the riches of Peru.

Shortly thereafter word came from Spain that Enciso had lodged a complaint with the King, and that Balboa had been condemned and was to be summoned to Spain. Hoping to conciliate the King by a striking and profitable enterprise,

Balboa then resolved to attempt the crossing of the isthmus and the conquest of Peru.

The expedition of 190 Spaniards and 1000 natives set out on September 1, 1513. On September 25 or 26, Balboa stood "silent, upon a peak in Darien" and looked down upon the Gulf of San Miguel, an arm of the Pacific Ocean. Thus occurred the first crossing of America and the first sighting by a European of the South Sea, El Mar del Sur.

For the story of Balboa's historic expedition we have chosen Alonso de Ovalle's account, which is included in a history of Chile that was first published in Rome in 1649. It was translated from Spanish into English and published at London in 1703. The English version bears the title *An Historical Relation of the Kingdom of Chile, by Alonso de Ovalle of the Company of Jesus, a Native of St. Jago of Chile, and Procurator at Rome for that Place.*

Ovalle's account needs no introduction beyond pointing out that, through striving for brevity or because of lack of information, he has telescoped the events of the last years of Balboa's life. For as Ovalle tells the story, it seems that Balboa met his tragic end upon his return from the expedition that is described.

Actually, Balboa returned to Darien in triumph, loaded with wealth and booty. He sent messages and rich gifts to the King, in acknowledgment of which he was named Adelantado of the South Sea and Governor of Panama and Coiba. At the same time Pedrarius Dávila (Don Pedro Arias de Avila) was dispatched to take over the governorship of the colony of Darien.

During the next four years Balboa made numerous trips across the isthmus, some say as many as twenty, and prepared for the conquest of Peru. To this end he built and launched ships on the Pacific shore. With these he sailed to and took formal possession of the Pearl Islands (Archipelago de las Perlas), which he had visited on his first trip. Unfavorable weather prevented him from reaching Peru.

Then, in 1517, lured to Acla, near Darien, by deceptive messages from the jealous Pedrarius, Balboa was arrested, condemned, and executed.

The story of Balboa as told by Alonso de Ovalle follows:

Balboa Discovers the Pacific

To further what the Admiral Columbus had begun, God raised an instrument in the person of Vasco Nunnes [Núñez] de Balboa, one of the first discoverers of this New World, a man of a good understanding, as he showed upon the occasion which I shall now relate.

He was, with others, upon the discovery with General Enciso, the Governor. They came to a place called Urabá, and as they entered the port, by negligence of the steersman the Governor's ship struck upon a sand, and was lost, nothing being saved out of her but the lives of the men, who got into the boats, but naked and in danger of perishing for want of provision.

Vasco de Núñez said that he remembered there was not far off a river the banks of which were inhabited by much people. He guided them thither, and the thing being found to be as he had said, he gained great reputation among them all. They came thither and found the Indians in arms against the Castilians, whose name was already become odious to those nations.

They made a vow to Our Lady to dedicate to her the first settlement and church to the honor of her image, under the title of Sancta Maria la Antigua, or the Ancient St. Mary, which to this day is venerated in Seville; and to send her many rich gifts of gold and silver, which one of them, as a pilgrim, should carry in the name of the rest.

Being encouraged by this vow, they fell upon the Indians, and obtained the victory.

Presently they made a settlement, and built a town dedicated to the Virgin, calling it Sancta Maria el Antigua of Dairen [Darien] because that was the name of that river. After this, to accomplish their vow, they sent the promised presents to the devout image of the Virgin.

The good opinion of Vasco de Núñez increasing thus daily, and having cunningly ordered it so that Enciso resigned his government, they chose Vasco Núñez in his room; at first with an associate, but he found means in time to be alone, as it was necessary he should, in point of command, being to overcome such difficulties as were to be met with at every turn. And

indeed he knew how to make himself be both feared and beloved, having a very good spirit of government.

In the new discoveries he undertook, he came first to the
lands of the Cacique Ponea, and not finding him at home, he
destroyed them. He passed on to the lands of the Cacique
Careta, who, not caring to enter into war, received him peace-
fully, and treated him as a friend.

This Cacique Careta had a kinsman who was a lord that
lived further in the country, and his name was Suran, who
persuaded another neighboring Prince called Comagre to make
a friendship with the Castilians. This Prince had a very fine
palace, which astonished them, and particularly when they saw,
in a kind of chapel or oratory, some dead bodies lying covered
with rich mantles, and many jewels of gold and pearls. And
being asked whose bodies those were, they answered, of their
predecessors, and that to preserve them from corruption they
had dried them with fire.

The King caressed the Castilians and gave them great
presents. He had seven sons, and one of them, more liberal,
gave the Spaniards a regalo of near 4000 pesos of fine gold, and
some pieces of rare workmanship. They weighed it, and taking
the King's fifth, they began to divide the remainder.

In the division, two soldiers fell out about their share. The
Cacique's son who had made the present, hearing the noise,
could not bear it, but coming to them, struck the balance where
the gold was weighing and threw it all upon the ground, saying: "Is it possible you should value so much a thing that so
little deserves your esteem? And that you should leave the
repose of your houses, and pass so many seas, exposed to such
dangers, to trouble those who live quiet in their own country?
Have some shame, Christians, and do not value these things;
but if you are resolved to search gold, I'll show you a country
where you may satisfy yourselves."

And pointing with his finger to the south, he told them they
should see there another sea, when they had passed over certain high mountains, where they should see other people who
could go with sails and oars as they did; and that passing that
sea, they should meet with vast quantities of gold, whereof the
natives made all their utensils; and that he would be their guide,

and conduct them with his father's vassals; but that it would be requisite they should be more in number, because there were powerful kings who could hinder their passage; giving them by this the first notice of Peru and its riches.

This was the first knowledge and light which the Spaniards got of the South Sea, and of the gold and riches of its coasts, which gave them all great joy, so that they were impatient to see the hour of breaking through all obstacles to see that sea never before heard of, and enjoy the riches of it.

Vasco Núñez immediately disposed all things, and went out of Darien in the beginning of September, in the year 1513. And going along the seaside to the habitation of the friendly Cacique Careta, he went toward the mountains, by the lands of the Cacique Ponea. Who, though at first he endeavored to oppose their passage, yet being advised by the Indians of Careta, who accompanied the Castilians, he presented them with gold and provisions, and gave them guides, they in return giving him looking-glasses, needles, knives, and other baubles, which they valued very much.

Then they began to mount the mountain, through the country of a Cacique called Quareca, who appeared in arms and attacked the Spaniards. He had a long robe of cotton, but all his men were naked. They began to skirmish, and threaten by their actions to hinder the passage; but no sooner did they hear the noise and feel the effects of the muskets, and find some to fall, but they turned their backs, flying like a herd of deer, frighted to see the fire and hear the sound of the volleys, which appeared thunder to them, and thought the Spaniards had thunderbolts at their command. So they left the passage free for them.

The Indians of Careca had said that from their country to the top of the highest mountain there was the time of six suns, for by that they meant so many days' journey. But the ways were so bad that they employed five and twenty days to get to the top.

A little before they were at the highest, Vasco Núñez de Balboa caused a halt to be made, desiring to have the glory of having himself been the first man that ever saw the South Sea, and so it was. He goes alone, discovers that vast ocean, and the large bays of the South Sea called Pacific; and upon his knees, with tears in his eyes, lifts up his eyes to Heaven, giving thanks to the great Creator of all things for having brought him from such remote parts to contemplate that which none of his ancestors had ever seen.

He made a sign after this to his companions to come up, and so they all run in haste, pushing one another on. And when they were on the top, where there is a full prospect of the sea, 'tis not to be imagined the content they all received in admiring that vast and smooth liquid crystal, which, not being animated, did not on its side give leaps of joy, nor go out of its bed to the tops of the mountains, to welcome those who came to deliver it from the tyranny the Devil exercised over it by infecting the air with the breath of idolatry; which was breathed in all those parts, both east, west, north, and south. . . .

Vasco Núñez de Balboa, having performed his devotion, and thanked Our Lord, with all his companions, for so great a favor done them as to bring them to that place—and for the favor he was about to show to that New World by the means of the preachers of the Gospel, to whom he thus opened a way to publish it—he then bethought himself of his second obligation, which was to his King, in conformity to which he took possession in His Majesty's name, for the crowns of Castile and León, of the place where he was and of the sea which he discovered from thence, cutting for this purpose many trees, and making great crosses, which he set up, and writ upon them the names of Their Majesties.

After this, they began to go down from the mountain, marching always prepared for any encounter that they might have with the caciques in their way. So, though the Cacique Chiapes opposed them with his people, who were stout and many, yet by setting the dogs at them, and beginning to fire their muskets, they were soon routed.

This made the Cacique offer terms of peace, and receive and make much of the Castilians, presenting them with gold; and he proved so good a friend that he pacified many other caciques who were in arms to hinder the passage, who likewise made their presents of gold.

From the town of Chiapes, [Chiapas], Vasco Núñez sent out to discover the coasts of the South Sea, the Captains Francisco Pizarro, Juan de Escara, and Alonso Martín, each to a different place. This last found two canoes dry on the shore, and the sea below them about half a league. He wondered to see them so far from the sea, and as he was considering it, he perceived the sea coming very fast in, and did not stay long before it set the canoes on float. He entered into one of them, and took witness that he was the first European that had ever been upon that sea.

The tides on that coast ebb and flow every six hours, so as great ships will be left on shore, the water retiring so fast that it gives great admiration when it returns, to see so great a space covered so fast that it appears an inundation.

Vasco Núñez having advice of this, came down also to the coast, and going into the sea up to the mid-leg with a naked sword in his hand, said that he took possession of it, and all the coasts and bays of it, for the crowns of Castile and León, and that he was ready with that sword, as often as it should be necessary, to make good that claim against all that should oppose him.

The Indians were in great amaze at this new ceremony; and they were more surprised when they saw him, against their advice and that of the caciques, venture to cross the Gulf of Pearls, to discover the riches of it in that commodity—though it had like to have cost him dear, for he was near perishing in crossing that arm of the sea.

Now let us see (in order to undeceive those who shall read this) how little this courage and boldness availed this generous conqueror of the New World, and the great things his invincible mind had brought to pass. All his military prudence and cunning, by which he made himself be respected by unknown nations, availed him little; for this so fortunate a great captain had a tragical end. He lost his life in Darien at his return, finding there the Governor Pedrarias [Pedrarius], who came to succeed him. The King in sending this man had recommended to him the person of Vasco Núñez de Balboa, and ordered him to make use of his counsel, as one who had honored him by his bold undertakings, and to whom for a reward he ordered the governments of Panama and Coiba, and the Admiralship of the South Sea, which he had discovered and on which he had already built four ships, and got together 300 men to go upon the discovery of Peru.

But the said Pedrarius commanded him onshore, and there seizing him, caused him to be beheaded publicly as a traitor. The crier went before him, crying, as is customary, that he was a traitor, which when Vasco Núñez heard, he said it was a lie, and that no man had served the King with more zeal, nor more fidelity, than he, nor more desired to extend his monarchy. But all his complaints were like voices in the desert, which were of no force against envy and emulation, which had prevailed in his enemies and which can never fail against those who govern.

His death was much resented, and appeared very unjust in Spain, because, indeed, the King lost one of his bravest captains, and one who would have discovered Peru with more facility, and without all those tumults which since happened. For his prudence, valor, and zeal were above the ordinary size.

It cannot be denied but that the sentence may be justified according to the depositions of witnesses; but yet it was a great argument of his innocency that which he himself said to the Governor Pedrarius, which was that if he had in his heart to make himself master and independent, as they accused him, he would not have obeyed his call as he did, and leave his ship without any difficulty; for he had then 300 men all at his devotion, and four vessels, with which he might have been safe, and gone upon new discoveries, if his conscience had accused him.

They add here that an astrologer had told him that that year he should see something extraordinary in the heavens, he should be in guard against some great misfortune that threatened him, and that if he escaped from it, he should be the most powerful and happy man in the whole Indies; and that accordingly he did see this sign, but laughed at it, as thinking himself in so high a state.

NORTH
AMERICA

Seville

1522

Atlantic

Pacific   Ocean

Cape Verde
Islands

Ocean

1519

EQUATOR

Magellan
1519-22

SOUTH
AMERICA

Tuamotu

Río de la
Plata

San Julián

1520

Strait of Magellan

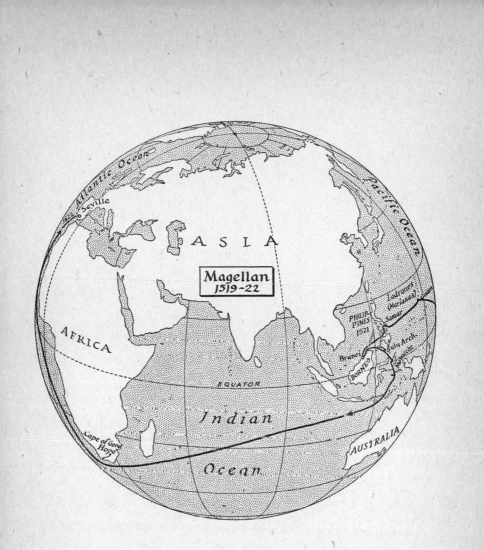

Europe Proves That the World Is Round

EUROPE PROVES THAT THE WORLD IS ROUND

CHAPTER 9

THE roundness of the world may have been discovered before the Greeks, for they were borrowers and preservers as well as originators. But the farthest back we have as yet been able to trace the sphericity idea is to the Pythagorean school that flourished among the Greek colonies in Asia Minor around 600 B.C.

The philosophers do not seem to have deduced the globular nature of the earth from observation, as from noting that the hull disappears first and the sails later when a vessel stands out to sea. They seem to have reached the sphericity concept rather by speculation, which we may perhaps oversimplify as having run:

The earth is a heavenly body, the heavenly bodies are perfect, the perfect shape is a sphere, therefore the earth is spherical.

With this concept once in mind, the philosophers, using it as a working hypothesis, began to search for and presently did find the evidence to prove that what they believed was true—such things as the gradual disappearance of a ship below the horizon and the circular shadow cast by the earth upon the moon at eclipse.

With the knowledge once in hand, the Greeks began to apply it. From the progress of geometry it soon became evident that by observing the sun's position in the sky accurately you could fix the distance of any given place north from the middle of the earth, a process we call the determination of latitude. Incidentally it was the same Pytheas who was discussed in relation to the Greek discovery of the Arctic who first of known

237

mathematicians determined accurately the latitude of a place, that of Massilia [Marseille] on the south coast of France.

The supreme practical achievement in this line was the measurement of the circumference of the earth, within 5 per cent of error, by Eratosthenes around 200 B.C. He was living at Alexandria on the lower Nile, and learned from travelers that the sun is not seen straight overhead, as observed from the bottom of a well, farther north than the vicinity of the First Nile Cataract. So he measured how far south of the vertical the sun appears from Alexandria at the solstice, around our June 22, and found the angle between this and the vertical. Then he assembled a great many measurements of the distance from Alexandria to the First Cataract and took the mean. Knowing the angle and this distance, he could get, by simple figuring, the complete circumference of the earth, assuming it to be truly spherical.

When we say that the result of Eratosthenes gave him the distance around the earth within one-twentieth of what we now believe it to be, we are of course waiving the disputes on whether it is possible at this date to convert Greek measurements into miles or meters exactly. The error may have been 10 per cent or it may have been zero; the point made is that even before Eratosthenes the philosophers possessed the right method for determining the circumference of the earth, and that the concept of a spherical earth was firmly established by them in the thinking of Europe.

Nor was that knowledge lost. Writers have said that there was no generation from before Aristotle until after Magellan during which the cosmographers, the men who thought, taught, and wrote about such things as the shape of the earth, did not maintain that the earth is spherical. This line of scholars naturally includes many of the Church fathers.

But while the geographers and cosmographers mostly agreed that the world was round, they presently went wrong on the size of it. The chief villain of that piece was the cosmographer Ptolemy, who wrote in the span A.D. 120-150. His geography secured dominance in European thinking, and retained it till the voyage of Magellan. Part of that dominance was clamping on Europe the idea that Eratosthenes had been wrong about the circumference of the earth, which Ptolemy scaled down to about two-thirds. It was this Ptolemaic concept, among other things, that made Columbus think the West Indies were the East Indies; for according to the Ptolemy scheme the eastern edge of Asia, as reported by Marco Polo, should not have been very far west from Europe.

It is of course maintained by some that this was a lucky break—that Columbus would not have sailed west except that he thought Asia so near. But this is maintained only by those who still follow the pristine Columbus myth, clinging even to that one of its details which claims Europe knew nothing of countries west beyond the Atlantic until after October 12, 1492.

The 1492 "discovery of the New World" is perhaps history's best case of robbing Peter to pay Paul. For in adding glory to Columbus by this device the claimants take from the inheritors of the mantle of Saint Peter the credit for an important part of the knowledge which the Church preserved from antiquity and gathered from its contemporaries. More than that, as is shown elsewhere in this book, the disciples of a 1492 discovery try to deprive the Church of the credit of maintaining both temporal and spiritual relation with lands beyond the Atlantic from early in the eleventh century to late in the fifteenth, indeed up to and including that Pope, Alexander VI, who came to the Throne of Peter in 1492, and made it one of his first official acts to remind Europe that the Church had obligations to the faraway bishopric of Greenland.

However it be with cosmographic and historical theorizing, to the layman the correctness of scholarly thinking for two thousand years was not demonstrated until the sixteenth century. The sailor who proved the philosophers right was Magellan.

Ferdinand Magellan (Fernando or Fernandez de Magalhãcs, Magallanes; c. 1480-1521), whose expedition made the first circumnavigation of the globe, was a Portuguese nobleman who had served his country with distinction in India and the Indies during the years 1505-12. He was at the taking of Malacca, a city in what is now the Malay States, and then accompanied an expedition sent to examine the Spice Islands, or Moluccas, in the eastern part of what is now the Netherlands East Indies.

After returning to Portugal, Magellan incurred the displeasure of the King. There being no hope of further employment by Portugal, he renounced his nationality, and in 1517 went to Spain to offer his services and to try to get support for a plan he had formulated.

Magellan proposed to reach the Moluccas by sailing westward through a strait which he hoped to discover at the southern end of South America. He further proposed to settle the controversy between Spain and Portugal as to the limits of the spheres that had been allotted to each country by the bull of Pope Alexander VI in 1493, by which the world was practically divided in half, the eastern half (as seen from Europe) going to Portugal and the western to Spain. The dividing line, which passed through the two poles, was vague enough in the west, where it ran through the Atlantic; its position in the east was a matter of conjecture and argument, for no one had yet sailed across the Pacific, and its extent was unknown.

Magellan urged that not only would he be able to mark off the boundaries between Portugal and Spain in the Pacific, but he would also be able to prove that the Moluccas, with their abundance of valuable spices, lay within the Spanish sphere.

Magellan's plan was sure-fire to arouse the interest of Spain, for the route to the East around the Cape of Good Hope was long, and was, moreover, largely controlled by Portugal. Ever since Columbus and his successors had shown that the Americas blocked the hoped-for short westward route between Europe and the riches of the Indies, the Spaniards had eagerly sought for such a strait as Magellan now proposed to find.

But while all hoped that a connecting passage would be found, there were nevertheless many who doubted its existence, believing instead that the southern end of South America spread out into a great continent, Terra Australis Incognita, which perhaps stretched all the way to the South Pole and thence nearly to Africa.

After Balboa's crossing of Panama in 1513, there had even been talk of cutting a canal through the isthmus if no strait could be found.

That Magellan had no great difficulty in convincing the Spaniards of the soundness of his plan is shown by the speed with which things moved. Magellan arrived in Spain on October 20, 1517. He quickly obtained the support of a number of wealthy and influential men, which enabled him to reach Charles V. An agreement with the King was signed on March 22, 1518, setting forth the terms under which the proposed expedition would be undertaken.

On August 10, 1519, five ships under Magellan's command set sail from Seville on the most remarkable voyage in the history of geographical discovery.

After crossing the Atlantic, the expedition put in briefly at what is now Rio de Janeiro. In January 1520 they entered the previously discovered Rio de la Plata (Plata River or River Plate), and examined it in the hope that it might provide a passage westward. Thence, coasting southward, they established winter quarters in Port St. Julian, where, during their stay of several months, they became acquainted with those natives whom Magellan named Patagonians (Big Feet).

On October 21, 1520, about two months after leaving Port St. Julian, Magellan sighted the eastern entrance to the strait which he named the Patagonian Strait and which now bears Magellan's name. The land on the southern side of the passage was named Tierra del Fuego, from the many fires burning there. The passage of more than 300 miles through the strait took about five and a half weeks. Thence the expedition, now consisting of three vessels (one had been wrecked and another had deserted), sailed on across the unknown waters of the Pacific.

The broad outline of the rest of the Magellan story is well known: that the ships reached and discovered the Philippines, that Magellan died there (April 27, 1521), and that one ship reached home. The *Vittoria* returned to Spain (September 8, 1522) around the Cape of Good Hope, thereby circumnavigating the globe for the first time.

Accompanying Magellan's expedition was Antonio Pigafetta, an Italian, who has left the best history of the voyage. His full, detailed account is a clear and seemingly unprejudiced recital of the events of the voyage, even if there is a tendency at times to exaggerate, as, for instance, in the description of the size of the Patagonians. Here extracts are used from only those parts

of Pigafetta's narrative which tell of new discoveries—the
voyage across the Atlantic from Spain to the coast of Brazil
had already been made many times, and the route of the return
voyage, around Africa, was of course well known.

There are four early manuscripts of Pigafetta's account. The
extracts that follow are from an English translation which was
included in Pinkerton's collection of voyages and travels, London, 1812. The account as published by Pinkerton bears the
title *Voyage Round the World, by the Cavallero Antonio Pigafetta, a Gentleman of Vicenza. Published originally in Italian
from a Manuscript in the Ambrosian Library at Milan, with
Notes by Charles Amoretti, One of the Librarians and Doctors
of the Ambrosian College; formerly Secretary of the Patriotic
Society of Agriculture and the Arts; one of the XL of the Italian
Society; Member of the Institute of Bologna, &c. And afterwards translated by him into French.*

Pigafetta's narrative begins:

Magellan and the Circumnavigation of the World

As there are men whose curiosity would not be satisfied with
merely hearing related the marvelous things I have seen, and
the difficulties I experienced in the course of the perilous expedition I am about to describe, and who are anxious to know
by what means I was enabled to surmount them; and as due
credit by such would not be given to the success of a similar
undertaking if they were left ignorant of its most minute details, I have deemed it expedient briefly to relate what gave
origin to my voyage, and the means by which I was so fortunate
as to bring it to a successful termination.

In the year 1519, I was in Spain at the court of Charles V,
King of the Romans, in company with Signor Chiericato, then
apostolical prothonotary and orator of Pope Leo X of holy
memory, who by his merits was raised to the dignity of Bishop
and Prince of Teramo. Now as from the books I had read, and
from the conversation of the learned men who frequented the
house of this prelate, I knew that by navigating the ocean
wonderful things were to be seen, I determined to be convinced of them by my own eyes, that I might be enabled to give

to others the narrative of my voyage, as well for their amusement as advantage, and at the same time acquire a name which should be handed down to posterity.

An opportunity soon presented itself. I learned that a squadron of five vessels was under equipment at Sevilla, destined for the discovery of the Molucca Islands, whence we derive our spices; and that Fernandez [Ferdinand] Magellan, a Portuguese gentleman, and commander of the order of St. Jago [Santiago] de la Spata, who had already more than once traversed the ocean with great reputation, was nominated Captain General of the expedition. I therefore immediately repaired to Barcelona, to request permission of His Majesty to be one on this voyage, which permission was granted. Thence, provided with letters of recommendation, I went by sea to Malaga, and from that city overland to Sevilla, where I waited three months before the expedition was in readiness to sail. . . .

The Captain General Ferdinand Magellan had resolved on undertaking a long voyage over the ocean, where the winds blow with violence and storms are very frequent. He had also determined on taking a course as yet unexplored by any navigator; but this bold attempt he was cautious of disclosing, lest anyone should strive to dissuade him from it by magnifying the risk he would have to encounter, and thus dishearten his crew. To the perils naturally incident on a similar voyage was joined the unfavorable circumstance of the four other vessels he commanded besides his own being under the direction of captains who were inimical to him, merely on account of his being a Portuguese, they themselves being Spaniards. . . .

Monday morning the tenth of August 1519, the squadron having every thing requisite on board and a complement of 237 men, its departure [from Seville] was announced by a discharge of artillery, and the foresail was set. . . .

The twentieth of September we sailed from San Lucar, steering toward the southwest, and on the twenty-sixth reached one of the Canary Islands called Teneriffe, situate in 28 degrees of latitude north. We stopped here for three days, at a spot where we could take in wood and water. . . .

On Monday, the third of October, we made sail directly toward the south. We passed between Cape Verd [Verde] and its islands in latitude 14 degrees 30 minutes north. After coasting along the shores of Guinea for several days, we arrived in latitude 8 degrees north, where is a mountain called Sierra Leona. . . .

After we had passed the equinoctial line, we lost sight of the polar star. We then steered south-southwest, making for the Terra di Verzino (Brazil), in latitude 23 degrees 30 minutes south. This land is a continuation of that on which Cape Augustin [St. Augustine] is situated in latitude 8 degrees 30 minutes south.

Here we laid in a good stock of fowls, potatoes, a kind of fruit which resembles the cone of a pine tree (the anana or pineapple), but which is very sweet and of an exquisite flavor, sweet reeds, the flesh of the anta, which resembles that of a cow, etc. We made excellent bargains here. For a hook or a knife we purchased five or six fowls; a comb brought us two geese; and a small looking-glass, or a pair of scissors, as much fish as would serve ten people; the inhabitants for a little bell or a ribbon gave a basket of potatoes, which is the name they give to roots somewhat resembling our turnips, and which are nearly like chestnuts in taste.

Our playing cards were an equally advantageous object of barter; for a king of spades I obtained half a dozen fowls, and the hawker even deemed his bargain an excellent one.

We entered this port [Rio de Janeiro] on Saint Lucy's day, the thirteenth of December. The sun at noon was vertical, and we suffered much more from the heat than on passing the line.

The land of Brazil, which abounds in all kinds of productions, is as extensive as Spain, France, and Italy united. It belongs to Portugal. . . .

We stayed thirteen days at this port; after which, resuming our course, we coasted along this country as far as 34 degrees 40 minutes south, where we found a large river of fresh water. . . .

This river [Rio de la Plata] contains seven small islands. In the largest, called Santa Maria, precious stones are found. It was formerly imagined that this was not a river, but a channel which communicated with the South Sea; but it was shortly found to be truly a river, which at its mouth is 17 leagues across.

Here John [Juan Diaz] de Solis, while on a voyage of discovery like us, was with sixty of his crew devoured by cannibals, in whom they placed too great confidence.

Coasting constantly along this land toward the Antarctic Pole, we stopped at two islands, which we found peopled by geese [penguins] and sea wolves [seals] alone. The former are so numerous and so little wild that we caught a sufficient store for the five ships in the space of a single hour. They are black, and seem to be covered alike over every part of the body with short feathers, without having wings with which to fly; in fact they cannot fly, and live entirely on fish. They are so fat that we were obliged to singe them, as we could not pluck their feathers. Their beak is curved like a horn.

The sea wolves are of different color, and nearly the size of a calf, with a head much like the head of that animal. Their ears are round and short, and their teeth very long. They have no legs, and their paws, which adhere to the body, somewhat resemble our hands, having also small nails. They are, however, web-footed like a duck. Were these animals capable of running, they would be much to be dreaded, for they seem very ferocious. They swim with great swiftness, and subsist on fish.

We experienced a dreadful storm between these islands, during which the lights of Saint Elmo, Saint Nicholas, and Saint Clare were oftentimes perceived at the tops of the masts. Instantly as they disappeared, the fury of the tempest abated.

On leaving these islands to continue our course, we ascended as high as 49 degrees 30 minutes south, where we discovered an excellent port [Port St. Julian], and as winter approached [the month was May], we thought best to take shelter here during the bad weather.

Two months elapsed without our perceiving any inhabitant of the country. One day when the least we expected anything of the kind, a man of gigantic figure presented himself before us. He capered almost naked on the sands, and was singing and dancing, at the same time casting dust on his head. The Captain sent one of our seamen onshore with orders to make similar gestures as a token of friendship and peace, which were well understood, and the giant suffered himself to be quietly led to a small island where the Captain had landed. I likewise went on shore there, with many others. He testified great surprise on seeing us, and holding up his finger, undoubtedly signified to us that he thought us descended from Heaven.

This man was of such immense stature that our heads scarcely reached to his waist. He was of handsome appearance, his face broad and painted red, except a rim of yellow round his eyes and two spots in shape of a heart on his cheeks. His hair, which was thin, appeared whitened with some kind of powder. His coat, or rather his cloak, was made of furs, well sewed together, taken from an animal which, as we had afterward an opportunity of seeing, abounds in this country. This animal [guanaco] has the head and ears of a mule, the body of a camel, the legs of a stag, and the tail of a horse, and like this last animal, it neighs.

This man likewise wore a sort of shoe, made of the same skin.[1] He held in his left hand a short and massive bow, the string of which, somewhat thicker than that of a lute, was made of the intestines of the same animal. In the other hand he held arrows made of short reeds, with feathers at one end, similar to ours, and at the other, instead of iron, a white-and-black flint stone. With the same stone they likewise form instruments to work wood with.

The Captain General gave him victuals and drink, and among other trifles presented him with a large steel mirror. The giant, who had not the least conception of this trinket, and who saw his likeness now perhaps for the first time, started back in so much fright as to knock down four of our men who happened to stand behind him. We gave him some little bells, a small looking-glass, a comb, and some glass beads; after which he was set on shore, accompanied by four men well armed.

His comrade, who had objected to coming on board the ship, seeing him return, ran to advise his comrades, who, perceiving that our armed men advanced toward them, ranged themselves in file without arms, and almost naked. They immediately began dancing and singing, in the course of which

---

[1] Amoretti remarks that it was because of this shoe, which made the man's foot resemble the foot of a bear, that Magellan called the people Patagonians.

they raised the forefinger to Heaven, to make us comprehend that it was thence they reckoned us to have descended. They at the same time showed us a white powder, in clay pans, and presented it to us, having nothing else to offer us to eat. Our people invited them by signs to come on board our ship, and proffered to carry on board with them whatever they might wish. They accepted the invitation, but the men, who merely carried a bow and arrow, loaded everything on the women as if they had been so many beasts of burden.

The women are not of equal size with the men, but in recompense they are much more lusty. Their breasts, which hang down, are more than a foot in length. They paint, and dress in the same manner as their husbands, but they have a thin skin of some animal with which they cover their nudity. They were, in our contemplation, far from handsome; nevertheless their husbands seemed very jealous.

The women led four of the animals of which I have previously spoken, in a string, but they were young ones. They make use of these young to catch the old ones. They fasten them to a tree, the old ones come to play with them, when from their concealment the men kill them with their arrows. The inhabitants of the country, both men and women, being invited by our people to repair to the vicinage of the ships, divided themselves into two parties, one on each side the port, and diverted us with an exhibition of the mode of hunting before recited.

Six days afterward, while our people were employed in felling wood for the ships, they saw another giant, dressed like those we had parted with and like them armed with a bow and arrow. On approaching our people he touched his head and body, afterward raising his hands to Heaven, gestures which the men imitated. The Captain General, informed of this circumstance, sent the skiff onshore to conduct him to the islet in the port, on which a house had been erected to serve as a forge, and a magazine for different articles of merchandise.

This man was of higher stature and better made than the others, he was moreover of gentler manners. He danced and sprang so high, and with such might, that his feet sunk several inches deep into the sand. He remained with us some days.

We taught him to pronounce the name of Jesus, to say the Lord's Prayer, etc., which he did with equal ease with ourselves, but in a much stronger tone of voice. Finally, we baptized him by the name of John. The Captain General made him a present of a shirt, a vest, cloth drawers, a cap, a looking-glass, comb, some little bells, and other trifling things. He returned toward his own people, apparently well contented.

The next day he brought us one of the large animals of which we have made mention, and received other presents to induce him to repeat his gift; but from that day we saw nothing of him, and suspected his companions had killed him on account of his attachment to us.

At the end of a fortnight four other of these men repaired to us. They were without arms, but we afterward found they had concealed them behind some bushes, where they were pointed out to us by two of the party, whom we detained. They were all of them painted, but in a different manner to those we had seen before.

The Captain wished to keep the two youngest, who as well were of handsomest form, to carry them with us on our voyage, and even take them to Spain; but, aware of the difficulty of securing them by forcible means, he made use of the following artifice.

He presented them a number of knives, mirrors, glass beads, etc., so that both their hands were full. He afterward offered them two of those iron rings used for chaining felons, and when he saw their anxiety to be possessed of them (for they are passionately fond of iron), and moreover that they could not hold them in their hands, he proposed to fasten them to their legs, that they might more easily carry them home, to which they consented. Upon this our people put on the irons and fastened the rings, by which means they were securely chained.

As soon as they became aware of the treachery used toward them they were violently enraged, and puffed and roared aloud, invoking Setebos, their chief demon, to come to their assistance.

Not content with having these men, the Captain was anxious of securing their wives also, in order to transport a race of giants to Europe. With this view he ordered the two others to be arrested, to oblige them to conduct our people to the spot where they were. Nine of our strongest men were scarcely able to cast them to the ground and bind them, and still even one of them succeeded in freeing himself, while the other exerted himself so much that he received a slight wound in the head from one of the men; but they were in the end obliged to show our people the way to the abode of the wives of our two prisoners. These women, on learning what had happened to their husbands, made such loud outcries as to be heard at a great distance.

Johan Carvajo, the pilot, who was at the head of our people, as night was drawing on, did not choose to bring away at that time the women to whose house he had been conducted, but remained there till morning, keeping a good guard. In the meantime came there two other men, who without expressing any dissatisfaction or surprise continued all night in the hut; but soon as dawn began to break, upon saying a few words, in an instant every one took to flight, man, woman, and child, the children even scampering away with greater speed than the rest. They abandoned their hut to us, and all that it contained. In the meantime one of the men drove off to a distance the little animals which they used in hunting, while another, concealed behind a bush, wounded one of our men in the thigh, who died immediately.

Though our people fired on the runaways, they were unable to hit any, on account of their not escaping in a straight line, but leaping from one side to another, and getting on as swiftly as horses at a full gallop. Our people burned the hut of these savages, and buried their dead companion.

Savage as they are, these Indians are yet not without their medicaments. When they have a pain in the stomach, for example, in lieu of an operative medicine they thrust an arrow pretty deeply down the throat, to excite a vomit, and throw up a matter of a greenish color, mixed with blood. The green is occasioned by a sort of thistle, on which they feed. If they have the headache, they make a gash in their forehead, and do the same with the other parts of their body where they experience pain, in order to draw from the affected part a considerable quantity of blood. Their theory, as explained to us by one of those we had taken, is on a par with their practice. Pain, they say, proceeds from the reluctance of the blood to abide any longer in the part where it is felt; by releasing it, consequently, the pain is removed.

Their hair is cut circularly like that of monks, but is longer, and supported round the head by a cotton string, in which they place their arrows when they go hunting. When the weather is very cold, they tie their private parts closely to the body. It appears that their religion is limited to adoring the Devil. They pretend that when one of them is on the point of death, ten or twelve demons appear dancing and singing around him. One of these, who makes a greater noise than the rest, is termed Setebos, the inferior imps are called Cheleule; they are painted like the people of the country. Our giant pretends to have once seen a devil, with horns, and hair of such length as to cover his feet; he cast out flames, added he, from his mouth and his posteriors.

These people, as I have already noticed, clothe themselves in the skin of an animal, and with the same kind of skin do they cover their huts, which they transport whither suits them best, having no fixed place of abode, but wandering about from spot to spot like gypsies. They generally live upon raw meat, and a sweet root called *capac*. They are great feeders; the two we took daily consumed a basketful of bread each, and drank half a pail of water at a draught. They eat mice raw, and without even slaying them. Our Captain gave these people the name of Patagonians.

We spent five months in this port, to which we gave the denomination of St. Julian, and met with no accidents onshore during the whole of our stay, save what I have noticed.

Scarcely had we anchored in this port before the four captains of the other vessels plotted to murder the Captain General. These traitors were Juan of Carthagena, *vehador* of the squadron; Lewis de Mendoza, the treasurer; Antonio Cocca, the paymaster; and Gaspar de Casada. The plot was discovered, the first was flayed alive, and the second was stabbed to the heart. Gaspar de Casada was forgiven, but a few days after he meditated treason anew. The Captain General then—who dared not take his life, as he was created a captain by the Emperor himself—drove him from the squadron, and left him in the country of the Patagonians, together with a priest, his accomplice.[2]

Another mishap befell part of the squadron while we remained at this station. The ship *St. Jago [Santiago]* which had been detached to survey the coast, was cast upon rocks; nevertheless, as if by a miracle, the whole of the crew were saved. Two seamen came overland to the port where we were to acquaint us of this disaster, and the Captain General sent men to the spot immediately, with some sacks of biscuit.

The crew stopped two months near the place where the vessel was stranded, to collect the wreck and merchandise which the sea successively cast onshore; and during all this time means of subsistence was transported them overland, although 100 miles distant from the port of St. Julian, and by a very bad and fatiguing road, through thickets and briers, among which the bearers of provision were obliged to pass the whole night without any other beverage than what they obtained from the ice they found, and which they were able with difficulty to break.

As for us, we fared tolerably in this port, though certain shellfish of great length, some of which contained pearls, but of very small size, were not edible. We found ostriches [rheas] here, foxes, rabbits much smaller than ours, and sparrows. The trees yield frankincense.

We planted a cross on the summit of a neighboring mountain, which we termed Monte Christo, and took possession of the country in the name of the King of Spain.

We at length left this port (the twenty-first of August) and keeping along the coast, in latitude 50 degrees 40 minutes south, discovered a river of fresh water [the Santa Cruz], into which we entered. The whole squadron nearly experienced shipwreck here, owing to the furious winds with which it was assailed, and which occasioned a very rough sea; but God and the *corpora*

---

[2] When Gómez, who commanded the *San Antonio*, deserted the squadron in the strait and returned to St. Julian, he took them both on board again, and carried them back to Spain.

sancta [the lights which shone on the summits of the masts] brought us succor and saved us from harm.

We spent two months here, to stock our vessels with wood and water. We laid in provision also of a species of fish nearly 2 feet in length and covered with scales; it was tolerable eating, but we were unable to take a sufficient number of them. Before we quitted this spot our Captain ordered all of us to make confession, and, like good Christians, to receive the communion.

Continuing our course toward the south, on the twenty-first of October, in latitude 52 degrees, we discovered a strait which we denominated the strait of the Eleven Thousand Virgins, in honor of the day. This strait, as will appear in the sequel, is 440 miles, or 110 maritime leagues, in length; it is half a league in breadth, sometimes more, sometimes less, and terminates in another sea, which we denominated the Pacific Ocean. This strait is enclosed between lofty mountains covered with snow, and it is likewise very deep, so that we were unable to anchor except quite close to shore, where was from 25 to 30 fathoms of water.

The whole of the crew were so firmly persuaded that this strait had no western outlet that we should not, but for the deep science of the Captain General, have ventured on its exploration. This man, as skillful as he was intrepid, knew that he would have to pass by a strait very little known, but which he had seen laid down on a chart of Martin de Boheme [Martin Behaim], a most excellent cosmographer, in the treasury of the King of Portugal.

As soon as we entered on this water, imagined to be only a bay, the Captain sent forward two vessels, the *San Antonio*, and *La Concepción [Concepción]* to examine where it terminated, or whither it led, while we in the *Trinidad* and the *Vittoria* awaited them in the mouth of it.

At night came on a terrible hurricane, which lasted six and thirty hours, and forced us to quit our anchors and leave our vessels to the mercy of the winds and waves in the gulf.

The two other vessels, equally buffeted, were unable to double a cape in order to rejoin us; so that by abandoning themselves to the gale, which drove them constantly toward what they conceived to be the bottom of a bay, they were apprehensive momentarily of being driven onshore. But at the instant they gave themselves up for lost, they saw a small opening, which they took for an inlet of the bay. Into this they entered, and perceiving that this channel was not closed, they threaded it, and found themselves in another, through which they pursued their course to another strait leading into a third bay still larger than the preceding. Then, in lieu of following up their exploration, they deemed it most prudent to return and render account of what they had observed to the Captain General.

Two days passed without the two vessels returning, sent to examine the bottom of the bay, so that we reckoned they had been swallowed up during the tempest; and seeing smoke on shore, we conjectured that those who had had the good fortune to escape had kindled those fires to inform us of their existence and distress.

But while in this painful incertitude as to their fate, we saw them advancing toward us under full sail, and their flags flying; and when sufficiently near, heard the report of their bombards and their loud exclamations of joy. We repeated the salutation, and when we learnt from them that they had seen the prolongation of the bay, or, better speaking, the strait, we made toward them, to continue our voyage in this course, if possible.

When we had entered into the third bay, which I have before noticed, we saw two openings, or channels, the one running to the southeast, the other to the southwest. The Captain General sent the two vessels, the *Sant' Antonio* and *La Concepción* to the southeast, to examine whether or not this channel terminated in an open sea. The first set sail immediately, under press of canvas, not choosing to wait for the second, which the pilot wished to leave behind, as he had intention to avail himself of the darkness of the night to retrace his course, and return to Spain by the same way we came.

This pilot was Emanuel Gómez, who hated Magellan, for the sole reason that when he came to Spain to lay his project before the Emperor of proceeding to the Moluccas by a western passage, Gómez himself had requested, and was on the point of obtaining, some caravels for an expedition of which he would have had the command. This expedition had for its object to make new discoveries; but the arrival of Magellan prevented his request from being complied with, and he could only obtain the subaltern situation of his serving under a Portuguese. In the course of the night he conspired with the other Spaniards on board the ship. They put in irons, and even wounded, the captain, Alvaro de Meschita, the cousin german of the Captain General, and carried him thus to Spain. They reckoned likewise on transporting thither one of the two giants we had taken, and who was on board their ship; but we learnt on our return that he died on approaching the equinoctial line, unable to bear the heat of the tropical regions.

The vessel, *La Concepción*, which could not keep up with the *Sant' Antonio*, continued to cruise in the channel to await its return, but in vain.

We, with the two other vessels, entered the remaining channel, on the southwest, and continuing our course, came to a river which we called Sardine River, on account of the vast number of the fish of this denomination we found in it. We anchored here to wait for the two other ships, and remained in the river four days; but in the interim we dispatched a boat, well manned, to reconnoiter the cape of this channel, which promised to terminate in another sea. On the third day the sailors sent on this expedition returned, and announced their having seen the cape where the strait ended, and with it a great sea—that is to say, the ocean. We wept for joy. This cape was denominated Il Capo Deseado [The Wished-for Cape; Cape of Good Hope] for in truth we had long wished to see it.

We returned to join the two other vessels of the squadron, and found the *Concepción* alone. On inquiring of the pilot, Johan Serano, what had become of the other vessel, we learnt that he conceived it to be lost, as he had not once seen it since he entered the channel. The Captain General then ordered it to be sought for everywhere, but especially in the channel into which it had penetrated. He sent back the *Vittoria* to the mouth of the strait, with directions if they should not find it, to hoist a standard on some eminent spot at the foot of which, in a small pot, should be placed a letter pointing out the course the Captain General would take in order to enable the missing ship to follow the squadron. This mode of communication, in case of a division, was concerted at the instant of our departure.

Two other signals were hoisted in the same manner on eminent sites in the first bay, and on a small island of the third bay, on which we saw a number of sea wolves and birds. The Captain General, with the *Concepción*, awaited the return of the *Vittoria* near the River of Sardines, and erected a cross on a small island, at the foot of two mountains covered with snow, where the river had its source.

Had we not discovered this strait leading from one sea to the other, it was the intention of the Captain General to continue his course toward the south, as high as 75 degrees, where in summer there is no night, or very little, as in winter there is scarcely any day. While we were in the strait, in the month of October, there were but three hours' night.

The shore in this strait, which on the left turns to the southeast, is low. We called it the Strait of the Patagonians [Strait of Magellan]. At every half-league it contains a safe port, with excellent water, cedarwood, sardines, and a great abundance of shellfish. There were here also some vegetables, part of them of bitter taste but others fit to eat, especially a species of sweet celery, which grows on the margin of springs and which, for want of other, served us for food.

In short, I do not think the world contains a better strait than this. . . .

On Wednesday, the twenty-eighth of November, we left the strait and entered the ocean to which we afterward gave the denomination of Pacific, and in which we sailed the space of three months and twenty days, without tasting any fresh provisions. The biscuit we were eating no longer deserved the name of bread; it was nothing but dust, and worms which had consumed the substance; and what is more, it smelled intolerably, being impregnated with the urine of mice. The water we were obliged to drink was equally putrid and offensive.

We were even so far reduced, that we might not die of hunger, to eat pieces of the leather with which the mainyard was covered to prevent it from wearing the rope. These pieces of leather, constantly exposed to the water, sun, and wind, were so hard that they required being soaked four or five days in the sea in order to render them supple; after this we broiled them to eat. Frequently indeed we were obliged to subsist on sawdust, and even mice, a food so disgusting, were sought after with such avidity that they sold for half a ducat apiece.

Nor was this all. Our greatest misfortune was being attacked by a malady in which the gums swelled so as to hide the teeth, as well in the upper as the lower jaw, whence those affected were thus incapable of chewing their food. Nineteen of our number died of this complaint [scurvy], among whom was the Patagonian giant, and a Brazilian whom we had brought with us from his own country. Besides those who died, we had from 25 to 30 sailors ill, who suffered dreadful pains in their arms, legs, and other parts of the body; but these all of them recovered. As for myself, I cannot be too grateful to God for the continued health I enjoyed; though surrounded with sick, I experienced not the slightest illness.

In the course of these three months and twenty days we traversed nearly 4000 leagues in the ocean denominated by us Pacific, on account of our not having experienced throughout the whole of this period any the least tempestuous weather. We did not either in this whole length of time discover any land, except two desert islands; on these we saw nothing but birds and trees, for which reason we named them Las Islas Desdichados (The Unfortunate Islands). We found no bottom along their shores, and saw no fish but sharks. The two islands are 200 leagues apart. The first lies in latitude 15 degrees south, the second in latitude 9 degrees.

From the run of our ship, as estimated by the log, we traversed a space of from 60 to 70 leagues a day; and if God and His Holy Mother had not granted us a fortunate voyage, we should all have perished of hunger in so vast a sea. I do not think that anyone for the future will venture upon a similar voyage.

If on leaving the straits we had continued a western course under the same parallel, we should have made the tour of the world; and without seeing any land should have returned by Wished-for Cape [Cape of Good Hope] to the cape of the

Eleven Thousand Virgins, both of which are in latitude 52 degrees south.

The Antarctic has not the same stars as the Arctic Pole; but here are seen two clusters of small nebulous stars which look like small clouds, and are but little distant the one from the other.[3] In midst of these clusters of small stars two are distinguished very large and very brilliant, but of which the motion is scarcely apparent. These indicate the Antarctic Pole.

Though the needle declined somewhat from the North Pole, it yet oscillated toward it, but not with equal force as in the Northern Hemisphere. When out at sea, the Captain General directed the course the pilots should steer, and inquired how they pointed. They unanimously replied they bore in that direction he ordered them. He then informed them that their course was wrong, and directed them to correct the needle, because, being in the Southern, it had not an equal power to designate the true north as in the Northern Hemisphere.

When in midst of the ocean, we discovered in the west five stars of great brilliancy, in form of a cross.

We steered northwest by west till we reached the equinoctial line in 122 degrees of longitude, west of the line of demarcation [laid down by Pope Alexander VI]. This line is 30 degrees west of the meridian, and 3 degrees west of Cape Verde. . . .

After we had crossed the line we steered west by north. We then ran 200 leagues toward the west; when, changing our course again, we ran west by south until in the latitude of 13 degrees north. We trusted by this course to reach Cape Gatticara, which cosmographers have placed in this latitude; but they are mistaken, this cape lying 12 degrees more toward the north. They must, however, be excused the error in their plan, as they have not like us had the advantage of visiting these parts.

When we had run 70 leagues in this direction and were in latitude 12 degrees north, longitude 146 degrees, on Wednesday, the sixth of March, we discovered in the northwest a small island, and afterward two others in the southwest. The first was more lofty and larger than the other two.

The Captain General meant to stop at the largest to victual

---

[3] These are now called the Magellanic Clouds.

and refresh, but this was rendered impossible, as the islanders came on board our ships and stole first one thing and then another, without our being able to prevent them. They invited us to take in our sails and come on shore, and even had the address to steal the skiff which hung astern of our vessel.

Exasperated at length, our Captain landed with forty men, burnt forty or fifty of their houses and several of their boats, and killed seven of the people. By acting thus he recovered his skiffs, but he did not deem it prudent to stop any longer after such acts of hostility. We therefore continued our course in the same direction as before.[4] . . .

The sixteenth of March, at sunrise we found ourselves near an elevated land 300 leagues from the islands De los Ladrones. We soon discovered it to be an island. It is called Zamal [Samar]. Behind this island is another not inhabited, and we afterward learnt that its name is Humunu. Here the Captain General resolved on landing the next day to take in water in greater security, and take some rest after so long and tedious a voyage. Here likewise he caused two tents to be erected for the sick, and ordered a sow to be killed. . . .

Perceiving around us a number of islands on the fifth Sunday of Lent, which also is the feast of Saint Lazarus, we called the archipelago by the name of that saint. ▨

Thus is recorded the first sighting by Europeans of the Philippines, which name was afterward given to the islands in honor of Philip of Austria, son of Charles V. The natives proved to be friendly and helpful, and in return the Spaniards treated them with consideration.

On March 29, the vessels moved to an anchorage off the island of Mindanao, and here the expedition stayed for a week. Friendly relations were established with two local kings, the King of Massana and the King of Butuan, a brisk trade was carried on, and the kings were converted to Christianity.

---

[4] Although the expedition had only this brief encounter, Pigafetta felt able to describe in some detail the manners and customs of these natives. In the course of his remarks he states: "The inhabitants of these islands are poor, but very dexterous, and above all at thieving; for this reason we gave the name of De los Ladrones to the islands." The group which received this uncomplimentary name was later called the Marianas, by which name these islands are still known.

On April 5, the expedition, accompanied by the King of Massana, sailed from Mindanao, threading a way between the islands of the archipelago and ariving two days later at the island of Cebu as here recorded:

On Sunday, the seventh of April, we entered the port of Zubu [Cebu]. We passed by several villages, in which we saw houses built upon trees. When near the town, the Captain ordered all our colors to be hoisted and all our sails to be taken in; and a general salute was fired, which caused great alarm among the islanders.

The Captain then sent one of his pupils, with the interpreter, as ambassador to the King of Cebu. On arriving at the town they found the King surrounded by an immense concourse of people alarmed at the noise occasioned by the discharge of our bombards. The interpreter began with removing the apprehension of the monarch, informing him that this was a custom with us, and meant as a mark of respect toward him, and as a token of friendship and peace. Upon this assurance the fears of all were dissipated.

The King inquired by his Minister what brought us to his island, and what we wanted. The interpreter answered that his master, who commanded the squadron, was a captain in the service of the greatest monarch upon earth, and that the object of his voyage was to proceed to Malucho [the Moluccas]; but that the King of Massana, at whose island we had touched, having spoken very highly of him, he had come hither to pay him his respects, and at the same time to take in provisions and give merchandise in exchange.

The King replied he was welcome, but at the same time he advised him that all vessels which might enter his port in view of trading were subject previously to pay duties. In proof of the truth of which he added that four days had not yet elapsed since his having received port dues for a junk from Ciam [Siam], which had come thither to take in slaves and gold; he moreover sent for a Moorish [Mohammedan] merchant, who came from Siam with the same view, to bear witness to what he stated.

The interpreter answered that his master, being the captain of so great a king, could not consent to pay duty to any monarch upon earth; that if the King of Cebu wished for peace, he brought peace with him, but if he wished to be hostile, he was prepared for war.

The merchant from Siam then, approaching the King, said to him in his own language, *"Cata rajah chita"*—that is to say, "Take care, Sire, of that." "These people," added he, for he thought us Portuguese, "are those who conquered Calicut, Malacca, and all Upper India."

The interpreter, who comprehended what the Moor said, then remarked that his monarch was one vastly more powerful than the King of Portugal, to whom the Siamese alluded, as well by sea as by land; that it was the King of Spain, the Emperor of the whole Christian world; and that if he had preferred to have him for an enemy rather than a friend he would have sent a sufficient number of men and vessels entirely to destroy his island.

The Moor confirmed what the interpreter said. The King then, finding himself embarrassed, said he would advise with his Ministers, and return an answer the next day. In the meantime he ordered a breakfast, consisting of several dishes, to be set before the deputy of the Captain General and the interpreter, all the dishes consisting of meat served up in porcelain.

After breakfast our deputies returned and reported what had taken place. The King of Massana, who next to that of Cebu was the most powerful monarch of these islands, went on shore to announce to the King the friendly intentions of our Captain General with respect to him. . . .

Tuesday, in the morning, the King of Massana came on board our vessel, in company with the Moorish merchant, and after saluting the Captain on the part of the King of Cebu, told him he was authorized to communicate that the King was busied in collecting all the provisions he could to make a present to him, and that in the afternoon he would send his nephew with some of his Ministers to confirm a treaty of peace. The Captain thanked the deputation, and at the same time exhibited to them a man armed cap-à-pie, observing in case of a necessity to fight, we should all of us be armed in the same manner.

The Moor was terribly frightened at sight of a man armed

in this manner; but the Captain tranquilized him with the assurance that our arms were as advantageous to our friends as fatal to our enemies; and that we were able as readily to disperse all the enemies of our sovereign and our faith as to wipe the sweat from our brows.

The Captain made use of this lofty and threatening tone purposely, that the Moor might make report of it to the King. . . .

[When the treaty with the King of Cebu had been concluded, European goods were carried ashore and placed in a house that had been turned over to the Spaniards for this purpose.]

On Friday, we opened our warehouse and exhibited our different merchandise, which excited much admiration among the islanders. For brass, iron, and other weighty articles, they gave us gold in exchange. Our trinkets, and articles of a lighter kind, were bartered for rice, hogs, goats, and other edibles. For 14 pounds of iron we received 10 pieces of gold, of the value of a ducat and a half. The Captain General forbade too great an anxiety for receiving gold, without which order every sailor would have parted with all he had to obtain this metal, which would have ruined our commerce forever.

Throughout the negotiations Magellan had urged upon the King of Cebu the spiritual and temporal advantages that would result from conversion to Christianity. The King expressed willingness to embrace the faith, particularly, he said, since it would better enable him to enforce respect from his various chiefs. A great ceremony was held at which the King and Queen, the principal chiefs, and many of the people were baptized. Thereafter the conversion of most of the neighboring islands was quickly accomplished. Only one village had to be burned because of refusal to obey the commands of the King and Magellan.

Then came resistance from a powerful chief, as a result of which Magellan met his tragic end, a fate which might have been avoided had he been less zealous in the use of the sword for spreading the faith and in trying to impress the islanders with the superiority of Spanish arms.

The battle in which Magellan lost his life took place on April 27, 1521, "a day chosen by the Captain himself, being that which he held most propitious to his enterprise." Pigafetta took part in the battle, as the following tells:

🔖 Contiguous to the island Cebu is another called Matan [Mactan], which has a port of the same name, in which our vessels laid at anchor. The chief village of this island is likewise called Mactan, over which Zula and Cilapulapu presided as chiefs. In this island the village of Bulaia was situate, which we burnt.

On Friday, the twenty-sixth of April, Zula, one of these chiefs, sent one of his sons with two goats to the Captain General and observed that if he did not send him the whole of what he had promised, the blame was not to be imputed to himself, but to the other chief, Cilapulapu, who would not acknowledge the authority of the King of Spain. He further stated that if the Captain General would only send to his assistance the following night a boat with some armed men, he would engage to beat and entirely subjugate his rival.

On receiving this message the Captain General determined on going himself with these boats. We entreated him not to hazard his person on this adventure, but he answered that as a good pastor he ought not to be far away from his flock.

At midnight we left the ship, 60 in number, armed with helmets and cuirasses. The Christian King, the Prince, his nephew, and several chiefs of Cebu, with a number of armed men, followed us in twenty or thirty balangays. We reached Mactan three hours before day. The Captain would not then begin the attack; but he sent the Moor on shore to inform Cilapulapu and his people that if he would acknowledge the sovereignty of the King of Spain, obey the Christian King of Cebu, and pay the tribute he demanded, they should be looked upon as friends. Otherwise they should experience the strength of our lances.

The islanders, nothing intimidated, replied they had lances as well as we, although they were only sticks of bamboo pointed at the end, and staves hardened in the fire. They merely requested that they might not be attacked in the night, as they expected reinforcements, and should then be better able to cope with us. This they said designedly to induce us to attack them immediately, in hope that thus we should fall in the dikes they had dug between the sea and their houses.

We accordingly waited daylight, when we jumped into the water up to our thighs, the boats not being able to approach near enough to land, on account of the rocks and shallows. The number which landed was 49 only, as 11 were left in charge of the boats. We were obliged to wade some distance through the water before we reached the shore.

We found the islanders, 1500 in number, formed into three battalions, who immediately on our landing fell upon us, making horrible shouts. Two of these battalions attacked us in flank, and the third in front.

Our Captain divided his company into two platoons. The musketeers and crossbowmen fired from a distance the space of half an hour without making the least impression on the enemy; for though the balls and arrows penetrated their bucklers made of thin wood, and even wounded them at times in their arms, this did not make them halt, as the wounds failed of occasioning them instant death, as they expected; on the contrary, it only made them more bold and furious.

Moreover, trusting to the superiority of their numbers, they showered on us such clouds of bamboo lances, staves hardened in the fire, stones, and even dirt, that it was with difficulty we defended ourselves. Some even threw spears headed with iron at our Captain General, who to intimidate and cause them to disperse, ordered away a party of our men to set fire to their houses, which they immediately effected.

The sight of the flames served only to increase their exasperation. Some of them even ran to the village which was set on fire, and in which twenty or thirty houses were consumed, and killed two of our men on the spot. They seemed momently to increase in number and impetuosity. A poisoned arrow struck the Captain in the leg, who on this ordered a retreat in slow and regular order; but the majority of our men took to flight precipitately, so that only 7 or 8 remained about the Captain.

The Indians, perceiving their blows were ineffectual when aimed at our body or head, on account of our armor, and noticing at the same time that our legs were uncovered, directed against these their arrows, javelins, and stones, and these in such abundance that we could not guard against them. The bombards we had in our boats were of no utility, as the levelness of the strand would not admit of the boats' being brought sufficiently close inshore.

We retreated gradually, still continuing to fight, and were now at a bowshot from the islanders, and in the water up to our knees, when they renewed their attack with fury, throwing at us the same lance five or six times over as they picked it up on advancing. As they knew our Captain, they chiefly aimed at him, so that his helmet was twice struck from his head. Still he did not give himself up to despair, and we continued in a very small number fighting by his side.

This combat, so unequal, lasted more than an hour.

An islander at length succeeded in thrusting the end of his lance through the bars of his helmet, and wounding the Captain in the forehead, who, irritated on the occasion, immediately ran the assailant through the body with his lance, the lance remaining in the wound. He now attempted to draw his sword, but was unable, owing to his right arm being greviously wounded. The Indians, who perceived this, pressed in crowds upon him, and one of them having given him a violent cut with a sword on the left leg, he fell on his face. On this they immediately fell upon him.

Thus perished our guide, our light, and our support. On falling, and seeing himself surrounded by the enemy, he turned toward us several times, as if to know whether we had been able to save ourselves. As there was not one of those who remained with him but was wounded, and as we were consequently in no condition either to afford him succor or revenge his death, we instantly made for our boats, which were on the point of putting off. To our Captain indeed did we owe our deliverance, as the instant he fell, all the islanders rushed toward the spot where he lay.

The Christian King had it in his power to render us assistance, and this he would no doubt have done; but the Captain General, far from foreseeing what was about to happen when he landed with his people, had ordered him not to leave his balangay, but merely to remain a spectator of our manner of fighting. His Majesty bitterly bewailed his fate on seeing him fall.

But the glory of Magellan will survive him. He was adorned with every virtue; in midst of the greatest adversity he constantly possessed an immovable firmness. At sea he subjected himself to the same privations as his men. Better skilled than anyone in the knowledge of nautical charts, he was a perfect master of navigation, as he proved in making the tour of the world, an attempt on which none before him had ventured. ⱶ

In one way of looking at it, Magellan himself did not make the full "tour of the world." That was physically accomplished only by the survivors, among them Pigafetta himself. What the chronicler evidently had in mind was that Magellan did reach, by sailing west around South America, the lands already familiar to those Europeans who had reached them by sailing east around Africa.

For more than fifty years no other ships than Magellan's sailed around the world. The next circumnavigation was not accomplished until Drake's voyage of 1577.

The Discovery of the Amazon and the
First Crossing of South America

THE DISCOVERY OF THE AMAZON
AND THE FIRST CROSSING
OF SOUTH AMERICA

CHAPTER 10

THE Spanish expedition of Vicente Yáñez Pinzón entered the mouth of the Amazon in 1500 and went upstream perhaps 50 miles. He called it Río Santa Maria de la Mar Dulce, which was abbreviated to Mar Dulce. Somewhat later it was known as Río Grande and as El Río Marañón. But the Amazon was first effectively explored, and in that sense discovered, by Orellana, who traversed its length from the foothills of the Andes to the sea and who reported the Country of the Amazons.

Francisco de Orellana, first navigator if not discoverer of the greatest river in the world, and the first to cross the South American continent, was born in Trujillo, Estremadura, in about the year 1511. Like many another young adventure- and fortune-seeking Spaniard, he crossed to the new Indies in his youth, perhaps as early as 1527.

There is uncertainty as to the activities and whereabouts of Orellana during the first years of his stay in the New World, but from about 1534 on his fortunes were intimately tied in with those of Francisco Pizarro, his kinsman and fellow Estremadurian. Pizzaro, the great conquistador, had accompanied Balboa in the discovery of the Pacific, had later gone on to discover Peru, and had received in 1529 the royal appointment to be Governor and Captain General of New Castile, as the freshly-discovered land was named.

These were turbulent days; for in addition to the conquest of the native peoples, there was a succession of plots and counterplots among the rival Spanish governors and their followers, many of them involving open warfare. Orellana says of himself that he fought with honor, and with the loss of an eye, "in the conquests of Lima and Trujillo and Cuzco and in the pursuit of the Inca and in the conquest of Puerto Viejo and its outlying territory."

Commissioned by Francisco Pizarro in 1538 to conquer the province of La Culata, Orellana triumphed over the Indians and, at his own expense, founded the city of Santiago de Guayaquil (the present Guayaquil, Ecuador). In recognition of these services, Pizarro in the following year appointed him Captain General and Lieutenant Governor of the newly founded city, as well as of Villa Nueva de Puerto Viejo (Porto-viejo, Ecuador).

Then, in 1540, Gonzalo Pizarro arrived from Spain to take over from its former incumbent the post of Governor of the provinces of Quito, including La Culata and Puerto Viejo, a position to which he had been appointed by his half-brother Francisco. The idea behind this was that Gonzalo should head a great expedition to explore the interior of the country, and especially to seek the fabulous lands of El Dorado and La Canela (Land of Cinnamon).

Orellana, hearing of Gonzalo Pizarro's arrival, immediately went to Quito to turn over possession of his territory to the new chief and to offer his services on the forthcoming expedition. That he might the better serve His Majesty on this great undertaking, Orellana proposed not only to take his friends along but to spend his personal fortune as well. Pizarro accepted the offer, and Orellana retired to Guayaquil to recruit men and equipment. Arriving in Quito, he found he had missed Pizarro, who had set out with his party toward the end of February 1541.

It was an imposing array that Gonzalo Pizarro commanded. In his company were about 220 Spaniards, and nearly 4000 Indians who had been impressed into the service of their conquerors. The equipment was on a similarly grand scale—weapons and munitions of all kinds; horses (worth at least their weight in gold) for the Spaniards; llamas, for beasts of burden and to eke out the food supply; live hogs, variously estimated at from 2000 to 5000 in number; and thousands of dogs, both for hunting game and to use against the people that were to be conquered.

At Quito the Spaniards tried to dissuade Orellana from following Pizarro's route, for the country was "rough" and "hostile," and the natives would surely kill him, as they had others before him. Nevertheless, Orellana went ahead, with 23 companions.

Difficulties were encountered almost immediately. Not only were they under frequent attack by Indians, but as their food supply dwindled, they discovered that Pizarro's men had stripped their path of any possible food supply. When, after great privation, Orellana finally staggered into Pizarro's camp, "he still had left only a sword and a shield, and his companions likewise."

Pizarro was delighted to see Orellana and promptly made him his Lieutenant General.

As Orellana and his men were worn-out, they rested in the valley of Zumaco, about 30 leagues distant from Quito, while Pizarro, with 80 men, explored the country to the eastward. The journey was on foot, for horses were unable to get through the thick woods. After seventy days of marching, Pizzaro found, along the Napo River, the cinnamon trees he was looking for, but they were sparsely scattered over vast stretches of land.

Pizarro realized that trading in cinnamon would never bring him wealth. So he questioned some primitive local Indians about the contour of the land beyond, as to whether there were valleys and plains suitable for his horses, and riches for the taking. When the Indians could not give the answers he craved, Pizarro delivered some over "to be torn to pieces by the dogs, while others he caused to be burned alive."

Later, apprehensive and discouraged, the party turned back. As they neared a junction with the main expedition, they came upon a group of Indians at a large river, some paddling their canoes while others watched from the far bank. To these Pizarro called out to have no fear and to approach. Some fifteen or twenty of them did so, headed by their chief Delicola.

The usual query was put as to what riches lay beyond, be it ever so far distant. Delicola knew what had been the fate of his fellow Indians when they had been too truthful on being similarly questioned, so he painted a highly colored picture of rich lands, magnificent settlements, ruled by powerful over-lords, waiting to be conquered by the Spaniards. Pizarro, by way of reward for this cheering information, refrained from having Delicola torn by dogs or burned; instead he made him a slave, so that he might in the future serve as guide.

When the two parties of the expedition had joined up, the campmaster, returning with 50 soldiers from a fifteen-day reconnaissance, reported a great river on the shores of which lived Indians who wore clothes and were civilized. The expedition proceeded to this river and found some settlements that were "not very large," where they rested.

Mindful that the friendship of natives could be translated into food for his troops, Pizarro decided to remain at peace here. The Indians "bartered agreeably" with the Spaniards at first; "but presently they got angry and the greater part of them disappeared." In view of Pizarro's treatment of Indians he had met farther west, it seems not unlikely that news from upriver had reached the community, prompting those of discretion to flee.

Hostilities developed. The Spaniards had secured a few canoes in which to search for food, but dared not now venture abroad for fear of meeting Indian canoes, which they could not hope to equal in maneuver or in speed.

The Spaniards had reached the "Great River," but with considerably depleted forces, for all the Indian slaves brought from Quito had died. They considered that "this was the result of their having taken highland Indians." They came to the general conclusion that lowland natives could not live in the mountains nor the mountain people if brought to the lowlands.

It was decided to build a large river boat, called a brigantine, on which munitions, tools, and supplies could be carried, the horses keeping abreast on land. For since the slaves had died, there were no men to do any carrying—the tenor of the narra-tive is that it would have demeaned a soldier to carry anything but his own weapons.

This procedure adopted, the party descended the Coca (?) River forty-three marches. They found little food and no people. Finally their herd of swine brought from Quito was eaten up and the men started getting hungry. They had come from the Pacific Ocean, had crossed the Andes, but were still separated from the Atlantic by most of the width of South America. In a letter to the King, dated September 3, 1542, Pizarro relates:

Gonzalo Pizarro's Letter[1]

Pushing on down the river by the route which the guides told us [to follow], being now 70 leagues inside this province [ahead of us was] a great uninhabited region in which there was no food whatsoever to be had. Learning this, I gave orders for the expedition to halt and for us to lay in all the food that could be obtained.

The men being thus engaged in searching for foodstuffs, there came to me Captain Francisco de Orellana, and he told me how [he had questioned] the guides that I had placed in his charge for better protection and in order that he might talk to them and from them get information regarding the country beyond, as he had nothing to do, for it was I who looked after matters pertaining to fighting. He told me that the guides said that the uninhabited region was a vast one and there was no food whatsoever to be had this side of a spot where another great river joined up with the one down which we were proceeding, and that from this junction one day's journey up the [other] river there was an abundant supply of food.

From the said guides I in turn sought information, and they told me the same as they had told Captain Orellana. And Captain Orellana told me that in order to serve Your Majesty and for love of me, he was willing to take upon himself the task of going in search of food where the Indians said, for he was sure that there would be some there; and that if I would give him the brigantine and the canoes manned by 60 men, he would go in search of food and would bring it for the relief of the expeditionary force; and that, as I was to continue on

---

[1] From José Toribio Medina, *The Discovery of the Amazon, According to the Account of Friar de Carvajal and Other Documents,* translated from the Spanish by Bertram T. Lee, edited by H. C. Heaton, American Geographical Society, New York, 1934.

down and he was to come back with the food, the relief would be quick, and that within ten or twelve days he would get back to the expeditionary force.

Being confident that Captain Orellana would do as he said, because he was my lieutenant, I told him that I was pleased at the idea of his going for the food, and that he should see to it that he returned within the twelve days and in no case went beyond the junction of the rivers, but brought the food and gave his attention to nothing else, inasmuch as he had the men to do it with. He answered me saying that by no means would he exceed what I had told him, and that he would come with the food within the time that he had stated.

With this confidence that I had in him, I gave him the brigantine and the canoes and 60 men, because it was reported that there were many Indians going about the river in canoes; telling him also, inasmuch as the guides had said that at the beginning of the uninhabited region there were two very large rivers that could not be bridged over, to leave there four or five canoes to ferry the expeditionary force over. He promised me that he would do so, and so departed.

Paying no heed to what he owed to the services of Your Majesty and to what it was his duty to do as he had been told by me, his captain, and to the well-being of the expeditionary force and of the enterprise, instead of bringing the food, he went down the river without leaving any arrangements [for the aid of those who were to follow on], leaving only the signs and choppings showing how they had been on land and had stopped at the junction of the rivers and in other parts, without there having come in any news of him at all up to the present time; he thus displaying toward the whole expeditionary force the greatest cruelty that ever faithless men have shown, aware that it was left so unprovided with food and caught in such a vast uninhabited region and among such great rivers, carrying off all the arquebuses and crossbows and munitions and iron materials of the whole expeditionary force.[2]

---

[2] Medina says that Pizarro gravely exaggerates, for Orellana had on board only three arquebuses and four or five crossbows, according to Carvajal's *Relación*, published in Oviedo's *Historia de las Indias*.

After great hardship the expeditionary force arrived at the junction where he was to await me.

When the members of the expeditionary force, having gone that far, saw the junction and realized [that there was no relief] for them in the way of food, because he had gone on and there was no way of finding any food whatsoever, they became greatly discouraged, because for many days the whole expeditionary force had eaten nothing but palm shoots and some fruit stones which they found on the ground which had fallen from the trees, together with all the various kinds of noxious wild beasts which they had been able to find. They had eaten in this wild country more than one thousand dogs and more than one hundred horses, without any other kind of food whatsoever, from which cause many members of the expeditionary force had become sick, and some were weak, while others died of hunger and from not being in a condition to go on any farther. ✠

True, Orellana did not return in the twelve-day period allotted him by Pizarro. The story of why he did not, and of what happened to him and his men, is the story of the discovery of most of the Amazon River and of the first crossing of South America.

Friar Gaspar de Carvajal, who went along with Orellana, and doubtless was present at the leave-taking of the two men, tells a different story from that of Pizarro. He says the latter did not specify a twelve-day period for the expedition but allowed Orellana to use his discretion. He insists that Orellana had no choice about returning to the junction of the two rivers, the agreed meeting-place, once they had traveled a certain distance—that finding no food, their only chance of survival lay in pushing on still farther, whereupon it soon became impossible for them to retrace their steps. For it would have meant backtracking through a foodless country, with the added difficulty of a river current which would then have been against them.

Carvajal maintains that, far from being guilty of treason, Orellana was ever mindful of his duty to the King, that he was a brave man and a sound leader. But here the good Friar shall speak for himself.

Like both Orellana and Pizarro, Father Gaspar de Carvajal, the chronicler of Orellana's expedition, was born in Trujillo. When a royal decree ordered ten members of the Dominican order to go to Peru in 1535, Carvajal was in command of eight of them.

When Gonzalo Pizarro passed through Lima, Peru, on his way to Quito, the young and courageous Carvajal, who had already acquired considerable prestige, was there. It was natural for Pizarro to invite him to come along, as Medina says, "on an enterprise in which God and King could be served so well."

He set out from Quito with Pizarro. When, toward the end of 1541, the latter resolved to send Orellana down the waters of the Coca with the sick to search for food, Carvajal and another cleric in the party, doubtless with respect to their calling, were given places aboard the brigantine.

Carvajal's is the only document which gives in full the account of Orellana's voyage. According to Medina, "even if it is written without art, it is the faithful reflection of his own impressions and of what he saw."

This section has been paraphrased and condensed from José Toribio Medina's *The Discovery of the Amazon*, first published in Seville in 1894, and republished in 1934 by the American Geographical Society, translated by Bertram T. Lee and edited by H. C. Heaton. This edition is used also to pick up the only narrative written by an eyewitness to the first navigation of the Amazon. Carvajal's narrative has the title:

Account Written by Friar Gaspar de Carvajal, a friar of the Order of Saint Dominic of Guzman, of the recent voyage of discovery down the famous great river which Captain Francisco de Orellana, by a very great piece of good fortune, discovered, starting at its source and coming out at the sea, accompanied by fifty-seven men whom he took along with him, having launched forth at random upon the said river, which from the name of the captain who discovered it came to be called the Orellana River.

We take up the narrative as Carvajal tells how Orellana

came to leave the main body of the expedition and go off with 57 men to follow an unknown river.

Orellana and the Amazon

🖎 The said Captain Orellana picked out 57 men, with whom he embarked in the aforesaid boat and in certain canoes which they had taken away from the Indians, and he began to proceed down his river with the idea of promptly turning back if food was found; all of which turned out just the reverse of what we all expected, because we did not find food for a distance of 200 leagues,[3] nor were we finding any [for ourselves], from which cause we suffered very great privation, as will be stated farther on, and so we kept going on, beseeching Our Lord to see fit to guide us on that journey in such a way that we might return to our companions.

On the second day after we had set out and separated from our companions, we were almost wrecked in the middle of the river because the boat struck a log and it stove in one of its planks, so that if we had not been close to land we should have ended our journey there. But matters were soon remedied [thanks to the energy of the men] in hauling the boat out of water and fastening a piece of plank on it, and we promptly started off on our way with very great haste.

As the river flowed fast, we proceeded on at the rate of from 20 to 25 leagues, for now the river was high and [its power] increased, owing to the effect of many other rivers which emptied into it on the right, from a southerly direction. We journeyed on for three days without [finding] any inhabited country at all.

Seeing that we had come far away from where our companions had stopped and that we had used up what little food we had brought along, [too little] for so uncertain a journey as the one that we were pursuing, the Captain and the companions conferred about the difficulty, and the [question of] turning back, and the lack of food; for as we had expected to return quickly, we had not laid in a supply of food. But, con-

---

[3] The Spanish league is here probably about 3.75 miles, so 200 leagues would be about 750 miles.

fident that we could not be far off [from some settlement], we decided to go ahead, and this at the cost of no little hardship for all.

As neither on the next day nor on the following one was any food found, nor any sign of a settlement, in accordance with the view of the Captain I said mass as it is said at sea, commending to Our Lord our persons and our lives, beseeching Him, as an unworthy man, to deliver us from such manifest hardship and [eventual] destruction, for that's what it was coming to look like to us now, since although we did wish to go back up the river, that was not possible on account of the heavy current, [and there was no alternative], for to attempt to go by land was out of the question, so that we were in great danger of death because of the great hunger we endured.

So, after taking counsel as to what should be done, talking over our affliction and hardships, it was decided that we should choose of two evils the one which to the Captain and to all should appear to be the lesser, which was to go forward and follow the river, [and thus] either die or see what there was along it, trusting in Our Lord that He would see fit to preserve our lives until we should see our way out.

In the meantime, lacking other victuals, we reached a privation so great that we were eating nothing but leather, belts and soles of shoes, cooked with certain herbs, with the result that so great was our weakness that we could not remain standing, for some on all fours and others with staffs went into the woods to search for a few roots to eat, and some there were who ate certain herbs with which they were not familiar. They were at the point of death, because they were like madmen and did not possess sense, but as Our Lord was pleased that we should continue on our journey, no one died.

Because of this suffering, as stated, a number of the companions were quite disheartened, to whom the Captain spoke words of cheer, and he told them to exert themselves and have confidence in Our Lord, for since He had cast us upon that river He would see fit to bring us out to a haven of safety. In such a way did he cheer up the companions that they accepted that hardship. . . .

So it was that, it being Monday evening, which by count

was the eighth of the month of January [1542], while eating certain forest roots they heard drums very plainly very far from where we were. The Captain was the one who heard them first and announced it to the other companions, and they all listened, and they being convinced of the fact, such was the happiness which they all felt that they cast out of their memories all the past suffering, because we were now in an inhabited country and no longer could die of hunger.

The Captain straightway ordered us to keep watch by quarters with great care, because . . . [torn] it might be that the Indians had caught sight of us and would come at night and attack the party, as is their custom. So that night a very heavy watch was kept, the Captain not sleeping, it being considered that that night transcended all the rest, because all were so eager for day to come, for they had had their fill of [living on] roots.

No sooner had morning come than the Captain ordered the powder and arquebuses and crossbows to be made ready and all the men to be alert for arming themselves, because in truth not one of the companions here was without great worry as to how to do what they had to. The Captain had his own [worry] and that of all. And so in the morning, everything being made quite ready and put in order, we started to go in search of the village.

At the end of 2 leagues of advancing down the river we saw coming up the river to look over and reconnoiter the land four canoes filled with Indians. When they saw us, they turned about at great speed, giving the alarm in such a manner that in less than a quarter of an hour we heard in the villages many drums that were calling the country to arms, because they are heard from very far off and are so well attuned that they have their bass and tenor and treble.

At once the Captain ordered the companions who were at the oars to row with all speed, so that we might arrive at the first village before the natives had gathered together.

So it was that at very great haste we began to move on. We arrived at the village, where the Indians were all waiting to defend and guard their homes. The Captain commanded that in very good order his men should all leap out on land, and that all should look after one another, and that no one should exceed orders, and [that] as good [soldiers] they should look to what they had in hand to do, and that each one should .do what he was supposed to do. So great was the courage which they all gained on seeing the village that they forgot all the past toils, and the Indians left the village and all the food that there was in it, which was no small relief and support for us.

Before the companions should eat, although they had great need, the Captain ordered them all to scout about the village in order that afterward, while they were gathering food together and resting, the Indians might not turn back on us and do us some harm. And it was so done.

Here the companions set about to make up for the past, because they did nothing but eat of that which the Indians had prepared for themselves and drink of their beverages, and this with so much eagerness that they thought that they would never satisfy themselves. This was not done all unguardedly, because, although they ate like men all that they needed, they did not forget to take all precautions in everything that was incumbent upon them for the defense of their persons; for they all remained alert, their shields on their shoulders and their swords under their arms, watching to see if the Indians were turning back on us. In this way we earned this rest, for such it may be called for us after all the hardship we had endured, until two hours past midday, when the Indians began to come on the water to see what was going on. Thus they kept moving about on the river like simpletons.

This having been observed by the Captain, he got up on the bank of the river and in their language (for to a certain extent he could understand them) he began to speak with them and tell them to have no fear and to come near, for he wished to speak to them. So two Indians came right up to where the Captain was, and he cajoled them and took away their fear and gave them something from his supplies and told them to go get the overlord (for he wished to speak to him) and to have no fear that he would do him any harm whatsoever.

So the Indians took what was given them and went at once to inform their overlord, who came right away, very much decked out, to where the Captain and the companions were, and was very well received by the Captain and by all; and they embraced him, and the Chief himself manifested great contentment at seeing the good reception that was given him. At once the Captain ordered that he be given clothes and other things, with which he was much pleased, and thereafter he became so happy that he told the Captain to decide on what he needed, for he would give it to him.

The Captain told him to order nothing to be furnished him but food; and straightway the Chief ordered his Indians to bring food, and in a very short time they brought in abundance all that was needed, including meats, partridges, turkeys, and fish of many sorts. After this, the Captain thanked the Chief heartily and told him to depart with God's blessing and to summon to him all the overlords of that land, of whom there were thirteen, because he wished to speak to them all together and announce the reason for his coming.

Although he the [Chief] said that the next day they would all be with the Captain and that he was going to send for them, and went away quite content, the Captain continued to put things in order as best befitted the welfare of himself and his companions, arranging the watches in such a way that both by day and by night every precaution should be taken in order that the Indians might not fall upon us, and that there should be no oversight or laxity in consequence of which they might be encouraged to attack us either by night or by day.

The next day, at the hour of vespers, the afore-mentioned Chief came and brought with him three or four other overlords, for the rest were unable to come, as they were far away, but would come the next day. The Captain extended to them the same reception as to the first and spoke to them at great length on behalf of His Majesty, and in the latter's name took possession of the said land. He did the same with all the others who afterward came [to him] in this province, for, as I have said, there were thirteen of them, and in the case of all of them he took possession in the name of His Majesty.

When the Captain perceived that he [now] had all the inhabitants and the overlords accepting peace and friendly toward him [and] that kind treatment was the proper procedure to be followed, [he took advantage of the fact that] they were all glad to come with peaceful intentions. In this way he took possession of them and of the said land in the name of His Majesty.

When this was done, he commanded all his companions to gather together so that he might talk to them on the subject of what steps it was proper to take in the interests of their expedition and their salvation and [even the saving of] their lives, giving them a long talk, bolstering up their courage with very strong words.

After the Captain had given them this talk, the companions were very happy to see the good courage that the Captain had within him, and to see with what patience he bore up under the hardships which were falling to his lot, and they spoke to him also some very kind words, and with the words which the Captain spoke to them they went about so happy that they were not conscious of any of the hardships that they had endured.

After the companions had somewhat recovered from the effects of the hunger and suffering that they had undergone, being [now] in a mood to work, the Captain, seeing that it was necessary to make plans for what was ahead, gave orders to call all the companions together, and repeated to them that they could see that with the boat which we were using and the canoes, if God saw fit to guide us to the sea, we could not go on out to a place of rescue, and [that] for this reason it was necessary to apply our wits to building another brigantine of greater burden, so that we might sail on the sea. This [he advised] in spite of the fact that among us there was no skilled craftsman who knew that trade, for what we found most diffi- cult was how to make the nails.

Meanwhile the Indians did not stop offering aid and coming to the Captain and bringing to him foodstuffs in abundance, and all with as much orderliness as if all their lives they had been servants. They came wearing their jewels and gold medal- lions. Never did the Captain permit that anything be taken [away from them], or even merely looked at, in order that the Indians might not conceive the idea that we valued such things, and the more indifference we showed in this matter, the more gold did they put on.

It was here that they informed us of the existence of the Amazons and of the wealth farther down the river. The one who gave us this information was an Indian overlord named Aparia, an old man who said he had been in that country. He also told us about another overlord who lived at some distance from the river, far inland, who he said possessed very great wealth in gold. This overlord's name is Ica. Never did we get to see him, because, as I say, he kept away from the river where we were.

In order not to lose time nor waste the food in vain, the Captain decided that a start should at once be made on what was to be done. So he gave orders to prepare the necessary materials, and the companions said that they wanted to begin their task at once.

There were among us two men to whom not a little [credit] is due for having done something which they had never learned [to do]. They came before the Captain and told him that they, with the help of Our Lord, would make the nails that were needed, and asked [him] to order others to make charcoal. The names of these two companions were, the one, Juan de Alcántara, a hidalgo hailing from the town of Alcántara, and the other, Sebastián Rodríguez, a native of Galicia. The Captain thanked them, promising them reward and payment for such an important piece of work.

He at once ordered some bellows to be made out of buskins, and in a like manner all the other tools. The other companions he commanded in groups of three to prepare good kilnfuls of charcoal. All of this was promptly put into execution. Each one took his own tool, and they went off to the woods to cut wood and bring it on their shoulders from the woods to the village, [a distance] which must have been about half a league.

They made their pits, and this with very great toil. As they were weak and not expert in that line of work, they could not bear up under the burden. And the other companions who had not the strength to cut wood worked the bellows, and others carted water, while the Captain worked at everything, so that we all had something to which to give our attention.

Our company gave such a good account of itself in this village, in the organization of this task, that in twenty days, with the help of God, two thousand very good nails and other things were made. The Captain put off the construction of the brigantine for some other place where he might find a greater need for it and better facilities.

We stayed in this village longer than we should have stayed, eating up all we had. This was the cause of our suffering great hardship from this point on, which was [due to a desire] to see if in some way or manner we could get news from the expeditionary force.

Seeing that none could be had, the Captain decided to give 1000 castellanos to six companions if they would form a group and take the news to the Governor Gonzalo Pizarro. In addition to this he would give them two Negroes to help them row and a few Indians, in order that they might carry letters to him and give to the Governor on his [Orellana's] behalf news of what was happening. Among them all only three were found, because all feared the death that was sure [to come] to them, in view of the long time that it was bound to take them to get back to where they had left the said Governor. They thought he had probably turned back, because they had gone 150 leagues since they had left the Governor in the nine days that they had used up in going on [as far as here].

The task being finished, and in view of the fact that our food was becoming exhausted, and that 7 of our companions had died from the hunger endured, we departed on the day of Our Lady of Candlemas. We laid in what foodstuffs we could, because this was not the time to stay any longer in that village—on the one hand because, so it seemed, this was beginning to become irksome to the natives and they [Orellana's men] wished to leave them content, and on the other hand because of our desire not to lose time and use up our food without advantage, because we did not know whether we should need it. So we began to move on through this said province.

We had not gone a distance of 20 leagues when there joined with our river another one from the right, not very wide, on which river an important overlord named Irrimorrany had his abode. Because he was an Indian and overlord of much intelligence and because he had come to see the Captain and bring him food, he [the Captain] wanted to go to his country; but [in addition to other difficulties in the way of doing so] there was also the reason that the river came down very strong and with a great onrush.

Here we were on the point of perishing, because, right there where this river flowed into the one on which we were navigating, the one stream battled with the other and sent large pieces of driftwood from one side to the other, so that it was hard work to navigate up it, because it [the river] formed many whirlpools and carried us from one bank to the other.

By dint of hard work we got out of this danger, [though] without being able to reach the village, and we passed on toward where we had heard [was] the village, and we passed on toward where we had heard that there was another village which they told us was 200 leagues farther on from there, all the country between being barren. So we covered this distance at the cost of a great deal of suffering for our bodies, passing through many hardships and very extraordinary dangers.

For example, there befell us a certain mishap and [one which caused us] no small worry for the time that we were held up by it. This was that two canoes carrying 11 Spaniards of ours became lost among some islands without knowing where we were and without our being able to find them. They were lost for two days without being able to locate us, and we, expecting never to see them again, for the time being experienced very great grief.

But at the end of the aforesaid time Our Lord was pleased that we should come together, so that there was no little rejoicing among [us] all. In this way we were so overcome with happiness that it seemed to us that all the suffering endured had passed out of our memories.

After resting a day at the spot where we found them, the Captain ordered us to continue on our journey. . . .

As we were going along one Sunday morning, at a fork which the river made—for it divided into two parts—there came upstream to see us some Indians in four or five canoes which were laden with much food. They came close to where the Captain was and asked for permission to approach because they wished to speak with the said Captain, who ordered them to approach.

So they did approach. They told him that they were prominent persons and vassals of Aparia, and that it was at his command that they were coming to bring us food. They began to take out of their canoes many partridges like those of our *apin*, save that they are larger, and many turtles, which are as large as leather shields, and fish also of various kinds.

The Captain thanked them and gave them something taken from his supplies. After he had sold [given] it to them, the Indians remained very happy to see the kind treatment that was being extended to them and to see that the Captain understood their tongue, a fact which was of no little consequence in connection with our getting to a haven of clear understanding. For had he not understood it, we should have found our final escape to be a difficult one.

As the Indians were desirous of taking leave, they told the Captain to go to the village where their chief overlord resided, whose name, as I have said, was Aparia. The Captain asked them down which of the two arms he ought to proceed. They replied that they would guide us, [telling us] to follow them. So within a short time we saw the settlements where the said overlord was.

Proceeding toward that place, the Captain again asked the Indians to whom these settlements belonged. The Indians replied that there dwelt the above-mentioned overlord of theirs. Then they set off toward the village to give the message that we were coming. It was not long before we saw many Indians come out of the aforesaid village and get into their canoes, in the attitude of warriors.

It looked as if they were getting ready to attack us. The Captain ordered his companions, who saw the manifestation [of hostility] that the Indians were making, to be alert, with their weapons ready, so that in case they attacked us they might not be able to harm us.

In good order, rowing and with full power, we put into shore, and the Indians seemed to get out of the way. The Captain leaped out on land all armed, and after him all the others. At this the Indians became frightened and came in closer to land. Inasmuch as the Captain understood them—for, as I have already said, his understanding of the language was, next to God, the deciding factor by virtue of which we did not perish [somewhere] along the river—[we got out of this difficult situation]; for had he not understood it, neither would the Indians have come forward with peaceful intentions nor should we have met with success in these settlements.

As Our Lord was pleased that such a great [venture into the] unknown and [feat of] discovery should be carried out and brought to the notice of His Caesarean Majesty, and at the cost of so much hardship, the discovery *was* made, and [it is certain] that by no other method or force of human energy could the discovery have been made, had not God put His hand to it [then], or until many centuries and years had elapsed.

After the Captain had called the Indians to him, he told them to have no fear, [but] to step out on land. They proceeded to do so, for they came close into land, showing on their faces that they rejoiced at our coming. The overlord leaped out on land, and with him many important personages and overlords who accompanied him, and he asked permission of the Captain to sit down.

He seated himself, and all his followers [remained] standing. He ordered to be brought from his canoes a great quantity of foodstuffs, not only turtles, but also manatees and other fish, and roasted partridges and cats and monkeys.

The Captain, perceiving the polite manners of the overlord, addressed a few words to him, giving him to understand that we were Christians and worshiped a single God, who was the Creator of all created things, and that we were not like them who walked in the paths of error worshiping stones and images made [by man]. In this connection he told them many other things, and explained to them also how we were servants and vassals of the Emperor of the Christians, the great King of Spain, and [that] he was called Don Carlos our master, to whom belonged the territory of all the Indies and many other dominions and kingdoms existing throughout the world, and that we were going to make a report to him on what we had seen in it.

They were very attentive and with keen interest [went on] listening to what the Captain was saying to them. They told him that if we were going to visit the Amurians, whom they call Coniupuyara in their tongue, which means "grand mistresses," to be careful about what we were doing, for we were few in number and they many, for they would kill us. They counseled us not to stop in their country, for right here they would give us everything that we might need. The Captain told them that he could not avoid at least passing by at a distance, in order to give an account to him who was sending him, who was his King and master.

After the Captain had spoken and it seemed as if the listeners were very content, that chief overlord asked who he was; and as, by way of seeing if the Captain showed any discrepancy in his words, he [also] asked to be better informed about what was being told to him, the latter told him in reply the same things that he had [just] explained to him. And he told him more; namely, that we were children of the sun and that the object of our journey was to go down that river, as he had already told him. At this the Indians marveled greatly and manifested great joy, taking us to be saints or celestial beings, because they worship the sun and hold it to be their god, whom they themselves call Chise.

They then told the Captain that they were his [the Captain's] servants and that they wished to serve him, and [told him] to look into the matter of just what he and his companions had need of, for he [the overlord] would give it to him very willingly. The Captain thanked him well and then ordered many things to be given [to him] and to the other important personages, and in consequence thereof they were so pleased that henceforth not a single thing did the Captain ask for that they did not at once give to him.

They all stood up and told the Captain to take up lodgings in the village, for they would leave it free for them, and [then announced] that they wished to go to their homes and that each day they would come to bring us food. The Captain directed them to have all the overlords come to visit him, because he wished to give them something out of what he had [brought along with him].

The overlord said that the next day they would come, and so they did all come with a very great supply of food, and were all well received and treated by the Captain. To all of them together he repeated what he had first told the principal overlord.

He took possession of them all in the name of His Majesty. There were twenty-six overlords. As a token of possession he ordered a very tall cross to be set up, in which the Indians took delight. Thenceforth the Indians came every day to bring us food, and to speak with the Captain, for in this they took great delight.

When the Captain perceived the excellent conveniences and resources of the country and the favorable attitude of the Indians, he commanded all his comrades to come together and told them that since there was a good supply of materials here as well as good will on the part of the Indians, it would be well to build a brigantine. So the work got under way. . . .

Such great haste was applied to the building of the brigantine that in thirty-five days it was constructed and launched, calked with cotton and tarred with pitch, all of which the Indians brought because the Captain asked them for these things. Great was the joy of our companions over having accomplished that thing which they so much desired to do.

There were so many mosquitoes in this village that we were unable to aid one another either by day or by night, being thus at a loss as to what to do for one another, [yet we managed to get along], because with the good lodgings and the desire we had of seeing the end of our expedition we did not [fully] realize our hardships.

In the meantime, while we were engaged in this task there came to see the Captain four Indians, who approached us. They were of such a stature that each one was taller by a span than the tallest Christian. They were quite white and had very fine hair which reached down to their waists, [and they came] all decked out in gold and [splendid] attire. They brought much food; and they approached with such humbleness that we were all amazed at their manners and good breeding.

They took out a great quantity of food and placed it before the Captain and told him how they were vassals of a very great overlord, and that it was by his command that they came to see who we were or what we wanted or where we were going. The Captain received them very nicely. Before conversing with them, he commanded that they be given many trinkets, which they esteemed highly, and they were greatly pleased.

The Captain told them all that he had told the overlord Aparia, whereat the Indians were not a little astonished, and the Indians said to the Captain that they wished to go and make a report to their overlord [and begged the Captain] to give them permission to depart. The Captain gave it to them, and [told them] to depart with his best wishes, and gave them many things for them to present to their principal overlord, and [asked them] to tell him that the Captain earnestly requested him to come to pay him a visit, because he would get a great deal of pleasure out of meeting him. They said that they would do so.

They left, and nevermore did we learn anything as to where they were from or from what country they had come. . . .

The small boat was also put in condition, because it had begun to rot. So, everything being now well repaired and put in shape, the Captain ordered that all be ready and make up their ship stores, because with the help of Our Lord he wished to depart the following Monday. . . .

When twelve days of the month of May had gone by, we arrived in the provinces belonging to Machiparo, who is a very great overlord and one having many people under him, and is a neighbor of another overlord just as great, named Omaga. They are friends who join together to make war on other overlords who are inland, for they [the latter] come each day to drive them from their homes.

This Machiparo has his headquarters near the river upon a small hill, and holds sway over many settlements and very large ones, which together contribute for fighting purposes 50,000 men of the age of from thirty years up to seventy, because the young men do not go to war. In all the fights that we had with them we did not see any but it was the old men, and these [were] quite expert; and they have thin mustaches but no beards.

Before we had come within 2 leagues of this village, we saw

the villages glimmering white. We had not proceeded far when we saw coming up the river a great many canoes, all equipped for fighting, gaily colored, and [the men] with their shields on, which are made out of the shell-like skins of lizards and the hides of manatees and of tapirs, as tall as a man, for they cover them entirely. They were coming on with a great yell, playing on many drums and wooden trumpets, threatening us as if they were going to devour us.

Immediately the Captain gave orders to the effect that the two brigantines should join together so that the one might aid the other, and that all should take their weapons and look to what they had before them and take heed of the necessity on their part of defending their persons and fighting with the determination to come through to a haven of safety, and that all should commend themselves to God, for He would help us in that serious plight in which we were.

In the meantime the Indians kept coming closer, with their squadrons formed to catch us in the center. Thus they were coming on in such orderly fashion and with so much arrogance that it seemed as if they already had us in their hands. Our companions were all [filled] with so much courage that it seemed to them that four Indians to each one of them were not enough. So the Indians drew near to the point where they began to attack us. Immediately the Captain gave the command to make ready the arquebuses and crossbows.

Here there happened to us a misfortune by no means slight when one considers the situation in which we were at the time, which was that the arquebusiers found their powder damp, in consequence whereof they turned out to be of no use, and it was necessary for the crossbows to make up for the deficiency of the arquebuses. So our crossbowmen began to inflict some damage on the enemy, as they were close up and we [were] fear-inspiring.

When it was seen [by] the Indians that so much damage was being done to them, they began to hold back, [yet] not showing any sign of cowardice; rather it seemed as if their courage were increasing. There kept coming to them many reinforcements, and every time that some came they set about to attack us so boldly that it seemed as if they wanted to seize hold of the brigantines with their hands. In this manner we kept on fighting until we came to the village, where there were a great number of men stationed on the high banks to defend their homes. Here we engaged in a perilous battle, because there were many Indians on the water and on land and from all sides they gave us a hard fight.

So, of necessity, although seemingly at the risk of the lives of all of us, we attacked and captured the first spot [we could] where the Indians did not cease to leap out on land at our companions, because they continued to defend it [the land] courageously. Had it not been for the crossbows, which effected some remarkable shots here, the landing would not have been won.

With this help already mentioned, the brigantines were beached, and one half of our companions jumped into the water and fell upon the Indians in such a manner that they made them flee. The other half stayed on the brigantines defending them from the other warriors who were out on the water, for they did not cease, even though the land was won, to fight on, and although damage was being done to them by the crossbows, they nevertheless did not give up [their attempt] to carry out their evil design.

The beginning of the settlement being won, the Captain ordered the Lieutenant with 25 men to run through the settlement and drive the Indians out of it, and look to see if there was any food [there], because he intended to rest in the said village five or six days in order to let us recover from the hardships which we had endured. So the Lieutenant went and made a foray for a distance of half a league out through the village. This [he did] not without difficulty, for although the Indians were in retreat, they kept up a defensive fight, like men whom it vexed to abandon their homes.

As the Indians, when they do not meet with success in their intentions at the beginning, always run away until they feel the second impulse to return to a normal state of mind, they were, as I say, still fleeing. When the aforesaid Lieutenant had perceived the great extent of the settlement and of its population, he decided not to go on farther but to turn back and tell the Captain what the situation was. Thus he did turn back before the Indians could do him any damage.

Having got back to the beginning of the settlement, he found that the Captain was lodged in the houses and that the Indians were still attacking him from the river. He [the Lieutenant] told him exactly how things were and [informed him] that there was a great quantity of food, such as turtles in pens and pools of water, and a great deal of meat and fish and biscuit, and all this in such abundance that there was enough to feed an expeditionary force of 1000 men for one year.

The Captain, having observed what a good harbor it was, decided to gather food together in order to recuperate, as I have said, and for this purpose he sent for Cristóbal Maldonado and told him to take a dozen companions and go and seize all the food that he could. So he went, and when he arrived there he found that the Indians were going about the village carrying off the food that they had.

The said Cristóbal Maldonado toiled hard to collect the food. When he had gathered together more than a thousand turtles, the Indians returned, and this second time there came a great number of men, and very determined [they were] to kill Maldonado and his men and push on to strike at the place where we were with the Captain.

When the said Cristóbal Maldonado saw the Indians coming back, he rallied his companions and attacked the enemy, and here they [Maldonado's party] were held in check for a long time, because there were more than 2000 Indians. Of the companions who were with Cristóbal Maldonado there were only 10, and they had much to do to defend themselves. In the end such superior skill was displayed that the Indians were routed. Maldonado's men again started to collect the food. Two companions came out of this second fight wounded.

As the country was very thickly settled and the Indians were constantly re-forming and replenishing their ranks, they again came back at the said Cristóbal Maldonado, so resolutely that [it was evident that] they sought (and actually started) to seize them all with their hands. In this assault they wounded 6 companions very badly, some being pierced through the arms and others through the legs. They wounded the said Cristóbal

Maldonado to the extent of piercing one of his arms and giving him a blow in the face with a stick.

Here the companions found themselves in a very serious plight and need of help, for as they were wounded and very tired . . . [torn] they could not go backward nor forward. So they all considered themselves as good as dead and kept saying that they ought to return to where their Captain was.

The said Cristóbal Maldonado told them not to think of such a thing, because he for one had no intention of returning to where his Captain was, whereby the Indians would carry off the victory. So he rallied around him those of the companions who were in a condition to fight, and put himself on the defensive, and fought so courageously that he was the means of preventing the Indians from killing all of our companions.

[Here a long account of how the battle continued with varying fortunes is omitted. Eighteen Spaniards were wounded, of whom one soon died.]

[When the battle was over], after the men had been called in, the Captain harangued them, recalling to them the hardships already endured and bolstering them up for those to come, instructing them to refrain from provoking the attacks of the Indians, because of the dangers that might arise therefrom. He determined still to continue on down the river, and he began to load food on board.

As soon as it was on board the Captain commanded that the wounded be placed on board. Those who were unable to go on their own feet he ordered to be wrapped in blankets and be carried aboard on the backs of other men, as if these latter were carrying loads of maize, so that they might not embark limping and so that the Indians on perceiving this might not regain so much courage that they would not let us embark.

After this had been done, the brigantines being ready and unmoored and the oars in hand, the Captain with the companions in good order went down [to the river], and they embarked, and he put off, and was not a stone's throw away when there came more than 400 Indians on the water and along the land.

As those on the land could not get at us, they served no purpose but to call and shout; and those on the water attacked again and again, like men who had been wronged, with great fury.

But our companions with their crossbows [and] arquebuses defended the brigantines so well that they turned away those wicked people.

This was around sundown, and in this manner, attacking us every little while, [they kept] following us all the night. For not one moment did they allow us a respite, because they had us headed off. In this way we kept on until it was day, when we saw ourselves in the midst of numerous and very large settlements, whence fresh Indians were constantly coming out, while those who were fatigued dropped out.

About midday, when our companions were no longer able to row, we were all thoroughly exhausted from the cruel night and from the fighting which the Indians had forced upon us. The Captain, in order that the men might get a little rest and eat something, gave orders that we put in on an uninhabited island which was in the middle of the river. Just as they began to cook something to eat there came along a great number of canoes. They attacked us three times, so that they put us in great distress.

It having become evident to the Indians that from the water they could not put us to rout, they decided to attack us by land and by water, because, as there were many Indians, there were enough of them for anything. The Captain, seeing what the Indians were making ready to do, decided not to wait for them on land, and hence embarked again and pulled out into the river, because there he thought he could better fight back.

Thus we began to move on, with the Indians still not ceasing to follow us and force upon us many combats, because from these settlements there had gathered together many Indians and on the land the men who appeared were beyond count. There went about among these men and the war canoes four or five sorcerers, all daubed with whitewash and with their mouths full of ashes, which they blew into the air, having in their hands a pair of aspergills, with which as they moved along they kept throwing water about the river as a form of enchantment.

[Here follow several pages about a running fight as the Spaniards drifted and rowed downstream. Finally they captured a village.]

So we remained resting, regaling ourselves with good lodgings, eating all we wanted, and we stayed three days in this village. There were many roads here that entered into the interior of the land, very fine highways, for which reason the Captain was wary and commanded us to get ready, because he did not wish to stay there any longer, for it might come about that from our staying there some harm would result.

This idea having been voiced by the Captain, all began to get ready to depart when they should be ordered to do so.

We had gone, from the time we left Aparia to this said village, 340 leagues, of which 200 were without any settlements.

We found in this village a very great quantity of very good biscuit which the Indians make out of maize and yucca, and much fruit of all kinds.

To return to the story, I [next] state that on Sunday after the Ascension of Our Lord we set out from this village and began to move on. We had not gone more than 2 leagues when we saw emptying into the river another very powerful and wider river on the right. So wide is it that at the place where it emptied in it formed three islands, in view of which we gave it the name of Trinity River. At this junction there were numerous and very large settlements and very pretty country and very fruitful land. All this now lay in the dominion and land of Omagua.

Because the villages were so numerous and so large and because there were so many inhabitants, the Captain did not wish to make port. So all that day we passed through settled country with occasional fighting. On the water they attacked us so pitilessly that they made us go down mid-river. Many times the Indians started to converse with us, and as we did not understand them, we did not know what they were saying to us.

At the hour of vespers we came to a village that was on a high bank. As it appeared small to us, the Captain ordered us to capture it, and also because it looked so nice that it seemed as if it might be a recreation spot of some overlord of the inland. So we directed our course with a view to capturing it. The Indians put up a defense for more than an hour, but in the end they were beaten and we were masters of the village, where we found very great quantities of food, of which we laid in a supply.

In this village there was a villa in which there was a great deal of porcelain ware of various makes, both jars and pitchers, very large, with a capacity of more than 25 arrobas, and other small pieces, such as plates and bowls and candelabra of this porcelain of the best that has ever been seen in the world, for that of Malaga is not its equal, because it [this porcelain which we found] is all glazed and embellished with all colors, and so bright that they astonish. More than this, the drawings and paintings which they make on them are so accurately worked out that [one wonders how] with [only] natural skill they manufacture and decorate all these things [making them look just] like Roman [articles].

Here the Indians told us that as much as there was made out of clay in this house, so much there was back in the country in gold and silver, and [they said] that they would take us there, for it was near. . . .

From this village there went out many roads, fine highways to the inland country. The Captain wished to find out where they led to. For this purpose he took with him Cristóbal Maldonado and the Lieutenant and some other companions, and started to follow the roads. He had not gone half a league when the roads became more like royal highways, and wider.

When the Captain perceived this, he decided to turn back, because he saw that it was not prudent to go on any farther. So he did return to where the brigantines were. When he got back the sun was now going down, and the Captain said to the companions that it would be well to depart at once from there, because it was not wise to sleep at night in a land so thickly populated. . . .

We left this village and went on journeying past a very large inhabited region. There was one day when we passed more than twenty villages, and this on the side where we were steering our course. The other side we could not see, for the reason that the river was so wide. So we traveled on for two days along the right side, and afterward we crossed over and proceeded for two days more along the left side, for during the time we could sight one [side] we could not see the other. . . .

On Saturday, the eve of Holy Trinity, the Captain gave orders to make port at a village where the Indians put themselves on the defensive. In spite of that we drove them from their homes and here we procured supplies, and there were even a few fowl to be found.

This same day, on leaving there, pursuing our voyage, we saw the mouth of another great river on the left, which emptied into the one which we were navigating [and] the water of which was as black as ink. For this reason we gave it the name of Río Negro, which river flowed so abundantly and with such violence that for more than twenty leagues it formed a streak down through the other water, the one [water] not mixing with the other. . . .

On Monday, we continued our way from there, all the time passing by very large settlements and provinces, procuring food as best we could whenever we lacked it. On this day we made port at a medium-sized village, where the inhabitants let us come right up to them. In this village there was a very large public square, and in the center of the square was a hewn tree trunk 10 feet in girth, there being represented and carved in relief a walled city with its enclosure and with a gate.

At this gate were two towers, very tall and having windows, and each tower had a door, the two facing each other, and at each door were two columns; and this entire structure that I am telling about rested upon two very fierce lions, which turned their glances backward as though suspicious of each other, holding between their forepaws and claws the entire structure, in the middle of which there was a round open space. In the center of this space there was a hole through which they offered and poured out chicha for the sun, for this is the wine which they drink, and the sun is the one whom they worship and consider as their god.

In short, the construction was a thing well worth seeing, and the Captain and all of us, marveling at such a great thing, asked an Indian who was seized here [by us] what that was, or as a reminder of what they kept that thing in the square. The Indian answered that they were subjects and tributaries of the Amazons and that the only service which they rendered them consisted in supplying them with plumes of parrots and macaws for the linings of the roofs of the buildings which constitute their places of worship, and that [all] the villages which they had were of that kind, and that they had that thing there as a reminder, and that they worshiped it as a thing which was the emblem of their mistress, who is the one who rules over all the land of the aforesaid women. . . .

Having departed from here, we passed by many more villages where the Indians stood waiting for us ready to fight, like a warlike people, with their arms and shields in their hands, crying out to us, asking why we were fleeing, for they were waiting for us there. But the Captain did not wish to attack where he saw that we could win no honor, particularly as we had a certain amount of food on hand. Whenever there was some on hand, nowhere would he risk his life and those of the companions.

That is why in some places we fought, they from the land and we from the water. Whenever the Indians were in great numbers, they formed a wall and our arquebuses and crossbows inflicted damage upon them.

On Wednesday, the day before Corpus Christi, the seventh of June, the Captain gave orders to make port at a small settlement that was on the aforesaid river. It was seized without resistance. There we found much food, particularly fish, for of this there was found such a variety and so plentifully that we could have loaded our brigantines up well. This [fish] the Indians had drying, to be transported into the interior to be sold.

All the companions, seeing that the village was a small one, begged the Captain to celebrate there, since it was the eve of such a great festival. The Captain, as a man who was familiar with the ways of the Indians, said that they must not speak of such a thing, because he had no intention of doing it, for

although the village seemed small to them, it had a large outlying district whence the inhabitants could come to give aid
and inflict injury upon us. Rather we should go on as we were
accustomed to doing and get to the wilderness to sleep.

Our companions again asked as a favor that he celebrate
there. The Captain, seeing that all were making the request,
although against his will, consented to what they requested. So
we stayed in this village resting until the hour when the sun
was going down, when the Indians came to see their houses,
because when we went ashore there were none but women,
inasmuch as the Indian men had gone off to attend to their
field occupations. So, it being the proper time, they were
now coming back.

When they found their homes in the possession of someone whom they did not know, they were greatly astonished
and began to tell us to get out of them. At the same time that
they said this they came to an understanding among themselves and got ready to attack us, and this they did. But at
the moment when they started to penetrate the camp, there
stood facing the Indians four or five companions, who fought
so well that they succeeded in bringing it about that the Indians
did not care to enter where our men were. Our men made
them take to flight, and when the Captain came out there was
nothing left to be done.

Night had now fallen, and the Captain, suspecting what
might happen, gave orders that the guards be doubled and that
all sleep with their armor on, and that was done. At midnight,
at the hour when the moon came out, the Indians came back
in great numbers upon us and fell upon our party from three
sides. When they were discovered, they had wounded the
sentinels and were in among us. As the alarm was given, the
Captain came out shouting, saying: "Shame, shame, gentlemen!
They are nobody! At them!" And so our companions rose up
and with very great fury attacked those men, so that, although
it was night, they were dispersed because they could not with-
stand our companions, and so they fled.

The Captain, thinking that they were bound to come back,
commanded that an ambuscade be laid along the way by
which they would have to come and that the others should not

sleep, and gave orders that the wounded should have their wounds dressed. It was I who dressed them, because the Captain was busy going from one place to another, attending to everything necessary for the saving of our lives, for in this he was always very zealous. If he had not been so expert in things pertaining to fighting (for it seemed as if Our Lord was guiding him in what he was to do), many times they would have killed us.

In this manner we were occupied all the night, and the day having come, the Captain commanded us to get into our boats and to go on, but [first] ordered certain persons whom we had captured there to be hanged. This [was done] in order that the Indians from here on might acquire fear of us and not attack us.

We got into our boats. When we were out on the river, there arrived at the village many Indians with the intention of falling upon us. Also by water there came many canoes; but as we were proceeding well off from shore, they no longer had any opportunity to put into effect their wicked intention.

On this day we penetrated into a forest, and rested on the following [day]. The next day we continued our voyage. We had not gone 4 leagues when we saw emptying in on the right side a very great and powerful river, indeed greater than the one which we were following. Because of its being so wide, we gave it the name of Río Grande.

We continued on, and on the left side we saw some very large settlements standing on a slope which reached down to the river. In order to get a look at them the Captain gave orders that we steer toward there, and we did. It being observed by the Indians that we were going toward that place, they decided, so it seemed, not to show themselves but to stay in hiding, thinking that we would leap out on land. For this reason they kept the roads that came down to the river cleared.

The Captain and a few companions understood the base action that they had planned, and ordered us to continue on, keeping well away from shore. The Indians, seeing that we were passing by well out from shore, rose up more than 5000 strong, armed, and they began to shout at us and challenge us and strike their weapons one against another. With this they made such a great noise that it seemed as if the river were sinking [from under us].

We moved on, and [having gone] something like half a league, we came upon another larger village, but here we steered our course well out in the river. This is a temperate land and one of very great productiveness. We did not get acquainted with their manners and customs, because they did not furnish us any opportunity for that.

Here this race of people came to an end, and we came upon another that gave us little trouble.

We continued onward in our journey, and always through settled country. One morning at eight o'clock we saw on a high spot a fine-looking settlement, which, from appearances, must have been the capital of some great overlord. In order to examine it we should have liked, although at a risk, to pull in close; but it was not possible, because it had an island in front of it. By the time we decided to try to go in there we had already left the entrance behind us upstream. For this reason we passed by in sight of it, looking at it.

In this village there were seven gibbets at certain distances apart from one another throughout the village, and on the gibbets [were] nailed many dead men's heads, because of which we gave to this province the name of Province of the Gibbets [Pictas], which extended down the river 70 leagues.

There came down to the river from this village roads made by hand. On the one side and on the other [were] planted fruit trees, wherefore it seemed probable that it was a great overlord who ruled over this land.

We proceeded onward, and the next day we came upon another village of the same sort. As we were in need of food, we were forced to attack it. The Indians hid in order to let us leap out on land. So our companions did leap out. As soon as the Indians saw that they were on land, they came out from their ambuscade with very great fury. At their head came their captain or overlord, spurring them on with a very loud yell. A crossbowman of ours took aim at this overlord and shot him and killed him. Some of the Indians, on seeing that,

decided not to wait but to flee, and others to fortify themselves in their houses. There they put themselves on the defensive and fought like wounded dogs.

The Captain, seeing that they did not want to surrender and
that they had done us injury and wounded some of our companions, gave the order to set fire to the houses where the
Indians were. Consequently they came out from them and fled
and gave us a chance to collect some food. For in this village,
praised be Our Lord, there was no lack of it. There were many
turtles of the kind already mentioned and many turkeys and
parrots and a very great abundance [of many things], for
bread and maize do not require any special mention. We departed from here and straightway went off to an island to
rest and enjoy what we had seized.

There was captured in this village an Indian girl of much
intelligence. She said that near by and back in the interior
there were many Christians like ourselves, and that they were
under the rule of an overlord who had brought them down the
river. She told us how there were two white women among
them [as wives of two of these Christians], and that others
had Indian wives, and children by them. These are the people
who got lost out of Diego de Ordaz's party, so it is thought
from the indications which were at hand regarding them, for it
was off to the north of the river.[4]

We proceeded on down our river without seizing any village,
because we had food on board, and at the end of a few days we
moved out of this province, at the extreme limit of which
stood a very large settlement through which the Indian girl
told us we had to go to get to where the Christians were. But
as we were not concerned with this matter, we decided to press
forward, for as to rescuing them from where they were, the
time for that will come. . . .

We were proceeding on our way searching for a peaceful
spot to celebrate and to gladden the feast of the blessed Saint
John the Baptist, herald of Christ, when God willed that on
rounding a bend which the river made, we should see on the
shore ahead many villages, and very large ones, which shone

---

[4] Most critics do not take this story seriously, although there was a De
Ordaz party who were shipwrecked near the mouth of the Amazon in 1531.

white. Here we came suddenly upon the excellent land and dominion of the Amazons.

These said villages had been forewarned and knew of our coming, in consequence whereof the inhabitants came out on the water to meet us, in no friendly mood. When they had come close to the Captain, he would have liked to induce them to accept peace, and so he began to speak to them and call them, but they laughed, and mocked us, and came up close to us and told us to keep on going, and that down below they were waiting for us, and that there they were to seize us all and take us to the Amazons.

The Captain, angered at the arrogance of the Indians, gave orders to shoot at them with the crossbows and arquebuses, so that they might reflect and become aware that we had where-with to assail them. In this way damage was inflicted on them and they turned about toward the village to give the news of what they had seen.

As for us, we did not fail to proceed and to draw close to the villages. Before we were within half a league of putting in, there were along the edge of the water, at intervals, many squadrons of Indians. In proportion as we kept on going ahead, they gradually came together and drew close to their living-quarters.

There was in the center of this village a very great horde of fighters, formed in a good squadron. The Captain gave the order to have the brigantines beached right there where these men were, in order to go look for food. So it came about that as we began to come in close to land, the Indians started to defend their village and to shoot arrows at us.

As the fighters were in great numbers, it seemed as if it rained arrows; but our arquebusiers and crossbowmen were not idle, because they did nothing but shoot. And although they killed many, the Indians did not become aware of this, for in spite of the damage that was being done to them they kept it up, some fighting and others dancing. Here we all came very close to perishing, because as there were so many arrows, our companions had all they could do to protect themselves from them, without being able to row, in consequence whereof they did [so much] damage to us that before we could jump out on land they had wounded five of us, of whom I was one, for they hit me in one side with an arrow, which went in as far as the hollow region. If it had not been for [the thickness of] my clothes, that would have been the end of me.

In view of the danger that we were in, the Captain began to cheer up the men at the oars and urge them to make haste to beach the brigantines. So, although with hard work, we succeeded in beaching the boats. Our companions jumped into the water, which came up to their chests.

Here was fought a very serious and hazardous battle, because the Indians were there mixed in among our Spaniards, who defended themselves so courageously that it was a marvelous thing to behold. More than an hour was taken up by this fight, for the Indians did not lose spirit—rather it seemed as if it was being doubled in them, although they saw many of their own number killed, and they passed over their bodies, and they merely kept retreating and coming back again.

I want it to be known what the reason was why these Indians defended themselves in this manner. It must be explained that they are the subjects of, and tributaries to, the Amazons, and our coming having been made known to them, they went to them to ask help, and there came as many as ten or twelve of them.

For we ourselves saw these women, who were there fighting in front of all the Indian men as women captains, and these latter fought so courageously that the Indian men did not dare to turn their backs; anyone who did turn his back they killed with clubs right there before us. This is the reason why the Indians kept up their defense for so long.

These women are very white and tall, and have hair very long, and braided and wound about the head, and they are very robust, and go about naked [but] with their privy parts covered, with their bows and arrows in their hands, doing as much fighting as ten Indian men. Indeed there was one woman among these who shot an arrow a span deep into one of the brigantines, and others less deep, so that our brigantines looked like porcupines. . . .

We had now traveled, from the spot from which we had started and at which we had left Gonzalo Pizarro, 1400 leagues, rather more than less, and we did not know how much there still remained from here to the sea. . . .

[In one of the fights, a little downstream from where they met the Amazons, Orellana lost an eye.]

[The country was now densely populated.] One village was not half a league away from another, and still less than that along that whole bank of the river on the right, which is the south bank; and I can add that inland from the river, at a distance of 2 leagues, more or less, there could be seen some very large cities that glistened in white. This the land is as good, as fertile, and as normal in appearance as our Spain, for we entered upon it on Saint John's day and already the Indians were beginning to burn over their fields.

It is a temperate land, where much wheat may be harvested and all kinds of fruit trees may be grown. Besides this, it is suitable for the breeding of all sorts of livestock, because on it there are many kinds of grass, just as in our Spain, such as wild marjoram and thistles of a colored sort and scored, and many other very good herbs. The woods of this country are groves of evergreen oaks and plantations of cork trees bearing acorns (for we ourselves saw them) and groves of hard oak. The land is high and makes rolling savannas, the grass not higher than up to the knees, and there is a great deal of game of all sorts. . . .

The twenty-fifth of June we went in among some islands which we [at first] thought uninhabited; but after we got to be in among them, so numerous were the settlements which came into sight and which we distinguished on the said islands that we were grieved. When their inhabitants saw us, there came out to meet us on the river over two hundred pirogues, [so large] that each one carries twenty or thirty Indians and some forty, and of these there were many. They were quite colorfully decorated with various emblems, and those manning them had with them many trumpets and drums, and pipes on which they play with their mouths, and rebecs, which among these people have three strings.

They came on with so much noise and shouting and in

such good order that we were astonished. They surrounded our two brigantines and attacked us like men who expected to carry us off. But it resulted in just the reverse for them, for our arquebusiers and crossbowmen made it so uncomfortable for them that, many as they were, they were glad to stand off.

On land a marvelous thing to see were the squadron formations that were in the villages, all playing on instruments and dancing about, [each] with a pair of palm leaves in his hands, manifesting very great joy upon seeing that we were passing beyond their villages.

These islands are high, although not particularly so, and have level land, apparently very fertile, and so pleasing to the sight that although we were worn-out they did not fail to gladden us. Along the shore of this island, which is the largest, we kept skirting. It must be about 6 leagues long, it being in the middle of the river; what its width is we cannot say.

And still the Indians kept following us until they drove us out of this province of San Juan, whose length, as I have said, is 150 leagues, all of which we covered while enduring much hardship from hunger, avoiding fighting, because, as it was thickly populated, there was no opportunity to go on land.

All along this island the aforesaid pirogues and canoes still continued in pursuit of us, attacking us whenever they felt like doing so. But as they were constantly tasting the fruit of our shots, they accompanied us [only] for a distance.

At the end of this island there was a district much more thickly settled, from which there came forth, as a reinforcement, many more pirogues to attack us. Here the Captain, seeing himself in such a desperate plight and desiring peace with these people, endeavoring to see if we could take some time to rest, decided to speak to the Indians and appeal to them for peace, and in order to bring them around to this [attitude of mind], he gave orders to place a certain quantity of barter goods in a gourd and to throw it into the water. The Indians picked it up, but they valued it so little that they made fun of it. But for all that they did not cease

following us until they drove us from their villages, which,
as we have said, were very numerous.

That night we managed to get to a place to sleep, now
outside of this whole settled region, in an oak grove which
was on a large flat space near the river, where we were not
without fearful apprehensions, because Indians came to spy
on us. Toward the interior there were many well-populated
districts and [there were] roads which led into it [the interior],
for which reason the Captain and all the rest of us stayed on
guard waiting for whatever might happen to us.

In this stopping-place the Captain took [aside] the Indian
who had been captured farther back, because he now understood him by means of a list of words that he had made, and
asked him of what place he was a native. The Indian answered
that he was from that village where he had been seized. The
Captain asked him what the name of the overlord of this
land was, and the Indian replied that his name was Couynco
and that he was a very great overlord; and that his rule extended to where we were, and that, as I have already said, was
150 leagues.

The Captain asked him what women those were [who] had
come to help them and fight against us. The Indian said that
they were certain women who resided in the interior of the
country, a seven-day journey from the shore.

The Captain asked him if these women were married. The
Indian said they were not. The Captain asked him about how
they lived. The Indian replied that, as he had already said,
they were off in the interior of the land and that he had
been there many times and had seen their customs and mode
of living, for as their vassal he was in the habit of going
there to carry the tribute whenever the overlord sent him.

The Captain asked if these women were numerous. The
Indian said that they were, and that he knew by name seventy
villages, and named them before those of us who were there
present, and that he had been in several of them.

The Captain asked him if these villages were built of straw.
The Indian said they were not, but out of stone and with
regular doors, and that from one village to another went roads
closed off on one side and on the other and with guards

stationed at intervals along them so that no one might enter without paying duties.

The Captain asked if these women bore children. The Indian answered that they did.

The Captain asked him how, not being married and there being no man residing among them, they became pregnant. He said that these Indian women consorted with Indian men at times. When that desire came to them, they assembled a great horde of warriors and went off to make war on a very great overlord whose residence is not far from that of these women, and by force they brought them to their own country and kept them with them for the time that suited their caprice.

After they found themselves pregnant they sent them back to their country without doing them any harm. Afterward, when the time came for them to have children, if they gave birth to male children, they killed them and sent them to their fathers; if female children, they raised them with great solemnity and instructed them in the arts of war.

He said furthermore that among all these women there was one ruling mistress who subjected and held under her hand and jurisdiction all the rest, which mistress went by the name of Conori. He said that they had a very great wealth of gold and silver and that [in the case of] all the mistresses of rank and distinction their eating utensils were nothing but gold or silver, while the other women, belonging to the plebeian class, used a service of wooden vessels, except what was brought in contact with fire, which was of clay.

He said that in the capital and principal city in which the ruling mistress resided there were five very large buildings which were places of worship and houses dedicated to the sun, which they called *caranain,* and [that] inside, from half a man's height above the ground up, these buildings were lined with heavy wooden ceilings covered with paint of various colors; and that in these buildings they had many gold and silver pieces for the service of the sun; and these women were dressed in clothing of very fine wool, because in this land there are many sheep of the same sort as those of Peru [llamas]. Their dress consisted of blankets girded about them [covering their bodies] from the breasts down, [in some cases merely] thrown over [the shoulders], and in others clasped together in front, like a cloak, by means of a pair of cords. They wore their hair reaching down to the ground at their feet, and upon their heads [were] placed crowns of gold, as wide as two fingers, and their individual colors.

He said in addition that in this land, as we understood him, there were camels that carried the inhabitants on their backs, and he said that there were other animals, which we did not succeed in understanding about, which were as big as horses and which had hair a span long, and cloven hoofs, and that people kept them tied up, and that of these there were few. He said that there were in this land two salt-water lakes, from which the women obtained salt.

He related that they had a rule to the effect that when the sun went down no male Indian was to remain in all of these cities, but that any such must depart and go to his country. He said in addition that many Indian provinces bordering on them were held in subjection by them and made to pay tribute and to serve them, while there were other [provinces] with which they carried on war, in particular with the one which we have mentioned, and that they brought the men [of this province] there to have relations with them. These were said to be of very great stature and white and numerous, and [he claimed that] all that he had told here he had seen many times as a man who went back and forth every day.

All that this Indian told us and more besides had been told to us 6 leagues from Quito, because concerning these women there were a great many reports. In order to see them many Indian men came down the river 1400 leagues. Likewise the Indians farther up had told us that anyone who should take it into his head to go down to the country of these women was destined to go a boy and return an old man.

The country, the captive Indian said, was cold and there was very little firewood there, and [it was] very rich in all kinds of foods. Also he told many other things, and [said] that every day he kept finding out more, because he was an Indian of much intelligence and very quick to comprehend; and so are all the rest [in that] land, as we have stated.

This account of the Amazons is one of the chief reasons why, uncharitably and incorrectly, the Carvajal narrative has been denominated "full of lies." These same Amazon stories are the reason, too, why the river ceased to bear any of its former names, and also the reason why it was not renamed Orellana's River, as proposed by Carvajal. People just forgot everything else about the stream in their passion to hear more about this discovery-at-last of a nation of women such as had been described in Greek and other European folklore through the ages.

The reasons for the "nonsense" about the Amazons are, it would seem, mainly three: that the Spaniards misunderstood their Indian informants; that the Indians had discovered the Spaniards loved tall tales, especially about wealth and women; and that Carvajal actually saw women fighting with their men in defense of their homes. The last of these reasons is, indeed, given in explanation by the more charitable of the early commentators, for instance, Antonio de Herrera:

"In regard to the Amazons, many have expressed the opinion that Captain Orellana ought not to have given this name to those women who fought, nor have affirmed on such slender evidence that they were Amazons; for in the Indies it was not an unusual thing that the women fought and drew their bows, as has been seen in the Windward Islands and in Cartagena and its neighborhood, where they showed themselves to be as valorous as the men."

Carvajal's narrative continues:

🖎 The next day, in the morning we departed from this stopping-place in the oak grove, not a little delighted, thinking that we were leaving all the settled country behind us and that we were going to have an opportunity to rest from our hardships, past and present. So we started off again on our customary way. But we had not gone far when on the left we saw some very large provinces and settlements. These lay in the pleasantest and brightest land that we had seen anywhere along the river, because it was high land with hills and valleys thickly populated, from which said provinces there came out toward us in midstream a very great number of pirogues to attack us and lead us into a fight.

These people are as tall as, and [even] taller than, very tall men, and they keep their hair clipped short. They all came forth stained black, for which reason we called this the Province of the Black Men [Provincia de los Negros]. They came forth very gaily decked out and attacked us many times; but they did no damage to us, while they themselves did not get away without some.

We captured none of the said villages, the Captain not giving us an opportunity to do so on account of the excessively large number of inhabitants that were there.

The Captain asked the Indian already mentioned to whom that land belonged and who held it in subjection. He said that the land and the settlements which were in sight, together with many others that we could not see, belonged to a very great overlord whose name was Arripuna, who ruled over a great expanse of country; that in a direction back up the river and across country he possessed [territory so vast as to require] eighty days of journeying [to cross it] as far as a lake which was off to the north, [the country about] which was very populous, and that this was ruled over by another overlord whose name was Tinamoston.

He said that Arripuna was a very great warrior, and that his subjects ate human flesh, which was not eaten in all the rest of the land that we had gone through up to here.

This aforesaid overlord [Arripuna] is not [the ruler] of the lake, but he is [the overlord] of a distinct territory. It is he who holds under his control and in his country the Christians whom we learned about farther back, because this said Indian had seen them. He said that the said overlord possessed and controlled a very great wealth of silver, and that they used silver in all this land, but [that] gold they were not familiar with. In truth the very land warrants one in believing all that is reported, according to the [general] aspect and appearance that it has.

We went on pursuing our course down the river, and at the end of two days we came upon a small village where the Indians offered resistance to us, but we routed them and seized the food supplies and [then] continued on, and [we captured] another [village] that was close to it, a larger one.

Here the Indians put up a resistance and fought for the space of half an hour, so well and with such bravery that before we had had a chance to leap out on land they killed on board the larger brigantine a companion whose name was Antonio de Carranza, a native of Burgos.

In this village the Indians were familiar with some kind of poisonous plant, for this became evident from the wound of the aforesaid man, because at the end of twenty-four hours he surrendered his soul to God.

To return to our story, I have to state that the village was captured. We collected all the maize that the brigantines could hold, because when we saw [the effects of] the poison, we proposed not to put foot on land in a settled district unless it was from sheer necessity. So we proceeded with more prudence than we had been exercising up to now. . . .

Here [in a village somewhat farther downstream] was noticed a thing of no little amazement and augury to those of us who heard it. At the hour of vespers there alighted upon a tree under which we were quartered a bird whose cry was all that we ever got to know about it, and this it uttered rapidly, and it said distinctly: "*Hui*" [hut, house]. This it said three times, in very rapid succession. I can also relate that this same bird, or another [like it], we heard in our midst from [the time we reached] the first village, where we made the nails. It was accurate [in giving its warning] to the extent that, noticing that we were close to an inhabited spot, at the watch of dawn it used to tell us so in this manner: "*Hui!*" This [happened] many times. This means that this bird was so reliable with its cry that we now considered the fact that there was an inhabited district near by as sure as if we had seen it. So it was that when its cry was heard our companions were cheered, and particularly if there was a shortage of food, and they made ready to go all prepared for fighting. Here this bird left us, for nevermore did we hear it. . . .

[After some further adventures with Indians, and after] Our Lord blinded them in order that they might not see us, we recognized that we were not very far from the sea, because the

flowing of the tide extended to where we were, whereat we rejoiced not a little in the realization that now we could not fail
to reach the sea.

As we started to move on, as I have said, within a short time
we discovered an arm of a river, not very wide, out of which
we saw coming forth two squadrons of pirogues with a very
great clamor and outcry. Each one of these squadrons headed
for the brigantines and began to attack us and to fight like
ravenous dogs. If it had not been for the railings that had been
built farther back, we should have come out of this skirmish
decidedly decimated; but with this protection and with the
damage that our crossbowmen and arquebusiers did to them,
we managed, with the help of Our Lord, to defend ourselves.

But after all we did not escape without damage, because
they killed another companion of ours, named Garciá de Soria,
a native of Logrono. In truth the arrow did not penetrate half
a finger, but as it had poison on it, he did not linger twenty-
four hours, and he gave up his soul to Our Lord.

We went on fighting in this manner from the time the sun
came up until it was somewhat past ten o'clock, for they did not
let us rest one moment. On the contrary, there were more and
more warriors every hour; indeed the river was all cluttered
up with pirogues, and this [was] because we were in a land
thickly inhabited and one belonging to an overlord whose
name was Nurandaluguaburabara. . . .

[The party crossed the river and followed a shore little inhabited; but it was seemingly fertile, and the Spaniards conjectured the inhabitants resided well inland.]

When we had gone on a little farther, the Captain ordered
us to go on shore to get some recreation and see the resources
of that land which was so pleasing to our sight. So we stopped
[a number of] days at this aforesaid place, whence the Captain
ordered [some men] to go and reconnoiter the country toward
the interior for a distance of 1 league in order to see and
determine what [sort of] country it was. So they went, and
they had not advanced a league when they turned back. They

told the Captain how the country kept getting better and better because it was all savannas and woodlands of the type which we have stated, and that there had been seen many traces of people who came there to hunt game, and that it was not wise to go on farther. The Captain was delighted at their having turned back.

Here we began to leave [behind us] the good country and the savannas and the high land and began to enter into low country with many islands, although not so thickly inhabited as those farther back. Here the Captain turned away from the mainland and went in among the islands, among which he gradually made his way, seizing food wherever we saw that this could be done without damage [to us].

Owing to the fact that the islands were numerous and very large, never again did we manage to reach the mainland either on the one side or on the other all the way down to the sea, during which [part of our voyage] we covered, in and out among the islands, a distance of some 200 leagues, over the full length of which, and 100 more, the tide comes up with great fury, so that in all there are 300 of tidewater and 1500 without tides. Consequently the total number of leagues that we have covered on this river, from where we started out as far as the sea, is 1800 leagues, rather more than less.

Continuing on our journey in our customary way, as we were getting to be very weak and in great need of sustenance we set out to capture a village which was situated on an estuary. . . .

[So they had another battle, or series of them. But] it pleased Our Lord Jesus Christ to help us and favor us as He had always done on this voyage, and [to watch over us as one] who had brought us here like lost people, without our knowing where we were or whither we were going or what was to become of us. . . .

Once again [some days later], while we were in the midst of this suffering, Our Lord manifested the special care which He was exercising over us sinners, for He saw fit to provide [for us] in this [time of] shortage of food, as in all other instances I have quoted. It happened as follows:

One day toward evening there was seen floating down the

river a dead tapir, the size of a mule. When the Captain saw it, he ordered certain companions to go after it for him and to take a canoe to bring it in. They did bring it, and it was divided up among all the companions in such a way that for each one there turned out to be enough to eat for five or six days, which was no small help, but on the contrary a great one, for all.

This tapir had been dead for only a short time, because it was [still] warm, and it had no wound whatsoever on it. . . .

[Both brigantines had been damaged.] The repairing of the [small] brigantine and [the making of] the nails being completed, in order to repair the large one, we departed from this spot and kept pushing ahead and looking for [proper] facilities or a beach to haul it out of the water and repair it as it needed to be.

On Holy Saviour's Day, which is the Transfiguration of Our Redeemer Jesus Christ, we found the said beach that we were looking for, where both brigantines were entirely repaired, and rigging for them was made out of vines, as well as the cordage for the sea [voyage], and sails out of the blankets in which we had been sleeping. Their masts were set up.

The said work took fourteen days of continuous and regular penance, due to our great hunger and to the little food that was to be had, for we did not eat anything but what could be picked up on the strand at the water's edge, which was a few small snails and a few crabs of a reddish color of the size of frogs. These one half of the companions went to catch while the other half remained working.

In this manner and amidst hardships of this sort we finished the aforesaid task, which was no small joy for our companions, who had had so difficult a task put upon them.

We departed from this stopping-place on the eighth of the month of August, fitted out none too well [but] in proportion to the limited means at our disposal, because we lacked many things that we really needed. But as we were in a spot where we could not secure them, we put up with our hardships as best we could.

From here on we proceeded under sail, watching the tide, tacking from one side to the other, for there was a very considerable tide when one took into consideration the fact that it was at a place where the river was wide, although we were passing among islands. To be sure, we were in no small danger whenever we expected the tide; but as we had no anchors, we would fasten to stones.

We kept steering our course through places where the water was shallow enough to allow us to make use of our anchors, and we held on so poorly that it happened to us very frequently to drag our [stone] anchors along the bottom and go back upstream in one hour a greater distance than we had covered during the whole day. Our Lord saw fit, not looking upon our sins, to bring us out of these dangers and to do us so many favors that He did not permit us to die of hunger or suffer shipwreck, which we were very close to many times, finding ourselves aground, we being now all out in the water, asking God for His mercy. And when one considers the [number of] times that bottom was struck and knocks were received, it may well be believed that God with His absolute power chose to save us so that we might mend our ways, or for some other mysterious purpose that His Divine Majesty [held] in store, which we mortals, consequently, did not grasp.

We went on in our journey, continually passing by settled country, where we secured a certain amount of food, although only a small amount, because the Indians had carried it off, but we found a few roots which they call *inanes* [yams], [and so we remained alive], for if we had not found these, we should all have perished from hunger. Thus we came out of there very short of supplies. In all these villages the Indians met us without weapons, because they are a very docile people, and they gave us to understand by signs that they had seen Christians [before]. These Indians are at the mouth of the river through which we came out, where we took on water, each one a jarful, and some half an almud of roasted maize and others less, and others [supplied themselves] with roots.

In this manner we got ready to navigate by sea wherever fortune might guide us and cast us, because we had no pilot, nor compass, nor navigator's chart of any sort, and we did not even know in what direction or toward what point we ought to head. For all these things Our Master and Redeemer

Jesus Christ made up, to Whom we looked as to our true pilot and guide, trusting in His Most Holy Majesty and He would place us on the right way and bring us to a land of Christians.

All the tribes that there are along this river down which we have passed, as we have said, are people of great intelligence and [are] skillful men, according to what we saw and to what they appeared to be from all the tasks which they perform, not only in carving but also in drawing and in painting in all colors, very bright, such that it is a marvelous thing to see.

We passed out of the mouth of this river from between two islands, the distance from the one to the other being 4 leagues measured across the stream, and the whole [width], as we saw farther back, from point to point must be over 50 leagues. It sends out into the sea fresh water for more than 25 leagues; it rises and falls 6 or 7 fathoms.

We passed out, as I have said, on the twenty-sixth of the month of August, on Saint Louis' day. We [always had such good weather that] never in our course down the river or on the sea did we have squalls, and that was no small miracle which Our Lord worked for us. We began to proceed on our way with both brigantines at times in sight of land and then again [so far out] that we could see it, but not so [plainly] that we could determine where [we were].

On the very day of the Beheading of Saint John, at night, one brigantine got separated from the other, so that never again did we succeed in sighting each other, wherefore we concluded that those on the other brigantine had got lost. At the end of nine days that we had been sailing along, our sins drove us into the Gulf of Paria, we believing that that was our route. When we found ourselves within it we tried to go out to sea again. Getting out was so difficult that it took us seven days to do so, during all of which [time] our companions never dropped the oars from their hands. During all these seven days we ate nothing but some fruit resembling plums, which are called *hogos*. Thus it was that with great toil we got out of the Mouths of the Dragon (for so this may [well] be called for us), because we came very close to staying inside there [forever].

We got out of this prison. We proceeded onward for two days along the coast, at the end of which [time], without knowing where we were nor whither we were going nor what was to become of us, we made port on the island of Cubagua and in the city of Nueva Cádiz, where we found our company and the small brigantine, which had arrived two days before, because they arrived on the ninth of September and we arrived on the eleventh of the month with the large brigantine, on board which was our Captain. So great was the joy which we felt, the ones at the sight of the others, that I shall not be able to express it, because they considered us to be lost and we [so considered] them.

Of one thing I am persuaded and assured: that both to them and to us God granted great favors, and very special ones, in having us under His care at this time of year, for at any other the fallen trees that float along this coast would not have permitted us to navigate, because it is the most dangerous coast that has ever been seen.

We were as well received by the citizens of this city as if we had been their sons, because they sheltered us and gave us all that we were in need of.

From this island the Captain decided to go and give an account to His Majesty of this new and great discovery and of this river, which we hold to be the Marañon, because the distance from the mouth as far as the island of Cubagua is 450 leagues by latitude, for so we figured it out after we arrived. Although there are along the entire coast many rivers, they are [relatively] small ones.

I, Brother Gaspar de Carvajal, the least of the friars of the order of our brother and friar, Father Saint Dominic, have chosen to take upon myself this little task and [recount] the progress and outcome of our journey and navigation, not only in order to tell about it and make known the truth in the whole matter, but also in order to remove the temptation from many persons who may wish to relate this peregrination of ours or [publish] just the opposite of what we have experienced and seen.

What I have written and related is the truth throughout.

Because profuseness engenders distaste, so I have related
sketchily and summarily all that has happened to Captain Francisco de Orellana and to the hidalgos of his company and to us
companions of his who went off with him [after separating] from
the expeditionary corps of Gonzalo Pizarro, brother of Don
Francisco Pizarro, the Marquis, and Governor of Peru. God
be praised. Amen. ✠

Chapter 11

The First Crossing of North America

THE FIRST CROSSING OF
NORTH AMERICA

CHAPTER 11

NORTH AMERICA where it is broad, as distinguished from the narrow parts between the Gulf of Mexico and the Pacific, was first crossed by the Scotsman Alexander Mackenzie. This crossing was well north of the United States in what is now Canada.

Mackenzie was born at Inverness, Scotland, probably in 1755. He seems to have entered North America through the port of New York. He lived for some time near Johnstown in that state, and was sent to Montreal for education and to get him away from the rebellion then brewing, which turned into a revolution.

In 1779 Mackenzie was in a Toronto countinghouse. By 1783 he was in the fur business connected with the North West Company, incipient but rapidly developing competitors of the monopolistic Hudson's Bay Company, which was at that time practically the government of much of what is now Canada, their power extending down into the present United States, as in the Red River Valley of Minnesota-Dakota and on the Pacific coast as far south as San Francisco.

Competition with the "Great Company," which had had a legal monopoly of the fur trade for more than a century—ever since its organization in 1670—was a strenuous and threatened to become a bloody business. Indeed, it became bloody within Mackenzie's time, for he lived till 1820, and there started in 1814 the Pemmican War, a sanguinary struggle thought of as being for the control of pemmican, but which was more broadly the culminating phase of that business competition which Mackenzie helped to inaugurate.

The North West Company, and Mackenzie with it, were led

into the field of geographic exploration by the necessities of the case, the handicap they were under because the Great Company had both a legal advantage and a shorter and cheaper route from Europe to the fur countries—through Hudson Bay—whereas the Nor'westers were compelled to use the more roundabout and longer route through the St. Lawrence Gulf and River.

To counterbalance these advantages of the Great Company, the Nor'westers had to find better inland routes than were then known, they had to work out better methods of transport, and they had to develop a superior provisioning. For they saw that one of the weaknesses of the Great Company was that they clung to the use of a typically British diet, which was costly, heavy, bulky, and not particularly conducive to such robust health as was necessary in poling boats up rivers, carrying burdens over portages, and in general for the covering of great distances at the best speed and with the maximum pay loads.

In all three departments of this competition Mackenzie was among the leaders. He does not seem to have contributed markedly to the improvement of overland back-packing or of canoe technique; but his success as an explorer helped to confirm the Nor'westers in the use of pemmican to take the place of the heavier, bulkier porridge, bread, and salted meats. And he found for his partners superior trading routes that led from the already known middle of the continent both to the Arctic Sea in the north and to the Pacific Ocean in the west.

In order to understand the facility with which Mackenzie, and the rest of the commercial explorers of the North West Company, such as David Thompson, made their journeys of thousands of miles through country that was unknown till then to Europeans, we need to consider two main things: the attitude of the fur traders toward the Indians, and their manner of provisioning themselves.

"The only good Indian is a dead Indian" is the slogan of the immigrant farmer who wants to dispossess a hunting people in order that he may raise wheat, corn, and cotton. It was therefore almost exclusively a United States slogan; Canada did not act upon it except to a degree along the St. Lawrence

and around Lakes Huron and Erie, and also very slightly in
the wheatlands of Manitoba. For the pioneers who opened up
for Europeans the continent farther north than the Great Lakes
were in the main fur traders, to whom the only good Indian
was a live Indian, for only live Indians could bring in furs
to trade.

Even beyond the Hudson's Bay Company, the Nor'westers
were single-minded fur traders. The former company had a
fine record in their relation to the Indian, at least better than
almost anything we can point to in the United States; still, they
were excelled by the Free Traders, as the Nor'westers were
called, together with all others who ventured to compete with
the Governor and Company of Adventurers of England Trading into Hudson's Bay.

One handicap of the Great Company was that they were
a bit racistic in such things as feeding Indian guests at tables
other than those where they themselves ate, and usually taking women on a concubinage basis, at most, where the Nor'-
westers usually married them. The Nor'westers did nothing, or
at any rate less, to hurt the pride of the Indian; they did even
more than the Great Company to make it clear that they were
friends.

Before Mackenzie's time the men of the Hudson's Bay Company had been traveling freely throughout the interior of North
America for generations, practically without risk to their lives,
because it was known to all that they wanted every Indian to
live as long as possible. The Nor'westers traveled with, if possible, even greater ease and freedom. About the only trouble
with local people which they had was when the competition
with the Hudson's Bay Company had reached that bitterness
which finally led to the Pemmican War, and then the difficulty
had been stirred up against the Nor'westers by the other company—or, as that company would say it, they were forced to
enlist the help of the Indians in an effort to protect themselves
against the unfair competition of the Nor'westers.

With the Indians disposed to be not only friendly but helpful,
the Nor'westers were able to dispense with European foods and
all forms of provisions that needed to be brought along from
eastern Canada or New England. They got along in three ways

—by their own hunting and fishing, by the purchase of fresh meat from Indians, and by the purchase of jerky and its end product, pemmican. Of these things only the pemmican needs explaining; for though once known to practically every American as the best of condensed foods, we are by now so far away from our own frontier, and its need for concentrated rations, that there are many today who have never even heard of this stand-by of the early plainsman.

Naturally it was not the established Western farmer who needed condensed foods, but rather the explorer, the pioneer, and the fur trader. The largest users were the fur people; for to them the difference between profit and loss could well hinge on that decrease in pay load which resulted from a man's eating, and therefore needing to carry on his own back or in a canoe, three pounds of food for each day instead of a pound and a half. This is no place to argue such a point, and it is established here by quoting an average finding of the historians of the frontier, the selection being from Dr. Frederick Merk, professor of American history and head of the Department of History at Harvard. He says in the Introduction to Sir George Simpson's *Fur Trade and Empire* (Harvard University Press, 1932):

"Pemmican made possible the interior communication system of the North West Company, and it was on this foundation also that [Sir George] Simpson [later] built the remarkable transportation system of the Hudson's Bay Company."

Originally pemmican was in the main a summer ration; for the journeys of the Indians who invented it, and of the overland travelers who borrowed it, were chiefly in summer. Surely more than 95 per cent of the pemmican use known to us from the records, perhaps 99 per cent, was in temperatures that ranged from the moderate warmth of early spring and late autumn to the intense heat of midsummer when the thermometer (for instance in North Dakota, the very center of the pemmican industry of the early nineteenth century) went as high on occasions as 120° in the shade.

As already implied, the need for condensed foods disappeared when the farmer took the place of the trader on the Plains, and the use of pemmican was naturally transferred to sportsmen, mountaineers, and explorers—chiefly polar explorers, for the rest of the earth was pretty well known by the late nineteenth century. So if we want a recent authority on the chief merits of pemmican—compactness, lightness, wholesomeness, sustaining power, and palatability in the long run—we must almost of necessity go to a polar explorer. The authority chosen here is Admiral Robert E. Peary, for he is better known than most of those who have written on pemmican within the last few decades. His statement is so brief and unequivocal that one cannot think of a better explanation than he implies for the ease with which Mackenzie and the overland men of his time were able to travel, the speed and simplicity of their journeys.

Peary used pemmican as chief travel ration on all his journeys from 1886 to his attainment of the North Pole in 1909. Some of these journeys were even longer and harder than the striking march of nearly 1000 miles in sixty-three days to the pole and back, when the party not merely walked but also had to assist the dogs, managing and pulling the sledges. Peary's companions on this his last journey were, as usual with him, young Americans of college type, sailors and hunters; racially they were whites, Eskimos, and one Negro, the party thus differing in composition from those of the fur traders of Mackenzie's day, who were Yankees of the early pioneer type, French Canadians, Scotsmen, Plains Indians, and Forest Indians.

Note first that Peary on his journeys usually ate only twice a day, then read from his *Secrets of Polar Travel* (Century, 1917):

"Of all foods that I am acquainted with, pemmican is the only one that, under appropriate conditions, a man can eat twice a day for three hundred and sixty-five days in the year and have the last mouthful taste as good as the first.

"And it is the most satisfying food I know. I recall innumerable marches in bitter temperatures when men and dogs had been working to the limit and I reached the place for camp feeling as if I could eat my weight of anything. When the pemmican ration was dealt out and I saw my little half-pound lump, about as large as the bottom third of an ordinary drinking-glass, I have often felt a sullen rage that life should contain such situations. By the time I had finished the last morsel I would not have walked round the completed igloo for anything and everything the St. Regis, the Blackstone, or the Palace Hotel could have put before me."

One reason for Peary to be so explicit and emphatic was that by the time he wrote (1917) the age of pioneering in North America had receded into the past so far that he knew most of his readers would be unfamiliar with all forms of concentrated rations, among them pemmican.

When Mackenzie wrote about his 1793 journey to the Pacific the case was different. In Britain pemmican was known by everybody from hearsay, for it was a period when travel books were eagerly read and when, although pemmican attained its greatest European fame later, the public already knew that serious overland journeys would normally depend on pemmican to cover stretches where game was scarce. Still, this American food invention was, Mackenzie evidently thought, vague enough with his readers as to its precise nature so that a description of it would be useful to them. He tells:

"The provision called pemmican, on which the Chepewyans [Chipewyans], as well as the other savages of this country, chiefly subsist in their journeys, is prepared in the following manner:

"The lean parts of the flesh of the larger animals are cut in thin slices, and are placed on a wooden grate over a slow fire, or exposed to the sun, and sometimes to the frost. These operations dry it, and in that state it is pounded between two stones. It will then keep with care for several years. . . .

"The inside fat, and that of the rump, which is much thicker in these wild than our domestic animals, is melted down and mixed, in a boiling state, with the pounded meat, in equal proportions. It is then put in baskets or bags for the convenience of carrying it. Thus it becomes a nutritious food, and is eaten without any further preparation, or the addition of spice, salt, or any vegetable or farinaceous substance."

Mackenzie adds that "a little time reconciles it to the palate." It is the normal experience that men neither like nor dislike pemmican at first, for it is nearly tasteless, after the fashion of a beefsteak or a roast, the flavor developing slowly in the mouth as one chews. However, fondness usually grew with the months, and certainly with the years, as we can infer from Peary's cited verdict. That this holds to the present may be worth showing, and Principal (President) Raymond Priestley of the University of Birmingham, England, writes, after three years of intermittent use, in his book *Antarctic Adventure* (Dutton, 1915):

"I have taken all sorts of delicacies on short trips when the food allowance is elastic, I have picked up similar delicacies at depots along the line of march, and I have even taken a small plum pudding or a piece of wedding cake for a Christmas treat, but on every such occasion I would willingly have given either of these luxuries for half its weight of the regulation pemmican.

"It can therefore be imagined how we looked forward to a resumption of pemmican after a six months' enforced abstinence."

Such, as stated by Peary and Priestley, was the food on which Mackenzie depended to take him through any sections of game scarcity on his way to the Pacific.

By Mackenzie's time the country from Hudson Bay to what now is the Province of Alberta, and between the St. Lawrence and Alberta, was sprinkled with Hudson's Bay Company trading posts, and with an increasing number of the posts of their rivals. The competition was the most aggressive on the prairies between where now are North Dakota and north-central Alberta.

In addition to developing better ways of transport and provisioning for this mid-continental region of severe business strife, the Nor'westers wanted to push into country that had not as yet been reached by the Great Company. So they asked Mackenzie, then one of their newer associates, to seek a feasible commercial route from Lake Athabaska to the Pacific, with a view of laying under tribute both the country traversed and the shores of the western sea.

At this stage it was known that a river flowed from Lake Athabaska to Slave Lake. The presumption was, it then seemed, that an augmented stream would flow thence to the Pacific. So Mackenzie in 1789 followed this river, which now bears his name, and found it to lead not to the Pacific but northwest into the Arctic Sea.

Successful in having made a great discovery, but a failure in not having reached the Pacific, Mackenzie spent the winter 1789-90 in the Athabaska district. The next three years were passed in trading, in acquiring astronomical skill for determining his geographical position, and in other preparations.

The location of the Pacific coast was known, as well as its general nature; for Captain James Cook, among others, had been there, making a good chart and publishing a lucid account of the land and the people. Mackenzie's problem was to connect the known fur country of the Athabaska and Peace valleys with these coastal discoveries, and to find a trade route so advantageous that, whether from the Pacific or from Lake Athabaska, the whole intervening country might be laid under commercial tribute by the Nor'westers.

There were political complications. The then famous fur country of Nootka Sound, in what is now British Columbia, had been visited in 1774 by both the Spanish and the British. In 1788 the British had built a post there; but this was taken from them in 1789 by the Spanish, who still held it as Mackenzie was preparing for his journey. He must not fall into their clutches, and would therefore turn back before colliding with them, or would at least plan to do so.

Mackenzie started on his journey late in the summer, because he had no intention of going that year beyond the country known to Europeans, which appears to have been about halfway up the Peace River. In that vicinity, a few miles upstream from where the Smoky joins the Peace, Mackenzie spent the winter 1792-93, at Fort Forks in log cabins built by himself and his men. This was near where now is the town of Peace River. Game was plentiful and they lived on it, chiefly buffalo, elk, and deer. There was fish, too.

Unlike the sea voyagers of the time, and indeed unlike the fur traders who lived partly on European food at or near the coast of Hudson Bay, the Mackenzie party had no illness during the winter. Just over a hundred years later, a good many overland travelers in the same country, on their way to the Klondike in the Yukon gold rush of 1897-99, sickened with scurvy and died from it—all the way down the Mackenzie, too, and into the valley of the Yukon.

The difference was, of course, that the gold-rush people depended in the main on foods they brought along. Mackenzie wintered on fresh meat, the pemmican being saved for the travel of next summer; but there are records from the fur country to show that in winters of little game, when white men and local Indians had to live on pemmican which had been stored against famine, there was also complete absence of scurvy. It seems, then, that dried meat differs from salted, and from bread and porridge, in being an antiscorbutic.

On his journey to the Arctic four years before, Mackenzie had been told by Indians of the lower Mackenzie concerning a great river to the west on which were Russian traders, thus the Yukon. When Peace River Indians now told him that by continuing west over the Rockies he would find a great river, he thought this would be the one he had heard of before, that had Russians at its mouth. He was mistaken, of course. There are two great rivers west of the Rockies that head near the Peace—the ones now called Fraser and Columbia.

On May 9, 1793, Mackenzie started to ascend the Peace River, on that section of his journey which involved country wholly new to Europeans. The account is from his *Voyage from Montreal on the River St. Laurence through the Continent of North America to the Frozen and Pacific Oceans* (London, 1801):

Mackenzie's Journey to the Pacific

🐾 [May 9, 1793] The canoe was put into the water: her dimensions were 25 feet long within, exclusive of the curves of stem and stern, 26 inches hold, and 4 feet 9 inches beam. At the same time she was so light that two men could carry her on a good road 3 or 4 miles without resting.

In this slender vessel, we shipped provisions, goods for presents, arms, ammunition, and baggage, to the weight of 3000 pounds, and an equipage of ten people; viz., Alexander Mackay, Joseph Landry, Charles Ducette, François Beaulieux, Baptiste Bisson, François Courtois, and Jacques Beauchamp, with two Indians as hunters and interpreters. One of them, when a boy, was used to be so idle that he obtained the reputable name of Cancre [Crab], which he still possesses.

With these persons I embarked at seven in the evening.

My winter interpreter, with another person, whom I left here to take care of the fort and supply the natives with ammunition during the summer, shed tears on the reflection of those dangers which we might encounter in our expedition, while my own people offered up their prayers that we might return in safety from it.

We began our voyage with a course south by west against a strong current 1¾ miles, southwest by south 1 mile, and landed before eight on an island for the night.

[May 10] The weather was clear and pleasant, though there was a keenness in the air; and at a quarter past three in the morning we continued our voyage, steering southwest ¾ mile, southwest by south 1¼ miles, south ¾ mile, southwest by south ¼ mile, southwest by west 1 mile, southwest by south 3 miles, south by west ¾ mile, and southwest 1 mile.

[This is given as a sample of how Mackenzie reports the changes of course as he works upstream along the Peace; most of the later course descriptions are omitted, only the distance made good each day being given in brackets.]

The canoe, being strained from its having been very heavily laden, became so leaky that we were obliged to land, unload, and gum it [with spruce gum]. As this circumstance took place about twelve, I had an opportunity of taking an altitude, which made our latitude 55 degrees, 58 minutes, 48 seconds.

When the canoe was repaired, we continued our course, steering southwest by west 1½ miles, when I had the misfortune to drop my pocket compass into the water; west ½ mile, west-southwest 4½ miles. Here the banks are steep and hilly, and in some parts undermined by the river.

Where the earth has given way, the face of the cliffs discovers numerous strata, consisting of reddish earth and small stones, bitumen, and a grayish earth below which, near the water edge, is a red stone. Water issues from most of the banks, and the ground on which it spreads is covered with a thin white scurf, or particles of a saline substance. There are several of these salt springs.

At half-past six in the afternoon the young men landed, when they killed an elk and wounded a buffalo. In this spot we formed our encampment for the night.

From the place which we quitted this morning, the west side of the river displayed a succession of the most beautiful scenery I had ever beheld.

The ground rises at intervals to a considerable height, and stretching inward to a considerable distance, at every interval or pause in the rise, there is a very gently ascending space or lawn, which is alternate with abrupt precipices to the summit of the whole, or at least as far as the eye could distinguish. This magnificent theater of nature has all the decorations which the trees and animals of the country can afford it. Groves of poplars in every shape vary the scene, and their intervals are enlivened with vast herds of elks and buffaloes—the former choosing the steeps and uplands and the latter preferring the plains. At this time the buffaloes were attended with their young ones, who were frisking about them, and it appeared that the elks would soon exhibit the same enlivening circumstance.

The whole country displayed an exuberant verdure. The trees that bear a blossom were advancing fast to that delightful appearance, and the velvet rind of their branches, reflecting the oblique rays of a rising or setting sun, added a splendid gaiety to the scene, which no expressions of mine are qualified to describe. The east side of the river consists of a range of high land covered with the white spruce and the soft birch, while the banks abound with the alder and the willow. The water continued to rise and, the current being proportionably strong, we made a greater use of setting poles than paddles.

[May 11] The weather was overcast. With a strong wind ahead, we embarked at four in the morning, and left all the fresh meat behind us but the portion which had been assigned to the kettle, the canoe being already too heavily laden.

[Of food, they thus had with them only pemmican or its components, dried lean meat and suet. They proceeded about 11 miles and stopped when they found "the wind so strong ahead that it occasioned the (birchbark) canoe to take in water."]

We now proceeded west-southwest, 1¼ miles, where we found a chief of the Beaver Indians on an hunting party. I remained, however, in my canoe, and though it was getting late, I did not choose to encamp with these people, lest the friends of my hunters might discourage them from proceeding on the voyage.

We therefore continued our course, but several Indians kept company with us, running along the bank and conversing with my people, who were so attentive to them that they drove the canoe on a stony flat, so that we were under the necessity of landing to repair the damages and put up for the night, though very contrary to my wishes. My hunters obtained permission to proceed with some of these people to their lodges, on the promise of being back by the break of day though I was not without some apprehension respecting them.

The chief, however, and another man, as well as several people from the lodges, joined us before we had completed the repair of the canoe. And they made out a melancholy story that they had neither ammunition nor tobacco sufficient for their necessary supply during the summer. I accordingly referred him to the fort, where plenty of those articles were left in the care of my interpreter, by whom they would be abundantly furnished, if they were active and industrious in pursuing their occupations. I did not fail, on this occasion, to magnify the advantages of the present expedition, observing at the same time that its success would depend on the fidelity and conduct of the young men who were retained by me to hunt.

The chief also proposed to borrow my canoe, in order to transport himself and family across the river. Several plausible reasons, it is true, suggested themselves for resisting his proposition; but when I stated to him that as the canoe was intended for a voyage of such consequence, no woman could be permitted to be embarked in it, he acquiesced in the refusal.

It was near twelve at night when he took his leave, after I had gratified him with a present of tobacco.

[May 12] Some of the Indians passed the night with us, and

I was informed by them that, according to our mode of proceeding, we should in ten days get as far as the Rocky Mountains. The young men now returned, to my great satisfaction,
and with the appearance of contentment, though I was not
pleased when they dressed themselves in the clothes which I
had given them before we left the fort, as it betrayed some
latent design.

At four in the morning we proceeded on our voyage [making
good 18 miles]. We landed for the night on an island, where
several of the Indians visited us, but unattended by their
women, who remained in their camp, which was at some distance from us.

The land on both sides of the river, during the two last days,
is very much elevated, but particularly in the latter part of it,
and on the western side presents in different places white,
steep, and lofty cliffs. Our view being confined by these
circumstances, we did not see so many animals as on the
tenth. Between these lofty boundaries, the river becomes narrow, and in a great measure free from islands, for we had
passed only four. The stream, indeed, was not more than from
200 to 300 yards broad, whereas before these cliffs pressed
upon it, its breadth was twice that extent and besprinkled with
islands.

We killed an elk, and fired several shots at animals from the
canoe.

The greater part of this band being Rocky Mountain Indians,
I endeavored to obtain some intelligence of our intended route,
but they all pleaded ignorance, and uniformly declared that
they knew nothing of the country beyond the first mountain.
At the same time they were of opinion that, from the strength
of the current and the rapids, we should not get there by
water, though they did not hesitate to express their surprise
at the expedition we had already made.

I inquired, with some anxiety, after an old man who had
already given me an account of the country beyond the limits
of his tribe, and was very much disappointed at being informed
that he had not been seen for upward of a moon.

This man had been at war on another large river beyond
the Rocky Mountains, and described to me a fork of it be-

tween the mountains, the southern branch of which he directed me to take. From thence, he said, there was a carrying-place of about a day's march for a young man to get to the other river.

To prove the truth of his relation, he consented that his son, who had been with him in those parts, should accompany me, and he accordingly sent him to the fort some days before my departure. But the preceding night he deserted with another young man, whose application to attend me as a hunter being refused, he persuaded the other to leave me.

I now thought it right to repeat to them what I had said to the chief of the first band respecting the advantages which would be derived from the voyage, that the young men might be encouraged to remain with me, as without them I should not have attempted to proceed.

[May 13] The first object that presented itself to me this morning was the young man whom I have already mentioned as having seduced away my intended guide. At any other time or place I should have chastised him for his past conduct, but in my situation it was necessary to pass over his offense, lest he should endeavor to exercise the same influence over those who were so essential to my service. Of the deserter he gave no satisfactory account, but continued to express his wish to attend me in his place, for which he did not possess any necessary qualifications.

The weather was cloudy, with an appearance of rain, and the Indians pressed me with great earnestness to pass the day with them, and hoped to prolong my stay among them by assuring me that the winter yet lingered in the Rocky Mountains. But my object was to lose no time, and having given the chief some tobacco for a small quantity of meat, we embarked at four, when my young men could not conceal their chagrin at parting with their friends for so long a period as the voyage threatened to occupy.

When I had assured them that in three moons we should return to them, we proceeded on our course [making good some 9 miles]. Here the land lowered on both sides, with an increase of wood, and displayed great numbers of animals. The river also widened from 300 to 500 yards, and was full of islands and flats. Having continued our course 3 miles, we made for the shore at seven, to pass the night.

At the place from whence we proceeded this morning, a river falls in from the north. There are also several islands, and many rivulets on either side, which are too small to deserve particular notice.

We perceived along the river tracks of large bears, some of which were 9 inches wide, and of a proportionate length. We saw one of their dens, or winter quarters, called *watee*, in an island, which was 10 feet deep, 5 feet high, and 6 feet wide, but we had not yet seen one of those animals.

The Indians entertain great apprehension of this kind of bear, which is called the grizzly bear, and they never venture to attack it but in a party of at least three or four.

Our hunters, though they had been much higher than this part of our voyage by land, knew nothing of the river. One of them mentioned that having been engaged in a war expedition, his party on their return made their canoes at some distance below us. The wind was north throughout the day, and at times blew with considerable violence.

The apprehensions which I had felt respecting the young men were not altogether groundless, for the eldest of them told me that his uncle had last night addressed him in the following manner:

"My nephew, your departure makes my heart painful. The white people may be said to rob us of you. They are about to conduct you into the midst of our enemies, and you may never more return to us. Were you not with the Chief [the ordinary word for a white fur trader], I know not what I should do, but he requires your attendance, and you must follow him."

[May 14] The weather was clear, and the air sharp, when we embarked at half-past four. Our course was south by west 1½ miles, southwest by south ¼ mile, southwest. We here found it necessary to unload and gum the canoe, in which operation we lost an hour, when we proceeded on the last course 1½ miles. I now took a meridian altitude, which gave 56 degrees, 11 minutes, 19 seconds north latitude, and continued to proceed west-southwest 2½ miles. Here the Bear River, which is of a large appearance, falls in from the east; west 3½ miles, south-southwest 1½ miles, and southwest 4½ miles, when we encamped upon an island about seven in the evening.

During the early part of the day, the current was not so strong as we had generally found it, but toward the evening it became very rapid, and was broken by numerous islands. We were gratified, as usual, with the sight of animals. The land on the west side is very irregular, but has the appearance of being a good beaver country; indeed we saw some of those animals in the river. Wood is in great plenty, and several rivulets added their streams to the main river.

A goose was the only article of provision which we procured today. Smoke was seen, but at a great distance before us.

[May 15] The rain prevented us from continuing our route till past six in the morning, when [we started, making good some 14 miles].

In the preceding night the water rose upward of 2 inches, and had risen in this proportion since our departure. The wind, which was west-southwest, blew very hard throughout the day, and with the strength of the current, greatly impeded our progress. The river, in this part of it, is full of islands, and the land on the south or left side is thick with wood. Several rivulets also fall in from that quarter. At the entrance of the last river which we passed, there was a quantity of wood, which had been cut down by axes, and some by the beaver. This fall, however, was not made, in the opinion of my people, by any of the Indians with whom we were acquainted.

The land to the right is of a very irregular elevation and appearance, composed in some places of clay and rocky cliffs, and others exhibiting stratas of red, green, and yellow colors. Some parts, indeed, offer a beautiful scenery, in some degree similar to that which we passed on the second day of our voyage, and equally enlivened with the elk and the buffalo, who were feeding in great numbers, and unmolested by the hunter.

In an island which we passed, there was a large quantity of white birch, whose bark might be employed in the construction of canoes.

[May 16] The weather being clear, we re-embarked at four

in the morning, and proceeded west by north 3 miles. Here the land again appeared as if it run across our course, and a considerable river discharged itself by various streams. According to the Rocky Mountain Indian, it is called the Sinew River.

This spot would be an excellent situation for a fort or factory, as there is plenty of wood, and every reason to believe that the country abounds in beaver. As for the other animals, they are in evident abundance, as in every direction the elk and the buffalo are seen in possession of the hills and the plains. [Made good 12 miles.]

Mr. Mackay, and one of the young men, killed two elks, and mortally wounded a buffalo, but we only took a part of the flesh of the former.

The land above the spot where we encamped spreads into an extensive plain, and stretches on to a very high ridge, which in some parts presents a face of rock, but is principally covered with verdure, and varied with the poplar and white birch tree.

The country is so crowded with animals as to have the appearance in some places of a stall yard, from the state of the ground and the quantity of dung which is scattered over it. The soil is black and light. We this day saw two grizzly and hideous bears.

[May 17] It froze during the night, and the air was sharp in the morning, when we continued our course [making good 11 miles during the forenoon]. At two in the afternoon the Rocky Mountains appeared in light, with their summits covered with snow, bearing southwest by south. They formed a very agreeable object to every person in the canoe, as we attained the view of them much sooner than we expected.

A small river was seen on our right, and we continued our progress southwest by south 6 miles, when we landed at seven, which was our usual hour of encampment.

Mr. Mackay, who was walking along the side of the river, discharged his piece at buffalo, when it burst near the muzzle, but without any mischievous consequences.

On the high grounds, which were on the opposite side of the river, we saw a buffalo tearing up and down with great fury, but could not discern the cause of his impetuous motions. My hunters conjectured that he had been wounded with an arrow by some of the natives.

We ascended several rapids in the course of the day, and saw one bear.

[May 18] It again froze very hard during the night, and at four in the morning we continued our voyage, but we had not proceeded 200 yards before an accident happened to the canoe, which did not, however, employ more than three-quarters of an hour to complete the repair.

[After paddling about 10 miles we came to] where there is a small run of water from the right 3½ miles, when the canoe struck on the stump of a tree, and unfortunately where the banks were so steep that there was no place to unload except a small spot, on which we contrived to dispose the lading in the bow, which lightened the canoe so as to raise the broken part of it above the surface of the water; by which contrivance we reached a convenient situation.

It required, however, two hours to complete the repair, when the weather became dark and cloudy, with thunder, lightning, and rain. We however continued the last course ½ mile, and at six in the evening we were compelled by the rain to land for the night.

About noon we had landed on an island where there were eight lodges of last year. The natives had prepared bark here for five canoes, and there is a road along the hills where they had passed. Branches were cut and broken along it, and they had also stripped off the bark of the trees to get the interior rind, which forms a part of their food.

The current was very strong through the whole of the day, and the coming up along some of the banks was rendered very dangerous from the continual falling of large stones from the upper parts of them. This place appears to be a particular pass for animals across the river, as there are paths to it on both sides, every 10 yards.

In the course of the day we saw a ground hog and two cormorants. The earth also appeared in several places to have been turned up by the bears, in search of roots.

[May 19] It rained very hard in the early part of the night, but the weather became clear toward the morning, when we embarked at our usual hour. As the current threatened to be very strong, Mr. Mackay, the two hunters, and myself went on shore, in order to lighten the canoe, and ascended the hills, which are covered with cypress and but little encumbered with underwood.

We found a beaten path, and before we had walked a mile fell in with a herd of buffaloes, with their young ones. But I would not suffer the Indians to fire on them, from an apprehension that the report of their fowling pieces would alarm the natives that might be in the neighborhood; for we were at this time so near the mountains as to justify our expectation of seeing some of them. We however sent our dog after the herd, and a calf was soon secured by him.

While the young men were skinning the animal, we heard two reports of firearms from the canoe, which we answered, as it was a signal for my return. We then heard another, and immediately hastened down the hill, with our veal, through a very close wood.

There we met one of the men, who informed us that the canoe was at a small distance below, at the foot of a very strong rapid, and that as several waterfalls appeared up the river, we should be obliged to unload and carry. I accordingly hastened to the canoe, and was greatly displeased that so much time had been lost, as I had given previous directions that the river should be followed as long as it was practicable.

The last Indians whom we saw had informed us that at the first mountain there was a considerable succession of rapids, cascades, and falls, which they never attempted to ascend, and where they always passed overland the length of a day's march. My men imagined that the carrying-place was at a small distance below us, as a path appeared to ascend a hill where there were several lodges of the last year's construction.

The account which had been given me of the rapids was perfectly correct, though by crossing to the other side, I must acknowledge with some risk in such a heavy-laden canoe, the river appeared to me to be practicable as far as we could see. The traverse, therefore, was attempted, and proved successful.

We now towed the canoe along an island, and proceeded without any considerable difficulty till we reached the extremity of it, when the line [for towing the canoe behind men walking on the bank] could be no longer employed; and in endeavoring to clear the point of the island, the canoe was driven with such violence on a stony shore as to receive considerable injury.

We now employed every exertion in our power to repair the breach that had been made, as well as to dry such articles of our loading as more immediately required it. We then transported the whole across the point, when we reloaded, and continued our course about three-quarters of a mile.

We could now proceed no further on this side of the water, and the traverse was rendered extremely dangerous, not only from the strength of the current, but by the cascades just below us, which, if we had got among them, would have involved us and the canoe in one common destruction. We had no other alternative than to return by the same course we came or to hazard the traverse, the river on this side being bounded by a range of steep, overhanging rocks, beneath which the current was driven on with resistless impetuosity from the cascades. Here are several islands of solid rock, covered with a small portion of verdure, which have been worn away by the constant force of the current, and occasionally, as I presume, of ice, at the water's edge, so as to be reduced in that part to one-fourth the extent of the upper surface—presenting, as it were, so many large tables, each of which was supported by a pedestal of a more circumscribed projection. They are very elevated for such a situation, and afford an asylum for geese, which were at this time breeding on them.

By crossing from one to the other of these islands, we came at length to the main traverse, on which we ventured, and were successful in our passage.

Mr. Mackay and the Indians, who observed our maneuvers from the top of a rock, were in continual alarm for our safety, with which their own indeed may be said to have been nearly connected. However, the dangers that we encountered were very much augmented by the heavy loading of the canoe.

When we had effected our passage, the current on the west side was almost equally violent with that from whence we had just escaped, but the craggy bank being somewhat lower, we were enabled, with a line of 60 fathoms, to tow the canoe till we came to the foot of the most rapid cascade we had hitherto seen. Here we unloaded, and carried everything over a rocky point of 120 paces.

When the canoe was reloaded, I, with those of my people who were not immediately employed, ascended the bank, which was there, and indeed as far as we could see it, composed of clay, stone, and a yellow gravel. My present situation was so elevated that the men who were coming up a strong point could not hear me, though I called to them with the utmost strength of my voice to lighten the canoe of part of its lading.

And here I could not but reflect, with infinite anxiety, on the hazard of my enterprise. One false step of those who were attached to the line, or the breaking of the line itself, would have at once consigned the canoe, and everything it contained, to instant destruction. It however ascended the rapid in perfect security. But new dangers immediately presented themselves, for stones, both small and great, were continually rolling from the bank, so as to render the situation of those who were dragging the canoe beneath it extremely perilous. Besides, they were at every step in danger, from the steepness of the ground, of falling into the water. Nor was my solicitude diminished by my being necessarily removed at times from the sight of them.

In our passage through the woods we came to an enclosure which had been formed by the natives for the purpose of setting snares for the elk, and of which we could not discover the extent.

After we had traveled for some hours through the forest, which consisted of the spruce, birch, and the largest poplars I had ever seen, we sunk down upon the river where the bank is low, and near the foot of a mountain; between which and a high ridge the river flows in a channel of about 100 yards broad, though at a small distance below it rushes on between perpendicular rocks, where it is not much more than half that breadth.

Here I remained, in great anxiety, expecting the arrival of the canoe, and after some time I sent Mr. Mackay with one of the Indians down the river in search of it, and with the other I went up it to examine what we might expect in that quarter. In about a mile and a half I came to a part where the river washes the feet of lofty precipices, and presented, in the form of rapids and cascades, a succession of difficulties to our navigation.

As the canoe did not come in sight, we returned, and from the place where I had separated with Mr. Mackay we saw the men carrying it over a small rocky point. We met them at the entrance of the narrow channel already mentioned. Their difficulties had been great indeed, and the canoe had been broken, but they had persevered with success, and having passed the carrying-place, we proceeded with the line as far as I had already been, when we crossed over and encamped on the opposite beach. But there was no wood on this side of the water, as the adjacent country had been entirely overrun by fire.

We saw several elks feeding on the edge of the opposite precipice, which was upward of 300 feet in height.

I now dispatched a man with an Indian to visit the rapids above, when the latter soon left him to pursue a beaver which was seen in the shallow water on the inside of a stony island; and though Mr. Mackay and the other Indian joined him, the animal at length escaped from their pursuit. Several others were seen in the course of the day, which I by no means expected, as the banks are almost everywhere so much elevated above the channel of the river.

Just as the obscurity of the night drew on, the man returned with an account that it would be impracticable to pass several points, as well as the superimpending promontories.

[May 20] The weather was clear with a sharp air, and we renewed our voyage at a quarter past four, on a course southwest by west ¾ mile. We now, with infinite difficulty, passed along the foot of a rock which, fortunately, was not a hard stone, so that we were enabled to cut steps in it for the distance of 20 feet; from which, at the hazard of my life, I leaped on a small rock below, where I received those who followed me on my shoulders. In this manner four of us passed, and dragged up the canoe, in which attempt we broke her.

Very luckily, a dry tree had fallen from the rock above us, without which we could not have made a fire [to melt spruce gum for repairing the canoe], as no wood was to be procured within a mile of the place.

When the canoe was repaired, we continued towing it along the rocks to the next point, when we embarked, as we could not at present make any further use of the line, but got along the rocks of a round high island of stone till we came to a small sandy bay.

As we had already damaged the canoe, and had every reason to think that she soon would risk much greater injury, it became necessary for us to supply ourselves with bark, as our provision of that material article was almost exhausted. Two men were accordingly sent to procure it, who soon returned with the necessary store.

Mr. Mackay and the Indians, who had been on shore since we broke the canoe, were prevented from coming to us by the rugged and impassable state of the ground. We therefore again resumed our course with the assistance of poles, with which we pushed onward till we came beneath a precipice, where we could not find any bottom; so that we were again obliged to have recourse to the line, the management of which was rendered not only difficult but dangerous, as the men employed in towing were under the necessity of passing on the outside of trees that grew on the edge of the precipice.

We however surmounted this difficulty, as we had done many others, and the people who had been walking overland now joined us. They also had met with their obstacles in passing the mountain.

It now became necessary for us to make a traverse where the water was so rapid that some of the people stripped themselves to their shirts that they might be the better prepared for swimming, in case any accident happened to the canoe, which they seriously apprehended. But we succeeded in our attempt without any other inconvenience except that of taking in water. We now came to a cascade, when it was thought necessary to take out part of the lading.

At noon we stopped to take an altitude, opposite to a small river that flowed in from the left. While I was thus engaged, the men went on shore to fasten the canoe, but as the current was not very strong, they had been negligent in performing this office. It proved, however, sufficiently powerful to sheer her off, and if it had not happened that one of the men, from absolute fatigue, had remained and held the end of the line, we should have been deprived of every means of prosecuting our voyage, as well as of present subsistence.

But notwithstanding the state of my mind on such an alarming circumstance, and an intervening cloud that interrupted me, the altitude which I took has been since proved to be tolerably correct, and gave 56 degrees north latitude. Our last course was south-southwest 2¼ miles.

We now continued our toilsome and perilous progress with the line west by north, and as we proceeded the rapidity of the current increased, so that in the distance of 2 miles we were obliged to unload four times, and carry everything but the canoe. Indeed, in many places it was with the utmost difficulty that we could prevent her from being dashed to pieces against the rocks by the violence of the eddies.

At five we had proceeded to where the river was one continued rapid. Here we again took everything out of the canoe, in order to tow her up with the line, though the rocks were so shelving as greatly to increase the toil and hazard of that operation. At length, however, the agitation of the water was so great that a wave striking on the bow of the canoe broke the line, and filled us with inexpressible dismay, as it appeared impossible that the vessel could escape from being dashed to pieces, and those who were in her from perishing.

Another wave, however, more propitious than the former, drove her out of the tumbling water, so that the men were enabled to bring her ashore, and though she had been carried over rocks by these swells which left them naked a moment after, the canoe had received no material injury.

The men were, however, in such a state from their late alarm that it would not only have been unavailing but imprudent to have proposed any further progress at present, particularly as the river above us as far as we could see was one white sheet of foaming water.

That the discouragements, difficulties, and dangers which

had hitherto attended the progress of our enterprise should have excited a wish in several of those who were engaged in it to discontinue the pursuit, might be naturally expected; and indeed it began to be muttered on all sides that there was no alternative but to return.

Instead of paying any attention to these murmurs, I desired those who had uttered them to exert themselves in gaining an ascent of the hill, and encamp there for the night. In the meantime I set off with one of the Indians, and though I continued my examination of the river almost as long as there was any light to assist me, I could see no end of the rapids and cascades. I was therefore perfectly satisfied that it would be impracticable to proceed any further by water.

We returned from this reconnoitering excursion very much fatigued, with our shoes worn-out and wounded feet, when I found that, by felling trees on the declivity of the first hill, my people had contrived to ascend it.

From the place where I had taken the altitude at noon to the place where we made our landing, the river is not more than 50 yards wide, and flows between stupendous rocks, from whence huge fragments sometimes tumble down, and falling from such an height, dash into small stones with sharp points, and form the beach between the rocky projections. Along the face of some of these precipices, there appears a stratum of a bituminous substance which resembles coal, though while some of the pieces of it appeared to be excellent fuel, others resisted for a considerable time the action of fire, and did not emit the least flame.

The whole of this day's course would have been altogether impracticable if the water had been higher, which must be the case at certain seasons.

We saw also several encampments of the Knisteneaux along the river, which must have been formed by them on their war excursions: a decided proof of the savage, bloodthirsty disposition of that people, as nothing less than such a spirit could impel them to encounter the difficulties of this almost inaccessible country, whose natives are equally unoffending and defenseless.

Mr. Mackay informed me that in passing over the mountains

he observed several chasms in the earth that emitted heat and smoke, which diffused a strong sulphurous stench. I should certainly have visited this phenomenon if I had been sufficiently qualified as a naturalist to have offered scientific conjectures or observations thereon.

[May 21] It rained in the morning, and did not cease till about eight, and as the men had been very fatigued and disheartened, I suffered them to continue their rest till that hour.

Such was the state of the river, as I have already observed, that no alternative was left us; nor did any means of proceeding present themselves to us but the passage of the mountain over which we were to carry the canoe as well as the baggage. As this was a very alarming enterprise, I dispatched Mr. Mackay with three men and the two Indians to proceed in a straight course from the top of the mountain, and to keep the line of the river till they should find it navigable. If it should be their opinion that there was no practicable passage in that direction, two of them were instructed to return in order to make their report, while the others were to go in search of the Indian carrying-place.

While they were engaged in this excursion, the people who remained with me were employed in gumming the canoe and making handles for the axes.

At sunset, Mr. Mackay returned with one of the men, and in about two hours was followed by the others. They had penetrated thick woods, ascended hills, and sunk into valleys till they got beyond the rapids, which according to their calculation was a distance of 3 leagues. The two parties returned by different routes, but they both agreed that with all its difficulties, and they were of a very alarming nature, the outward course was that which must be preferred.

Unpromising, however, as the account of their expedition appeared, it did not sink them into a state of discouragement; and a kettle of wild rice sweetened with sugar, which had been prepared for their return, with their usual regale of rum, soon renewed that courage which disdained all obstacles that threatened our progress, and they went to rest with a full determination to surmount them on the morrow.

I sat up, in the hope of getting an observation of Jupiter

and his first satellite, but the cloudy weather prevented my obtaining it.

[May 22] At break of day we entered on the extraordinary journey which was to occupy the remaining part of it.

The men began, without delay, to cut a road up the mountain, and as the trees were but of small growth, I ordered them to fell those which they found convenient in such a manner that they might fall parallel with the road, but at the same time not separate them entirely from the stumps, so that they might form a kind of railing on either side.

The baggage was now brought from the waterside to our encampment. This was likewise, from the steep shelving of the rocks, a very perilous undertaking, as one false step of any of the people employed in it would have been instantly followed by falling headlong into the water.

When this important object was attained, the whole of the party proceeded, with no small degree of apprehension, to fetch the canoe, which in a short time was also brought to the encampment. And as soon as we had recovered from our fatigue, we advanced with it up the mountain, having the line doubled and fastened successively, as we went on, to the stumps, while a man at the end of it hauled it round a tree, holding it on and shifting it as we proceeded. So that we may be said, with strict truth, to have warped the canoe up the mountain. Indeed by a general and most laborious exertion, we got everything to the summit by two in the afternoon.

At noon, the latitude was 56 degrees, 0 minutes, 47 seconds north. At five, I sent the men to cut the road onward, which they effected for about a mile, when they returned.

The weather was cloudy at intervals, with showers and thunder. At about ten, I observed an emersion of Jupiter's second satellite; time by the achrometer 8:32:20, by which I found the longitude to be 120 degrees, 29 minutes, 30 seconds west from Greenwich.

[May 23] The weather was clear at four this morning, when the men began to carry. I joined Mr. Mackay and the two Indians in the labor of cutting a road.

The ground continued rising gently till noon, when it began to decline; but though on such an elevated situation, we could

see but little, as mountains of a still higher elevation and covered with snow were seen far above us in every direction. In
the afternoon the ground became very uneven; hills and deep
defiles alternately presented themselves to us. Our progress,
however, exceeded my expectation, and it was not till four in
the afternoon that the carriers overtook us.

At five, in a state of fatigue that may be more readily conceived than expressed, we encamped near a rivulet or spring
that issued from beneath a large mass of ice and snow.

Our toilsome journey of this day I compute at about 3 miles,
along the first of which the land is covered with plenty of wood,
consisting of large trees encumbered with little underwood,
through which it was by no means difficult to open a road
by following a well-beaten elk path. For the 2 succeeding miles
we found the country overspread with the trunks of trees laid
low by fire some years ago, among which large copses had
sprung up of a close growth and intermixed with briers so as to
render the passage through them painful and tedious.

The soil in the woods is light and of a dusky color; that in
the burned country is a mixture of sand and clay with small
stones. The trees are spruce, red pine, cypress, poplar, white
birch, willow, alder, arrowwood, redwood, *liard*, service tree,
bois-picant, etc. I never saw any of the last kind before. It rises
to about 9 feet in height, grows in joints without branches, and
is tufted at the extremity. The stem is of an equal size from
the bottom to the top, and does not exceed an inch in diameter;
it is covered with small prickles, which caught our trousers and
working through them, sometimes found their way to the flesh.
The shrubs are the gooseberry, the currant, and several kinds
of briers.

[May 24] We continued our very laborious journey, which led
us down some steep hills and through a wood of tall pines. After
much toil and trouble in bearing the canoe through the difficult passages which we encountered, at four in the afternoon
we arrived at the river, some hundred yards above the rapids or
falls, with all our baggage.

I compute the distance of this day's progress to be about 4
miles; indeed I should have measured the whole of the way
if I had not been obliged to engage personally in the labor

of making the road. But after all, the Indian carrying-way, whatever may be its length—and I think it cannot exceed 10 miles—will always be found more safe and expeditious than the passage which our toil and perseverance formed and sur- mounted.

Those of my people who visited this place on the twenty- first were of opinion that the water had risen very much since that time. About 200 yards below us the stream rushed with an astonishing but silent velocity between perpendicular rocks which are not more than 35 yards asunder. When the water is high, it runs over those rocks in a channel three times that breadth, where it is bounded by far more elevated precipices. In the former are deep round holes, some of which are full of water while others are empty, in whose bottom are small round stones, as smooth as marbles. Some of these natural cylinders would contain 200 gallons.

At a small distance below the first of these rocks, the channel widens in a kind of zigzag progression, and it was really awful to behold with what infinite force the water drives against the rocks on one side, and with what impetuous strength it is repelled to the other. It then falls back, as it were, into a more strait but rugged passage, over which it is tossed in high, foaming, half-formed billows as far as the eye could follow it.

The young men informed me that this was the place where their relations had told me that I should meet with a fall equal to that of Niagara. To exculpate them, however, from their ap- parent misinformation, they declared that their friends were not accustomed to utter falsehoods, and that the fall had probably been destroyed by the force of the water. It is however very evident that those people had not been here, or did not adhere to the truth.

By the number of trees which appeared to have been felled with axes, we discovered that the Knisteneaux, or some tribes who are known to employ that instrument, had passed this way. We passed through a snare enclosure, but saw no animals, though the country was very much intersected by their tracks.

[May 25] It rained throughout the night, and till twelve this day, while the business of preparing great and small poles, and putting the canoe in order, etc. caused us to remain here till five in the afternoon.

I now attached a knife, with a steel, flint, beads, and other trifling articles, to a pole, which I erected and left as a token of amity to the natives. When I was making this arrangement, one of my attendants, whom I have already described under the title of the Cancre, added to my assortment a small round piece of green wood, chewed at one end in the form of a brush, which the Indians use to pick the marrow out of bones. This he informed me was an emblem of a country abounding in animals.

The water had risen during our stay here 1½ feet perpendicular height.

[After proceeding on various courses westerly about 4 miles] we encamped for the night. The Cancre killed a small elk.

[May 26] The weather was clear and sharp, and between three and four in the morning we renewed our voyage, our first course being west by south 3½ miles, when the men complained of the cold in their fingers, as they were obliged to push on the canoe with the poles. Here a small river flowed in from the north. We now continued to steer west-southwest ¼ mile, west-northwest 1½ miles, and west 2 miles, when we found ourselves on a parallel with a chain of mountains on both sides the river, running south and north.

The river, both yesterday and the early part of today, was from 400 to 800 yards yide, and full of islands, but was at this time diminished to about 200 yards broad, and free from islands, with a smooth but strong current. Our next course was southwest 2 miles, when we encountered a rapid, and saw an encampment of the Knisteneaux.

We now proceeded [by various westerly courses about 7 miles]. Here a river poured in on the left, which was the most considerable that we had seen since we had passed the mountain. At seven in the evening we landed and encamped.

Though the sun had shone upon us throughout the day, the air was so cold that the men, though actively employed, could not resist it without the aid of their blanket coats. This circumstance might in some degree be expected from the surrounding mountains, which were covered with ice and snow.

But as they are not so high as to produce the extreme cold which we suffered, it must be more particularly attributed to the high situation of the country itself rather than to the local elevation of the mountains, the greatest height of which does not exceed 1500 feet—though in general they do not rise to half that altitude. But as I had not been able to take an exact measurement, I do not presume upon the accuracy of my conjecture.

Toward the bottom of these heights, which were clear of snow, the trees were putting forth their leaves, while those in their middle region still retained all the characteristics of winter, and on their upper parts there was little or no wood.

(From this day to the fourth of June the courses of my voyage are omitted, as I lost the book that contained them. I was in the habit of sometimes indulging myself with a short doze in the canoe, and I imagine that the branches of the trees brushed my book from me when I was in such a situation, which renders the account of these few days less distinct than usual.)

[May 27] The weather was clear, and we continued our voyage at the usual hour, when we successively found several rapids and points to impede our progress. At noon our latitude was 56 degrees, 5 minutes, 54 seconds north.

The Indians killed a stag, and one of the men who went to fetch it was very much endangered by the rolling down of a large stone from the heights above him.

[May 28] The day was very cloudy. The mountains on both sides of the river seemed to have sunk in their elevation during the voyage of yesterday. Today they resume their former altitude, and run so close on either side of the channel that all view was excluded of everything but themselves. This part of the current was not broken by islands, but in the afternoon we approached some cascades, which obliged us to carry our canoe and its lading for several hundred yards. Here we observed an encampment of the natives, though some time had elapsed since it had been inhabited.

The greater part of the day was divided between heavy showers and small rain, and we took our station on the shore about six in the evening, about 3 miles above the last rapid.

[May 29] The rain was so violent throughout the whole of this day that we did not venture to proceed. As we had almost expended the contents of a rum keg, and this being a day which allowed of no active employment, I amused myself with the experiment of enclosing a letter in it and dispatching it down the stream, to take its fate. I accordingly introduced a written account of all our hardships, etc., carefully enclosed in bark, into the small barrel by the bunghole, which being carefully secured, I consigned this epistolatory cargo to the mercy of the current.

[May 30] We were alarmed this morning at break of day by the continual barking of our dog, who never ceased from running backward and forward in the rear of our situation. When, however, the day advanced, we discovered the cause of our alarm to proceed from a wolf who was parading a ridge a few yards behind us, and had been most probably allured by the scent of our small portion of fresh meat.

The weather was cloudy, but it did not prevent us from renewing our progress at a very early hour. A considerable river appeared from the left, and we continued our course till seven in the evening, when we landed at night where there was an Indian encampment.

[May 31] The morning was clear and cold, and the current very powerful. On crossing the mouth of a river that flowed in from the right of us, we were very much endangered. Indeed all the rivers which I have lately seen appear to overflow their natural limits, as it may be supposed from the melting of the mountain snow. The water is almost white, the bed of the river being of limestone. The mountains are one solid mass of the same material, but without the least shade of trees or decoration of foliage.

At nine the men were so cold that we landed in order to kindle a fire, which was considered as a very uncommon circumstance at this season. A small quantity of rum, however, served as an adequate substitute, and the current being so smooth as to admit of the use of paddles, I encouraged them to proceed without any further delay.

In a short time an extensive view opened upon us, displaying a beautiful sheet of water that was heightened by the calmness of the weather, and a splendid sun. Here the mountains, which were covered with wood, opened on either side, so that we entertained the hope of soon leaving them behind us.

When we had got to the termination of this prospect, the river was barred with rocks, forming cascades and small islands. To proceed onward, we were under the necessity of clearing a narrow passage of the driftwood on the left shore. Here the view convinced us that our late hopes were without foundation, as there appeared a ridge or chain of mountains running south and north as far as the eye could reach.

On advancing 2 or 3 miles, we arrived at the fork, one branch running about west-northwest, and the other south-southeast. If I had been governed by my own judgment, I should have taken the former, as it appeared to me to be the most likely to bring us nearest to the part where I wished to fall on the Pacific Ocean, but the old man whom I have already mentioned as having been frequently on war expeditions in this country had warned me not on any account to follow it, as it was soon lost in various branches among the mountains, and that there was no great river that ran in any direction near it. But by following the latter, he said, we should arrive at a carrying-place to another large river that did not exceed a day's march, where the inhabitants build houses, and live upon islands.

There was so much apparent truth in the old man's narrative that I determined to be governed by it; for I did not entertain the least doubt, if I could get into the other river, that I should reach the ocean.

I accordingly ordered my steersman to proceed at once to the east branch, which appeared to be more rapid than the other, though it did not possess an equal breadth. These circumstances disposed my men and Indians, the latter in particular being very tired of the voyage, to express their wishes that I should take the western branch, especially when they perceived the difficulty of stemming the current in the direction on which I had determined.

Indeed the rush of water was so powerful that we were the greatest part of the afternoon in getting 2 or 3 miles—a very tardy and mortifying progress, and which, with the voyage, was openly execrated by many of those who were engaged in it. And the inexpressible toil these people had endured, as well as the dangers they had encountered, required some degree of consideration. I therefore employed those arguments which were the best calculated to calm their immediate discontents, as well as to encourage their future hopes, though at the same time I delivered my sentiments in such a manner as to convince them that I was determined to proceed.

[June 1, 1793] On the first of June we embarked at sunrise, and toward noon the current began to slacken. We then put to shore, in order to gum the canoe, when a meridian altitude gave me 55 degrees, 42 minutes, 16 seconds north latitude. We then continued our course, and toward the evening the current began to recover its former strength. Mr. Mackay and the Indians had already disembarked, to walk and lighten the boat.

At sunset we encamped on a point, being the first dry land which had been found on this side the river that was fit for our purpose since our people went on shore. In the morning we passed a large rapid river that flowed in from the right.

In no part of the Northwest did I see so much beaver work, within an equal distance, as in the course of this day. In some places they had cut down several acres of large poplars, and we saw also a great number of these active and sagacious animals. The time which these wonderful creatures allot for their labors, whether in erecting their curious habitations or providing food, is the whole of the interval between the setting and the rising sun.

Toward the dusky part of the evening we heard several discharges from the fowling pieces of our people, which we answered, to inform them of our situation, and sometime after it was dark, they arrived in an equal state of fatigue and alarm. They were also obliged to swim across a channel in order to get to us, as we were situated on an island, though we were ignorant of the circumstance till they came to inform us.

One of the Indians was positive that he heard the discharge of firearms above our encampment; and on comparing the number of our discharges with theirs, there appeared to be some foundation for his alarm, as we imagined that we had heard two reports more than they acknowledged, and in their turn they declared that they had heard twice the number of those which we knew had proceeded from us. The Indians were therefore certain that the Knisteneaux must be in our vicinity on a war expedition, and consequently, if they were numerous, we should have had no reason to expect the least mercy from them in this distant country.

Though I did not believe that circumstance, or that any of the natives could be in possession of firearms, I thought it right, at all events, we should be prepared. Our fuses were therefore primed and loaded, and having extinguished our fire, each of us took his station at the foot of a tree, where we passed an uneasy and restless night.

[June 2] The succeeding morning being clear and pleasant, we proceeded at an early hour against a rapid current, intersected by islands.

About eight we passed two large trees, whose roots having been undermined by the current, had recently fallen into the river, and in my opinion the crash of their fall had occasioned the noise which caused our late alarm. In this manner the water ravages the islands in these rivers, and by driving down great quantities of wood, forms the foundations of others.

The men were so oppressed with fatigue that it was necessary they should encamp at six in the afternoon. We therefore landed on a sandy island, which is a very uncommon object, as the greater part of the islands consist of a bottom of round stones and gravel covered from 3 to 10 feet with mud and old driftwood. Beaver work was as frequently seen as on the preceding day.

[June 3] On the third of June we renewed our voyage with the rising sun. At noon I obtained a meridian altitude, which gave 55 degrees, 22 minutes, 3 seconds north latitude.

[June 4] We embarked this morning at four in a very heavy fog. The water had been continually rising, and in many places overflowed its banks. The current also was so strong that our progress was very tedious, and required the most laborious exertions [to make good 12 miles]. We could not find a place fit for an encampment till nine at night, when we landed on a bank of gravel, of which little more appeared above water than the spot we occupied.

[June 5] This morning we found our canoe and baggage in the water, which had continued rising during the night. We then gummed the canoe, as we arrived at too late an hour to perform that operation on the preceding evening. This necessary business being completed, we traversed to the north shore, where I disembarked with Mr. Mackay and the hunters, in order to ascend an adjacent mountain, with the hope of obtaining a view of the interior part of the country.

I directed my people to proceed with all possible diligence, and that if they met with any accident, or found my return necessary, they should fire two guns. They also understood that when they should hear the same signal from me, they were to answer, and wait for me if I were behind them.

When we had ascended to the summit of the hill, we found that it extended onward in an even, level country, so that, encumbered as we were with the thick wood, no distant view could be obtained. I therefore climbed a very lofty tree, from whose top I discerned on the right a ridge of mountains covered with snow, bearing about northwest. From thence another ridge of high land, whereon no snow was visible, stretched toward the south, between which and the snowy hills on the east side there appeared to be an opening, which we determined to be the course of the river.

Having obtained all the satisfaction that the nature of the place would admit, we proceeded forward to overtake the canoe, and after a warm walk came down upon the river, when we discharged our pieces twice, but received no answering signal. I was of opinion that the canoe was before us, while the Indians entertained an opposite notion. I however crossed another point of land, and came again to the waterside about ten. Here we had a long view of the river, which circumstance excited in my mind some doubts of my former sentiments.

We repeated our signals, but without any return, and as every moment now increased my anxiety, I left Mr. Mackay and one of the Indians at this spot to make a large fire—and send branches adrift down the current as notices of our situation, if the canoe was behind us—and proceeded with the other

Indian across a very long point, where the river makes a considerable bend, in order that I might be satisfied if the canoe was ahead. Having been accustomed for the last fortnight to a very cold weather, I found the heat of this day almost insupportable, as our way lay over a dry sand, which was relieved by no shade but such as a few scattered cypresses could afford us.

About twelve we arrived once more at the river, and the discharge of our pieces was as unsuccessful as it had hitherto been. The water rushed before us with uncommon velocity, and we also tried the experiment of sending fresh branches down it. To add to the disagreeableness of our situation, the gnats and mosquitoes appeared in swarms to torment us.

When we returned to our companions, we found that they had not been contented with remaining in the position where I had left them, but had been 3 or 4 miles down the river, but were come back to their station without having made any discovery of the people on the water.

Various very unpleasing conjectures at once perplexed and distressed us. The Indians, who are inclined to magnify evils of any and every kind, had at once consigned the canoe and everyone on board it to the bottom, and were already settling a plan to return upon a raft, as well as calculating the number of nights that would be required to reach their home.

As for myself, it will be easily believed that my mind was in a state of extreme agitation. And the imprudence of my conduct in leaving the people in such a situation of danger and toilsome exertion added a very painful mortification to the severe apprehensions I already suffered. It was an act of indiscretion which might have put an end to the voyage that I had so much at heart, and compelled me at length to submit to the scheme which my hunters had already formed for our return.

At half-past six in the evening, Mr. Mackay and the Cancre set off to proceed down the river as far as they could before the night came on, and to continue their journey in the morning to the place where we had encamped the preceding evening. I also proposed to make my excursion upward, and if we both failed of success in meeting the canoe, it was agreed that we should return to the place where we now separated.

In this situation we had wherewithal to drink in plenty, but with solid food we were totally unprovided. We had not seen even a partridge throughout the day, and the tracks of reindeer that we had discovered were of an old date. We were, however, preparing to make a bed of the branches of trees, where we should have had no other canopy than that afforded us by the heavens, when we heard a shot, and soon after another, which was the notice agreed upon if Mr. Mackay and the Indian should see the canoe. That fortunate circumstance was also confirmed by a return of the signal from the people.

I was however so fatigued from the heat and exercise of the day, as well as incommoded from drinking so much cold water, that I did not wish to remove till the following morning. But the Indian made such bitter complaints of the cold and hunger which he suffered that I complied with his solicitations to depart, and it was almost dark when we reached the canoe, barefooted and drenched with rain.

But these inconveniences affected me very little when I saw myself once more surrounded with my people. They informed me that the canoe had been broken, and that they had this day experienced much greater toil and hardships than on any former occasion. I thought it prudent to affect a belief of every representation that they made, and even to comfort each of them with a consolatory dram. For however difficult the passage might have been, it was too short to have occupied the whole day if they had not relaxed in their exertions. The rain was accompanied with thunder and lightning.

It appeared from the various encampments which we had seen, and from several paddles we had found, that the natives frequent this part of the country at the latter end of the summer and the fall.

[June 6] At half-past four this morning we continued our voyage [about 3 miles]. The whole of this distance we proceeded by hauling the canoe from branch to branch. The current was so strong that it was impossible to stem it with the paddles; the depth was too great to receive any assistance from the poles; and the bank of the river was so closely lined with willows and other trees that it was impossible to employ the line.

As it was past twelve before we could find a place that would allow of our landing, I could not get a meridian altitude. We occupied the rest of the day in repairing the canoe, drying our clothes, and making paddles and poles to replace those which had been broken or lost.

[June 7] The canoe, which had been little better than a wreck, being now repaired, we proceeded [making good about 12 miles], and encamped at seven o'clock. Mr. Mackay and the hunters walked the greatest part of the day, and in the course of their excursion killed a porcupine. Here we found the bed of a very large bear, quite fresh. During the day several Indian encampments were seen which were of a late erection. The current had also lost some of its impetuosity during the greater part of the day.

[June 8] It rained and thundered through the night, and at four in the morning we again encountered the current. [We made good 17 miles], when the mountains were in full view in this direction, and eastward. For the three last days we could only see them at short intervals and long distances, but till then they were continually in sight on either side, from our entrance into the fork. Those to the left were at no great distance from us.

For the last two days we had been anxiously looking out for the carrying-place, but could not discover it, and our only hope was in such information as we should be able to procure from the natives. All that remained for us to do was to push forward till the river should be no longer navigable. It had now, indeed, overflowed its banks, so that it was eight at night before we could discover a place to encamp.

Having found plenty of wild parsnips, we gathered the tops and boiled them with pemmican for our supper.

[June 9] The rain of this morning terminated in a heavy mist at half-past five, when we embarked and [made good 16 miles]. Here we perceived a smell of fire, and in a short time heard people in the woods, as if in a state of great confusion— which was occasioned, as we afterward understood, by their discovery of us. At the same time this unexpected circumstance produced some little discomposure among ourselves, as our arms were not in a state of preparation, and we were as yet unable to ascertain the number of the party.

I considered that if there were but few, it would be needless to pursue them, as it would not be probable that we should overtake them in these thick woods; and if they were numerous, it would be an act of great imprudence to make the attempt, at least during their present alarm. I therefore ordered my people to strike off to the opposite side, that we might see if any of them had sufficient courage to remain. But before we were half over the river, which in this part is not more than 100 yards wide, two men appeared on a rising ground over against us, brandishing their spears, displaying their bows and arrows, and accompanying their hostile gestures with loud vociferations.

My interpreter did not hesitate to assure them that they might dispel their apprehensions, as we were white people, who meditated no injury, but were, on the contrary, desirous of demonstrating every mark of kindness and friendship. They did not, however, seem disposed to confide in our declarations, and actually threatened if we came over before they were more fully satisfied of our peaceable intentions, that they would discharge their arrows at us.

This was a decided kind of conduct which I did not expect. At the same time I readily complied with their proposition, and after some time had passed in hearing and answering their questions, they consented to our landing, though not without betraying very evident symptoms of fear and distrust. They however laid aside their weapons, and when I stepped forward and took each of them by the hand, one of them, but with a very tremulous action, drew his knife from his sleeve and presented it to me as a mark of his submission to my will and pleasure.

On our first hearing the noise of these people in the woods, we displayed our flag, which was now shown to them as a token of friendship. They examined us, and everything about us, with a minute and suspicious attention. They had heard, indeed, of white men, but this was the first time they had ever seen a human being of a complexion different from their own.

The party had been here but a few hours, nor had they yet erected their sheds, and except the two men now with us, they had all fled, leaving their little property behind them. To those which had given us such a proof of their confidence, we paid the most conciliating attentions in our power. One of them I sent to recall his people, and the other, for very obvious reasons, we kept with us.

In the meantime the canoe was unloaded, the necessary baggage carried up the hill, and the tents pitched.

Here I determined to remain till the Indians became so familiarized with us as to give all the intelligence which we imagined might be obtained from them. In fact, it had been my intention to land where I might most probably discover the carrying-place, which was our more immediate object, and undertake marches of two or three days, in different directions, in search of another river.

If unsuccessful in this attempt, it was my purpose to continue my progress up the present river as far as it was navigable, and if we did not meet with natives to instruct us in our further progress, I had determined to return to the fork and take the other branch, with the hope of better fortune.

It was about three in the afternoon when we landed, and at five the whole party of Indians were assembled. It consisted only of three men, three women, and seven or eight boys and girls. With their scratched legs, bleeding feet, and disheveled hair, as in the hurry of their flight they had left their shoes and leggings behind them, they displayed a most wretched appearance. They were consoled, however, with beads and other trifles which seemed to please them. They had pemmican also given them to eat, which was not unwelcome, and in our opinion, at least, superior to their own provision, which consisted entirely of dried fish.

When I thought that they were sufficiently composed, I sent for the men to my tent, to gain such information respecting the country as I concluded it was in their power to afford me. But my expectations were by no means satisfied. They said that they were not acquainted with any river to the westward, but that there was one from whence they were just arrived, over a carrying-place of eleven days' march, which they represented as being a branch only of the river before us.

Their ironwork they obtained from the people who inhabit the bank of that river and an adjacent lake, in exchange for beaver skins and dressed moose skins. They represented the latter as traveling during a moon to get to the country of other tribes, who live in houses, with whom they traffic for the same commodities; and that these also extend their journeys in the same manner to the seacoast, or, to use their expression, the Stiking Lake, where they trade with people like us, that come there in vessels as big as islands.

They added that the people to the westward, as they have been told, are very numerous. Those who inhabit the other branch they stated as consisting of about forty families, while they themselves did not amount to more than a fourth of that number, and were almost continually compelled to remain in their strongholds, where they sometimes perished with cold and hunger, to secure themselves from their enemies, who never failed to attack them whenever an opportunity presented itself.

This account of the country, from a people who I had every reason to suppose were well acquainted with every part of it, threatened to disconcert the project on which my heart was set, and in which my whole mind was occupied.

It occurred to me, however, that from fear, or other motives, they might be tardy in their communication. I therefore assured them that if they would direct me to the river which I described to them, I would come in large vessels, like those that their neighbors had described, to the mouth of it, and bring them arms and ammunition in exchange for the produce of their country, so that they might be able to defend themselves against their enemies and no longer remain in that abject, distressed, and fugitive state in which they then lived.

I added also that in the meantime if they would on my return accompany me below the mountains to a country which was very abundant in animals, I would furnish them, and their companions, with everything they might want, and make peace between them and the Beaver Indians.

But all these promises did not appear to advance the object of my inquiries, and they still persisted in their ignorance of any such river as I had mentioned, that discharged itself into the sea.

In this state of perplexity and disappointment, various projects presented themselves to my mind, which were no sooner formed than they were discovered to be impracticable, and were consequently abandoned. At one time I thought of leaving the canoe, and everything it contained, to go overland, and pursue that chain of connection by which these people obtain their ironwork. But a very brief course of reflection convinced me that it would be impossible for us to carry provisions for support through any considerable part of such a journey, as well as presents to secure us a kind reception among the natives, and ammunition for the service of the hunters and to defend ourselves against any act of hostility.

At another time my solicitude for the success of the expedition incited a wish to remain with the natives, and go to the sea by the way they had described. But the accomplishment of such a journey, even if no accident should interpose, would have required a portion of time which it was not in my power to bestow. In my present state of information, to proceed further up the river was considered as a fruitless waste of toilsome exertion; and to return unsuccessful, after all our labor, sufferings, and dangers, was an idea too painful to indulge.

Besides, I could not yet abandon the hope that the Indians might not yet be sufficiently composed and confident to disclose their real knowledge of the country freely and fully to me. Nor was I altogether without my doubts respecting the fidelity of my interpreter, who, being very much tired of the voyage, might be induced to withhold those communications which would induce me to continue it. I therefore continued my attentions to the natives, regaled them with such provisions as I had, indulged their children with a taste of sugar, and determined to suspend my conversation with them till the following morning.

On my expressing a desire to partake of their fish, they brought me a few dried trout, well cured, that had been taken in the river which they lately left. One of the men also brought me five beaver skins, as a present.

[June 10] The solicitude that possessed my mind interrupted my repose. When the dawn appeared I had already quitted my bed, and was waiting with impatience for another conference with the natives. The sun, however, had risen before they left their leafy bowers, whither they had retired with their children, having most hospitably resigned their beds, and the partners of them, to the solicitations of my young men.

I now repeated my inquiries, but my perplexity was not removed by any favorable variation in their answers. About nine, however, one of them still remaining at my fire in conversation with the interpreters, I understood enough of his language to know that he mentioned something about a great river, at the same time pointing significantly up that which was before us.

On my inquiring of the interpreter respecting that expression, I was informed that he knew of a large river that runs toward the midday sun, a branch of which flowed near the source of that which we were now navigating; and that there were only three small lakes, and as many carrying-places, leading to a small river which discharges itself into the great river, but that the latter did not empty itself into the sea. The inhabitants, he said, built houses, lived on islands, and were a numerous and warlike people.

I desired him to describe the road to the other river by delineating it with a piece of coal on a strip of bark, which he accomplished to my satisfaction. The opinion that the river did not discharge itself into the sea I very confidently imputed to his ignorance of the country.

My hopes were now renewed, and an object presented itself which awakened my utmost impatience. To facilitate its attainment, one of the Indians was induced by presents to accompany me as a guide to the first inhabitants, which we might expect to meet on the small lakes in our way. I accordingly resolved to depart with all expedition, and while my people were making every necessary preparation, I employed myself in writing the following description of the natives around me:

They are low in stature, not exceeding 5 feet 6 or 7 inches, and they are of that meager appearance which might be expected in a people whose life is one succession of difficulties in procuring subsistence. Their faces are round, with high cheekbones, and their eyes, which are small, are of a dark brown color. The cartilage of their nose is perforated, but without any ornaments suspended from it. Their hair is of a dingy black, hanging loose and in disorder over their shoulders, but irregularly cut in the front, so as not to obstruct the sight. Their beards are eradicated, with the exception of a few straggling hairs, and their complexion is a swarthy yellow.

Their dress consists of robes made of the skins of the beaver, the ground hog, and the reindeer dressed in the hair, and of the moose skin without it. All of them are ornamented with a fringe, while some of them have tassels hanging down the seams; those of the ground hog are decorated on the fur side with the tails of the animal, which they do not separate from them.

Their garments they tie over the shoulders, and fasten them round the middle with a belt of green skin, which is as stiff as horn. Their leggings are long, and if they were topped with a waistband, might be called trousers; they, as well as their shoes, are made of dressed moose, elk, or reindeer skin. The organs of generation they leave uncovered.

The women differ little in their dress from the men, except in the addition of an apron, which is fastened round the waist and hangs down to the knees. They are in general of a more lusty make than the other sex, and taller in proportion, but infinitely their inferiors in cleanliness. A black artificial stripe crosses the face beneath the eye from ear to ear, which I first took for scabs, from the accumulation of dirt on it.

Their hair, which is longer than that of the men, is divided from the forehead to the crown, and drawn back in long plaits behind the ears. They have also a few white beads, which they get where they procure their iron; they are from a line to an inch in length, and are worn in their ears, but are not of European manufacture. These, with bracelets made of horn and bone, compose all the ornaments which decorate their persons. Necklaces of the grizzly or white bear's claws are worn exclusively by the men.

Their arms consist of bows made of cedar, 6 feet in length, with a short iron spike at one end, and serve occasionally as a spear. Their arrows are well made, barbed, and pointed with

iron, flint, stone, or bone; they are feathered, and from 2 to
2½ feet in length. They have two kinds of spears, but both
are double-edged, and of well-polished iron. One of them is
about 12 inches long, and 2 wide, the other about half the
width and two-thirds of the length. The shafts of the first are
8 feet in length, and the latter 6. They have also spears made
of bone.

Their knives consist of pieces of iron shaped and handled
by themselves. Their axes are something like our adze, and
they use them in the same manner as we employ that instrument. They were, indeed, furnished with iron in a manner that
I could not have supposed, and plainly proved to me that
their communication with those who communicate with the
inhabitants of the seacoast cannot be very difficult, and from
their ample provision of iron weapons, the means of procuring
it must be of a more distant origin than I had at first conjectured.

They have snares made of green skin, which they cut to the
size of sturgeon twine, and twist a certain number of them
together. And though when completed they do not exceed the
thickness of a cod line, their strength is sufficient to hold a
moose deer; they are from 1½ to 2 fathoms in length. Their
nets and fishing lines are made of willow bark and nettles;
those made of the latter are finer and smoother than if made
with hempen thread. Their hooks are small bones, fixed in
pieces of wood split for that purpose and tied round with fine
watap, which has been particularly described in the former
voyage.

Their kettles are also made of watap, which is so closely
woven that they never leak, and they heat water in them by
putting red-hot stones into it. There is one kind of them, made
of spruce bark, which they hang over the fire, but at such a
distance as to receive the heat without being within reach of
the blaze—a very tedious operation.

They have various dishes of wood and bark; spoons of horn
and wood, and buckets; bags of leather and network; and
baskets of bark, some of which hold their fishing tackle while
others are contrived to be carried on the back. They have a
brown kind of earth in great abundance, with which they rub

their clothes, not only for ornament but utility, as it prevents the leather from becoming hard after it has been wetted.

They have spruce bark in great plenty, with which they make their canoes, an operation that does not require any great portion of skill or ingenuity, and is managed in the following manner:

The bark is taken off the tree the whole length of the intended canoe, which is commonly about 18 feet, and is sewed with watap at both ends. Two laths are then laid and fixed along the edge of the bark which forms the gunwale. In these are fixed the bars, and against them bear the ribs or timbers, that are cut to the length to which the bark can be stretched. And to give additional strength, strips of wood are laid between them. To make the whole watertight, gum is abundantly employed. These vessels carry from two to five people.

Canoes of a similar construction were used by the Beaver Indians within these few years, but they now very generally employ those made of the bark of the birch tree, which are by far more durable.

Their paddles are about 6 feet long, and about 1 foot is occupied by the blade, which is in the shape of a heart.

Previous to our departure, the natives had caught a couple of trout of about 6 pounds weight, which they brought me, and I paid them with beads. They likewise gave me a net made of nettles, the skin of a moose deer, dressed, and a white horn in the shape of a spoon, which resembles the horn of the buffalo [musk ox] of the Coppermine River; but their description of the animal to which it belongs does not answer to that.

My young men also got two quivers of excellent arrows, a collar of white bear's claws, of a great length, horn bracelets, and other articles, for which they received an ample remuneration.

[June 10] At ten we were ready to embark. I then took leave of the Indians, but encouraged them to expect us in two moons, and expressed a hope that I should find them on the road with any of their relations whom they might meet. I also returned the beaver skins to the man who had presented them to me, desiring him to take care of them till I came back, when I would purchase them of him. Our guide expressed much less concern about the undertaking in which he had engaged than his companions, who appeared to be affected with great solicitude for his safety.

We now pushed off the canoe from the bank, and proceeded east ½ mile, when a river flowed in from the left, about half as large as that which we were navigating. We continued the same course ¾ mile, when we missed two of our fowling pieces, which had been forgotten, and I sent their owners back for them, who were absent on this errand upward of an hour.

We now proceeded northeast by east ½ mile, northeast by north ¾ mile, when the current slackened. There was a verdant spot on the left, where, from the remains of some Indian timber-work, it appeared that the natives have frequently encamped.

Our next course was east 1 mile, and we saw a ridge of mountains covered with snow to the southeast. The land on our right was low and marshy for 3 or 4 miles, when it rose into a range of heights that extended to the mountains. We proceeded [about 15 miles in a generally southern direction], when we landed at seven o'clock and encamped. During the greatest part of the distance we came today, the river runs close under the mountains on the left.

[June 11] The morning was clear and cold. On my interpreter's encouraging the guide to dispel all apprehension, to maintain his fidelity to me, and not to desert in the night, "How is it possible for me," he replied, "to leave the lodge of the Great Spirit!—When he tells me that he has no further occasion for me, I will then return to my children." As we proceeded, however, he soon lost, and with good reason, his exalted notions of me.

At four we continued our voyage, steering east by south 1½ miles, east-southeast ½ mile. A river appeared on the left, at the foot of a mountain which, from its conical form, my young Indian called the Beaver Lodge Mountain. Having proceeded south-southeast ½ mile, another river appeared from the right. We now came in a line with the beginning of the mountains we saw yesterday. Others of the same kind ran parallel with them on the left side of the river, which was reduced to the breadth of 15 yards, and with a moderate current.

[Good progress was made this day along a very crooked river.] In the afternoon we quitted the main branch, which, according to the information of our guide, terminates at a short distance, where it is supplied by the snow which covers the mountains. In the same direction is a valley which appears to be of very great depth, and is full of snow that rises nearly to the height of the land, and forms a reservoir of itself sufficient to furnish a river whenever there is a moderate degree of heat.

The branch which we left was not at this time more than 10 yards broad, while that which we entered was still less. Here the current was very trifling, and the channel so meandering that we sometimes found it difficult to work the canoe forward. The straight course from this to the entrance of a small lake or pond is about east 1 mile.

This entrance by the river into the lake was almost choked up by a quantity of driftwood, which appeared to me to be an extraordinary circumstance; but I afterward found that it falls down from the mountains. The water, however, was so high that the country was entirely overflowed, and we passed with the canoe among the branches of trees. The principal wood along the banks is spruce, intermixed with a few white birch growing on detached spots, the intervening spaces being covered with willow and alder.

We advanced about 1 mile in the lake, and took up our station for the night at an old Indian encampment. Here we expected to meet with natives, but were disappointed; but our guide encouraged us with the hope of seeing some on the morrow.

We saw beaver in the course of the afternoon, but did not discharge our pieces, from the fear of alarming the inhabitants. There were also swans in great numbers, with geese and ducks, which we did not disturb for the same reason. We observed also the tracks of moose deer that had crossed the river. And wild parsnips grew here in abundance, which have been already mentioned as a grateful vegetable. Of birds, we saw bluejays, yellow birds, and one beautiful hummingbird. Of the first and last, I had not seen any since I had been in the Northwest.

[June 12] The weather was the same as yesterday, and we proceeded between three and four in the morning. We took up the net which we had set the preceding evening, when it contained a trout, one white fish, one carp, and three chub.

The lake is about 2 miles in length, east by south, and from 300 to 500 yards wide. This I consider as the highest and southernmost source of the Unjigah or Peace River, latitude 54 degrees, 24 minutes north, longitude 121 degrees west of Greenwich, which, after a winding course through a vast extent of country, receiving many large rivers in its progress and passing through the Slave Lake, empties itself into the Frozen Ocean in 70 degrees north latitude, and about 135 degrees west longitude.

We landed and unloaded, where we found a beaten path leading over a low ridge of land of 817 paces in length to another small lake. The distance between the two mountains at this place is about ¼ mile, rocky precipices presenting themselves on both sides. A few large spruce trees and *liards* were scattered over the carrying-place. There were also willows along the side of the water, with plenty of grass and weeds.

The natives had left their old canoes here, with baskets hanging on the trees, which contained various articles. From the latter I took a net, some hooks, a goat's horn, and a kind of wooden trap, in which, as our guide informed me, the ground hog is taken. I left, however, in exchange a knife, some fire steels, beads, awls, etc.

Here two streams tumble down the rocks from the right and lose themselves in the lake which we had left, while two others fall from the opposite heights and glide into the lake which we were approaching; this being the highest point of land dividing these waters, and we are now going with the stream.

This lake runs in the same course as the last, but is rather narrower, and not more than half the length. We were obliged to clear away some floating driftwood to get to the carrying-place, over which is a beaten path of only 175 paces long.

The lake empties itself by a small river, which if the channel were not interrupted by large trees that had fallen across it, would have admitted of our canoe with all its lading. The impediment, indeed, might have been removed by two axmen in a few hours. On the edge of the water, we observed a large quantity of thick yellow scum or froth, of an acrid taste and smell.

We embarked on this lake, which is in the same course and about the same size as that which we had just left, and from whence we passed into a small river that was so full of fallen wood as to employ some time and require some exertion to force a passage. At the entrance, it afforded no more water than was just sufficient to bear the canoe, but it was soon increased by many small streams which came in broken rills down the rugged sides of the mountains, and were furnished, as I suppose, by the melting of the snow. These accessory streamlets had all the coldness of ice.

Our course continued to be obstructed by banks of gravel, as well as trees which had fallen across the river. We were obliged to force our way through the one and to cut through the other, at a great expense of time and trouble. In many places the current was also very rapid and meandering.

At four in the afternoon, we stopped to unload and carry, and at five we entered a small round lake of about ⅓ mile in diameter. From the last lake to this is, I think, in a straight line east by south 6 miles, though it is twice that distance by the winding of the river.

We again entered the river, which soon ran with great rapidity, and rushed impetuously over a bed of flat stones. At half-past six we were stopped by two large trees that lay across the river, and it was with great difficulty that the canoe was prevented from driving against them. Here we unloaded and formed our encampment.

The weather was cloudy and raw, and as the circumstances of this day's voyage had compelled us to be frequently in the water, which was cold as ice, we were almost in a benumbed state. Some of the people who had gone ashore to lighten the canoe experienced great difficulty in reaching us, from the rugged state of the country. It was indeed almost dark when they arrived.

We had no sooner landed than I sent two men down the river to bring me some account of its circumstances, that I might form a judgment of the difficulties which might await us on the morrow, and they brought back a fearful detail of rapid currents, fallen trees, and large stones.

At this place our guide manifested evident symptoms of discontent. He had been very much alarmed in going down some of the rapids with us, and expressed an anxiety to return. He showed us a mountain, at no great distance, which he represented as being on the other side of a river into which this empties itself.

[June 13] At an early hour of this morning the men began to cut a road, in order to carry the canoe and lading beyond the rapid, and by seven they were ready. That business was soon effected, and the canoe reladen, to proceed with the current, which ran with great rapidity. In order to lighten her, it was my intention to walk with some of the people; but those in the boat with great earnestness requested me to embark, declaring at the same time that if they perished, I should perish with them. I did not then imagine in how short a period their apprehension would be justified.

We accordingly pushed off, and had proceeded but a very short way when the canoe struck, and notwithstanding all our exertions, the violence of the current was so great as to drive her sideways down the river, and break her by the first bar, when I instantly jumped into the water and the men followed my example. But before we could set her straight, or stop her, we came to deeper water, so that we were obliged to re-embark with the utmost precipitation. One of the men who was not sufficiently active was left to get on shore in the best manner in his power.

We had hardly regained our situations when we drove against a rock which shattered the stern of the canoe in such a manner that it held only by the gunwales, so that the steersman could no longer keep his place. The violence of this stroke drove us to the opposite side of the river, which is but narrow, when the bow met with the same fate as the stern.

At this moment the foreman seized on some branches of a small tree in the hope of bringing up the canoe, but such was their elasticity that, in a manner not easily described, he was jerked on shore in an instant, and with a degree of violence that threatened his destruction.

But we had no time to turn from our own situation to inquire what had befallen him; for in a few moments we came across a cascade which broke several large holes in the bottom of the canoe, and started all the bars except one behind the scooping seat. If this accident, however, had not happened, the vessel must have been irretrievably overset.

The wreck becoming flat on the water, we all jumped out, while the steersman, who had been compelled to abandon his place and had not recovered from his fright, called out to his companions to save themselves. My peremptory commands superseded the effects of his fear, and they all held fast to the wreck; to which fortunate resolution we owed our safety, as we should otherwise have been dashed against the rocks by the force of the water, or driven over the cascades.

In this condition we were forced several hundred yards, and every yard on the verge of destruction; but at length we most fortunately arrived in shallow water and a small eddy, where we were enabled to make a stand, from the weight of the canoe resting on the stones rather than from any exertions of our exhausted strength. For though our efforts were short, they were pushed to the utmost, as life or death depended on them.

This alarming scene, with all its terrors and dangers, occupied only a few minutes; and in the present suspension of it, we called to the people on shore to come to our assistance, and they immediately obeyed the summons. The foreman, however, was the first with us. He had escaped unhurt from the extraordinary jerk with which he was thrown out of the boat, and just as we were beginning to take our effects out of the water, he appeared to give his assistance.

The Indians, when they saw our deplorable situation, instead of making the least effort to help us, sat down and gave vent to their tears. I was on the outside of the canoe, where I remained till everything was got on shore, in a state of great pain from the extreme cold of the water, so that at length it was with difficulty I could stand, from the benumbed state of my limbs.

The loss was considerable and important, for it consisted of our whole flock of balls [bullets], and some of our furniture; but these considerations were forgotten in the impressions of our miraculous escape. Our first inquiry was after the absent man, whom in the first moment of danger we had left to get on shore, and in a short time his appearance removed our anxiety. We had, however, sustained no personal injury of consequence, and my bruises seemed to be in the greater proportion.

All the different articles were now spread out to dry. The powder had fortunately received no damage, and all my instruments had escaped. Indeed, when my people began to recover from their alarm and to enjoy a sense of safety, some of them, if not all, were by no means sorry for our late misfortune, from the hope that it must put a period to our voyage, particularly as we were without a canoe, and all the bullets sunk in the river.

It did not, indeed, seem possible to them that we could proceed under these circumstances. I listened, however, to the observations that were made on the occasion without replying to them, till their panic was dispelled and they had got themselves warm and comfortable, with a hearty meal, and rum enough to raise their spirits.

I then addressed them by recommending them all to be thankful for their late very narrow escape. I also stated that the navigation was not impracticable in itself, but from our ignorance of its course, and that our late experience would enable us to pursue our voyage with greater security.

I brought to their recollection that I did not deceive them, and that they were made acquainted with the difficulties and dangers they must expect to encounter before they engaged to accompany me. I also urged the honor of conquering disasters, and the disgrace that would attend them on their return home without having attained the object of the expedition.

Nor did I fail to mention the courage and resolution which was the peculiar boast of the Northmen; and that I depended on them, at that moment, for the maintenance of their character. I quieted their apprehension as to the loss of the bullets by bringing to their recollection that we still had shot from which they might be manufactured. I at the same time acknowledged the difficulty of restoring the wreck of the canoe, but confided in our skill and exertion to put it in such a state as would carry us on to where we might procure bark, and build a new one.

In short, my harangue produced the desired effect, and a very general assent appeared, to go wherever I should lead the way.

Various opinions were offered in the present posture of affairs, and it was rather a general wish that the wreck should be abandoned, and all the lading carried to the river, which our guide informed us was at no great distance, and in the vicinity of woods where he believed there was plenty of bark. This project seemed not to promise that certainty to which I looked in my present operations; besides, I had my doubts respecting the views of my guide, and consequently could not confide in the representation he made to me.

I therefore dispatched two of the men at nine in the morning, with one of the young Indians—for I did not venture to trust the guide out of my sight—in search of bark, and to endeavor, if it were possible, in the course of the day to penetrate to the great river into which that before us discharges itself in the direction which the guide had communicated. I now joined my people in order to repair, as well as circumstances would admit, our wreck of a canoe, and I began to set them the example.

It now grew late, and the people who had been sent out on the excursion already mentioned were not yet returned. About ten o'clock, however, I heard a man halloo, and I very gladly returned the signal. In a short time our young Indian arrived with a small roll of indifferent bark. He was oppressed with fatigue and hunger, and his clothes torn to rags. He had parted with the other two men at sunset, who had walked the whole day, in a dreadful country, without procuring any good bark or being able to get to the large river. His account of the river on whose banks we were could not be more unfavorable or discouraging. It had appeared to him to be little more than a succession of falls and rapids, with occasional interruptions of fallen trees.

Our guide became so dissatisfied and troubled in mind that we could not obtain from him any regular account of the country before us. All we could collect from him was that the river into which this empties itself is but a branch of a large river, the great fork being at no great distance from the confluence of this; and that he knew of no lake, or large body of still water, in the vicinity of these rivers. To this account of the country, he added some strange, fanciful, but terrifying descriptions of the natives.

We had an escape this day which I must add to the many instances of good fortune which I experienced in this perilous expedition. The powder had been spread out, to the amount of 80 pounds' weight, to receive the air; and in this situation one of the men carelessly and composedly walked across it with a lighted pipe in his mouth, but without any ill consequence resulting from such an act of criminal negligence. I need not add that one spark might have put a period to all my anxiety and ambition.

I observed several trees and plants on the banks of this river which I had not seen to the north of the latitude 52 degrees, such as the cedar, maple, hemlock, etc. At this time the water rose fast, and passed on with the rapidity of an arrow shot from a bow.

[June 14] The weather was fine, clear, and warm, and at an early hour of the morning we resumed our repair of the canoe.

At half-past seven our two men returned hungry and cold, not having tasted food or enjoyed the least repose for twenty-four hours, with their clothes torn into tatters and their skin lacerated in passing through the woods. Their account was the same as that brought by the Indian, with this exception, that they had reason to think they saw the river or branch which our guide had mentioned; but they were of opinion that from the frequent obstructions in this river, we should have to carry the whole way to it, through a dreadful country, where much time and labor would be required to open a passage through it.

Discouraging as these accounts were, they did not, however, interrupt for a moment the task in which we were engaged, of repairing the canoe, and this work we contrived to complete by the conclusion of the day. The bark which was brought by the Indian, with some pieces of oilcloth and plenty of gum, enabled us to put our shattered vessel in a condition to answer our present purposes.

The guide, who has been mentioned as manifesting continual signs of dissatisfaction, now assumed an air of contentment, which I attributed to a smoke that was visible in the direction of the river, as he naturally expected, if we should fall in with any natives, which was now very probable from such a circumstance, that he should be released from a service which he had found so irksome and full of danger.

[June 15] The weather continued the same as the preceding day, and according to the directions which I had previously given, my people began at a very early hour to open a road through which we might carry a part of our lading, as I was fearful of risking the whole of it in the canoe in its present weak state, and in a part of the river which is full of shoals and rapids. Four men were employed to conduct her, lightened as she was of twelve packages. They passed several dangerous places, and met with various obstructions, the current of the river being frequently stopped by rafts of driftwood and fallen trees, so that after fourteen hours' hard labor we had not made more than 3 miles. Our course was southeast by east, and as we had not met with any accident, the men appeared to feel a renewed courage to continue their voyage.

In the morning, however, one of the crew, whose name was Beauchamp, peremptorily refused to embark in the canoe. This being the first example of absolute disobedience which had yet appeared during the course of our expedition, I should not have passed it over without taking some very severe means to prevent a repetition of it; but as he had the general character of a simple fellow among his companions, and had been frightened out of what little sense he possessed by our late dangers, I rather preferred to consider him as unworthy of accompanying us, and to represent him as an object of ridicule and contempt for his pusillanimous behavior—though in fact he was a very useful, active, and laborious man.

At the close of the day we assembled round a blazing fire, and the whole party, being enlivened with the usual beverage which I supplied on these occasions, forgot their fatigues and apprehensions. Nor did they fail to anticipate the pleasure they should enjoy in getting clear of their present difficulties, and gliding onward with a strong and steady stream, which our guide had described as the characteristic of the large river we soon expected to enter.

[June 16] The fine weather continued, and we began our work, as we had done the preceding days. Some were occupied in opening a road, others were carrying, and the rest employed in conducting the canoe. I was of the first party, and soon discovered that we had encamped about ½ mile above several falls, over which we could not attempt to run the canoe, lightened even as she was. This circumstance rendered it necessary that the road should be made sufficiently wide to admit the canoe to pass—a tedious and toilsome work. In running her down a rapid above the falls, a hole was broken in her bottom, which occasioned a considerable delay, as we were destitute of the materials necessary for her effectual reparation.

On my being informed of this misfortune, I returned, and ordered Mr. Mackay, with two Indians, to quit their occupation in making the road and endeavor to penetrate to the great river, according to the direction which the guide had communicated, without paying any attention to the course of the river before us.

When the people had repaired the canoe in the best manner they were able, we conducted her to the head of the falls. She was then unloaded and taken out of the water, when we carried her for a considerable distance through a low, swampy country. I appointed four men to this laborious office, which they executed at the peril of their lives, for the canoe was now become so heavy, from the additional quantity of bark and gum necessary to patch her up, that two men could not carry her more than 100 yards without being relieved; and as their way lay through deep mud, which was rendered more difficult by the roots and prostrate trunks of trees, they were every moment in danger of falling, and beneath such a weight, one false step might have been attended with fatal consequences. The other two men and myself followed as fast as we could, with the lading.

Thus did we toil till seven o'clock in the evening, to get to the termination of the road that had been made in the morning. Here Mr. Mackay and the Indians joined us, after having been at the river, which they represented as rather large. They had also observed that the lower part of the river before us was so full of fallen wood that the attempt to clear a passage through it would be an unavailing labor.

The country through which they had passed was morass and almost impenetrable wood. In passing over one of the embarras, our dog, which was following them, fell in, and it was with very great difficulty that he was saved, as the current had carried him under the drift. They brought with them two geese, which had been shot in the course of their expedition.

To add to our perplexities and embarrassments, we were persecuted by mosquitoes and sand flies through the whole of the day.

The extent of our journey was not more than 2 miles southeast, and so much fatigue and pain had been suffered in the course of it that my people, as might be expected, looked forward to a continuance of it with discouragement and dismay. I was, indeed, informed that murmurs prevailed among them, of which I took no notice. When we were assembled together for the night, I gave each of them a dram, and in a short time they retired to the repose which they so much required.

We could discover the termination of the mountains at a considerable distance on either side of us, which, according to my conjecture, marked the course of the great river. On the mountains to the east there were several fires, as their smokes were very visible to us. Excessive heat prevailed throughout the day.

Having sat up till twelve last night, which had been my constant practice since we had taken our present guide, I awoke Mr. Mackay to watch him in turn. I then laid down to rest, and at three I was awakened to be informed that he had deserted. Mr. Mackay, with whom I was displeased on this occasion, and the Cancre, accompanied by the dog, went in search of him, but he had made his escape—a design which he had for some time meditated, though I had done everything in my power to induce him to remain with me.

This misfortune did not produce any relaxation in our exertions. At an early hour of the morning we were all employed in cutting a passage at ¾ mile, through which we carried our canoe and cargo, when we put her into the water with her lading, but in a very short time were stopped by the driftwood, and were obliged to land and carry.

In short, we pursued our alternate journeys, by land and water, till noon, when we could proceed no further, from the various small unnavigable channels into which the river branched in every direction; and no other mode of getting forward now remained for us but by cutting a road across a neck of land. I accordingly dispatched two men to ascertain the exact distance, and we employed the interval of their absence in unloading and getting the canoe out of the water.

It was eight in the evening when we arrived at the bank of the great river. At length we enjoyed, after all our toil and anxiety, the inexpressible satisfaction of finding ourselves on the bank of a navigable river on the west side of the first great range of mountains. ✇

A great discoverer, Mackenzie lacked the gifts of the writer, as the reader may have discovered. He is therefore, not quoted further, but summarized:

The big river of his discovery was taken by Mackenzie to be the Columbia, the mouth of which was already known and the upper reaches of which he thought he had traversed, so reporting in his quarto narrative of 1801, which has been quoted here. In reality he had added to his triumphs by the discovery of a river which has proved to be nearly 785 miles in length. It was not explored for the main part of its length till 1808, by Simon Fraser, after whom it was named.

For Mackenzie did not follow his supposed Columbia more than a few days, which was because the local Indians frightened him off it by tales of dangerous rapids and canyons and of more dangerous people who dwelt along its banks and would be sure to kill him and all his companions, white and Indian.

So the party struck off overland, westward from this temporarily south-flowing stream, and descended by various portages and minor rivers to the Pacific, which they reached in the Bella Coola neighborhood, a little north and east of the north end of Vancouver Island. This was on June 22, 1793. They returned that same autumn to the Peace and reached Fort Chipewyan, on Lake Athabaska, August 23.

From the time they reached the vicinity of the headwaters of the Peace, on the east side of the Rocky Mountain divide, in the neighborhood of the present Yellowhead Pass that carries the Canadian National Railway, Mackenzie was among Indians who had never seen a white man, and he so continued till he was in the vicinity of the Pacific. Luckily, these were Indians who had heard more about those white men who wanted to purchase furs than of the others, farther south, who desired farms and to whom "the only good Indian is a dead Indian." The people therefore hindered Mackenzie little, and then only through misunderstanding; they helped him a great deal. However, he came near being killed by coastal natives, who were familiar, at least by hearsay, with Spaniards and Russians as well as Yankees and Britishers.

Mackenzie's journey in birchbark canoes that were carried over portages, repaired with spruce gum and with bark patches, and discarded for others new-built from the trees along the way—this epochal first crossing of North America is typical of how a large section of the forested part of the continent was explored, from Atlantic to Pacific. His dependence on game, reliance on pemmican for the crossing of gameless areas, use of rum for coaxing and bribing and the like use of sugar, were equally typical.

Socially the most interesting to the historian is Mackenzie's reliance upon the friendliness of local people. In this he was typical of the explorers of Canada, not so typical of the men who opened up the United States, rather untypical of the

Spaniards in Mexico and the Russians in Alaska. That the Spanish were in the main different follows from their attitude that they were conquerors, entitled to plunder the vanquished. They were not to any extent traders, dependent on free customers, but more likely miners or planters, requiring slave labor.

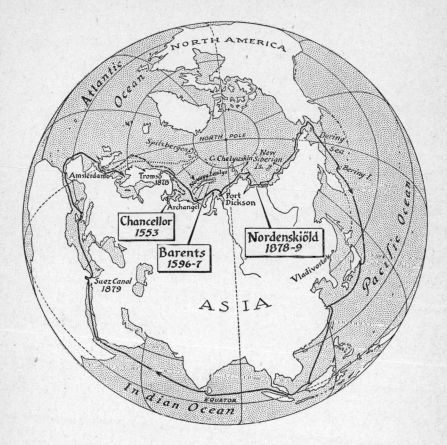

Discovery of the Northeast Passage

DISCOVERY OF THE NORTHEAST PASSAGE

CHAPTER 12

Sᴉxᴛᴇᴇɴᴛʜ-ᴄᴇɴᴛᴜʀʏ England, its maritime strength not yet developed, was enviously aware of the rich traffic in gold and jewels, spices and perfumes, that was being carried on by the Portuguese and the Spanish. But the navies of Spain and Portugal were so strong, and their determination so firm to keep out all competitors, that it was impossible for the English to challenge them on the established routes to the Orient. Hence the zeal with which the English, and later the Dutch, sought again and again to find a new way to India and China. There were three directions in which to make such attempts: northward by way of the Pole, northwestward along the Arctic shore of the New World by what came to be known as the Northwest Passage, and northeastward along the north coast of the Old World by the route called the Northeast Passage. The searches for the northern and northwestern routes are considered elsewhere in this book.

As early as about 870, Europeans had discovered the western end of the Northeast Passage, when the Norwegian Ottar (Octher, Ohthere) sailed northeastward to the White Sea. Thereafter during their great period of maritime activity the Norsemen extended their voyages northeastward as far as Novaya Zemlya.

In telling of discoveries along the course of the Northeast Passage, the point of view is that of western Europe. Much of the coast and many of the islands had of course long been familiar to the Russians, and before them to the nomadic Mongolian peoples, such as the Finns, the Lapps, and the Nentsi.

Sigismund von Heberstein, ambassador from the Roman Emperor, visited Russia in 1517 and again in 1525. On the basis of these journeys he published in 1549 his *Rerum Moscoviticarum Commentarii* . . . by which the empire of the Czar first became extensively known to western Europe. In this book, under the subtitle *Navigatio per Mare Glaciale*, Von Heberstein tells of the voyage of Gregory Istoma and the envoy David from the White Sea to Trondheim in the year 1496. These Russians, and others, sailed around the northern extremity of Norway in boats which, when necessary, could be carried overland. From this and other evidence Nordenskjöld concludes "it may be considered certain that Norwegians, Russians, and Karelians often traveled in boats on peaceful or warlike errands, during the fifteenth and the beginning of the sixteenth century, from the west coast of Norway to the White Sea, and in the opposite direction."

In this field also, as in so many other parts of the world, there are rumors that the Portuguese were among the early western-European pioneers, for they are believed to have sent out an expedition toward Novaya Zemlya in 1484 to search for a passage to India. Here as elsewhere they are deprived of the credit which history might give them through that obsession with secrecy which it almost seems as if they had inherited from the Phoenician explorers of Portugal two and three thousand years before.

In England during the first half of the sixteenth century there was much talk of such a northeastern venture by England as the rumor attributes to the Portuguese; but the design did not crystallize until after the founding, on December 18, 1551, of the company of Merchant Adventurers. Of this company, Sebastian Cabot, then resident in England and receiving a liberal pension from the King, was made Governor for life. The company's first attempt to find a passage northward of the Old World was made in 1553, when three ships were sent out under the command of Sir Hugh Willoughby.

The contemporary documents relating to this expedition are so detailed and clear that a bare outline of the voyage is sufficient to introduce them.

The three ships and 112 men sailed from England in May

1553, carrying an open letter from Edward VI, written in Latin, Greek, and several other languages. The letter, which stated that discoveries and the making of commercial treaties were the sole objects of the expedition, was addressed to "the Kings, Princes, and other Potentates inhabiting the northeast parts of the world, toward the mighty Empire of Cathay."

In August one of the vessels, commanded by Richard Chancellor, was separated from the others in a gale off northern Norway. Willoughby's two ships, as shown by his brief journal, sailed back and forth in what is now the Barents Sea, probably sighted Kolguev Island, and finally went into winter quarters at a harbor on the north coast of the Kola Peninsula. The harbor was at the mouth of the river Arzina, "near Kegor," probably at the site of the present Varsinskoe. Here Willoughby and all of his companions perished, doubtless of scurvy.

Chancellor was more fortunate than Willoughby. His vessel reached the mouth of the Dvina River in the White Sea, where Archangel was built later. Thence he journeyed overland to Moscow and made arrangements for trade with Russia, and the following summer returned with his ship to England. His voyage, while contributing little new to knowledge of the Northeast Passage, was of great importance in establishing commercial relations with Muscovy, as Russia was then normally called by the English.

Of the several contemporary documents relating to the Willoughby expedition, three have been chosen with which to tell the story here, taken from Hakluyt's *Principall Navigations, Voiages, Traffiques and Discoveries of the English Nation*. These are: Cabot's instructions to the expedition, Willoughby's note that was found with his ship, and Chancellor's account of the voyage.

The full text of Sebastian Cabot's instructions to the Willoughby-Chancellor expedition is used, partly because it was (apart from the doubtful Portuguese attempt) the first of that long series of western-European expeditions which, taken up eventually by the Russians, led to the opening of a seaway around the north of the Old World. An even more cogent reason for not substituting a briefer and possibly more readable abridgment is that this document, if read as a whole, presents an unexcelled view of how things were intended to be, and how they often were, in that series of discovery voyages which, through four centuries, had so large a part in making Britain a world power.

🔖 *Ordinances, instructions, and advertisements of and for the direction of the intended voyage for Cathay, compiled, made, and delivered by the right worshipful M. Sebastian Cabota Esquier, governour of the mysterie and companie of the Marchants adventurers for the discoverie of Regions, Dominions, Islands and places unknowen, the 9. day of May, in the yere of our Lord God 1553. and in the 7. yeere of the reigne of our most dread soveraigne Lord Edward the 6. by the grace of God, king of England, Fraunce and Ireland, defender of the faith, and of the Church of England and Ireland, in earth supreame head.*

First, the Captain General, with the pilot major, the masters, merchants, and other officers, to be so knit and accorded in unity, love, conformity, and obedience in every degree on all sides that no dissension, variance, or contention may rise or spring betwixt them and the mariners of this company, to the damage or hindrance of the voyage; for that dissension (by many experiences) hath overthrown many notable intended and likely enterprises and exploits.

2. *Item*, for as much as every person hath given an oath to be true, faithful, and loyal subjects and liegemen to the King's Most Excellent Majesty, his heirs and successors, and for the observation of all laws and statutes made for the preservation of His Most Excellent Majesty, and his crown imperial of his realms of England and Ireland, and to serve His Grace, the realm, and this present voyage truly, and not to give up, intermit, or leave off the said voyage and enterprise until it shall be accomplished, so far forth as possibility and life of man may serve or extend. Therefore it behooveth every person in his degree, as well for conscience as for duty's sake, to remember his said charge, and the accomplishment thereof.

3. *Item*, where furthermore every mariner or passenger in his ship hath given like oath to be obedient to the Captain General,

and to every captain and master in his ship, for the observation of these present orders contained in this book and all other which hereafter shall be made by the twelve counselors in this present book named, or the most part of them, for the better conduction and preservation of the fleet and achieving of the voyage, and to be prompt, ready, and obedient in all acts and feats of honesty, reason, and duty to be ministered, showed, and executed in advancement and preferment of the voyage and exploit. Therefore it is convenient that this present book shall once every week (by the discretion of the captain) be read to the said company, to the intent that every man may the better remember his oath, conscience, duty, and charge.

4. *Item*, every person by virtue of his oath to do effectually and with goodwill (as far forth as him shall comply) all and every such act and acts, deed and deeds, as shall be to him or them from time to time commanded, committed, and enjoined (during the voyage) by the Captain General, with the assent of the Council and assistants, as well in and during the whole navigation and voyage as also in discovering and landing, as cases and occasions shall require.

5. *Item*, all courses in navigation to be set and kept, by the advice of the captain, pilot major, masters, and master's mates, with the assents of the counselors and the most number of them, and in voices uniformly agreeing in one to prevail and take place, so that the Captain General shall in all counsels and assemblies have a double voice.

6. *Item*, that the fleet shall keep together, and not separate themselves asunder, as much as by wind and weather may be done or permitted, and that the captains, pilots, and masters shall speedily come aboard the Admiral when and as often as he shall seem to have just cause to assemble them for counsel or consultation to be had concerning the affairs of the fleet and voyage.

7. *Item*, that the merchants, and other skillful persons in writing, shall daily write, describe, and put in memory the navigation of every day and night, with the points and observation of the lands, tides, elements, altitude of the sun, course of the moon and stars; and the same so noted by the order of the master and pilot of every ship to be put in writing, the

Captain General assembling the masters together once every week (if wind and weather shall serve) to confer all the observations and notes of the said ships, to the intent it may appear wherein the notes do agree, and wherein they dissent, and upon good debatement, deliberation, and conclusion determined, to put the same into a common ledger, to remain of record for the company. The like order to be kept in proportioning of the cards, astrolabes, and other instruments prepared for the voyage, at the charge of the company.

8. *Item*, that all enterprises and exploits of discovering or landing to search islands, regions, and suchlike, to be searched, attempted, and enterprised by good deliberation and common assent, determined advisedly. And that in all enterprises, notable embassages, suites, requests, or presentment of gifts, or presents to Princes, to be done and executed by the Captain General in person or by such other as he by common assent shall appoint or assign to do or cause to be done in the same.

9. *Item*, the steward and cook of every ship, and their associates, to give and render to the captain and other head officers of their ship weekly (or oftener if it shall seem requisite), a just and plain and perfect account of expenses of the victuals, as well as flesh, fish, biscuit, meat, or bread, as also of beer, wine, oil, or vinegar, and all other kind of victualing under their charge; and they, and every of them, so to order and dispense the same that no waste or unprofitable excess be made otherwise than reason and necessity shall command.

10. *Item*, when any inferior or mean officer, of what degree or condition he shall be, shall be tried [proved] untrue, remiss, negligent, or unprofitable in or about his office in the voyage, or not to use himself in his charge accordingly, then every such officer to be punished or removed at the discretion of the captain and assistants, or the most part of them; and the person so removed not to be reputed, accepted, or taken from the time of his remove any more for an officer, but to remain in such condition and place as he shall be assigned unto; and none of the company to resist such chastisement or worthy punishment as shall be ministered unto him moderately, according to the fault or desert of his offense, after the laws and common cus-

toms of the seas, in such cases heretofore used and observed.

11. *Item*, if any mariner or officer inferior shall be found by his labor not meet nor worthy the place that he is presently shipped for, such person may be unshipped and put on land at any place within the King's Majesty's realm and dominion, and one other person more able and worthy to be put in his place, at the discretion of the captain and masters; and order to be taken that the party dismissed shall be allowed proportionably the value of that he shall have deserved to the time of his dismission or discharge, and he to give order with sureties, pawn, or other assurance to repay the overplus of that he shall have received which he shall not have deserved; and such wages to be made with the party newly placed as shall be thought reasonable, and he to have the furniture of all such necessaries as were prepared for the party dismissed, according to right and conscience.

12. *Item*, that no blaspheming of God, or detestable swearing, be used in any ship, nor communication of ribaldry, filthy tales, or ungodly talk to be suffered in the company of any ship, neither dicing, carding, tabling, nor other devilish games to be frequented, whereby ensueth not only poverty to the players, but also strife, variance, brawling, fighting, and oftentimes murder, to the utter destruction of the parties and provoking of God's most just wrath and sword of vengeance. These and all suchlike pestilences and contagions of vices and sins to be eschewed, and the offenders once monished and not reforming, to be punished at the discretion of the captain and master, as appertaineth.

13. *Item*, that morning and evening prayer, with other common services appointed by the King's Majesty and laws of this realm to be read and said in every ship daily by the minister in the Admiral [the *Bona Esperanza*] and the merchant or some other person learned in other ships, and the Bible or paraphrases to be read devoutly and Christianly to God's honor, and for His grace to be obtained and had by humble and hearty prayer of the navigants accordingly.

14. *Item*, that every officer is to be charged by inventory with the particulars of his charge, and to render a perfect account of the defraying of the same, together with modest and temper-

ate dispensing of powder, shot, and use of all kind of artillery, which is not to be misused, but diligently to be preserved for the necessary defense of the fleet and voyage, together with due keeping of all instruments of your navigation, and other requisites.

15. *Item*, no liquor to be spilt on the ballast, nor filthiness to be left withinboard. The cookroom and all other places to be kept clean for the better health of the company. . . .

16. *Item*, the liveries in apparel given to the mariners to be kept by the merchants, and not to be worn but by the order of the captain, when he shall see cause to muster or show them in good array, for the advancement and honor of the voyage; and the liveries to be redelivered to the keeping of the merchants until it shall be thought convenient for every person to have the full use of his garment.

17. *Item*, when any mariner or any other passenger shall have need of any necessary furniture of apparel for his body, and conservation of his health, the same shall be delivered him by the merchant, at the assignment of the captain and master of that ship wherein such needy person shall be, at such reasonable price as the same cost, without any gain to be exacted by the merchants, the value therof to be entered by the merchant in his books, and the same to be discounted off the party's wages that so shall receive and wear the same.

18. *Item*, the sick, diseased, weak, and visited person withinboard, to be tendered, relieved, comforted, and holpen in the time of his infirmity, and every manner of person, without respect, to bear another's burden, and no man to refuse such labor as shall be put to him, for the most benefit and public wealth of the voyage and enterprise to be achieved exactly.

19. *Item*, if any person shall fortune to die or miscarry in the voyage, such apparel and other goods as he shall have at the time of his death is to be kept by the order of the captain and master of the ship, and an inventory to be made of it, and conserved to the use of his wife and children, or otherwise according to his mind and will; and the day of his death to be entered in the merchants' and stewards' books, to the intent it may be known what wages he shall have deserved to his death, and what shall rest due to him.

20. *Item*, that the merchants appointed for this present voyage shall not make any show or sale of any kind of merchandises, or open their commodities to any foreign princes or any of their subjects, without the consent, privity, or agreement of the captains, the cape merchants [supercargoes], and the assistants, or four of them, whereof the Captain General, the pilot major, and cape merchant to be three, and every of the petty merchants to show his reckoning to the cape merchant, when they, or any of them, shall be required. And no commutation or truck to be made by any of the petty merchants without the assent above-said. And all wares and commodities trucked, bought, or given to the company, by way of merchandise, truck, or any other respect, to be booked by the merchants, and to be well ordered, packed, and conserved in one mass entirely, and not to be broken or altered until the ships shall return to the right discharges; and inventory of all goods, wares, and merchandises so trucked, bought, or otherwise dispensed to be presented to the Governor, consuls, and assistants in London, in good order, to the intent the King's Majesty may be truly answered of that which to His Grace by his grant of corporation is limited, according to our most bound duties, and the whole company also to have that which by right unto them appertaineth, and no embezzlement shall be used, but the truth of the whole voyage to be opened, to the common wealth and benefit of the whole company and mystery, as appertaineth, without guile, fraud, or male engine [malignance].

21. *Item*, no particular person to hinder or prejudice the common stock of the company, in sale or preferment of his own proper wares and things, and no particular emergent or purchase to be employed to any several profit until the common stock of the company shall be furnished; and no person to hinder the common benefit in such purchases or contingents as shall fortune to any one of them by his own proper policy, industry, or chance; nor no contention to rise in that behalf, by any occasion of jewel, stone, pearls, precious metals, or other things of the region where it shall chance the same to rise, or to be found, bought, trucked, permuted, or given. But every person to be bounden in such case, and upon such occasion, by order and direction, as the General Captain and the Council

shall establish and determine, to whose order and discretion the same is left; for that of things uncertain, no certain rules may or can be given.

22. *Item*, not to disclose to any nation the state of our religion, but to pass it over in silence, without any declaration of it, seeming to bear with such laws and rites as the place hath where you shall arrive.

23. *Item*, for as much as our people and ships may appear unto them strange and wondrous, and theirs also to ours, it is to be considered how they may be used, learning much of their natures and dispositions, by some one such person as you may first either allure or take to be brought aboard your ships, and there to learn as you may, without violence or force; and no woman to be tempted or entreated to incontinency or dishonesty.

24. *Item*, the person so taken to be well entertained, used, and appareled, to be set on land, to the intent that he or she may allure other to draw nigh to show the commodities. And if the person taken may be made drunk with your beer or wine, you shall know the secrets of his heart.

25. *Item*, our people may not pass further into a land than that they may be able to recover their pinnaces or ships; and not to credit the fair words of the strange people, which be many times tried subtle and false, nor to be drawn into peril of loss for the desire of gold, silver, or riches. And esteem your own commodities above all other, and in countenance show not much to desire the foreign commodities; nevertheless take them as for friendship, or by way of permutation.

26. *Item*, every nation and region is to be considered advisedly, and not to provoke them by any disdain, laughing, contempt, or suchlike, but to use them with prudent circumspection, with all gentleness and courtesy. And not to tarry long in one place, until you shall have attained the most worthy place that may be found, in such sort as you may return with victuals sufficient prosperously.

27. *Item*, the names of the people of every island are to be taken in writing, with the commodities and incommodities of the same, their natures, qualities, and dispositions, the site of the same, and what things they are most desirous of, and what

commodities they will most willingly depart with, and what metals they have in hills, mountains, streams, or rivers, in or under the earth.

28. *Item*, if people shall appear gathering of stones, gold, metal, or other like on the sand, your pinnaces may draw nigh, marking what things they gather, using or playing upon the drum or such other instruments as may allure them to harkening, to fantasy, or desire to see and hear your instruments and voices. But keep you out of danger, and show to them no point or sign of rigor and hostility.

29. *Item*, if you shall be invited into any lord's or ruler's house, to dinner or other parlance, go in such order of strength that you may be stronger than they; and be wary of woods and ambushes, and that your weapons be not out of your possessions.

30. *Item*, if you shall see them wear lions' or bears' skins, having long bows, and arrows, be not afraid of that sight; for such be worn oftentimes more to fear [frighten] strangers than for any other cause.

31. *Item*, there are people that can swim in the sea, havens, and rivers naked, having bows and shafts, coveting to draw nigh your ships, which if they shall find not well watched or warded, they will assault, desirous of the bodies of men, which they covet for meat. If you resist them, they dive, and so will flee; and therefore diligent watch is to be kept both day and night, in some islands.

32. *Item*, if occasion shall serve that you may give advertisements of your proceedings in such things as may correspond to the expectation of the company, and likelihood of success in the voyage, passing such dangers of the seas, perils of ice, intolerable colds, and other impediments, which by sundry authors and writers have ministered matter of suspicion in some heads that this voyage could not succeed for the extremity of the North Pole, lack of passage, and suchlike, which have caused wavering minds and doubtful heads not only to withdraw themselves from the adventure of this voyage, but also dissuaded others from the same; the certainty whereof, when you shall have tried by experience (most certain master of all worldly knowledge), then for declaration of the truth,

which you shall have experted, you may by common assent of counsel send either by land or otherwise such two or one person, to bring the same by credit as you shall think may pass in safety. Which sending is not to be done but upon urgent causes, in likely success of the voyage, in finding of passage, in towardliness of beneficial traffic, or such other like, whereby the company, being advertised of your estates and proceedings may further provide, foresee, and determine that which may seem most good and beneficial for the public wealth of the same, either providing beforehand such things as shall be requisite for the continuance of the voyage, or else otherwise to dispose as occasion shall serve: In which things your wisdoms and discretions are to be used and showed, and the contents of this capitule by you much to be pondered, for that you be not ignorant how many persons, as well as the King's Majesty, the lords of his honorable Council, this whole company, as also your wives, children, kinsfolks, allies, friends, and familiars, be replenished in their hearts with ardent desire to learn and know your estates, conditions, and welfares; and in what likelihood you be in to obtain this notable enterprise, which is hoped no less to succeed to you than the Orient or Occident Indies have to the high benefit of the Emperor and Kings of Portugal, whose subjects' industries and travails by sea have enriched them by those lands and islands which were to all cosmographers and other writers both unknown and also by appearances of reason void of experience thought and reputed unhabitable for extremities of heats, and colds, and yet indeed tried [proved] most rich, peopled, temperate, and so commodious as all Europe hath not the like.

33. *Item,* no conspiracies, partakings, factions, false tales, untrue reports, which be the very seeds and fruits of contention, discord, and confusion, by evil tongues to be suffered, but the same, and all other ungodliness, to be chastened charitably with brotherly love, and always obedience to be used and practiced by all persons in their degrees, not only for duty and conscience' sake toward God, under whose merciful hand navigants above all other creatures naturally be most nigh and vicine, but also for prudent and worldly policy and public weal, considering and always having present in your minds that

you be all one most royal King's subjects and naturals, with daily remembrance of the great importance of the voyage, the honor, glory, praise, and benefit that depend of and upon the same, toward the common wealth of this noble realm, the advancement of you the travailers therein, your wives and children, and so to endeavor yourselves as that you may satisfy the expectation of them who at their great costs, charges, and expenses have so furnished you in good sort and plenty of all necessaries as the like was never in any realm seen, used, or known requisite and needful for such an exploit, which is most likely to be achieved and brought to good effect if every person in his vocation shall endeavor himself according to his charge and most bounden duty; praying the living God to give you His grace to accomplish your charge to His glory, whose merciful hand shall prosper your voyage and preserve you from all dangers.

In witness whereof I, Sebastian Cabota, Governor aforesaid, to these present ordinances have subscribed my name and put my seal, the day and year above-written. 🐦

🐦 *The true copie of a note found written in one of the two ships, to wit, the* Speranza, *which wintred in Lappia, where sir Hugh Willoughby and all his companie died, being frozen to death. Anno 1553.*

The voyage intended for the discovery of Cathay, and divers other regions, dominions, islands, and places unknown, set forth by the right worshipful master Sebastian Cabota [Cabot], Esquire, and Governor of the mystery and company of the Merchants Adventurers of the City of London; which fleet, being furnished, did set forth the tenth day of May 1553, and in the seventh year of our Most Dread Sovereign Lord and King, Edward the Sixth.

The names of the ships of the fleet, and of their burden, together with the names of the captains and counselors, pilot major, masters of the ships, merchants, with other officers, and mariners, as hereafter followeth.

The *Bona Esperanza* [usually called the *Speranza*], Admiral of the fleet, of 120 tons, having with her a pinnace and a boat.

Sir Hugh Willoughby, Knight, Captain General of the fleet. William Gefferson, master of the ship. [Here, as with later-mentioned ships of the fleet, names of the other officers and men are omitted.]

The *Edward Bonaventure*, of 160 tons, with her a pinnace and a boat. Richard Chancelor [Chancellor], captain and pilot major of the fleet. Stephen Borowgh, master of the ship. [The master of the *Edward Bonaventure* is that Stephen Burrough (Borrough, Borowgh, Burrowe) whose voyage in 1556 is described hereafter.]

The *Bona Confidentia*, of 90 tons, having with her a pinnace and a boat. Cornelius Durfoorth, master of the ship.

[Here follow in Willoughby's note the long oaths which were required of the officers and men of the expedition. These are entitled "The juramentum, or oath, ministered to the captain," and "The oath ministered to the master of the ship, etc." The Willoughby note continues:]

These foresaid ships being fully furnished with their pinnaces and boats, well appointed with all manner of artillery and other things necessary for their defense, with all the men aforesaid, departed from Ratcliffe [Ratcliff], and valed unto Detford [Deptford], the tenth day of May 1553.

The eleventh day about two of the clock, we departed from Deptford, passing by Greenwich, saluting the King's Majesty then being there, shooting off our ordinance, and so valed unto Blackwall, and there remained until the seventeenth day. And that day in the morning we went from Blackwall, and came to Woolwich by nine of the clock, and there remained one tide, and so the same night unto Heyreth.

The eighteenth day from Heyreth unto Gravesend, and there remained until the twentieth day. That day being Saturday, from Gravesend unto Tilberie Hope [Tilbury Harbor], remaining there until the two and twentieth day.

[Such delays as the six days at Blackwell and the two at Gravesend were repeated throughout May—frequent calls for one day at a port, several calls for several days each—so that the last of May found them not beyond Orwell, where they remained fifteen days. From June 15 to 19 they made some progress, but "The nineteenth day at eight of the clock in the morning we went back to Orwell, and abode there three days tarrying for the wind," so the total time lost at or near Orwell became twenty-two days. Thus it was more than six weeks after the departure from Ratcliff before they were at last well off on their voyage, heading for the Shetlands. There may have been any number of contributory circumstances and goodish excuses; but still this tardiness must indicate that Willoughby did not realize how brief the season would be during which the climate left him free to navigate the waters north of Russia. Moreover, the season was farther advanced than indicated by the narrative, which is based on the old calendar; according to the new reckoning, it was July 3, not June 23, when they finally set out for the Shetlands.]

The twenty-third day of June, the wind being fair in the southwest, we hailed into the seas to Orfordnesse, and from thence into the seas 10 leagues northeast. Then, being past the sands, we changed our course 6 leagues north-northeast. About midnight we changed our course again and went due north, continuing in the same unto the twenty-seventh day.

The twenty-seventh day about seven of the clock, north-northwest 42 leagues to the end to fall with Shotland. Then the wind veered to the west, so that we could lie but north and by west, continuing in the same course 40 leagues, whereby we could not fetch Shotland. Then we sailed north 16 leagues by estimation, after that north and by west and north-northwest, then southeast, with divers other courses, traversing and tracing the seas, by reason of sundry and manifold contrary winds, until the fourteenth day of July. And then, the sun entering into Leo, we discovered land eastward of us, unto the which we sailed that night as much as we might. And after, we went on shore with our pinnace, and found little houses to the number of thirty, where we knew that it was inhabited, but the people were fled away, as we judged for fear of us.

The land was all full of little islands, and that innumerable, which were called (as we learned afterward) Aegeland and

Halgeland, which lieth from Orfordnesse north and by east, being in the latitude of 66 degrees. The distance between Orfordnesse and Aegeland 250 leagues. Then we sailed from thence 12 leagues northwest, and found many other islands, and there came to anchor the nineteenth day, and manned our pinnace and went on shore to the islands, and found people mowing and making hay, which came to the shore and welcomed us. In which place were an innumerable sort of islands which were called the Isles of Rost, being under the dominion of the King of Denmark, which place was in latitude 66 degrees and 30 minutes. The wind being contrary, we remained there three days, and there was an innumerable sort of fowls of divers kinds, of which we took very many.

The twenty-second day, the wind coming fair, we departed from Rost, sailing north-northeast, keeping the sea until the twenty-seventh day, and then we drew near unto the land, which was still east of us. Then went forth our pinnace to seek harbor, and found many good harbors, of the which we entered into one with our ships, which was called Stanfew, and the land being islands, were called Lewfoot, or Lofoot [Lofoten], which were plentifully inhabited, and very gentle people, being also under the King of Denmark. But we could not learn how far it was from the mainland. And we remained there until the thirtieth day, being in latitude 68 degrees, and from the foresaid Rost about 30 leagues north-northeast.

The thirtieth day of July about noon we weighed our anchors, and went into the seas, and sailed along these islands northnortheast, keeping the land still in sight until the second day of August. Then hauling in close aboard the land, to the intent to know what land it was, there came a skiff of the island aboard of us, of whom we asked many questions, who showed unto us that the island was called Seynam, which is the latitude of 70 degrees, and from Stanfew 30 leagues, being also under the King of Denmark, and that there was no merchandise there, but only dried fish and train oil.

Then we, being purposed to go unto Finmarke [Finmark], inquired of him if we might have a pilot to bring us unto Finmark, and he said that if we could bear in, we should have a good harbor, and on the next day a pilot to bring us to Fin-

mark, unto the Wardhouse,[1] which is the strongest hold in
Finmark, and most resorted to by report. But when we would
have entered into a harbor, the land being very high on every
side, there came such flaws of wind and terrible whirlwinds
that we were not able to bear in, but by violence were constrained to take the sea again, our pinnace being unshipped.
We sailed north and by east, the wind increasing so sore that
we were not able to bear any sail, but took them in and lay
adrift, to the end to let the storm overpass. And that night, by
violence of wind and thickness of mists, we were not able to
keep together within sight, and then about midnight we lost
our pinnace, which was a discomfort unto us.

As soon as it was day, and the fog overpast, we looked about,
and at the last we descried one of our ships to leeward of us.
Then we spread a hullock of our foresail, and bare room with
her, which was the *Confidence*, but the *Edward* we could
not see. Then, the flaw something abating, we and the *Confidence* hoisted up our sails the fourth day, sailing northeast and by north, to the end to fall with the Wardhouse,
as we did consult to do before, in case we should part company. Thus running northeast and by north and northeast 50
leagues, then we sounded, and had 160 fathoms, whereby we
thought to be far from land, and perceived that the land lay not
as the globe made mention. Wherefore we changed our course
the sixth day, and sailed southeast and by south 48 leagues,
thinking thereby to find the Wardhouse.

The eighth day, much wind rising at the west-northwest, we,
not knowing how the coast lay, struck our sails and lay adrift,
where we sounded and found 160 fathoms as afore.

The ninth day, the wind veering to the south-southeast, we
sailed northeast 25 leagues.

The tenth day, we sounded and could get no ground, neither
yet could see any land, whereat we wondered. Then, the wind
coming at the northeast, we ran southeast about 48 leagues.

The eleventh day, the wind being at south, we sounded, and
found 40 fathoms, and fair sand.

---

[1] Vardö (Vardöhus), an island lying off the northeastern extremity of Norway.

The twelfth day, the wind being at south and by east, we lay with our sail east and east by north 30 leagues.

The fourteenth day, early in the morning we descried land [probably Kolguev Island], which land we bare withal, hoisting out our boat to discover what land it might be. But the boat could not come to land, the water was so shoal, where was very much ice also, but there was no similitude of habitation. And this land lieth from Seynam east and by north 160 leagues, being in latitude 72 degrees. Then we plied to the northward the fifteenth, sixteenth, and seventeenth days.

The eighteenth day, the wind coming at the northeast, and the *Confidence* being troubled with bilge water and stocked, we thought it good to seek harbor for her redress. Then we bare room the eighteenth day south-southeast, about 70 leagues.

The twenty-first day, we sounded and found 10 fathoms. After that we sounded again and found but 7 fathoms, so shoaler and shoaler water, and yet could see no land, whereat we marveled greatly. To avoid this danger, we bare roomer into the sea eleven that night, northwest and by west.

The next day we sounded and had 20 fathoms, then shaped our course and ran west-southwest until the second day. Then we descried low land, unto which we bare as nigh as we could, and it appeared unto us unhabitable. Then we plied westward along by that land, which lieth west-southwest and east-northeast, and, much wind blowing at the west, we hauled into the sea north and by east 30 leagues. Then, the wind coming about at the northeast, we sailed west-northwest. After that, the wind bearing to the northwest, we lay with our sails west-southwest, about 14 leagues, and then descried land and bare in with it, being the twenty-eighth day, finding shoal water, and bare it till we came to 3 fathoms. Then, perceiving it to be shoal water, and also seeing dry sands, we hauled out again northeast along that land until we came to the point thereof. That land turning to the westward, we ran along 16 leagues northwest. Then, coming into a fair bay, we went on land with our boat, which place was unhabited, but yet it appeared unto us that the people had been there, by crosses and other signs. From thence we went all along the coast westward.

The fourth day of September, we lost sight of land, by reason of contrary winds, and the eighth day we descried land again. Within two days after, we lost the sight of it. Then, running west and by south about 30 leagues, we got the sight of land again and bare in with it until night. Then, perceiving it to be a lee shore, we got us into the sea, to the end to have sea room.

The twelfth of September, we hauled to shoreward again, having then indifferent wind and weather. Then, being near unto the shore, and the tide almost spent, we came to an anchor in 30 fathoms water.

The thirteenth day, we came along the coast, which lay northwest and by west and southeast and by east.

The fourteenth day, we came to an anchor within 2 leagues of the shore, having 60 fathoms.

There we went ashore with our boat, and found two or three good harbors, the land being rocky and high, but as for people could we see none. The fifteenth day, we ran still along the coast until the seventeenth day. Then, the wind being contrary unto us, we thought it best to return unto the harbor which we had found before, and so we bare roomer with the same, howbeit we could not accomplish our desire that day. The next day, being the eighteenth of September, we entered into the haven, and there came to an anchor at 6 fathoms. This haven runneth into the main[land] about 2 leagues, and is in breadth half a league, wherein were very many seal fishes and other great fishes, and upon the main we saw bears, great deer, foxes, with divers strange beasts, as guloines and such other which were to us unknown, and also wonderful. Thus remaining in this haven the space of a week, seeing the year far spent, and also very evil weather, as frost, snow, and hail, as though it had been the deep of winter, we thought best to winter there. Wherefore we sent out three men south-southwest, to search if they could find people, who went three days' journey, but could find none. After that, we sent other three westward four days' journey, which also returned without finding any people. Then sent we three men southeast three days' journey, who in like sort returned without finding of people, or any similitude of habitation.

Here endeth Sir Hugh Willoughbie his note, which was written with his owne hand. 🖦

Willoughby's note came to light in 1554 when some Russian fishermen found the ships and the bodies of the company, where they had died. The two vessels, one of them carrying Willoughby's corpse, were sent to England in 1555 by the merchant George Killingworth. Hakluyt, after quoting the Willoughby journal, says further:

🖦 These two notes following were written upon the outside of this pamphlet, or book.

1. The proceedings of Sir Hugh Willoughby after he was separated from the *Edward Bonaventure*.

2. Our ship being at an anchor in the harbor called Sterfier in the Island Lofoten.

The river or haven wherein Sir Hugh Willoughby with the company of his two ships perished for cold is called Arzina in Lapland, near unto Kegor. But it appeareth by a will found in the ship that Sir Hugh Willoughby and most of the company were alive in January 1554. 🖦

We turn now to the fuller Chancellor account, which Hakluyt prefaces with the testimony of Richard Eden to the effect that the book was "largely and faithfully written in the Latin tongue, by that learned young man Clement Adams, schoolmaster to the Queen's henchmen, as he received it at the mouth of the said Richard Chancellor."

Samuel Purchas, who presents an extract from this work in his collection of voyages, displays, in a marginal note, the true passion of the booklover and collector when he says: "I have this book of Clement Adams, in Latin, written in a very elegant hand and eloquent style to King Philip, (as I think) the very original."

🖦 *The newe Navigation and discoverie of the kingdome of Moscovia, by the Northeast, in the yeere 1553: Enterprised by Sir Hugh Willoughbie knight, and perfourmed by Richard*

Chancelor Pilot major of the voyage: Written in Latine by Clement Adams.

At what time our merchants perceived the commodities and wares of England to be in small request with the countries and people about us, and near unto us, and that those merchandises which strangers in the time and memory of our ancestors did earnestly seek and desire were now neglected, and the price thereof abated, although by us carried to their own ports, and all foreign merchandises in great account and their prices wonderfully raised—certain grave citizens of London, and men of great wisdom and careful for the good of their country, began to think with themselves how this mischief might be remedied. Neither was a remedy (as it then appeared) wanting to their desires, for the avoiding of so great an inconvenience. For seeing that the wealth of the Spaniards and Portuguese by the discovery and search of new trades and countries was marvelously increased, supposing the same to be a course and mean for them also to obtain the like, they thereupon resolved upon a new and strange navigation.

And whereas at the same time one Sebastian Cabota [Cabot], a man in those days very renowned, happened to be in London, they began first of all to deal and consult diligently with him, and after much speech and conference together, it was at last concluded that three ships should be prepared and furnished out, for the search and discovery of the northern part of the world, to open a way and passage to our men for travel to new and unknown kingdoms.

And whereas many things seemed necessary to be regarded in this so hard and difficult a matter, they first make choice of certain grave and wise persons in manner of a Senate or company, which should lay their heads together, and give their judgments, and provide things requisite and profitable for all occasions. By this company it was thought expedient that a certain sum of money should publicly be collected to serve for the furnishing of so many ships. And lest any private man should be too much oppressed and charged, a course was taken that every man willing to be of the society should disburse the portion of £25 apiece. So that in short time by this means the sum of £6000 being gathered, the three ships were bought, the most part whereof they provided to be newly built and trimmed.

But in this action, I wot not whether I may more admire the care of the merchants or the diligence of the shipwrights. For the merchants, they get very strong and well-seasoned planks for the building; the shipwrights, they with daily travail and their greatest skill do fit them for the dispatch of the ships. They calk them, pitch them, and among the rest, they make one most stanch and firm by an excellent and ingenious invention.

For they had heard that in certain parts of the ocean, a kind of worm is bred which many times pierceth and eateth through the strongest oak that is; and therefore that the mariners, and the rest to be employed in this voyage, might be free and safe from this danger, they cover a piece of the keel of the ship with thin sheets of lead. And having thus built the ships, and furnished them with armor and artillery, then followed a second care no less troublesome and necessary than the former; namely, the provision of victuals, which was to be made according to the time and length of the voyage.

And whereas they afore determined to have the east part of the world sailed unto, and yet that the sea toward the same was not open except they kept the northern tract, whereas yet it was doubtful whether there were any passage yea or no, they resolved to victual the ships for eighteen months, which they did for this reason. For our men being to pass that huge and cold part of the world, they, wisely foreseeing it, allow them six months victual to sail to the place, so much more to remain there if the extremity of the winter hindered their return, and so much more also for the time of their coming home.

Now this provision being made and carried aboard, with armor and munition of all sorts, sufficient captains and governors of so great an enterprise were as yet wanting: To which office and place, although many men (and some void of experience) offered themselves, yet one Sir Hugh Willoughby, a most valiant gentleman, and well-born, very earnestly requested to have that care and charge committed unto him; of whom before all others, both by reason of his goodly personage (for he was of a tall stature) as also for his singular skill in the services of war, the company of the merchants made greatest account; so that at the last they concluded and made choice of him for the general of this voyage, and appointed to him the Admiral with authority and command over all the rest.

And for the government of other ships, although divers men seemed willing and made offers of themselves thereunto, yet by a common consent one Richard Chancellor, a man of great estimation for many good parts of wit in him, was elected, in whom alone great hope for the performance of this business rested. This man was brought up by one Master Henry Sidney, a noble young gentleman and very much beloved of King Edward, who at this time, coming to the place where the merchants were gathered together, began a very eloquent speech or oration, and spake to them after this manner following.

"My very worshipful friends, I cannot but greatly commend your present godly and virtuous intention in the serious enterprising (for the singular love you bear to your country) a matter which (I hope) will prove profitable for this nation, and honorable to this our land. Which intention of yours we also of the nobility are ready to our power to help and further. Neither do we hold anything so dear and precious unto us which we will not willingly forgo and lay out in so commendable a cause. But principally I rejoice in myself that I have nourished and maintained that wit which is like by some means, and in some measure, to profit and stead you in this worthy action.

"But yet I would not have you ignorant of this one thing, that I do now part with Chancellor not because I make little reckoning of the man, or that his maintenance is burdenous and chargeable unto me, but that you might conceive and understand my goodwill and promptitude for the furtherance of this business, and that the authority and estimation which he deserveth may be given him. You know the man by report, I by experience; you by words, I by deeds; you by speech and company, but I by the daily trial of his life have a full and perfect knowledge of him.

"And you are also to remember into how many perils for your

sakes, and his country's love, he is now to run; whereof it is requisite that we be not unmindful, if it please God to send him good success.

"We commit a little money to the chance and hazard of fortune. He commits his life (a thing to a man of all things most dear) to the raging sea, and the uncertainties of many dangers. We shall here live and rest at home quietly with our friends and acquaintance; but he in the meantime, laboring to keep the ignorant and unruly mariners in good order and obedience, with how many cares shall he trouble and vex himself? With how many troubles shall he break himself? And how many disquietings shall he be forced to sustain? We shall keep our own coasts and country, he shall seek strange and unknown kingdoms. He shall commit his safety to barbarous and cruel people, and shall hazard his life amongst the monstrous and terrible beasts of the sea.

"Wherefore in respect of the greatness of the dangers, and the excellency of his charge, you are to favor and love the man thus departing from us. And if it fall so happily out that he return again, it is your part and duty also liberally to reward him."

After that this noble young gentleman had delivered this or some suchlike speech, much more eloquently than I can possibly report it, the company then present began one to look upon another, one to question and confer with another. And some (to whom the virtue and sufficiency of the man was known) began secretly to rejoice with themselves, and to conceive a special hope that the man would prove in time very rare and excellent, and that his virtues already appearing and shining to the world would grow, to the great honor and advancement of this kingdom.

After all this, the company growing to some silence, it seemed good to them that were of greatest gravity amongst them to inquire, search, and seek what might be learned and known concerning the easterly part or tract of the world. For such cause two Tartarians [Tatars], which were then of the King's stable, were sent for, and an interpreter was gotten to be present, by whom they were demanded touching their country and the manners of their nation. But they were able to answer nothing to the purpose, being indeed more acquainted (as one there merrily and openly said) to toss pots than to learn the states and dispositions of people.

But after much ado and many things passed about this matter, they grew at last to this issue, to set down and appoint a time for the departure of the ships; because divers were of opinion that a great part of the best time of the year was already spent, and if the delay grew longer, the way would be stopped and barred by the force of the ice and the cold climate. And therefore it was thought best by the opinion of them all that by the twentieth day of May, the captains and mariners should take shipping, and depart from Radcliffe upon the ebb, if it pleased God.

They, having saluted their acquaintance, one his wife, another his children, another his kinsfolks, and another his friends dearer than his kinsfolks, were present and ready at the day appointed; and having weighed anchor, they departed with the turning of the water, and sailing easily, came first to Greenwich. The greater ships are towed down with boats and oars, and the mariners, being all appareled in watchet or sky-colored cloth, rowed amain, and made way with diligence.

And being come near to Greenwich (where the Court then lay), presently upon the news thereof the courtiers came running out, and the common people flocked together, standing very thick upon the shore. The Privy Council, they looked out at the windows of the Court, and the rest ran up to the tops of the towers. The ships hereupon discharge their ordinance, and shoot off their pieces after the manner of war and of the sea, insomuch that the tops of the hills sounded therewith, the valleys and the waters gave an echo.

And the mariners, they shouted in such sort that the sky rang again with the noise thereof. One stood in the poop of the ship, and by his gesture bids farewell to his friends in the best manner he could. Another walks upon the hatches, another climbs the shrouds, another stands upon the mainyard, and another in the top of the ship.

To be short, it was a very triumph (after a sort) in all respects to the beholders.

But (alas) the good King Edward (in respect of whom principally all this was prepared), he only by reason of his sickness was absent from this show, and not long after the departure of these ships, the lamentable and most sorrowful accident of his death followed.

But to proceed in the matter.

The ships, going down with the tide, came at last to Woolwich, where they stayed and cast anchor, with purpose to depart therehence again as soon as the turning of the water and a better wind should draw them to set sail. After this they departed and came in to Harwich, in which port they stayed long, not without great loss and consuming of time. Yet at the last, with a good wind they hoisted up sail and committed themselves to the sea, giving their last adieu to their native country, which they knew not whether they should ever return to see again or not. Many of them looked oftentimes back, and could not refrain from tears, considering into what hazards they were to fall and what uncertainties of the sea they were to make trial of.

Amongst the rest, Richard Chancellor, the Captain of the *Edward Bonaventure*, was not a little grieved with the fear of wanting victuals, part whereof was found to be corrupt and putrefied at Harwich, and the hogsheads of wine also leaked, and were not stanch. His natural and fatherly affection also somewhat troubled him, for he left behind him his two little sons, which were in the case of orphans if he sped not well. The estate also of his company moved him to care, being in the former respects after a sort unhappy, and were to abide with himself every good or bad accident.

But in the meantime while his mind was thus tormented with the multiplicity of sorrows and cares, after many days sailing, they kenned land afar off, whereunto the pilots directed the ships. And being come to it, they land, and find it to be Rost Island, where they stayed certain days, and afterward set sail again, and proceeding toward the north, they espied certain other islands, which were called the Crosse of Islands.

From which places when they were a little departed, Sir Hugh Willoughby, the General, a man of good foresight and providence in all his actions, erected and set out his flag, by which he called together the chiefest men of the other ships, that by the help and assistance of their counsels, the order of the government and conduction of the ships in the whole voyage might be the better. Who being come together accordingly, they conclude and agree that if any great tempest should arise at any time and happen to disperse and scatter them, every ship should endeavor his best to go to Wardhouse, a haven or castle of some name in the kingdom of Norway, and that they that arrived there first in safety should stay and expect the coming of the rest.

The very same day in the afternoon, about four of the clock, so great a tempest suddenly arose, and the seas were so outrageous, that the ships could not keep their intended course, but some were perforce driven one way and some another way, to their great peril and hazard. The General with his loudest voice cried out to Richard Chancellor, and earnestly requested him not to go far from him. But he neither would nor could keep company with him if he sailed still so fast; for the Admiral [the *Speranza*] was of better sail than his ship. But the said Admiral (I know not by what means), bearing all his sails, was carried away with so great force and swiftness that not long after he was quite out of sight, and the third ship also with the same storm and like rage was dispersed and lost us.

The ship boat of the Admiral (striking against the ship) was overwhelmed in the sight and view of the mariners of the *Bonaventure*. And as for them that are already returned and arrived, they know nothing of the rest of the ships, what was become of them.

But if it be so that any miserable mishap have overtaken them, if the rage and fury of the sea have devoured those good men, or if as yet they live and wander up and down in strange countries, I must needs say that they were men worthy of better fortune, and if they be living, let us wish them safety and a good return. But if the cruelty of death hath taken hold of them, God send them a Christian grave and sepulcher.[2]

Now Richard Chancellor, with his ship and company, being thus left alone, and become very pensive, heavy, and sorrow-

---

[2] This appears to have been written by Adams before the fate of Willoughby and his crew became known in England.

ful by this dispersion of the fleet, he (according to the order
before taken) shapeth his course for Wardhouse in Norway,
there to expect and bide the arrival of the rest of the ships.
And being come thither, and having stayed there the space of
seven days and looked in vain for their coming, he determined
at length to proceed alone in the purposed voyage.

And as he was preparing himself to depart, it happened
that he fell in company and speech with certain Scottishmen,
who having understanding of his intention, and wishing well to
his actions, began earnestly to dissuade him from the further
prosecution of the discovery by amplifying the dangers which
he was to fall into, and omitted no reason that might serve
to that purpose.

But he, holding nothing so ignominious and reproachful as
inconstancy and levity of mind, and persuading himself that
a man of valor could not commit a more dishonorable part
than for fear of danger to avoid and shun great attempts, was
nothing at all changed or discouraged with the speeches and
words of the Scots, remaining steadfast and immutable in his
first resolution—determining either to bring that to pass which
was intended, or else to die the death.

And as for them which were with Master Chancellor in his
ship, although they had great cause of discomfort by the loss
of their company (whom the foresaid tempest had separated
from them) and were not a little troubled with cogitations and
perturbations of mind in respect of their doubtful course, yet
notwithstanding, they were of such consent and agreement of
mind with Master Chancellor that they were resolute, and
prepared, under his direction and government, to make proof
and trial of all adventures, without all fear or mistrust of future
dangers. Which constancy of mind in all the company did
exceedingly increase their Captain's carefulness; for he, being
swallowed up with like goodwill and love toward them, feared
lest through any error of his the safety of the company should
be endangered.

To conclude, when they saw their desire and hope of the
arrival of the rest of the ships to be every day more and more
frustrated, they provided to sea again, and Master Chancellor
held on his course toward that unknown part of the world, and

sailed so far that he came at last to the place where he found no night at all, but a continual light and brightness of the sun shining clearly upon the huge and mighty sea. And having the benefit of this perpetual light for certain days, at the length it pleased God to bring them into a certain great bay, which was of 100 miles or thereabout over.[3]

Whereinto they entered, and somewhat far within it cast anchor, and looking every way about them, it happened that they espied afar off a certain fisher boat, which Master Chancellor, accompanied with a few of his men, went toward to commune with the fishermen that were in it, and to know of them what country it was, and what people, and of what manner of living they were. But they, being amazed with the strange greatness of his ship (for in those parts before that time they had never seen the like), began presently to avoid and to flee. But he, still following them, at last overtook them, and being come to them, they (being in great fear, as men half-dead) prostrated themselves before him, offering to kiss his feet. But he (according to his great and singular courtesy) looked pleasantly upon them, comforting them by signs and gestures, refusing those duties and deferences of theirs, and taking them up in all loving sort from the ground.

And it is strange to consider how much favor afterward in that place this humanity of his did purchase to himself. For they, being dismissed, spread by and by a report abroad of the arrival of a strange nation, of a singular gentleness and courtesy. Whereupon the common people came together offering to these new-come guests victuals freely, and not refusing to traffic with them, except they had been bound by a certain religious use and custom not to buy any foreign commodities without the knowledge and consent of the King.

By this time our men had learned that this country was called Russia, or Muscovie [Muscovy], and that Ivan Vasilivich [Ivan IV, the Terrible] (which was at that time their King's name) ruled and governed far and wide in those places. And the barbarous Russians (Russes) asked likewise of our men whence they were, and what they came for. Whereunto answer was

___

[3] This was the White Sea. Anchorage was taken at the mouth of the Dvina, near the site of the present city of Archangel.

made that they were Englishmen sent into those coasts from the Most Excellent King Edward the Sixth, having from him in commandment certain things to deliver to their King, and seeking nothing else but his amity and friendship, and traffic with his people, whereby they doubted not but that great commodity and profit would grow to the subjects of both kingdoms.

The barbarians heard these things very gladly, and promised their aid and furtherance to acquaint their King out of hand with so honest and reasonable a request.

In the meantime Master Chancellor entreated victuals for his money of the governor of that place (who together with others came aboard him), and required hostages of them likewise for the more assurance of safety to himself and his company. To whom the governors answered that they knew not in that case the will of their King, but yet were willing in such things as they might lawfully do, to pleasure him; which was as then to afford him the benefit of victuals.

Now while these things were a-doing, they secretly sent a messenger unto the Emperor, to certify him of the arrival of a strange nation, and withal to know his pleasure concerning them. Which message was very welcome unto him, insomuch that voluntarily he invited them to come to his Court. But if by reason of the tediousness of so long a journey they thought it not best so to do, then he granted liberty to his subjects to bargain and to traffic with them; and further promised that if it would please them to come to him, he himself would bear the whole charges of post horses.

In the meantime the governors of the place deferred the matter from day to day, pretending divers excuses, and saying one while that the consent of all the governors, and another while, that the great and weighty affairs of the kingdom, compelled them to defer their answers. And this they did of purpose, so long to protract the time until the messenger (sent before to the King) did return with relation of his will and pleasure.

But Master Chancellor (seeing himself held in this suspense with long and vain expectation, and thinking that of intention to delude him they posted the matter off so often) was very instant with them to perform their promise. Which if they would not do, he told them that he would depart and proceed in his voyage. So that the Muscovites (although as yet they knew not the mind of their King), yet fearing the departure indeed of our men, who had such wares and commodities as they greatly desired, they at last resolved to furnish our people with all things necessary, and to conduct them by land to the presence of their King.

And so Master Chancellor began his journey, which was very long and most troublesome, wherein he had the use of certain sleds, which in that country are very common, for they are carried themselves upon sleds, and all their carriages are in the same sort, the people almost not knowing any other manner of carriage. The cause whereof is the exceeding hardness of the ground congealed in the wintertime by the force of the cold, which in those places is very extreme and horrible, where-of hereafter we will say something.

But now they, having passed the greater part of their journey, met at last with the sledman (of whom I spake before) sent to the King secretly from the justices or governors, who by some ill hap had lost his way and had gone to the seaside, which is near to the country of the Tatars, thinking there to have found our ship.

But having long erred and wandered out of his way, at the last in his direct return he met (as he was coming) our Captain on the way. To whom he by and by delivered the Emperor's letters, which were written to him with all courtesy and in the most loving manner that could be; wherein express commandment was given that post horses should be gotten for him and the rest of his company without any money. Which thing was of all the Russes [Russians] in the rest of their journey so willingly done that they began to quarrel, yea, and to fight also, in striving and contending which of them should put their post horses to the sleds. So that after much ado and great pains taken in this long and weary journey (for they had traveled very near 1500 miles) Master Chancellor came at last to Mosco [Moscow], the chief city of the kingdom and the seat of the King; of which city, and of the Emperor himself, and of the principal cities of Muscovy, we will speak immediately more at large in this discourse. ✍

The remainder of Clement Adams' discourse tells "Of Moscovie, which is also called Russia," and describes the country, the principal cities, the Court, the manners, and the religion of the people ruled by the "great Duke Ivan Vasilivich, by the grace of God great lord and Emperor of all Russia, great Duke of Volodemer, Mosco, and Novograd, King of Kazan, King of Astracan, lord of Plesko, and a great duke of Smolensko, of Twerria, Joughoria, Permia, Vadska, Bulghoria, and others, lord and great duke of Novograd in the low country, of Chernigo, Rezan, Polotskoy, Rostove, Yaruslavely, Bealozera, Liefland, Oudoria, Obdoria, and Condensa, Commander of all Siberia, and of the north parts, and lord of many other countries."

This account, fascinating as it is and important as it was in providing England with the first eyewitness description of the great Muscovite Empire, lies outside the scope of this work.

Chancellor was sumptuously entertained at the court. When he returned to England the following summer, he carried with him a cordial letter from the Emperor to the King of England, opening the way to the formal establishment of trade relations.

There was great delight in London at the prospect of this new commercial connection, and as early as 1555 a charter was granted by Philip and Mary to the company of "merchants adventurers of England, for the discovery of lands, territories, isles, dominions, and seigniories unknown," commonly called the Muscovy Company. The aged Sebastian Cabot, as the "chiefest setter-forth" of the project, was appointed Governor, "to have and enjoy the said office . . . during his natural life, without amoving or dismissing from the same room."

That year, 1555, the company sent emissaries and merchants to Russia to negotiate a commercial treaty and to examine more closely the vast new field of trade. Chancellor himself, together with George Killingworth, the company's first agent in Muscovy, and several other merchants, went again to Russia by way of his former route through the White Sea. This was Chancellor's last mission, for on the return trip to England in the summer of 1556, the *Edward Bonaventure*, in which he was escorting the Russian Ambassador to London, was wrecked off the coast of Scotland, with considerable loss of life. The Ambassador survived, but Chancellor and his wife were drowned.

The Muscovy Company did not, however, concern themselves merely with the Russian trade, were it ever so lucrative. They looked upon this as merely the first step in the grand plan for opening the Northeast Passage so that the wealth of India and China might flow by this channel from the Pacific to the Atlantic. For this purpose the small vessel *Searchthrift* was dispatched in 1556, under command of that Stephen Burrough who had been master of the *Edward Bonaventure* on the Willoughby expedition of 1553.

A. E. Nordenskiöld, in his great work *The Voyage of the Vega round Asia and Europe* (Macmillan, 1881), interprets the Burrough voyage:

"To the inhabitants of western Europe the islands Novaya Zemlya and Vaygats first became known through Stephen Burrough's voyage of discovery in 1556. Burrough therefore is often called the discoverer of Novaya Zemlya, but incorrectly. For when he came thither he found Russian vessels, manned by hunters well acquainted with the navigable waters and the land. It is clear from this that Novaya Zemlya had then already been known to the inhabitants of northern Russia for such a length of time that a very actively prosecuted hunting could arise there.

"It is even probable that in the same way as the northernmost part of Norway was already known for a thousand years back, not only to wandering Lapps, but also to Norwegians and Quaens, the land round Yugor Schar and Vaygats [Vaigach Island] was known several centuries before Burrough's time, not only to the nomad Samoyeds [Nentsi] on the mainland, but also to various Beorma or Finnish tribes. Probably the Samoyeds then, as now, drove their reindeer herds up thither to pasture on the grassy plains along the coasts of the Polar Sea, where they were less troubled by the mosquito and the reindeer fly than further to the south, and probably the wild nomads were accompanied then, as now, by merchants from the more civilized races settled in northern Russia. The name Novaya

Zemlya (New Land) indicates that it was discovered at a later period, probably by Russians, but we know neither when nor how.

"The narrative of Stephen Burrough's voyage, which like so many others has been preserved from oblivion by Hakluyt's famous collection, thus not only forms a sketch of the first expedition of western Europeans to Novaya Zemlya, but is also the principal source of our knowledge of the earliest Russian voyages to these regions."

The following are some of the most pertinent passages from the discourse in Hakluyt that bears the title

The navigation and discoverie toward the river of Ob, made by Master Steven Burrough, Master of the Pinnesse called the Serchthrift, *with divers things worth the noting, passed in the yere 1556.*

We departed from Ratcliffe to Blackwall the twenty-third of April. Saturday being Saint Mark's day, we departed from Blackwall to Gray's.

The twenty-seventh, being Monday, the Right Worshipful Sebastian Cabot came aboard our pinnace at Gravesend, accompanied with divers gentlemen and gentlewomen, who after that they had viewed our pinnace, and tasted of such cheer as we could make them aboard, they went on shore, giving to our mariners right liberal rewards. And the good old gentleman Master Cabot gave to the poor most liberal alms, wishing them to pray for the good fortune and prosperous success of the *Searchthrift,* our pinnace.

And then at the sign of the Christopher, he and his friends banqueted, and made me and them that were in the company great cheer. And for very joy that he had to see the towardness of our intended discovery, he entered into the dance himself, amongst the rest of the young and lusty company. Which being ended, he and his friends departed most gently, commending us to the governance of Almighty God.

Tuesday, we rode still at Gravesend, making provision for such things as we wanted.

Wednesday, in the morning we departed from Gravesend,

the wind being at southwest; that night we came to an anchor thwart Our Lady of Hollands.

Thursday, at three of the clock in the morning, we weighed, and by eight of the clock we were at an anchor in Orwell wannes, and then incontinent I went aboard the *Edward Bonaventure*, where the worshipful company of merchants appointed me to be, until the said good ship arrived at Wardhouse. Then I returned again into the pinnace.

[Burrough then relates the events of the crossing to Norway; at the end of May "the North Cape (which I so named the first voyage) was thwart of us." On June 7, he was aboard the *Searchthrift* once more and exchanging farewell salutes with the *Edward Bonaventure*; on the ninth, anchorage was taken at the mouth of the Kola River, where the *Searchthrift* stayed for nearly two weeks.]

[June 11, at Kola River] Thursday, at six of the clock in the morning, there came aboard of us one of the Russian *lodias*, rowing with twenty oars, and there were four and twenty men in her. The master of the boat presented me with a great loaf of bread, and six rings of bread, which they call kolaches, and four dried pikes, and a peck of fine oatmeal, and I gave unto the master of the boat a comb and a small glass. And he declared unto me that he was bound to Pechora, and after that I made them to drink, the tide being somewhat broken, they gently departed. The master's name was Pheodor. . . .

[June 18] As we rode in this river, we saw daily coming down the river many of their *lodias*, and they that had least had four and twenty men in them, and at the last they grew to thirty sail of them. And amongst the rest, there was one of them whose name was Gabriel, who shewed me very much friendship. And he declared unto me that all they were bound to Pechora, a fishing for salmons and morses [walruses]; insomuch that he shewed me by demonstrations that with a fair wind we have seven or eight days' sailing to the river Pechora, so that I was glad of their company. This Gabriel promised to give me warning of shoals, as he did indeed. . . .

[June 22] Monday, we departed from the river Cola [Kola],

with all the rest of the said *lodias*, but, sailing before the wind, they were all too good for us. But according to promise, this Gabriel and his friend did often strike their sails, and tarried for us, forsaking their own company.

[Here are omitted Burrough's accounts of his voyage eastward to the mouth of the Pechora and of his difficulty with shoals in spite of the guidance and help of Gabriel (for the English vessel was of deeper draft than the native boats). His narrative is resumed as he leaves the mouth of the Pechora bound for Novaya Zemlya.]

[July 20] Monday at a north and by east sun, we weighed, and came out over the said dangerous bar [at the mouth of the Pechora], where we had but 5 foot water, insomuch that we found a foot less water coming out than we did going in. I think the reason was, because when we went in the wind was off the sea, which caused the sands to break on either side of us, and we kept in the smoothest between the breaches, which we durst not have done except we had seen the Russians to have gone in before us; and at our coming out the wind was off the shore, and fair weather, and then the sands did not appear with breaches, as at our going in. We thank God that our ship did draw so little water.

When we were a-seaboard the bar, the wind scanted upon us, and was at east-southeast, insomuch that we stopped the ebbs, and plied all the floods to the windward and made our way east-northeast.

Tuesday at a northwest sun we thought that we had seen land at east, or east and by north of us; which afterward proved to be a monstrous heap of ice.

Within a little more than half an hour after we first saw this ice, we were enclosed within it before we were aware of it, which was a fearful sight to see. For, for the space of six hours, it was as much as we could do to keep our ship aloof from one heap of ice, and bear roomer from another with as much wind as we might bear a course. And when we had passed from the danger of this ice, we lay to the eastward close by the wind.

The next day we were again troubled with the ice.

Thursday, being calm, we plied to the windward, the wind being northerly. We had the latitude this day at noon in 70 degrees 11 minutes.

We had not run past two hours northwest, the wind being at north-northeast and northeast and by north a good gale, but we met again with another heap of ice. We weathered the head of it, and lay a time to the seaward, and made way west 6 leagues.

Friday, at a southeast sun we cast about to the eastward, the wind being at north-northeast. The latitude this day at noon was 70 degrees 15 minutes.

On Saint James his day, bolting to the windward, we had the latitude at noon in 70 degrees 20 minutes. The same day, at a southwest sun, there was a monstrous whale aboard of us, so near to our side that we might have thrust a sword or any other weapon in him, which we durst not do for fear he should have overthrown our ship. And then I called my company together, and all of us shouted, and with the cry that we made he departed from us. There was as much above-water of his back as the breadth of our pinnace, and at his falling down he made such a terrible noise in the water that a man would greatly have marveled, except he had known the cause of it. But God be thanked, we were quietly delivered of him. And a little after we spied certain islands [near the southern extremity of Novaya Zemlya], with which we bare, and found good harbor in 15 or 18 fathoms, and black ooze. We came to an anchor at a northeast sun, and named the island Saint James his Island, where we found fresh water. . . .

[July 28] Tuesday, we plied to the westward along the shore, the wind being at northwest, and as I was about to come to anchor we saw a sail coming about the point whereunder we thought to have anchored. Then I sent a skiff aboard of him, and at their coming aboard, they took acquaintance of them, and the chief man said he had been in our company in the river Kola, and also declared unto them that we were past the way which should bring us to the Ob.

This land, said he, is called Nova Zembla [Novaya Zemlya], that is to say, the New Land. And then he came aboard himself with his skiff, and at his coming aboard he told me the

like, and said further that in this Novaya Zemlya is the highest
mountain in the world.[4] as he thought, and that Camen Bold-
shay, which is on the main of Pechora, is not to be compared
to this mountain, but I saw it not. He made me also certain
demonstrations of the way to the Ob, and seemed to make
haste on his own way, being very loathe to tarry, because
the year was far past, and his neighbor had fet [fetched]
Pechora, and not he. So I gave him a steel glass, two pewter
·spoons, and a pair of velvet-sheathed knives; and then he
seemed somewhat the more willing to tarry, and showed me
as much as he knew for our purpose. He also gave me seventeen wild geese, and showed me that four of their *lodias* were
driven perforce from Caninoze [Kanin Nos or Cape] to this
Novaya Zemlya. This man's name was Loshak. . . .

[July 31] Friday, the gale of wind began to increase, and
came westerly withal, so that by a northwest sun we were at
an anchor among the islands of Vaigats [Vaigach], where we
saw two small *lodias*. The one of them came aboard of us, and
presented me with a great loaf of bread. And they told me that
they were all of Colmogro [Kholmogory, Archangel], except
one man that dwelt at Pechora, who seemed to be the chiefest
among them in killing of the morse.

There were some of their company on shore which did chase
a white bear over the high cliffs into the water, which bear
the *lodia* that was aboard of us killed in our sight.

This day there was a great gale of wind at north, and we
saw so much ice driving a-seaboard that it was then no going
to sea. . . .

[August 1] Saturday, I went ashore, and there I saw three
morses that they had killed. They held one tooth of a morse,
which was not great, at a ruble, and one white bearskin at 3
rubles and 2 rubles. They further told me that there were
people called Samoeds [Samoyeds] on the great island,[5] and
that they would not abide them nor us, who have no houses,
but only coverings made of deers' skins, set over them with

---

[4] So far as is known, the highest peaks in Novaya Zemlya attain an elevation of no more than about 4500 feet.

[5] This is one of the earliest English accounts of the people formerly known
as Samoyeds, now called Nentsi.

stakes. They are men expert in shooting, and have great plenty of deer [reindeer]. . . .

[August 3] Monday, we weighed and went room with another island, which was 5 leagues east-northeast from us. And there I met again with Loshak, and went on shore with him, and he brought me to a heap of the Samoyeds' idols, which were in number above three hundred, the worst and the most unartificial work that ever I saw. The eyes and mouths of sundry of them were bloody; they had the shape of men, women, and children, very grossly wrought, and that which they had made for other parts was also sprinkled with blood. Some of their idols were an old stick with two or three notches made with a knife in it.

I saw much of the footing of the said Samoyeds, and of the sleds that they ride in. There was one of their sleds broken, and lay by the heap of idols, and there I saw a deer's skin which the fowls had spoiled. And before certain of their idols, blocks were made as high as their mouths; being all bloody, I thought that to be the table whereon they offered their sacrifice. I saw also the instruments whereupon they had roasted flesh, and as far as I could perceive, they make their fire directly under the spit.

Loshak, being there present, told me that these Samoyeds were not so hurtful as they of Ob are, and that they have no houses, as indeed I saw none, but only tents made of deers' skins, which they underprop with stakes and poles. Their boats are made of deers' skins, and when they come onshore they carry their boats with them upon their backs. For their carriages they have no other beasts to serve them, but deer only. As for bread and corn, they have none, except the Russians bring it to them. Their knowledge is very base, for they know no letter.

[August 4] Tuesday, we turned for the harbor where Loshak's bark lay, whereas before we rode under an island. And there he came aboard of us and said unto me: "If God send wind and weather to serve, I will go to the Ob with you," because the morses were scant at these islands of Vaigach. But if he could not get to the river of Ob, then he said he would go to the river of Naramzay, where the people were not altogether so savage as the Samoyeds of the Ob are. He showed me that they will shoot at all men, to the uttermost of their power, that cannot speak their speech.

Wednesday, we saw a terrible heap of ice approach near unto us, and therefore we thought good with all speed possible to depart from thence, and so I returned to the westward again, to the island where we were the thirty-first of July.

[Plagued by drifting ice and by fierce storms, the *Searchthrift* was unable to proceed into the Kara Sea and on to the Ob.]

[August 22] And thus, we being out of all hope to discover any more to the eastward this year, we thought it best to return, and that for three causes:

The first, the continual northeast and northerly winds, which have more power after a man is passed to the eastward of Kanin Nos than in any place that I do know in these northerly regions.

Second, because of great and terrible abundance of ice which we saw with our eyes, and we doubt greater store abideth in those parts. I adventured already somewhat too far in it, but I thank God for my safe deliverance from it.

Third, because the nights waxed dark, and the winter began to draw on with his storms;[6] and therefore I resolved to take the first best wind that God should send, and ply toward the Bay of Saint Nicholas, and to see if we might do any good there, if God would permit it. ⚐

On September 11, Burrough finally arrived at Archangel, where he spent the winter, intending to continue his voyage to the Ob the following summer. This plan was abandoned, however, when it became necessary for him to turn westward instead, to search for ships of the Muscovy Company that had been lost the summer of 1556 on the return trip to England from Archangel.

Nearly a quarter of a century elapsed before there was another English attempt to find the Northeast Passage. The dis-

---

[6] The difference between the old and new calendars must be taken into account. When Burrough made his decision to turn back, it was by modern reckoning September 1, not August 22.

couraging reports brought back by Burrough no doubt were influential in causing the lapse, and besides, there was preoccupation with expanding the Muscovy trade and with fitting out Frobisher's three expeditions to the northwest.

In fact, there was only one more English attempt to find the passage during the sixteenth century. This was in 1580, when the Muscovy Company sent out Arthur Pet in the 40-ton *George*, accompanied by Charles Jackman in the 20-ton *William*. The tiny ships safely navigated the route to Novaya Zemlya, and eventually to the eastern side of Vaigach Island, thus being the first western-European vessels known to have entered the Kara Sea. The entrance to the sea was made by Yugorski Shar (Proliv Yugorski Shar, or Yugor Strait), which separates Vaigach Island from the mainland to the southward. The channel then was known locally by the name which it still retains, although it was frequently referred to thereafter by the English as Pet Strait, and by the Dutch as Vaigach Strait (spelled in many different ways) or Nassau Strait. To Pet and Jackman goes the credit also of being the first explorers in this region to venture deliberately into the drifting pack. This was perhaps the result of their previous northern experience, for Pet had been with Chancellor to the White Sea, and Jackman had served with Frobisher to the northwest with such distinction that Jackman Sound in Frobisher Bay was named for him.

After 1580 there was no further English attempt to discover a Northeast Passage until the disastrous expedition of Wood and Flawes in 1676, mentioned hereafter.

The torch was now taken up by the Netherlanders. With the successful conclusion of the war for independence against Spain, the United Provinces began to expand their maritime power and to seek ways and means of sharing in the fabulous profits of the East. "Now in order to reach these countries, they were obliged to avoid the meeting the Spaniards, or the Portuguese; and that difficulty seemed to be in a manner unsurmountable. But after all, they found out ways and means to compass their end." [7] How this end was achieved on the

[7] *Collection of Voyages Undertaken by the Dutch East-India Company*, London, 1703.

southern route, and with what glorious success, is related in connection with the discovery of Australia.

The Dutch plans, however, also included a search for a northern route, for "They conceived that by steering northeast, they might afterward run along the coast of Tartary, and so reach Cathay, China, Japan, India, and the Philippine and Molucca islands." [8]

That Dutch interest should turn toward the northeast may have been due largely to the efforts of Oliver Brunel, a shadowy figure in history, who as early as 1565 appears to have played a leading part in establishing a Dutch settlement in Kola and thereafter in developing the White Sea trade of the Netherlanders. He had traveled extensively along this coast, had visited Novaya Zemlya, and on an overland journey had reached the Ob, the first known western European to get that far east. During the 1580's he organized the first Dutch expedition for discovery of the Northeast Passage, a voyage of which little is known except that there appears to have been an unsuccessful attempt to sail through Yugorski Shar, and that later the ship was wrecked on the shoals of Pechora Bay.

Despite Brunel's failure, Dutch efforts in this direction continued, resulting finally in the dispatch during the period 1594-97 of three successive expeditions, the most ambitious and large-scale of the many attempts to discover the Northeast Passage. In all three ventures the outstanding figure was Willem Barents, accomplished mariner and skillful navigator.

The narrative of Barents's three voyages was written by Gerrit de Veer, a member of the second and third expeditions, and was first published in 1598 at Amsterdam in a Dutch, a Latin, and a French edition. The work was translated into English by William Phillip and published at London in 1609; summaries of his translation were included in Purchas and other collections of travels. The complete work, under the title *The Three Voyages of William Barents to the Arctic Regions*, was reissued at London by the Hakluyt Society in 1853, with an introduction and editorial notes by Charles T. Beke; a second edition, published in 1876, has an additional introduction by Lieutenant Koolemans Beynen.

---

[8] *Ibid.*

The first of the Dutch expeditions was sent out in 1594, and consisted of four vessels. A large ship commanded by Barents, accompanied by a small fishing sloop, attempted a passage around the northern end of Novaya Zemlya. The other two vessels, commanded by Cornelis Corneliszoon Nai (Nay) and Brant Tetgales, otherwise known as Brant Ysbrandtszoon, were to proceed to Vaigach Island and thence to the Kara Sea.

Parting from Nai and Tetgales at Kildin, an island lying off the Murmansk coast just eastward of the mouth of the Kola River, Barents sailed for Novaya Zemlya, which was first sighted on July 4. Thence he proceeded northward and northeastward along the western side of Novaya Zemlya, locating prominent features of the coast so accurately that they can still be identified. For July 9, Gerrit de Veer describes a remarkable chase of a polar bear, to commemorate which the place was called Bear Cape. Thence they sailed past Cross Island (named for two large crosses found there) and on to Cape Nassau, 76 degrees, 15 minutes north latitude, a name that has been retained on many recent maps.

So far there had been smooth going; but on the night of July 15 they found "great store of ice, as much as they could descry out of the top [crow's nest, at the top of the mast], that lay as if it had been a plain field of ice." For two weeks thereafter Barents struggled to find a way through or around the pack, at times progressing and at others losing his small gains through being driven back by wind and ice. Finally, halted by the ice in the vicinity of Novaya Zemlya's northern extremity, which he named Ice Cape (a name which is retained in the present Mys Zhelaniya), he became convinced that further progress by this route would be impossible. He then turned south to head for Vaigach Island, where he hoped to meet the other vessels of the expedition. From the journal entries it is estimated that in the interval between July 10, when he first passed Cape Nassau, and August 3, when he began the homeward voyage, Barents turned his ship about no less than eighty-one times and covered more than 1500 miles, what with drifting and tacking in various directions.

The return voyage gives the first reference to Matochkin Shar, the strait that divides Novaya Zemlya into two islands, a reference which provides also a glimpse into the peregrinations of Oliver Brunel. The journal tells that on August 8 they came to an island which they named Black Island. "There W. Barents took the height of the sun, it being under 71 degrees and 1/3; and there they found a great creek, which William Barents judged to be the place where Oliver Brunel had been before, called Costincsarth."

Meantime Nai and Tetgales had sailed eastward along the mainland coast. They passed through Yugorski Shar into the Kara Sea, bestowing the names Nassau Strait upon the channel and North Tartaric Ocean upon the sea. After some difficulties with ice, they sailed on and, entering an open sea, came on August 10 to the mouth of the Kara River, which they mistook for the Ob.

Here they determined to turn home, believing that the problem of the Northeast Passage was now solved, that from the point they had reached it would be easy to sail on around the Taimir Peninsula and thence to China. They were joined by Barents on August 15, close outside the western end of Yugorski Shar at three small islands called by the explorers Mauritius, Orange, and New Walcheren.

Convinced by the reports of Nai and Tetgales that the sea route to the Indies had actually been discovered, the United Provinces sent out seven vessels the following year, with Nai as admiral, Tetgales, Barents, and others as captains, and Jacob van Heemskerck, Jan Huyghen van Linschoten,[9] Jan Corneliszoon Rijp and others as lieutenants.

The vessels, laden with trade goods, arrived at Vaigach Island on August 12, 1595, and found the strait between the island and the mainland filled with ice. After a delay of about ten days they succeeded in passing through Yugorski Shar, but the Kara Sea was so choked with ice that they were forced to anchor at Staten (Mestni) Island, close off the mainland shore at the eastern end of the strait. This was the farthest point reached, and on September 15 the fleet turned homeward.

[9] Linschoten had been with Nai and Tetgales on the 1594 expedition; that voyage and the one of 1595 are sketched by him in *Voyagie, ofte Schip Vaert, van Jan Huyghen van Linschoten, van by Noorden om langes Noorwegen de Noortcaep, Laplant, Vinlant, Ruslandt . . . tot voorby de revier Oby,* Franeker, 1601.

On both the first and the second of these expeditions the Dutch received valuable information and advice on navigation and ice conditions, and on the length of the season, from Russian fishermen whom they met en route and from the Nentsi whom they talked with at Vaigach Island. They learned that Russian trading and fishing vessels sailed every year through Yukorski Shar, and thence on past the Ob to the Yenisei River, where they would usually pass the winter.

The Nentsi gave detailed information as to the Kara Sea, its extent and navigability, which events proved correct, but the advice was received with supercilious skepticism by the Europeans as coming from "barbarians, who had greater skill in managing their bow than a nautical gnomon, and could give better information regarding their hunting than about the navigable water." More credence was placed in the natives' descriptions of the extent and direction of the coast line, descriptions which showed the familiarity of these hunters with the Taimir Peninsula. For this fitted in nicely with the explorers' own theories and ambitions, since they were told that the land extended beyond the Ob to a cape which projected toward Novaya Zemlya, and that beyond this promontory was a great sea which extended along Tartary to warm regions.

The results of the 1594 and 1595 expeditions are summed up by Nordenskiöld: "This [the second] expedition did not yield any new contribution to the knowledge of our globe. But it deserves to be noted that we can state with certainty, with the knowledge we now possess of the ice conditions of the Kara Sea, that the Dutch during both their first and second voyages had the way open to the Obi and Yenisei. If they had availed themselves of this and continued their voyage till they came to inhabited regions on either of these rivers, a considerable commerce would certainly have arisen between Middle Asia and Europe by this route as early as the beginning of the seventeenth century."

The lack of success of the 1595 expedition cooled the ardor of the Dutch somewhat, but not enough to prevent the outfitting, under private auspices, of a third expedition the next year. The manner in which this came about is described by Gerrit de Veer:

"After that the seven ships were returned back again from their north voyage, with less benefit than was expected, the General States of the United Provinces consulted together to send certain ships thither again a third time, to see if they might bring the said voyage to a good end, if it were possible to be done. But after much consultation had, they could not agree thereon; yet they were content to cause a proclamation to be made that if any, either town or merchants, were disposed to venture to make further search that way at their own charges, if the voyage were accomplished, and that thereby it might be made apparent that the said passage was to be sailed, they were content to give them a good reward in the country's behalf, naming a certain sum of money."

Under these conditions two vessels set out from Amsterdam in May of 1596, one commanded by Jacob van Heemskerck, with Barents as chief pilot, the other commanded by Jan Corneliszoon Rijp.

It has seemed strange to many commentators that Barents, a skillful and experienced mariner, should have held, on the 1596-97 voyage, a position subordinate to that of a man who was not a sailor. But Heemskerck was of noble birth, which weighed in the selection of a leader. Similar influence had prevailed in giving the command of the English expedition of 1553 to Sir Hugh Willoughby,[10] inexperienced in nautical matters, but a knight of "goodly personage" and possessed of "singular skill in the services of war."

It has been suggested that the financial backers of the expedition may have feared that if Barents were in command, his enthusiasm might lead him into taking undue risks, and that Barents had so set his heart upon the venture that he was willing to go in almost any capacity. Moreover, he had had opportunity on the 1595 expedition of appraising Heemskerck's many fine qualities, and may not have minded holding a nominally subordinate position to such a man. For, as Beke points out, "while Heemskerck thus held the superior rank of captain, Barents's relation to him was evidently that of an equal."

The last expedition of William Barents failed not only to

10 For an account of the Willoughby expedition, see pages 388-418.

discover the Northeast Passage but to make any material contribution toward the solution of the problem. Unlike the earlier
expeditions, however, the 1596-97 venture added tremendously
to Europe's gradually expanding knowledge of the northern
regions, and is ranked as one of the great voyages in the annals
of Arctic exploration. Important also were the commercial
results of the expedition, for the discovery, on the outbound
voyage the summer of 1596, of Bear Island and Spitsbergen
opened the way for the cultivation of the whale, seal, and
walrus fisheries in those waters that were later to pay the
Hollanders rich dividends.

The discovery of these islands came about through a disagreement early in the outward voyage between Barents and
Corneliszoon. As De Veer puts it:

"John Cornelis' ship held aloof from us and would not keep
with us, but we made toward him, and sailed northeast, bating
a point of our compass, for we thought that we were too far
westward, as after it appeared, otherwise we should have held
our course northeast. And in the evening when we were together, we told him that we were best to keep more easterly
because we were too far westward; but his pilot made answer
that they desired not to go into the Straits of Weygates
[Vaigach Strait, Yugorski Shar] . . . but whatsoever we said and
sought to counsel them for the best, they would hold no course
but north-northeast, for they alleged that if we went any
more easterly that then we should enter into the Vaigach Strait.
But we, being not able (with many hard words) to persuade
them, altered our course one point of the compass, to meet
them, and sailed northeast and by north, and should otherwise
have sailed northeast and somewhat more east."

So it was that on June 9, 1596, "we found the island [Bear
Island] that lay under 75 degrees and 30 minutes, and (as
we guessed) it was about 5 [20] miles long." This island which
lies to the south of the Spitsbergen group, is shown on modern
charts in virtually the latitude at which Barents, with his rude
instruments, placed it three and a half centuries ago.

"The nineteenth of June we saw land again. . . . This land
was very great, and we sailed westward along by it till we
were under 79 degrees and a half." In this passage De Veer

is reporting the achievement of two new records in exploration—the highest northing that had yet been attained by ships,
and the discovery of the group of islands usually called Spitsbergen, from its largest island.

For ten days the two ships cruised about in the vicinity of
Spitsbergen (which the explorers at first supposed to be Greenland), pushing north beyond the 80th degree of latitude and
trying unsuccessfully to sail around the northern end of the
group. Barents then resolved to try to work eastward by a
more southerly route, a decision which, on July 1 in the vicinity
of Bear Island, revived the disagreement between the two
skippers, as shown by the journal entry for that day:

"John Cornelison and his officers came aboard of our ship, to
speak with us about altering of our course. But we being of
a contrary opinion, it was agreed that we should follow on our
course and he his; which was, that he (according to his desire)
should sail unto 80 degrees again; for he was of opinion that
there he should find a passage through, on the east side of the
land that lay under 80 degrees [that is, Spitsbergen]. And upon
that agreement we left each other, they sailing northward, and
we southward because of the ice, the wind being east-southeast."

Novaya Zemlya was first sighted on July 17, and the course
was then altered to north-northeast. As on the earlier voyage,
much heavy ice was encountered; but eventually Barents succeeded in rounding the northern end of Novaya Zemlya, and
on August 21 he entered the indentation which he named Ice
Haven, near the northeastern extremity of Novaya Zemlya,
in about 76 degrees north latitude. All attempts to sail eastward
were failures, and it was decided to return to Holland. After
vainly trying to sail southwestward along the eastern side of
Novaya Zemlya, Barents turned about to try to return by the
way he had come.

But when, on August 26, "we had past by the Ice Haven,
the ice began to drive with such force that we were enclosed
round about therewith, and yet we sought all the means we
could to get out, but it was all in vain. . . . The same day in
the evening we got to the west side of the Ice Haven, where

we were forced, in great cold, poverty, misery, and grief, to stay all that winter."

The first days at Ice Haven were frightening to these Arctic novices, for the ice in their haven was in constant motion, so that on frequent occasions the vessel was squeezed and lifted up between the grinding floes. Between these onslaughts the ice would slacken, the ship would settle back into the water in better condition than the men had thought possible, and hope would rise that perhaps they could escape and resume their homeward journey after all. One of their worst experiences came on August 30, when the pressure on the ship was so great that it was "most fearful both to see and hear, and made all the hair of our heads to rise upright with fear."

So began the second Arctic wintering by Europeans. Through the published narrative of the stay of the expedition at Ice Haven, as written by Gerrit de Veer, the natural conditions of the northern regions during winter first became known to Europe. Many of the astronomical and geographical observations remain unchallenged to this day.

Along certain lines there is exaggeration in the narrative, as, for instance, in the constant references to the extreme cold throughout the winter at the northern end of Novaya Zemlya. Still, the cold no doubt did seem bitter to the inexperienced Hollanders, with their inadequate clothing and the drafty, badly designed house that they built of driftwood and timbers from the ship.

Moreover, the English translation of William Phillip tends to exaggerate upon the original Dutch account. For example, in his journal entry for March 23, 1597, De Veer describes the weather as *helle bittere koude,* a phrase which Phillip translated as "infernal bitter cold," but which Beke translates as "with a clear sharp cold." In this connection Beke remarks that De Veer "is not open to the reproach of having, in the whole course of his narrative, made use of such an expression as that which the translator has here erroneously attributed to him."

Inexperienced the party may have been, but lazy they were not. The driftwood for housebuilding was about 4 miles distant from the site chosen for the camp, and throughout the latter

half of September and well into October the regular procedure
was to make two round trips a day, hauling wood for the
house on two rude sledges which they had constructed.

The building of the house and the sledging of driftwood were
frequently interrupted by encounters with polar bears, which
showed little respect for the human interlopers, whose weapons
and technique were unsuitable against the huge beasts. The
bears prowled constantly about the ship, coming on board when
no one was there and being chased away amid much excitement
when the crew were about.

Apparently the men of Barents's party never looked upon the
occasional bears that were killed as sources of food, not even
in their greatest extremity the following spring, when food
was scarce and they were suffering from scurvy. Perhaps they
were not able to rid themselves of the distaste for bear meat
they had acquired when, having killed a bear at Bear Island
on the outward voyage, they ate some of the flesh, "but we
brooked it not well." Thereafter when they succeeded in killing a bear it was looked upon chiefly as a deliverance from
danger or as a curiosity, as when, having removed the entrails
from a dead bear, "we set her upon her forefeet, so that she
might freeze as she stood, intending to carry her with us into
Holland if we might get our ship loose."

While the journal has no further mention of the eating of
bear meat after the incident at Bear Island, the party did on
one occasion sample the liver of a bear, with unfortunate results, perhaps through overeating.[11]

De Veer reported in November that "the bears left us at
the setting of the sun, and came not again before it rose, [while]
the foxes to the contrary came abroad when they were gone."
On January 21, a short time before the sun was seen to rise
above the horizon, he noted: "At that time taking of foxes
began to fail us, which was a sign that the bears would soon
come again, as not long after we found it to be true; for as
long as the bears stayed away the foxes came abroad, and not
much before the bears came abroad the foxes were but little
seen."

While the foxes were about, the men trapped them ener-

[11] For the edibility of polar-bear liver, see footnote, p. 553.

getically, securing sometimes two or three a day. Of these good use was made, for the foxes "served us not only for meat, but of the skins we made caps to wear upon our heads, therewith to keep them warm."

Had it not been for the fox meat, scurvy would no doubt have made even greater inroads upon the party than it did. As it was, 5 out of the expedition's 17 members died before the return to Holland the summer of 1597, most if not all of them victims of scurvy.

In December we have from De Veer the first case of carbon-monoxide poisoning to be reported from the Arctic. His account of this incident follows. Note that heretofore they had been burning driftwood.

Carbon Monoxide Poisons the Crew

The seventh of December . . . we had a great storm with a northeast wind, which brought an extreme cold with it. At which time we knew not what to do, and while we sat consulting together what were best for us to do, one of our companions gave us counsel to burn some of the sea coals that we had brought out of the ship, which would cast a great heat and continue long; and so at evening we made a great fire thereof, which cast a great heat.

At which time we were very careful to keep it in, for that the heat being so great a comfort unto us, we took care how to make it continue long: whereupon we agreed to stop up all the doors and the chimney, thereby to keep in the heat, and so went into our cabins to sleep, well comforted with the heat, and so lay a great while talking together. But at last we were taken with a great swooning and dazzling in our heads, yet some more than other some, which we first perceived by a sick man and therefore the less able to bear it, and found ourselves to be very ill at ease, so that some of us that were strongest started out of their cabins, and first opened the chimney and then the doors, but he that opened the door fell down in a swoon [with much groaning] upon the snow; which I hearing, as lying in my cabin next to the door, started up, and casting vinegar in his face recovered him again, and so he rose up.

And when the doors were open, we all recovered our healths

again by reason of the cold air; and so the cold, which before had been so great an enemy unto us, was then the only relief that we had; otherwise without doubt we had died in a sudden swoon. After that, the master, when we were come to ourselves again, gave every one of us a little wine to comfort our hearts.

The eighth of December it was foul weather, the wind northerly, very sharp and cold, but we durst lay no more coals on as we did the day before, for that our misfortune had taught us to shun one danger we should not run into an other. ⚑

In May it was decided that if the ship were not freed from the ice by the end of that month, the party should return in boats. The men at once set about preparing for departure. On June 13, 1597, the two boats started on the homeward journey, most of the crew, among them Barents, by this time much weakened by scurvy.

Before taking final leave of the house, Heemskerck drew up two documents outlining the principal events of the expedition; to these most of the men subscribed their names, and one document was placed in each boat. At the same time Barents wrote a letter which he placed in a "musket's charge and hanged it up in the chimney." Nearly three centuries later (in 1876) the Barents letter, still readable in part, was recovered from the ruins of the old Dutch house at Ice Haven by the British yachtsman Charles L. W. Gardiner.

So weak was Barents that on June 16, as they rounded the northern tip of Novaya Zemlya, he said to De Veer: "Gerrit, if we are near the Ice Point, just lift me up again. I must see that point once more." But before the others he maintained an attitude of confidence, for when Heemskerck on the same day asked him how he felt, he replied, "Quite well, mate, I still hope to be able to run before we get to Warehouse [Wardhouse]."

The most difficult experience of the return voyage came soon after they had passed Ice Cape, and here let De Veer tell the story:

The Death of Barents

The seventeenth of June in the morning, when we had broken our fasts, the ice came so fast upon us that it made our hairs start upright upon our heads, it was so fearful to behold; by which means we could not make fast our scutes [boats] so that we thought verily that it was a foreshowing of our last end. For we drave away so hard with the ice, and were so sore pressed between a flake of ice, that we thought verily the scutes would burst in a hundred pieces, which made us look pitifully one upon the other, for no counsel nor advice was to be found, but every minute of an hour we saw death before our eyes.

At last, being in this discomfort and extreme necessity, the master said if we could take hold with a rope upon the fast ice, we might therewith draw the scute up, and so get it out of the great drift of ice. But as this counsel was good, yet it was so full of danger that it was the hazard of his life that should take upon him to do it; and without doing it, was it most certain that it would cost us all our lives. This counsel (as I said) was good, but no man (like to the tale of the mice) durst hang the bell about the cat's neck, fearing to be drowned. Yet necessity required to have it done, and the most danger made us choose the least.

So that being in that perplexity (and as a drowned calf may safely be risked), I, being the lightest of all our company, took on me to fasten a rope upon the fast ice; and so creeping from one piece of driving ice to another, by God's help got to the fast ice, where I made a rope fast to a high howel. And they that were in the scute drew it thereby unto the said fast ice, and then one man alone could draw more than all of them could have done before.

And when we had gotten thither, in all haste we took our sick men out and laid them upon the ice, laying clothes and other things under them, and then took all our goods out of the scutes, and so drew them upon the ice, whereby for that time we were delivered from that great danger, making account that we had escaped out of death's claws, as it was most true. . . .

[On June 20, while they were still encamped on the fast ice], William Barents spake and said, "I think I shall not live long after him [Claes Adrianson, another invalid]." And yet we did not judge William Barents to be so sick, for we sat talking one with the other, and spake of many things, and William Barents read in my card which I had made touching our voyage. At last he laid away the card and spake unto me, saying, "Gerrit, give me some drink," and he had no sooner drunk but he was taken with so sudden a qualm that he turned his eyes in his head and died presently. . . . The death of William Barents put us in no small discomfort, as being the chief guide and only pilot on whom we reposed ourselves next under God; but we could not strive against God, and therefore we must of force be content. ✠

Two other members of the crew died as the open boats made their way southward. While there was little decrease in the navigational dangers, there was improvement in the food supply, for birds and eggs in considerable quantities were secured at several places along the west coast of Novaya Zemlya.

At last, on July 28 at St. Laurens Bay, they fell in with two Russian vessels, manned by hunters whom they had met the year before. Two days later the boats arrived at Vaigach Island, where, at the suggestion of the Russians, they went ashore and gathered and ate a quantity of scurvy grass, and what with this and with the fish and other provisions they secured along the way, the party arrived at Kola a month later in restored health and spirits.

Here, to their surprise and joy, they met Jan Corneliszoon Rijp, from whom they had parted the previous year at Bear Island. In his vessel the twelve survivors of the Heemskerck-Barents expedition took passage home.

The return to Holland of Heemskerck and his companions in 1597 coincided with that of Houtman from the East Indies. The fortunate issue of the latter venture, especially when contrasted with the hardships and disappointments of the northern undertaking, lessened the necessity as well as the desire for finding a northeastern commercial route to the Indies. The problem of the Northeast Passage was, therefore, not seriously taken up again for a long time. However, attempts were not wholly wanting.

The further attempts by the Dutch were chiefly motivated by business competition, rivals trying to find a way to break their own East India Company's monopoly of the Eastern trade, and that company wanting the route for themselves if there was a northern passage to China. None of these undertakings added materially to the existing knowledge.

Summing up the sixteenth-century attempts of the Dutch to solve the problem of the Northeast Passage, Nordenskiöld has said:

"These expeditions did not, indeed, attain the intended goal —the discovery of a northeastern sea route to eastern Asia— but they not only gained for themselves a prominent place in the history of geographical discovery, but also repaid a hundredfold the money that had been spent on them, in part directly through the whale fishing to which they gave rise, and which was so profitable to Holland, and in part indirectly through the elevation they gave to the self-respect and national feeling of the people. They compared the achievements of their countrymen among the ice and snow of the polar lands to the voyage of the Argonauts, to Hannibal's passage of the Alps, and to the campaign of the Macedonians in Asia and the deserts of Libya."

English interest in finding the Northeast Passage flared briefly in the ill-starred expedition of Wood and Flawes of 1676, after a lapse of nearly a century, following the 1580 voyage of Pet and Jackman. The 1676 voyage was preceded by much discussion of the suitability of the Polar Sea for navigation. John Wood, its principal advocate, supported his opinions largely with unconfirmed statements of very high latitudes which it was claimed had been reached by Dutch navigators.

The expedition, consisting of the *Speedwell*, commanded by Wood, and the *Prosperous*, under William Flawes, set out with great hopes of easy success. The voyage was, however, without any advance in knowledge, and is mentioned here only because of its adverse influence upon similar attempts thereafter.

A. E. Nordenskiöld, commander of the first expedition to

navigate the full course of the Northeast Passage, summarizes the 1676 voyage:

"Wood did not penetrate so far, either to the north or east, as his predecessors or as the whalers, who appear to have at that time frequently visited North Novaya Zemlya. Wood had previously accompanied Sir John Narborough during a voyage through the dangerous Magellan Straits, in the course of which he became known as a bold and skillful seaman; but he not only wanted experience in sailing amongst ice, but also the endurance and the coolness that are required for voyages in the High North. He thereby showed himself to be quite unfit for the command which he undertook. Before his departure he was unreasonably certain of success; and when his vessel was wrecked on the coast of Novaya Zemyla, he knew no other way to keep up the courage of his men and prevent mutiny than to send the brandy bottle round.[12] Finally, after his return he made Barents and other distinguished seafarers in the Arctic regions answerable for all the skipper tales collected from quite other quarters, which he before his departure held to be proved undoubtedly true. . . .

". . . it is certain that the ignominious result of Wood's voyage exerted so great a deterring influence from all new undertakings in the same direction that nearly two hundred years elapsed before an expedition was again sent out with the distinctly declared intention . . . of achieving a northeast passage. This was the famous Austrian expedition of Payer and Weyprecht in 1872-74, which failed indeed in penetrating far to the eastward, but which in any case formed an epoch in the history of Arctic exploration by the discovery of Franz Josef Land and by many valuable researches on the natural conditions of the polar lands."

Meantime the Russians were extending their knowledge of the northern coast of Siberia. As has already been stated, trading voyages along the coast from the White Sea at least as far as the Yenisei were commonplace with the Russians at

---

[12] "All I could do in this exigency was to let the brandy bottle go round, which kept them always foxed, till the eighth of July Captain Flawes came so seasonably to our relief."—Sir John Barrow, A *Chronological History of Voyages into the Arctic Regions*, London, 1818, p. 268.

the time of the first visits to Muscovy of western Europeans. As the conquest of Siberia proceeded, more and more of the coast line became known, though the voyages along it were for trade or the collection of tribute rather than for the definite purpose of finding a passage leading from the Atlantic to the Pacific.

The discoverer of Bering Strait, an important link in the route between the oceans, may have been Simon Dezhnev, in 1648, his party coming by boat eastward from the mouth of the Kolima, rounding East Cape (now Cape Dezhnev), and proceeding southwesterly to the mouth of the Anadyr. At the time of Dezhnev's journey a brisk trade was being carried on by the natives on the Siberian side of the strait and those on the American side. But Dezhnev's report, with its implication that the continents were separated by a strait, was destined through carelessness or design, to a century of oblivion, and speculation continued as to whether Asia and America were one piece of land or separate continents with a strait between.

It is probable that rumors of the strait [13] and of the trade with Alaska reached Peter the Great (1672-1725) and influenced him in initiating that series of notable exploratory journeys, called the Great Northern Expeditions, which revealed the entire north coast of the Old World through formal exploration. Rumors of a strait would have interested Peter more than the prospect of trade with Alaska. What he hoped, no doubt, was that the strait would be there, navigable and forming a connection between his most easterly territories in Asia and his most northwesterly territories in Europe; in other words, that the long-sought Northeast Passage might finally be revealed.

Culminating this series of exploratory journeys was the seventeen-year effort (1725-42) of Vitus Bering, from whom the strait derives its name, an undertaking that had been planned by Peter and which was carried out after his death.

In midsummer of 1728 Bering sailed northeasterly along the shore of Kamchatka, discovered St. Lawrence Island, and pro-

---

[13] On many old maps a channel called the Strait of Anian is shown in this general vicinity. On what authority it came to be placed there has long been a matter of scholarly controversy. The problem is too complicated for discussion here.

ceeded so far north—now and then in sight of the coast to his left—that we feel sure he passed through the strait that Dezhnev, unknown to Bering, had navigated eighty years before. Although Bering himself believed that by going so far north (to 69 degrees 18 minutes north latitude) he had created the presumption that America and Asia were not united, there still was doubt as to their separateness, a doubt that was only gradually dispelled by the work of numerous Russian and British expeditions in the late eighteenth century and the early nineteenth.

Thus bit by bit the whole of the Northeast Passage became known, while at the same time the belief grew that its use as a continuous seaway was impracticable for cargo ships.

The doctrine of the impassability of the northeastern route for ships was challenged and eventually disproved by Baron Nils Adolf Erik Nordenskiöld, distinguished explorer, scientist, and geographical historian.

Born in Helsingfors, Finland, in 1832, and educated as a chemist and mineralogist, Nordenskiöld moved to Stockholm in 1857, where he was soon caught up by the lure of the Arctic. His early work was centered in Spitsbergen. On the basis of surveys undertaken there in the summers of 1858, 1861, and 1864, he produced an accurate map of this hitherto incompletely known group of islands.

Next he organized the Swedish North Polar expeditions of 1868 and 1872-73, both of which used Spitsbergen as a base. On the first voyage he reached 81 degrees, 42 minutes north latitude, 17 degrees, 30 minutes east longitude, in the *Sofia*—the highest latitude attained to that date by any ship. On the second of these expeditions Nordenskiöld wintered in Spitsbergen, and in the spring attempted to reach the North Pole with reindeer teams and sledges, but the sea ice proved too rough to be crossed by this means and he was forced to retreat. In returning to his ship he made the first crossing of the inland ice of Northeast Land, the northernmost island of the Spitsbergen group. This was not his first experience at this kind of travel, for in 1870, in the interval between his polar expeditions, he had made his first journey up on the Inland Ice of Greenland, this being the forerunner of a similar but more extended journey undertaken in 1883.

In 1875, with a background of six Arctic expeditions, Nordenskiöld turned his attention to the problem of the Northeast Passage. His thorough knowledge of the literature pertaining to this region, from the earliest times to his own day, led him to the belief, contrary to the then accepted opinion, that the route held great promise of becoming a regular commercial trade route.

Before attempting to navigate the entire passage, however, he made two reconnoitering trips, in 1875 and in 1876, both times crossing the Kara Sea to the mouth of the Yenisei.

To digress, on the first of these voyages Nordenskiöld discovered at the mouth of the Yenisei a well-sheltered harbor in an island lying close off the mainland coast. Both the island and the harbor were named for Baron Oscar Dickson, a Swedish merchant who had generously supported much of Nordenskiöld's work. Port Dickson, which was revisited by Nordenskiöld on his Northeast Passage expedition of 1878, was described by him in 1881 as "the best-known haven on the whole north coast of Asia, and will certainly in the future be of great importance for the foreign commerce of Siberia . . . I am convinced that the day will come when great warehouses and many dwellings inhabited all the year round will be found at Port Dickson. Now the region is entirely uninhabited."

Nordenskiöld wrote with the insight of the true prophet. Port Dickson is today one of the most important harbors on the Northern Sea Route, the name applied by the Soviet Union to the commercial seaway that utilizes the Northeast Passage. The great warehouses and dwellings which Nordenskiöld foresaw are now there, with wharves and docks and all the paraphernalia of an up-to-date mechanized port, together with a polar station for scientific studies and an airport for an air line that connects Dickson Island with the mainland cities of the Soviet Union. In 1939, Dickson was described as one of the liveliest points in the Arctic, with a population of from 3000 to 4000 during the navigation season.

So favorable were the results of the two preliminary voyages that by 1877 Nordenskiöld felt he was ready to launch the great project, which he outlines in the Introduction to his narrative, *The Voyage of the Vega*:

"After my return from the latter [1876] voyage, I came to the conclusion that on the ground of the experience thereby gained, and of the knowledge which, under the light of that experience, it was possible to obtain from old, especially from Russian, explorations of the north coast of Asia, I was warranted in asserting that the open navigable water, which two years in succession had carried me across the Kara Sea, formerly of so bad repute, to the mouth of the Yenisei, extended in all probability as far as Bering Strait, and that a circumnavigation of the Old World was thus within the bounds of possibility.

"It was natural that I should endeavor to take advantage of the opportunity for making new and important discoveries which thus presented itself. An opportunity had arisen for solving a geographical problem—the forcing a northeast passage to China and Japan—which for more than three hundred years had been a subject of competition between the world's foremost commercial states and most daring navigators, and which, if we view it in the light of a circumnavigation of the Old World, had for thousands of years back been an object of desire for geographers."

In July 1877 a plan of the expedition was presented to the King of Sweden and Norway. The arguments therein set forth proved convincing, and the expedition was organized with the financial support of the King, Baron Dickson, and A. Sibiriakov, a Russian merchant. Two vessels were provided; the 300-ton *Vega*, provisioned for two years, was to make the full voyage, and the smaller *Lena* was to proceed only as far as the Lena River.

Nordenskiöld's monumental two-volume work describing the voyage was published at Stockholm in 1881; the same year a translation into English by Alexander Leslie was published at London, also in two volumes, under the title *The Voyage of the Vega round Asia and Europe, with a Historical Review of Previous Journeys along the North Coast of the Old World.*

As the title suggests, this is no mere narrative of daily events. As he tells of the *Vega*'s progress to the eastward, the author from time to time interpolates the historical material, tracing the successes and failures of earlier ventures along the portion of the route which he has just traversed.

The title does not, however, suggest the wealth and variety of other material that is included in *The Voyage of the Vega*. There are the results of the studies of the scientists who accompanied the expedition, including such things as meteorological, hydrological, and oceanographical observations. Always there is close attention to ice conditions, both as to what Nordenskiöld could see for himself and what he could learn from the Russians and the natives. Everything interested him, and there are frequent digressions, as for example pages of scholarly speculation on some dust particles that were found on a piece of drift ice—were they of cosmic origin or were they volcanic ash, perhaps thrown out by the volcanoes of Iceland? And of course careful notes are taken of the manners and customs of the native peoples with whom he came in touch, the Nentsi at Vaigach Island in the west near Europe and the Chukchis in the Far East near Alaska.

To summarize adequately a work like *The Voyage of the Vega* is manifestly impossible. No more can be attempted here than to give the high points of the narrative as Nordenskiöld proceeds eastward along the Northeast Passage. On July 21, 1878, the *Vega* and the *Lena* left Tromsö. On July 30, Yugorski Shar was reached without a trace of ice having been seen; the strait too was free of ice. Here the *Vega* and the *Lena* were joined by the *Fraser* and the *Express*, two of Sibiriakov's cargo vessels that were bound for the Yenisei. Crossing the Kara Sea without difficulty, the expedition arrived at Port Dickson on August 6, and departing thence on August 10, began the exploratory part of the voyage. We take up Nordenskiöld's narrative as he was approaching Cape Chelyuskin, the northern extremity of Asia:

The Voyage of the Vega

On the nineteenth August we continued to sail and steam along the coast, mostly in a very close fog, which only at intervals dispersed so much that the lie of the coast could be made out. In order that they might not be separated, both vessels had often to signal to each other with the steam whistle. The sea was bright as a mirror. Drift ice was seen now and then, but only in small quantity and very rotten; but in the course of the day we steamed past an extensive unbroken ice field, fast to the land, which occupied a bay on the west side of the Chelyuskin peninsula. . . .

The fog prevented all view far across the ice, and I already feared that the northernmost promontory of Asia would be so surrounded with ice that we could not land upon it. But soon a dark ice-free cape peeped out of the mist in the northeast. A bay open to the north here cuts into the land, and in this bay both the vessels anchored on the nineteenth August at 6 o'clock P.M.

We had now reached a great goal, which for centuries had been the object of unsuccessful struggles. For the first time a vessel lay at anchor off the northernmost cape of the Old World. No wonder then that the occurrence was celebrated by a display of flags and the firing of salutes, and when we returned from our excursion on land, by festivities on board, by wine and toasts. . . .

According to the plan of the voyage, I now wished to steam from this point right eastward toward the New Siberian Islands, in order to see if we should fall in with land on the way. On the twentieth and twenty-first we went forward in this direction among scattered drift ice, which was heavier and less broken-up than that which we had met with on the other side of Taimur [Taimir] Land, but without meeting with any serious obstacles. We fell in also with some very large ice floes, but not with any icebergs. We were besides again attended by so close a mist that we could only see ice fields and pieces of ice in the immediate neighborhood of the vessel. . . .

The night before the twenty-second we steamed through pretty close ice. The whole day so thick a fog still prevailed that we could not see the extent of the ice fields in the neighborhood of the vessel. Toward noon we were therefore compelled to take a more southerly course. When we found that we could not advance in this direction, we lay to at a large ice floe, waiting for clear weather, until in the afternoon the fog again lightened somewhat, so that we could continue our voyage.

But it was not long before the fog again became so thick that, as the sailors say, you could cut it with a knife. There was now evidently a risk that the *Vega*, while thus continuing to "box the compass" in the ice labyrinth in which we had entangled ourselves, would meet with the same fate that befell the *Tegetthoff*. In order to avoid this, it became necessary to abandon our attempt to sail from Cape Chelyuskin straight to the New Siberian Islands, and to endeavor to reach as soon as possible the open water at the coast.

When it cleared on the morning of the twenty-third, we therefore began again to steam forward among the fields of drift ice, but now not with the intention of advancing in a given direction, but only of getting to open water. The ice fields we now met with were very much broken-up, which was an indication that we could not be very far from the edge of the pack. But notwithstanding this, all our attempts to find penetrable ice in an easterly, westerly, or southerly direction were unsuccessful. We had thus to search in a northerly direction for the opening by which we had sailed in. . . . It was not until 6:30 P.M. that we at last came to the sack-formed opening in the ice through which we had sailed in at noon of the previous day. . . .

When we got out of the ice, we steamed toward the land, which was sighted on the twenty-third at 8:45 P.M. The land was low and free from snow. . . . The coast here stretched from north to south . . . [and] on the twenty-fourth August we still sailed along the land toward the south. . . .

During the last two days we had been sailing over a region which on recent maps [that is, recent in 1878] is marked as land. This shows that a considerable change must be made on the map of North Siberia. . . .

On the twenty-fifth, twenty-sixth, and twenty-seventh August we had for the most part calm, fine weather, and the sea was completely free of ice. . . . But the depth now decreased so much that, for instance, on the night before the twenty-sixth we had great difficulty in getting past some shoals lying west of the delta of the Lena, off the mouth of the Olonek.

It had originally been my intention to let the *Vega* separate from the *Lena* at some anchorage in one of the mouth arms of the Lena River. But on account of the shallowness of the water, the favorable wind, and the ice-free sea that now lay before us to the eastward, I determined to part from the *Lena* in the open sea off Tumat Island. This parting took place on the night between the twenty-seventh and twenty-eighth August. . . . As a salute to our trusty little attendant during our voyage round the north point of Asia, some rockets were fired, on which we steamed or sailed on, each to his destination.

During our passage from Norway to the Lena we had been much troubled with fog, but it was only when we left the navigable water along the coast to the east of Cape Chelyuskin that we fell in with ice in such quantity that it was an obstacle to our voyage. If the coast had been followed the whole time, if the weather had been clear, and the navigable water sufficiently surveyed so that it had been possible to keep the course of the vessel near the land, the voyage of the *Vega* to the mouth of the Lena *would never have been obstructed by ice*, and I am convinced that this will happen year after year during the close of August, at least between the Yenisej [Yenisei] and the Lena. For I believe that the place where ice obstacles will perhaps be met with most frequently will not be the north point of Asia, but the region east of the entrance to the Kara Sea. . . .

After the parting the *Lena* shaped her course toward the land; the *Vega* continued her voyage in a northeasterly direction toward the New Siberian Islands.

These have, from the time of their discovery,[14] been renowned among the Russian ivory collectors for their extraordinary richness in tusks and portions of skeletons of the extinct northern species of elephant known by the name of mammoth.

We know . . . that the mammoth was a peculiar northern species of elephant with a covering of hair, which, at least during certain seasons of year, lived under natural conditions closely resembling those which now prevail in middle and even in northern Siberia. The widely extended grassy plains and forests of North Asia were the proper homeland of this animal,

---

[14] The New Siberian Islands were first visited in 1770, by Lyakhov. They had been seen from a distance by a number of earlier Russian travelers who were following the mainland coast at some distance offshore.

and there it must at one time have wandered about in large herds.

 . The same, or a closely allied, species of elephant also occurred in North America, in England, France, Switzerland, Germany, and North Russia. . . . But while in Europe only some more or less inconsiderable remains of bones are commonly to be found, in Siberia we meet not only with whole skeletons, but also whole animals frozen in the earth, with solidified blood, flesh, hide, and hair. Hence we may draw the conclusion that the mammoth died out, speaking geologically, not so very long ago. . . .

I have not, indeed, been successful during the voyage of the *Vega* in making any remarkable discovery that would throw light on the mode of life of the mammoth; but as we now sail forward between shores probably richer in such remains than any other on the surface of the globe, and over a sea from whose bottom our dredge brought up, along with pieces of driftwood, half-decayed portions of mammoth tusks, and as the savages with whom we came in contact several times offered us very fine mammoth tusks or tools made of mammoth ivory, it may not perhaps be out of place here to give a brief account of some of the most important mammoth finds which have been preserved for science. We can only refer to the discovery of mammoth mummies [carcasses], for the finds of mammoth tusks sufficiently well preserved to be used for carving are so frequent as to defy enumeration.

Middendorff reckons the number of the tusks which yearly come into the market as at least a hundred pairs, whence we may infer that during the years that have elapsed since the conquest of Siberia useful tusks from more than 20,000 animals have been collected.

[Here follows a description of the most important finds of mammoth carcasses from 1692 on. Since Nordenskiöld's day numerous others have been discovered, many of them in an almost perfect state of preservation. The last find mentioned by Nordenskiöld was the carcass of a rhinoceros, and on this his remarks are quoted.]

A new and important find was made 'in 1877 on a tributary of the Lena . . . in 69 degrees north latitude. For there was found there an exceedingly well-preserved carcass of a rhinoçeros. . . . From the find Schrenck draws the conclusion that this rhinoceros belonged to a high-northern species, adapted to a cold climate, and living in, or at least occasionally wandering to, the regions where the carcass was found. There the mean temperature of the year is now very low, the winter exceedingly cold . . . and the short summer exceedingly warm.

Nowhere on earth does the temperature show extremes so widely separated as here. Although the trees in winter often split with tremendous noise, and the ground is rent with the cold, the wood is luxuriant and extends to the neighborhood of the Polar Sea, where, besides, the winter is much milder than farther in the interior. With respect to the possibility of these large animals' finding sufficient pasture in the regions in question, it ought not to be overlooked that in sheltered places overflowed by the spring inundations there are found, still far north of the limit of trees, luxuriant bushy thickets, whose newly expanded juicy leaves, burned up by no tropical sun, perhaps form a special luxury for grass-eating animals, and that *even the bleakest stretches of land in the High North are fertile in comparison with many regions where at least the camel can find nourishment, for instance the east coast of the Red Sea.*

The nearer we come to the coast of the Polar Sea, the more common are the remains of the mammoth, especially at places where there have been great landslips at the riverbanks when the ice breaks up in spring. Nowhere, however, are they found in such numbers as on the New Siberian Islands. . . .

It was not until the thirtieth of August that we were off the west side of Ljachoff's Island [Lyakhov Island, the southernmost of the New Siberian Islands], on which I intended to land. The north coast, and as it appeared the day after the east coast, was clear of ice, but the winds recently prevailing had heaped a mass of rotten ice on the west coast. . . . [This ice] did not indeed form any very serious obstacle to the advance of the *Vega*, but in case we had attempted to land there . . . it might even, if a sudden frost had occurred, have become a fetter which would have confined us to that spot for the winter. Even a storm arising hastily might in this shallow water have been actually dangerous to the vessel anchored in an open road. The prospect of wandering about for some days on the island did not appear to me to outweigh the danger of the possible failure of the main object of the expedition. I therefore gave up for the time my intention of landing. The course was shaped southward toward the sound [Dmitri Laptev Strait], of so bad repute in the history of the Siberian Polar Sea, which separates Lyakov Island from the mainland. . . .

On the mainland side it [Laptev Strait] is bounded by a rocky headland projecting far into the sea, which often formed the turning point in attempts to penetrate eastward from the mouth of the river Lena, and perhaps just on that account, like many other headlands dangerous to the navigator on the north coast of Russia, was called Svjatoinos [Svjatoi Nos, The Holy Cape], a name which for the oldest Russian Polar Sea navigators appears to have had the same significance as "the cape that can be passed with difficulty." No one however now thinks with any apprehension of the two "holy capes," which in former times limited the voyages of the Russians and Finns living on the White Sea to the east and west, and this, I am quite convinced, will some time be the case with this and all other holy capes in the Siberian Polar Sea.[15] . . .

The whole day [August 31] we continued our voyage eastward with glorious weather over a smooth ice-free sea, and in the same way on the first September. . . .

East of the Bear Islands [lying off the mouth of the Kolima] heavy sea ice in pretty compact masses had drifted down toward the coast, but still left an open ice-free channel along the land. . . .

On the third September, after we had sailed past the Bear Islands, the course was shaped right for Cape Chelagskoj [Shelagski]. This course, as will be seen by a glance at the map, carried us far from the coast, and thus out of the channel next the land, in which we had hitherto sailed. The ice was heavy and close, although at first so distributed that it was navigable. But with a north wind, which began to blow on the night before

---

[15] This prophecy was made good about half a century later through the opening of a routine seaway by the government of the Soviet Union that utilizes the Northeast Passage for both commercial and military traffic. This recent development is summarized at the close of the Nordenskiöld narrative.

the first September, the temperature fell below the freezing-point, and the water between the pieces of drift ice was covered with a very thick crust of ice, and the drift ice came closer and closer together. It thus became impossible to continue the course which we had taken.

We therefore turned toward the land, and at 6 o'clock P.M., after various bends in the ice and a few concussions against the pieces of ice that barred our way, again reached the ice-free channel, 8 to 12 kilometers broad, next the land. While we lay a little way in among the drift-ice fields we could see no sign of open water, but it appeared as if the compact ice extended all the way to land, a circumstance which shows how careful the navigator ought to be in expressing an opinion as to the nature of the pack beyond the immediate neighborhood of the vessel.[16] . . .

Cape Baranov was passed on the night before the fifth September, the mouth of Chaun Bay on the night before the sixth September, and Cape Shelagski was reached on the sixth at 4 o'clock P.M. The distance in a right line between this headland and the Bear Islands is 180 miles. In consequence of the many detours in the ice we had required two and one-half days to traverse this distance, which corresponds to 72 miles per day, or 3 per hour, a speed which in a voyage in unknown, and for the most part ice-bestrewed, waters must yet be considered very satisfactory.

But after this our progress began to be much slower. At midnight the sun was already 12 degrees to 13 degrees below the horizon, and the nights were now so dark that at that time of day we were compelled to lie still anchored to some large ground ice. A further loss of time was caused by the dense fog, which often prevailed by day, and which in the unknown shallow water next the land compelled Captain Palander to advance with extreme caution. The navigation along the north coast of Asia began to get somewhat monotonous. Even the most zealous polar traveler may tire at last of mere ice, shallow water, and fog; and mere fog, shallow water, and ice.

Now, however, a pleasant change began, by our coming at

---

[16] This difficulty vanishes when scouting airplanes are used, as in the present technique of navigating the Northeast Passage.

last in contact with natives. In the whole stretch from Yugor Schar [Yugorski Shar] to Cape Shelagski we had seen neither men nor human habitations, if I except the old uninhabited hut between Cape Chelyuskin and the Chatanga [Khatanga River]. But on the sixth September, when we were a little way off Cape Shelagski, two boats were sighted. Every man, with the exception of the cook, who could be induced by no catastrophe to leave his pots and pans and who had circumnavigated Asia and Europe perhaps without having been once on land, rushed on deck. The boats were of skin, built in the same way as the umiaks or women's boats of the [Greenland] Eskimo. They were fully laden with laughing and chattering natives, men, women and children, who indicated by cries and gesticulations that they wished to come on board.

The engine was stopped, the boats lay to, and a large number of skin-clad, bareheaded beings climbed up over the gunwale in a way that clearly indicated that they had seen vessels before. A lively talk began, but we soon became aware that none of the crew of the boats or the vessel knew any language common to both. It was an unfortunate circumstance, but signs were employed as far as possible. This did not prevent the chatter from going on, and great gladness soon came to prevail, especially when some presents began to be distributed, mainly consisting of tobacco and Dutch clay pipes.

It was remarkable that none of them could speak a single word of Russian, while a boy could count tolerably well up to ten in English, which shows that the natives here come into closer contact with American whalers than with Russian traders. They acknowledged the name Chukch or Chautchu [Chukchi].

Many of them were tall, well-grown men. They were clothed in close-fitting skin trousers and "pesks" of reindeer skin. The head was bare, the hair always clipped short, with the exception of a small fringe in front, where the hair had a length of 4 centimeters and was combed down over the brow. Some had a cap of the sort used by the Russians at Chabarova [Khabarovo, a village on the southern side of Yugorski Shar] stuck into the belt behind, but they appeared to consider the weather still too warm for the use of this head covering. . . .

In a little we continued our voyage, after the Chukchis had

returned to their boats, evidently well pleased with the gifts they had received and the leaf tobacco I had dealt out in bundles—along with the clay pipes, of which every one got as many as he could carry between his fingers—with the finery and old clothes which my comrades and the crew strewed around them with generous hand. For we were all convinced that after some days we should come to waters where winter clothes would be altogether unnecessary, where our want of any article could easily be supplied at the nearest port, and where the means of exchange would not consist of goods, but of stamped pieces of metal and slips of paper.

On the seventh September, we steamed the whole day along the coast in pretty open ice. At night we lay to at a floe. . . . But in the morning we found ourselves again so surrounded by ice and fog that, after several unsuccessful attempts to make an immediate advance, we were compelled to lie to at a large piece of drift ice near the shore. When the fog had lightened so much that the vessel could be seen from the land, we were again visited by a large number of natives, whom as before we entertained as best we could. They invited us by evident signs to land and visit their tents. As it was in any case impossible immediately to continue our voyage, I accepted the invitation, ordered a boat to put out, and landed along with most of my comrades.

The beach here is formed of a low bank of sand which runs between the sea and a small shallow lagoon or fresh-water lake, whose surface is nearly on a level with that of the sea. Farther into the interior the land rises gradually to bare hills, clear of snow or only covered with a thin coating of powdered snow from the fall of the last few days. . . .

The villages of the Chukchis commonly stand on the bank of sand which separates the lagoon from the sea. The dwellings consist of roomy skin tents, which enclose a sleeping chamber of the form of a parallelepiped surrounded by warm well-prepared reindeer skins, and lighted and warmed by one or more train-oil lamps. It is here that the family sleep during summer, and here most of them live day and night during winter. In summer, less frequently in winter, a fire is lighted besides in the outer tent, with wood, for which purpose a hole is opened in the top of the raised tent roof. But to be compelled to use wood for heating the inner tent the Chukchis consider the extremity of scarcity of fuel.

We were received everywhere in a very friendly way, and were offered whatever the house afforded. At the time the supply of food was abundant. In one tent reindeer beef was being boiled in a large cast-iron pot. At another two recently shot or slaughtered reindeer were being cut in pieces. At a third an old woman was employed in taking out of the paunch of the reindeer the green spinachlike contents and cramming them into a sealskin bag, evidently to be preserved for green food during winter. . . . Other skin sacks filled with train oil stood in rows along the walls of the tent.

The Chukchis offered train oil for sale, and appeared to be surprised that we would not purchase any. In all the tents were found seals cut in pieces, a proof that the catch of seals had recently been abundant. At one tent lay two fresh walrus heads with large beautiful tusks. I tried without success to purchase these heads, but next day the tusks were offered to us. The Chukchis appear to have a prejudice against disposing of the heads of slain animals. According to older travelers, they even pay the walrus head a sort of worship.

Children were met with in great numbers, healthy and thriving. In the inner tent the older children went nearly naked, and I saw them go out from it without shoes or other covering and run between the tents on the hoarfrost-covered ground. The younger were carried on the shoulders both of men and women, and were then so wrapped up that they resembled balls of skin. The children were treated with marked friendliness, and the older ones were never heard to utter an angry word. . . .

On the morning of the ninth September we endeavored to steam on, but were soon compelled by the dense fog to lie to again at a ground ice, which, when the fog lightened, was found to have stranded quite close to land. . . . At this place we lay till the morning of the tenth. . . .

This was the first time that any vessel had lain to on this coast. Our arrival was therefore evidently considered by the natives a very remarkable occurrence, and the report of it appears to have spread very rapidly. For though there were no tents in the neighborhood, we had many visitors. I still availed myself of the opportunity of procuring by barter a large number of articles distinctive of the Chukchis' mode of life. Eight years before I had collected and purchased a large number of ethnographical articles, and I was now surprised at the close correspondence there was between the household articles purchased from the Chukchis and those found in Greenland in old Eskimo graves.

My traffic with the natives was on this occasion attended with great difficulty. For I suffered from a sensible want of the first condition for the successful prosecution of a commercial undertaking—goods in demand. Because during the expeditions of 1875 and 1876 I found myself unable to make use of the small wares I carried with me for barter with the natives, and found that Russian paper money was readily taken, I had, at the departure of the *Vega* from Sweden, taken with me only money, not wares intended for barter. But money was of little use here. . . .

The only proper wares for barter I now had were tobacco and Dutch clay pipes. . . . Certain as I was of reaching the Pacific this autumn, I scattered my stock of tobacco around me with so liberal a hand that it was soon exhausted, and my Chukchi friends' wants satisfied for several weeks. I therefore, as far as this currency was concerned, already when the *Vega* was beset suffered the prodigal's fate of being soon left with an empty purse. . . .

During the night before the tenth September, the surface of the sea was covered with a very thick sheet of newly frozen ice, which was broken up again in the neighborhood of the vessel by blocks of old ice drifting about. The pack itself appeared to have scattered a little. We therefore weighed anchor to continue our voyage. At first a detour toward the west was necessary to get round a field of drift ice. Here too, however, our way was barred by a belt of old ice, which was bound together so firmly by the ice that had formed in the course of the night that a couple of hours' work with axes and ice hatchets was required to open a channel through it.

On the other side of this belt of ice we came again into pretty open water, but the fog, instead, became so dense that we had again to lie to at a ground ice, lying farther out to the sea but more to the west than our former resting-place. On the night before the eleventh there was a violent motion among the ice. Fortunately the air cleared in the morning, so that we could hold on our course among pretty open ice, until on the approach of night we were obliged as usual to lie to at a ground ice.

The following day, the twelfth September, when we had passed Irkaipij or Cape North [now Cape Schmidt] a good way, we fell in with so close ice that there was no possibility of penetrating farther. We were therefore compelled to return, and were able to make our way with great difficulty among the closely packed masses of drift ice. Here the vessel was anchored in the lee of a ground ice which had stranded near the northernmost spur of Irkaipij, until a strong tidal current began to carry large pieces of drift ice past the vessel's anchorage. She was now removed and anchored anew in a little bay open to the north, which was formed by two rocky points jutting out from the mainland. Unfortunately we were detained here, waiting for a better state of the ice, until the eighteenth September. It was this involuntary delay which must be considered the main cause of our wintering.

Irkaipij is the northernmost promontory in that part of Asia which was seen by Cook in 1778. It was therefore called by him Cape North, a name which has since been adopted in most maps, although it is apt to lead to confusion from capes similarly named being found in most countries. It is also incorrect, because the cape does not form the northernmost promontory either of the whole of Siberia or of any considerable portion of it. For the northernmost point of the mainland of Siberia is Cape Chelyuskin, the northernmost in the land east of the Lena, Svyatoi Nos, the northernmost in the stretch of coast east of Chaun Bay, Cape Shelagski, and so on. Cape North ought, therefore, to be replaced by the original name Irkaipij, which is well known to all the natives between Chaun Bay and Behring [Bering] Strait.[17]

[17] As stated, the name has been changed by the Soviet authorities to Cape Schmidt, in honor of Otto J. Schmidt, who was director of the Administration of the Northern Sea Route in the 1930's when the Northeast Passage was first developed as a regular commercial seaway.

On the neck of land which connects Irkaipij with the mainland, there was at the time of our visit a village consisting of
sixteen tents. We saw here also ruins; viz., the remains of a
large number of old house sites. . . .

Between us and the inhabitants of the present Chukchi
village at Irkaipij there soon arose very friendly relations. A
somewhat stout, well-grown, tall, and handsome man named
Chepurin we took at first to be chief. He was therefore repeatedly entertained in the gunroom, on which occasions small gifts
were given him to secure his friendship. . . . Already on our
arrival he was better clothed than the others, his tent was
larger and provided with two sleeping apartments, one for
each of his wives. But notwithstanding all this we soon found
that we had made a mistake when, thinking that a society
could not exist without government, we assigned to him so
exalted a position. Here, as in all Chukchi villages which we
afterward visited, absolute anarchy prevailed.[18]

At the same time the greatest unanimity reigned in the little
headless community. Children, healthy and thriving, tenderly
cared for by the inhabitants, were found in large numbers. A
good word to them was sufficient to pave the way for a friendly
reception in the tent. The women were treated as the equals
of the men, and the wife was always consulted by the husband
when a more important bargain than usual was to be made.
. . . One of the children had round his neck a band of pearls
with a Chinese coin having a square hole in the middle suspended from it; another bore a perforated American cent piece.
None knew a word of Russian, but here too a youngster could
count ten in English. They also knew the word "ship." . . .

On the eighteenth September the state of the ice was quite
unchanged. If a wintering was to be avoided, it was, however,
not advisable to remain longer here. It had besides appeared
from the hilltop which I visited the day before that an open-
water channel, only interrupted at two places by ice, was still
to be found along the coast. The anchor accordingly was
weighed, and the *Vega* steamed on, but in a depth of only 6 to
8 meters. As the *Vega's* draught is from 4.8 to 5 meters, we had

---

[18] The same was true of all North American Eskimos when first reached by
Europeans—they were found to be communistic anarchists.

only a little water under the keel, and that among ice in quite unknown waters. . . .

On the nineteenth we continued our voyage in the same way as before, in still and for the most part shallow water near the coast, between high masses of ground ice, which frequently had the most picturesque forms. . . .

After having been moored during the night to a large ground ice, the *Vega* continued her course on the twentieth September. . . . We soon came to a place where the ice was packed so close to land that an open channel only 3½ to 4½ meters deep remained close to the shore. We were therefore compelled after some hours' sailing to lie to at a ground ice to await more favorable circumstances. . . .

On the twenty-second, I made, along with Captain Palander, an excursion in the steam launch to take soundings farther to the east. We soon succeeded in discovering a channel of sufficient depth and not too much blocked with ice, and on the twenty-third the *Vega* was able to resume her voyage among very closely packed drift ice, often so near the land that she had only a fourth of a meter of water under her keel. We went forward however, if slowly. . . .

On the evening of the twenty-third September, we lay to at a ground ice in a pretty large opening of the ice field. This opening closed in the course of the night, so that on the twenty-fourth and twenty-fifth we could make only very little progress, but on the twenty-sixth we continued our course, at first with difficulty but afterward in pretty open water, to the headland which on the maps is called Cape Onman. . . .

On the twenty-seventh we continued our course in somewhat open water to Kolyutschin [Kolyuchin] bay. . . . The mouth of the bay was filled with very closely packed drift ice that had gathered round the island situated there, which was inhabited by a large number of Chukchi families. In order to avoid this ice the *Vega* made a considerable detour up the fjord. The weather was calm and fine, but new ice was formed everywhere among the old drift ice where it was closely packed. Small seals swarmed by hundreds among the ice, following the wake of the vessel with curiosity. . . .

When on the following day, the twenty-eighth September,

we had sailed past the headland which bounds Kolyuchin Bay on the east, the channel next the coast, clear of drift ice but covered with newly formed ice, became suddenly shallow. The depth was too small for the *Vega*, for which we had now to seek a course among the blocks of ground ice and fields of drift ice in the offing. The night's frost had bound these so firmly together that the attempt failed. We were thus compelled to lie to at a ground ice so much the more certain of getting off with the first shift of the wind, and of being able to traverse the few miles that separated us from the open water at Bering Strait, as whalers on several occasions had not left this region until the middle of October.

[Nordenskiöld here reviews the experience of American whaling vessels in these waters, from which it appeared there were good grounds for considering that the sea between Kolyuchin Bay and Bering Strait should remain open until after the end of September.]

Whether our sailing along the north coast of Asia to Kolyuchin Bay was a fortunate accident or not, the future will show. I for my part believe it was a fortunate accident which will often happen. Certain it is, in any case, that when we had come so far as to this point, our being frozen in was a quite accidental misfortune brought about by an unusual state of the ice in the autumn of 1878 in the North Bering Sea.

Assured that a few hours' southerly wind would be sufficient to break up the belt of ice, scarcely a Swedish mile [6.64 English miles] in breadth, that barred our way, and rendered confident by the above-quoted communications from experts in America concerning the state of the ice in the sea north of Bering Strait, I was not at first very uneasy at the delay. . . . When day after day passed without any change taking place, it became clear to me that we must make preparations for wintering just on the threshold between the Arctic and the Pacific oceans [that is, only about 120 miles from Cape Dezhnev, the northeastern extremity of the Asiatic continent].

It was an unexpected disappointment, which it was more difficult to bear with equanimity as it was evident that we would have avoided it if we had come some hours earlier to the eastern side of Kolyuchin Bay. There were numerous occasions during the preceding part of our voyage on which these hours might have been saved: the *Vega* did not require to stay so long at Port Dickson, we might have saved a day at Taimir Island, have dredged somewhat less west of the New Siberian Islands, and so on; and above all, our long stay at Irkaipij waiting for an improvement in the state of the ice was fatal, because at least three days were lost there without any change for the better taking place. . . .

. . . Up to a distance of about 6 kilometers from the shore the ice . . . lay during the course of the whole winter nearly undisturbed. . . . Farther out to sea, on the other hand, it was in constant motion. So-called polynias, or open places, probably occur here all the year round, and when the weather was favorable we could therefore nearly always see a blue water sky at the horizon from true northwest to east.

A southerly wind after some days brought the open-water channel so near the vessel that it was possible to walk to it in a few hours. It then swarmed with seals—an indication that it was in connection with a sea that was constantly open. The neighborhood of such a sea perhaps also accounts for the circumstance that we did not see a single seal hole in the ice fields that surrounded the vessel.

The ground ice to which the *Vega* was moored on the twenty-ninth September, and under which she lay during the course of the winter, was about 40 meters long and 25 meters broad; its highest point lay 6 meters above the surface of the water. It was thus not very large, but gave the vessel good shelter. . . .

The violent motion which took place in the ice during the night before the fifteenth December gave us a sharp warning that our position in the open road was by no means so secure as was desirable, but that there was a possibility that the vessel might be nipped suddenly and without any previous warning. If such a misfortune had happened, the crew of the *Vega* would certainly have had no difficulty in getting to land over the ice. . . .

In order as far as possible to secure ourselves against the consequences of such a misfortune [as the crushing of the ship through ice pressure], a depot of provisions, guns, ammunition, etc., reckoned for thirty men and one hundred days, was formed on land. Fortunately we did not require to depend upon it. The stores were laid up on the beach without the protection of lock or bolt, covered only with sails and oars, and no watch was kept at the place. Notwithstanding this, and the want of food which occasionally prevailed among the natives, it remained untouched both by the Chukchis who lived in the neighborhood and by those who daily drove past the place from distant regions. All knew very well the contents of the sail-covered heap. . . .

Most of those who for the first time took part in a wintering in the High North were, when the first cold occurred, more or less frostbitten, on several occasions . . . but fortunately never to such a degree that any serious bad results followed. After we, newcomers to the polar regions, warned by experience, became more careful, such frostbites occurred but seldom. Nor did there occur a single case of frostbite in the feet. To this conduced our clothing, which was adapted to the climate. . . .

On board the vessel in our cabins and collection rooms it was besides by no means so cold as many would suppose. . . . Much greater inconvenience than from cold did we in the cabins suffer from the excessive heat and the fumes which firing in large cast-iron stoves is wont to cause in small close rooms. . . .

The state of health on board during the course of the winter was exceedingly good. Dr. Almquist's report enumerates only a few serious maladies, all successfully cured . . . but not a single case of that insidious disease, scurvy, which formerly raged in such a frightful way among the crews in all long voyages, and which is still wont to gather so many victims from among polar travelers.[19]

When we were beset, the ice next the shore . . . was too weak to carry a foot passenger, and the difficulty of reaching the vessel from the land with the means which the Chukchis had at their disposal was thus very great. When the natives observed us, there was in any case immediately a great commotion among them. Men, women, children, and dogs were seen running

---

[19] The chief elements in the diet were preserved meat and fish, dried fish, salt pork, preserved vegetables, butter, sugar. There were also small amounts fresh fish and local red meat in the Nordenskiöld commissariat.

up and down the beach in eager confusion. . . . [After several unsuccessful attempts] a large skin boat was put out, which was filled brimful of men and women, regardless of the evident danger of navigating such a boat, heavily laden, through sharp newly formed ice. They rowed immediately to the vessel, and on reaching it most of them climbed without the least hesitation over the gunwale with jests and laughter. . . .

Our first meeting with the inhabitants of this region, where we afterward passed ten long months, was on both sides very hearty, and formed the starting-point of a very friendly relation between the Chukchis and ourselves, which remained unaltered during the whole of our stay. . . .

Our hunters [in October] made hunting excursions in different directions, but the supply of game was scanty. The openings in the ice probably swarmed with seals, but they were too distant, and without a boat it was impossible to carry on any hunting there.[20] Not a single polar bear now appeared to be visible in the neighborhood, although bears' skulls are found at several places on the beach. . . .

In the beginning of March there passed us a large number of sledges laden with reindeer skins, and drawn by eight to ten dogs each. . . . These trains were on a commercial journey from Irkaipij to Päk at Bering Strait. . . .

Sledges of considerable size, drawn by reindeer, began after the middle of March to pass the *Vega* in pretty large numbers. They were laden with reindeer skins and goods bought at the Russian market places, and intended for barter at Bering Strait.

The reindeer Chukchis [who live in the interior] are better clothed, and appear to be in better circumstances and more independent, than the coast Chukchis. . . . As every one owns a reindeer herd, all must follow the nomad mode of living, but at the same time they carried on traffic between the savages in the northernmost parts of America [Alaska] and the Russian fur-dealers in Siberia, and many pass their whole lives in commercial journeys. . . .

---

[20] This confirms what is otherwise clear, that the men of the *Vega* did not understand hunting methods of the Eskimo type, through which they could have secured abundant fresh meat.

[July] On the seventeenth the "year's ice" next the land at last broke up, so that an extensive land clearing arose. But the ground ices were still undisturbed, and between these the "year's ice" even lay so fast that all were agreed that at least fourteen days must still pass before there was any prospect of getting free. . . . So certain was I, however, that the ice barrier would not yet for a long time be broken up that I immediately . . . made arrangements for a new journey [into the interior]. . . .

While we were thus employed the forenoon of the eighteenth passed. We sat down to dinner at the usual time, without any suspicion that the time of our release was now at hand. During dinner it was suddenly observed that the vessel was moving slightly. Palander rushed on deck, saw that the ice was in motion, ordered the boiler fires to be lighted—the engine having long ago been put in order in expectation of this moment—and in two hours, by 3:30 P.M. on the eighteenth July, the *Vega*, decked with flags, was under steam and sail again on the way to her destination. . . .

The course was shaped at first for the northwest in order to make a detour round the drift-ice fields lying nearest us, then along the coast for Bering Strait. On the height at Yinretlen there stood as we passed the men, women, and children of the village all assembled, looking out to sea at the fire horse—the Chukchis would perhaps say fire dog or fire reindeer—which carried their friends of the long winter months forever away from their cold, bleak shores. Whether they shed tears, as they often said they would, we could not see from the distance which now parted us from them. But it may readily have happened that the easily moved disposition of the savage led them to do this. Certain it is that in many of us the sadness of separation mingled with the feelings of tempestuous joy which now rushed through the breast of every *Vega* man.

The *Vega* met no more ice obstacles on her course to the Pacific. . . . The sea was mirror-bright and nearly clear of ice, a walrus or two stuck up his head, strangely magnified by the fog, in our neighborhood, seals swam round us in large numbers, and flocks of birds, which probably breed on the steep cliffs of Serdze Kamen, swarmed round the vessel. The trawl net repeatedly brought up from the sea bottom a very abundant yield of worms, molluscs, crustacea, etc. A zoologist would here have had a rich working-field.

The fog continued, so that on the other side of Serdze Kamen we lost all sight of land, until on the morning of the twentieth dark heights again began to peep out. These were the mountain summits of the easternmost promontory of Asia, East Cape, an unsuitable name, for which I have substituted on the map that of Cape Deschnev after the gallant Cossack who for the first time two hundred and thirty years ago circumnavigated it.[20]

By 11 A.M. we were in the middle of the sound which unites the North Polar Sea with the Pacific, and from this point the *Vega* greeted the Old and New worlds by a display of flags and the firing of a Swedish salute.

Thus finally was reached the goal toward which so many nations had struggled, all along from the time [1553] when Sir Hugh Willoughby, with the firing of salutes from cannon and with hurrahs from the festive-clad seamen, in the presence of an innumerable crowd of jubilant men certain of success, ushered in the long series of northeast voyages. But, as I have before related, their hopes were grimly disappointed. Sir Hugh and all his men perished as pioneers of England's navigation and of voyages to the ice-encumbered sea which bounds Europe and Asia on the north.

Innumerable other marine expeditions have since then trodden the same path, always without success, and generally with the sacrifice of the vessel and of the life and health of many brave seamen.

Now for the first time, after the lapse of three hundred and twenty-six years, and when most men experienced in sea matters had declared the undertaking impossible, was the Northeast Passage at last achieved. This has taken place thanks to the discipline, zeal, and ability of our man-of-war's men and their officers, without the sacrifice of a single human life, without sickness among those who took part in the undertaking, without the slightest damage to the vessel, and under circumstances which show that the same thing may be done again in most, perhaps in all, years in the course of a few weeks.

---

[20] Cape Dezhnev is the name now formally applied to the cape.

The optimism of Nordenskiöld, with which this quotation closes, did not echo far down the corridors of the pessimistic time in which he wrote. For the centuries-old and world-wide faith in the commercial advantages of a Northwest and a Northeast Passage had died with Sir John Franklin a quarter century before the *Vega* expedition. It was not destined for rebirth until a half-century after the publication of *The Voyage of the Vega,* a book through which an optimistic generation could so reasonably have justified a program of immediate development. It required two wars and a revolution to ripen the time for this development.

In the first of these, the Russo-Japanese War of 1904-05, the defeat of Imperial Russia, traceable no doubt to many causes, was frequently blamed on an inadequacy of transportation, and in special on the insufficiency of the Trans-Siberian Railway as an overland connecting link between Europe and the Pacific. Obviously, a second war in the Far East would require not merely a double-tracking of the transcontinental railway but also the building of other railways and the opening of seaways.

When World War I came in 1914, nothing adequate had as yet been done for increasing the carrying power of the railway or to open seaways. The need did not arise, for Japan was fighting on the same side with Russia.

But in 1917 came the Bolshevik Revolution with developments such that, among other things, the United States and Japan undertook joint military operations from the east against the Soviet Union, which had replaced Imperial Russia.

Now developed the Soviet doctrine of capitalist encirclement. It was to the effect that the capitalist lands would at first expect the sprawling socialistic nation to disintegrate from internal weaknesses; that when the capitalists realized this was not going to happen, they would try to stop the spread of socialism through a military operation which would take the form of an attack from the west by Europe and from the east by Japan, this attack perhaps helped on both fronts by the United States.

To prepare against the visualized struggle, and for other reasons, the Soviet Union not merely pressed the double-tracking of its transcontinental railway but also started the construction of other railways. And to decrease the transportation problem eastward (as well as to guard by distance against attacks from Europe), they further began to create industrial and manufacturing centers remote from Europe, nearer to Japan, at various points in Asia.

These preparations involved logically the development of sea freighting to complement the overland traffic. The Suez and Panama canals would be closed to the USSR in the postulated War of Capitalist Encirclement; the distances around either Cape Horn or the Cape of Good Hope were too long, and besides, the "capitalists" would obviously possess control of those oceans. Only through the Northeast Passage was there any chance of success. Therefore the Northeast Passage had to be made a success.

The general preparations for the visualized coming struggle developed additional needs for a seaway around the north of Asia. For moving factories and populations away from Europe, in accord with the principle of defense in depth, involved the colonization of Siberia, a region so large that even that section of it which lies north of the Trans-Siberian Railway is bigger than the United States.

This vast field of colonization is devoid of natural transportation routes except for its great rivers, nearly all of which flow north into the waters of the Northeast Passage. Three streams the size of the Mississippi—the Ob, the Yenisei, and the Lena —rise in the heart of Asia and furnish during summer through their liquid water steamboat highways of 2000 miles each, leading from the rich interior to the sea. During winter they furnish, through the ice that forms on them, level tractor highways of similar length and ramifications. Then there are many other considerable north-flowing rivers which, except for being larger, correspond to our Hudson, Rio Grande, and Columbia.

There was a double must in the peremptory order that fate presented to the Soviet Union. They had to have a successful Northeast Passage both for through transport from Atlantic to Pacific and for developing and making accessible the resources of three valleys, each comparable to the Mississippi basin of the United States, and many basins of lesser rivers.

Accordingly, the Five Year Plans of the Soviet Government contemplated and provided for a twentieth-century northward movement of population comparable to the nineteenth-century westward movement of Americans across the United States and southern Canada. In step with this colonization they created traffic eastward from the Atlantic side along the northern coasts of the Soviet Union to tap the Ob, the Yenisei, and other rivers that reach the Polar Sea west of Cape Chelyuskin, with corresponding westward traffic from the Pacific side to serve the Lena and other streams that have their mouths east of Chelyuskin. There was also through traffic, but this was less emphasized.

In 1937, the last year for which Northern Sea Route information was released before the war secrecy descended, about 20 ships were engaged in through voyaging while around 200 shuttled back and forth between Atlantic or Pacific and their logically assigned river ports. Usually a through ship made only one voyage per summer between an Atlantic and a Pacific base, such as Murmansk and Archangel on the West, Petropavlovsk and Vladivostok on the east. One ship made a return voyage, traversing the Northeast Passage twice in one season.

Naturally the ships that ply the waters of the Northern Sea Route during its open season are not idle the rest of the year, but are used on other runs.

Although Nordenskiöld did forecast success for the Northeast Passage, in case its developments were attempted, he could not have foreseen the present relative ease of navigation, unless he indeed foresaw both the radio and the airplane. For it is by the use of these, and through the progress of weather forecasting, that what was previously difficult and haphazard has now become precise and relatively easy.

The sea ice of the Northeast Passage is in constant motion at varying though sluggish speeds which are controlled by the wind both as to direction and as to velocity. By observing the drift ice and reporting its location today, its speed, and its direction, we can forecast its location tomorrow or the next day, through applying the current weather forecast. In some cases a vessel can therefore steer with confidence on Monday toward an area that is jammed with ice, knowing that by arrival time Tuesday the floes are going to be miles away.

The weather reporting upon which the navigation forecasts of the Northern Sea Route are based is chiefly from stations located on the mainland or on islands, but some is from ships and planes. As to character, location, and drift of ice, the reporting is mainly from airplanes that scout every relevant part of the seaway constantly during the navigation season. The combining of weather and ice information, so as to foretell where the ice is going to be at a given time, is done partly in central forecast clearing-stations and partly in chartrooms by the commanders of ships or convoys.

The result of the ice forecasting, and of the scouting of planes in advance of ships, is a safety and a regularity of navigation in the Northeast Passage far beyond Nordénskiöld's optimism, based though it was on a knowledge which he considered adequate for the prediction of successful use of these waters. This knowledge had been brought gradually to the attention of Europe through the centuries by prehistoric and dimly historical voyagers, by the well-known Great Northern Expeditions of the Emperor Peter, and by the long line of explorers, chiefly Russian, who prepared the way for the Swedish Finn who was not merely the first to take an oceangoing ship through the whole passage, but who was also in his day the most consistent prophet of its coming usefulness.

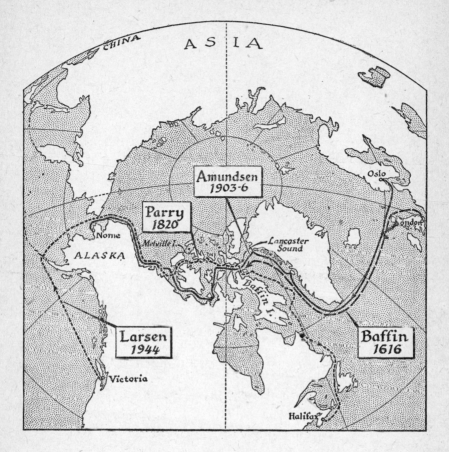

Discovery of the Northwest Passage

DISCOVERY OF THE
NORTHWEST PASSAGE

CHAPTER 13

No one knows when the search for the Northwest Passage began, or at least there is no agreement as to the date.

Some maintain that John Cabot realized before Columbus did that the Americas were not the Indies. Cabot may, then, have been in search of a passage around America by the northwest in 1497 when he visited the Newfoundland region, and still more likely in 1498 when, as some believe, he went far north on the west side of Greenland, perhaps discovering Hudson Strait and Davis Strait—remembering, of course, that the Icelanders had discovered both these straits and their surroundings in connection with their colonization of Greenland, just before and just after the year 1000.

Little is known of John Cabot's voyages, indeed much less than what we know of the Icelandic and Greenlandic voyages of five hundred years earlier. So we are not on solid ground, in post-Columbian times, with regard to the Northwest Passage until we come to the voyages of the Cortereal brothers, just after 1500, which have been dealt with in an earlier section of this book. From them no connected narrative has survived.

There is, indeed, no connected story from any search for the Northwest Passage until 1576, when Sir Martin Frobisher, privateer if not pirate, was commissioned by the Government of Queen Elizabeth to seek a near way to the Far East by way of the northwest. For fifteen years before that time he had been striving to organize this discovery voyage, not merely because he believed access to the Pacific feasible by the northwest but also, as his colleague George Best tells us, because he considered that discovering the passage was "the only thing

475

of the world that was left yet undone whereby a notable mind might be made famous and fortunate."

There are several of these Northwest Passage narratives, but none of them by Sir Martin himself. Here the account by George Best is used.

The Best narrative describes the voyages from personal knowledge, for the author was with Frobisher on all three, being finally Captain of the *Jane Anne* of the third expedition.

Since this book deals in narratives, it must of necessity omit what is perhaps the most interesting section of Book One, wherein Best outlines the philosophy or cosmography that supported the geographic thinking and the exploratory plans of the Elizabethan age. What strikes us most today in reading his *True Discourse*, is how "advanced" they were more than three centuries ago. For Britain understood in Shakespeare's time many things which some of us pride ourselves on having learned since that recent beginning of the current air age which has made travel in the polar regions a commonplace.

For instance, it has been until within the last one or two decades a common idea that the most extreme heat is found in the tropics, that moderate temperatures characterize the "Temperate" Zone, and that the most extreme cold is found in the Arctic.

Countering such "vulgar errors" of his time, Best points out that concepts like these rest upon a wrong view of the shape of the earth and of its relation to the sun. He says that from a true conception of earth and sun it follows of necessity that the most extreme heat will not occur in the tropics, for the days are not long enough; that the greatest heat must occur in the Temperate Zone, where the hot midsummer days are longer and the cooling nights shorter; and that warmth comparable to that of the tropics is to be expected within the Arctic during its short summers, because the warming day is twenty-four hours long and the cool night missing. These deductions, says Best, had been verified before his time by travelers and were to be accepted by his contemporaries as basic knowledge if they wanted to foresee what was to be expected on a discovery voyage into the Arctic.

Having made it clear, among other things, that the tropics

have heat which is uniform but not extreme, that the Temperate Zone has the greatest extremes of heat and cold, and that the Arctic, though it has long and cold winters, must of necessity have summers that are hot if you get away from ocean and mountains into the interior of some land—after having made such things clear, Best furnishes a short introduction to the expedition narratives and then presents in condensed form the account of the first voyage:[1]

Frobisher and the Northwest Passage

◢ The [Arctic] summers are warm and fruitful, and the winter's nights under the pole are tolerable to living creatures.

And if it be so that the winter and time of darkness there be very cold, yet hath not nature left them unprovided therefor. For there the beasts are covered with hair so much the thicker in how much the vehemency of cold is greater, by reason whereof the best and richest furs are brought out of the coldest regions. Also the fowls of these cold countries have thicker skins, thicker feathers, and more store of down than in other hot places.

Our Englishmen that travel to St. Nicholas, and go afishing to Wardhouse, enter far within the Circle Arctic, and so are in the frozen zone; and yet there, as well as in Iseland [Iceland], and all along those northern seas, they find the greatest store of the greatest fishes that are, as whales, etc., and also abundance of mean fishes, as herrings, cods, haddocks, brets, etc., which argueth that the sea as well as the land may be and is well frequented and inhabited in the cold countries.

But some, perhaps, will marvel there should be such temperate places in the regions about the poles, when at under —[2] degrees in latitude, our Captain Frobisher and his company were troubled with so many and so great mountains of fleeting ice with so great storms of cold, with such continual snow on tops of mountains, and with such barren soil, there being

---

[1] Richard Collinson, *The Three Voyages of Martin Frobisher in Search of a Passage to Cathaia and India by the North-West*, A.D. 1576-8, Hakluyt Society, London, 1867.

[2] For reasons of state secrecy, the latitudes and longitudes of the Frobisher voyages were at first deleted from published narratives.

neither wood or trees, but low shrubs and such like. To all which objections may be answered thus:

First, those infinite islands of ice were engendered and congealed in time of winter, and now by the great heat of summer were thawed, and then by ebbs, floods, winds, and currents were driven to and fro, and troubled the fleet, so that this is an argument to prove the heat in summer there to be great, that was able to thaw so monstrous mountains of ice. As for continual snow on tops of mountains, it is there no otherwise than is in the hottest part of the middle [equatorial] zone, where also lieth great snow all the summer long upon tops of mountains, because there is not sufficient space for the sun's reflection whereby the snow should be molten.

Touching the cold stormy winds, and the barrenness of the country, it is there as it is in Cornwall and Devonshire in England, which parts, though we know to be fruitful and fertile, yet on the north side thereof all along the coast within 7 or 8 miles of the sea, there can neither hedge nor tree grow, although they be diligently by art husbanded and seen unto; and the cause thereof are the northern driving winds, which, coming from the sea, are so bitter and sharp that they kill all the young and tender plants, and suffer scarce anything to grow; and so is it in the islands of Meta Incognita [Baffin Island], which are subject most to east and northern winds, which the last were choked up the passage so with ice that the fleet could hardly recover their port. Yet, notwithstanding all the objections that may be, the country is habitable, for there are men, women, children, and sundry kind of beasts in great plenty, as bears, deer, hares, foxes, and dogs; all kinds of flying fowls, as ducks, sea mews, wilmots, partridges, larks, crows, hawks, and suchlike, as in the Third Book you shall understand more at large.

Then it appeareth that not only the middle zone but also the zones about the poles are habitable, which thing being well considered and familiarly known to our General Captain Frobisher, as well for that he is thoroughly furnished of the knowledge of the sphere, and all other skills appertaining to the art of navigation, as also for the confirmation he hath of the same by many years' experience, both by sea and land, and being persuaded of a new and nearer passage to Cataya [Cathay, China], than by Capo d'Buona Speranza [Cape of Good Hope], which the Portuguese yearly use. He began first with himself to devise, and then with his friends to confer, and laid a plain plat [plan] unto them, that that voyage was not only possible by the northwest, but also, as he could prove, easy to be performed.

And further, he determined and resolved with himself to go make full proof thereof, and to accomplish, or bring true certificate of the truth, or else never to return again, knowing this to be the only thing of the world that was left yet undone whereby a notable mind might be made famous and fortunate.

But although his will were great to perform this notable voyage, whereof he had conceived in his mind a great hope, by sundry sure reasons and secret intelligence which here, for sundry causes, I leave untouched—yet he wanted altogether means and ability to set forward and perform the same. Long time he conferred with his private friends of these secrets, and made also many offers for the performing of the same in effect unto sundry merchants of our country, above fifteen years before he attempted the same, as by good witness shall well appear (albeit some evil-willers which challenge to themselves the fruits of other men's labors have greatly injured him in the report of the same, saying that they have been the first authors of that action, and they have learned him the way, which themselves as yet have never gone).

But perceiving that hardly he was hearkened unto of the merchants, which never regard virtue without sure, certain, and present gains, he repaired to the Court (from whence, as from the fountain of our commonwealth, all good causes have their chief increase and maintenance), and there laid open to many great estates and learned men the plot and sum of his device. And amongst many honorable minds which favored his honest and commendable enterprise, he was specially bound and beholding to the Right Honorable Ambrose Dudley, Earl of Warwick, whose favorable mind and good disposition hath always been ready to countenance and advance all honest actions with the authors and executors of the same. And so by means of my lord his honorable countenance, he received some comfort of his cause, and by little and little, with no small expense and pain, brought his cause to some perfection, and had drawn together so many adventurers and such sums of money as might well defray a reasonable charge, to furnish himself to sea withal.

He prepared two small barks of 25 and 20 ton apiece, wherein he intended to accomplish his pretended voyage. Wherefore, being furnished with the foresaid two barks and one small pinnace of 10 ton burthen, having therein victuals and other necessaries for twelve months provision, he departed upon the said voyage from Blackewall the fifteenth of June, Anno Domini 1576.

One of the barks wherein he went was named the *Gabriel* and the other the *Michael*, and sailing northwest from England upon the first of July, at length he had sight of a high and ragged land, which he judged Freeselande (whereof some authors have made mention), but durst not approach the same by reason of the great store of ice that lay along the coasts, and the great mists that troubled them not a little.[3]

Not far from thence he lost company of his small pinnace, which, by means of the great storm, he supposed to be swallowed up of the sea, wherein he lost only four men.

Also the other bark named the *Michael*, mistrusting the matter, conveyed themselves privily away from him, and returned home with great report that he was cast away.

The worthy Captain, notwithstanding these discomforts, although his mast was sprung and his topmast blown overboard with extreme foul weather, continued his course toward the northwest, knowing that the sea at length must needs have an ending, and that some land should have a beginning that way; and determined, therefore, at the least, to bring true proof what land and sea the same might be, so far to the northwestward, beyond any man that hath heretofore discovered.

And the twentieth of July he had sight of a high land, which he called Queen Elizabeth's Foreland [Baffin Island, southeast tip] after Her Majesty's name, and sailing more northerly along

---

[3] This must have been the south tip of Greenland.

the coast, he descried another foreland with a great gut, bay, or passage dividing, as it were, two mainlands or continents asunder. There he met with store of exceeding great ice all this coast along, and coveting still to continue his course to the northward, was always by contrary wind detained overthwart these straits, and could not get beyond.

Within few days after, he perceived the ice to be well consumed and gone, either there engulfed in by some swift currents or in drafts carried more to the southward of the same straits, or else conveyed some other way. Wherefore he determined to make proof of this place to see how far that gut had continuance, and whether he might carry himself through the same into some open sea on the back side, whereof he conceived no small hope, and so entered the same the one and twentieth of July, and passed above 50 leagues therein, as he reported, having upon either hand a great main or continent. And that land upon his right hand as he sailed westward, he judged to be the continent of Asia, and there to be divided from the firm of America, which lieth upon the left hand over against the same.

This place he named after his name Frobisher's Strait, like as Magellan at the southwest end of the world, having discovered the passage to the South Sea (where America is divided from the continent of that land which lieth under the South Pole) and called the same strait Magellan Straits. After he had passed 60 leagues into this foresaid strait, he went ashore, and found sign where fire had been made.

He saw mighty deer that seemed to be mankind, which ran at him, and hardly he escaped with his life in a narrow way, where he was fain to use defense and policy to save his life.

In this place he saw and perceived sundry tokens of the peoples resorting thither, and being ashore upon the top of a hill, he perceived a number of small things fleeting in the sea afar off which he supposed to be porpoises or seals, or some kind of strange fish; but coming nearer, he discovered them to be men in small boats made of leather. And before he could descend down from the hill certain of those people had almost cut off his boat from him, having stolen secretly behind the rocks for that purpose, where he speedily hasted to his boat and bent himself to his holbert [halberd], and narrowly escaped the danger and saved his boat.

Afterward he had sundry conferences with them, and they came aboard his ship, and brought him salmon and raw flesh and fish, and greedily devoured the same before our men's faces. And to show their agility, they tried many masteries upon the ropes of the ship after our mariners' fashion, and appeared to be very strong of their arms and nimble of their bodies. They exchanged coats of seal and bear skins and suchlike with our men, and received bells, looking-glasses, and other toys in recompense thereof again.

After great courtesy and many meetings, our mariners, contrary to their Captain's direction, began more easily to trust them, and five of our men, going ashore, were by them intercepted with their boat, and were never since heard of to this day again. So that the Captain, being destitute of boat, bark, and all company, had scarcely sufficient number to conduct back his bark again. He could now neither convey himself ashore to rescue his men (if he had been able), for want of a boat, and again, the subtle traitors were so wary as they would after that never come within our men's danger.

The Captain, notwithstanding, desirous to bring some token from thence of his being there, was greatly discontented that he had not before apprehended some of them. And therefore to deceive the deceivers he wrought a pretty policy; for knowing well how they greatly delighted in our toys, and specially in bells, he rang a pretty lowbell, making wise that he would give him the same that would come and fetch it. And because they would not come within his danger for fear, he flung one bell unto them, which of purpose he threw short that it might fall into the sea and be lost.

And to make them more greedy of the matter, he rang a louder bell, so that in the end one of them came near the ship side to receive the bell, which, when he thought to take at the Captain's hand, he was thereby taken himself; for the Captain, being readily provided, let the bell fall and caught the man fast, and plucked him with main force, boat and all, into his bark out of the sea. Whereupon, when he found himself in captivity, for very choler and disdain he bit his tongue in twain within his mouth. Notwithstanding, he died not therof, but lived until he came in England, and then he died of cold which he had taken at sea.

Now with this new prey (which was a sufficient witness of the Captain's far and tedious travel toward the unknown parts of the world, as did well appear by this strange infidel, whose like was never seen, read, nor heard of before, and whose language was neither known nor understood of any) the said Captain Frobisher returned homeward, and arrived in England in August following, anno 1576, where he was highly commended of all men for his great and notable attempt, but specially famous for the great hope he brought of the passage to Cathay, which he doubted nothing at all to find and pass through in those parts, as he reporteth.

And it is especially to be remembered at the first arrival in those parts, there lay so great store of ice all the coast along so thick together that hardly his boat could pass unto the shore. At length, after divers attempts, he commanded his company, if by any possible means they could get ashore, to bring him whatsoever thing they could first find, whether it were living or dead, stock or stone, in token of Christian possession, which thereby he took in behalf of the Queen's Most Excellent Majesty, thinking that thereby he might justify the having and enjoying of the same things that grew in these unknown parts.

Some of his company brought flowers, some green grass, and one brought a piece of black stone, much like to a sea coal in color, which by the weight seemed to be some kind of metal or mineral. This was a thing of no account in the judgment of the Captain at the first sight. And yet for novelty it was kept, in respect of the place from whence it came.

After his arrival in London, being demanded of sundry his friends what thing he had brought them home of that country, he had nothing left to present them withal but a piece of this black stone. And it fortuned a gentlewoman, one of the adventurers' wives, to have a piece thereof, which by chance she threw and burned in the fire, so long that at the length being taken forth and quenched in a little vinegar, it glistened with a bright marcasite of gold.

Whereupon, the matter being called in some question, it was

brought to certain gold-finders [assayers] in London to make assay thereof, who indeed found it to hold gold, and that very richly for the quantity. Afterward, the same gold-finders promised great matters thereof if there were any store to be found, and offered themselves to adventure for the searching of those parts from whence the same was brought. Some that had great hope of the matter sought secretly to have a lease at Her Majesty's hands of those places, whereby to enjoy the mass of so great a public profit unto their own private gains.

In conclusion, the hope of the same gold ore to be found kindled a greater opinion in the hearts of many to advance the voyage again. Whereupon preparation was made for a new voyage against the year following, and the Captain more specially directed by commission for the searching more of this gold ore than for the searching any further of the passage. And being well accompanied with divers resolute and forward gentlemen, Her Majesty then lying at the Right Honorable the Lord of Warwick's house in Essex, came to take their leaves, and kissing Her Highness's hands, with gracious countenance and comfortable words departed towards their charge. ✄

On his third expedition, in 1578, Frobisher entered Hudson Strait, thus thirty-two years before Henry Hudson. This strait Frobisher may have taken for a passage to the southern ocean, as indeed it was thought to be by Hudson and a number of others. But what Frobisher definitely took for an entrance to the Pacific was not a strait at all, but one of the largest and widest bays in the world, now called Frobisher Bay. Sir Martin and his colleagues apparently knew that the land on its shores, their Meta Incognita, lay farther west than Greenland. It was not he but later speculators who developed the theory that the Frobisher expedition had really discovered a strait cutting through Greenland. So it was in Greenland that Frobisher Strait appeared on the maps for some time after the voyages.

It was only secondary with Frobisher to discover a way to the riches of the Indies; the objective was riches, just any riches. Therefore, as Best has related, when the rocks he picked up on his first voyage were identified in Britain as gold or heavily gold-bearing ore (really iron pyrites or other rocks containing mica),

the Queen and the Court, the knights and the gentry, lost their
interest in going farther. Why should they go farther and certainly fare worse? All they had to do on Frobisher Strait was
to shovel rock from the beach into cargo vessels. And that is
what they did.

Frobisher took three ships and a complement of 120 men to
his gold mine in 1577. He returned once more in 1578, with
plans for colonizing the new land, this time with fifteen vessels.
It was on this large and, as it proved, final expedition that the
fleet, driven off its course by stormy weather and drifting ice,
mistook the entrance to Hudson Strait for that of Frobisher Bay
and sailed some distance into the strait before turning back and
proceeding to the "gold" mines of Meta Incognita.

For a variety of reasons the plan for founding a settlement in
Frobisher Bay was abandoned, and at the end of the summer of
1578 the vessels of the third expedition returned to England,
carrying a large quantity of ore.

Then the bubble finally burst, a rather substantial bubble of
many hundreds of tons of iron ore. In a contemporary publication, Camden's *Annals of Elizabeth*, it is stated that the "stones,
when neither gold nor silver nor any other metal could be
extracted from them, we have seen cast forth to mend the highways." Within our generation some of the pyrites dumped by
Frobisher into Dartford harbor in England have been dredged
up in connection with harbor improvements, so that specimens
are now available in museums.

Although it was only through a few decades that cartog-
raphers placed Frobisher Strait in Greenland, it was centuries
before the "strait" was definitely identified as the bay that now
carries the name of Frobisher. The discovery was made by
Charles Francis Hall of Cincinnati, Ohio, in 1861-62, on his
Franklin Search expedition. He found a number of relics that
were beyond dispute English and Elizabethan. For greater
safety he split the collection in half, giving a part to the Royal
Geographical Society of London and part to the Smithsonian
Institution of Washington. Both collections are now missing, and
nobody seems to know what happened to them. Some Frobisher
relics from the Smithsonian collection were exhibited by the
United States Naval Observatory at the International Exhibition

of 1876 in Philadelphia, but their disposition after the close of that exhibition is unknown.

There has been the hope that when memorabilia were removed from British libraries and museums to avoid their loss by bombing in World War II, there might come to light some boxes containing the Frobisher relics. If this has happened, the press has not as yet carried the news. There had been no corresponding hope for a rediscovery of the Smithsonian part of the collection.

Hall made his discovery of the Frobisher relics on an island about a third of the way into Frobisher Bay, which has a total length of nearly 175 miles. This tends to confirm what we had no reason to doubt in any case, that Frobisher's vessels turned back before they saw the head of the bay.

Since this is not a history, no attempt is made to list even the famous names and considerable discoveries of the next two hundred years in connection with the search for the Northwest Passage; we come at once to the greatest single forward stride, made in 1819-20 by the ships *Hecla* and *Griper* under the command of Sir Edward Parry. It was not merely a long stride but was also the discovery of the potentially most valuable of the five or more variants by which a seaway between Atlantic and Pacific can be laid out around the north of America.

In 1818, Parry had been an officer in the expedition of Sir John Ross. As they proceeded west through Lancaster Sound, a dispute arose when the commander and some others felt sure they descried a range of mountains lying athwart their path, forming the head of a bay, while Parry and a number of others claimed that this was a mirage, or other false identification, and that for all they knew when they turned back there might have been an open road to the Pacific. On this basis Parry was made commander of the 1819-20 expedition, which he described in a huge quarto volume that has a number of appendices by scientific and other members of his staff. This volume, published at London in 1821, bears the title: *Journal of a Voyage for the Discovery of a North-West Passage from the Atlantic to the Pacific; performed in the years 1819-20 in His Majesty's Ships Hecla and Griper, under the orders of William Edward Parry,*

R. N., F. R. S., and commander of the Expedition. The following extract begins after the vessels had sailed through Davis Strait and well into Baffin Bay, and when they were standing off the entrance to Lancaster Sound, the east-west passage that separates the northern end of Baffin Island from Devon Island.

Parry and the Northwest Passage

◢ [August 1, 1819] We were now about to enter and to explore that great sound or inlet which has obtained a degree of celebrity beyond what it might otherwise have been considered to possess, from the very opposite opinions which have been held with regard to it. To us it was peculiarly interesting, as being the point to which our instructions more particularly directed our attention; and I may add—what I believe we all felt—it was that point of the voyage which was to determine the success or failure of the expedition, according as one or other of the opposite opinions alluded to should be corroborated.

It will readily be conceived, then, how great our anxiety was for a change of the westerly wind and swell, which, on the first of August, set down Sir James Lancaster's Sound [Lancaster Sound], and prevented our making much progress. We experienced also another source of anxiety. The relative sailing qualities of the two ships were found to have altered so much that we were obliged to keep the *Hecla* under easy sail the whole day to allow the *Griper* to keep up with us, although the latter had hitherto kept way with her consort when sailing by the wind.

The ships stretched to the northward across the entrance of the sound, meeting occasionally with some loose and heavy streams of ice, and were at noon in latitude, by observation, 73 degrees 55 minutes 18 seconds, and in longitude, by the chronometers, 77 degrees 40 minutes.[4] Several whales were seen in the course of the day, and Mr. Allison remarked that this was the only part of Baffin's Bay in which he had ever seen young whales; for it is a matter of surprise to the whalers in general

---

[4] Like most seafaring narratives of the time, Parry's is encumbered with positional figures, courses, and wind directions. Most of these are omitted hereafter.

that they seldom or never meet with young ones on this fishery, as they are accustomed to do in the seas of Spitsbergen.

The *Griper* continued to detain us so much that I determined on making the best of our way to the westward, that no more time than was necessary might be occupied in the examination of the bottom of Lancaster Sound, provided it should be found to be an inlet surrounded by land. I was the more inclined to do this from the circumstance of the sea being so clear of ice as to offer no impediment to the navigation, which rendered it next to impossible that the two ships should not meet each other again. And it seemed to me to be of considerable importance to obtain as early information as possible whether a passage did or did not exist there, as in the latter event, we should have to proceed still further to the northward in search of one through some of the other sounds of Baffin; besides, the farther north we had to go, the shorter would the navigable season be to allow us to explore these sounds.

On these considerations I ordered the *Hecla* to be hove to in the evening, and sent Lieutenant Liddon an instruction, with some signals which might facilitate our meeting in case of fog. And I appointed as a place of rendezvous the meridian of 85 degrees west, and as near the middle of the sound as circumstances would permit. As soon, therefore, as the boat returned from the *Griper*, we carried a press of sail, and in the course of the evening saw the northern shore of the sound looming through the clouds which hung over it.

[August 2] It fell calm on the morning of the second, and at 9 A.M. we sounded with the deep-sea clams, and found 1050 fathoms by the line, on a bottom of mud and small stones; but I believe the depth of water did not exceed 800 or 900 fathoms, the ship's drift being considerable on account of the swell. It should be remarked, also, that where the soundings exceed 500 or 600 fathoms, even in very calm weather, the actual depth must, in the usual way of obtaining it, be a matter of some uncertainty, for the weight of the line causes it to run out with a velocity not perceptibly diminished, long after the lead or the clams have struck the ground.

The clams being now down, we were about to try the set of the current by mooring a boat to the line when the breeze again sprung up from the westward and prevented it. At noon we were in latitude by observation 74 degrees 30 minutes 3 seconds and in longitude 78 degrees 1 minute, Cape Osborn being north 79 degrees west, distant 41 miles.

The weather being clear in the evening, we had the first distinct view of both sides of the sound, and the difference in the character of the two shores was very apparent, that on the south consisting of high and peaked mountains, completely snow-clad except on the lower parts, while the northern coast has generally a smoother outline, and had, comparatively with the other, little snow upon it, the difference in this last respect appearing to depend principally on the difference in their absolute height. The sea was open before us, free from ice or land; and the *Hecla* pitched so much from the westerly swell in the course of the day as to throw the water once or twice into the stern windows, a circumstance which, together with other appearances, we were willing to attribute to an open sea in the desired direction. More than forty black whales were seen during the day.

[August 3] We had alternately fresh breezes from the westward and calms on the morning of the third, when we had only gained 8 or 9 miles upon the *Griper*, which we observed coming up the sound before an easterly wind, with all her studding sails set, while we had a fresh breeze from the westward. In the forenoon we were between Capes Warrender and Osborn, and had a good view of Sir George Hope's Monument, which proved to be a dark-looking and conspicuous hill on the mainland, and not an island, as it appeared to be when at a distance, on our former voyage.

A solitary iceberg being near us, Captain Sabine, Lieutenant Beechey, and Mr. Hooper were sent upon it to observe the variation of the needle and the longitude, and to take angles for the survey, a base being measured by Massey's log between the ship and the berg. We here obtained soundings in 373 fathoms, the bottom consisting of mud and small stones, of which a small quantity was brought up in the clams. By a boat moored to this instrument, a tide or current was found to set north 65 degrees east, at the rate of ⅝ mile per hour; the variation observed upon the iceberg was 106 degrees 58 minutes 5 seconds westerly.

Being favored at length by the easterly breeze which was bringing up the *Griper*, and for which we had long been looking with much impatience, a crowd of sail was set to carry us with all rapidity to the westward. It is more easy to imagine than to describe the almost breathless anxiety which was now visible in every countenance while, as the breeze increased to a fresh gale, we ran quickly up the sound. The mastheads were crowded by the officers and men during the whole afternoon, and an unconcerned observer, if any could have been unconcerned on such an occasion, would have been amused by the eagerness with which the various reports from the crow's-nest were received, all, however, hitherto favorable to our most sanguine hopes.

Between 4 and 6 P.M., we passed several ripplings on the water, as if occasioned by a weather tide, but no bottom could be found with the hand leads. Being now abreast of Cape Castlereagh, more distant land was seen to open out to the westward of it, and between the cape and this land was perceived an inlet, to which I have given the name of the Navy Board's Inlet. We saw points of land apparently all round this inlet, but being at a very great distance from it, we were unable to determine whether it was continuous or not. But as the land on the western side appeared so much lower and smoother than that on the opposite side near Cape Castlereagh, and came down so near the horizon about the center of the inlet, the general impression was that it is not continuous in that part. As our business lay to the westward, however, and not to the south, the whole of this extensive inlet was in a few hours lost in distance.

In the meantime the land had opened out on the opposite shore to the northward and westward of Cape Warrender, consisting of high mountains, and in some parts of tableland. Several headlands were here distinctly made out, of which the northernmost and most conspicuous was named after Captain Nicholas Lechmere Pateshall, of the Royal Navy. The extensive bay into which Cape Pateshall extends, and which, at the distance we passed it, appeared to be broken or detached in many parts, was named Croker's Bay, in honor of Mr. Croker, Secretary of the Admiralty. I have called this large opening a bay, though the quickness with which we sailed past it did not allow us to determine the absolute continuity of land round the bottom of it. It is therefore by no means improbable that a passage may here be one day found from Lancaster Sound into the northern sea. The cape which lies on the western side of Croker Bay was named after Sir Everard Home.

Our course was nearly due west, and the wind, still continuing to freshen, took us in a few hours nearly out of sight of the *Griper*. The only ice which we met with consisted of a few large bergs very much washed by the sea. And, the weather being remarkably clear, so as to enable us to run with perfect safety, we were by midnight in a great measure relieved from our anxiety respecting the supposed continuity of land at the bottom of this magnificent inlet, having reached the longitude of 83 degrees 12 minutes, where the two shores are still above 13 leagues apart, without the slightest appearance of any land to the westward of us for four or five points of the compass.

The color of the water having become rather lighter, we hove to at this time for the *Griper*, and obtained soundings in 150 fathoms, on a muddy bottom. The wind increased so much as to make it necessary to close-reef the sails, and to get the topgallant yards down, and there was a breaking sea from the eastward. A great number of whales were seen in the course of this day's run.

[August 4] Having made the ship snug, so as to be in readiness to round to should the land be seen ahead, and the *Griper* having come up within a few miles of us, we again bore up at 1 A.M. At half-past three, Lieutenant Beechey, who had relieved me on deck, discovered from the crow's-nest a reef of rocks inshore of us to the northward, on which the sea was breaking. These breakers appeared to lie directly off a cape, which we named after Rear-Admiral Joseph Bullan, and which lies immediately to the eastward of an inlet that I named Brooking Cuming Inlet.

As the sea had now become high, and the water appeared discolored at some distance without the breakers, the *Hecla* was immediately rounded to, for the purpose of sounding. We could find no bottom with 50 fathoms of line, but the *Griper*, coming up shortly after, obtained soundings in 75 fathoms, on a bottom of sand and mud.

We here met with innumerable loose masses of ice, upon which the sea was constantly breaking in a manner so much resembling the breakers on shoals as to make it a matter of some little uncertainty at the time whether those of which I have spoken above might not also have been caused by ice. It is possible, therefore, that shoal water may not be found to exist in this place; but I thought it right to mark the spot on the chart to warn future navigators when approaching this part of the coast. That there is something out of the common way in this neighborhood appears, however, more than probable, from the soundings obtained by the *Griper*, which are much less than we found them in any other part of the sound at the same distance from land.

At 7 A.M., there being less sea and no appearance of broken or discolored water, we again bore away to the westward, the *Griper* having joined us about the meridian of 85 degrees, which had been appointed as our place of rendezvous. Since the preceding evening, a thick haze had been hanging over the horizon to the southward, which prevented our seeing the land in that direction, to the westward of 87 degrees, while the whole of the northern shore—though, as it afterward proved, at a greater distance from us—was distinctly visible.

At noon, being in latitude 74 degrees 15 minutes 53 seconds north, longitude, by chronometers, 86 degrees 30 minutes 30 seconds, we were near two inlets, of which the easternmost was named Burnet Inlet and the other Stratton Inlet. The land between these two had very much the appearance of an island. We rounded to, for the purpose of sounding as well as to wait for our consort, and found no bottom with 170 fathoms of line, the water being of a dirty light-green color.

The cliffs on this part of the coast present a singular appearance, being stratified horizontally, and having a number of regular projecting masses of rock, broad at the bottom and coming to a point at the top, resembling so many buttresses raised by art at equal intervals. This very remarkable construction continues with little variation along the whole of this northern shore. . . .

After lying to for an hour, we again bore up to the westward, and soon after discovered a cape, afterward named by Captain Sabine, Cape Fellfoot, which appeared to form the termination of this coast. And as the haze which still prevailed to the south prevented our seeing any land in that quarter, and the sea was literally as free from ice as any part of the Atlantic, we began to flatter ourselves that we had fairly entered the Polar Sea, and some of the most sanguine among us had even calculated the bearing and distance of Icy Cape as a matter of no very difficult or improbable accomplishment.[5] This pleasing prospect was rendered the more flattering by the sea having, as we thought, regained the usual oceanic color, and by a long swell which was rolling in from the southward and eastward.

At 8 P.M., we came to some ice of no great breadth or thickness, extending several miles in a direction nearly parallel to our course; and as we could see clear water over it to the southward, I was for some time in the hope that it would prove a detached stream, from which no obstruction to our progress westerly was to be apprehended. At twenty minutes past ten, however, the weather having become hazy and the wind light, we perceived that the ice along which we had been sailing for the last two hours was joined, at the distance of half a mile to the westward of us, to a compact and impenetrable body of floes which lay across the whole breadth of the strait formed by the island and the western point of Maxwell Bay. We hauled our wind to the northward, just in time to avoid being embayed in the ice, on the outer edge of which a considerable surf, the effect of the late gale, was then rolling.

A second island was discovered to the southward of the former, to both of which I gave the name of Prince Leopold's Isles, in honor of his Royal Highness Prince Leopold of Saxe-Coburg. Immediately to the eastward of these islands there was a strong water sky, indicating a considerable extent of open sea, but a bright ice blink to the westward afforded little hope, for the present, of finding a passage in the desired direction. We saw today for the first time, a number of white whales

---

[5] The reference is to Icy Cape, Alaska, discovered by Captain James Cook in 1778.

(*Delphinus albicans*); guillemots, fulmar petrels, and kitti-wakes were also numerous near the ice.

[August 5] The easterly wind died away on the morning of the fifth and was succeeded by light and variable airs, with thick, snowy weather. At noon we were in latitude 74 degrees 19 minutes 38 seconds, longitude 89 degrees 18 minutes 40 seconds, the soundings being 135 fathoms, on a muddy bottom. At half-past ten we tried whether there were any current, and if so, in what direction it might be setting, by mooring a boat to the bottom with the deep-sea clams; but none could be detected. An hour before, the same experiment had been tried on board the *Griper*, when Lieutenant Liddon found the current to be setting east, at the rate of 9 miles per day.

While the calm and thick weather lasted, a number of the officers and men amused themselves in the boats in endeavoring to kill some of the white whales which were swimming about the ships in great numbers; but the animals were so wary that they would scarcely suffer the boats to approach them within 30 or 40 yards without diving. Mr. Fisher described them to be generally from 18 to 20 feet in length, and he stated that he had several times heard them emit a shrill, ringing sound, not unlike that of musical glasses when badly played. This sound, he further observed, was most distinctly heard when they happened to swim directly beneath the boat, even when they were several feet under water, and ceased altogether on their coming to the surface.

We saw also, for the first time, one or two shoals of narwhals (*Monodon monoceros*), called by the sailors sea unicorns.

A steady breeze springing up from the west-northwest in the afternoon, the ships stood to the northward till we had distinctly made out that no passage to the westward could at present be found between the ice and the land. The weather having become clear about this time, we perceived that there was a large open space to the southward, where no land was visible, and for this opening, over which there was a dark water sky,[6] our course was now directed.

---

[6] When the sky is cloudy, especially if uniformly overcast, it mirrors what is beneath it, forming a map in the sky. On this sky map ice or snow will show white, and the patches are called ice blink or snow blink. Water or

[August 6] It fell calm again, however, in a few hours, so that at noon on the sixth we were still abreast of Prince Leopold's Isles, which were so surrounded by ice that we could not approach them nearer than 4 or 5 miles. The appearance of these islands is not less remarkable than that of the northern shore of the strait, being also stratified horizontally, but having none of those buttress-like projections before described. The different strata form so many shelves, as it were, on which the snow lodges, so that immediately after a fall of snow, the islands appear to be striped with white and brown alternately. The northernmost island, when seen from the east-northeast, appears like a level piece of tableland, being quite perpendicular at each extreme.

The *Griper* having unfortunately sprung both her topmasts, Lieutenant Liddon took advantage of the calm weather to shift them. The *Hecla's* boats were at the same time employed in bringing on board ice, to be used as water—a measure to which it is occasionally necessary to resort in these regions when no pools or ponds are to be found upon the floes. In this case, berg ice, when at hand, is generally preferred; but that of floes, which is in fact the ice of sea water, is also abundantly used for this purpose, the only precaution which it is necessary to observe being that of allowing the salt water to drain off before it is dissolved for use. One of our boats was upset by the fall of a mass of ice which the men were breaking, but fortunately no injury was sustained.

A breeze sprung up from the north-northwest in the evening, and the *Griper* being ready to make sail, we stood to the southward. The land which now became visible to the southeast discovered to us that we were entering a large inlet, not less than 10 leagues wide at its mouth, and in the center of which no land could be distinguished. The western shore of the inlet, which extended as far as we could see to the south-southwest, was so encumbered with ice that there was no possibility of sailing

---

snowless land shows black, and is a water sky or a land sky. If covered with faded grass, land will show yellow in the clouds. In navigating icy waters the sky map is so useful that the navigator prefers an overcast day, with its map in the heavens, to a clear day when dependence must be wholly on direct vision. (Some claim that even on a clear day there is a slight ice sheen on the horizon to show pack ice or snowy land beyond the sky lines.)

near it. I therefore ran along the edge of the ice, between which
and the eastern shore there was a broad and open channel, with
the intention of seeking, in a lower latitude, a clearer passage
to the westward than that which we had just been obliged to
abandon lying between Prince Leopold's Isles and Maxwell
Bay. . . .

Since the time we first entered Lancaster Sound, the sluggish-
ness of the compasses, as well as the amount of their irregularity
produced by the attraction of the ship's iron, had been found
very rapidly, though uniformly, to increase as we proceeded
to the westward—so much, indeed, that for the last two days
we had been under the necessity of giving up altogether the
usual observations for determining the variation of the needle
on board the ships.

This irregularity became more and more obvious as we now
advanced to the southward. The rough magnetic bearing of
the sun at noon, or at midnight, or when on the prime vertical,
as compared with its true azimuth, was sufficient to render this
increasing inefficiency of the compass quite apparent. For
example, at noon this day, while we were observing the meridian altitude, the bearing of the sun was two points on the
Hecla's larboard bow, and consequently her true course was
about south-southwest. The binnacle and azimuth compasses
at the same time agreed in showing north-northwest ½ west,
making the variation to be allowed on that course 11½ points
westerly, corresponding nearly with an azimuth taken on the
following morning, which gave 137 degrees 12 minutes.

It was evident, therefore, that a very material change had
taken place in the dip, or the variation, or in both these phenomena since we had last an opportunity of obtaining observations upon them, which rendered it not improbable that we were
now making a very near approach to the magnetic pole. This
supposition was further strengthened on the morning of the
seventh when, having decreased our latitude to about 73
degrees, we found that no alteration whatever in the absolute
course on which the *Hecla* was steering produced a change of
more than three or four points in the direction indicated by the
compass, which continued uniformly from north-northeast to

north-northwest, according as the ship's head was placed on one side or the other of the magnetic meridian.

We now therefore witnessed, for the first time, the curious phenomenon of the directive power of the needle becoming so weak as to be completely overcome by the attraction of the ship; so that the needle might now be properly said to point to the north pole of the ship.

[As Parry moved south into Prince Regent Inlet the compasses became wholly useless, were removed from their positions, and were stored in the lumber room, there to remain the rest of the season. Parry conjectured that the magnetic pole was near. It was located slightly to the south and west, on Boothia Peninsula, by Sir John Ross's second expedition in 1829-33.

After penetrating 100 miles south into Regent Inlet, Parry concluded the chances of reaching the Pacific would be better if he turned back to Lancaster Sound and resumed his westward attempts. Later experience, his and that of others, has confirmed the soundness of the decision.

The ships were back in Lancaster Sound by August 13, but were unable to proceed westward because of dense, drifting ice. Parry made the mistake of persisting in this quarter for some time, for later experience has shown that open water is more to be expected along the northern shores. The narrative is picked up when the ships were at last ready to give up trying to force their way west along the southern edge of the strait.]

[August 18] There being still no prospect of getting a single mile to the westward in the neighborhood of Leopold Islands, and a breeze having freshened up from the eastward in the afternoon, I determined to stand over once more toward the northern shore, in order to try what could there be done toward effecting our passage; and at 9 P.M., after beating for several hours among floes and streams of ice, we got into clear water near that coast, where we found some swell from the eastward. There was just light enough at midnight to enable us to read and write in the cabin.

The wind and sea increased on the nineteenth, with a heavy

fall of snow, which, together with the uselessness of the compasses and the narrow space in which we were working between the ice and the land, combined to make our situation for several hours a very unpleasant one. At 2 P.M., the weather being still so thick that we could at times scarcely see the ship's length ahead, we suddenly found ourselves close under the land, and had not much room to spare in wearing round. . . .

[August 20] The snow was succeeded by rain at night, after which the wind fell and the weather became clear, so that on the morning of the twentieth, when we found ourselves off Stratton Inlet, we were enabled to bear up alongshore to the westward. The points of ice led us occasionally within 2 miles of the land, which allowed us to look into several small bays or inlets, with which this coast appears indented, but which it would require more time than we could afford thoroughly to survey or examine.

The remarkable structure of this land, which I have before attempted to describe, is peculiarly striking about Cape Fellfoot, where the horizontal strata very much resemble two parallel tiers of batteries placed at regular intervals from the top to the bottom of the cliff, affording a grand and imposing appearance.

There is a low point running off some distance from Cape Fellfoot, which is not visible till approached within 5 or 6 miles. We passed along this point at the distance of 4 miles, finding no bottom with from 50 to 65 fathoms of line. Maxwell Bay is a very noble one, having several islands in it, and a number of, openings on its northern shore, which we could not turn aside to explore. It was, however, quite free from ice, and might easily have been examined had it been our object to do so, and time would have permitted. A remarkable headland on the western side I named after Sir William Herschel. . . .

[August 21] On the twenty-first we had nothing to impede our progress but the want of wind, the great opening through which we had hitherto proceeded from Baffin Bay being now so perfectly clear of ice that it was almost impossible to believe it to be the same part of the sea which, but a day or two before, had been completely covered with floes to the utmost extent of our view. . . .

A thick fog came on at night, which, together with the light-ness of the wind and the caution necessary in navigating an unknown sea under such circumstances, rendered our progress to the westward extremely slow, though we had fortunately no ice to obstruct us. The narwhals were blowing about us in all directions, and two walruses with a young one were seen upon a piece of ice.

[August 22] The fog clearing up on the following day, we found ourselves abreast a bay, to which the name of Radstock Bay was subsequently given by Lieutenant Liddon's desire, in compliment to the Earl of Radstock. . . . Immediately to the westward of us we discovered more land, occupying several points of the horizon, which renewed in us considerable ap-prehension lest we should still find no passage open into the Polar Sea.

As we advanced slowly to the westward, the land appeared to be nearly insular. . . .

In the afternoon, the weather became very clear and fine, the wind being light from the westward. As this latter circumstance rendered our progress very slow, the opportunity was taken to dispatch the boats on shore for the purpose of making observa-tions; and at the same time a boat from each ship, under the respective command of Lieutenants Beechey and Hoppner, was sent to examine a bay at no great distance to the northward and westward of us.

The first party landed at the foot of a bluff headland which forms the eastern point of this bay, and which I named after my friend Mr. Richard Riley, of the Admiralty. They had scarcely landed ten minutes when a fresh breeze unexpectedly sprung up from the eastward, and their signal of recall was immediately made.

As soon as the boats returned, all sail was made to the west-ward, where the prospect began to wear a more and more in-teresting appearance. We soon perceived, as we proceeded, that the land along which we were sailing, and which, with the exception of some small inlets, had appeared to be hitherto continuous from Baffin Bay, began now to trend much to the northward, beyond Beechey Island [at the southwestern ex-tremity of Devon Island], leaving a large open space between that coast and the distant land to the westward, which now appeared like an island, of which the extremes to the north and south were distinctly visible. . . .

At sunset we had a clear and extensive view to the northward, between Cape Hotham and the eastern land. On the latter several headlands were discovered and named. Between the northernmost of these, called Cape Bowden, and the island to the westward there was a channel of more than 8 leagues in width, in which neither land nor ice could be seen from the masthead. To this noble channel I gave the name of Wellington, after His Grace the Master General of the Ordnance.

The arrival off this grand opening was an event for which we had long been looking with much anxiety and impatience; for the continuity of land to the northward had always been a source of uneasiness to us, principally from the possibility that it might take a turn to the southward and unite with the coast of America. The appearance of this broad opening, free from ice, and of the land on each side of it, more especially that on the west, leaving scarcely a doubt on our minds of the latter being an island, relieved us from all anxiety on that score; and everyone felt that we were now finally disentangled from the land which forms the western side of Baffin Bay, and that, in fact, we had actually entered the Polar Sea.

Fully impressed with this idea, I ventured to distinguish the magnificent opening through which our passage had been effected from Baffin Bay to Wellington Channel by the name of Barrow's Strait, after my friend Mr. Barrow, Secretary of the Admiralty, both as a private testimony of my esteem for that gentleman and as a public acknowledgment due to him for his zeal and exertions in the promotion of northern discovery. To the land on which Cape Hotham is situated, and which is the easternmost of the group of islands (as we found them to be by subsequent discovery) in the Polar Sea, I gave the name of Cornwallis Island, after Admiral the Honorable Sir William Cornwallis, my first naval friend and patron; and an inlet 7 miles to the northward of Cape Hotham was called Barlow Inlet, as a testimony of my respect for Sir Robert Barlow, one of the Commissioners of His Majesty's Navy.

Though two-thirds of the month of August had now elapsed,

I had every reason to be satisfied with the progress which we had hitherto made. I calculated upon the sea being still navigable for six weeks to come, and probably more if the state of the ice would permit us to edge away to the southward in our progress westerly. Our prospects, indeed, were truly exhilarating: the ships had suffered no injury; we had plenty of provisions; crews in high health and spirits; a sea, if not open, at least navigable; and a zealous and unanimous determination in both officers and men to accomplish, by all possible means, the grand object on which we had the happiness to be employed.

[August 23] A calm which prevailed during the night kept us nearly stationary off Beechey Island till 3 A.M. on the twenty-third, when a fresh breeze sprung up from the northward, and all sail was made for Cape Hotham, to the southward of which it was now my intention to seek a direct passage toward Bering Strait. Wellington Channel, to the northward of us, was as open and navigable, to the utmost extent of our view, as any part of the Atlantic, but as it lay at right angles to our course, and there was still an opening at least 10 leagues wide to the southward of Cornwallis Island, I could fortunately have no hesitation in deciding which of the two it was our business to pursue. . . .

It is impossible to conceive anything more animating than the quick and unobstructed run with which we were favored from Beechey Island across to Cape Hotham. Most men have probably, at one time or another, experienced that elevation of spirits which is usually produced by rapid motion of any kind; and it will readily be conceived how much this feeling was heightened in us, in the few instances in which it occurred, by the slow and tedious manner in which the greater part of our navigation had been performed in these seas.

Our disappointment may therefore be imagined when, in the midst of these favorable appearances and of the hope with which they had induced us to flatter ourselves, it was suddenly and unexpectedly reported from the crow's-nest that a body of ice lay directly across the passage between Cornwallis Island and the land to the southward. As we approached this obstruction, which commenced about Cape Hotham, we found that there was, for the present, no opening in it through which a passage could be attempted.

After lying to for an hour, however, Lieutenant Beechey discovered from the crow's-nest that one narrow neck appeared to consist of loose pieces of heavy ice detached from the main floes which composed the barrier, and that beyond this there was a considerable extent of open water. The *Hecla* was immediately pushed into this part of the ice, and after a quarter of an hour's "boring," during which the breeze had, as usual, nearly deserted us, succeeded in forcing her way through the neck. The *Griper* followed in the opening which the *Hecla* had made, and we continued our course to the westward, having once more a navigable sea before us.

We now remarked that a very decided change had taken place in the character of the land to the northward of us since leaving Beechey Island, the coast near the latter being bold and precipitous next the sea, with very deep water close to it, while the shores of Cornwallis Island rise with a gradual ascent from a beach which appeared to be composed of sand. . . .

At noon, we had reached the longitude of 94 degrees 43 minutes 15 seconds, the latitude, by observation, being 74 degrees 20 minutes 52 seconds, when we found that the land which then formed the western extreme of this side was a second island, which, after Rear-Admiral Edward Griffith, I called Griffith Island. . . .

At 2 P.M., having reached the longitude of 95 degrees 7 minutes, we came to some heavy and extensive floes of ice, which obliged us to tack, there being no passage between them. We beat to the northward during the whole of the afternoon, with a fresh breeze from that quarter, in the hope of finding a narrow channel under the lee of Griffith Island. In this expectation we were, however, disappointed, for at 8 P.M. we were near enough to perceive not only that the ice was quite close to the shore, but that it appeared not to have been detached from it at all during this season. We therefore bore up, and ran again to the southward, where the sea by this time had become rather more clear along the lee margin of a large field of ice extending far to the westward. . . .

After various unsuccessful attempts to get through the ice

which now lay in our way, we were at length so fortunate as to accomplish this object by "boring" through several heavy "streams," which occasioned the ships to receive many severe shocks; and at half an hour before midnight we were enabled to pursue our course, through "sailing ice," to the westward.

[August 24] A fog came on on the morning of the twenty-fourth, which once more reduced us to the necessity of depending on the steadiness of the wind for a knowledge of the direction in which we were steering, or of having recourse to the unpleasant alternative of heaving to till the weather should become clear. The former was of course preferred, and we pushed on with all the canvas which the *Griper's* bad sailing would allow us to carry, using the very necessary precaution of keeping the hand leads constantly going. We passed one field of ice of immense length, the distance which we ran along it without meeting a single break in it being, according to the report of the officers, from 8 to 10 miles, and its general thickness about 8 feet.

In this manner we had sailed between 15 and 20 miles in a tolerably clear sea when, on the fog clearing away at 7 A.M., we found by the bearings of the sun that the wind had not deceived us, and that we had made nearly all westing during the night's run. We also saw land to the northward of us, at the distance of 9 or 10 miles, appearing like an island, which it afterward proved to be, and which I named after Viscount Lowther, one of the lords of His Majesty's Treasury. Shortly after, we also saw land to the south, so that we could not but consider ourselves fortunate in having steered so directly in the proper course for sailing in this channel during the continuance of the foggy weather. . . . We here obtained soundings in 63 fathoms, on a bottom of sand and small stones, with some pieces of coral.

The wind, drawing more to the westward soon after the clearing up of the fog, obliged us to beat to windward during the rest of the day between the two lands, that to the southward being loaded with ice while the shores of Lowther Island were perfectly clear and accessible. . . .

It now became evident that all the land around us consisted of islands, and the comparative shoalness of the water made great caution necessary in proceeding, surrounded as we were by both land and ice in almost every direction. In the course of the evening, more land came in sight to the northward, but the distance was at this time too great to enable us to distinguish its situation and extent.

The nearest land which we had seen to the northward on the preceding evening proved to be another island, 4 or 5 miles long from east to west, which I distinguished by the name of Garrett Island, out of respect to my much-esteemed friend Captain Henry Garrett of the Royal Navy, to whose kind offices and friendly attention during the time of our equipment I must ever feel highly indebted. The land to the northward of Garrett Island was found to be another island of considerable extent, having toward its eastern end a remarkable peaked hillock, very conspicuous when seen from the southward. I named this Bathurst Island, in honor of the Earl of Bathurst, one of His Majesty's principal Secretaries of State, and a bay near its southeastern point was called Bedford Bay.

The islands which we had discovered during this day's navigation—among which I have not ventured to include the land to the southward of Lowther Island, of which we obtained a very imperfect view—are generally of a moderate height, not exceeding perhaps 400 or 500 feet above the level of the sea. With the exception of some parts of Bathurst Island, which have a more rugged aspect and which rise to a greater elevation than this, we found them entirely clear of snow, and when the sun was shining upon them, they exhibited a brown appearance. . . .

[August 26] We had seen no whales nor narwhals since leaving Cape Riley on the morning of the twenty-third; and it was now remarked, not without some degree of unpleasant feeling, that not a single bird, nor any other living creature, had for the whole of this day made its appearance. It was, however, encouraging to find, while advancing to the westward as fast as an unfavorable wind would permit, that although the sea beyond us was for the most part covered with a compact and undivided body of ice, yet that a channel of sufficient breadth was still left open for us between it and the shore, under the lee of Bathurst Island. . . .

[August 27] We gained so little ground during the night and in the early part of the following morning, notwithstanding the smoothness of the water and a fine working breeze, that I am confident there must have been a tide setting against us off Cape Cockburn; but as it was of material importance to get round this headland before a change of wind should set the ice in upon the shore, I did not deem it proper to heave to for the purpose of trying the direction in which it was running. After 3 A.M., the ships began to make much better way, so that I considered it likely that the tide had slackened between three and four o'clock. . . .

While beating round Cape Cockburn, our soundings were from 33 to 21 fathoms, on a bottom of small broken shells and coral; and some starfish (*Asterias*) came up on the lead. After rounding this headland, the wind favored us by coming to the south-southwest; and as we stood on to the westward, the water deepened very gradually till noon, when being in latitude, by observation, 75 degrees 1 minute 51 seconds and longitude, by chronometers, 101 degrees 39 minutes 9 seconds, we sounded in 68 fathoms, on a bottom of mud of a peculiar flesh-color. . . .

The weather was at this time remarkably serene and clear, and, although we saw a line of ice to the southward of us, lying in a direction nearly east and west or parallel to the course on which we were steering, and some more land appeared to the westward, yet the space of open water was still so broad, and the prospect from the masthead, upon the whole, so flattering, that I thought the chances of our separation had now become greater than before; and I therefore considered it right to furnish Lieutenant Liddon with fresh instructions, and to appoint some new place of rendezvous in case of unavoidable separation from the *Hecla*. A boat was therefore dropped on board the *Griper* for that purpose, without her heaving to; and the same opportunity was taken to obtain a comparison between our chronometers.

About 7 P.M., we were sufficiently near to the western land to ascertain that it was part of another island, which I named after Vice-Admiral Sir Thomas Byam Martin, Comptroller of His Majesty's Navy. . . .

[From August 27 to the end of the month a combination of dense fogs and light winds kept the ships from making headway except now and then in such brief clear spells as were not also calms. On August 29, they passed the line where the north tip of the compass needle points straight south. Finally, on September 1, they got away from the vicinity of Byam Martin Island and sighted, at Cape Griffiths, the shore of Melville Island, destined to be the winter quarters of Parry's expedition and of a series of northern expeditions, the last of which, to date, was a 1916-17 wintering by the third Stefansson expedition.]

At ten o'clock the weather became clear enough to allow us to see our way through a narrow part in a patch of ice which lay ahead, and beyond which there was some appearance of a "water sky." There is, however, nothing more deceitful than this appearance during a fog, which, by the same optical illusion whereby all other objects become magnified, causes every small "hole" of clear water to appear like a considerable extent of open and navigable sea. We continued running till 11 P.M., when the fog came on again, making the night so dark that it was no longer possible to proceed in any tolerable security. I therefore directed the ships to be made fast to a floe, having sailed, by our account, 12 miles, the depth of water being 44 fathoms.

The fog continued till 5 A.M. on the thirtieth, when it cleared sufficiently to give us a sight of the land, and of the heavy ice aground off Cape Gillman, the latter being 5 or 6 miles to the northward of us, in which situation we had deepened our soundings to 50 fathoms during the night's drift. The state of the ice, and of the weather, not permitting us to move, Captain Sabine, being desirous of making some use of this unavoidable detention, and considering it at all times important to confirm magnetic observations obtained on shore in these high latitudes by others taken upon the ice, employed himself in repeating his series of observations on the dip of the needle. . . .

[September 1] The wind died away on the morning of the first of September, and the fog was succeeded by snow and sleet, which still rendered the atmosphere extremely thick. At a quarter before 4 A.M., I was informed by the officer of the watch that a breeze had sprung up, and that there was very little ice near the ships. Anxious to take advantage of these favorable circumstances, I directed all sail to be made to the westward. There was no difficulty in complying with the first part of this order, but to ascertain which way the wind was blowing, and to which quarter of the horizon the ship's head was to be directed, was a matter of no such easy accomplishment [because the compass was not working well]; nor could we devise any means of determining this question till five o'clock, when we obtained a sight of the sun through the fog, and were thus enabled to shape our course, the wind being moderate from the northward.

In standing to the southward, we had gradually deepened the water to 105 fathoms, and our soundings now as gradually decreased as we stood to the westward, giving us reason to believe, as on the preceding night, and from the experience we had acquired of the navigation among these islands, that we were approaching land in that direction. In this supposition we were not deceived, for at half-past eight, the fog having suddenly cleared up, we found ourselves within 4 or 5 miles of a low point of land which was named after Mr. Griffiths, and which, being at the distance of 6 or 7 leagues from Byam Martin Island, we considered to be part of another of the same group.

We sailed along the shore at the distance of 2 to 4 miles in a southwest-by-west direction, and having dropped a boat to obtain observations upon the ice, without heaving to for that purpose, we found ourselves to be at noon in latitude 74 degrees 59 minutes 35 seconds and longitude, by chronometers, 106 degrees 7 minutes 36 seconds. This land very much resembled, in height and general character, the other islands which we had lately passed, being in most parts of a brownish color, among which we also imagined a little green to be here and there discernible. We had some small rain in the afternoon, which was succeeded by snow toward midnight.

[September 2] At 1 A.M. on the second, a star was seen, being the first that had been visible to us for more than two months.

The fog came on again this morning, which, together with the lightness of the wind preventing the ships getting sufficient way to keep them under command, occasioned them some of the heaviest blows which they had yet received during the voyage, although the ice was generally so loose and broken as to have allowed an easy passage with a moderate and leading wind. As none of the pieces near us were large enough for securing the ships in the usual manner, we could only heave to to windward of one of the heaviest masses, and allow the ship to drive with it till some favorable change should take place.

After lying for an hour in this inactive and helpless situation, we again made sail, the weather being rather more clear, which discovered to us that the main body of the ice was about 3 miles distant from the land, the intermediate space being very thickly covered with loose pieces, through which our passage was to be sought. As we stood in for the land in the forenoon, we decreased our soundings uniformly from 27 to 11 fathoms at 1½ or 2 miles from the beach, and a boat which I sent to sound inshore found the water to shoal very regularly to 6 fathoms at about ½ mile.

At this distance from the beach, there were many large masses of ice aground; and it was here that the method so often resorted to in the subsequent part of the voyage, of placing the ships between these masses and the land, in case of the ice closing suddenly upon us, first suggested itself to our minds.

As we were making no way to the westward, I directed two boats to be prepared from each ship, for the purpose of making the usual observations on shore, as well as to endeavor to kill deer; and at 1 P.M., I left the ship, accompanied by a large party of officers and men, and was soon after joined by the *Griper's* boats. We landed on a very flat sandy beach, which did not allow the boats to come nearer than their own length, and we were immediately struck with the general resemblance in the character of this island [Melville Island] to that of Byam Martin Island, which we had lately visited. The basis of this land is sandstone, but we met with limestone also, occurring in loose pieces on the surface, and several lumps of coal were brought in by the parties who had traversed the island in different directions.

Our sportsmen were by no means successful, having seen only two deer, which were too wild to allow them to get near them. The dung of these animals, however, as well as that of the musk ox, was very abundant, especially in those places where the moss was most luxuriant. Every here and there we came to a spot of this kind, consisting of one or two acres of ground covered with a rich vegetation, and which was evidently the feeding-place of those animals, there being quantities of their hair and wool lying scattered about.

Several heads of the musk ox were picked up, and one of the *Hecla*'s seamen brought to the boat a narwhal's horn which he found on a hill more than a mile from the sea, and which must have been carried thither by Eskimo or by bears. Three or four brace of ptarmigan (*Tetrao lagopus*) were killed, and these were the only supply of this kind which we obtained. Sergeant Martin of the artillery and Captain Sabine's servant brought down to the beach several pieces of a large fir tree, which they found nearly buried in the sand at the distance of 300 or 400 yards from the present high-water mark, and not less than 30 feet above the level of the sea. We found no indication of this part of the island having been inhabited, unless the narwhal's horn above alluded to be considered as such.

The latitude of the place of observation here, which was within 100 yards of the beach, was 74 degrees 58 minutes, the longitude, by chronometers, 107 degrees 3 minutes 31.7 seconds, and the variation of the magnetic needle 151 degrees 30 minutes 3 seconds easterly. . . . At the top of a hill, immediately above the place of observation and about a mile from the sea, a bottle was buried, containing the usual information. A mound of sand and stones was raised over it, and a boarding-pike fixed in the middle. We returned on board at half-past eight, and found that Lieutenant Beechey had in the meantime taken a number of useful soundings, and made other hydrographical remarks for carrying on the survey of the coast.

[Along southern Melville Island the westward progress was slow, due to fogs, calms, and unfavorable wind directions. Still, on September 4 they reached one of the goals of their expedition, as Parry tells:]

At a quarter-past 9 P.M., we had the satisfaction of crossing the meridian of 110 degrees west from Greenwich, in the latitude of 74 degrees 44 minutes 20 seconds, by which His Majesty's ships, under my orders, became entitled to the sum of £5000, being the reward offered by the King's Order in Council, grounded on a late Act of Parliament, to such of His Majesty's subjects as might succeed in penetrating thus far to the westward within the Arctic Circle. In order to commemorate the success which had hitherto attended our exertions, the bluff headland which we had just passed was subseqently called by the men Bounty Cape, by which name I have therefore distinguished it on the chart. . . .

[The winds kept blowing from directions such that the pack of Melville Sound, to the south, was being pressed northward up against the south shores of Melville Island. But on September 6 Parry had not lost hope of reaching the Pacific Ocean that year.]

I was beginning once more to indulge in those flattering hopes, of which often-repeated disappointments cannot altogether deprive us, when I perceived, from the crow's-nest, a compact body of ice extending completely in to the shore near the point which formed the western extreme. We ran sufficiently close to be assured that no passage to the westward could at present be effected, the floes being literally upon the beach, and not a drop of clear water being visible beyond them. I then ordered the ships to be made fast to a floe, being in 80 fathoms' water at the distance of 4 or 5 miles from the beach. The season had now so far advanced as to make it absolutely necessary to secure the ships every night from ten till two o'clock, the weather being too dark during that interval to allow of our keeping under way in such a navigation as this, deprived as we were of the use of the compasses.

But, however anxious the hours of darkness must necessarily be under such circumstances, the experience of the former voyage had given us every reason to believe that the month of September would prove the most valuable period of the year for prosecuting our discoveries in these regions, on account of the sea being more clear from ice at this time than at any other. Feeling, therefore, as I did, a strong conviction that the ultimate accomplishment of our object must depend, in a great measure, on the further progress we should make this season, I determined to extend our operations to the latest possible period.

[When Parry wrote this he was near Cape Hearne on the middle south coast of Melville Island. On September 8 a shore party discovered "several lumps of coal on the beach." For September 9 Parry writes:]

Impatient and anxious as we were to make the most of the short remainder of the present season, our mortification will easily be imagined at perceiving, on the morning of the ninth, not only that the ice was as close as ever to the westward, but that the floes in our immediate neighborhood were sensibly approaching the shore. As there was no chance, therefore, of our being enabled to move, I sent a party on shore at daylight to collect what coal they could find, and in the course of the day nearly two-thirds of a bushel, being about equal to the *Hecla's* daily expenditure, was brought on board. Our sportsmen, who were out for several hours, could only procure us a hare, and a few ducks.

[The winds continued unfavorable till the sixteenth, when Parry writes:]

It was observed, for the first time, that a strong current was setting to the westward during the whole of the last night, directly against a fresh gale from that quarter. At 9 A.M., the wind being much more moderate as well as more off the land, and the weather fine and clear, we cast off, and made all sail to the westward, running along the land at the distance of 2 or 3 miles from it. At a quarter before noon, we were abreast of Cape Providence, beyond which, at the distance of 3 or 4 leagues, another headland, still more high and bold in its appearance, was discovered, and named after Mr. Hay, private secretary to the First Lord of the Admiralty.

At the place which we left in the morning, the ice had been driven from the shore to the distance of 6 or 7 miles; but we found as we proceeded that the channel became gradually more and more contracted, till at length the ice was observed to extend, in a solid and impenetrable body, completely in to the very shore, a little to the eastward of Cape Hay. Our latitude, by account at noon, was 74 degrees 23 minutes 25 seconds, longitude 112 degrees 29 minutes 30 seconds.

The wind again freshened to a strong gale in the afternoon, reducing us to our close-reefed topsails, which were as much as the ship would bear, the squalls blowing out of the ravines with extreme violence. It became necessary, therefore, to look out for a secure situation for the ships during the ensuing night, which threatened to be a tempestuous one; but no such situation presented itself in this neighborhood, the whole of the coast to the westward of Cape Providence being so steep that the heaviest ice can find no ground to rest upon. I was therefore reduced to the disagreeable necessity of running back to the lower shore 3½ miles to the eastward of Cape Providence, where alone the ships could, under present circumstances, be placed in tolerable security during six or seven hours of darkness. . . .

[September 17] At 9 A.M. on the seventeenth, the wind being more moderate and the weather fine, we cast off and ran along the land, but had not proceeded far when it was perceived that the ice, in very heavy and compact floes of more than usual dimensions, still extended close into the shore near Cape Hay. . . .

Finding that no further progress could possibly be made at present, and the wind again freshening up from the westward, with heavy squalls of snow, I was once more under the necessity of returning to the eastward till some land ice could be met with to which the ships might be secured for the night. They were accordingly made fast in a proper berth of this kind, not far from that which we had occupied the preceding night, in 15 fathoms water and at 150 yards from the beach. . . .

At 8 P.M., while it was fortunately yet light enough to see about us, it was perceived that a large floe to the southeast had very much neared the shore since we anchored, rendering it necessary immediately to leave our present situation, where there was not a single mass of grounded ice on the outside to afford the smallest shelter to the ships. I determined, therefore, to stand back to the eastward, and as the night was, for the first time this fortnight past, very fine and moderate, to keep the ships under way and to regulate our course, in the best manner we could, by the stars.

[September 18] We had at this time a fine working breeze off the land, but it gradually died away toward midnight, after which the "young" ice began to form so rapidly on the surface of the sea that we could scarcely get the ships to move through the water; and at 6 A.M., on the eighteenth, when we were within ¼ mile of the shore, their way was altogether stopped. . . .

[The next day the wind continued unfavorable while the chills of autumn grew more severe. For September 20, Parry writes:]

The advanced period of the season, the unpromising appearance of the ice to the westward, and the risk to the ships with which the navigation had been attended for some days past, naturally led me to the conclusion that, under these circumstances, the time had arrived when it became absolutely necessary to look out for winter quarters. Among the circumstances which now rendered this navigation more than usually perilous, and the hope of success proportionally less, there was none which gave more reasonable ground for apprehension than the incredible rapidity with which the young ice formed upon the surface of the sea during the greater part of the twenty-four hours.

It had become evident, indeed, that it could only be attributed to the strong winds which had lately prevailed that the sea was not at this time permanently frozen over; for whenever the wind blew less than a gale, that formation took place immediately, and went on with such astonishing rapidity that had the weather continued calm for more than four and twenty hours together, it seemed to me extremely probable that we must have passed the winter in our present exposed and insecure situation.

[They had noted a little to the eastward a bay that would be a good wintering-place. It has since been called Winter Harbour, for the ships were able to work back to it and to spend there the season 1819-20 in fair health and relative comfort. They reached Britain the autumn of 1820. In his concluding remarks, Parry sums up the accomplishments of the expedition:]

Of the existence of such a passage [a Northwest Passage into the Pacific Ocean], and that the outlet will be found at Bering Strait, it is scarcely possible, on an inspection of the map, with the addition of our late discoveries and in conjunction with those of Cook and Mackenzie, any longer to entertain a reasonable doubt.

In discovering one outlet from Baffin Bay into the Polar Sea, and finding that sea studded with numerous islands, another link has at least been added to the chain of evidence upon which geographers have long ventured to delineate the northern coast of America . . . while at the same time considerable progress has been made toward the actual accomplishment of the desired passage, which has for nearly three centuries engaged the attention of the maritime nations of Europe. 🖝

Parry had explored the most favorable of the several routes by which the Northwest Passage can be navigated. We know this now, but he did not know it then, and believed that a superior passage might be found through a less northerly channel. On this view he based his second and third expeditions, which were successful in terms of discovery of lands, channels, and other facts of geographic worth, but which did not contribute as much as the first expedition to the problem of finding a commercial seaway between the Atlantic and Pacific oceans around the north of the Americas.

Meantime there had been developed in Canada a fur empire, ruled by a corporation styled The Governor and Company of Adventurers of England Trading into Hudson's Bay (generally known as the Hudson's Bay Company), which received its charter from Charles II in 1670. It was a provision of the charter that, as one of the returns for the many privileges that were granted them by the Crown, they should search for a Northwest Passage.

This search was never pushed with energy; rather its non-performance was defended by numerous explanations and excuses. Indeed, it is the opinion of many historians that during the first hundred years, while as yet the Company had scarce the knowledge or power for carrying on the search, there developed among its leaders the conviction that finding the passage would be to the disadvantage of the Company. In a commercial sense this may have been right, especially if there is postulated a narrowness of vision which prevented the Governor and Company in London from realizing that they did not necessarily have to remain forever just fur traders, but could enter into various other developments.

As mere fur traders, the Honorable Company were clear-sighted in thinking that if a commercial seaway were developed leading from Europe around the northern shores of Canada to the Indies, then cities would grow up, and there would be a farming colonization spreading southward. Now the European farm colonist destroys native peoples, though not necessarily under the open slogan of our frontiersmen of the nineteenth century that "the only good Indian is a dead Indian." The farmer destroys or drives away the fur animals. So the Company were shrewd in a business way, and perhaps even humane, when they desired to keep alive as many as possible of their fur hunters and to save on their behalf the lands that were basic to the fur trade. Their slogan was, in effect, "The only good Indian is a live Indian," for only he can be a customer.

However, there was constant prodding from Britain regarding a seaway, and the Hudson's Bay Company did send out search parties. Notable was the journey of Samuel Hearne northwestward from Churchill, on Hudson Bay, to the vicinity of Coronation Gulf, on the middle north coast of North America. In 1770-71 he tagged along with a band of Indians who knew about and valued the copper of the region between Great Bear Lake and the sea. Perhaps it was more the copper than the Northwest Passage that Hearne was seeking. He found the copper lands and saw, or reported from the hearsay of his native companions, the waters of Coronation Gulf, one of the links of the eventual sea route.

The greatest single contribution of the Hudson's Bay Company to the discovery of the Northwest Passage was made by Thomas Simpson, a young Scot in their employ and nephew to that Sir George Simpson, then Resident or Deputy Governor of the Company, who has been called the "empire-builder" and who is a remarkable figure in the history of North American commercial development.

It is difficult to unravel the tangled, and it would seem deliberately tangled, relation between uncle and nephew. It is enough here to mention that when Thomas either committed suicide or was murdered, in June of 1840, it was general talk throughout the fur countries that it was probably murder, and that a contributing reason, if not the cause, was the knowledge of those who did the killing that Sir George would welcome it and would make no special effort against the perpetrators.[7]

The suicide or murder of Thomas Simpson occurred when he was on his way back to England from his expedition of 1836-39, in buoyant spirits, according to at least some of the evidence, through being convinced that he had practically discovered the Northwest Passage, that he needed only a few more steps for the completion of the discovery.

The western section of the passage was known. Dezhnev had found its Pacific entrance in 1648 when he discovered the channel later named after Bering. Through the 1778 voyage of Captain James Cook north and east from Bering Strait, knowledge was extended as far to the northeast as Icy Cape, Alaska. That discovery was continued eastward to Point Barrow, by Thomas Elson of Frederick William Beechey's expedition, in 1826. In the same year, Sir John Franklin made a small-boat journey westward from the mouth of the Mackenzie to Return Reef, which lies some 150 miles to the eastward of Point Barrow.

On Franklin's second expedition, 1825-27, Sir John Richardson, his second in command, had mapped the passage, in the summer of 1826, from the mouth of the Mackenzie eastward to Coronation Gulf. On his first expedition Franklin had, in 1821, descended the Coppermine and surveyed eastward along the south shore of Coronation Gulf to Turnagain Point.

At this stage Thomas Simpson took over, with a discovery journey which General A. W. Greely, himself both a distinguished polar explorer and a discriminating student of the history of exploration, has referred to as one of the greatest feats in the history of discovery.

In 1836 Simpson, outfitted perhaps with some reluctance by the Hudson's Bay Company and as the active leader of an expedition where Peter Warren Dease was the figurehead, was sent out by the Company to survey the northern shores of the continent. In 1837 he descended the Mackenzie to its mouth, duplicated the 1826 voyage of Franklin westward to Return Reef, and thence, by boat and afoot, made good the rest of the

---

[7] See the chapter "The Strange Fate of Thomas Simpson," in *Unsolved Mysteries of the Arctic,* by Vilhjalmur Stefansson, Macmillan, 1938.

way to Point Barrow, joining the Northwest Passage discovery from the Mackenzie with that part of it which had been done from Bering Strait.

Having connected his discoveries westward in 1837 with those of Franklin and Elson, in the spring of 1838 Simpson left his winter quarters near Slave Lake and descended the Coppermine to its mouth in Coronation Gulf. He used small boats which his men were able to drag across sandspits or narrow blockades of sea ice. He was the first effective Arctic user of pemmican, lightest and most satisfying of travel rations; with men in his party who were competent hunters the pemmican could be supplemented by fresh meat to make it last even longer.

A comparison of Simpson's description of his journey along this coast with that of Franklin, who had been before him, and with those of travelers who have been there since, will show that Simpson was dealing with one of the most unfavorable years. Still, by August 9 the party were only 3 miles short of Franklin's farthest of 1821 at Point Turnagain. Here the boats were stopped and had to remain icebound until the nineteenth.

From the vicinity of Point Turnagain, on the northen shore of Kent Peninsula, the story is taken from Simpson's own narrative, as given in the *Life and Travels of Thomas Simpson*, by Alexander Simpson, London, 1845.

Simpson and the Northwest Passage

On Monday the twentieth of August, at 8 A.M., we set out on our journey of discovery.

My companions were five of the Company's servants and the two Indians. Each man's load at starting weighed about half a hundredweight, comprehending a tent for the nightly shelter of the whole party, a canvas canoe, with frame and cords, to ferry us across rivers, a box of astronomical instruments, a copper kettle, two axes, guns, ammunition, and provisions [pemmican] for ten days; in short, our food, lodging, bedding, arms, and equipage.

As for myself, my trusty double-barrel slung at my back, a telescope, compass, and dagger, formed my own encumbrance;

so that I might at pleasure ascend the rising grounds, to take bearings and view the coast.

The plan of march I adopted was as follows: We set out at 7 or 8 A.M., after breakfasting (which lessened the loads) and obtaining observations for longitude, and traveled for ten hours, exclusive of a halt of half an hour at noon to procure the latitude and variation. With their burdens the men advanced fully 2 miles an hour, our daily progress thus averaging 20 geographical or 23 English miles.

A fatigue party of three men attended us to our first encampment. About the middle of this day's journey we passed the extreme point to which Sir John Franklin and his officers walked in 1821. A little farther we found several old Eskimo camping-places, and human skulls and bones were seen in various situations. One skeleton lay alongside that of a musk bull, in such a manner as rendered it extremely probable that the dying beast had gored the hapless hunter.

The coast line continued low, our road alternately leading over sand, sharp stones, through swamps and rivulets. Large boulder rocks rose here and there upon the shore and acclivities. The ice all along was forcibly crushed upon the beach, the edging of water being so shallow that the gulls waded betwixt the ice and the sand. During the greater part of the day we were drenched with rain.

The land preserved its north-northeast direction to our encampment—on the pitch of a flat cape—in latitude 68 degrees 37 minutes north, longitude 108 degrees 58 minutes west. This spot I named Cape Franklin, as a tribute of respect, from a perfect stranger, to that enterprising and justly celebrated officer. Land, 20 or 25 miles off, high, and covered with snow, stretched from west to northeast, and raised apprehensions that we were entering a deep inlet or sound.

We had no sooner turned Cape Franklin on the twenty-first than we came in view of a very distant hill, bearing north 82 degrees east, which I rightly conjectured to stand not far back from the coast. The latter is remarkably straight; but the walking was very fatiguing, the shore consisting chiefly of soft, wet sands traversed by a multitude of brooks. These descend from a range of low, stony hills, which, at the distance of 2 or 3 miles, close the inland view, and were partially clothed with moss and scanty herbage.

The ice was everywhere grounded on the shore; but the weather had by this time improved, and continued so clear and moderate during the rest of the outward journey that I daily obtained astronomical observations.

A flight of white geese passed us, led on, or officered, by three large grey ones (*Anser Canadensis*). Numerous flocks of these fowl were luxuriating in the fine feeding that the marshes and little bays afforded. The young geese were large and strong, but having not yet acquired the perfect command of their wings, we captured several upon the ice. Two white wolves were skulking on the hillside, and a brace of Alpine hares were shot.

Just before encamping, we forded Hargrave River—so named by me after a particular friend; it is about 100 yards wide. Our tent in the evening wore the semblance of a tailor's and cobbler's shop, everyone being engaged in repairing the injuries his habiliments had received during the day. At this place we secured, under a heap of stones, two days' provisions, to serve for our return to the boats.

The shore next day maintained nearly the same character, and was intersected by many small streams, none of which, on our choosing proper crossing places, reached more than waist-high. They flow over a bed of stones or sand. Their waters were at this time low and clear, but their deep and rugged channels showed that at the melting of the snows not a few of them become formidable torrents.

The ice grew heavier as we advanced, and had been driven ashore with such violence by the gales as to plow up the shingle and raise it in heaps upon the beach. The stranded fragments were from 3 to 6 feet thick, but no icebergs were anywhere to be seen.

I hoped, from this strong evidence of winds and tides, that we were not engaged in exploring a bay; though the northern land [island visible to the north] still stretched out before us, appearing in some places scarcely 20 miles distant.

We found today the bones of a large whale and the skull of a polar bear, and sea wrack and shells strewed the beach. No deer were seen, but the recent print of their hoofs often appeared in the sand.

In the afternoon we passed, at a distance of 6 miles, the conspicuous hill mentioned yesterday. It is about 600 feet high, and received the name of Mount George, after my respected relative, Governor Simpson. Driftwood was become so scarce that we made a practice of picking up every piece we could find, an hour or two before camping time, to prepare our supper and breakfast. Some of the men's legs were much swelled and inflamed this evening from the fatigue of their burdens, the inequalities of the ground, and the constant immersion in icy-cold water.

The tide fell 16 or 18 inches during our stay at Point Ballenden; but as it had been subsiding for some time previously, I think the whole rise and fall must exceed 2 feet. Strong new ice formed in every open spot during the calm of the night.

On the twenty-third the coast led somewhat more to the northward. The traveling was exceedingly painful, the beach and slopes of the hills being formed of loose stones, varied here and there by moss and an ample number of brooks and streams. We however advanced with spirit, all hands being in eager expectation respecting the great northern land, which seemed interminable. Along its distant shore the beams of the declining sun were reflected from a broad channel of open water, while on the coast we were tracing the ice still lay immovable, and extended many miles to seaward.

As we drew near in the evening an elevated cape, land appeared all round, and our worst fears seemed confirmed. With bitter disappointment I ascended the height, from whence a vast and splendid prospect burst suddenly upon me. The sea, as if transformed by enchantment, rolled its free waves at my feet, and beyond the reach of vision to the eastward. [This was the water area now called Queen Maud Gulf.] Islands of various shape and size overspread its surface, and the northern land terminated to the eye in a bold and lofty cape bearing east-northeast, 30 or 40 miles distant, while the continental coast trended away southeast.

I stood, in fact, on a remarkable headland, at the eastern outlet of an ice-obstructed strait. On the extensive land to the northward I bestowed the name of our most gracious sovereign Queen Victoria. Its eastern visible extremity I called Cape Pelly, in compliment to the Governor of the Hudson's Bay Company; and the promontory where we encamped, Cape Alexander, after an only brother, who would give his right hand to be the sharer of my journeys.

Cape Alexander is a rounded, rocky ridge covered with loose stones, 4 miles in width, and 200 or 300 feet high. Its western part is situated in latitude 68 degrees 56 minutes north, longitude 106 degrees 40 minutes west. The rise and fall of the tide here was little short of 3 feet, being the greatest yet observed by us in the Arctic seas.

The weather was calm, and the tide falling, when we halted. A considerable quantity of loose ice passed to the westward, and floated back again as the water rose in the morning, affording a seeming presumption that the flood came from that quarter.

A solitary deer [caribou] bounded up the ascent, and along the shore ran a path beaten by those animals. Sinclair wounded one of a small herd of musk cattle that were grazing on the banks of a lake behind the cape, but it escaped. Eskimo marks stood upon the heights, but no recent traces of inhabitants could be found.

We next morning cut across the eastern shoulder of Cape Alexander to Musk Ox Lake, which lies in a valley. It is ½ mile long, and empties itself by a subterraneous channel through a steep ridge of shingle into another basin, about half its size, which was frozen to the bottom. Crossing the ice, we forded the little stream below, which, like many others, still retained drifts of snow on its banks.

Our rough route led amongst large boulders, and through wet mossy tracts producing dwarf willows. The immediate coast line continued flat, but skirted as before by low stony hills. Some ice lingered in the bays, but the sea was quite open.

At the distance of 9 miles we crossed another bluff cape, composed of traprocks, where an observation gave the latitude 68 degrees 52 minutes 19 seconds north, variation 63 degrees east. This was the greatest deviation of the compass from the true meridian. From Boathaven to Cape Franklin the variation increased very fast, since only 9 miles beyond that cape it was found to be 60 degrees. Thence advancing eastward, it fell off to 56 degrees 30 minutes, and again augmented as the coast trended more northerly; while from Trap Cape to our extreme point—only 11 miles in a southeasterly direction—it diminished nearly 1½ degrees.

Where the direction of our journey crossed that of Ross's magnetic pole at large angles, the change of variation was rapid; when we traveled nearly in the line of that pole, the change was slow. The farther east we went, the more sluggish did the compass become; the pocket one, especially, often had to be shaken before it would traverse at all, and when set upon the rocks, would sometimes remain pointing just as it was placed.

At 6 p.m. we opened what appeared a very extensive bay, running far away southward and studded with islands. We proceeded on to a projecting point, where we encamped. From thence I could trace part of the western shores of the bay, formed by a bold curve of granitic hills; other land blending with the horizon in the east-southeast, apparently very remote.

As the time allotted for outgoing was now expired, this great bay, which would have consumed many days to walk round, seemed an appropriate limit to our journey. Under any circumstances, the continued and increasing lameness of two or three of my men must have rendered my return hence imperative.

I had, indeed, at one time hoped to fall in with Eskimos, and with their assistance to reach Ross's Pillar [that is, completing the Northwest Passage by connecting with the farthest of Ross, who came from the east], but we had already explored a hundred miles of coast without encountering an inhabitant. . . .

The morning of the twenty-fifth was devoted to the determination of our position, and the erection of a pillar of stones on the most elevated part of the point; then, hoisting our union jack, I took formal possession of the country in Her Majesty's name. In the pillar I deposited a brief sketch of our proceedings. It is in latitude 68 degrees 43 minutes 39 seconds north, longitude (reduced by the watch from Boathaven) 106 degrees 3 minutes west, and the variation was 60 degrees 38 minutes 23 seconds east.

Our present discoveries were in themselves not unimportant,

but their value was much enhanced by the disclosure of an open sea to the eastward, and the suggestion of a new route—along the southern coast of Victoria Land—by which that open sea might be attained while the shores of the continent were yet environed by an impenetrable barrier of ice, as they were this season.

Our portable canoe, which we had not had occasion to use, was buried in the sand at the foot of a huge round rock on the beach, and with lighter burdens we commenced retracing our steps. . . .

[The following year, 1839, the third one of his expedition, Simpson came again from his winter quarters in the interior, where his men had been living either by their own hunting or on meat purchased from local hunters. By July 26 they had reached Cape Alexander, the farthest of the previous summer. The narrative of his further progress eastward by canoe skirting the large body of water that is now called Queen Maud Gulf, and thence through Simpson Strait to Castor and Pollux Bay, on the mainland east of King William Island, is taken from Simpson's journal:]

Our course was first directed to the highest island of the Minto group seen by me the previous season, from whence we now obtained a commanding prospect of the bold rocky indented shores, running away much farther southward than I could have anticipated, and skirted by numerous islands. I at the same time discovered that what I had before taken for the opposite side of the great bay that so aptly bounded our pedestrian journey was only the outer end of a very large island, which afterward formed a prominent object for several days, and was distinguished by the name of the Prime Minister of England, Viscount Melbourne.

Our first encampment was near a very bluff rocky cape that afforded another extensive view, and was named by Mr. Dease after the noble family of Roxborough. Beyond it opened Labyrinth Bay—a perfect maze of islands, from whence a range of picturesque rocky hills, about 500 feet high, extended away southward till they became lost in distance.

It would be an endless task to attempt to enumerate the

bays, islands, and long, narrow, projecting points that followed. The coast continued to stretch south and southeast, but lost its bold character and became low and stony. This lowness of the land increased the intricacies and perplexity of the route, rendering it necessary to ascend every elevation that presented itself to ascertain where to make for next.

We had the disadvantage, too, of some bad foggy weather; but as long as we could pick our way through the open water among the bays and islands, we made tolerable progress. Close without, the main body of ice lay firm and heavy.

So confused were our people by the devious course we were obliged to pursue as to lose all idea of the true direction, few of them being able to indicate it within eight points of the compass. I even overheard one stoutly maintaining, in a cloudy day, that west was east!

Our Indian companions were quite as wide of the mark as the rest; and I was now fully convinced that their peculiar faculty of finding their way over pathless wilds has its origin in memory, in the habitual observation and retention of local objects, even the most trifling, which a white man, less interested in storing up such knowledge, would pass without notice.

On the last day of July we encamped near the mouth of a river, much larger than the Coppermine,[8] with a strong current, that freshened the water among the reefs for some distance from the shore. Its banks appeared much frequented at this season by reindeer and musk cattle, and no fewer than five fat bucks were killed by some of the party while the rest were pitching the tents and preparing supper.

A couple of Eskimo sledges lay by the riverside; and as we had found many old stone caches, both upon islands and points of the mainland, it seemed more than probable that, like the natives near the Coppermine, the people to whom they belonged had come from their winter stations over the ice in June to ascend this fine stream. It falls into the sea in latitude 68 degrees 2 minutes north, longitude 104 degrees 15 minutes west, and was named after the Right Honorable Edward Ellice. As we found nothing but drift willows on its banks, it must be entirely

---

[8] This is an error. The Coppermine is much larger, but has a small and unimpressive mouth.

destitute of wood, and probably takes its rise in large lakes not far from Lake Beechey, discovered by Sir George Back.

The bordering country consisted of green flats varied by little lakes and rocky knolls. The latter, with low intervening beaches, form the general features of this part of the coast, and render it very difficult, at any distance, to distinguish the line of the mainland from a chain of islands. Our most useful rule in such cases was that while the former presented patches of green, the latter were in general perfectly barren. The bottom is a soft mud, and the water is discolored and shallow, as will be seen by the soundings on the map. But even were it otherwise, no ship would ever steer for shores so beset with hidden dangers; the first point of the mainland that she durst approach would be Cape Alexander. . . .

From the first to the fifth of August we were detained, by a crush of very heavy ice, on a point that jutted out beyond all the islands. . . . On this point we found the bones of a whale, and marks of the recent tents of a family or two of natives, who had left behind them the skin of a polar bear, from which circumstance we called the spot White Bear Point.

On the fifth we worked our way out through the ice, and at half-past ten at night, while in the act of encamping on an island in latitude 67 degrees 56 minutes, saw the first stars, the atmosphere being beautifully clear. Several days of remarkably fine weather succeeded, and enabled us rapidly to unravel our intricate path.

Had we been enveloped in continual fogs, as in 1837, success on such a coast as this must have been hopeless, as, in addition to the perplexity of the route, the compass, from our increasing proximity to the magnetic pole, soon became totally useless. The daily recurrence of astronomical observations was therefore of inestimable value, and no words can express our deep sense of gratitude to Providence for its great goodness toward us.

The coast, with its succession of bays and numberless islands, still kept edging away southeastward, as far as Ogden Bay, in latitude 67 degrees 36 minutes north, longitude 101 degrees 15 minutes west, and then made a turn to the northeast. The rocks had again become somewhat bolder, with a striped and variegated surface; but the color of the water still merited the epithet

of the Red Sea, bestowed by our men upon the southern part
of this stupendous bay, till near Point Johnson, when the variegated rocks gave place to a very low line of granite or gneiss,
extending from east to east-southeast, bordered with very small
isles of the same formation, amongst which the sea became
clear as crystal. As for the main ice, it hung close upon the
island fringe, but within, we generally had the benefit of open
water.

On the eighth the coast suddenly turned up northward in a
fine curve, in latitude 67 degrees 43 minutes north, longitude
99 degrees 15 minutes west, which we denominated McLough-
lin Bay, out of respect for the officer in charge of the Columbia
[River] Department [of the Hudson's Bay Company]. We next
reached a space clear of islands, but much encumbered with
ice, with 11 and 12 fathoms water; and then there appeared
green sloping hills and large islands, the favorite resort of
reindeer. This, after a short interval of sand, was in its turn
succeeded (at Point Grant) by a large tract of shingle and limestone.

It was here that the traces of Eskimos became frequent. Not
a point nor an island could we land upon but exhibited old
caches, camping-places, or graves. One of their tent sites—an
oval—measured 20 feet the longest way, and in another place
we found several deposits of marrowbones!

On the tenth we proceeded northeastward all day among the
islands, and some began to apprehend that we had lost the
continent altogether, till in the evening we opened a strait
running in to the southward of east, whilst the rapid rush of the
tide from that quarter left no longer any room to doubt the
neighborhood of an open sea, leading to the mouth of Back's
Great Fish River.

The ebb left on the sandy beach many little fish, which Oolig-
buck called *oonglak*, and which he said are highly relished by
the Churchill and Ungava Eskimos, on whose coasts they are
caught of a much larger size. In this strait too we saw the first
salmon since crossing Coronation Gulf. They came from under
a heavy mass of ice, behind which the men were resting on their
oars; and as seals were exceedingly numerous, there can be no

question that various fish on which they prey abound in these transparent waters.

I must candidly acknowledge that we were not prepared to find so southerly a strait leading to the estuary of the Great Fish River, but rather expected *first* to double Cape Felix of Captain James Ross, toward which the coast had been latterly trending. The extensive land on which that conspicuous cape stands forms the northern shore of the strait through which we passed on the eleventh, and which led us the same afternoon, by an outlet only 3 miles wide, to the much-desired eastern sea.

That glorious sight was first beheld by myself from the top of one of the high limestone islands, and I had the satisfaction of announcing it to some of the men, who, incited by curiousity, followed me thither. The joyful news was soon conveyed to Mr. Dease, who was with the boats at the end of the island, about ½ mile off; and even the most desponding of our people forgot, for the time, the great distance we should have to return to winter quarters, though a wish that a party had been appointed to meet us somewhere on the Great Fish River, or even at Fort Reliance, was frequently expressed. Point Seaforth—the eastern outlet of this remarkable strait—is situated in latitude 68 degrees 32 minutes north, longitude 97 degrees 35 minutes west.

On the continent on Ross's Land, and on the larger islands, reindeer were seen browsing the scanty herbage that springs up amongst the shingle; and stone marks, set up by the natives to deceive or decoy them, appeared in many well-chosen places. While pursuing a small herd seen from our encampment about 12 miles south-southeast of the strait, I had a fine view, from an eminence, of the inland country, rising into stony elevations, shaded with green and diversified by many small lakes.

The twelfth of August was signalized by the most tremendous thunderstorm I ever witnessed in these northern regions, accompanied by torrents of rain and some heavy showers of hail. I afterward ascertained that this storm passed violently over Great Slave Lake, and lightly over Fort Simpson on Mackenzie River, the day before—the eleventh—appearing in both cases to come from the northeast while with us it came in the opposite direction. It must, therefore, have traveled from southwest to northeast, with a rotary motion, agreeably to the theory of

Colonel Reid. Toward evening, when its fury was somewhat spent, I took advantage of the impossibility of proceeding to make a set of observations with the dipping needle. . . .

On the thirteenth it blew strongly from the westward, with a very dense cold fog that prevented our starting till 8 A.M. We then ran rapidly southeast and east, and at the end of 15 or 20 miles got clear of the countless islands that had all along, from my last year's pedestrian limit, embarrassed us beyond measure, and hailed with real transport the open sea, though mantled in fog.

After rounding a long point, we sailed some distance down a seemingly deep bay, which, as soon as we could make out land on the opposite side, we crossed, and then coasted along the flat shore, which was bristled with shoals and breakers. On doubling a very sharp point that offered a lee spot for the boats, I landed, and saw before me a perfect sandy desert. It was Back's Point Sir C. Ogle that we had at length reached.

M'Kay and Sinclair did not at first recognize the place, in consequence of the thick fog; nor could I venture at the time to assert its identity, as we had made a long run from Thunder Cove without either sun or compass to direct us, having for our only guide the direction of the wind when we set out in the morning, with the various tacks we had made, and the time occupied on each. We continued on to the southward till past 10 P.M., when the darkness, the rocks, and the increasing gale compelled us to put ashore—as it afterward proved—beyond Point Pechell.

Our long shivering fast was not compensated by the usual warm evening meal. The little store of wood we had carefully hoarded up in the boats being entirely spent, pemmican and cold water formed, for some time, our standing fare. The want of even good water had been not unfrequently felt, particularly whilst we were amongst the rocky and shingle islands.

A genuine northeaster raged during the two following days, when our new hands first beheld the northern ocean in its majesty, rolling in a heavy surf upon the beach.

On the fifteenth the storm chased away the fog, and two deer were killed; but, as might have been expected from the surrounding sterility, they were very lean. A young Arctic fox was caught by one of the Indians, and after being fondled and fed, the pretty little creature was restored to liberty.

The weather becoming moderate on the sixteenth, we directed our course, with flags flying, to the Montreal Island, which had been distinguished from the main shore. Shortly before noon we landed in a little bay where Sir George Back encamped on his return from Point Ogle to the Great Fish River. Directed by M'Kay, our people soon found a deposit among the rocks, containing two bags of pemmican, several pounds of chocolate, two canisters of gunpowder, a box of percussion caps, and an old japanned tin vasculum enclosing three large fish-hooks.

The pemmican, or *taureau*, as the voyageurs called it, was literally *alive*, and it was wittily remarked, *"L'isle de Montréal sera bientôt peuplée de jeunes taureaux."* The chocolate, though wrapped in oilskin, was so rotten that our men could scarcely extract "a kettleful" out of it to celebrate the grand event of the day. As for the minor articles, Mr. Dease and I took possession of them, as memorials of our having breakfasted on the identical spot where the tent of our gallant, though less successful, precursor stood that very day five years before.

Finding it impossible to reconcile Back's longitude of the Montreal Island with that assigned by Franklin to Point Turnagain, I have adhered to my own observations, which agree closely with the latter. The longitude of the island will thus be 96 degrees 24 minutes 45 seconds, instead of 95 degrees 18 minutes 15 seconds, and the extent of our discoveries be diminished by about 25 miles.[9]

All the objects for which the expedition was so generously instituted were now accomplished, but Mr. Dease and myself were not quite satisfied. We had determined the northern limits of America to the *westward* of the Great Fish River; it still remained a question whether Boothia Felix might not be united to the continent on the other side of the estuary. The men, who had never dreamed of going any further, were therefore summoned, and the importance of proceeding some distance to the eastward explained to them, when, to their honor, all assented without a murmur.

[9] Simpson's longitude is approximately the one now used on maps.

A fog that had come on dispersed toward evening, and unfolded a full view of the picturesque shores of the estuary. Far in the southeast, Victoria Headland stood out, so boldly defined that even without the help of the chart we should have instantly recognized it from Back's exquisite drawing. Cape Beaufort we almost seemed to touch; rocky islets here and there studded the gulf, and with the telescope we were able to discern a continuous line of high land, as far round as northeast, about two points more northerly than Cape Hay, the extreme eastern point seen by Sir George Back.

This being ascertained, and the men having had their supper, we struck out for the farthest visible land, at 9 P.M., or about half an hour after sunset.

It was a lovely night. The fury of the North lay chained in repose. The Harp, the Eagle, the Charioteer, and many other bright constellations gemmed the sky and sparkled on the waters, while the high Polar Star seemed to crown the glorious vault above us. The passage occupied six hours' unremitting labor at the oar, and long before morning we were almost drenched with the heavy dew, whilst the rising swell indicated the approach of another gale.

Just at sunrise on the seventeenth I climbed the bluff cape to which our course had been directed, and saw the coast turn off sharply and decidedly eastward. Thence, round to the northwest, stretched a sea free from ice and devoid of all land, except what looked like two very distant islands. On the rocky summit, above 200 feet in height, the natives of this barren region had erected a ponderous stone slab for a landmark. Some of their old encampments were found in the valley below, also several stone forms for building skin canoes. A line of blue hills rose, and spread away, in the south.

Observations were obtained, placing this remarkable and singularly shaped cape in latitude 68 degrees 3 minutes 52 seconds north, longitude 95 degrees 41 minutes 30 seconds west. . . . The promontory was . . . [called] Cape Britannia, in affectionate remembrance of our native land, whose glory we trust may never know change or decay.

The cruel northeast wind having again arisen, we were only

able to attain the farthest angle of the cape, about 3 miles distant, where we remained wind-bound for two days. . . .

A couple of deer shot by our hunters were in wretched condition. The refuse of the meat soon attracted several white wolves, one of which attempted to drag off a head and antlers entire as I came up, but dropped his heavy booty before I got within sure distance.

The interior country is checkered with little lakes, and green swamps interpose between the hills of naked granite. On the beetling rock that sheltered our little camp from the sea, and forms the most commanding station on this part of the coast, we erected a conical pile of ponderous stones, 14 feet high, which, if it be not pulled down by the natives, may defy the rage of a thousand storms. In it was placed a sealed bottle containing an outline of our proceedings, and possession was taken of our extensive discoveries, in the name of Victoria the First, amidst the firing of guns and the enthusiastic cheers of the whole party. It was only on occasions like this that we regretted the want of any kind of liquor with which to treat our faithful crews.

At this time we were not a little concerned at Sinclair's being attacked by a fit of illness. This man, active, careful, and ambitious in the discharge of his duty, proved unable to endure the deprivation of fire and warm food. Some medicines, seasonably administered, brought him round, and in fair weather we managed to gather moss and dry seaweed enough for the preparation of our meals, which happily prevented others of the party from being laid up.

On the nineteenth, the wind having shifted to east-southeast, we set out at an early hour. Crossing a small inlet adjoining our encampment, we opened a fine bay, where the sea ran strong and high. For three hours our poor fellows pulled into the bay with great spirit, hoping to gain some shelter from the land, while Mr. Dease and myself had no sinecure in bailing out our old and leaky boats.

At last, finding that we receded instead of advancing, sail was hoisted, not in the expectation of gaining the opposite point, but with the resolution of at least *seeing* beyond it, and then putting about for Cape Britannia, should it be found impossible to land. As we advanced, the coast began to rise more and more outward, till at last it assumed a northeast bearing, and after a fine cool run of 30 miles, we made the land to breakfast at 4 P.M. on a cape called Cape Selkirk, after the noble Earl of that name.

This point is formed of lime and sandstone, through which protrude huge granite boulders of every grain and hue. We then advanced 6 miles farther, with the oars, along the shore, which now trended east-northeast, a flat barren limestone tract. In the night some flocks of Canada geese flew over the tents southward, a sure sign of an approaching change in the season.

Next day (twentieth) the wind returned to its old quarter, and after buffeting the waves, among shoals and breakers, for 3 miles, we were compelled to put into a small river that opportunely presented a deep channel.

It was now quite evident to us, even in our most sanguine mood, that the time was come for commencing our return to the distant Coppermine River, and that any further foolhardy perseverance could only lead to the loss of the whole party, and also of the great object which we had so successfully achieved. The men were therefore directed to construct another monument in commemoration of our visit, while Mr. Dease and I walked to an eminence 3 miles off, to see the farther trending of the coast. Our view of the low main shore was limited to about 5 miles, when it seemed to turn off more to the right.

Far without lay several lofty islands, and in the northeast, more distant still, appeared some high blue land—this, which we designated Cape Sir John Ross, is in all probability one of the southeastern promontories of Boothia. We could therefore hardly doubt being now arrived at that large gulf, uniformly described by the Eskimos as containing many islands and, with numerous indentations, running down to the southward till it approaches within 40 miles of Repulse and Wager bays.

The exploration of such a gulf to the Strait of the Fury and Hecla would necessarily demand the whole time and energies of another expedition, having some point of retreat much nearer to the scene of operations than Great Bear Lake; and we felt assured that the Honorable Company, who had already done so much in the cause of discovery, would not abandon their munificent work till the precise limits of this great continent were fully and finally established.

I must here be allowed to express our admiration of Sir John Ross's extraordinary escape from this neighborhood, after the protracted endurance of hardships unparalleled in Arctic story.

The mouth of the stream which bounded the last career of our admirable little boats, and received their name, lies in latitude 68 degrees 28 minutes 23 seconds north, longitude 94 degrees 14 minutes west, variation 16 degrees 20 minutes west. Here, as indeed wherever we landed, appeared old stone circles, traps, and caches, but no *recent* traces of inhabitants were discoverable.

The strong wind, that had forbidden our advance, gave wings to our retreat, and bore us the same night back to Cape Britannia. ▰

Those who consider that Simpson did not prove a continuous waterway around the north of Canada usually feel that the credit should go to Sir John Franklin's third expedition.

Franklin sailed from Britain in 1845, with Francis Rawdon Moira Crozier as second in command, with two ships, the *Erebus* and the *Terror*, manned by 129 selected officers and men. They were last seen by a whaling vessel off the west coast of Greenland, waiting to cross for Lancaster Sound. Then the entire party disappeared from the knowledge of Europe.

It was a decade before a series of expeditions from a number of countries finally gave us the outline of a tragedy that shocked the world beyond anything else in the annals of exploration.

· The ships had spent the first winter at Beechey Island, in Erebus Bay, near the western end of Devon Island. During the summer of 1846 they proceeded south and west until they were beset off the northern end of Victoria Strait, in the pack between King William and Victoria islands, thus practically in sight of those waters which had been explored by Simpson.

The vessels remained fast in the pack throughout the winter of 1846-47, and the summer of 1847 passed without the ice breaking up. Sir John died, apparently of heart failure, on June 11, 1847. Scurvy began to make its inroads, and 24 men had died by the spring of 1848 when the decision was made to abandon the ships, which by then had drifted about 19 miles southwest of their place of besetment, thus still closer to the known Simpson waters.

On April 25, 1848, the survivors, under the leadership of Crozier, started south, apparently planning to reach Back River, which had been explored by and named for Sir George Back, Franklin's companion of his earlier work along the mainland. The purpose would have been to ascend this river and to reach a post of the Hudson's Bay Company.

As viewed from our time, we have in this retreat an appalling case of failure to adapt oneself to conditions. For two years the expedition had been in close touch with Eskimos who were living by seal-hunting, but it does not appear that any of the Europeans learned how to hunt seals, nor, indeed, that they learned any of the elements of northern self-preservation. Instead of seeking the big game of the region, they carried fowling pieces and shot birds. Then they began to eat each other, for cannibalism is not peculiar to any race, nationality, or social class. There is no indication, of course, that any of the Franklin party were killed for food, but merely that when some died the others ate them, and then died in their turn until all had perished.

The dismay at the loss of a whole expedition, the largest and most heralded of the century, combined with the horror of the reports of cannibalism, finally shocked the world out of its optimistic belief of three hundred years that a practical Northwest Passage would be discovered.

Although it is now clear that Franklin's last expedition discovered the passage (if Simpson did not), the knowledge of these facts had not reached Britain until a formal award for the discovery had been made to Sir Robert McClure, captain of the ship *Investigator* and second in command to Admiral Sir Richard Collinson, who commanded one of the Franklin search expeditions.

The *Enterprise* of Collinson and the *Investigator* of McClure had come north in 1850 through the Pacific and were supposed to meet off northwestern Alaska. They missed each other, and came east separately, each believing that the other had failed to reach the northern sea. After penetrating eastward between the mainland and Victoria Island, McClure turned west and then north into Prince of Wales Strait, wintering at Princess Royal Islands, halfway up the strait. In the autumn a journey was made by sledge to the northeast corner of Banks Island, whence they could see Melville Island, where Parry had wintered.

McClure accordingly wrote down on paper that he had discovered the Northwest Passage, and left the document in a cylinder at the discovery point. Although originally placed in a beacon, there was no sign of this in 1917 when members of the third Stefansson expedition came by sledge across Melville Sound and discovered the cylinder on a sandy flat. It had not been tight, and was filled with damp sand so that parts of the document were missing.[10] As deciphered, it reads:

✄ This notice was deposited by a traveling party from Her Britannic Majesty's discovery ship *Investigator*, who were in search of the expedition under Sir John Franklin which up to this date has not been heard of.

The *Investigator* wintered in the pack northeast 4 miles from the Princess Royal Isles; upon the southwest side of the large [word missing, paper torn] left a depot of provisions.

The crews are all well and in excellent spirits, having escaped any sickness during the winter.

A party discovered the Northwest Pasage by traveling over the ice upon the twenty-sixth October last in latitude 73 degrees 31 minutes north, longitude (by lunar) 114 degrees 14 minutes west.

It is requested whoever may find this will communicate the same to the Secretary of the Admiralty, London.

Dated [several words illegible—perhaps "safe and sound"] *Investigator* frozen in the pack, latitude 72 degrees 50 minutes north, longitude 117 degrees, 55 minutes west.

21 April, 1851

—— McClure [signature partly illegible],
Commander ✄

---

[10] A photograph of this document is published opposite page 637 of *The Friendly Arctic*, by Vilhjalmur Stefansson, Macmillan, 1921.

The winter of 1851-52 was spent by McClure at Mercy Bay, on the northeastern coast of Banks Island, and here the ship remained throughout the summer and the following winter. In the spring of 1853 the crew abandoned the *Investigator* and crossed the ice of Melville Sound to Melville Island to join the *Resolute*, commanded by Captain Henry Kellett.

The *Resolute*, one of the five ships of the Franklin searching expedition that was sent out from England in 1852 under command of Sir Edward Belcher, was not destined to carry home her own crew and that of the *Investigator*. Instead, at Belcher's orders, she was abandoned during the summer of 1853, together with three of the other vessels of the expedition, and the combined crews of all the ships were crowded together on the remaining ship, the *North Star*, for passage to England.

Upon his return to Britain, McClure and his men received the formal award of £10,000 for the discovery of the Northwest Passage. Whether McClure discovered it or not, he and his crew were the first of all men to travel all the way around the continents of North and South America. They had gone south and west through the Atlantic, north through the Pacific, and east through waters of the Polar Sea to reach Britain from the northwest.

There is dispute, although not serious, about whether the navigability of the Northwest Pasage by ships of considerable draft had now been demonstrated. It really had been, when the evidence is pieced together; for the ships of the Franklin expedition, drawing more than 20 feet, had reached Victoria Strait, between King William and Victoria islands, while Collinson's *Enterprise*, of comparable size, had reached the same waters from the west.

But the passage had never been traversed in one direction by any ship. To accomplish this, and for other purposes, an expedition was organized by Roald Amundsen. Leaving Norway in 1903 in the *Gjöa*, they sailed west through Lancaster Sound and Barrow Strait, then south through Peel Sound, Franklin Strait, and James Ross Strait to enter a bay in the southeastern part of King William Island, where they spent two winters.

In the spring of 1905, Godfred Hansen, Amundsen's second in command, made a sledge journey west from King William

Island which completed about one-third of the unfinished mapping of Victoria Island, doing the east coast up to what he named Cape Fridtjof Nansen. This is mentioned here because on the journey the sledges, traveling on the sea ice, connected up the tracks of Franklin's and Collinson's ships, showing that the ocean channel between them is unbroken.

The summer of 1905 the *Gjöa* proceeded westward, and on August 17 had reached the wide portion of Dease Strait, off the entrance to Cambridge Bay, which Collinson had reached from the west in the *Enterprise* in 1852. After traversing Coronation Gulf and Dolphin and Union Strait, Amundsen recognized that he was already in waters frequented by the Yankee whaling fleet.

In the western part of the passage, 1905 was an unfavorable season, and the *Gjöa* was beset at King Point, just west of the Mackenzie, where she wintered. She reached the Pacific through Bering Strait the summer of 1906.

During the second and third decades of the twentieth century the Hudson's Bay Company, with renewed activity, spread its trading posts north and east beyond their previous limits. They erected them not only at Arctic mainland points but also on Victoria and King William islands. Because of this development, and for other reasons, the Dominion Government extended northward and eastward correspondingly the service of the Royal Canadian Mounted Police. These activities necessitated the development of shipping along the Northwest Passage.

At first the Hudson's Bay Company supplied its northern posts by two ships, one going north through the Atlantic and west through Lancaster Sound, the other north through the Pacific and Bering Strait and thence eastward along the north coasts of Alaska and Canada. Later the Pacific service was discontinued in favor of shipments down the Mackenzie River from Edmonton which were picked up by an ocean-going vessel at the eastern edge of the Mackenzie delta. In any case, traffic from west and east met at Fort Ross, one of the Company's new posts which had been established on Bellot Strait. The ships, then, did not complete the Northwest Passage either eastward or westward, but met at Fort Ross, each returning the way it had come.

The first voyage east through the Northwest Passage was made in the year 1941-42 by the R.C.M.P. schooner *St. Roch*, commanded by Sergeant (now Inspector) H. A. Larsen. The length of time, two summers, required for this voyage has been commonly misinterpreted as showing difficulties, so it is well to point out that the operation was not looked upon by the Mounted Police as a through voyage, but was merely a routine service to revisit posts and do various chores. The case was merely that a ship that had come in from the west and was doing its job in the north, year after year, finally decided to return south by way of the east.

At this stage there were five or more channels or variants in making the Northwest Passage, all known to be feasible in certain years, although not necessarily all feasible during any one season. For, as was pointed out in connection with the Northeast Passage, the ice is during summer in constant motion, so that when it vacates Channel A it is likely to jam Channel B.

The Northwest Passage route thus far most cultivated was the most southerly, hugging the mainland, for it served the best interests of the fur traders and the natives. However, it has long been known that this is the shallowest of the channels and the most devious, filled with rocks and other dangers, thus requiring vessels of shallow draft prepared for intricate navigation, and necessitating careful sounding of channels, with buoys and things of that sort, if it were to be thought of as an active freighting highway.

The best of the five or more channels was obviously the most northerly one, which had been opened by Parry. In all the years since his time there have been few cases when a vessel tried to reach Melville Island from the Atlantic and failed to do so, even square-rigged sailing ships, in many cases commanded by inexperienced men.

Then it had been discovered, in particular by the third Stefansson expedition, that the pack from the Beaufort Sea to the west of Prince Patrick and Banks islands is always pushing eastward through the relatively narrow McClure Strait. This ice that has been under grinding pressure as it crowds through the strait necessarily slackens out in the roomy waters of the sound, permitting ships to pass between Melville Island and

Prince of Wales Strait, except perhaps for a few days now and then when strong easterly winds are blowing that neutralize the current and press the ice from the sound westward against the incoming McClure Strait stream.

Aware of these conditions, the Royal Canadian Mounted Police decided to send Larsen westward through Lancaster Sound, Melville Sound, and Prince of Wales Strait in 1944. Several variant accounts of this notable voyage have been published. The one used here by permission is the version written up from interviews and other material by Clifford Wilson and published in the Hudson's Bay Company's *Beaver* of March 1945, under the title "Arctic Odyssey." The extract begins where Larsen, having proceeded through Lancaster Sound and Barrow Strait, has entered Melville Sound and is approaching Winter Harbour, on the south coast of Melville Island.

Larsen and the Northwest Passage

Westward from Dealy Island lay Winter Harbour, named by Parry, who spent the winter of 1819-20 there.

On the twenty-ninth [of August, 1944] the *St. Roch* anchored in the harbor, and going ashore, the men found a storehouse built by Bernier in 1910, still in reasonably good condition. From one of the rafters they found a bottle hanging, and opening it they found—doubtless with mixed feelings—a piece of paper bearing a record of a visit made in 1929 by one of the greatest of modern Arctic travelers, the late Inspector A. H. Joy, R.C.M.P.

Before leaving the next day, they deposited a record of their own at Parry Rock.

Fortune favored them, and the ice opened up to permit a run of 30 miles to the south. Then the mist descended, and they had to throw out grapnels to a large floe and wait. Meanwhile they took advantage of the situation and filled up their fresh-water tanks from pools lying in the hollows of the floe.

On the last day of August they met ice heavier than any they had experienced that season. It was driving in from the west through McClure Strait. Fog came down intermittently and lowered visibility to zero, and at such times the little *St. Roch* could only drift helplessly as the great growlers swirled her about, pounding and grinding against her sides.

For the next two days they alternately drifted and steamed between enormous floes which appeared to have broken up or split only a few days before. But late in the afternoon of the third day, land loomed ahead through the lifting fog. It was the entrance to Prince of Wales Strait, between Banks and Victoria islands—but which side of the entrance, no one knew. If it were the northern [western] side, passing to the north of it would lead them away from their course and into McClure Strait. If it were the south [east] side, passing to the south could only lead them into Collinson Inlet, which would soon be recognizable.

Larsen decided to try the latter course—and soon found that he was in the inlet. The head of this inlet has never been explored, but as it was choked with ice, with more coming in abaft, the skipper put her about and headed for Prince of Wales Strait.

He was now coming to what might prove the most difficult part of the voyage.[11] Since leaving Navy Board Inlet, at the entrance to the Northwest Passage, the sea lanes he had threaded between the islands of the archipelago had been reasonably wide. Now, however, there lay ahead of him a strait 175 miles long, with the land masses converging in some places to within 10 miles of each other.

But luck was with him. The long narrow passage stretched away under the sunlight between its rocky shores, almost completely free of ice. Steadily the *St. Roch* plowed southward, and before nightfall she was through the strait and out into the wide expanse of Amundsen Gulf. She had made the Northwest Passage in eighteen days!

[In speaking of the passage as an eighteen-day voyage, Wilson is measuring from the eastern mouth of Lancaster Sound to the southwestern mouth of Wales Strait, which is right in the

---

[11] This is, of course, the comment of the author, Mr. Clifford Wilson. The third Stefansson expedition had a ship wintering in Prince of Wales Strait two years, 1915-17, and gathered facts which tended to show that the strait would be on the average one of the best links in this variant of the Northwest Passage—the one by Barrow Strait, Melville Sound, Prince of Wales Strait.

sense that the waters at either end of this stretch have long been cultivated by ships from both Atlantic and Pacific, so that familiarity has bred contempt for such difficulties as there are. Inspector Larsen has said, however, that he considers more difficult on the average the section of the passage that is west of Banks Island than the one east of it. Wilson's narrative for this western section, based on interviews with Inspector Larsen and on other sources, tends to bear this out as the quotation continues:]

Larsen radioed the good news to R.C.M.P. headquarters at Ottawa, and received in reply congratulations, and instructions to try for Herschel Island and Vancouver. At Holman Island, the next day, the *St. Roch* men called at the H.B.C. post and gave the news of their success to the astounded post manager, Leonard Coates.

On September 5, they set off for Herschel Island, but by reason of the ice in Amundsen Gulf had to follow the coast line of the mainland westward from Cape Parry. Near Tuktuk (Port Brabant) their progress was arrested by tightly packed ice. They tied up to a grounded floe 10 miles north of Toker Point, and remained thus for twenty hours while more and more ice pressed down from the northwest. But storm clouds were gathering, and rather than be caught in such an exposed condition, Larsen decided to head in for Tuktuk.

There, however, trouble of another sort lay in wait for them. It was dark when they reached Tuktuk harbor, and trying to find anchorage there, they ran aground. Hardly had they freed themselves when a gale of hurricane force swept down upon them from out of the northwest, and for two days they had to ride out the storm at anchor. So great were the waves that some of the Company buildings were washed away.

When at last the gale abated, Mackenzie Bay between Tuktuk and Herschel Island was jam-packed with ice. For a week the *St. Roch* waited for a lead to open up. Then on September 17 she made a try for Herschel Island, and by steaming between the pack and the shore in fairly shallow water, through the heaviest ice of the voyage, reached it the next day.

Vancouver was still a long way off, the season was late, and many leagues of ice-filled seas beset her course. To all appearances, the *St. Roch* would have to winter at Herschel Island. The Eskimo family, with food and supplies, were put ashore, and the crew prepared to meet the winter.

On the twenty-first, however, Larsen radioed Ottawa that he was going to make a dash for it. Three days later he was past the point of extreme danger—Point Barrow—and heading southwest for Bering Strait. At Wainwright Inlet they saw the last of the ice, and from then on—save for a two-day storm in early October—it was all plain sailing.

The unique part of the *St. Roch* voyage is the crossing of Melville Sound from Melville Island to Prince of Wales Strait. In interviews other than those with Mr. Wilson, Inspector Larsen has said that he has studied all accounts he has been able to find about voyages from eastern Lancaster Sound to Winter Harbour, Melville Island, and again from northern Prince of Wales Strait to Bering Strait. On comparison of these narratives with his own experience, it appears to him that his voyage was made in a more difficult navigation season, as to weather and ice, than most of the others—that he had to deal with nearly or quite the worst year on record.

From all Larsen has been able to learn, the section most frequently difficult to navigate on the whole Northwest Passage is probably the one from Herschel Island to Point Barrow. That is because that sector of coast is exposed to the main Polar Sea, just as are many parts of the Northeast Passage. What makes easier the section from eastern Lancaster Sound to western Prince of Wales Strait is that the various Canadian islands block the main Arctic pack, protecting a ship from its steady pressure.

Inspector Larsen considers that the most southerly variant of the passage, the one that has so far been chiefly used by the Hudson's Bay Company and the Royal Canadian Mounted Police, is too shoal and too crowded with rocks and other dangers to be suitable for ships drawing more than 15 or 20 feet—a 10-foot draft is better. This means ships of only a few hundred tons. The Lancaster-Barrow-Melville-Prince of Wales route, the one he used in 1944, he considers suitable for ships of any size—say 10,000 or 15,000 tons. These would be vessels of the type now used by Norway in Antarctic whaling, and some of them are ordinary tankers purchased from Standard Oil or other companies that used them on the Atlantic. They have been reconditioned only slightly when transferred to the icy waters of the Antarctic.

To generalize, it may be said that mile for mile the Northwest Passage around Canada is no more difficult than the Northeast Passage around Siberia. Since the mileage is less than half, the difficulty should be less than half. It ought to be as easy to make two round-trip voyages per season around the north of Canada as to make one around the north of Asia, which latter has been done.

It does not follow, however, that the Northwest Passage is going to be twice as much used as the northeastern. The Soviet Union is eager to use its own passage, for it wants to divert freight from the Trans-Siberian Railway. Canada is reciprocally anxious not to use its own, for it wants to concentrate as much freight as possible on its present transcontinental lines, the Canadian National and the Canadian Pacific railways, which start on the Gulf of St. Lawrence, follow the southern edge of Canada, and end in British Columbia.

Since the national policies differ so fundamentally, we may expect a steady and perhaps a rapid growth in traffic through the Northeast Passage without corresponding growth in utilization of the Northwest Passage.

It remains true, however, that Canada has demonstrated the feasibility of its own passage, and that it can now keep that in reserve, to use in case of such an emergency as a war, somewhat as the Soviet Union did with the Northeast Passage during World War II. For then there would no doubt be a congestion of traffic on Canada's transcontinental railways, driving that country to seek relief by a sea route. This, between such ports as Montreal and Vancouver, is much shorter by way of the north than the alternative southern route through the Panama Canal, and thus preferable during the navigation period.

As the Norwegians have proved with whaling ships in the Antarctic, and as the Soviet Union has proved with freighting ships in the Northeast Passage, nothing special in the way of a strengthened ship is required for the Northwest Passage. Nor is strengthening even desirable; for it has been found that when a ship is buttressed its cargo capacity is decreased more than its safety is increased, or the reliability of its performance.

The dream of four centuries has come true. The Old World is using its passage; the New World will use its own whenever the need develops.

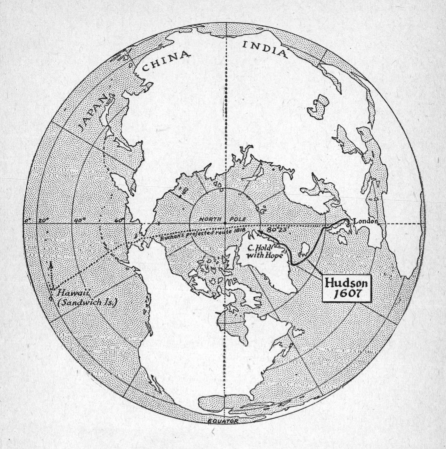

North to the Indies

NORTH TO THE INDIES

CHAPTER 14

THE centuries that immediately followed Columbus and Cabot were too practical for such vain glories as the strife for credit through having reached a remarkable spot, such as the top of a mountain or the top of the world. The chief romance of early modern exploration was in finding a road to riches. Columbus believed that such a road might lie by way of the North Pole, a shorter passage to the wealth of the Indies. Men of that time, unconcerned about reaching the pole as an achievement, were much concerned to find by way of the pole a near way to the Far East.

So far as is known, the first aggressive planner that took up the Columbus suggestion of a polar way to China was Robert Thorne of England, who succeeded in getting a vessel dispatched for the Indies by way of the pole in 1527. As with John Cabot's second voyage, all we know about Thorne's venture is that the ship sailed.

The first try for the Indies by way of the pole of which the details are known is Henry Hudson's voyage of 1607. He sailed from London (where, apparently, he had been born), touched at the Shetlands, and passed Iceland without seeing it. On reaching Greenland, 50 or 75 miles north of the Arctic Circle, he thought he might be on the coast of one of the islands with which the fabrications of the Zenos had filled the maps of the northwestern Atlantic. So when he left that coast and headed northeast, he was not in a position to know that it was the coast of the same great land which he reached 200 or 250 miles north of the Arctic Circle, near where the name Hold with Hope, which he gave, is still on our maps—though perhaps not exactly where Hudson placed it.

547

Hudson's was already one of the greatest discovery voyages ever made in the Arctic before he began the first known attempt to penetrate northward beyond the lands through the Polar Sea toward the Indies. He knew of Spitsbergen to the northeast, for he had with him the Barents maps. So what he attempted was to find a way toward the Pacific by passing north between the land he was now discovering, on his left, and the islands that would lie to his right. The following quotation is from *Henry Hudson the Navigator*, published by the Hakluyt Society in 1860 under the editorship of G. M. Asher. The text used by Asher is from *Purchas His Pilgrimes* where it has the heading:

> *Diverse Voyages and Northerne Discoveries of that worthy irrecoverable Discoverer Master Henry Hudson. His Discoverie toward the North Pole, set forth at the charge of certaine Worshipfull Merchants of London, in May 1607. Written partly by John Playse one of the Company, and partly by H. Hudson.*

The more southerly coastal stretch of Greenland skirted by Hudson is reported by him as land mainly covered by ice, the more northerly as free of snow in late June. It has been confirmed by later exploration that the Blosseville Coast, immediately to the northwest of Iceland, has little ice-free land, but that Jameson Land, directly north from Iceland, is free of permanent ice and also snow-free during midsummer.

Here is the portion of Hudson record where he has passed Scoresby Sound, without discovering it, and is working northeasterly along the shore.

Henry Hudson in the Arctic

On the one and twentieth day [of June, 1607], in the morning, while we steered our course north-northeast, we thought we had embayed ourselves, finding land on our larboard and ice upon it, and many great pieces of drift ice. We steered away northeast, with diligent looking out every clear for land, having a desire to know whether it would leave us to the east, both to know the breath of the sea, and also to shape a more northerly course.

And considering we knew no name given to this land, we thought good to name it Hold-with-Hope, lying in 73 degrees of latitude.

The sun was on the meridian on the south part of the compass, nearest-hand. Here it is to be noted that when we made the Mount of God's Mercie [Mercy Mount] and Young's Cape, the land was covered with snow for the most part, and extreme cold when we approached near it; but this land was very temperate to our feeling.

And this likewise is to be noted, that being two days without observation, notwithstanding our lying ahull by reason of much contrary wind, yet our observation and dead reckoning were within 8 leagues together, our ship being before us 8 leagues. This night, until next morning, proved little wind.

The three and twentieth, in the morning, we had a hard gale on head of us, with much rain that fell in very great drops, much like our thundershowers in England. We tacked about and stood east northerly with a short sail; to our feeling it was not so cold as before we had it. It was calm from noon to three of the clock, with fog.

After the wind came up at east and east-southeast, we steered away northeast with the fog and rain. About seven or eight of the clock, the wind increased with extreme fog, we steered away with short sail east-northeast and sometimes east and by north. About twelve at midnight the wind came up at southwest; we steered away north, being reasonable clear weather.

The four and twentieth, in the morning, about two of the clock, the master's mate thought he saw land on the larboard, trending north and northwest westerly, and the longer we ran north, the more it fell away to the west, and did think it to be a main highland.

This day, the wind being westerly, we steered away north, and by observation we were in 73 degrees nearest-hand. At noon we changed our course, and steered away north and by east; and at our last observation, and also at this, we found the meridian all leeward on the south and by west, westerly part of the compass, when we had sailed two watches, 8 leagues.

The five and twentieth, the wind scanted and came up at north-northwest; we lay northeast two watches, 8 leagues. After the wind became variable between the northeast and the north, we steered away east and by north and sometimes east. We had thick fog.

About noon three granpasses [whales] played about our ship.

This afternoon the wind veered to the east and southeast; we hauled away north and by east. This night was close weather, but small fog. (We use the word night for distinction of time, but long before this the sun was always above the horizon, but as yet we could never see him upon the meridian north.)

This night, being by our account in the latitude of 75 degrees, we saw small flocks of birds with black backs and white bellies, and long spear tails. We supposed that land was not far off, but we could not descry any, with all the diligence which we could use, being so close weather that many times we could not see 6 or 7 leagues off.

The six and twentieth, in the morning was close weather; we had our wind and held our course as afore. This day our observation was 76 degrees 38 minutes, and we had birds of the same sort as afore, and divers other of that color, having red heads, that we saw when we first made the Mount of God's Mercy in Greenland, but not so many. After we steered away north and by east, two watches, 10 leagues, with purpose to fall with the southern part of Newland [Spitsbergen], accounting ourselves 10 or 12 leagues from the land. Then we stood away northeast, one watch, 5 leagues.

The seven and twentieth, about one or two of the clock in the morning we made Newland, being clear weather on the sea; but the land was covered with fog, the ice lying very thick all along the shore for 15 or 16 leagues, which we saw. Having fair wind, we coasted it in a very pleasing smooth sea, and had no ground at 100 fathoms 4 leagues from the shore.

This day at noon, we accounted we were in 78 degrees, and we stood along the shore. This day was so foggy that we were hardly able to see the land many times, but by our account we were near Vogel Hooke. About eight of the clock this evening, we purposed to shape our course from thence northwest.

Here is to be noted that although we ran along near the shore, we found no great cold, which made us think that if we had been on shore the place is temperate.

Holding this northwest course, about ten of the clock at night we saw great store of ice on head off us, bearing westerly off us, which we could not go clear of with the foresaid course. Then we tacked about, and stood away between the south and the southeast, as much desirous to leave this land as we were to see it.

The eight and twentieth was a hard gale of wind all the forenoon, between the south and the southwest. We shaped our course [blank in original]; we did it to be farther from the ice and land. It pleased God that about twelve of the clock this night it cleared up, and we found that we were between the land and the ice, Vogel Hooke then bearing nearest-hand east off us. Then we tacked about and stood in for the shore, having sea room between the ice and the land.

The nine and twentieth, at four in the morning, the wind at northeast, a pretty gale, we thought best to shorten our way; so we tacked about and stood north-northwest, the wind a little increasing. About twelve at noon, we saw ice ahead off us; we cast about again and stood away east-southeast with very much wind, so that we shortened our sails for the space of two watches. Then about eight this evening we struck ahull, and it proved the hardest storm that we had in this voyage.

The thirtieth, in the morning, was stormy; about noon it ceased; at seven in the evening it proved almost calm.

The first of July, all the forenoon the wind was at southeast; we stood northeast for the shore, hoping to find an open sea between the shore and the ice. About noon we were embayed with ice, lying between the land and us. By our observation we were in 78 degrees 42 minutes, whereby we accounted we were thwart of the great indraught.

And to free ourselves of the ice, we steered between the southeast and south, and to the westward, as we could have sea. And about six this evening it pleased God to give us clear weather, and we found we were shot far into the inlet, being almost a bay, and environed with very high mountains, with low land lying between them. We had no ground in this bay at 100 fathoms. Then, being sure where we were, we steered away west, the wind at southeast and calm, and found all our ice on the northern shore and a clear sea to the southward.

The second, it pleased God to give us the wind at northeast, a fair gale with clear weather, the ice being to the northward of us and the weather shore, and an open sea to the southward under our lee. We held on our course northwest till twelve of the clock. Having sailed in that course 10 leagues, and finding the ice to fall from us to the [blank in original], we gave thanks to God who marvelously preserved us from so many dangers amongst so huge a quantity of ice and fog.

We steered away northwest, hoping to be free from ice; we had observation 78 degrees, 56 minutes. We fell with ice again, and trended it as it lay between the west and south-southeast.

The third, we had observation 78 degrees, 33 minutes. This day we had our shrouds frozen; it was searching cold. We also trended the ice, not knowing whether we were clear or not, the wind being at north.

The fourth was very cold, and our shrouds and sails frozen. We found we were far in the inlet. The wind being at north, we bore up and stood south-southeast, and south and southwest by west till ten this night.

The fifth, was very much wind at northeasterly; at twelve we struck ahull, having brought ourselves near the mouth of the inlet.

The sixth, in the morning the wind was as before, and the sea grown. This morning we came into a very green sea; we had our observation 77 degrees, 30 minutes. This afternoon the wind and sea assuaged. About four of the clock we set sail, and steered northwest and by west, the wind being at north-northeast. This day proved the clearest day we had long before.

The seventh, at four in the morning, was very clear weather, and the fairest morning that we saw in three weeks before. We steered as afore, being by our account in 78 degrees nearest-hand, and out of the sack. We found we were compassed in with land and ice, and were again entered into a black sea, which by proof we found to be an open passage.

Now, having the wind at north-northeast, we steered away south and by east, with purpose to fall with the southernmost part of this land [Spitsbergen] which we saw, hoping by this mean either to defray the charge of the voyage, or else, if it pleased God in time to give us a fair wind to the northeast, to satisfy expectation. All this day and night afterward proved calm.

The eighth, all the forenoon proved calm, and very thick fog. This morning we saw many pieces of driftwood drive by us. We heaved out our boat to stop a leak, and mended our riggings. This day we saw many seals, and two fishes which we judged to be sea horses or morses [walrus, that is, whale horse]. At twelve this night we had the wind at east and by south; we stood away northeast.

The ninth, all the forenoon was little wind at southeast, with thick fog. This day we were in amongst islands of ice, where we saw many seals.

The tenth, in the morning, was foggy; afterward it proved clear. We found we were compassed with ice every way about us; we tacked about, and stood south and by west, and south-southwest, one watch, 5 leagues, hoping to get more sea room and to stand for the northeast; we had the wind at northwest.

The eleventh, very clear weather, with the wind at southeast-south. We were come out of the blue sea into our green sea again, where we saw whales. Now, having a fresh gale of wind at south-southeast, it behooved me to change my course, and to sail to the northeast, by the southern end of Newland. But being come into a green sea, praying God to direct me, I steered away north 10 leagues.

After that we saw ice on our larboard, we steered away east and by north 3 leagues, and left the ice behind us. Then we steered away north till noon. This day we had the sun on the meridian south and by west, westerly; his greatest height was 37 degrees, 20 minutes. By this observation we were in 79 degrees, 17 minutes. We had a fresh gale of wind and a smooth sea, by means whereof our ship had outrun us.

At ten this evening clear weather, and then we had the company of our troublesome neighbors, ice with fog. The wind was at south-southwest. Here we saw plenty of seals, and we supposed bears had been here, by their footing and dung upon the ice. This day, many of my company were sick with eating of bear's flesh the day before, unsalted.[1]

---

[1] Unless you overeat, you do not become ill from polar-bear meat. But illness from bear liver is frequently reported, so it is supposed Hudson's men ate the livers. A recent theory has it that such illness is from an excessive intake of vitamins, in which certain livers are notably rich.

The twelfth, for the most part, was thick fog. We steered between south and by east, and south-southeast 2½ leagues, to clear us of the ice. Then we had the wind at south; we steered till noon northeast 5 leagues.

This morning we had our shrouds frozen. At noon, by our account we were in 80 degrees, being little wind at west-south-west, almost calm with thick fog. This afternoon we steered away north and sometimes northeast. Then we saw ice ahead of us. We cast about and stood southeast, with little wind and fog.

Before we cast about by means of the thick fog, we were very near ice, being calm, and the sea setting onto the ice, which was very dangerous. It pleased God at the very instant to give us a small gale, which was the means of our deliverance; to Him be praise therefor.

At twelve this night it cleared up, and out of the top William Collins, our boatswain, saw the land called Newland by the Hollanders, bearing south-southwest 12 leagues from us.

The thirteenth, in the morning, the wind at south and by east, a good gale, we cast about and stood northeast and by east, and by observation we were in 80 degrees, 23 minutes. This day we saw many whales.

This forenoon proved clear weather, and we could not see any sign of ice out of the top. Between noon and three of the clock, we steered away northeast and by east 5 leagues, then we saw ice on head of us. We steered east two glasses, 1 league, and could not be clear of the ice with that course. Then we steered away southeast 2½ leagues. After, we sailed east and by north, and east 4 leagues, till eight the next morning.

The fourteenth, in the morning, was calm with fog. At nine, the wind at east, a small gale with thick fog. We steered south-east and by east, and running this course we found our green sea again, which by proof we found to be freest from ice, and our azure-blue sea to be our icy sea. At this time we had more birds than we usually found.

At noon, being a thick fog, we found ourselves near land [Spitsbergen], bearing east of us. And running farther, we found a bay open to the west and by north northerly, the bottom and sides thereof being to our sight very high and ragged land. The northern side of this bay's mouth, being high land, is a small island, the which we called Collins Cape, by the name of our boatswain, who first saw it.

In this bay we saw many whales, and one of our company having a hook and line overboard to try for fish, a whale came under the keel of our ship and made her held; yet by God's mercy we had no harm but the loss of the hook and three parts of the line.

At a southwest sun from the northwest and by north, a flood set into the bay. At the mouth of this bay we had sounding 30 fathoms, and after, 26 fathoms, but being farther in, we had no ground at 100 fathoms, and therefore judged it rather a sound than a bay. Between this high ragged [land] in the swamps and valleys lay much snow.

Here we found it hot. On the southern side of this bay lie three or four small islands or rocks.

In the bottom of this bay, John Colman, my mate, and William Collins, my boatswain, with two others of our company, went on shore, and there they found and brought aboard a pair of morses' teeth in the jaw. They likewise found whales' bones, and some dozen or more of deers' horns. They saw the footings of beasts of other sorts; they also saw rote geese. They saw much driftwood on the shore, and found a stream or two of fresh water.

Here they found it hot on the shore,[2] and drank water to cool their thirst, which they also commended.

Here we found the want of a better ship boat. As they certified me, they were not on the shore past half an hour, and among other things brought aboard a stone of the country. When they went from us it was calm, but presently after we had a gale of wind at northeast, which came with the flood with fog. We plied to and again in the bay, waiting their coming. But after they came aboard we had the wind at east and

[2] As was pointed out before, the explorers from Prince Henry to Sir John Franklin were always looking for profit in trade, mining, or such. There was a pull toward optimism, and favorable signs were reported, emphasized, even exaggerated. This remained true until about 1850 when the commercial-optimist period was replaced by one of modest heroism, whereupon difficulties and dangers began to be emphasized in Arctic travel narratives.

by south a fine gale; we, minding our voyage and the time to perform it, steered away northeast and north-northeast.

This night proved clear, and we had the sun on the meridian, on the north and by east part of the compass. From the upper edge of the horizon, with the cross-staff, we found his height 10 degrees 40 minutes, without allowing anything for the semi-diameter of the sun, or the distance of the end of the staff from the center in the eye. From a north sun to an east sun, we sailed between north and north-northeast, 8 leagues.

The fifteenth, in the morning was very clear weather, the sun shining warm, but little wind at east southerly. By a southeast sun we had brought Collins Cape to bear off us southeast, and we saw the high land of Newland, that part by us discovered on our starboard, 8 or 10 leagues from us, trending northeast and by east, and southwest and by west, 18 or 20 leagues from us to the northeast, being a very high mountainous land, like ragged rocks with snow between them.

By mine account, the northern part of this land which now we saw stretched into 81 degrees. All this day proved clear weather, little wind, and reasonable warm.

The sixteenth, in the morning warm and clear weather, the wind at north. This morning we saw that we were compassed in with ice in abundance, lying to the north, to the northwest, the east, and southeast. And being run toward the farthest part of the land by us discovered, which for the most part trendeth nearest-hand northeast and southwest, we saw more land joining to the same, trending north in our sight, by means of the clearness of the weather, stretching far into 82 degrees, and by the bowing or showing of the sky much farther.

Which when I first saw, I hoped to have had a free sea between the land and the ice, and meant to have compassed this land by the north. By now, finding by proof it was impossible, by means of the abundance of ice compassing us about by the north and joining to the land, and seeing God did bless us with a fair wind to sail by the south of this land to the northeast, we returned, bearing up the helm, minding to hold that part of the land which the Hollanders had discovered in our sight; and if contrary winds should take us, to harbor there, and to try what we could find to the charge of our voyage, and to proceed on our discovery as soon as God should bless us with wind.

And this I can assure at this present, that between 78½ degrees and 82 degrees, by this way there is no passage; but I think this land may be profitable to those that will adventure it. In this bay before spoken of, and about this coast, we saw more abundance of seals then we had seen any time before, swimming in the water.

At noon this day, having a stiff gale of wind at north, we were thwart of Collins Cape, standing in 81½ degrees, and at one of the clock the cape bore northeast of us. From thence I set our course west-southwest, with purpose to keep in the open sea free from ice, and sailed in that course 16 leagues. At ten this night we steered away southwest, with the wind at north, a hard gale, until eight the next morning, 18 leagues.

The seventeenth, in the morning a good gale at north. At eight we altered our course, and steered away south till eight in the evening, and ran 12 leagues. This day proved reasonable clear and warm.

The eighteenth, in the morning the wind increased at south and by east, with thick fog. All this afternoon and night proved close weather, little fog, and reasonable warm.

The nineteenth, at eight in the morning the wind at south, with thick fog. We steered southeast 4 leagues till noon, then the wind veered more large. We steered southeast and by east 4 leagues till four, then we veered sheet and steered east and by southeasterly 15 leagues, till eight the next morning. This day, after the morning, proved reasonable clear and warm.

The twentieth, in the morning little wind. At eight this morning we saw land ahead of us under our lee and to weatherward of us, distant from us 12 leagues, being part of Newland. It is very high mountainous land, the highest that we had seen until now. As we sailed near it, we saw a sound ahead of us, lying east and west.

The land on the northern side of this sound's mouth trendeth nearest-hand west-northwest and east-southeast 12 leagues, in our sight, being 10 leagues from us. And the land on the southern side, being 8 or 10 leagues in our sight, at this time trendeth south-southeast and north-northwest. From eight to noon was calm. This day, by observation, we were in 77 degrees 26 minutes.

On the northern side of the mouth of this inlet lie three islands not far the one from the other, being very high mountainous land. The farthest of the three to the northwest hath four very high mounts, like heaps of corn. That island next the inlet's mouth hath one very high mount on the southern end. Here one of our company killed a red-billed bird.

All this day after the morning, and all night, proved calm, inclining rather to heat than cold. This night we had some warm rain.

The one and twentieth, all the forenoon calm. At four in the afternoon we had a small gale of wind at south-southeast, with fog. We steered away east to stand in with the land, and sailed 3 leagues until midnight. Then the wind came at northeast, we cast about, and steered south 10 leagues till eight the next morning.

The two and twentieth, at eight in the morning much wind at east, and variable, with short sail we steered 3 leagues south and by east. Then came down very much wind; we struck ahull. All this afternoon and night proved very much wind with rain.

The three and twentieth, all the forenoon was very much wind at south, with rain and fog. At four this afternoon we saw land bearing northeast of us, 6 leagues from us. Then we had the wind at south-southwest. We steered away southeast and southeast and by east 4 leagues, the sea being very much grown. We accounted we had hulled northwest and by north 22 leagues, and north 3 leagues. Then, fearing with much wind to be set on a lee shore, we tacked about and made our way good west and by north, half a point northerly, all this night with much wind.

The four and twentieth, in the morning much wind as afore, and the sea grown. This morning we struck our main-topmast to ease our ship, and sailed from the last evening 8, to this noon, 15, leagues west and by north half a point northerly. From twelve to eight, 6 leagues as afore, with the wind at south and by west. At eight we tacked about with the wind at south-southwest, and lay southeast and by east, with much wind, and the sea grown.

The five and twentieth was a clear morning. We set our main-topmast. We saw land bearing north of us, and under our lee, we sailing southeast and by east. Then the wind scanted. We cast about, and lay southwest and by west 2½ leagues till noon. Then it began to overcast, and the wind to scant again. We cast about, and lay southeast and by south, the wind at southwest and by west, and sailed in that course 3 leagues, till four in the afternoon. Then the wind scanted again, and we sailed 3 leagues south.

Now, seeing how contrary the wind proved to do the good which we desired this way, I thought to prove our fortunes by the west once again; and this evening at eight, we being in the latitude of 78, and from land 15 leagues—which leagues part whereof bear from the northeast to the east off us—we steered away west, with the wind at southeast, and clear weather.

The six and twentieth, all this day proved rain with thick fog, and a hard gale of wind at east and by north and east-northeast. From the last evening at eight to this noon, we ran 25 leagues; from noon till midnight, 19 leagues, the wind at east and by south; from midnight till two and the next morning, 2 leagues west.

The seven and twentieth, extreme thick fog, and little wind, at east and by south. Then it proved calm, and the sea very lofty. We heard a great rut or noise with the ice and sea—which was the first ice we heard or saw since we were at Collins Cape—the sea heaving us westward toward the ice. We heaved out our boat, and rowed to tow out our ship farther from the danger, which would have been to small purpose, by means the sea went so high. But in this extremity it pleased God to give us a small gale at northwest and by west; we steered away southeast, 4 leagues, till noon.

Here we had finished our discovery if the wind had continued that brought us hither, or if it had continued calm; but it pleased God to make this northwest and by west wind the mean of our deliverance, which wind we had not found common in this voyage. God give us thankful hearts for so great deliverance.

Here we found the want of a good ship boat, as once we had

done before at Whales Bay. We wanted also half a dozen long oars to row in our ship.

At noon the day cleared up, and we saw by the sky ice bearing off us, from west-southwest to the north and north-northeast. Then we had a good gale at west. We steered away south till four, 7 leagues. From four to six, south 4 leagues, and found by the icy sky and our nearness to Groneland [Greenland] that there is no passage that way; which, if there had been, I meant to have made my return by the north of Groneland to Davis his Straits, and so for England.

Here, finding we had the benefit of a westerly wind, which all this voyage we had found scant, we altered our course and steered to the eastward, and ran southeast 4 leagues. From eight this evening till noon the next day, east-southeast, 30 leagues. All this day and night proved very cold, by means, as I suppose, of the winds coming off so much ice.

The eight and twentieth, very cold, the wind at west, not very foggy. At noon this day we steered away southeast and by east, and by observation we were 76 degrees 36 minutes. From noon to eight, 10 leagues. Then the wind scanted to southeast and by south; we steered away east and by north 18 leagues, till the next day noon.

The nine and twentieth, all the forenoon a thick fog and wet, the wind at southeast and by east, nearest-hand, and raw cold. From noon to four we sailed 3 leagues east and by north, half a point northerly. Then the wind veered more large; we steered east and by south 8 leagues till twelve at night.

At this time, to windward we heard the rut of land, which I knew to be so by the color of the sea. It was extreme thick fog, so that we could hardly see a cable's length from our ship. We had ground 25 fathoms, small black pebble stones. We sounded again, and had ground at 30 fathoms, small stones like beans; at the next cast no ground at 60 fathoms. I cast about again and steered southwest 6 leagues, west and by north 2 leagues, till the next day noon. All this day and night extreme thick fog.

The thirtieth, all the forenoon very thick fog. At noon almost calm. After, we had little wind, and steered north-northwest till two. Then it cleared up, so that we could see from us 2 leagues, with the wind at northwest. Then we steered east-southeast; after, it cleared. At south, in the evening, we saw an island bearing off us northwest, from us 5 leagues, and we saw land bearing off from us 7 leagues. We had land likewise bearing off us from east-southeast to southeast and by east, as we judged, 10 leagues.

Then, having the wind at west-northwest, we steered south and by east. It presently proved calm till ten this evening; then we had a little gale at southwest and by west. We steered away south-southeast till twelve this night, and accounted ourselves in 76, from land 10 leagues; which was the likeliest land that we had seen on all parts of Newland, being plain riggie land of a mean height and not ragged, as all the rest was that we had seen this voyage, nor covered with snow.

At twelve this night we saw two morses in the sea near us, swimming to land. From twelve at night to four, calm.

The one and thirtieth, at four this morning we had the wind at southeast; we steered south-southwest. Then it proved calm, and so continued all the forenoon. The afternoon we had the wind at east-southeast; we steered south, 8 leagues.

Then, being like to prove much wind contrary to our purpose, and finding our fog more thick and troublesome then before, divers things necessary wanting, and our time well-nigh spent to do further good this year, I commanded to bear up for our return for England, and steered away south-southwest. ⚑

By August 15 Hudson was in the Faeroes, "and the fifteenth of September I arrived in Tilberie Hope in the Thames."

Only by a comparison with what went before and came after can we see the greatness of this discovery voyage; but we must also discount it somewhat, as Hudson did himself. For he has been quoted to the effect that he did not know what names belonged to the land he saw to the northwest and north of Iceland, and that implies his awareness that ships of his own and other countries plied this coast in former days, as we now know from Icelandic reports that (in the late Middle Ages) the Bristol men and others used to sail northwesterly from Iceland to disappear over the horizon, at which point Greenland would be heaving into sight on days of clear weather.

That Hudson knew of the still earlier navigators of Iceland and Norway who had frequented Greenland seas is no inference, for we have it by Hudson's own statement that he carried with him the sailing directions of the Norwegian Ivar Bardarson, which were written down in Norway around 1370, after Ivar had spent many years in Greenland (on which see further pages 82-83 of the present volume).

But in comparison with the well-known explorers, Hudson stands high as a pioneer. Latitude 74 degrees on the Greenland east coast does not appear to have been reached, following his voyage, until 1831, or two hundred and twenty-four years later. Hudson's farthest north of 80 degrees 23 minutes was not excelled for a hundred and sixty-six years and then (1773) only by 30 miles. It was not until after a hundred and ninety-nine years that the great whaling master William Scoresby made a substantial northing over Hudson when, in 1806, he reached 81 degrees 30 minutes, some 75 miles beyond the farthest point reached by the great Londoner.

Hudson's opinion in the July 16 diary entry is wrong where he thinks there is no northward passage between Spitsbergen and Greenland—herein he falls into the prevalent error of his time in thinking that Greenland extended in a wide curve northeast, east, and finally southeast to a point north of Norway. But another entry for the same day proved magnificently right, where he says of Spitsbergen (Newland): "I think this land may be profitable to those that will adventure it."

The context shows that Hudson's optimistic forecast on Spitsbergen refers to the waters surrounding the island group—he had in mind a "fishery" of seal, walrus, and whale to supply oil for the lamps of Europe. Those waters soon were adventured, chiefly by the British and the Dutch, from which ventures grew up not merely the greatest oil business of two centuries, not to cease till the arrival of kerosene, but also a bitter rivalry between two neighbor nations, Britain and the Netherlands. The story is fascinating, but complicated.

The next formal voyage to reach the Indies by way of the pole was that of C. J. Phipps in 1773, the one that surpassed Hudson by 30 miles. The last noteworthy attempt was under David Buchan, who sailed from Britain in 1818 with instructions to proceed by way of the pole to the Sandwich (Hawaiian) Islands, where he would spend the winter. He was to return the following summer by way of the pole, or by another route which he might prefer. But he reached only 80 degrees 37 minutes in the Spitsbergen vicinity, thus about midway between the farthest points of Hudson and Phipps. His ships were back safe in the autumn; they had been on the voyage from April to October.

The Attainment of the North Pole

THE ATTAINMENT OF
THE NORTH POLE

CHAPTER 15

W<small>HEN</small> men ceased thinking of reaching the Indies by way of the pole, they started thinking about reaching the pole. Nine years after Buchan returned from the last formal attempt to reach the Pacific by way of north latitude 90 degrees, Sir Edward Parry made the first attempt on the pole, a word which thereafter tended to be spelled in the accounts of explorers with a capital P, as the supreme goal of northward endeavor.

For reasons explained and implied in our section on the Northwest Passage, Parry was in his time the commanding figure of Arctic exploration, to remain permanently a giant among the giants. With the experience of four Arctic voyages, three of which he had commanded, he decided to attempt the Pole, and selected the Spitsbergen approach, for there he could sail farther north than on any other margin of the Arctic— thanks to the great bay northward into the floating sea ice which is created by the melting power of the Gulf Stream or warm North Atlantic drift. Then, using boats shod along their keels with strips of iron and dragged by sturdy British tars, he would advance northward, using the boats as sledges whenever he faced ice, using them as boats again when he came to water.

Here Parry tells his own story from the point where his ship could go no further, taken from the London, 1828, quarto edition of his *Narrative of an Attempt to Reach the North Pole in Boats Fitted for the Purpose, and Attached to His Majesty's Ship* Hecla, *in the year MDCCCXXVII.*

567

Parry and the North Pole

On the evening of the eighteenth [of June, 1827], while standing in for the high land to the eastward of Verlegen Hook [Spitsbergen], which, with due attention to the lead, may be approached with safety, we perceived from the crow's-nest what appeared a low point, possibly affording some shelter for the ship, and which seemed to answer to an indentation of the coast laid down in an old Dutch chart, and there called Treurenburg Bay.

[June 19] On the following morning I proceeded to examine the place, accompanied by Lieutenant Ross in a second boat, and, to our great joy, found it a considerable bay, with one part affording excellent landlocked anchorage, and, what was equally fortunate, sufficiently clear of ice to allow the ship to enter. Having sounded the entrance, and determined on the anchorage, we returned to the ship to bring her in; and I cannot describe the satisfaction which the information of our success communicated to every individual on board.

The main object of our enterprise now appeared almost within our grasp, and everybody seemed anxious to make up by renewed exertions for the time we had unavoidably lost.

[June 20] The ship was towed and warped in with the greatest alacrity, and at 1.40 A.M. on the twentieth, we dropped the anchor in Hecla Cove, in thirteen fathoms, on a bottom of very tenacious blue clay, and made some hawsers fast to the land ice which still filled all the upper part of the bay. After resting a few hours, we sawed a canal ¼ mile in length, through which the ship was removed into a better situation, a bower cable taken on shore and secured to the rocks, and an anchor with the chain cable laid out the other way.

[June 21] On the morning of the twenty-first, we hauled the launch up on the beach, it being my intention to direct such resources of every kind to be landed as would render our party wholly independent of the ship, either for returning to England or for wintering, in case of the ship being driven to sea by the ice—a contingency against which, in these regions, no precaution can altogether provide.

I directed Lieutenant Foster, upon whom the charge of the *Hecla* was now to devolve, to land without delay the necessary stores, keeping the ship seaworthy by taking in an equal weight of ballast; and as soon as he should be satisfied of her security from ice, to proceed on the survey of the eastern coast; but should he see reason to doubt her safety with a still further diminution of her crew, to relinquish the survey, and attend exclusively to the ship. I also gave directions that notices should be sent in the course of the summer to the various stations where our depots of provisions were established, acquainting me with the situation and state of the ship, and giving me any other information which might be necessary for my guidance on our return from the northward.

These and other arrangements being completed, I left the ship at 5 P.M., with our two boats, which we named the *Enterprise* and *Endeavour*, Mr. Beverly being attached to my own, and Lieutenant Ross, accompanied by Mr. Bird, in the other. Besides these, I took Lieutenant Crozier in one of the ship's cutters, for the purpose of carrying some of our weight as far as Walden Island, and also a third store of provisions to be deposited on Low Island, as an intermediate station between Walden Island and the ship.

As it was still necessary not to delay our return beyond the end of August, the time originally intended, I took with me only seventy-one days' provisions, which, including the boats and every other article, made up a weight of 260 pounds per man. And as it appeared highly improbable, from what we had seen of the very rugged nature of the ice we should first have to encounter, that either the reindeer, the snowshoes, or the wheels would prove of any service for some time to come, I gave up the idea of taking them.

We however constructed out of the snowshoes four excellent sledges, for dragging a part of our baggage over the ice; and these proved of invaluable service to us, while the rest of the things just mentioned would only have been an incumbrance.

Having received the usual salutation of three cheers from those we left behind, we paddled through a quantity of loose ice at the entrance of the bay, and then steered, in a perfectly open sea and with calm and beautiful weather, for the western part of Low Island, which we reached at half-past two on the morning of the twenty-second.

[June 22] The low beach on which we landed was principally

composed of rounded fragments of limestone, intermixed with some of clay-slate, and several small rounded pieces of pumice stone were also found. The driftwood lined the beach in great quantities, the whole being of the pine tribe, as usual, and a Greenland whaler's harpoon was found lying among it.

Having deposited the provisions, we set off at 4 A.M., paddling watch and watch, to give the people a little rest. It was still quite calm, but there being much ice about the island, and a thick fog coming on, we were several hours groping our way clear of it.

The walruses were here very numerous, lying in herds upon the ice, and plunging into the water to follow us as we passed. The sound they utter is something between bellowing and very loud snorting, which, together with their grim, bearded countenances and long tusks, make them appear, as indeed they are, rather formidable enemies to contend with. Under our present circumstances, we were very well satisfied not to molest them, for they would soon have destroyed our boats if one had been wounded; but I believe they are never the first to make the attack.

[June 23] We landed upon the ice still attached to Walden Island at 3:30 A.M. on the twenty-third. Our flat-bottomed boats rowed heavily with their loads, but proved perfectly safe and very comfortable. The men being much fatigued, we rested here some hours, and after making our final arrangements with Lieutenant Crozier, parted with him at three in the afternoon, and set off for Little Table Island. Finding there was likely to be so much open water in this neighborhood in the autumn, I sent directions to Lieutenant Foster to have a spare boat deposited at Walden Island, in time for our return, in case of any accident happening to ours.

The land ice, which still adhered to the Seven Islands, was very little more broken off than when the *Hecla* had been here a week before, and we rowed along its margin a part of the way to Little Table Island, where we arrived at 10 P.M. We here examined and resecured the provisions left on shore, having found our depot at Walden Island disturbed by the bears.

The prospect to the northward at this time was very favorable, there being only a small quantity of loose ice in sight; and the weather still continuing calm and clear, with the sea as smooth as a mirror, we set out without delay at half-past ten, taking our final leave of the Spitsbergen shores, as we hoped, for at least two months.

Steering due north, we made good progress, our latitude by the sun's meridian altitude at midnight being 80 degrees 51 minutes 13 seconds. A beautifully colored rainbow appeared for some time, without any appearance of rain falling.

We observed that a considerable current was setting us to the eastward just after leaving the land, so that we had made a north-northeast course, distance about 10 miles, when we met with some ice, which soon becoming too close for further progress, we landed upon a high hummock to obtain a better view. We here perceived that the ice was close to the northward, but to the westward discovered some open water, which we reached after two or three hours' paddling, and found it a wide expanse, in which we sailed to the northward without obstruction, a fresh breeze having sprung up from the southwest.

The weather soon after became very thick, with continued snow, requiring great care in looking out for the ice, which made its appearance after two hours' run, and gradually became closer, till at length we were stopped by it at noon, and obliged to haul the boats upon a small floe piece, our latitude by observation being 81 degrees 12 minutes 51 seconds.

Our plan of traveling being nearly the same throughout this excursion after we first entered upon the ice, I may at once give some account of our usual mode of proceeding.

It was my intention to travel wholly at night, and to rest by day, there being, of course, constant daylight in these regions during the summer season. The advantages of this plan, which was occasionally deranged by circumstances, consisted first, in our avoiding the intense and oppressive glare from the snow during the time of the sun's greatest altitude, so as to prevent, in some degree, the painful inflammation in the eyes called snow blindness, which is common in all snowy countries. We also thus enjoyed greater warmth during the hours of rest, and had a better chance of drying our clothes; besides which, no small advantage was derived from the snow being harder at night for traveling.

The only disadvantage of this plan was that the fogs were somewhat more frequent and more thick by night than by day, though even in this respect there was less difference than might have been supposed, the temperature during the twenty-four hours undergoing but little variation.

This traveling by night and sleeping by day so completely inverted the natural order of things that it was difficult to persuade ourselves of the reality. Even the officers and myself, who were all furnished with pocket chronometers, could not always bear in mind at what part of the twenty-four hours we had arrived; and there were several of the men who declared, and I believe truly, that they never knew night from day during the whole excursion.

When we rose in the evening, we commenced our day by prayers, after which we took off our fur sleeping dresses, and put on those for traveling, the former being made of camlet lined with raccoon skin, and the latter of strong blue box cloth. We made a point of always putting on the same stockings and boots for traveling in, whether they had dried during the day or not; and I believe it was only in five or six instances at the most that they were not either still wet or hard-frozen. This indeed, was of no consequence, beyond the discomfort of first putting them on in this state, as they were sure to be thoroughly wet in a quarter of an hour after commencing our journey; while on the other hand, it was of vital importance to keep dry things for sleeping in.

Being "rigged" for traveling, we breakfasted upon warm cocoa and biscuit, and after stowing the things in the boats and on the sledges, so as to secure them as much as possible from wet, we set off on our day's journey, and usually traveled from five to five and a half hours, then stopped an hour to dine, and again traveled four, five, or even six hours, according to circumstances.

After this we halted for the night—as we called it, though it was usually early in the morning—selecting the largest surface of ice we happened to be near for hauling the boats on, in order to avoid the danger of its breaking up by coming in contact with other masses, and also to prevent drift as much as possible. The boats were placed close alongside each other, with their sterns to the wind, the snow or wet cleared out of them, and the sails, supported by the bamboo masts and three paddles, placed over them as awnings, an entrance being left at the bow.

Every man then immediately put on dry stockings and fur boots, after which we set about the necessary repairs of boats, sledges, or clothes; and after serving the provisions for the succeeding day, we went to supper. Most of the officers and men then smoked their pipes, which served to dry the boats and awnings very much, and usually raised the temperature of our lodgings 10° or 15°.

This part of the twenty-four hours was often a time, and the only one, of real enjoyment to us; the men told their stories and "fought all their battles o'er again," and the labors of the day, unsuccessful as they too often were, were forgotten. A regular watch was set during our resting time, to look out for bears or for the ice breaking up round us, as well as to attend to the drying of the clothes, each man alternately taking this duty for one hour.

We then concluded our day with prayers, and having put on our fur dresses, lay down to sleep with a degree of comfort which perhaps few persons would imagine possible under such circumstances, our chief inconvenience being that we were somewhat pinched for room, and therefore obliged to stow rather closer than was quite agreeable.

The temperature while we slept was usually from 36° to 45°, according to the state of the external atmosphere; but on one or two occasions, in calm and warm weather, it rose as high as 60° to 66°, obliging us to throw off a part of our fur dress.

After we had slept seven hours, the man appointed to boil the cocoa roused us, when it was ready, by the sound of a bugle, when we commenced our day in the manner before described.

Our allowance of provisions for each man per day was as follows:

Biscuit . . . . 10 ounces
Pemmican[1] . . . . 9 ounces

---

[1] This appears to be the first recorded use of pemmican on a polar expedition outside North America. The first use in polar exploration appears to have been by Parry's friend Sir John Franklin on his Canadian overland expedition

Sweetened cocoa powder .... 1 ounce to make 1 pint
Rum .... 1 gill
Tobacco .... 3 ounces per week

Our fuel consisted entirely of spirits of wine, of which 2 pints formed our daily allowance, the cocoa being cooked in an iron boiler over a shallow iron lamp with seven wicks—a simple apparatus which answered our purpose remarkably well. We usually found 1 pint of the spirits of wine sufficient for preparing our breakfast, that is for heating 26 pints of water, though it always commenced from the temperature of 32°.

If the weather was calm and fair, this quantity of fuel brought it to the boiling point in about an hour and a quarter; but more generally the wicks began to go out before it had reached 200°. This, however, made a very comfortable meal to persons situated as we were. Such, with very little variation, was our regular routine during the whole of this excursion.

[June 24] We set off on our first journey over the ice at 10 P.M. on the twenty-fourth, Table Island bearing south-southwest, and a fresh breeze blowing from west-southwest, with thick fog, which afterward changed to rain. The bags of pemmican were placed upon the sledges, and the bread in the boats, with the intention of securing the latter from wet; but this plan we were very soon obliged to relinquish.

We now commenced upon very slow and laborious traveling, the pieces of ice being of small extent and very rugged, obliging us to make three journeys, and sometimes four, with the boats and baggage, and to launch several times across narrow pools of water. This, however, was nothing more than we had expected to encounter at the margin of the ice and for some distance within it and every individual exerted himself to the very utmost, with the hope of the sooner reaching the main or field ice.

[June 25] We stopped to dine at 5 A.M. on the twenty-fifth, having made, by our log (which we kept very carefully, mark-

---

of 1825-27. These were all summer journeys, and pemmican (extensively used by the North American fur trade after about 1780) was, indeed, even long after Parry, employed chiefly as a summer food. Its first use on an exploratory winter journey may have been by Dr. John Rae of the Hudson's Bay Company in 1846-47 during his search for the lost third Franklin expedition.

ing the courses by compass, and estimating the distances), about 2½ miles of northing; and again setting forward, proceeded till 11 A.M., when we halted to rest, our latitude by observation at noon being 81 degrees 15 minutes 13 seconds.

Setting out again at half-past nine in the evening, we found our way to lie over nothing but small loose rugged masses of ice, separated by little pools of water, obliging us constantly to launch and haul up the boats, each of which operations required them to be unloaded, and occupied nearly a quarter of an hour.

[June 26] It came on to rain very hard on the morning of the twenty-sixth; and finding we were making very little progress (having advanced not more than half a mile in four hours), and that our clothes would be soon wet through, we halted at half-past one and took shelter under the awnings. The weather improving at six o'clock, we again moved forward, and traveled till a quarter past eleven, when we hauled the boats up on the only tolerably large floe piece in sight.

The rain had very much increased the quantity of water lying upon the ice, of which nearly half the surface was now covered with numberless little ponds of various shapes and extent. It is a remarkable fact that we had already experienced in the course of this summer more rain than during the whole of seven previous summers *taken together*, though passed in latitudes from 7 degrees to 15 degrees lower than this.

A great deal of the ice over which we passed today presented a very curious appearance and structure, being composed on its upper surface of numberless irregular needlclike crystals placed vertically and nearly close together, their length varying, in different pieces of ice, from 5 to 10 inches, and their breadth in the middle about ½ inch, but pointed at both ends. The upper surface of ice having this structure sometimes looks like greenish velvet; a vertical section of it, which frequently occurs at the margin of floes, resembles, while it remains compact, the most beautiful satin spar, and asbestos, when falling to pieces.

At this early part of the season, this kind of ice afforded pretty firm footing, but as the summer advanced, the needles became more loose and movable, rendering it extremely fatiguing to walk over them, besides cutting our boots and feet, on which account the men called them "penknives" [now usually called candle ice].

It appeared probable to us that this peculiarity might be produced by the heavy drops of rain piercing their way downward through the ice, and thus separating the latter into needles of the form above described, rather than to any regular crystallization when in the act of freezing; which supposition seemed the more reasonable as the needles are always placed in a vertical position, and never occur except from the upper surface downward.

We pursued our journey at 9:30 P.M., with the wind at northeast and thick weather, the ice being so much in motion as to make it very dangerous to cross with loaded boats, the masses being all very small. Indeed, when we came to the margin of the floe piece on which we had slept, we saw no road by which we could safely proceed, and therefore preferred remaining where we were to the risk of driving back to the southward on one of the smaller masses.

On this account we halted at midnight, having waded three-quarters of a mile through water from 2 to 5 inches deep upon the ice. The thermometer was at 33°. In the course of this short journey, we saw several rotges and dovekies, and a few kittiwakes, ivory gulls, and mallemucks.

[June 27] The weather continued so thick that we could only see a few yards around us; but the wind backing to the southward, and beginning to open out the loose ice at the edge of the floe, we proceeded at 10:30 P.M., and after crossing several small pieces, came to the first tolerably heavy ice we had yet seen, but all broken up into masses of small extent.

[June 28] At 7 A.M. on the twenty-eighth, we came to a floe covered with high and rugged hummocks, which opposed a formidable obstacle to our progress, occurring in two or three successive tiers, so that we had no sooner crossed one than another presented itself. Over one of these we hauled the boats with extreme difficulty, by a "standing pull," and the weather being then so thick that we could see no pass across the next tier, we were obliged to stop at 9 A.M.

While performing this laborious work, which required the boats to be got up and down places almost perpendicular,

James Parker, my coxswain, received a severe contusion in his back, by the boat falling upon him from a hummock; and the boats were constantly subject to very heavy blows, but sustained no damage.

The weather continued very foggy during the day, but a small lane of water opening out at no great distance from the margin of the floe, we launched the boats, at eight in the evening, among loose drift ice, and after some time landed on a small floe to the eastward, the only one in sight, with the hope of its leading to the northward. It proved so rugged that we were obliged to make three and sometimes four journeys with the boats and provisions, and this by a very circuitous route; so that the road by which we made a mile of northing was full 1½ miles in length, and over this we had to travel at least five and sometimes seven times.

[June 29] Thus, when we halted to dine at 2 A.M., after six hours' severe toil and much risk to the men and boats, we had only accomplished about 1¼ miles in a north-northeast direction.

After dining we proceeded again till half-past six, and then halted, very much fatigued with our day's work, and having made 2½ miles of northing.

One of the carpenter's mates was a good deal hurt by a loaded sledge running against him, which laid him up for a day or two.

We were here in latitude, by account, 81 degrees 23 minutes, and in longitude, by the chronometers, 21 degrees 32 minutes 34 seconds east, in which situation the variation of the magnetic needle was observed to be 15 degrees 31 minutes, westerly. We now enjoyed the first sunshine since our entering the ice, and a great enjoyment it was after so much thick and wet weather.

We rose at 4:30 P.M., in the hope of pursuing our journey, but after hauling the boats to the edge of the floe, found such a quantity of loose rugged ice to the northward of us that there was no possibility, for the present, of getting across or through it. Soon afterward the whole of it became in motion, and driving down upon the floe, obliged us to retreat from the margin, and wait for some favorable change. We here tried for soundings, but found no bottom with 200 fathoms of line.

The weather was beautifully clear, and the wind moderate from the southwest. From this situation we saw the easternmost of the Seven Islands, bearing south by west, but Little Table Island, though more to the northward, yet being less high, was not in sight. Observing a small opening at 10:30 P.M., we launched the boats, and hauled them across several pieces of ice, some of them being very light and much decayed.

Our latitude by the sun's meridian altitude at midnight was 81 degrees 23 minutes, so that we had made only eight miles of northing since our last observation at noon on the twenty-fifth.

[Parry does not seem to realize it yet, but they are being defeated by the southward current. Part of what they make good through travel is being taken from them by the drift while they are in camp on the moving floes.]

[June 30] The thirtieth commenced with snowy and inclement weather, which soon rendered the atmosphere so thick that we could no longer see our way, obliging us to halt till 2 P.M., when we crossed several small pools with great labor and loss of time. We had generally very light ice this day, with some heavy rugged pieces intermixed; and when hauling across these we had sometimes to cut with axes a passage for the boats among the hummocks. We also dragged them through a great many pools of fresh water, to avoid the necessity of going round them.

The wind freshening up from the south-southwest, we afterward found the ice gradually more and more open, so that in the course of the day we made by rowing, though by a very winding channel, 5 miles of northing; but were again stopped by the ice soon after midnight, and obliged to haul up on the first mass that we could gain, the ice having so much motion that we narrowly escaped being "nipped."

We had passed, during this day's journey, a great deal of light ice, but for the first time one heavy floe, from 2 to 3 miles in length, under the lee of which we found the most open water. A number of rotges and ivory gulls were seen about the "holes" of water, and now and then a very small seal.

[July 1] We set out again at 11:30 A.M., the wind still fresh from the southwest, and some snow falling; but it was more than an hour before we could get away from the small piece of ice on which we slept, the masses beyond being so broken up, and so much in motion, that we could not at first venture to launch the boats. Our latitude, observed at noon, was 81 degrees 30 minutes 41 seconds.

After crossing several pieces, we at length got into a good "lead" of water, 4 or 5 miles in length, two or three of which, as on the preceding day, occurred under the lee of a floe, being the second we had yet seen that deserved that name. We then passed over four or five small floes, and across the pools of water that lay betwixt them.

The ice was now less broken up, and sometimes tolerably level; but from 6 to 18 inches of soft snow lay upon it in every part, making the traveling very fatiguing, and obliging us to make at least two and sometimes three journeys with our loads. We now find it absolutely necessary to lighten the boats as much as possible by putting the bread bags on the sledges, on account of the "runners" of the boats sinking so much deeper into the snow; but our bread ran a great risk of being wetted by this plan.

As soon as we landed on a floe piece, Lieutenant Ross and myself generally went on ahead, while the boats were unloading and hauling up, in order to select the easiest road for them. The sledges then followed in our track, Messrs. Beverly and Bird accompanying them, by which the snow was much trodden down, and the road thus improved for the boats.

As soon as we arrived at the other end of the floe, or came to any difficult place, we mounted one of the highest hummocks of ice near at hand (many of which were from 15 to 25 feet above the sea) in order to obtain a better view around us; and nothing could well exceed the dreariness which such a view presented. The eye wearied itself in vain to find any object but ice and sky to rest upon, and even the latter was often hidden from our view by the dense and dismal fogs which so generously prevailed.

For want of variety, the most trifling circumstance engaged a more than ordinary share of our attention—a passing gull, or a mass of ice of unusual form, became objects which our situation and circumstances magnified into ridiculous importance—and we have since often smiled to remember the eager interest with which we regarded many insignificant occurrences. It may well be imagined, then, how cheering it was to turn from this scene of inanimate desolation to our two little boats in the distance, to see the moving figures of our men winding with their sledges among the hummocks, and to hear once more the sound of human voices breaking the stillness of this icy wilderness.

In some cases Lieutenant Ross and myself took separate routes to try the ground, which kept us almost continually floundering among deep snow and water.

The sledges having then been brought up as far as we had explored, we all went back for the boats, each boat's crew, when the road was tolerable, dragging their own, and the officers laboring equally hard with the men. It was thus we proceeded for 9 miles out of every 10 that we traveled over ice; for it was very rarely indeed that we met with a surface sufficiently level and hard to drag all our loads at one journey, and in a great many instances during the first fortnight, we had to make three journeys with the boats and baggage; that is, to traverse the same road five times over.

We halted at 11 P.M. on the first, having traversed from 10 to 11 miles, and made good, by our account, 7½ in a north by west direction.

[July 2] We again set forward at 10 A.M. on the second, the weather being calm and the sun oppressively warm, though with a thick fog. The temperature in the shade was 35° at noon, and only 47° in the sun; but this, together with the glare from the snow, produced so painful a sensation in most of our eyes as to make it necessary to halt at 1 P.M., to avoid being blinded. We therefore took advantage of this warm weather to let the men wash themselves, and mend and dry their clothes, and then set out again at half-past three. The snow was, however, so soft as to take us up to our knees at almost every other step, and frequently still deeper; so that we were sometimes five minutes together in moving a single empty boat with all our united strength.

It being impossible to proceed under these circumstances, I determined, by degrees, to fall into our night traveling again, from which we had of late insensibly deviated. We therefore halted at half-past five, the weather being now very clear and warm, and many of the people's eyes beginning to fail.

[July 3] We did not set out again till after midnight, with the intention of giving the snow time to harden after so warm a day; but we found it still so soft as to make the traveling very fatiguing.

Our way lay at first across a number of small loose pieces, most of which were from 5 to 20 yards apart, or just sufficiently separated to give us all the labor of launching and hauling up the boats without the advantage of making any progress by water; while we crossed, in other instances, from mass to mass by laying the boats over, as bridges, by which the men and baggage passed. By these means, we at length reached a floe about a mile in length, in a northern direction; but it would be difficult to convey an adequate idea of the labor required to traverse it.

The average depth of snow upon the level parts was about 5 inches, under which lay water 4 or 5 inches deep; but the moment we approached a hummock, the depth to which we sank increased to 3 feet or more, rendering it difficult at times to obtain sufficient footing for one leg to enable us to extricate the other.

The pools of fresh water had now also become very large, some of them being ¼ mile in length, and their depth above our knees. Through these we were prevented taking the sledges, for fear of wetting all our provisions; but we preferred transporting the boats across them, notwithstanding the severe cold of the snow water, the bottom being harder for the "runners" to slide upon. On this kind of road we were, in one instance, above two hours in proceeding a distance of 100 yards.

We halted at 6:30 A.M. to dine, and to empty our boots and wring our stockings—which, to *our* feelings, was almost like putting on dry ones—and again set out in an hour, getting at length into a "lane" of water 1¼ miles long, in a north-northeast direction. We halted for the night at half an hour before midnight, the people being almost exhausted with a laborious day's work, and our distance made good to the northward not exceeding 2¼ miles.

We allowed ourselves this night a hot supper, consisting of a pint of soup per man, made of an ounce of pemmican each, and eight or ten birds which we had killed in the course of the last week; and this was a luxury which persons thus situated could perhaps alone duly appreciate. We had seen in the course of the day a few rotges, a dovekie, a loon, a mallemuck, and two or three very small seals.

We rose and breakfasted at 9 P.M.; but the weather had gradually become so inclement and thick, with snow, sleet, and a fresh breeze from the eastward, that we could neither have seen our way nor have avoided getting wet through, had we moved.

[July 4] We therefore remained under cover; and it was as well that we did so, for the snow soon after changed to heavy rain, and the wind increased to a fresh gale, which unavoidably detained us till 7.30 P.M. on the fourth, when we found on setting out that there was nothing but loose drift ice for us to haul over; nor from the highest hummock could we discover a single floe, much less a field, toward which to direct our course. On two or three small floe pieces which we did cross, none of which were ¼ mile in extent, we found the hummocks occurring, ridge after ridge, with only 50 or 60 yards of level ice between them. The rain had produced even a greater effect than the sun in softening the snow.

Lieutenant Ross and myself, in performing our pioneering duty, were frequently so beset in it that sometimes, after trying in vain to extricate our legs, we were obliged to sit quietly down for a short time to rest ourselves, and then make another attempt; and the men in dragging the sledges were often under the necessity of crawling upon all fours to make any progress at all. Nor would any kind of snowshoes have been of the least service, but rather an incumbrance to us, for the surface was so irregular that they would have thrown us down at every other step.

We had hitherto made use of the Lapland shoes, or *kamoogas*, for walking in, which are excellent for dry snow; but there being now so much water upon the ice, we substituted the Eskimo boots which had been made in Greenland expressly for our use, and which are far superior to any others for this kind of traveling.

[July 5] Just before halting at 6 A.M. on the fifth, the ice at the margin of the floe broke while the men were handing the provisions out of the boats; and we narrowly escaped the loss of a bag of cocoa, which fell overboard, but fortunately rested on a "tongue." The bag being made of Mackintosh's waterproof canvas, the cocoa did not suffer the slightest injury.

We had seen, in the course of our last journey, a few rotges, a loon, an ivory gull, a mallemuck, and a tern (*Sterna Arctica*). We here observed the dip of the magnetic needle to be 82 degrees 4.7 minutes and the variation 13 degrees 16 minutes westerly, the latitude being 81 degrees 45 minutes 15 seconds and the longitude, by chronometers, 24 degrees 23 minutes east, by which we found that we had been drifted considerably to the eastward. In this situation we tried for soundings with 400 fathoms of line without reaching the bottom. The temperature at that depth, by Six's thermometer, was 30°, that at the surface, at the time, being 32½°, and of the air 34°.

We rose at 5 P.M., the weather being clear and fine, with a moderate breeze from the south. No land was in sight from the highest hummocks, nor could we perceive anything but broken loose ice in any direction. We hauled across several pieces which were scarcely fit to bear the weight of the boats, and in such places used the precaution of dividing our baggage, so that in case of the ice breaking or turning over, we should not lose all at once.

The farther we proceeded, the more the ice was broken; indeed, it was much more so here than we had found it since first entering the "pack." The labor required to drag the boats over the hummocks, and from one mass to another, was so great that we were obliged to have recourse to what seamen call a bowline haul for many minutes together, which so exhausted the men that it was necessary for them every now and then to sit down and take breath.

After stopping at midnight to dine, and to obtain the meridian altitude, we passed over a floe full of hummocks, 1½ miles in length; but any kind of floe was relief to us after the constant difficulty we had experienced in passing over loose ice. Many of the hummocks were smooth regular cones, much resembling in shape the aromatic pastilles sold by chemists. This roundness and regularity of form indicate age, all the more recent ones being sharp and angular.

We had now for several days ceased to observe any ice covered with mud or soil, called by the sailors dirty ice, which was frequently met with during the first week after our leaving the open water. We often, however, noticed parts of the ice which at a distance appeared of an iron-rust color; but on coming near it, and taking up some in the hand, we could detect nothing with a magnifying glass.[2]

[July 6] After several hours of very beautiful weather, a thick fog came on early on the morning of the sixth, and at 5 A.M. we halted, having got to the end of the floe and only made good 2½ miles to the northward. The men were greatly fatigued by this day's exertions, and we served an extra ounce of bread and one of pemmican for their supper, an addition to the original allowance which we were frequently obliged to make after this time to prevent our going to bed hungry.

The fog continued very thick all day; but being unwilling to stop on this account, we set out again at half-past six in the evening, and passed over several small flat pieces with no great difficulty, but with much loss of time in launching and hauling up the boats.

[July 7] The fog still continued very thick, and the ice of the same broken kind as before, till toward the end of our day's journey we landed on the only really level floe we had yet met with. It was, however, only ¾ mile in length, but being almost clear of snow, afforded such good traveling that although much fatigued at the time, we hauled the boats, and all the baggage, across it at one journey, at the rate of about 2 miles an hour, and halted at the northern margin at 5 A.M. on the seventh.

The prospect beyond was still very unfavorable, and at eight in the evening, when we again launched the boats, there

---

[2] What they were observing was "pink snow," produced by a tiny plant which grows in the snow both out at sea and on land. When the slant of the sun is right, a snowbank may look strongly pink at 10 to 30 or more yards, but will seem white when you reach it.

was not a piece of large or level ice to be seen in a northern direction. After an hour, we arrived at a very difficult pass, which required all our strength, as well as care, to accomplish. We had first to launch the boats into the water over a high and rugged margin, and then to haul them across a number of irregular and ill-connected masses, sometimes making bridges of them for the conveyance of ourselves and our provisions, and once having to cut a passage through a ridge of hummocks which lay across our path. We were thus more than two hours in proceeding a distance not exceeding 150 yards.

Notwithstanding · these discouraging difficulties, the men labored with great cheerfulness and good will, being animated with the hope of soon reaching the more continuous body which had been considered as composing the "main ice" to the northward of Spitsbergen, and which Captain Lutwidge [of the Phipps expedition], about the same meridian and more than a degree to the southward of this, describes as "one continued plain of smooth, unbroken ice, bounded only by the horizon."

They never did reach the "main ice," in the sense of finding any that gave them reasonable prospects of an advance that would amount to much.

The rest of the Parry tale, in its description, is more of the same. The rain fell in torrents they had not expected, the patches of open water that permitted rowing were seldom a mile wide, the ice between the leads and pools was broken, hummocky. The one improvement was in that the melting power of the rain continually lessened the depth of the snow in which they had been floundering between the pressure ridges. The water from the melting of the sea ice, and from the rain and snow, made lakes upon the larger floes through which they waded from ankle-deep to thigh-deep "and which always afforded us a pure and abundant supply" of drinking water.

The quantities of rain were a surprise. On July 15 "it rained so hard and so incessantly that it would have been impossible to move without a complete drenching. I had never before seen rain in the polar regions to be compared to this, which continued, without intermission, for twenty-one hours, sometimes falling with great violence and in large drops."

The warmth of the weather surprised him, too. On July 16 the thermometer stood at 38° in the shade, "the same thermometer held against the black painted side of the boat rose to 58½°." The next day "it was so warm in the sun, though the temperature in the shade [doubtless only a foot or two above the ice] was only 35°, that the tar was running out of the seams of the boat, and a blackened bulb held against the paintwork raised the thermometer to 72°."

By July 17 Parry was worrying about the drift that carried him back almost as fast as he could move forward. "The latitude, observed at midnight, was 82 degrees 32 minutes 15 seconds, nearly the same as at noon, though we had certainly walked 1 mile to the northward."

On July 18 we have an early step toward what eventually became a full-fledged technique of polar exploration—the method of living on the country, living by forage. On that day the exhausted men were "put into good spirits by our having killed a small seal which, the following night, gave us an excellent supper. . . . We also considered it a great prize, on account of its blubber, which gave us fuel sufficient for cooking six hot messes for our whole party, though the animal only weighed 30 pounds in the whole"—thus a baby seal.

Parry was conscious that the slow progress he was making would be neutralized or turned into a loss except for the continued good fortune that they had been having, southerly winds which inhibited the tendency of the ice to move south with the current. On July 19, a good month from the beginning of their struggle with the moving floes, Parry wrote:

"It is remarkable that we had hitherto been so much favored by the wind that only a single northerly one, and that very moderate and of short duration, appears upon our journals up to this day, when a breeze sprung up from that quarter, accompanied by a thick fog.

"Though this wind appeared to be the means of opening several lanes of water, of which we gladly took advantage when we set out at 8 P.M., yet we were aware that any such effect could only be produced by the ice drifting to the southward, and would therefore have willingly dispensed with this apparent facility in proceeding."

The foreboding came true. On July 20 Parry said in his diary: "How great was our mortification in finding that our latitude, by observation at noon, was . . . less than 5 miles to the northward of our place at noon on the seventeenth, since which time we had certainly traveled 12 in that direction."

Only one thing cheered them now, the confirmation of the discovery that they could contribute to their own support. On July 21 Parry wrote:

"Our sportsmen had the good fortune to kill another seal today, rather larger than the first, which again proved a most welcome addition to our provisions and fuel.

"Indeed, after this supply of the latter, we were enabled to allow ourselves every night a pint of warm water for supper, each man making his own soup from such a portion of his bread and pemmican as he could save from dinner."

There were temporary encouragements in good speed, canceled soon by difficult travel and by the southward drift. One of the good spells was July 22:

"Our traveling tonight was the very best we had during this excursion, for though we had to launch and haul up the boats frequently, an operation which under the most favorable circumstances necessarily occupies much time, yet the floes being large and tolerably level, and some good lanes of water occurring, we made, according to the most moderate calculation, between 10 and 11 miles in a north-northeast direction, and traversed a distance of about 17."

At first they rejoiced in this marvelous progress. "In proportion, then, to the hopes we had begun to entertain, was our disappointment in finding, at noon, that we were in latitude 82 degrees 43 minutes 5 seconds, or not quite 4 miles to the northward of yesterday's observation, instead of the 10 or 11 which we had traveled." Their sleep was restless from the feeling that as they slept they were losing the ground over which they had struggled wearily.

Soon they were losing more than they gained. On July 26, after four days of valiant struggle with difficult ice and small pools of water, they took the next observation and Parry found "we had lost by drift no less than 13½ miles; for we were now more than 3 miles to the *southward* of that observation, though we had certainly traveled between 10 and 11 due north in this interval."

Parry saw the handwriting on the wall and says for July 26:

More of Parry's Journey

It had for some time past been too evident that the nature of the ice with which we had to contend was such, and its drift to the southward, especially with a northerly wind, so great, as to put beyond our reach anything but a very moderate share of success in traveling to the northward. Still, however, we had been anxious to reach the highest latitude which our means would allow, and with this view, although our whole object had long become unattainable, had pushed on to the northward for thirty-five days, or until half our resources were expended and the middle of the season arrived. For the last few days, the 83d parallel was the limit to which we had ventured to extend our hopes; but even this expectation had become considerably weakened since the setting in of the last northerly wind, which continued to drive us to the southward during the necessary hours of rest nearly as much as we could gain by eleven or twelve hours of daily labor.

Had our success been at all proportionate to our exertions, it was my full intention to have proceeded a few days beyond the middle of the period for which we were provided, trusting to the resources we expected to find at Table Island. But this was so far from being the case that I could not but consider it as incurring useless fatigue to the officers and men, and unnecessary wear and tear for the boats, to persevere any longer in the attempt. I determined, therefore, on giving the people one entire day's rest, which they very much needed, and time to wash and mend their clothes while the officers were occupied in making all the observations which might be interesting in this latitude, and then to set out on our return on the following day.

Having communicated my intentions to the people, who were all much disappointed in finding how little their labors had effected, we set about our respective occupations, and were much favored by a remarkably fine day.

The dip of the magnetic needle was here 82 degrees 21.6 minutes, and the variation 18 degrees 10 minutes westerly, our latitude being 82 degrees 40 minutes 23 seconds and our longitude 19 degrees 25 minutes east of Greenwich.

The highest latitude we reached was probably at 7 A.M. on the twenty-third, when after the midnight observation we traveled, by our account, something more than 1½ miles, which would carry us a little beyond 82 degrees 45 minutes. . . .

At the extreme point of our journey, our distance from the *Hecla* was only 172 miles in a south-8 degrees west direction. To accomplish this distance we had traversed, by our reckoning, 292 miles, of which about 100 were performed by water, previously to our entering the ice.

As we traveled by far the greater part of our distance on the ice three and not infrequently five times over, we may safely multiply the length of the road by two and a half, so that our whole distance, on a very moderate calculation, amounted to 580 geographical or 668 statute miles, being nearly sufficient to have reached the pole in a direct line.

Up to this period we had been particularly fortunate in the preservation of our health. . . .

Our ensigns and pendants were displayed during the day; and sincerely as we regretted·not having been able to hoist the British flag in the highest latitude to which we had aspired, we shall perhaps be excused in having felt some little pride in being the bearers of it to a parallel considerably beyond that mentioned in any other well-authenticated record.

[On the way back the current was with them, and they had the satisfying knowledge that while they slept or rested they were usually moving in the direction of their ship. The ice as it drifted south into more open water also slackened out, with longer leads and wider pools, so that oars and sails were in more and more use, with increased and easier speed. There was additional proof that men can live here by forage. Parry wrote August 7:]

Some small rain fell during the night, but we were fortunate in getting housed before it came down more heavily, which it did the whole day.

A fat she-bear crossed over a lane of water to visit us, and approaching the boats within 20 yards, was killed by Lieutenant Ross. The scene which followed was laughable, even to us who participated in it.

Before the animal had done biting the snow, one of the men was alongside of him with an open knife, and being asked what he was about to do, replied that he was going to cut out his heart and liver to put into the pot, which happened to be then boiling for our supper. In short, before the bear had been dead an hour, all hands of us were employed, to our great satisfaction, in discussing the merits not only of the said heart and liver, but 1 pound per man of the flesh; besides which, some or other of the men were constantly frying steaks during the whole day, over a large fire made of the blubber.

The consequence of all this, and other similar indulgences, necessarily was that some of them complained for several days after of the pains usually arising from indigestion, though they all, amusingly enough, attributed this effect to the quality, and not the quantity, of meat they had eaten. The fact however is that the flesh of the bear is just as wholesome, though not quite as palatable, as any other, and had they eaten moderately of it, as the officers did, they would have suffered no inconvenience whatever.

However, notwithstanding these excesses at first, we were really thankful for this additional supply of meat; for we had observed for some time past that the men were evidently not so strong as before, and would be the better for more sustenance.

[On August 9 came a demonstration that heavy ice floats with the current, because of its lower projections that reach deep, while light ice is blown before the wind, since it is on the surface. Parry says:]

At nine o'clock, the wind having freshened from the southward, and there being only one floe in sight, with immense spaces of open water between the streams of loose ice, I thought it better to halt upon the floe than to incur the probable risk of being driven back should we be obliged to rest on any of the smaller pieces.

It was fortunate that we adopted this plan; for, the wind still increasing from the southward, the loose ice continued to drive past us to the northward during the whole of this and the following day, at the rate of 1½ miles an hour, and we were therefore very glad to retain our present quarters. The weather being wet, with fog, we occupied the men in making additional sails out of our empty bread bags, and in filling the empty vessels with water,[3] since it now appeared more than probable that we were close to the open sea.

At noon on the tenth, we observed in latitude 81 degrees 40 minutes 13 seconds, which was only 4 miles to the northward of our reckoning from the last observation, although there had been almost constantly southing in the wind ever since, and it had been blowing strong from that quarter for the last thirty hours.

This circumstance afforded a last and striking proof of the general tendency of the ice to drift southward, about the meridians on which we had been traveling.

Another bear came toward the boats in the course of the day, and was killed. We were now so abundantly supplied with meat that the men would again have eaten immoderately had we not interposed the necessary authority to prevent them.

[For their emergence upon the open sea Parry has a description enlightening in several ways. He writes for August 11:]

The wind falling toward midnight, we launched the boats at 1:30 A.M. on the eleventh, paddling alternately in large spaces of clear water, and among streams of loose "sailing ice."

We soon afterward observed such indications of an open sea as could not be mistaken, much of the ice being "washed" as by a heavy sea, with small rounded fragments thrown on the surface, and a good deal of "dirty ice" occurring. We also met

---

[3] Parry may have been the first polar explorer to say in a book (his account of an earlier expedition) that sea ice is salty when new, but it gradually freshens with age, and furnishes excellent drinking water when one or more years old.

with several pieces of driftwood and birchbark, the first since we had entered the ice; and the sea was crowded with shrimps and other sea insects, principally the *Clio borealis* and *Argonauta Arctica,* on which numerous birds were feeding.

After passing through a good deal of loose ice, it became gradually more and more open, till at length, at a quarter before 7 A.M., we heard the first sound of the swell under the hollow margins of the ice, and in a quarter of an hour had reached the open sea, which was dashing with heavy surges against the outer masses.

We hauled the boats up on one of these, to eat our last meal upon the ice, and to complete the necessary supply of water for our little voyage to Table Island, from which we were now distant 50 miles, our latitude being 81 degrees 34 minutes and longitude 18.25 degrees east. A light air springing up from the northwest, we again launched the boats, and at 8 A.M. finally quitted the ice, after having taken up our abode upon it for forty-eight days.

The wind dying away, our progress wholly depended on the paddles, which made it very laborious for the men. At 2 P.M. we came to some loose ice a mile or two wide, but so open as scarcely to oblige us to alter our course. At three the temperature of the sea had increased to 36°, the air being the same; and at 9 P.M. both had risen to 38°, not a piece of ice being in sight in any direction.

The weather continued quite calm, and the atmosphere very pleasant to our feelings. We saw a great many seals sporting about, as well as large flocks of rotges, the latter feeding on the *Argonauta Arctica,* which now swarmed in myriads. We also passed a great many pieces of driftwood, and laid in a stock as fuel, lest we should find none at Table Island.

We had some fog during the night, so that we steered entirely by compass, according to our last observations by the chronometers, which proved so correct that at 5 A.M. on the twelfth, on the clearing up of the haze, we made the island right ahead. At 10 A.M., when within 3 miles of it, the temperature of the air was as high as 41°, and the sea still continued at 38°.

At 11 A.M., we reached the island, or rather the rock to the northward of it, where our provisions had been deposited, and

I cannot describe the comfort we experienced in once more feeling a dry and solid footing.

We found that the bears had devoured all the bread (100 pounds), which occasioned a remark among the men, with reference to the quantity of these animals' flesh that we had eaten, that "Bruin was only square with us." We also found that Lieutenant Crozier had been here since we left the island, bringing some materials for repairing our boats, as well as various little luxuries to which we had lately been strangers, and depositing in a copper cylinder a letter from Lieutenant Foster giving me a detailed account of the proceedings of the ship up to the twenty-third of July. 🖌

The rest is fairly conventional detail of how the boat party rejoined their ship. They were safe aboard by the evening of August 21. The expedition spent the rest of the month in further scientific studies of the Spitsbergen islands and waters. Then when they wanted to leave at the end of August they were delayed two weeks by persistent head winds. By September 23 the *Hecla* was in the Orkneys; she was at home in the Thames October 6.

Parry's farthest north of 82 degrees 45 minutes, 445 miles short of the Pole, held the record forty-eight years. The record-breakers were the expedition of Sir George Nares, which, sledging along the north coast of Ellesmere Island in 1875, went 3 miles beyond Parry, to 82 degrees 48 minutes. Next year that party beat its own record by 48 geographical miles, sledging north to 83 degrees 20 minutes over the floating ice of the Polar Sea in winter, when conditions for such travel are relatively favorable, the ice being more sluggish in motion and consisting of larger fields.

The next northing record was established in 1882 by J. B. Lockwood and D. L. Brainard, of A. W. Greely's United States Army expedition, by sledging from Ellesmere Island northeastward along the north coast of Greenland to 83 degrees 24 minutes, thus 4 miles beyond the British record of Nares.

From Nares to Greely, all these advances were made through first proceeding as far north as possible by ship through the narrow waters between Ellesmere Island and Greenland and then sledging along those coasts or out upon the northern sea.

The next two records were made in the general Parry region. Fridtjof Nansen and Frederik Hjalmar Johansen, leaving the drifting *Fram* in the ice northeasterly from the Franz Josef group, sledged northward the winter of 1895 to 86 degrees 12 minutes, breaking the Greely record by 168 geographical miles. That achievement of the Norwegians was excelled five years later by the Italians under the Duke of the Abruzzi, who, led by Umberto Cagni, sledged from a Franz Josef island base to 86 degrees 34 minutes.

Now comes upon the stage the supreme sledge traveler among polar explorers, the determiner of the insularity of Greenland, the discoverer of earth's most northerly land, the establisher of several "farthest norths," the discoverer of the North Pole—Robert Edwin Peary.

By antithesis, Peary calls to mind Byron's verdict on critics that

> A man must serve his time at every trade
> Save censure; critics all are ready made.

This fits the explorers to the extent that most of them go into the field without any such special training as we expect if a man is to be successful as a farmer, a carpenter, or a sailor, let alone in professions like engineering, surgery, or the law. Not so Lieutenant Peary, whose ambition was northern exploration and who worked up through a long and grueling apprenticeship.

True, Peary's last tour of duty before going north was a survey for the Nicaragua Canal, but he had been detailed to that by his naval superiors. At the first opportunity he went north, in 1886, and made a summer excursion up onto the Inland Ice of Greenland, to learn something about conditions of polar work before starting on his own account seriously. What he had been reading for years and what he saw on this reconnaissance combined to make him decide that he would choose polar exploration for his lifework. He may have been the first man in history to make that formal decision.

For several years Peary was now confined to the routine of his naval job by the necessity of earning a living; but he kept reading, studying, lecturing, pulling wires to the end that he might go north again. In 1891 he was finally able to sail. That was the beginning of a series of expeditions during which he spent nine winters in the Arctic, traveled thousands of miles afoot, developed a school of disciples from the outside world, gained the friendship and respect of the local Eskimos, and became, among polar explorers, the first master of the technique of winter travel in cold weather.

Most revolutions have their antecedent causes and early stages that, in retrospect, look like the background to the culminating events. So it was in the revolution in method which Peary carried through to its triumphant conclusion.

In the earliest stage of modern polar exploration journeys were performed during summer, in fear of the northern cold and dread of the coming winter. The first winterings confirmed men's forebodings through the deaths of some or all of the crews. Then came safe winterings, like Parry's on Melville Island, where the men practically hibernated—dug themselves in during the fall to emerge in the spring from houses and housed-over ships.

It was known that Eskimos drove dogs and sledges over the snow, but in Parry's case, on his first expedition the explorers waited till the snow was gone and then dragged carts through the mud. In 1917 the ruts of their wheels could still be seen in the soil of Melville Island.

But gradually Europeans began to learn from the Eskimos. Instead of merely describing the curious native ways, the explorers started trying them, and with progressive success. Sledges took the place of carts, dogs took the place of sailors at the drag ropes, officers ceased to look upon hunting as a sport and began to see it as a means of livelihood. So they devoted less and less time to shooting birds on the wing with fowling pieces and more and more to securing caribou and seals with muskets.

The Hudson's Bay Company men, far to the south, had become expert providers of food through the hunt; but when one of them, Dr. John Rae, applied the technique to real polar work, in his 1846-47 search for the lost third Franklin expedition, and when he did without hardship and easily things which under the orthodox methods of that day would have ended in tragedy, the general feeling was of disapproval—he had demeaned if not disgraced the supersport of polar exploration by going native.

However, the tide was then turning; for when in the same Franklin search a few years later Captain Sir Francis Leopold McClintock applied substantially the Rae method, adapting it to differing conditions, the applause was universal.

There still remained far too much of a hangover of white man's superiority ideas. Eskimo methods were, it is true, used with great success by a few, notably Charles Francis Hall and Frederick Schwatka. But it remained for Peary to apply to Eskimo materials and methods what might perhaps be considered a blend of military-type planning with engineering procedure, and to combine this with systematic use of the Eskimos themselves.

Peary went over completely to the Eskimo view when he replaced the white man's preference for summer travel by the full use of winter. He went all the way over from the practice of the early northern explorers, who began their work in spring and closed it in the fall; for he laid it down as a principle that serious northern journeys should begin in midwinter and close before the thaws of spring.

To apply this principle, he also went over completely to Eskimo ways. The snow house took the place of the tents used formerly. His sledges were of the Eskimo type (though improved through superior materials brought in from the south, as well as lengthened for the special business of crossing narrow leads or traveling on thin ice). His hauling power was Eskimo dogs working in Eskimo harness and hitched the local way. His clothes were of Eskimo cut, made of local skins and worn Eskimo style.

A few things were non-Eskimo, such as glass instead of slits in the snow goggles, and spy glasses for visual aids. The rifle took the place of the Eskimo bow and arrow.

An element which Peary considered crucial in his plans, the food invention pemmican, was borrowed from cousins of the Eskimo Indians—from the Plains Indians of the Kansas-Dakota-Manitoba section of North America.

While Peary was acquiring his matchless polar technique, and making the various geographic discoveries upon which his early fame rested, he had incidentally chalked up three farthest norths—83 degrees 54 minutes in 1900, 84 degrees 17 minutes in 1902, and 87 degrees 6 minutes in 1906, all of them by sledge on the Polar Sea north of Ellesmere Island and Greenland. The last record had placed him only 186 miles short of the Pole.

With so great a master and pioneer there is temptation to go into a sketch of character and a delineation of method as well as a narrative of journeys made from 1891 to 1909. What must be done here is to take all else for granted and to introduce briefly Peary's own story of how, as the culmination of a life of struggle, he finally discovered the North Pole.

Peary's last expedition sailed from New York in the *Roosevelt*, with Robert A. Bartlett as captain, in July 1908. By superb management Bartlett took the ship north through the waters between Greenland and Ellesmere Island to 82 degrees 30 minutes, a world record for a ship under its own power. They wintered at Cape Sheridan on the Ellesmere coast and made forward depots of stores. On March 1, 1909, the journey toward the Pole was begun with 19 sledges, 24 men, and 133 dogs. Peary's companions were 17 Eskimos, 5 white men, and 1 Negro.

There is by now universal admiration for the "Peary method" as a whole, but there has been minor controversy on whether the sledges used were the best possible and whether the Greenland Eskimo type of hitching dogs is the most efficient. On one detail of the outfitting there has been violent controversy —the suitability of pemmican as a ration. Therefore let us listen to what Peary has to say on this food.[4]

Peary on Pemmican

🖎 My last two expeditions carried no food experiments, no wonderful preparations, no condensed products of astonishing powers. I had been through all this in earlier expeditions, and

---

[4] From *The Secrets of Polar Travel*, by Robert E. Peary, copyright 1917, D. Appleton-Century Company.

had tried preparation after preparation, only to find them of no value on the serious northern sledge journey, which was the object and climax of each expedition.

For that journey only the four tried articles—pemmican, tea, condensed milk, and hardtack—are necessary, and I could not change or better them for another expedition. On various expeditions I made and tried out several food mixtures, but discarded them all after trial. . . .

Of all the items which go to make up the list of supplies for a polar expedition, the one which ranks first in importance is pemmican. It is also the one which starts the most instant interrogation from the average person. . . .

Pemmican is understood to be of Indian origin, originally made of the meat and fat of the buffalo, and its name, from the Cree language, means "ground meat and grease." It is said that in the days when buffalo herds were numerous, the Indians and half-breeds made large quantities of pemmican in the autumn hunting, cutting the buffalo meat in long, thin strips, which were dried in the sun and wind, then, mixed with buffalo fat, were pounded into a mass.

Too much cannot be said of the importance of pemmican to a polar expedition. It is an absolute sine qua non. Without it a sledge party cannot compact its supplies within a limit of weight to make a serious polar journey successful. . . .

With pemmican, the most serious sledge journey can be undertaken and carried to a successful issue in the absence of all other foods.

And it is the most satisfying food I know. I recall innumerable marches in bitter temperatures when men and dogs had been worked to the limit and I reached the place for camp feeling as if I could eat my weight of anything. When the pemmican ration was dealt out, and I saw my little half-pound lump, about as large as the bottom third of an ordinary drinking glass, I have often felt a sullen rage that life should contain such situations. By the time I had finished the last morsel I would not have walked round the completed igloo for anything or everything that the St. Regis, the Blackstone, or the Palace Hotel could have put before me.

Even the Eskimo dogs were at times obliged to yield to the

filling qualities of pemmican, and anything that will stay the appetite of a healthy Eskimo dog must possess some body. . . .

Pemmican is the *only* food for dogs on a serious polar sledge journey; and there is nothing as good as walrus meat to keep dogs in good condition during the autumn and winter at headquarters previous to the sledge journey. . . .

In my various expeditions I have naturally had some experience with pemmican. In my first two journeys my pemmican supply was part of the pemmican made for the Greely relief expedition. A large amount of pemmican was made for this party; but as the few survivors of the unfortunate Greely expedition were rescued at Cape Sabine and brought home in a few weeks, virtually none of it was used. On the return of the rescue party this pemmican was bought in at auction by a dealer in such supplies, and my outfit was obtained from him.

This pemmican was more satisfactory than any I have ever had since. Nine-tenths of it was just as good as when made, and the fact that occasional tins of it were bad was no drawback and caused me no loss, as such tins were accepted by the dogs at their face value. . . .

When this supply was exhausted, I had some pemmican made for me; but it was not entirely satisfactory, and on a still later expedition I was persuaded to purchase some so-called pemmican of a foreign make. This, after I had sailed and it was too late to remedy the error, I found to be largely composed of pea flour. . . .

Next to insistent, minute, personal attention to the building of his ship, the polar explorer should give his personal, constant, and insistent attention to the making of his pemmican, and should know that very batch of it packed for him is made of the proper material in the proper proportion and in accordance with his specifications. ✠

In the above, Peary mentions four items of diet, but discusses only one of them, pemmican. The reason is stated and implied elsewhere, in a number of places.

Peary looked upon tea as a warming and mildly stimulating drink. A hot drink was more necessary for him than for many others. The British Antarctic men, for instance, used their pemmican in a warm stew, while the Peary meals had only one item that was heated, the tea; for they usually or always ate their pemmican cold, as if it were bread or a slab of chocolate.

The sugar and milk in the hot tea, while understood to have food value, were used by Peary in such small quantities that he looked upon them as flavoring rather than as significant dietetic items.

"With pemmican, the most serious sledge journey can be undertaken and carried to a successful issue *in the absence of all other food*." [Italics added.] As will appear in a number of places, this was Peary's considered view. Then why the pound of biscuit per day? He felt that a dietetic increase in bulk was hygienically desirable and thought of the biscuit as furnishing bulk, as well as an accustomed feature of diet that would fit in with the preconceptions of his white companions, who, unlike the Eskimos, were not used to an exclusive meat regimen.

It appears elsewhere, too, that Peary liked flavoring in his pemmican, as he did sweetening in his tea, and he speaks of a few raisins per pound as a good seasoning. There he is thinking of agreeableness in taste, as we can tell from his saying, in the above quotation, that the best pemmican he ever had was the army issue which he was able to get from the Greely rescue stores—and that was straight pemmican, a mixture of dehydrated lean and rendered fat, without fruit or other seasoning.

Peary's campaign plans on the North Pole trip required that after a few days out on the drifting pack ice some of the sledges should return home with the poorest dogs and Eskimos led by a single white man, who was needed on each party because Peary's Eskimos did not understand principles of navigation and could not have found their way home from a remote position at sea.

An attempt would be made by each returning party to follow the outward-bound sledge tracks back to land; but Peary knew from earlier journeys that the farther you are north from the land, the faster the ice drifts east. So it might not be possible to retrace the route—the trail might be broken through ice movement.

Peary had learned also that the farther east you are, the faster the ice drifts. This is why he started for the Pole from Cape Columbia on Ellesmere and not from the more northerly capes Bridgman or Jesup in Greenland—those capes are too near the open sea that is created to the eastward by the Gulf Stream (warm North Atlantic drift), into which opening Peary did not want to be carried, to have his floe melt under him.

We pick up the story where the last supporting party is about to turn back, near 88 degrees north latitude, thus a little farther north than Peary's own turning-point of three years before.[5]

Peary and the North Pole

After breakfast [April 1, 1909], Bartlett started to walk 5 or 6 miles to the north in order to make sure of reaching the 88th parallel. On his return he was to take a meridian observation to determine our position. While he was gone I culled the best dogs from his teams, replacing them with the poorer dogs from the teams of the main party. The dogs were on the whole in very good condition, far better than on any of my previous expeditions. I had been throwing the brunt of the dragging on the poorest dogs, those that I judged were going to fail, so as to keep the best dogs fresh for the final spurt.

My theory was to work the supporting parties to the limit, in order to keep the main party fresh; and those men who I expected from the beginning would form the main party at the last had things made as easy as possible for them all the way up. Ootah, Henson, and Egingwah were in this group. Whenever I could do so I had eased their loads for them, giving them the best dogs, and keeping the poorest dogs with the teams of those Eskimos who I knew were going back. It was a part of the deliberate plan to work the supporting parties as hard as possible, in order to keep the main party fresh up to the farthest possible point.

From the beginning there were certain Eskimos who I knew, barring some unforeseen accident, would go to the Pole with me. There were others who were assigned not to go anywhere

[5] From *The North Pole*, by Robert E. Peary, copyright 1910, 1937 by Josephine D. Peary, published by J. B. Lippincott Company.

near there, and others who were available for either course. If any accidents occurred to those men whom I had originally chosen, I planned to fill their places with the next-best ones who were all willing to go.

On Bartlett's return the Eskimos built the usual wind shelter already described, and Bartlett took a latitude observation, getting 87 degrees 46 minutes 49 seconds.

Bartlett was naturally much disappointed to find that even with his 5-mile northward march of the morning he was still short of the 88th parallel. Our latitude was the direct result of the northerly wind of the last two days, which had crowded the ice southward as we traveled over it northward. We had traveled fully 12 miles more than his observation showed in the last five marches, but had lost them by the crushing up of the young ice in our rear and the closing of the leads.

Bartlett took the observations here, as had Marvin five camps back, partly to save my eyes and partly to have independent observations by different members of the expedition. When the calculations were completed, two copies were made, one for Bartlett and one for me, and he got ready to start south on the back trail in command of my fourth supporting party, with his 2 Eskimos, 1 sledge and 18 dogs.

I felt a keen regret as I saw the Captain's broad shoulders grow smaller in the distance and finally disappear behind the ice hummocks of the white and glittering expanse toward the south. But it was no time for reverie, and I turned abruptly away and gave my attention to the work which was before me. I had no anxiety about Bartlett. I knew that I should see him again at the ship. My work was still ahead, not in the rear. Bartlett had been invaluable to me, and circumstances had thrust upon him the brunt of the pioneering instead of its being divided among several, as I had originally planned.

Though he was naturally disappointed at not having reached the 88th parallel, he had every reason to be proud, not only of his work in general, but that he had surpassed the Italian record by a degree and a quarter. I had given him the post of honor in command of my last supporting party for three reasons: first, because of his magnificent handling of the *Roosevelt*; second, because he had cheerfully and gladly stood between me and every possible minor annoyance from the start of the expedition to that day; third, because it seemed to me that, in view of the noble work of Great Britain in Arctic exploration, a British subject should, next to an American, be able to say that he had stood nearest the North Pole.

With the departure of Bartlett, the main party now consisted of my own division and Henson's. My men were Egingwah and Seegloo; Henson's men were Ootah and Ooqueah. We had 5 sledges and 40 dogs, the pick of 140 with which we had left the ship. With these we were ready now for the final lap of the journey.

We were now 133 nautical miles from the pole. Pacing back and forth in the lee of the pressure ridge near which our igloos were built, I made out my program. Every nerve must be strained to make five marches of at least 25 miles each, crowding these marches in such a way as to bring us to the end of the fifth march by noon, to permit an immediate latitude observation. Weather and leads permitting, I believed that I could do this. From the improving character of the ice, and in view of the recent northerly winds, I hoped that I should have no serious trouble with the going.

If for any reason I fell short of these proposed distances, I had two methods in reserve for making up the deficit. One was to double the last march—that is, make a good march, have tea and a hearty lunch, rest the dogs a little, and then go on again, without sleep. The other was, at the conclusion of my fifth march to push on with one light sledge, a double team of dogs, and one or two of the party, leaving the rest in camp. Even should the going be worse than was then anticipated, eight marches like the three from 85 degrees 48 minutes to 86 degrees 38 minutes, or six similar to our last one, would do the trick.

Underlying all these calculations was the ever-present knowledge that a twenty-four hours' gale would open leads of water which might be impassable, and that all these plans would be negatived.

As I paced to and fro, making out my plans, I remembered that three years ago that day we had crossed the "big lead" on our way north, April 1, 1906. A comparison of conditions now and then filled me with hope for the future.

This was the time for which I had reserved all my energies, the time for which I had worked for twenty-two years, for which I had lived the simple life and trained myself as for a race. In spite of my years [Peary was then 53], I felt fit for the demands of the coming days and was eager to be on the trail. As for my party, my equipment, and my supplies, they were perfect beyond my most sanguine dreams of earlier years. My party might be regarded as an ideal which had now come to realization—as loyal and responsive to my will as the fingers of my right hand.

My four Eskimos carried the technique of dogs, sledges, ice, and cold as their racial heritage. Henson and Ootah had been my companions at the farthest point on the expedition three years before. Egingwah and Seegloo had been in Clark's division, which had such a narrow escape at that time, having been obliged for several days to subsist upon their sealskin boots, all their other food being gone.

And the fifth was young Ooqueah, who had never before served in any expedition, but who was, if possible, even more willing and eager than the others to go with me wherever I should elect. For he was always thinking of the great treasures which I had promised each of the men who should go to the farthest point with me—whaleboat, rifle, shotgun, ammunition, knives, et cetera—wealth beyond the wildest dreams of Eskimos, which should win for him the daughter of old Ikwa of Cape York, on whom he had set his heart.

All these men had a blind confidence that I would somehow get them back to land. But I recognized fully that all the impetus of the party centered in me. Whatever pace I set, the others would make good; but if I played out, they would stop like a car with a punctured tire. I had no fault to find with the conditions, and I faced them with confidence.

At this time it may be appropriate to say a word regarding my reasons for selecting Henson as my fellow traveler to the Pole itself.[6] In this selection I acted exactly as I have done on all my expeditions for the last fifteen years. He has in those years always been with me at my point farthest north. More-

---

[6] At the time there was some press criticism of Peary for having taken a Negro with him to the Pole, and no white man.

over, Henson was the best man I had with me for this kind of work, with the exception of the Eskimos, who, with their racial inheritance of ice technique and their ability to handle sledges and dogs, were more necessary to me as members of my own individual party than any white man could have been. Of course they could not lead, but they could follow and drive dogs better than any white man.

Henson, with his years of Arctic experience, was almost as skillful at this work as an Eskimo. He could handle dogs and sledges. He was a part of the traveling machine. Had I taken another member of the expedition also, he would have been a passenger, necessitating the carrying of extra rations and other impedimenta. It would have amounted to an additional load on the sledges, while the taking of Henson was in the interest of economy of weight.

The second reason was that while Henson was more useful to me than any other member of my expedition when it came to traveling with my last party over the polar ice, he would not have been so competent as the white members of the expedition in getting himself and his party back to the land. If Henson had been sent back with one of the supporting parties from a distance far out on the ice, and if he had encountered conditions similar to those which we had to face on the return journey in 1906, he and his party would never have reached the land. While faithful to me, and when *with me* more effective in covering distance with a sledge than any of the others, he had not, as a racial inheritance, the daring and initiative of Bartlett, or Marvin, MacMillan, or Borup. I owed it to him not to subject him to dangers and responsibilities which he was temperamentally unfit to face.

As to the dogs, most of them were powerful males, as hard as iron, in good condition but without an ounce of superfluous fat; and, by reason of the care which I had taken of them up to this point, they were all in good spirits, like the men. The sledges, which were being repaired that day, were also in good condition. My food and fuel supplies were ample for forty days, and by the gradual utilization of the dogs themselves for reserve food, might be made to last for fifty days if it came to a pinch.

As the Eskimos worked away at repairing the sledges while we rested there on the first day of April, they stopped from time to time to eat some of the boiled dog which the surplus numbers in Bartlett's returning team had enabled them to have. They had killed one of the poorest dogs and boiled it, using the splinters of an extra broken sledge for fuel under their cooker. It was a change for them from the pemmican diet. It was fresh meat, it was hot, and they seemed thoroughly to enjoy it. But though I remembered many times when from sheer starvation I had been glad to eat dog meat raw, I did not feel inclined to join in the feast of my dusky friends.

A little after midnight on the morning of April 2, after a few hours of sound, warm, and refreshing sleep and a hearty breakfast, I started to lift the trail to the north, leaving the others to pack, hitch up, and follow. As I climbed the pressure ridge back of our igloo, I took up another hole in my belt, the third since I left the land—thirty-two days before. Every man and dog of us was as lean and flat-bellied as a board, and as hard.

Up to this time I had intentionally kept in the rear, to straighten out any little hitch or to encourage a man with a broken sledge, and to see that everything was in good marching order. Now I took my proper place in the lead. Though I held myself in check, I felt the keenest exhilaration, and even exultation, as I climbed over the pressure ridge and breasted the keen air sweeping over the mighty ice, pure and straight from the Pole itself.

These feelings were not in any way dampened when I plunged off the pressure ridge into water mid-thigh-deep, where the pressure had forced down the edge of the floe north of us and had allowed the water to flow in under the surface snow. My boots and trousers were tight, so that no water could get inside, and as the water froze on the fur of my trousers I scraped it off with the blade of the ice lance which I carried, and was no worse for my involuntary morning plunge. I thought of my unused bathtub on the *Roosevelt*, 330 nautical miles to the south, and smiled.

It was a fine marching morning, clear and sunlit, with a temperature of minus 25°, and the wind of the past few days had subsided to a gentle breeze. The going was the best we had

had since leaving the land. The floes were large and old, hard and level, with patches of sapphire-blue ice (the pools of the preceding summer). While the pressure ridges surrounding them were stupendous, some of them 50 feet high, they were not especially hard to negotiate, either through some gap or up the gradual slope of a huge drift of snow. The brilliant sunlight, the good going save for the pressure ridges, the consciousness that we were now well started on the last lap of our journey, and the joy of again being in the lead affected me like wine. The years seemed to drop from me, and I felt as I had felt in those days fifteen years before when I headed my little party across the great icecap of Greenland, leaving 20 and 25 miles behind my snowshoes day after day, and on a spurt stretching it to 30 or 40.

Perhaps a man always thinks of the very beginning of his work when he feels it is nearing its end. The appearance of the ice fields to the north this day, large and level, the brilliant blue of the sky, the biting character of the wind—everything excepting the surface of the ice, which on the great cap is absolutely dead level with a straight line for a horizon—reminded me of those marches of the long ago.

The most marked difference was the shadows, which on the icecap [of Greenland] are absent entirely, but on the polar ice, where the great pressure ridges stand out in bold relief, are deep and dark. Then, too, there are on the polar ice those little patches of sapphire-blue already mentioned, made from the water pools of the preceding summer. On the Greenland icecap years ago I had been spurred on by the necessity of reaching the musk oxen of Independence Bay before my supplies gave out. Now I was spurred on by the necessity of making my goal, if possible, before the round face of the coming full moon should stir the tides with unrest and open a network of leads across our path.

After some hours the sledges caught up with me. The dogs were so active that morning, after their day's rest, that I was frequently obliged to sit on a sledge for a few minutes or else run to keep up with them, which I did not care to do just yet. Our course was nearly, as the crow flies, due north, across floe after floe, pressure ridge after pressure ridge, headed straight for some hummock or pinnacle of ice which I had lined in with my compass.

In this way we traveled for ten hours without stopping, covering, I felt sure, 30 miles, though, to be conservative, I called it 25. My Eskimos said that we had come as far as from the *Roosevelt* to Porter Bay, which by our winter route scales 35 miles on the chart. Anyway, we were well over the 88th parallel, in a region where no human being had ever been before. And whatever distance we made, we were likely to retain it now that the wind had ceased to blow from the north. It was even possible that with the release of the wind pressure the ice might rebound more or less and return us some of the hard-earned miles which it had stolen from us during the previous three days.

Near the end of the march I came upon a lead which was just opening. It was 10 yards wide directly in front of me, but a few hundred yards to the east was an apparently practicable crossing where the single crack was divided into several. I signaled to the sledges to hurry; then, running to the place, I had time to pick a road across the moving ice cakes and return to help the teams across before the lead widened so as to be impassable. This passage was effected by my jumping from one cake to another, picking the way, and making sure that the cake would not tilt under the weight of the dogs and the sledge, returning to the former cake where the dogs were, encouraging the dogs ahead while the driver steered the sledge across from cake to cake and threw his weight from one side to the other so that it could not overturn. We got the sledges across several cracks so wide that while the dogs had no trouble in jumping, the men had to be pretty active in order to follow the long sledges. Fortunately the sledges were of the new Peary type, 12 feet long. Had they been of the old Eskimo type, 7 feet long, we might have had to use ropes and pull them across hand over hand on an ice cake.

It is always hard to make the dogs leap a widening crack, though some of the best dog-drivers can do it instantly, using the whip and the voice. A poor dog-driver would be likely to get everything into the water in the attempt. It is sometimes necessary to go ahead of the dogs, holding the hand low and shaking it as though it contained some dainty morsel of food, thus inspiring them with courage for the leap.

Perhaps a mile beyond this, the breaking of the ice at the edge of a narrow lead as I landed from a jump sent me into the water nearly to my hips; but as the water did not come above the waistband of my trousers, which were watertight, it was soon scraped and beaten off before it had time to freeze. This lead was not wide enough to bother the sledges.

As we stopped to make our camp near a huge pressure ridge, the sun, which was gradually getting higher, seemed almost to have some warmth. While we were building our igloos, we could see, by the water clouds lying to the east and southeast of us some miles distant, that a wide lead was opening in that direction. The approaching full moon was evidently getting in its work.

As we had traveled on, the moon had circled round and round the heavens opposite the sun, a disk of silver opposite a disk of gold. Looking at its pallid and spectral face, from which the brighter light of the sun had stolen the color, it seemed hard to realize that its presence there had power to stir the great ice fields around us with restlessness—power even now, when we were so near our goal, to interrupt our pathway with an impassable lead.

The moon had been our friend during the long winter, giving us light to hunt by for a week or two each month. Now it seemed no longer a friend, but a dangerous presence to be regarded with fear. Its power, which had before been beneficent, was now malevolent and incalculably potent for evil.

When we awoke early in the morning of April 3, after a few hours' sleep, we found the weather still clear and calm. There were some broad heavy pressure ridges in the beginning of this march, and we had to use pickaxes quite freely. This delayed us a little, but as soon as we struck the level of old floes we tried to make up for lost time. As the daylight was now continuous, we could travel as long as we pleased and sleep as little as we must. We hustled along for ten hours again, as we had before, making only 20 miles because of the early delay with the pickaxes and another brief delay at a narrow lead. We were now halfway to the 89th parallel, and I had been obliged to take up another hole in my belt.

Some gigantic rafters were seen during this march, but they were not in our path. All day long we had heard the ice grinding and groaning on all sides of us, but no motion was visible to our eyes. Either the ice was slacking back into equilibrium, sagging northward after its release from the wind pressure, or else it was feeling the influence of the spring tides of the full moon. On, on we pushed, and I am not ashamed to confess that my pulse beat high, for the breath of success seemed already in my nostrils.

With every passing day even the Eskimos were becoming more eager and interested, notwithstanding the fatigue of the long marches. As we stopped to make camp, they would climb to some pinnacle of ice and strain their eyes to the north, wondering if the Pole was in sight, for they were now certain that we should get there this time.

We slept only a few hours the next night, hitting the trail again a little before midnight between the third and fourth of April. The weather and the going were even better than the day before. The surface of the ice, except as interrupted by infrequent pressure ridges, was as level as the glacial fringe from Hecla to Cape Columbia, and harder. I rejoiced at the thought that if the weather held good I should be able to get in my five marches before noon of the sixth.

Again we traveled for ten hours straight ahead, the dogs often on the trot and occasionally on the run, and in those ten hours we reeled off at least 25 miles. I had a slight accident that day, a sledge runner having passed over the side of my right foot as I stumbled while running beside a team; but the hurt was not severe enough to keep me from traveling.

Near the end of the day we crossed a lead about 100 yards wide, on young ice so thin that as I ran ahead to guide the dogs, I was obliged to slide my feet and travel wide, bear-style, in order to distribute my weight, while the men let the sledges and dogs come over by themselves, gliding across where they could. The last two men came over on all fours.

I watched them from the other side with my heart in my mouth—watched the ice bending under the weight of the sledges and the men. As one of the sledges neared the north side, a runner cut clear through the ice, and I expected every moment that the whole thing, dogs and all, would go through the ice and down to the bottom. But it did not.

This dash reminded me of that day, nearly three years before, when in order to save our lives we had taken desperate chances in recrossing the "big lead" on ice similar to this—ice that buckled under us and through which my toe cut several times as I slid my long snowshoes over it. A man who should wait for the ice to be really safe would stand small chance of getting far in these latitudes. Traveling on the polar ice, one takes all kinds of chances. Often a man has the choice between the possibility of drowning by going on or starving to death by standing still, and challenges fate with the briefer and less painful chance.

That night we were all pretty tired, but satisfied with our progress so far. We were almost inside of the 89th parallel, and I wrote in my diary: "Give me three more days of this weather!" The temperature at the beginning of the march had been minus 40°. That night I put all the poorest dogs in one team and began to eliminate and feed them to the others, as it became necessary.

We stopped for only a short sleep, and early in the evening of the same day, the fourth, we struck on again. The temperature was then minus 35°, the going was the same, but the sledges always haul more easily when the temperature rises, and the dogs were on the trot much of the time. Toward the end of the march we came upon a lead running north and south, and as the young ice was thick enough to support the teams, we traveled on it for two hours, the dogs galloping along and reeling off the miles in a way that delighted my heart. The light air which had blown from the south during the first few hours of the march veered to the east and grew keener as the hours wore on.

I had not dared to hope for such progress as we were making. Still the biting cold would have been impossible to face by anyone not fortified by an inflexible purpose. The bitter wind burned our faces so that they cracked, and long after we got into camp each day they pained us so that we could hardly go to sleep. The Eskimos complained much, and at every camp fixed their fur clothing about their faces, waists, knees, and wrists. They also complained of their noses, which I had never known them to do before. The air was as keen and bitter as frozen steel.

At the next camp I had another of the dogs killed. It was now exactly six weeks since we left the *Roosevelt*, and I felt as if the goal were in sight. I intended the next day, weather and ice permitting, to make a long march, "boil the kettle" midway, and then go on again without sleep, trying to make up the 5 miles which we had lost on the third of April.

During the daily march my mind and body were too busy with the problem of covering as many miles of distance as possible to permit me to enjoy the beauty of the frozen wilderness through which we tramped. But at the end of the day's march, while the igloos were being built I usually had a few minutes in which to look about me and to realize the picturesqueness of our situation—we, the only living things in a trackless, colorless, inhospitable desert of ice. Nothing but the hostile ice, and far more hostile icy water, lay between our remote place on the world's map and the utmost tips of the lands of Mother Earth.

I knew of course that there was always a *possibility* that we might still end our lives up there, and that our conquest of the unknown spaces and silences of the polar void might remain forever unknown to the world which we had left behind. But it was hard to realize this. That hope which is said to spring eternal in the human breast always buoyed me up with the belief that, as a matter of course, we should be able to return along the white road by which we had come.

Sometimes I would climb to the top of a pinnacle of ice to the north of our camp and strain my eyes into the whiteness which lay beyond, trying to imagine myself already at the Pole. We had come so far, and the capricious ice had placed so few obstructions in our path, that now I dared to loose my fancy, to entertain the image which my will had heretofore forbidden to my imagination—the image of ourselves at the goal.

We had been very fortunate with the leads so far, but I was in constant and increasing dread lest we should encounter an impassable one toward the very end. With every successive march, my fear of such impassable leads had increased. At every pressure ridge I found myself hurrying breathlessly forward, fearing there might be a lead just beyond it, and when I arrived at the summit I would catch my breath with relief— only to find myself hurrying on in the same way at the next ridge.

At our camp on the fifth of April I gave the party a little more sleep than at the previous ones, as we were all pretty well played out and in need of rest. I took a latitude sight, and this indicated our position to be 89 degrees 25 minutes, or 35 miles from the Pole; but I determined to make the next camp in time for a noon observation, if the sun should be visible.

Before midnight on the fifth we were again on the trail. The weather was overcast, and there was the same gray and shadowless light as on the march after Marvin had turned back. The sky was a colorless pall gradually deepening to almost black at the horizon, and the ice was a ghastly and chalky white, like that of the Greenland icecap—just the colors which an imaginative artist would paint as a polar icescape. How different it seemed from the glittering fields, canopied with blue and lit by the sun and full moon, over which we had been traveling for the last four days.

The going was even better than before. There was hardly any snow on the hard granular surface of the old floes, and the sapphire-blue lakes were larger than ever. The temperature had risen to minus 15°, which, reducing the friction of the sledges, gave the dogs the appearance of having caught the high spirits of the party. Some of them even tossed their heads and barked and yelped as they traveled.

Notwithstanding the grayness of the day and the melancholy aspect of the surrounding world, by some strange shift of feeling the fear of the leads had fallen from me completely. I now felt that success was certain, and notwithstanding the physical exhaustion of the forced marches of the last five days, I went tirelessly on and on, the Eskimos following almost automatically, though I knew that they must feel the weariness which my excited brain made me incapable of feeling.

When we had covered, as I estimated, a good 15 miles, we halted, made tca, ate lunch, and rested the dogs. Then we went on for another estimated 15 miles. In twelve hours' actual traveling time we made 30 miles. Many laymen have wondered why we were able to travel faster after the sending back of each of the supporting parties, especially after the last one. To any man experienced in the handling of troops this will need no explanation. The larger the party and the greater the number of sledges, the greater is the chance of breakages or delay for one reason or another. A large party cannot be forced as rapidly as a small party.

Take a regiment, for instance. The regiment could not make as good an average daily march for a number of forced marches as could a picked company of that regiment. The picked company could not make as good an average for a number of forced marches as could a picked file of men from that particular company; and this file could not make the same average for a certain number of forced marches that the fastest traveler in the whole regiment could make.

So that with my party reduced to five picked men, every man, dog, and sledge under my individual eye, myself in the lead, and all recognizing that the moment had now come to let ourselves out for all there was in us, we naturally bettered our previous speed.

When Bartlett left us, the sledges had been practically rebuilt, all the best dogs were in our pack, and we all understood that we must attain our object and get back as quickly as we possibly could. The weather was in our favor. The average march for the whole journey from the land to the pole was over 15 miles. We had repeatedly made marches of 20 miles. Our average for five marches from the point where the last supporting party turned back was about 26 miles.

The last march northward ended at ten o'clock on the forenoon of April 6. I had now made the five marches planned from the point at which Bartlett turned back, and my reckoning showed that we were in the immediate neighborhood of the goal of all our striving. After usual arrangements for going into camp, at approximate local noon of the Columbia meridian, I made the first observation at our polar camp. It indicated our position as 89 degrees 57 minutes.

We were now at the end of the last long march of the upward journey. Yet with the Pole actually in sight I was too weary to take the last few steps. The accumulated weariness of all those days and nights of forced marches and insufficient sleep, constant peril and anxiety, seemed to roll across me all at once. I was actually too exhausted to realize at the moment that my life's purpose had been achieved. As soon as our igloos had been completed and we had eaten our dinner and double-rationed the dogs, I turned in for a few hours of absolutely necessary sleep, Henson and the Eskimos having unloaded the sledges and got them in readiness for such repairs as were necessary. But, weary though I was, I could not sleep long. It was therefore only a few hours later when I woke. The first thing I did after awaking was to write these words in my diary: "The Pole at last. The prize of three centuries. My dream and goal for twenty years. Mine at last! I cannot bring myself to realize it. It seems all so simple and commonplace."

Everything was in readiness for an observation at 6 P.M. Columbia meridian time, in case the sky should be clear, but at that hour it was, unfortunately, still overcast. But as there were indications that it would clear before long, two of the Eskimos and myself made ready a light sledge carrying only the instruments, a tin of pemmican, and one or two skins; and drawn by a double team of dogs, we pushed on an estimated distance of 10 miles. While we traveled, the sky cleared, and at the end of the journey, I was able to get a satisfactory series of observations at Columbia meridian midnight. These observations indicated that our position was then beyond the Pole.

Nearly everything in the circumstances which then surrounded us seemed too strange to be thoroughly realized; but one of the strangest of those circumstances seemed to me to be the fact that in a march of only a few hours I had passed from the western to the eastern hemisphere and had verified my position at the summit of the world. It was hard to realize that in the first miles of this brief march we had been traveling due north, while on the last few miles of the same march we had been traveling south, although we had all the time been traveling precisely in the same direction. It would be difficult to imagine a better illustration of the fact that most things are relative. Again, please consider the uncommon circumstance that in order to return to our camp, it now became necessary to turn and go north again for a few miles and then to go directly south, all the time traveling in the same direction.

As we passed back along that trail which none had ever seen before or would ever see again, certain reflections intruded themselves which, I think, may fairly be called unique. East, west, and north had disappeared for us. Only one direction remained, and that was south. Every breeze which could possibly blow upon us, no matter from what point of the horizon, must be a south wind. Where we were, one day and one night constituted a year, a hundred such days and nights constituted a century. Had we stood in that spot during the six months of the Arctic winter night, we should have seen every star of the northern hemisphere circling the sky at the same distance from the horizon, with Polaris (the North Star) practically in the zenith.

All during our march back to camp the sun was swinging around in its ever-moving circle. At six o'clock on the morning of April 7, having again arrived at Camp Jesup, I took another series of observations. These indicated our position as being 4 or 5 miles from the Pole, toward Bering Strait. Therefore, with a double team of dogs and a light sledge, I traveled directly toward the sun an estimated distance of 8 miles. Again I returned to the camp in time for a final and completely satisfactory series of observations on April 7 at noon Columbia meridian time. These observations gave results essentially the same as those made at the same spot twenty-four hours before.

I had now taken in all thirteen single, or six and one-half double, altitudes of the sun, at two different stations, in three different directions, at four different times. All were under satisfactory conditions, except for the first single altitude on the sixth. The temperature during these observations had been from minus 11° Fahrenheit to minus 30° Fahrenheit, with clear sky and calm weather (except as already noted for the single observation on the sixth). I give here a facsimile of a typical set of these observations. [Omitted]

In traversing the ice in these various directions as I had done, I had allowed approximately 10 miles for possible errors in my observations, and at some moment during these marches and countermarches, I had passed over or very near the point where north and south and east and west blend into one.

Of course there were some more or less informal ceremonies connected with our arrival at our difficult destination, but they were not of a very elaborate character. We planted five flags at the top of the world. The first one was a silk American flag which Mrs. Peary gave me fifteen years ago. That flag has done more traveling in high latitudes than any other ever made. I carried it wrapped about my body on every one of my expeditions northward after it came into my possession, and I left a fragment of it at each of my successive "farthest norths": Cape Morris K. Jesup, the northernmost point of land in the known world; Cape Thomas Hubbard, the northernmost known point of Jesup Land, west of Grant Land; Cape Columbia, the northernmost point of North American lands; and my farthest north in 1906, latitude 87 degrees 6 minutes in the ice of the Polar Sea. By the time it actually reached the Pole, therefore, it was somewhat worn and discolored.

A broad diagonal section of this ensign would now mark the farthest goal of earth—the place where I and my dusky companions stood.

It was also considered appropriate to raise the colors of the Delta Kappa Epsilon fraternity, in which I was initiated a member while an undergraduate student at Bowdoin College, the "World's Ensign of Liberty and Peace," with its red, white, and blue in a field of white, the Navy League flag, and the Red Cross flag.

After I had planted the American flag in the ice, I told Henson to time the Eskimos for three rousing cheers, which they gave with the greatest enthusiasm. Thereupon I shook hands with each member of the party—surely a sufficiently unceremonious affair to meet with the approval of the most democratic. The Eskimos were childishly delighted with our success. While of course they did not realize its importance fully, or its worldwide significance, they did understand that it meant the final achievement of a task upon which they had seen me engaged for many years.

Then, in a space between the ice blocks of a pressure ridge, I deposited a glass bottle containing a diagonal strip of my flag and records of which the following is a copy:

90 N. Lat., North Pole,
April 6, 1909

Arrived here today, 27 marches from C. Columbia.

I have with me 5 men, Matthew Henson, colored, Ootah, Egingwah, Seegloo, and Ookeah, Eskimos; 5 sledges and 38 dogs. My ship, the S. S. *Roosevelt*, is in winter quarters at C. Sheridan, 90 miles east of Columbia.

The expedition under my command which has succeeded in reaching the Pole is under the auspices of the Peary Arctic Club of New York City, and has been fitted out and sent north by the members and friends of the club for the purpose of securing this geographical prize, if possible, for the honor and prestige of the United States of America.

The officers of the club are Thomas H. Hubbard, of New York, President; Zenas Crane, of Mass., Vice-President; Herbert L. Bridgman, of New York, Secretary and Treasurer.

I start back for Cape Columbia tomorrow.

Robert E. Peary
United States Navy

90 N. Lat., North Pole,
April 6, 1909

I have today hoisted the national ensign of the United States of America at this place, which my observations indicate to be the North Polar axis of the earth, and have formally taken possession of the entire region, and adjacent, for and in the name of the President of the United States of America.

I leave this record and United States flag in possession.

Robert E. Peary
United States Navy

The formal quest of the North Pole, as distinguished from visiting it en route to the Indies, had begun with Parry in 1827 and was closed by Peary in 1909. The northern was the first of the earth's two poles to be attained and was found to lie in an ocean, or rather in a mediterranean sea, 391 geographical (about 450 statute) miles from the nearest land, Cape Morris Jesup, the north tip of Peary Land, which is the northernmost part of Greenland, discovered and first explored by Peary himself.

A sounding near the Pole gave 1500 fathoms, or about 1¾ miles, without bottom. (A sounding by Ivan Papanin, 1937, reached bottom near the Pole at about 2¼ miles.)

Peary had noticed his last seal near 86 degrees, "disporting himself in the open water" of a lead about 240 geographic miles short of the Pole. White bears, who live exclusively on seals, were there too; for 30 or 40 miles farther north than where he saw the seal Peary wrote: "Along the course of one of these leads we saw the fresh track of a polar bear going west, over 200 miles from land."

(In 1937 Papanin's Soviet expedition was camped on a drifting floe in the immediate vicinity of the North Pole and confirmed Peary's observations not merely as to the depth of water but also as to animal life. Indeed, they showed to be typical what from the reading of Peary's account one might think to be exceptional. For instance, Papanin was visited by a female bear with cubs so young they must have been born on the drifting ice right by the Pole. He saw seals paddling sluggishly along the surface of the leads there and gulping down shrimps. Upon lowering traps into the water, the Soviet scientists brought up small animals and plants from varying depths and demonstrated a life gradient, all the way to the bottom of the sea, similar to that of the North Atlantic—from which, indeed, the Polar Sea is a gulf.)

The morning of April 23, 1909, Peary was back at Cape Columbia. "Our return from the Pole was accomplished in sixteen marches. It had been, as a result of our experience and perfected clothing and equipment, an amazingly comfortable return, as compared with previous ones." Only one thing had worried them, the possibility of a gale from an untoward quarter that would have broken up the ice, separating the floes by leads of open water and speeding up the drift eastward in the direction of the tepid North Atlantic that would have melted the solid ice from beneath them. Peary says:

"There was no one in our party that was not delighted to have passed the treacherous lead and those wide expanses of young thin ice where a gale would have put an open sea between us and the land."

At the Cape Columbia camp Peary wrote:

"My lifework is accomplished. The thing which it was intended from the beginning that I should do, the thing which I believed could be done, and that I could do, I have done. I have got the North Pole out of my system after twenty-three years of effort, hard work, disappointments, hardships, privations, more or less suffering, and some risks. I have won the last great geographical prize, the North Pole, for the credit of the United States. This work is the finish, the cap and climax, of nearly four hundred years of effort, loss of life, and expenditure of fortunes by the civilized nations of the world, and it has been accomplished in a way that is thoroughly American. I am content."

During the next few years Peary made it clear repeatedly that he considered attainment of the North Pole to be the supreme geographic achievement, in terms of the difficulties involved. He also felt it to be the right thing to step aside for younger men. Those were the main reasons why he himself did not want to try for the South Pole and why he wanted to see his good friend, loyal supporter, and natural successor, Captain Robert Abram Bartlett, placed at the head of a United States expedition that would aim for 90 degrees south latitude. Peary had not as yet been successful in this organizational project when the Norwegians, under Amundsen, attained the South Pole.

An element in Peary's campaign on behalf of Bartlett was trying to make clear the difference between the northern and southern polar areas, and thus the necessary difference in exploratory procedure. He formulated a statement of the case which might have been entitled "Far as the Poles Apart."

Among the contrasting points made by Peary the central one is that the Arctic is a sea encompassed by lands, while the Antarctic is a continent surrounded by an ocean. The results of the first Scott expedition, and of Shackleton's expedition, were available to Peary, and he was able to bring out that the Antarctic Pole lies on a plateau 2 miles high, while the Arctic Pole is in a sea 2 miles deep. There would be a hardship in working at the great southern altitude—the shortness of breath familiar in high mountains—but there would be overcompensating advantages that make the South Pole relatively easy to reach. The chief of them are:

In attempting to reach the northern Pole you must sledge at the coldest time of year, for your chief northern handicap is open water, and this is bridged over by young ice the more rapidly the lower the thermometer. In striving for the southern Pole, the ice you walk upon is firm, resting on land; there is no open water and so you can travel at the warmest time of year. This means also that in northern work you contend with long nights in the beginning of a trip and have the twenty-four-hour daylight only later; in the south you have perpetual daylight for your whole journey, assuming (as always has been the case) that the sledge journeys begin in early summer and end in late summer.

Perhaps greatest of the many advantages of southern over northern conditions, from the sledging point of view, is that in the Antarctic you can make caches on the forward march and feel safe about picking them up when homeward bound. In the Arctic your northward journey is over moving ice and you can no more be sure of picking up a cake with its depot on a return march than you would be sure of finding on a westbound Atlantic crossing a dory you left behind when midway eastbound.

And on the Arctic sea, even if you took the chance of finding when southbound a depot left behind a month before, you still would face the risk that it might have been despoiled by foxes or bears. A polar bear can and will tear asunder practically any sort of package; and if he cannot break it open he may roll it away, possibly into water. By contrast, an Antarctic depot is thrice safe: it cannot float away because of the stability of land, it cannot spoil, for there is neither rain nor decay, and it cannot be plundered, for there is not, except on the very shores of the continent, any beast of whatever sort.

Peary was realistic about the difficulties of southern sledging and did not go beyond pointing out that, compared with the Arctic situation, the South Pole was relatively easy. For instance, the danger of falling into a crevasse that has been produced by the sluggish movement of the southern continental ice sheet, or of losing a sledge with its load into a crevasse, is considerably less than the danger of losing life or load in the turbulent movement of the drifting Arctic pack.

Peary's forecast of the relatively easy attainment of the South Pole was destined to be confirmed within three years, as will be seen in the last chapter of this book. It took hundreds of years of search to find the Antarctic mainland; but it was only sixteen years (1895-1911) from the first placing of human feet upon the shore of the southern continent until the first men stood at the southern Pole.

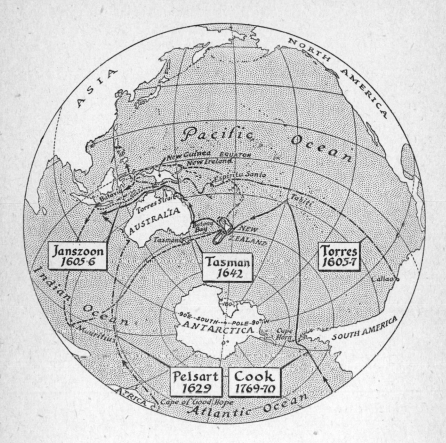

Discovery of Australia

DISCOVERY OF AUSTRALIA

CHAPTER 16

No RECORD exists of the earliest discovery of Australia from Europe or from Asia, but it must have occurred several centuries, at least, before the historical discovery. The Chinese are believed to have had some knowledge of this land as early as the thirteenth century, for Marco Polo, writing at this time, refers to the great southern continent. Some geographers are of opinion that, not counting the native Australians, the Malays were the true discoverers, and that they had sailed to the northwest shores of Australia centuries before relics of their visits were found by English explorers in the early part of the nineteenth century.

By the sixteenth century the belief in what came to be called Terra Australis Incognita, the Unknown Southland, was widely held, and the continent, in various shapes and sizes, began to appear on maps of the world. By the latter half of the sixteenth century many of the principal map-makers included a continental land mass in the southern sea, and on some of these a strait was shown between New Guinea and Terra Australis.

The basis for indicating such a channel appears to many geographers to have been hypothetical, probably founded on rumors and perhaps a result of wishful thinking, for the width and length of the strait, and the latitude in which it is laid down, vary from map to map and seldom approximate the location of the actual strait. Other scholars feel that there must have been a more solid foundation than mere rumor. One of the strongest arguments for this view is a passage in the text which accompanied the Wytfliet map of 1597: "The Australis Terra is the most southern of lands. It is separated from New Guinea by a narrow strait. Its shores are little known, since after one voyage and another that route has been deserted and seldom is the country visited unless when sailors are driven there by storms. The Australis Terra begins 2 or 3 degrees from the equator and is maintained . . . to be of so great an extent that if it were thoroughly explored it would be regarded as a fifth part of the world."

A number of claims have been advanced for the sighting of the continent in the sixteenth century, but as yet none of these have been fully substantiated. Binot de Gonneville (Paulmier), a Frenchman, claimed to have landed on the southern continent in 1503, and some French writers contend that Guillaume Le Testu sighted this mainland in 1531.

The Portuguese say they were the discoverers of Australia, but again there is no documentary evidence. Many scholars are, however, inclined to agree that the Portuguese had knowledge antedating that of their Dutch and Spanish rivals, knowledge which they kept secret to prevent competition.

With the turn of the century the situation altered greatly, and from about 1605 onward there are numerous accounts of the sighting of one part or another of what is now called Australia. So far as the north coast is concerned this was accomplished first and almost simultaneously by Dutch and Spanish expeditions, and later by English navigators.

The Dutch, besides probably being first to go ashore on the north coast, were first to discover the west coast of Australia, and then through successive sightings and landings they were first to lay down an approximate charting of the western shore line. The entry of the Hollanders into this region dates from Cornelis Houtman's expedition of 1595, a voyage important not only as marking the beginning of Dutch activities in the Indies but also as being indirectly responsible for an ever-increasing knowledge of the land that later came to be known as New Holland.

The compelling lure of the wealth of the East and the difficulties of challenging the established power here of Spain and Portugal are indicated in a book that was published in London in 1703. This translation into English from the original Dutch is entitled *A Collection of Voyages Undertaken by the Dutch East-Indies Company, for the Improvement of Trade and Navigation.* The Introduction presents the situation as it appeared to the Hollanders, and tells briefly of the Houtman voyage:

The Dutch and Australia

Though an infinity of evils attends the wars with which states and kingdoms are afflicted by the Divine permission, yet they oftentimes procure unexpected benefits. The same Providence that humbles the sinner furnishes means to raise him upon a due repentance. The scourge of war that punishes men may contribute, when the Divine Providence thinks fit, to whet their spirits, and render them capable of any enterprise.

This was the scourge that galled the United Provinces for so long a time; and constrained 'em to range o'er the remotest countries, in quest of the means of subsistence, of which the King of Spain had robbed 'em, not only by laying their country desolate with fire and sword and exercising the cruelest acts of tyranny upon their persons.

If the Spaniards had not seized their ships, and exposed their persons to the rigor of the Inquisition, probably they had never extended their navigation beyond the Baltic Sea, the northern countries, England, France, Spain, and its dependencies, the Mediterranean, and the Levant.

One would have thought that the tyrannical usage of the Spaniards would have ruined their country, and extirpated the people. But on the contrary, it occasioned the welfare and prosperity both of the one and the other. The people, being conducted by such sovereigns as were naturally wise and (if it be possible) become wiser by the sense of danger; being supported by the prudence and animated by the valor of their renowned General and Stadtholder, Prince Maurice of Nassau —the people, I say, under these encouragements, happily set out in order to find under another firmament, and among barbarous savages, the succors that were refused 'em by their neighbors.

Of all the countries that were visited in the way of this forced trade, none have contributed more toward the riches and present happiness of the United Provinces than the East and West Indies. Now in order to reach these countries, they were obliged to avoid the meeting with the Spaniards or the Portuguese; and that difficulty seemed to be in a manner unsurmountable. But after all, they found out ways and means to compass their end. . . .

They conceived that by steering northeast they might afterward run along the coast of Tartary, and so reach Cathai, China, Japan, India, and the Philippine and Molucca Islands. The execution of this project was committed to two excellent mariners—namely, William Barents and James Heemskirk—and divers others. . . . But hitherto the Almighty has not favored the discovery of that passage, or of the people that live in these climates.

While they were in quest of this northern passage, one Cornelis Houtman, a Hollander, happened to be in Portugal, and there satisfied his curiosity by a diligent inquiry into the state of the East Indies, and the course that one must steer in order to come at it. He had frequent conferences upon this subject with the Portuguese, who gave notice of it to the Court. At that time all foreigners were strictly prohibited to make such inquiries, and upon that score Houtman was put in prison, and ordered to lie there till he paid a severe fine.

In order to raise such a considerable sum of money, he addressed himself to the merchants of Amsterdam, and gave 'em to know that if they would pay his fine, he would discover to them all that related to the East Indies and the passage thither. Accordingly, they granted his request, and he performed his promise.

After a mature consideration of what he had offered, they resolved to erect another company, called the Company for Remote Countries. The Directors for this company . . . considering that 'twas as yet very uncertain whether the north passage was practicable—though at the same time they were sensible that 'twas the shortest and the surest passage, and withal the most healthy, in regard that in it they did not cross the equinoctial line—upon this consideration, I say, they came to a resolution, A.D. 1595, to send four vessels to the Indies by the way of the Cape of Good Hope.

Houtman and some others, who had the command in this expedition, were ordered to observe the course they steered very narrowly, and to settle with the Indians the commerce of spices and other goods, especially in those countries where the Portuguese had no settlement. They looked upon this commerce as a very valuable thing, especially considering that it would save 'em the trouble of fetching that sort of goods from Portugal, which they could not do without great hazard.

These ships returned to Holland in the space of two years and four months after their setting out; and though they had made no great profit of the voyage, yet their success animated their owners, and several other merchants, to carry on the design yet further. 🖪

Great, indeed, was the animation following this first Dutch intrusion on the route to the Indies by way of the Cape of Good Hope. Many rival commercial companies were formed in Holland almost immediately, but as early as 1602 these were merged in the Dutch East India Company (the General United East India Company). The rapid growth of this company is summarized by the Introduction from which we have just quoted, where it says:

The Dutch East India Company

🖪 In fine, the commerce to India became so common, and the forces of the company grew to that height, that in the years 1613 and 1614 they fitted out very near twenty-seven ships, at several times, under the command of several commodores. . . . In order to [get] a full view of their success, we need only to cast our eyes upon the following list of the dividends that were made.

	(1605 in June	15)	
	(1606 in April	75)	
	(1607 in July	40)	
An. D.	(1608 in April	20)	per cent
	(1609 in June	25)	
	(1610 in August	50)	
	(1613 in May	37)	

The Company being in such a flourishing condition, the next year, viz. 1615, the States joined with 'em in sending a strong squadron to the South Sea by the way of the Magellan Strait, upon the prospect of surprising the Spaniards, and weakening them on that side, after which they might have an easy passage to the Indies. ✠

The power of the Dutch grew in proportion to their commercial success, so that they rapidly took over the commanding position in the Indies formerly held by the Portuguese, a supremacy which they were to maintain until toward the end of the century. Along with their exploitation of known territories, the company engaged in active search for new lands with new sources of riches. The great southern continent provided the most hopeful field of operations, and throughout the first half of the seventeenth century one expedition after another was sent out to explore and report upon the unknown land.

North Coast

As indicated earlier, the discovery of the northern end of Australia was accomplished almost simultaneously by the Dutch and the Spanish. Although the Dutch explorations here probably antedated those of Spain by a few months, let us consider first the Spanish discovery.

So far as is known, Don Diego de Prado y Tovar and Luis Vaez de Torres were first to demonstrate, in 1606, the existence of a strait separating New Guinea from the land to the south, thus in effect discovering Australia. This was accomplished by vessels of the expedition of 1605-07, organized and originally commanded by Pedro Fernandez de Quiros.

Prado and Torres, bound for the Philippines, intended to pass northward of New Guinea. They sighted the coast of New Guinea in the vicinity of its southeastern extremity, and, unable to round the eastern tip, they turned westward and coasted along the island's southern shore. After crossing the Gulf of Papua they came to the strait that has been named for Torres. There is doubt as to which of the several channels Prado and Torres followed between the islands and reefs that encumber the tortuous Torres Strait, but the navigation was successful, and the voyage to the Philippines was continued.

This important expedition was, however, destined to an obscurity which only in recent years has been fully cleared away. For, in the almost routine fashion of the time, the documents relating to the voyage were first kept jealously secret by Spanish officialdom, and then forgotten.

One by one, at long intervals during the more than three centuries that have elapsed since the finding of the strait, the records have come to light, by accident or through the patient efforts of scholars. The last and most important of these, the journal of Prado, did not appear in print until 1930, a few years after the original manuscript had turned up in England.

Before the discovery of the Prado manuscript the chief source of information concerning the discovery of Torres Strait was a letter written by Torres to the King of Spain from Manila on July 12, 1607, but this was unknown to historians until its discovery in the archives of Manila by Alexander Dalrymple in 1762 and its publication in England in 1806.

The piecemeal manner in which the documents have been unearthed has created difficulties for those who have attempted to write chronological histories of the discovery of Australia. Necessarily basing their conclusions on incomplete information, scholars have engaged in warm and even acrimonious debate about the motives and the actions of the principal characters involved in the undertaking.

The most spirited of these debates has centered about Prado, who had generally been assumed to have occupied a minor position on the Quiros expedition. Among other things, it had been taken for granted that the command of the expedition had devolved upon Torres after Quiros had turned back to Mexico with one of the vessels. Not until 1930 was it learned that Prado was the true leader after the separation from the original commander. For his journal tells of sealed orders from the Viceroy of Peru, directing that, should the necessity arise, Prado should succeed to the command. Thus Prado became supreme commander for the remainder of the voyage while Torres continued as captain of his vessel.

Not only were the historians confounded by the suppression of evidence; the progress of discovery was also retarded. So successful was the Spanish policy of secrecy that later explorers in this region made their plans and prosecuted their search unaware of the discoveries of Prado and Torres. Thus while their voyage is extremely important from a historical stand-point, it had small influence upon the further discovery and exploration of Australia.

Moreover, now that the records are available, they still do not, as one might expect, contain the earliest reference to the Australian mainland. Whichever channel was used in the passage through Torres Strait, there is a strong probability that the mainland of Australia was sighted; but if so, this made no particular impression upon the explorers. Prado's journal and Torres's letter tell of numerous landings on the New Guinea coast, and there are descriptions of the country and of the natives at the various places where landings were made; there are frequent references to navigating conditions, to shoals, reefs, and islands. There is nothing that can be specifically related to Australia.

For this reason nothing is quoted from Prado and Torres here, but instead we turn to the better-documented voyages of the Dutch in this region.

The honor of first reporting clearly the discovery of any part of the Australian mainland seems to belong to the Dutch vessel *Duifken*, commanded by Willem Janszoon. This sighting probably antedated the discovery of Torres Strait by several months.

On her voyage of 1605-06, the *Duifken*, sailing from Bantam, passed eastward along the south coast of New Guinea as far as the western end of Torres Strait. Apparently not recognizing it as a strait, Janszoon here turned south into the Gulf of Carpentaria and coasted along the western side of the Cape York Peninsula as far as Cape Keerweer (Cape Turnagain). Janszoon appears to have been unaware of the significance of his discovery, for the Dutch writings of this period speak of the new land as if it were a part of New Guinea.

There is no firsthand account of the *Duifken's* voyage. Information regarding it is summarized in the official Dutch instructions issued to Tasman for his second voyage in 1644, a document which is important for the sketch it gives of Dutch exploration in the waters about Australia in the years between the voyages of Janszoon and Tasman.

The next exploratory venture in these waters was the 1623 voyage of the *Pera* and the *Aernem*. This expedition carried explicit orders from the Governor and Council of the Dutch East India Company to attempt to determine the extent of the southern continent, to make careful notes on navigation conditions, on the resources of the country, and on the possibilities for trade. "In a word, let nothing pass you unobserved, and whatever you find bring us a full and particular report of it, by which you will do the States of the United Netherlands a service and lay up special honor for yourself."

There was even a veiled reference to the capture of slaves: "In places where you meet with people, you will, by dexterity or otherwise, get hold of some adults, or still better, young lads or girls, to the end that they should be brought up here, and later, when opportunity offers, be broken in at the said quarters."

The journal of Jan Carstensz (Carstenszoon), skipper of the *Pera*, which was missing in 1644 when they were briefing Tasman, later turned up and was published in Dutch and English by Jan Ernst Heeres in *The Part Borne by the Dutch in the Discovery of Australia* (Leyden and London, 1899). From this journal it appears that the records of the *Duifken*, which are now missing, were available to Carstensz. Certainly he was familiar with the details of the earlier voyage, and he may even have had copies of the records with him.

In that part of the voyage of the *Pera* and the *Aernem* which concerns us here, the voyage along the northern side of Australia, the course appears to have been approximately the same as that of the *Duifken* as far as Cape Keerweer. Again there was failure to realize that New Guinea was a separate land, for because of its shoals and reefs, the western entrance to Torres Strait was believed to be only a "dry bight."

The western side of Cape York Peninsula was sighted on April 12, 1623. Three days later a party from the *Pera* went ashore in the vicinity of Cape Keerweer, and for a month thereafter, as they coasted southward and on the return voyage northward, frequent landings were made.

From Carstensz we have the first description of the aborigines of Australia and of the country of the Cape York Peninsula. Here are the pertinent extracts from his journal for the period April 15 to May 12, 1623:

Journal of Jan Carstensz

🐾 [April 15] . . . The land which we have hitherto seen and followed extends south and north. It is low-lying and without variety, having a fine sandy beach in various places. In the afternoon we dropped anchor owing to the calm, having sailed 11 miles south. Great volumes of smoke becoming visible on the land, the subcargo got orders to land with the two pinnaces, duly manned and armed, and was specially enjoined to use his utmost endeavors for the advantage of our masters. When the pinnaces returned at nightfall, the subcargo reported that the pinnaces could get no farther than a stone's throw from the land, owing to the muddy bottom, into which the men sunk to their waists; but that they had in various places seen blacks emerging from the wood, while others lay hid in the coppice. They therefore sent a man ashore with some pieces of iron and strings of beads tied to a stick, in order to attract the blacks; but as nothing could be effected and the night was coming on, they had been forced to return to the yachts. . . .

[April 17] . . . toward the evening, it fell a calm, so that we dropped anchor with the ebb, after which I went ashore myself with the two pinnaces duly provided with men and arms. We went a considerable distance into the interior, which we found to be a flat, fine country with few trees, and a good soil for planting and sowing, but so far as we could observe utterly destitute of fresh water. Nor did we see any human beings or even signs of them. Near the strand the coast was sandy, with a fine beach and plenty of excellent fish.

In the morning of the eighteenth the wind was east-north-east, course held south by west along the land. About noon, as we saw persons on the beach, we cast anchor in 3½ fathom clayey bottom. The skipper of the *Pera* got orders to row to land with the two pinnaces, duly provided for defense. In the afternoon when the pinnaces returned, we were informed by the skipper that as soon as he had landed with his men, a large number of blacks, some of them armed and others unarmed, had made up to them. These blacks showed no fear and were so bold as to touch the muskets of our men and to try to take the same off their shoulders, while they wanted to have whatever they could make use of. Our men accordingly diverted their attention by showing them iron and beads, and espying vantage, seized one of the blacks by a string which he wore round his neck and carried him off to the pinnace. The blacks who remained on the beach set up dreadful howls and made violent gestures, but the others who kept concealed in the wood remained there. These natives are coal-black, with lean bodies and stark-naked, having twisted baskets or nets round their heads. In hair and figure they are like the blacks of the Coromandel coast, but they seem to be less cunning, bold, and evil-natured than the blacks at the western extremity of Nova Guinea. . . .

On the nineteenth, the wind being southeast, we remained at anchor, and since the yachts were very poorly provided with firewood, the skipper of the *Pera* went ashore with the two pinnaces duly manned and armed. When the men were engaged in cutting wood, a large number of blacks, upward of two hundred, came upon them, and tried every means to surprise and overcome them, so that our men were compelled to fire two shots, upon which the blacks fled, one of the number having been hit and having fallen. Our men then proceeded somewhat farther up the country, where they found several weapons, of which they took some along with them by way of curiosities. During their march they observed in various places great quantities of divers human bones, from which it may be safely concluded that the blacks along the coast of Nova Guinea [Carstensz thought he was still in New Guinea] are man-eaters who do not spare each other when driven by hunger. . . .

[April 24] . . . This same day, the council having been convened, I submitted to them the question whether it would be advisable to run further south, and after various opinions had been expressed, it was agreed that this would involve divers difficulties, and that the idea better be given up. We might get into a vast bay, and it is evident that in these regions in the east monsoons north winds prevail, just as north (?) of the equator south winds prevail in the said monsoon. We should thus fall on a lee shore. For all of which reasons, and in order to act for the best advantage of the Lords Managers, it has been resolved and determined to turn back and follow the coast of Nova Guinea so long to northward as shall be found practicable; to touch at divers places which shall be examined with the utmost care; and finally to turn our course from there to Aru and Quey . . . it was furthermore proposed by me and ultimately approved by the council, to give 10 pieces of eight to the boatmen for every black they shall get hold of on shore and carry off to the yachts, to the end that the men may use greater care and diligence in this matter, and our masters may reap benefit from the capture of the blacks, which may afterward redound to certain advantage.

On the twenty-fifth the skipper of the *Pera* got orders to go ashore with the two pinnaces well manned and armed, in order to make special search for fresh water, with which we are very poorly provided by this time. About noon the skipper, having returned, informed us that he had caused pits to be dug in various places on the coast, but had found no fresh water. *Item*, that on the strand they had seen seven small huts made of dry hay, and also seven or eight blacks, who refused to hold parley with them. In the afternoon I went up a salt river for the space of about ½ mile [about 2⅓ English miles] with the two pinnaces. We then marched a considerable distance into the interior, which we found to be submerged in many places, thus somewhat resembling Waterland in Holland, from which it may be concluded that there must be large lakes farther inland. We also saw divers footprints of men and of large dogs, running from the south to the north; and since by resolution it has been determined to begin the return voyage at this point, we have, in default of stone, caused a wooden tablet to be nailed to a tree, the said tablet having the following words carved into it: *"Anno 1623 den 24n April sijn hier aen gecomen twee jachten wegen de Hooge Mogende Heeren Staten Gen."* [1]

---

[1] A.D. 1623, on April 24, there arrived here two yachts dispatched by their High Mightinesses of the States General.

On the twenty-sixth, seeing that there was no fresh water here, of which we stood in great need, that we could hold no parley with the natives, and that nothing of importance could be effected, we set sail again . . . at night we came to anchor in 4 fathoms close inshore.

Note that the yacht *Aernem*, owing to bad sailing, and to the small liking and desire which the skipper and the steersman have shown toward the voyage, has on various occasions and at different times been the cause of serious delay, seeing that the *Pera* (which had sprung a bad leak and had to be kept above water by more than eight thousand strokes of the pump every twenty-four hours) was every day obliged to seek and follow the *Aernem* for 1, 2, or even more miles to leeward.

On the twenty-seventh, the wind being east by south, with good weather, the skipper of the *Pera* rowed ashore with the two pinnaces duly provided for defense, in order to seek fresh water; but when he had caused several pits to be dug, no water was found. We therefore set sail forthwith, holding a southeast by east course along the land. At noon we were in latitude 16 degrees 30 minutes, and with a west by north wind made for the land, sailing with our foresail only fully two hours before sunset, in order to wait for the *Aernem*, which was a howitzer's shot astern of us. In the evening, having come to anchor in 3½ fathoms 1½ miles from the land, we hung out a lantern, that the *Aernem* might keep clear of us in dropping anchor; but this proved to be useless, for on purpose and with malice prepense [sic] she cut away from us against her instructions and our resolution, and seems to have set her course for Aru (to have a good time of it there), but we shall learn in time whether she has managed to reach it. . . .

[May] In the morning of the first the wind was east. The skipper once more rowed ashore with the pinnace, and having caused three pits to be dug, he at last found fresh water forcing its way through the sand. We used our best endeavors to take in a stock of the same. About 400 paces north of the farthest of the pits that had been dug they also found a small fresh-water lake, but the water that collected in the pits was found to be a good deal better. . . .

On the third we went on taking in water as before. . . . I

went ashore myself with 10 musketeers, and we advanced a long
way into the wood without seeing any human beings. The land
here is low-lying and without hills as before, in latitude 15
degrees 20 minutes. It is very dry and barren, for during all the
time we have searched and examined this part of the coast to
our best ability, we have not seen one fruit-bearing tree, nor
anything that man could make use of. There are no mountains,
or even hills, so that it may be safely concluded that the land
contains no metals, nor yields any precious woods, such as
sandalwood, aloes,. or columba. In our judgment this is the
most arid and barren region that could be found anywhere on
the earth. The inhabitants, too, are the most wretched and poorest creatures that I have ever seen in my age or time. As there
are no large trees anywhere on this coast, they have no boats or
canoes, whether large or small. This is near the place which we
touched at on the voyage out on Easter Day, April the sixteenth.
In the new chart we have given to this spot the name of Water-
plaets [Mitchell River?]. At this place the beach is very fine,
with excellent gravelly sand and plenty of delicious fish. . . .

In the morning of the fifth the wind was east, course held
north. At noon we were in 14 degrees 5 minutes latitude. Shortly
after, the wind went over to west, upon which we made for
the land and cast anchor in 2 fathom. I went ashore myself in
the pinnace, which was duly armed. The blacks here attacked
us with their weapons, but afterward took to flight; upon which
we went landinward for some distance, and found divers of
their weapons, such as assagais and callaways, leaning against
the trees. We took care not to damage these weapons, but tied
pieces of iron and strings of beads to some of them, in order to
attract the blacks, who, however, seemed indifferent to these
things, and repeatedly held up their shields with great boldness
and threw them at the muskets. These men are, like all the others
we have lately seen, of tall stature and very lean to look at, but
malignant and evil-natured. . . .

In the morning of the eighth, the wind being east-southeast,
with good weather, I went ashore myself with 10 musketeers.
We saw numerous footprints of men and dogs (running from
south to north). We accordingly spent some time there, following the footprints aforesaid to a river, where we gathered excel-

lent vegetables or potherbs. When we had got into the pinnace again, the blacks emerged with their arms from the wood at two different points. By showing them bits of iron and strings of beads we kept them on the beach until we had come near them, upon which one of them, who had lost his weapon, was by the skipper seized round the waist, while at the same time the quartermaster put a noose round his neck, by which he was dragged to the pinnace. The other blacks, seeing this, tried to rescue their captured brother by furiously assailing us with their assagais. In defending ourselves we shot one of them, after which the others took to flight, upon which we returned on board without further delay. . . .

In the morning of the eleventh, the wind being east-southeast, with good weather, we set sail again on a north-northeast course along the land. In the afternoon we sailed past a large river (which the men of the *Duifken* went up with a boat in 1606, and where one of them was killed by the arrows of the blacks). To this river, which is in 11 degrees 48 minutes latitude, we have given the name of Revier de Carpentier in the new chart.

In the morning of the twelfth, the wind was east-southeast, with pleasant weather. I went ashore myself with the skipper, and found upward of two hundred savages standing on the beach making a violent noise, threatening to throw their arrows at us, and evidently full of suspicion; for though we threw out to them pieces of iron and other things, they refused to come to parley, and used every possible means to wound one of our men and get him into their power. We were accordingly compelled to frighten them by firing one or two shots at them, by which one of the blacks was hit in the breast and carried to the pinnace by our men, upon which all the others retired to the hills or dunes. In their wretched huts on the beach we found nothing but a square-cut assagai, two or three small pebbles, and some human bones, which they use in constructing their weapons and scraping the same. We also found a quantity of black resin and a piece of metal, which the wounded man had in his net and which he had most probably got from the men of the *Duifken*. Since there was nothing further to be done here, we rowed back to the yacht, the wounded man dying before we had reached her.

[In a note to his journal entry for May 8, 1623, Carstensz sum-marizes his observations and conclusions regarding the new land and its aborigines:]

Note that in all places where we landed, we have treated the blacks or savages with especial kindness, offering them pieces of iron, strings of beads, and pieces of cloth, hoping by so doing to get their friendship and be allowed to penetrate to some consid-erable distance landinward, that we might be able to give a full account and description of the same. But in spite of all our kind-ness and our fair semblance, the blacks received us as enemies everywhere, so that in most places our landings were attended with great peril.

On this account, and for various other reasons afterward to be mentioned, we have not been able to learn anything about the population of Nova Guinea, and the nature of its inhabitants and its soil. Nor did we get any information touching its towns and villages, about the division of the land, the religion of the natives, their policy, wars, rivers, vessels, or fisheries; what commodities they have, what manufactures, what minerals, whether gold, silver, tin, iron, lead, copper, or quicksilver.

In the first place, in making further landings we should have been troubled by the rainy season, which might have seriously interfered with the use of our muskets, whereas it does no harm to the weapons of the savages. Secondly, we should first have been obliged to seek practicable paths or roads of which we knew nothing. Thirdly, we might easily have been surrounded by the crowds of blacks and been cut off from the boats, which would entail serious peril to the sailors with whom we always effected the landings, and who are imperfectly versed in the use of muskets. If on the contrary we had had well-drilled and experienced soldiers (the men best fitted to undertake such expeditions), we might have done a good deal of useful work. Still, in spite of all these difficulties and obstacles, we have shunned neither hard work, trouble, nor peril to make a thor-ough examination of everything with the means at our disposal, and to do whatever our good name and our honor demanded, the result of our investigation being as follows:

The land between 13 degrees and 17 degrees 8 minutes is a barren and arid tract, without any fruit trees and producing nothing fit for the use of man. It is low-lying and flat, without hills or mountains; in many places overgrown with brushwood and stunted wild trees. It has not much fresh water, and what little there is has to be collected in pits dug for the purpose. There is an utter absence of bays or inlets, with the exception of a few bights not sheltered from the sea wind. It extends mainly north by east and south by west, with shallows all along the coast, with a clayey and sandy bottom. It has numerous salt rivers extending into the interior, across which the natives drag their wives and children by means of dry sticks or boughs of trees.

The natives are in general utter barbarians, all resembling each other in shape and features, coal-black, and with twisted nets wound round their heads and necks, for keeping their food in. So far as we could make out, they chiefly live on certain ill-smelling roots which they dig out of the earth. We infer that during the eastern monsoon they live mainly on the beach, since we have there seen numerous small huts made of dry grass. We also saw great numbers of dogs, herons, and curlews, and other wild fowl, together with plenty of excellent fish, easily caught with a seine net. They are utterly unacquainted with gold, silver, tin, iron, lead, and copper, nor do they know anything about nutmegs, cloves, and pepper, all of which spices we repeatedly showed them without their evincing any signs of recognizing or valuing the same. From all which, together with the rest of our observations, it may safely be concluded that they are poor and abject wretches, caring mainly for bits of iron and strings of beads.

Their weapons are shields, assagais, and callaways of the length of 1½ fathom, made of light wood and cane, some with fishbones and others with human bones fastened to their tops. They are very expert in throwing the said weapons by means of a piece of wood, half a fathom in length, with a small hook tied to it in front, which they place upon the top of the callaway or assagai.

West Coast

The first landing along the west coast was that of Dirck Hartog, of the *Eendracht*, when he went ashore on October

25, 1616, on the island that now bears his name. At Cape Inscription, the northern end of the island, he left a tin platter or pewter dish with an inscription recording his visit. The platter, with the inscription still clear, was found by Vlamingh in 1697 and taken to Batavia; it is now in the States Museum at Amsterdam.

First to land on the western mainland of Australia and to describe the natives and the country was Francis Pelsart (Pelsert, Pelsaert), captain of the Dutch vessel *Batavia*, in 1629. His is largely a story of shipwreck, mutiny, and violence, but the brief descriptive remarks do include a reference to those characteristic and gigantic anthills that dot the landscape of northwestern Australia. Here is the English account of Pelsart's voyage from Pinkerton's collection of voyages and travels.

Voyage of Francis Pelsart to Australasia

The directors of the East India Company, animated by the return of five ships under General Carpenter, richly laden, caused, the very same year, 1628, eleven vessels to be equipped for the same voyage; amongst which there was one ship called the *Batavia*, commanded by Captain Francis Pelsart. They sailed out of the Texel on the twenty-eighth of October, 1628; and as it would be tedious and troublesome to the reader to set down a long account of things perfectly well known, I shall say nothing of the occurrences that happened in their passage to the Cape of Good Hope, but content myself with observing that on the fourth of June in the following year, 1629, this vessel, the *Batavia*, being separated from the fleet in a storm, was driven on the Abrollos, or shoals which lie in the latitude of 28 degrees south, and which have been since called by the Dutch the Abrollos of Frederic Houtman.

Captain Pelsart, who was sick in bed when this accident happened, perceiving that his ship had struck, ran immediately upon deck. It was night indeed, but the weather was fair, and the moon shone very bright. The sails were up, the course they steered was northeast by north, and the sea appeared as far as they could behold it covered with a white froth. The Captain called up the master, and charged him with the loss of the ship, who excused himself by saying he had taken all the care he could, and that having discerned this froth at a distance, he asked the steersman what he thought of it, who told him that the sea appeared white by its reflecting the rays of the moon. The Captain then asked him what was to be done, and in what part of the world he thought they were. The master replied that God only knew that, and that the ship was fast on a bank hitherto undiscovered.

Upon this they began to throw the lead, and found that they had 48 feet water before and much less behind the vessel. The crew immediately agreed to throw their cannon overboard, in hopes that when the ship was lightened, she might be brought to float again. They let fall an anchor, however, and while they were thus employed, a most dreadful storm arose of wind and rain, which soon convinced them of the danger they were in; for being surrounded with rocks and shoals, the ship was continually striking.

They then resolved to cut away the mainmast, which they did, and this augmented the shock, neither could they get clear of it, though they cut it close by the board, because it was much entangled with the rigging. They could see no land except an island, which was about the distance of 3 leagues, and two smaller islands, or rather rocks, which lay nearer. They immediately sent the master to examine them, who returned about nine in the morning and reported that the sea at high water did not cover them, but that the coast was so rocky and full of shoals that it would be very difficult to land upon them. They resolved, however, to run the risk, and to send most of their company on shore to pacify the women, children, sick people, and such as were out of their wits with fear, whose cries and noise served only to disturb them.

About ten o'clock they embarked these in their shallop and skiff and, perceiving their vessel began to break, they doubled their diligence. They likewise endeavored to get their bread up, but they did not take the same care of the water, not reflecting in their fright that they might be much distressed for want of it on shore. And what hindered them most of all was the brutal behavior of some of the crew that made themselves drunk with wine, of which no care was taken. In short, such was their confusion that they made but three trips that day, carrying over to the island 180 persons, twenty barrels of bread, and some small casks of water. The master returned on board toward evening, and told the Captain that it was to no purpose to send more provisions on shore, since the people only wasted those they had already. Upon this the Captain went in the shallop to put things in better order, and was then informed that there was not water to be found upon the island. He endeavored to return to the ship in order to bring off a supply, together with the most valuable part of their cargo, but a storm suddenly arising, he was forced to return.

The next day was spent in removing their water and most valuable goods on shore, and afterward the Captain in the skiff, and the master in the shallop, endeavored to return to the vessel, but found the sea run so high that it was impossible to get on board. In this extremity the carpenter threw himself out of the ship and swam to them, in order to inform them to what hardships those left in the vessel were reduced, and they sent him back with orders for them to make rafts by tying the planks together, and endeavor on these to reach the shallop and skiff. But before this could be done the weather became so rough that the Captain was obliged to return, leaving, with the utmost grief, his lieutenant and 70 men on the very point of perishing on board the vessel.

Those who were got on the little island were not in a much better condition, for upon taking an account of their water, they found they had not above 40 gallons for 40 people, and on the larger island, where there were 120, their stock was still less. Those on the little island began to murmur, and to complain of their officers because they did not go in search of water in the islands that were within sight of them, and they represented the necessity of this to Captain Pelsart, who agreed to their request, but insisted before he went to communicate his design to the rest of the people. They consented to this, but not till the Captain had declared that without the consent of the company on the large island, he would, rather than leave them, go and perish on board the ship.

When they were got pretty near the shore, he who commanded the boat told the Captain that if he had anything to say he must cry out to the people, for that they would not suffer him to go out of the boat. The Captain immediately attempted to throw himself overboard, in order to swim to the island. Those who were in the boat prevented him, and all that he could obtain from them was to throw on shore his table book, in which he wrote a line or two to inform them that he was gone in the skiff to look for water in the adjacent islands.

He accordingly coasted them [the islands] all with the greatest care, and found in most of them considerable quantities of water in the holes of the rocks, but so mixed with the sea water that it was unfit for use, and therefore they were obliged to go farther. The first thing they did was to make a deck to their boat, because they found it was impracticable to navigate those seas in an open vessel. Some of the crew joined them by that time the work was finished, and the Captain having obtained a paper signed by all his men importing that it was their desire that he should go in search of water, he immediately put to sea, having first taken an observation, by which he found they were in the latitude of 28 degrees 13 minutes south.

They had not been long at sea before they had sight of the continent, which appeared to them to lie about 16 miles north by west from the place they had suffered shipwreck. They found about 25 or 30 fathoms water; and as night drew on, they kept out to sea, and after midnight stood in for the land, that they might be near the coast in the morning.

On the ninth of June, they found themselves, as they reckoned, about 3 miles from the shore, on which they plied all that day, sailing sometimes north, sometimes west, the country appearing low, naked, and the coast excessively rocky, so that they thought it resembled the country near Dover. At last they saw a little creek into which they were willing to put because it appeared to have a sandy bottom; but when they attempted to enter it, the sea ran so high that they were forced to desist.

On the tenth, they remained on the same coast, plying to and again as they had done the day before. But, the weather growing worse and worse, they were obliged to abandon their shallop and even throw part of their bread overboard, because it hindered them from clearing themselves of the water, which their vessel began to make very fast. That night it rained most terribly, which, though it gave them much trouble, afforded them hopes that it would prove a great relief to the people they had left behind them on the islands. The wind began to sink on the eleventh, and as it blew from the west-southwest, they continued their course to the north, the sea running still so high that it was impossible to approach the shore.

On the twelfth, they had an observation, by which they found themselves in the latitude of 27 degrees. They sailed with a southeast wind all that day along the coast, which they found so steep that there was no getting on shore, inasmuch as there was no creek or low land without the rocks, as is commonly observed on seacoasts; which gave them the more pain because withinland the country appeared very fruitful and pleasant. They found themselves on the thirteenth in the latitude of 25 degrees 40 minutes, by which they discovered that the current set to the north. They were at this time over against an opening. The coast lying to the northeast, they continued a north course, but found the coast one continued rock of a red color, all of a height, against which the waves broke with such force that it was impossible for them to land.

The wind blew very fresh in the morning on the fourteenth, but toward noon it fell calm. They were then in the height of 24 degrees, with a small gale at east, but the tide still carried them further north than they desired, because their design was to make a descent as soon as possible; and with this view they sailed slowly along the coast till, perceiving a great deal of smoke at a distance, they rowed toward it as fast as they were able, in hopes of finding men, and water of course. When they came near the shore, they found it so steep, so full of rocks, and the sea beating over them with such fury, that it was impossible to land. Six of the men, however, trusting to their skill in swimming, threw themselves into the sea and resolved to get on shore at any rate, which with great difficulty and danger they at last effected, the boat remaining at anchor in 25 fathoms water.

The men on shore spent the whole day in looking for water, and while they were thus employed, they saw four men, who came up very near; but one of the Dutch sailors advancing toward them, they immediately ran away as fast as they were able, so that they were distinctly seen by those in the boat. These people were black savages, quite naked, not having so much as any covering about their middle. The sailors, finding no hopes of water on all the coast, swam on board again, much hurt and wounded by their being beat by the waves upon the rocks. And as soon as they were on board, they weighed anchor and continued their course along the shore, in hopes of finding some better landing-place.

On the fifteenth, in the morning, they discovered a cape, from the point of which there ran a ridge of rocks a mile into the sea, and behind it another ridge of rocks. They ventured between them, as the sea was pretty calm, but finding there was no passage, they soon returned. About noon, they saw another opening, and, the sea being still very smooth, they entered it, though the passage was very dangerous, inasmuch as they had but 2 feet water, and the bottom full of stones, the coast appearing a flat sand for about a mile.

As soon as they got on shore, they fell to digging in the sand, but the water that came into their wells was so brackish that they could not drink it, though they were on the very point of choking for thirst. At last in the hollows of the rocks they met with considerable quantities of rain water, which was a great relief to them, since they had been for some days at no better allowance than a pint apiece. They soon furnished themselves in the night with about 80 gallons, perceiving, in the place where they landed, that the savages had been there lately, by a large heap of ashes, and the remains of some crayfish.

On the sixteenth, in the morning, they returned on shore, in hopes of getting more water, but were disappointed. And having now time to observe the country, it gave them no great hopes of better success, even if they had traveled farther withinland, which appeared a thirsty barren plain, covered with anthills so high that they looked afar off like the huts of Negroes; and at the same time they were plagued with flies, and those in such multitudes that they were scarce able to defend themselves. They saw at a distance eight savages, with each a staff in his hand, who advanced toward them within musket shot; but as soon as they perceived the Dutch sailors moving toward them, they fled as fast as they were able.

It was by this time about noon and, perceiving no appearance either of getting water or entering into any correspondence with the natives, they resolved to go on board and continue their course toward the north, in hopes, as they were already in the latitude of 22 degrees 17 minutes, they might be able to find the river of Jacob Remmescens. But, the wind veering about to the northeast, they were not able to continue longer upon that coast, and therefore reflecting that they were now above 100 miles from the place where they were shipwrecked, and had scarce as much water as would serve them in their passage back, they came to a settled resolution of making the best of their way to Batavia, in order to acquaint the Governor General with their misfortunes, and to obtain such assistance as was necessary to get their people off the coast. . . .

We will now leave the Captain soliciting succors from the Governor General, in order to return to the crew who were left upon the islands, among whom there happened such transactions as, in their condition, the reader would little expect, and perhaps will hardly credit. In order to their being thoroughly understood, it is necessary to observe that they had for supercargo one Jerom Cornelis, who had been formerly an apothecary at Harlem. This man, when they were on the coast of Africa, had plotted with the pilot and some others to run away with the vessel, and either to carry her into Dunkirk, or to turn pirates in her on their own account. This supercargo had remained ten days on board the wreck, not being able in all that time to get on shore. Two whole days he spent on the mainmast, floating to and fro, till at last, by the help of one of the yards, he got to land.

When he was once on shore, the command, in the absence of Captain Pelsart, devolved of course upon him, which immediately revived in his mind his old design, insomuch that he resolved to lay hold of this opportunity to make himself master of all that could be saved out of the wreck, conceiving that it would be easy to surprise the Captain on his return, and determining to go on the account; that is to say, to turn pirate in the Captain's vessel. In order to carry this design into execution, he thought it necessary to rid themselves of such of the crew as were not like to come into their scheme; but before he proceeded to dip his hands in blood, he obliged all the conspirators to sign an instrument by which they engaged to stand by each other.

The whole ship's company were on shore in three islands, the greatest part of them in that where Cornelis was, which island they thought fit to call the burying-place of Batavia. One Mr. Weybhays was sent with another body into an adjacent island to look for water, which, after twenty days' search, he found, and made the appointed signal by lighting three fires, which, however, were not seen nor taken notice of by those under the command of Cornelis, because they were busy in butchering their companions, of whom they had murdered between 30 and 40. But some few, however, got off upon a raft of planks tied together, and went to the island where Mr. Weybhays was, in order to acquaint him with the dreadful accident that had happened.

Mr. Weybhays having with him 45 men, they all resolved to stand upon their guard, and to defend themselves to the last man in case these villains should attack them. This indeed was their design, for they were apprehensive both of this body and of those who were on the third island giving notice to the Captain on his return, and thereby preventing their intention of running away with his vessel. But as this third company was by much the weakest, they began with them first, and cut them all off except 5 women and 7 children, not in the least doubting that they should be able to do as much by Weybhays and his company. In the meantime, having broke open the merchant's chests which had been saved out of the wreck, they converted them to their own use without ceremony.

The traitor, Jerom Cornelis, was so much elevated with the success that had hitherto attended his villainy that he immediately began to fancy all difficulties were over, and gave a loose to his vicious inclinations in every respect. He ordered clothes to be made of rich stuffs that had been saved, for himself and his troop, and having chosen out of them a company of guards, he ordered them to have scarlet coats with a double lace of gold or silver. There were two minister's daughters among the women, one of whom he took for his own mistress, gave the second to a favorite of his, and ordered that the other three women should be common to the whole troop. He afterward drew up a set of regulations which were to be the laws of his new principality, taking to himself the style and title of Captain General, and obliging his party to sign an act or instrument by which they acknowledged him as such.

These points once settled, he resolved to carry on the war. He first of all embarked on board two shallops 22 men, well armed, with orders to destroy Mr. Weybhays and his company; and on their miscarrying, he undertook a like expedition with 37 men, in which, however, he had no better success; for Mr. Weybhays, with his people, though armed only with staves with nails drove into their heads, advanced even into the water to meet them, and after a brisk engagement, compelled these murderers to retire.

Cornelis then thought fit to enter into a negotiation, which was managed by the chaplain, who remained with Mr. Weybhays; and after several comings and goings from one party to the other, a treaty was concluded upon the following terms, viz., that Mr. Weybhays and his company should for the future remain undisturbed, provided they delivered up a little boat in which one of the sailors had made his escape from the island in which Cornelis was with his gang, in order to take shelter on that where Weybhays was with his company. It was also agreed that the latter should have a part of the stuffs and silks given them for clothes, of which they stood in great want. But while this affair was in agitation Cornelis took the opportunity of the correspondence between them being restored to write letters to some French soldiers that were in Weybhays's company, promising them 6000 livres apiece if they would comply with his demands, not doubting but by this artifice he should be able to accomplish his end.

His letters however had no effect; on the contrary, the soldiers to whom they were directed carried them immediately to Mr. Weybhays. Cornelis, not knowing that this piece of treachery was discovered, went over the next morning, with three or four of his people, to carry to Mr. Weybhays the clothes that had been promised him. As soon as they landed, Weybhays attacked them, killed two or three, and made Cornelis himself prisoner. One Wonterloss, who was the only man that made his escape, went immediately back to the conspirators, put himself at their head, and came the next day to attack Weybhays, but met with the same fate as before; that is to say, he and the villains that were with him were soundly beat.

Things were in this situation when Captain Pelsart arrived in the *Sardam* frigate. He sailed up to the wreck, and saw with great joy a cloud of smoke ascending from one of the islands, by which he knew that all his people were not dead. He came immediately to an anchor, and having ordered some wine and provisions to be put into the skiff, resolved to go in person with these refreshments to one of these islands. He had hardly quitted the ship before he was boarded by a boat from the island to which he was going. There were four men in the boat, of whom Weybhays was one, who immediately ran to the Captain, told him what had happened, and begged him to return to his ship immediately, for that the conspirators intended to surprise her; that they had already murdered 125 persons; and that they had attacked him and his company that very morning, with two shallops.

While they were talking the two shallops appeared, upon which the Captain rowed to his ship as fast as he could, and was hardly got on board before they arrived at the ship's side. The Captain was surprised to see men in red coats laced with gold and silver, with arms in their hands. He demanded what they meant by coming on board armed. They told him he should know when they were on board the ship. The Captain replied that they should come on board, but that they must first throw their arms into the sea, which if they did not do immediately, he would sink them as they lay. As they saw that disputes were to no purpose, and that they were entirely in the Captain's power, they were obliged to obey. They accordingly threw their arms overboard, and were then taken into the vessel, where they were instantly put in irons. One of them, whose name was John Bremen and who was first examined, owned that he had murdered with his own hands, or had assisted in murdering, no less than 27 persons. The same evening Weybhays brought his prisoner Cornelis on board, where he was put in irons and strictly guarded.

On the eighteenth of September, Captain Pelsart, with the master, went to take the rest of the conspirators in Cornelis's island. They went in two boats. The villains, as soon as they saw them land, lost all their courage and fled from them. They surrendered without a blow, and were put in irons with the rest. The Captain's first care was to recover the jewels which Cornelis had dispersed among his accomplices. They were, however, all of them soon found except a gold chain and a diamond ring; the latter was also found at last, but the former could not be recovered. They went next to examine the wreck, which they found staved into a hundred pieces. The keel lay on a bank of sand on one side, the fore part of the vessel stuck fast on a rock, and the rest of her lay here and there as the pieces had been driven by the waves, so that Captain Pelsart had very little hopes of saving any of the merchandise. One of the people belonging to Weybhays's company told him that one fair day, which was the only one they had in a month, as he was fishing near the wreck he had struck the pole in his hand against one of the chests of silver, which revived the Captain a little, as it gave him reason to expect that something might still be saved. They spent all the nineteenth in examining the rest of the prisoners, and in confronting them with those who escaped from the massacre.

On the twentieth, they sent several kinds of refreshments to Weybhays's company, and carried a good quantity of water from the isle. There was something very singular in finding this water. The people who were on shore there had subsisted near three weeks on rain water and what lodged in the clefts of the rocks, without thinking that the water of two wells which were on the island could be of any use, because they saw them constantly rise and fall with the tide, from whence they fancied they had a communication with the sea and consequently that the water must be brackish; but upon trial they found it to be very good, and so did the ship's company, who filled their casks with it.

On the twenty-first, the tide was so low, and an east-southeast wind blew so hard that during the whole day the boat could not get out. On the twenty-second, they attemped to fish upon the wreck, but the weather was so bad that even those who could swim well durst not approach it. On the twenty-fifth, the master and the pilot, the weather being fair, went off again to the wreck, and those who were left on shore, observing that they wanted hands to get anything out of her, sent off some to assist them. The Captain went also himself to encourage the men, who soon weighed one chest of silver and some time after, another. As soon as these were safe ashore they returned to their work, but the weather grew so bad that they were quickly obliged to desist, though some of their divers from Guzarat assured them they had found six more which might easily be weighed. On the twenty-sixth, in the afternoon, the weather being fair and the tide low, the master returned to the place where the chests lay and weighed three of them, leaving an anchor with a gun tied to it and a buoy to mark the place where the fourth lay, which, notwithstanding their utmost efforts, they were not able to recover.

On the twenty-seventh, the south wind blew very cold. On the twenty-eighth, the same wind blew stronger than the day before, and as there was no possibility of fishing in the wreck for the present, Captain Pelsart held a council to consider what they should do with the prisoners; that is to say, whether it would be best to try them there upon the spot, or to carry them to Batavia, in order to their being tried by the Company's officers. After mature deliberation, reflecting on the number of prisoners and the temptation that might arise from the vast quantity of silver on board the frigate, they at last came to a resolution to try and execute them there, which was accordingly done; and they embarked immediately afterwards for Batavia.

The rigid monopolistic practices of the Dutch in the East Indies, besides weakening the hold of the Spanish and the Portuguese, also restricted the activities of the English, who were beginning to compete for a portion of the trade of the East. In the Pinkerton volume the editorial comments that precede and follow the Pelsart narrative illustrate the resentment that existed in England at the Dutch policy of secrecy, and the suspicion with which the English viewed any Dutch information that was put out. An unfavorable report of any locality merely heightened the suspicion, for the English, like their contemporaries of other nationalities, believed what they wanted to believe, and what they wanted and therefore expected was that each new land discovered would be as rich in gold as Peru or in spices and other products as the Moluccas. Thus in prefacing the Pelsart story the translator remarks:

"It has appeared very strange to some very able judges of voyages that the Dutch should make so great account of the southern countries as to cause the map of them to be laid down in the pavement of the Stadthouse at Amsterdam, and yet publish no description of them. This mystery was a good deal heightened by one of the ships that first touched on Carpenter's Land [Carpentaria, as the land on the eastern side of the Gulf of Carpentaria was called], bringing home a considerable quantity of gold, spices, and other rich goods; in order to clear up which it was said that these were not the product of the country, but were fished out of the wreck of a large ship that had been lost upon the coast.

"But this story did not satisfy the inquisitive, because not attended with circumstances necessary to establish its credit; and therefore they suggested that instead of taking away the obscurity by relating the truth, this tale was invented in order to hide it more effectually."

The English comment on Pelsart's description of northwestern Australia concludes: ". . . it is very plain that the Dutch, or rather the Dutch East India Company, are fully persuaded that they have already as much or more territory in the East Indies than they can well manage, and therefore they neither do nor ever will think of settling New Guinea, Carpentaria, New Holland, or any of the adjacent islands, till either their trade declines in the East Indies or they are obliged to exert themselves on this side to prevent other nations from reaping the benefits that might accrue to them by planting those countries.

"But this is not all; for as the Dutch have no thought of settling these countries themselves, they have taken all imaginable pains to prevent any relations from being published which might invite or encourage any other nation to make attempts this way; and I am thoroughly persuaded that this very account of Captain Pelsart's shipwreck would never have come into the world if it had not been thought it would contribute to this end, or, in other words, would serve to frighten other nations from approaching such an inhospitable coast, everywhere beset with rocks, absolutely void of water, and inhabited by a race of savages more barbarous, and at the same time more miserable, than any other creatures in the world."

Gradually the puzzle that was Australia took some semblance of form as regards the north and west coasts, though there was still doubt as to whether these belonged to one land or to a group of islands. There was doubt also (the results of Torres's voyage not having been revealed) as to its relation to New Guinea. The greatest uncertainty existed regarding its southward extension. Did it reach all the way to the South Pole, as some contemporary maps showed, or was there a passage around it, as there was around Africa and South America? The solution of this problem was the object of the Tasman expedition of 1642-43.

Abel Janszoon Tasman (c. 1603-1659), the discoverer of Tasmania, New Zealand, and the Tonga and Fiji islands, was the greatest of the navigators in the service of the Dutch East India Company. Prior to his voyage of discovery he had made the passage several times to and from Holland and Java, and had made voyages as well to South America, China, Japan, India, the Philippines, and other Pacific islands. With so much experience to his credit, it appears natural that Tasman should have been chosen to command the expedition which Anton van Diemen, Governor of the Dutch East Indies, sent out in 1642 to explore the coast of the southern continent.

Leaving Batavia in August 1642 with the ships *Heemskerck* and *Zeehaen*, Tasman steered for Mauritius, and thence sailed first south and then east. On November 24 he sighted the west coast of the land which he named Van Diemen's Land, now called Tasmania. Rounding the southern end of the island, he anchored in Frederick Henry Bay, where he hoisted a flag on a pole with the company's mark carved in it, "that those who shall come after us may become aware that we have been here, and have taken possession of the said land as our lawful property."

Tasman's own journal is a valuable though on the whole rather dull account, typical of the experienced sailor, with its frequent references to winds and calms, anchoring conditions, variation of the compass, and other nautical matters.[2] In one of the more interesting passages, the entry for December 1, 1642, Tasman describes the new land as it appeared to a reconnaissance party, who reported to him:

First Description of Tasmania

🐚 That they had rowed the space of upward of a mile round the said point [in the bay where the vessels were anchored], where they had found high but level land, covered with vegetation (not cultivated, but growing naturally by the will of God), abundance of excellent timber, and a gently sloping watercourse in a barren valley, the said water, though of good quality, being difficult to procure, because the watercourse was so shallow that the water could be dipped with bowls only.

That they had heard certain human sounds, and also sounds nearly resembling the music of a trump, or a small gong, not far from them, though they had seen no one.

That they had seen two trees about 2 or 2½ fathom in thickness, measuring from 60 to 65 feet from the ground to the lowermost branches, which trees bore notches made with flint implements, the bark having been removed for the purpose. These notches, forming a kind of steps to enable persons to get up the trees and rob the birds' nests in their tops, were fully 5 feet apart, so that our men concluded that the natives here must be of very tall stature, or must be in possession of some sort of artifice for getting up the said trees. In one of the trees these notched steps were so fresh and new that they seemed to have been cut less than four days ago.

That on the ground they had observed certain footprints of

---

[2] The journal is included in a volume published at London in 1694, entitled *An Account of Several Late Voyages & Discoveries to the South and North,* by Sir John Narborough, Captain Jasmen Tasman, Captain John Wood, and Frederick Marten of Hamburgh.

animals, not unlike those of a tiger's claws. They also brought on board . . . a small quantity of gum of a seemingly very fine quality, which had exuded from trees, and bore some resemblance to gum-lac.

That round the eastern point of this bay they had sounded 13 or 14 feet at high water, there being about 3 feet at low tide.

That at the extremity of the said point they had seen large numbers of gulls, wild ducks, and geese, but had perceived none farther inward, though they had heard their cries, and had found no fish except different kinds of mussels forming small clusters in several places.

That the land is pretty generally covered with trees, standing so far apart that they allow a passage everywhere, and a look-out to a great distance, so that when landing our men could always get sight of natives or wild beasts, unhindered by dense shrubbery or underwood, which would prove a great advantage in exploring the country. ✍

From Tasmania the vessels turned east for the Solomon Islands, and on December 13 sighted a "large, high-lying land," the present New Zealand. On December 18 Tasman anchored at the entrance of a "large open bay" (Cook Strait), which he named Moordenaars (Massacre) Bay because several of his men were killed here by the natives. These people were the Maoris, now for the first time seen by Europeans. Tasman sailed eastward for some distance from his anchorage position, and then, having failed to discover that his large bay was in reality a strait dividing New Zealand into two islands, turned about and retraced his course. Thereafter he coasted the western side of the land to the northern extremity of the North Island, and then bore away to the north-northeast. To Tasman it seemed that the country he had found must be part of the great southern continent, for he says in his journal:

"This is the second land which we have sailed along and discovered. In honor of Their High Mightinesses the States-General we gave to this land the name of Staten Landt, since we deemed it quite possible that this land is part of the great Staten land, though this is not certain. This land seems to be a very fine country, and we trust that this is the mainland coast of the unknown Southland. To this course we have given the name of Abel Tasman Passage, because he has been the first to navigate it."

On the return of the expedition to Batavia there was considerable dissatisfaction among officials of the company at what was felt to be the meagerness of Tasman's results. In his report, dated June 19, 1643, Governor van Diemen reviews the achievements of Tasman: The expedition had, it is true, discovered two great lands, Van Diemen's Land and Staten Land, also various islands to the northeast (islands of the Tonga or Friendly group and the Fiji Islands), and had as well revealed "a convenient passage to the gold-bearing coast of Chile." But Tasman had failed to make a thorough investigation of his discoveries, so that "in point of fact no treasures or matters of great profit have as yet been found."

For a century and a half following its discovery, Tasmania was generally considered a part of a land of continental dimensions, the east coast of which on many maps was shown as extending southward in an unbroken line from the New Hebrides to the southern end of the Van Diemen's Land of Tasman. The location of the south coast of Australia was not determined until 1798, when Bass, accompanied by Flinders, discovered Bass Strait, thereby demonstrating the insularity of Tasmania.

East Coast

On his second voyage, begun in 1644, Tasman was instructed to determine whether a land connection existed between New Guinea and New Holland, for the demonstration by Prado and Torres that a strait lay between the two countries was still unknown to the Dutch. Tasman failed to achieve his purpose, and the numerous explorers who worked in these waters for more than a hundred years thereafter added to knowledge of the coasts that had already been discovered, but failed to solve the problem of what lay to the east of the land known to the Dutch as New Holland.

This problem, involving the discovery and exploration of the east coast of Australia, as well as a repetition of the discovery of the strait between New Guinea and Australia, awaited its solution until 1770, when along came a great English navigator.

James Cook (1728-1779), son of a Yorkshire farmer, entered the Royal Navy in 1755, after having first served an apprenticeship at sea, and within four years had risen to the position of master. For some time he was employed in a survey of the St. Lawrence River, and subsequently, as "marine surveyor of the coast of Newfoundland and Labrador," he compiled volumes of sailing directions for these coasts. In 1766 his published account of the solar eclipse of August 5 of that year called attention to his abilities as a mathematician and astronomer.

The latter achievement was, no doubt, a considerable factor in the British Admiralty's selection of Cook to lead an expedition to the South Pacific Ocean in 1768 for observing the transit of Venus. For this, the first of his three great voyages of discovery, Cook was commissioned as lieutenant; on the second, 1772-75, he was made a commander; and in 1776 he sailed with the rank of captain on the third and last expedition, from which he did not return, for he was killed in Hawaii on February 14, 1779, in a fight with the natives.

As a navigator Cook combined great skill with careful attention to detail, and he was, besides, a man of scrupulous honesty. In his journal he never fails to credit the discoveries of his predecessors, nor does he hesitate to criticize those who lack his own high standards. For example, there are the remarks on charts in his account of the first voyage:

"By our run from New Guinea [we] ought to be in sight of Wessels Isle, which according to the chart is laid down about 20 or 25 leagues from the coast of New Holland; but we saw nothing, by which I conclude that it is wrong laid down. And this is not to be wondered at when we consider that not only these islands, but the lands which bound this sea, have been discovered and explored by different people and at different times, and compiled and put together by others, perhaps some ages after the first discoveries were made.

"Navigation formerly wanted many of these helps toward keeping an accurate journal which the present age is possessed of. It is not they that are wholly to blame for the faultiness of the charts, but [of] the compilers and publishers, who publish to the world the rude sketches of the navigator as accurate surveys without telling what authority they have for so doing; for were they to do this, we should then be as good or better judge than they, and know where to depend upon the charts and where not.

"Neither can I clear seamen of this fault. Among the few I have known who are capable of drawing a chart or sketch of a seacoast I have generally, nay, almost always, observed them run into this error. I have known them lay down the line of a coast they have never seen, and put down soundings where they never have sounded; and, after all, are so fond of their performances as to pass the whole off as sterling under the title of a survey plan, etc. These things must in time be attended with bad consequences, and cannot fail of bringing the whole of their works in disrepute. If he is so modest as to say such-and-such parts, or the whole of his plan, is defective, the publishers or vendors will have it left out, because they say it hurts the sale of the work; so that between the one and the other we can hardly tell when we are possessed of a good sea chart until we ourselves have proved it."

The plan of the first expedition, 1768-71, was that Cook should first proceed to the island of Otaheite (Tahiti) for the observation of the transit of Venus, this site having been recommended by the British navigator Samuel Wallis, who had discovered the island in 1767. The orders from the Admiralty further directed that after observing the transit, Cook was to continue that exploration of the South Pacific Ocean in which Byron and Wallis had been engaged during the years immediately preceding.

This first voyage of Cook's has been described as being "to the English nation the most momentous voyage of discovery that has ever taken place," for the discovery and charting of the east coast of the land formerly known vaguely as New Holland opened the way for the English settlement of the new continent and the building of the great Commonwealth of Australia.

Scarcely less important were the scientific results of the expedition. The program for scientific research was financed by Joseph (later Sir Joseph) Banks, who took part in the voyage, accompanied by his librarian Dr. Daniel Charles Solander,

Swedish botanist and scholar. The arrangements for scientific study are set forth in a letter written to Linnaeus by the English naturalist John Ellis:

"I must now inform you that Joseph Banks, Esq., a gentleman of £6000 per annum estate, has prevailed on your pupil, Dr. Solander, to accompany him in the ship that carries the English astronomers to the new-discovered country in the South sea [that is, the Society Islands] . . . where they are to collect all the natural curiosities of the place, and after the astronomers have finished their observations on the transit of Venus, they are to proceed . . . on further discoveries. . . . No people ever went to sea better fitted out for the purpose of natural history, nor more elegantly. They have got a fine library of natural history; they have all sorts of machines for catching and preserving insects; all kinds of nets, trawls, drags, and hooks for coral fishing; they have even a curious contrivance of a telescope by which, put into the water, you can see the bottom at a great depth, where it is clear. . . . There are many people whose sole business it is to attend them for this very purpose. They have two painters and draughtsmen, several volunteers who have a tolerable notion of natural history. In short, Solander assured me this expedition would cost Mr. Banks £10,000."

The small vessel *Endeavour* set sail from England on August 25, 1768, to carry out this ambitious astronomical, scientific, and exploratory program. The transit of Venus was observed at Tahiti on June 3, 1769, and thence Cook sailed in quest of new lands. After exploring the Society Islands, he proceeded to New Zealand, where he spent six months circumnavigating the islands, examining and charting the coasts with great care. From New Zealand, Cook took a westerly course, and on April 19, 1770, sighted the east coast of Australia, probably in the vicinity of the present Cape Everard. Here the *Endeavour* turned northeastward, in pursuance of Cook's determination to "follow the direction of that coast to the northward, or what other direction it might take us, until we arrive at its northern extremity." The coast was thus explored and mapped, and finally, on Possession Island in Torres Strait, Cook "took posses-

662 GREAT ADVENTURES AND EXPLORATIONS

sion of the whole eastern coast" under the name of New South Wales.

Upon the return of the expedition to England in 1771, there was great public interest, and the printed narrative was eagerly awaited; but the official publication which appeared in 1773 was neither Cook's own journal nor that of Banks. Instead, Dr. John Hawkesworth, that "studious imitator of Dr. Johnson," as Boswell called him, was commissioned by Lord Sandwich, head of the Admiralty, to write a "literary" narrative based on the two journals. The result is said to have been satisfactory to neither Cook nor Banks, but more than a century was to elapse before the original journals were published, and during this time the Hawkesworth account, handsomely printed and illustrated, became firmly established as the authentic narrative. With the publication of Cook's journal in 1893 and of Banks's journal in 1896, it was at last possible to observe how Hawkesworth had woven together passages from both, at times changing the plain mariner's language of Cook into his own more florid style.

It is, then, more appropriate and satisfactory to take the account here of the discovery and exploration of the east coast of Australia direct from *Captain Cook's Journal during the First Voyage round the World Made in H. M. Bark "Endeavour," 1768-71, a literal transcription of the original MSS., with notes and introduction by Captain W. J. L. Wharton,* London, 1893.

It should be noted that, according to the nautical custom of the period, the days are reckoned from noon to noon, instead of from midnight to midnight, as in civil reckoning. By this method, which was known as ship time, the day begins at noon of the day before the civil date. Thus the entry for January 1, for example, begins with the P.M. of December 31, and is followed by the A.M. of January 1.

In his preface to the *Journal,* Wharton explains that a good many of the eccentricities of grammar appear to be due to the transcriber rather than to Cook.

Many of the nautical details have been omitted from the following extracts from Cook's *Journal,* so as to throw into higher relief the narrative of discovery and exploration.

The extracts begin with the journal entry for March 31, 1770, as the expedition prepares to leave New Zealand.

James Cook Discovers the East Coast of Australia

📝 [March 31, 1770] Being now resolved to quit this country [New Zealand] altogether, and to bend my thought toward returning home by such a route as might conduce most to the advantage of the service I am upon, I consulted with the officers upon the most eligible way of putting this in execution. To return by the way of Cape Horn was what I most wished, because by this route we should have been able to prove the existence or nonexistence of a southern continent, which yet remains doubtful. But in order to ascertain this we must have kept in a higher latitude in the very depth of winter; but the condition of the ship, in every respect, was not thought sufficient for such an undertaking. For the same reason the thought of proceeding directly to the Cape of Good Hope was laid aside, especially as no discovery of any moment could be hoped for in that route. It was therefore resolved to return by way of the East Indies by the following route: upon leaving this coast to steer to the westward until we fall in with the east coast of New Holland, and then to follow the direction of that coast to the northward, or what other direction it might take us, until we arrive at its northern extremity; and if this should be found impracticable, then to endeavor to fall in with the land or islands discovered by Quiros. . . .

Thursday, [April 19, 1770]. In the P.M. had fresh gales at south-southwest and cloudy squally weather, with a large southerly sea. . . . [At 6 A.M.] saw land extending from northeast to west, distance 5 to 6 leagues, having 80 fathoms, fine sandy bottom. We continued standing to the westward with the wind at south-southwest until eight, at which time we got topgallant yards across, made all sail, and bore away alongshore northeast for the easternmost land we had in sight, being at this time in the latitude of 37 degrees 58 minutes south, and longitude of 210 degrees 39 minutes west. The southernmost point of land we had in sight, which bore from us west ¼ south, I judged to lay in the latitude of 38 degrees south, and in the longitude of

211 degrees 7 minutes west from the meridian of Greenwich. I have named it Point Hicks,[3] because Lieutenant Hicks was the first who discovered this land.

To the southward of this point we could see no land, and yet it was clear in that quarter, and by our longitude compared with that of Tasman's, the body of Van Diemen's land [Tasmania] ought to have bore due south from us, and from the soon falling of the sea after the wind abated I had reason to think it did. But as we did not see it, and finding the coast to trend northeast and southwest, or rather more to the westward, makes me doubtful whether they are one land or no. However, everyone who compares this journal with that of Tasman's will be as good a judge as I am; but it is necessary to observe that I do not take the situation of Tasmania from the printed charts, but from the extract of Tasman's journal, published by Dirk Rembrantse. . . .

Friday, [April] 20. . . . At six, shortened sail and brought to for the night, having 56 fathoms, fine sandy bottom. The northernmost land in sight bore north by east ½ east, and a small island lying close to a point on the main bore west, distant 2 leagues. This point I have named Cape Howe. It may be known by the trending of the coast, which is north on the one side and southwest on the other. . . . It may likewise be known by some round hills upon the main just within it. . . . At noon . . . [the] course sailed alongshore since yesterday at noon was first north 52° east, 30 miles, then north by east and north by west, 41 miles.

The weather being clear gave us an opportunity to view the country, which had a very agreeable and promising aspect, diversified with hills, ridges, plains, and valleys, with some few small lawns; but for the most part the whole was covered with wood. The hills and ridges rise with a gentle slope; they are not high, neither are there many of them.

Saturday [April] 21. . . . In the P.M. we saw the smoke of fire in several places, a certain sign that the country is inhabited. . . . At 6 [A.M.], we were abreast of a pretty high mountain

---

[3] The land seen by Cook was not a point, but merely a rise in the coast line. The name Point Hicks Hill has been applied to an elevation that seems to agree with Cook's position.

laying near the shore, which, on account of its figure, I named Mount Dromedary. The shore under the foot of the mountain forms a point, which I have named Cape Dromedary, over which is a peaked hillock. . . . An open bay wherein lay three or four small islands . . . is the only likely anchoring place I have yet seen upon the coast.

Sunday, [April] 22. In the P.M. had a gentle breeze at south by west, with which we steered alongshore . . . at the distance of about 3 leagues. Saw the smoke of fire in several places near the sea beach. At five, we were abreast of a point of land which, on account of its perpendicular cliffs, I called Point Upright. . . . [In the morning] we steered alongshore north-northeast, having a gentle breeze at southwest, and were so near the shore as to distinguish several people upon the sea beach. They appeared to be of a very dark or black color; but whether this was the real color of their skins or the clothes they might have on I know not. . . .

A remarkable peaked hill laying inland, the top of which looked like a pigeon house and occasioned my giving it that name, bore north 32 degrees 33 minutes west, and a small low island, lying close under the shore, bore northwest, distance 2 or 3 leagues. . . .

When we first discovered this island in the morning, I was in hopes, from its appearance, that we should have found shelter for the ship behind it; but when we came to approach it near I did not think that there was even security for a boat to land. But this, I believe, I should have attempted had not the wind come on shore, after which I did not think it safe to send a boat from the ship, as we had a large hollow sea from the southeast rolling in upon the land, which beat everywhere very high upon the shore; and this we have had ever since we came upon the coast.

The land near the seacoast still continues of a moderate height, forming alternately rocky points and sandy beaches; but inland, between Mount Dromedary and the Pigeon House, are several pretty high mountains, two only of which we saw but what were covered with trees, and these lay inland behind the Pigeon House, and are remarkably flat atop, with steep rocky cliffs all around them. As far as we could see, the trees in this country hath all the appearance of being stout and lofty. . . .

[For several days Cook continued to sail along the shore, occasionally seeing the smoke of native fires, naming prominent features of the coast, but without seeing any bay that appeared "favorable enough to induce me to lose time in beating up to it."]

Saturday, [April] 28.—In the P.M. hoisted out the pinnace and yawl in order to attempt a landing, but the pinnace took in the water so fast that she was obliged to be hoisted in again to stop her leaks.

At this time we saw several people ashore, four of whom were carrying a small boat or canoe, which we imagined they were going to put into the water in order to come off to us; but in this we were mistaken. Being now not above 2 miles from the shore, Mr. Banks, Dr. Solander, Tupia [a native from Tahiti], and myself put off in the yawl and pulled in for the land to a place where we saw four or five of the natives, who took to the woods as we approached the shore; which disappointed us in the expectation we had of getting a near view of them, if not to speak to them. But our disappointment was heightened when we found that we nowhere could effect a landing, by reason of the great surf which beat everywhere upon the shore. We saw hauled up upon the beach three or four small canoes, which to us appeared not much unlike the small ones of New Zealand. In the wood were several trees of the palm kind, and no underwood; and this was all we were able to observe from the boat, after which we returned to the ship about five in the evening. . . . At daylight in the morning we discovered a bay [Botany Bay] which appeared to be tolerably well sheltered from all winds, into which I resolved to go with the ship, and with this view sent the master in the pinnace to sound the entrance, while we kept turning up with the ship, having the wind right out. At noon the entrance bore north-northwest, distance 1 mile.

Sunday, [April] 29.—In the P.M., wind southerly and clear weather, with which we stood into the bay and anchored under the south shore about 2 miles within the entrance, in 5 fathoms.

Saw, as we came in, on both points of the bay, several of the natives and a few huts; men, women, and children on the south shore abreast of the ship, to which place I went in the boats in hopes of speaking with them, accompanied by Mr. Banks, Dr. Solander, and Tupia. As we approached the shore they all made off except two men, who seemed resolved to oppose our landing. As soon as I saw this I ordered the boats to lay upon their oars, in order to speak to them; but this was to little purpose, for neither us nor Tupia could understand one word they said. We then threw them some nails, beads, etc. ashore, which they took up, and seemed not ill pleased with, insomuch that I thought they beckoned to us to come ashore. But in this we were mistaken, for as soon as we put the boat in they again came to oppose us, upon which I fired a musket between the two, which had no other effect than to make them retire back where bundles of their darts lay. And one of them took up a stone and threw at us, which caused my firing a second musket load with small shot; and although some of the shot struck the man, yet it had no other effect than making him lay hold on a target.

Immediately after this we landed, which we had no sooner done than they throwed two darts at us. This obliged me to fire a third shot, soon after which they both made off, but not in such haste but what we might have taken one. But Mr. Banks being of opinion that the darts were poisoned made me cautious how I advanced into the woods.

We found here a few small huts made of the bark of trees, in one of which were four or five small children, with whom we left some strings of beads, etc. A quantity of darts lay about the huts; these we took away with us. Three canoes lay upon the beach, the worst I think I ever saw. They were about 12 or 14 feet long, made of one piece of the bark of a tree, drawn or tied up at each end, and the middle kept open by means of pieces of stick by way of thwarts.

After searching for fresh water without success, except a little in a small hole dug in the sand, we embarked and went over to the north point of the bay, where in coming in we saw several people; but when we landed, now there were nobody to be seen. We found here some fresh water, which came trinkling down and stood in pools among the rocks; but as this was troublesome to come at, I sent a party of men ashore in the morning to the place where we first landed to dig holes in the sand, by which means and a small stream they found fresh water sufficient to water the ship.

The string of beads, etc., we left with the children last night were found laying in the huts this morning; probably the natives were afraid to take them away. After breakfast we sent some empty casks ashore and a party of men to cut wood, and I went myself in the pinnace to sound and explore the bay, in the doing of which I saw some of the natives; but they all fled at my approach. I landed in two places, one of which the people had but just left, as there were small fires and fresh mussels broiling upon them. Here likewise lay vast heaps of the largest oyster shells I ever saw.

Monday, [April] 30. As soon as the wooders and waterers were come on board to dinner, ten or twelve of the natives came to the watering-place and took away their canoes that lay there, but did not offer to touch any one of our casks that had been left ashore. And in the afternoon sixteen or eighteen of them came boldly up to within 100 yards of our people at the watering-place, and there made a stand. Mr. Hicks, who was the officer ashore, did all in his power to entice them to him by offering them presents; but it was to no purpose, all they seemed to want was for us to be gone. After staying a short time they went away. They were all armed with darts and wooden swords;[4] the darts have each four prongs, and pointed with fishbones. Those we have seen seem to be intended more for striking fish than offensive weapons; neither are they poisoned, as we at first thought.

After I had returned from sounding the bay I went over to a cove on the north side of the bay, where in three or four hauls with the seine we caught about 300 pounds' weight of fish,

---

[4] Later, when he had had more opportunity to observe the natives, Cook says these were throwing sticks rather than swords. "By the helps of these throwing sticks, as we call them, they will hit a mark [with a dart] at the distance of 40 or 50 yards, with almost, if not as much, certainty as we can do with a musket, and much more so than with a ball." Wharton says that "The invention of these throwing sticks, and of the boomerang, is sufficient to prove the intelligence of the Australian aborigines."

which I caused to be equally divided among the ship's company. In the A.M. I went in the pinnace to sound and explore the north side of the bay, where I neither met with inhabitants or anything remarkable. . . .

Tuesday, May 1. . . . This morning a party of us went ashore to some huts not far from the watering-place, where some of the natives are daily seen; here we left several articles, such as cloth, looking-glasses, combs, beads, nails, etc.

After this we made an excursion into the country, which we found diversified with woods, lawns, and marshes. The woods are free from underwood of every kind, and the trees are at such a distance from one another that the whole country, or at least great part of it, might be cultivated without being obliged to cut down a single tree. We found the soil everywhere except in the marshes to be a light white sand, and produceth a quantity of good grass, which grows in little tufts about as big as one can hold in one's hand, and pretty close to one another; in this manner the surface of the ground is coated.

In the woods between the trees Dr. Solander had a bare sight of a small animal something like a rabbit, and we found the dung of an animal [a kangaroo] which must feed upon grass, and which we judge could not be less than a deer. We also saw the track of a dog, or some suchlike animal.

We met with some huts and places where the natives had been, and at our first setting out one of them was seen; the others I suppose had fled upon our approach. I saw some trees that had been cut down by the natives with some sort of a blunt instrument, and several trees that were marked, the bark of which had been cut by the same instrument. In many of the trees, especially the palms, were cut steps of about 3 or 4 feet asunder for the conveniency of climbing them. We found two sorts of gum, one sort of which is like gum dragon, and is the same, I suppose, Tasman took for gum-lac; it is extracted from the largest tree in the woods.

Wednesday, [May] 2. Between three and four in the P.M. we returned out of the country, and after dinner went ashore to the watering-place, where we had not been long before seventeen or eighteen of the natives appeared in sight. In the morning I had sent Mr. Gore, with a boat, up to the head of the bay to dredge for oysters; in his return to the ship he and another person came by land, and met with these people, who followed him at the distance of 10 or 20 yards. Whenever Mr. Gore made a stand and faced them, they stood also, and notwithstanding they were all armed, they never offered to attack him; but after he had parted from them, and they were met by Dr. Monkhouse and one or two more, who, upon making a sham retreat, they throwed three darts after them, after which they began to retire. . . .

Thursday, [May] 3. Winds at southeast, a gentle breeze and fair weather. In the P.M., I made a little excursion along the seacoast to the southward, accompanied by Mr. Banks and Dr. Solander. At our first entering the woods we saw three of the natives, who made off as soon as they saw us; more of them were seen by others of our people, who likewise made off as soon as they found they were discovered.

In the A.M., I went in the pinnace to the head of the bay, accompanied by Drs. Solander and Monkhouse, in order to examine the country, and to try to form some connections with the natives. In our way thither we met with ten or twelve of them fishing, each in a small canoe, who retired into shoal water upon our approach. Others again we saw at the first place we landed at, who took to their canoes and fled before we came near them. After this we took water, and went almost to the head of the inlet, where we landed and traveled some distance inland.

We found the face of the country much the same as I have before described, but the land much richer; for instead of sand I found in many places a deep black soil, which we thought was capable of producing any kind of grain. At present it produceth, besides timber, as fine meadow as ever was seen. However, we found it not all like this; some few places were very rocky, but this I believe to be uncommon. The stone is sandy, and very proper for building, etc.

After we had sufficiently examined this part we returned to the boat, and seeing some smoke and canoes at another part, we went thither, in hopes of meeting with the people, but they made off as we approached. There were six canoes and six small fires near the shore, and mussels roasting upon them, and a few oysters laying near. From this we conjectured that there had been just six people, who had been out each in his canoe picking up the shellfish, and come ashore to eat them, where each had made his fire to dress them by. We tasted of their cheer, and left them in return strings of beads, etc. The day being now far spent, we set out on our return to the ship. . . .

Friday, [May] 4. Winds northerly, serene weather. Upon my return to the ship in the evening I found that none of the natives had appeared near the watering-place, but about twenty of them had been fishing in their canoes at no great distance from us.

In the A.M., as the wind would not permit us to sail, I sent out some parties into the country to try to form some connections with the natives. One of the midshipmen met with a very old man and woman and two small children; they were close to the waterside, and he, being alone, was afraid to make any stay with the two old people lest he should be discovered by those in the canoes. He gave them a bird he had shot, which they would not touch; neither did they speak one word, but seemed to be much frightened. They were quite naked; even the woman had nothing to cover her nudities. Dr. Monkhouse and another man, being in the woods not far from the watering-place, discovered six more of the natives, who at first seemed to wait his coming; but as he was going up to them he had a dart thrown at him out of a tree, which narrowly escaped him. As soon as the fellow had thrown the dart he descended the tree and made off, and with him all the rest, and these were all that were met with in the course of this day.

Saturday, [May] 5. In the P.M., I went with a party of men over to the north shore, and while some hands were hauling the seine, a party of us made an excursion of 3 or 4 miles into the country, or rather along the seacoast. We met with nothing remarkable; great part of the country for some distance inland from the seacoast is mostly a barren heath, diversified with marshes and morasses. Upon our return to the boat we found they had caught a great number of small fish, which the sailors call leatherjackets on account of their having a very thick skin; they are known in the West Indies. I had sent the yawl in the morning to fish for sting rays, who returned in the evening with upwards of four hundredweight; one single one weighed 240 pounds, exclusive of the entrails. In the A.M., as the wind continued northerly, I sent the yawl again afishing, and I went with a party of men into the country, but met with nothing extraordinary.

Sunday, [May] 6. In the evening, the yawl returned from fishing, having caught two sting rays weighing near 600 pounds. The great quantity of plants Mr. Banks and Dr. Solander found in this place occasioned my giving it the name of Botany Bay.[5] It is situated in the latitude of 34 degrees south, longitude 208 degrees 37 minutes west. It is capacious, safe, and commodious. [Here follow sailing directions for entering the bay.] We anchored near the south shore about a mile within the entrance, for the conveniency of sailing with a southerly wind and the getting of fresh water; but I afterward found a very fine stream of fresh water on the north shore in the first sandy cove within the island, before which the ship might lay almost landlocked, and wood for fuel may be got everywhere.

Although wood is here in great plenty, yet there is very little variety. The biggest trees are as large or larger than our oaks in England, and grows a good deal like them, and yields a reddish gum; the wood itself is heavy, hard, and black, like lignum vitae. . . .

In the wood are a variety of very beautiful birds, such as cockatoos, lorikeets, parrots, etc., and crows exactly like those we have in England. Waterfowl is no less plenty about the head of the harbor, where there is large flats of sand and mud, on which they seek their food. The most of these were unknown to us, one sort especially, which was black and white and as large as a goose, but most like a pelican. On the sand and mud banks are oysters, mussels, cockles, etc., which I believe are the chief

---

[5] The bay was at first called Stingray Bay, and this is the name that was used on Cook's plan of the bay. It is probable that it was only after the *Endeavour* had left, and when Banks had had time to examine his collections, that the name Botany Bay was decided upon.

In 1821 the place where Cook first landed, on the southern side of Botany Bay, was marked by a tablet, bearing an inscription which reads in part: "Under the Auspices of British Science These Shores Were Discovered by James Cook & Joseph Banks, the Columbus and Maecenas of Their Time. This Spot Once Saw Them, Ardent in the Pursuit of Knowledge."

support of the inhabitants, who go into shoal water with their little canoes and peck them out of the sand and mud with their hands, and sometimes roast and eat them in the canoe, having often a fire for that purpose—as I suppose, for I know no other it can be for.

The natives do not appear to be numerous, neither do they seem to live in large bodies, but dispersed in small parties along by the waterside. Those I saw were about as tall as Europeans, of a very dark brown color, but not black, nor had they woolly, frizzled hair, but black and lank like ours. No sort of clothing or ornaments were ever seen by any of us upon any of them, or in or about any of their huts, from which I conclude that they never wear any. Some that we saw had their faces and bodies painted with a sort of white paint or pigment.

Although I have said that shellfish is their chief support, yet they catch other sorts of fish, some of which we found roasting on the fire the first time we landed. Some of these they strike with gigs, and others they catch with hook and line; we have seen them strike fish with gigs, and hooks and lines are found in their huts. Sting rays, I believe, they do not eat, because I never saw the least remains of one near any of their huts or fireplaces. However, we could know but very little of their customs, as we never were able to form any connections with them. They had not so much as touched the things we had left in their huts on purpose for them to take away.

During our stay in this harbor I caused the English colors to be displayed ashore every day, and an inscription to be cut out upon one of the trees near the watering-place, setting forth the ship's name, date, etc. Having seen everything this place afforded, we, at daylight in the morning, weighed with a light breeze at northwest, and put to sea. . . . We steered alongshore north-northeast and at noon we were . . . about 2 or 3 miles from the land, and abreast of a bay, wherein there appeared to be safe anchorage, which I called Port Jackson. It lies 3 leagues to the northward of Botany Bay.

[Cook, eager to get on with his examination of the coast line, did not enter Port Jackson, and so missed the opportunity to explore one of the world's most magnificent harbors, where now stands Sydney, the capital of New South Wales. As the *Endeavour* proceeded northward, the journal is filled with careful notes of offshore depths and other navigation data, together with a description of the land as it appeared from the ship and the names applied to the principal features, either for their physical characteristics or for prominent Englishmen of the day. At places natives had assembled on headlands to watch the strange vessel pass by, and elsewhere the voyagers saw "smokes in the day and fires in the night." Cook's narrative is resumed with his journal entry for May 23, when the *Endeavour* again took anchorage.]

Wednesday, [May] 23.—Continued our course alongshore at the distance of about two miles off, having from 12 to 9, 8, and 7 fathoms, until five o'clock, at which time we were abreast of the south point of a large open bay [Bustard Bay], wherein I intended to anchor. Accordingly we hauled in close upon a wind, and sent a boat ahead to sound. After making some trips, we anchored at eight o'clock in 5 fathoms, a sandy bottom. . . .

Last night, some time in the middle watch, a very extraordinary affair happened to Mr. Orton, my clerk. He having been drinking in the evening, some malicious person or persons in the ship took advantage of his being drunk and cut off all the clothes from off his back; not being satisfied with this, they some time after went into his cabin and cut off a part of both his ears as he lay asleep in his bed.

The person whom he suspected to have done this was Mr. Magra, one of the midshipmen; but this did not appear to me. Upon inquiry, however, as I had been told that Magra had once or twice before this in their drunken frolics cut off his clothes, and had been heard to say (as I was told) that if it was not the law he would murder him, these things considered, induced me to think that Magra was not altogether innocent. I therefore for the present dismissed him the quarter-deck, and suspended him from doing any duty in the ship, he being one of those gentlemen frequently found on board King's ships that can very well be spared. Besides, it was necessary in me to show my immediate resentment against the person on whom the suspicion fell, lest they should not have stopped there.

With respect to Mr. Orton, he is a man not without faults; yet from all the inquiry I could make, it evidently appeared to me that so far from deserving such treatment, he had not designed injuring any person in the ship; so that I do—and shall always —look upon him as an injured man. Some reasons, however, might be given why this misfortune came upon him in which he himself was in some measure to blame; but as this is only conjecture, and would tend to fix it upon some people in the ship whom I would fain believe would hardly be guilty of such an action, I shall say nothing about it, unless I shall hereafter discover the offenders, which I shall take every method in my power to do; for I look upon such proceedings as highly dangerous in such voyages as this, and the greatest insult that could be offered to my authority in this ship, as I have always been ready to hear and redress every complaint that have been made against any person in the ship.

In the A.M., I went ashore with a party of men in order to examine the country, accompanied by Mr. Banks and the other gentlemen. . . .

As yet we had seen no people, but saw a great deal of smoke up and on the west side of the lagoon, which was all too far off for us to go by land excepting one. This we went to, and found ten small fires in a very small compass, and some cockleshells laying by them, but the people were gone. On the windward or south side of one of the fires was stuck up a little bark about 1½ feet high, and some few pieces lay about in other places. These we concluded were all the covering they had in the night, and many of them, I firmly believe, have not this, but, naked as they are, sleep in the open air. . . .

The country is visibly worse than at the last place we were at; the soil is dry and sandy, and the woods are free from underwoods of every kind. Here are some of the same sort of trees as we found in Botany Harbor, with a few other sorts. . . . About the skirts of the lagoon grows the true mangrove, such as are found in the West Indies, and which we have not seen during the voyage before. Here is likewise a sort of palm tree, which grows on low, barren, sandy places in the South Sea Islands.

All or most of the same sort of land and water fowl as we saw at Botany Harbor we saw here. Besides these we saw some bustards, such as we have in England, one of which we killed that weighed 17½ pounds, which occasioned my giving this place the Name of Bustard Bay. . . .

[On May 24 the *Endeavour* again stood out to sea. From Bustard Bay it was found that the coast assumed a north-westerly trend, all of it encumbered with shoals, which Cook prudently skirted. Some days later he found himself inside the long chain of islands and reefs known as the Great Barrier Reef, which lies off the northern half of the coast of Queens-land and stretches all the way up to Torres Strait. All of Cook's superb qualities of seamanship were needed to steer the ship through the dangerous waters of the passage between the reef and the shoals that stretch off the mainland coast. Again and again the ship was extricated from imminent peril, the dangers increasing to the northward as the Great Barrier Reef begins to close in on the land. Then, having passed Cape Grafton, the vessel went aground on Endeavour Reef; her narrow escape from complete destruction is best told in Cook's own words.]

Sunday, June 10. . . . The shore between Cape Grafton and the above northern point [northernmost point of land in sight] forms a large but not very deep bay, which I named Trinity Bay, after the day on which it was discovered, the north point, Cape Tribulation, because here began all our troubles. . . .

Monday, [June] 11. . . . My intention was to stretch off all night as well to avoid the danger we saw ahead [two low, woody islands, later named Hope Islands] as to see if any is-lands lay in the offing, especially as we now begun to draw near the latitude of those discovered by Quiros, which some geographers, for what reason I know not, have thought proper to tack to this land.

Having the advantage of a fine breeze of wind and a clear moonlight night in standing off from six until near 9 o'clock, we deepened our water from 14 to 21 fathoms, when all at once we fell into 12, 10, and 8 fathoms. At this time I had every-body at their stations to put about and come to an anchor; but in this I was not so fortunate, for meeting again with deep water, I thought there could be no danger in standing on.

Before ten o'clock we had 20 and 21 fathoms, and continued in that depth until a few minutes before eleven, when we had 17, and before the man at the lead could heave another cast, the ship struck and stuck fast.

Immediately upon this we took in all our sails, hoisted out the boats and sounded round the ship, and found that we had got upon the southeast edge of a reef of coral rocks, having in some place round the ship 3 and 4 fathoms water, and in other places not quite as many feet. . . . The ship being quite fast . . . we went to work to lighten her as fast as possible, which seemed to be the only means we had left to get her off.

As we went ashore about the top of high water we not only started water, but threw overboard our guns, iron, and stone ballast, casks, hoop staves, oil jars, decayed stores, etc.; many of these last articles lay in the way at coming at heavier. All this time the ship made little or no water. At 11 A.M., being high water as we thought, we tried to heave her off without success, she not being afloat by a foot or more, notwithstanding by this time we had thrown overboard 40 to 50 tons' weight. As this was not found sufficient, we continued to lighten her by every method we could think of. As the tide fell the ship began to make water as much as two pumps could free. . . .

Tuesday [June] 12. Fortunately we had little wind, fine weather, and a smooth sea, all this twenty-four hours. . . . At nine the ship righted, and the leak gained upon the pumps considerably. This was an alarming and I may say terrible circumstance, and threatened immediate destruction to us. However, I resolved to risk all and heave her off in case it was practical, and accordingly turned as many hands to the capstan and windlass as could be spared from the pumps. . . . At eleven got under sail, and stood in for the land, with a light breeze at east-southeast. Some hands employed sewing oakum, wool, etc. into a lower steering sail to fother the ship[6]; others employed at the pumps, which still gained upon the leak.

Wednesday, [June] 13. In the P.M. had light airs at east-southeast, with which we kept edging in for the land. Got up the main-topmast and main yard, and having got the sail ready

---

[6] In fothering, a sail covered thickly with oakum, rope yarn, and other loose material is drawn under the ship to stop a leak, the idea being that some of the loose material will be sucked into the hole.

for fothering of the ship, we put it over under the starboard fore chains, where we suspected the ship had suffered most, and soon after the leak decreased, so as to be kept clear with one pump with ease. This fortunate circumstance gave new life to everyone on board.

It is much easier to conceive than to describe the satisfaction felt by everybody on this occasion. But a few minutes before our utmost wishes were to get hold of some place upon the main, or an island, to run the ship ashore, where out of her materials we might build a vessel to carry us to the East Indies. No sooner were we made sensible that the outward application to the ship's bottom had taken effect than the field of every man's hopes enlarged, so that we thought of nothing but ranging along shore in search of a harbor, when we could repair the damages we had sustained. In justice to the ship's company, I must say that no men ever behaved better than they have done on this occasion; animated by the behavior of every gentleman on board, every man seemed to have a just sense of the danger we were in, and exerted himself to the very utmost. . . .

At 6 A.M., weighed and stood to the northwest, edging in for the land, having a gentle breeze at south-southeast. At nine we past close without two small low islands . . . about 4 leagues from the main. I have named them Hope Islands, because we were always in hopes of being able to reach these islands. . . .

Thursday, [June] 14. P.M. . . . sent the master, with two boats, as well to sound ahead of the ship as to look out for a harbor where we could repair our defects, and put the ship on a proper trim, both of which she now very much wanted. . . . At eight o'clock the pinnace, in which was one of the mates, returned on board, and reported that they had found a good harbor [Cook Harbor, Endeavour River] about 2 leagues to leeward. In consequence of this information, we at 6 A.M., weighed and run down to it. . . . (*Note.* This day I restored Mr. Magra to his duty, as I did not find him guilty of the crimes laid to his charge.)

[The entrance to the harbor was very narrow, and for several days the *Endeavour* lay offshore awaiting calm weather. The first attempt to enter was made on the seventeenth, but the vessel twice went aground. On the eighteenth she was refloated and warped in to the harbor, which was "much smaller than I had been told, but very convenient for our purpose." Here the party stayed until August 4, while the carpenters worked at repairing the ship, the armorers made bolts, nails, etc., and the naturalists ranged the countryside collecting specimens and making notes.]

Tuesday, [June] 19. . . . P.M., landed all the provisions and part of the stores; got the sick ashore, which amounted, at this time, to 8 or 9, afflicted with different disorders, but none very dangerously ill.[7] . . .

Friday, [June] 22. . . . At 2 A.M., the tide left her [the *Endeavour*], which gave us an opportunity to examine the leak, which we found to be at her floorheads, a little before the starboard fore chains. Here the rocks had made their way thro' four planks, quite to and even into the timbers, and wounded three more. The manner these planks were damaged—or cut out, as I may say—is hardly credible; scarce a splinter was to be seen, but the whole was cut away as if it had been done by the hands of man with a blunt-edge too. Fortunately for us, the timbers in this place were very close; otherwise it would have been impossible to have saved the ship, and even as it was it appeared very extraordinary that she made no more water than what she did. A large piece of coral rock was sticking in one hole, and several pieces of the fothering, small stones, etc., had made its way in, and lodged between the timbers, which had stopped the water from forcing its way in in great quantities. . . .

Saturday, [June] 23 and Sunday, [June] 24. . . . One of the men saw an animal something less than a greyhound; it was of a mouse-color, very slender made, and swift of foot. . . . I saw myself this [Sunday] morning, a little way from the ship, one of the animals before spoke of, it was of a light mouse-

---

[7] Some were no doubt suffering from scurvy, for Wharton points out that they had had nothing fresh but a little fish for four months, and scarcely any meat since they had left the Society Islands eleven months before. From this time on fresh food was more plentiful, and on his return to England in 1771 Cook had the satisfaction of reporting that he had not lost one man by illness during the whole voyage.

color and the full size of a greyhound, and shaped in every respect like one, with a long tail, which it carried like a greyhound; in short, I should have taken it for a wild dog but for its walking or running, in which it jumped like a hare or deer.[8]

Saturday, [June] 30. . . . I sent some of the young gentlemen to take a plan of the harbor, and went myself upon the hill which is near the south point, to take a view of the sea. At this time it was low water, and I saw what gave me no small uneasiness, which were a number of sandbanks and shoals laying all along the coast. The innermost lay about 3 or 4 miles from the shore, and the outermost extended off to sea as far as I could see without my glass; some just appeared above water. The only hopes I have of getting clear of them is to the northward, where there seems to be a passage, for as the wind blows constantly from the southeast, we shall find it difficult, if not impractical, to return to the southward. . . .

Sunday, [July] 1 P.M., the people returned from hauling the seine, having caught as much fish as came to 2½ pounds per man, no one on board having more than another. The few greens we got I caused to be boiled among the pease, and makes a very good mess, which, together with the fish, is a great refreshment to the people. A.M., a party of men, one from each mess, went again a-fishing, and all the rest I gave leave to go into the country, knowing that there was no danger from the natives. . . .

Monday, [July] 9. . . . In the evening, the master returned, having been several leagues out at sea, and at that distance off saw shoals without him, and was of opinion there was no getting out to sea that way. In his return he touched upon one of the shoals, the same as he was upon the first time he was out; he here saw a great number of turtle, three of which he caught, weighing 791 pounds. This occasioned my sending him out again provided with proper gear for striking them, he having before nothing but a boat hook. . . .

Tuesday, [July] 10. . . . In the A.M., four of the natives came down to the sandy point on the north side of the harbor, having along with them a small wooden canoe with outriggers, in which they seemed to be employed striking fish, etc. Some

---

[8] This was a kangaroo, the name of which Banks learned from the natives.

were for going over in a boat to them; but this I would not suffer, but let them alone, without seeming to take any notice of them. At length two of them came in the canoe so near the ship as to take some things we throwed them. After this they went away, and brought over the other two, and came again alongside, nearer than they had done before, and took such trifles as we gave them. After this they landed close to the ship, and all four went ashore, carrying their arms with them. But Tupia soon prevailed upon them to lay down their arms and come and set down by him, after which most of us went to them, made them again some presents, and stayed by them until dinnertime, when we made them understand that we were going to eat, and asked them by signals to go with us; but this they declined, and as soon as we left them they went away in their canoe.

One of the men was something above the middle age, the other three were young. None of them were above 5½ feet high, and all their limbs were proportionately small. They were wholly naked, their skins the color of wood soot, and this seemed to be their natural color. Their hair was black, lank, and cropped short, and neither woolly nor frizzled; nor did they want any of their fore-teeth, as Dampier has mentioned those did he saw on the western side of this country. Some parts of their bodies had been painted with red, and one of them had his upper lip and breast painted with streaks of white, which he called *carbanda*. Their features were far from being disagreeable; their voices were soft and tunable, and they could easily repeat any word after us, but neither us nor Tupia could understand one word they said.

Wednesday, [July] 11. Gentle land and sea breezes. Employed airing the bread, stowing away water, stores, etc. In the night the master and Mr. Gore returned with the longboat, and brought with them one turtle and a few shellfish. The yawl Mr. Gore left upon the shoal with six men, to endeavor to strike more turtle.

In the morning four of the natives made us another short visit; three of them had been with us the preceding day, the other was a stranger. One of these men had a hole through the bridge [cartilage] of his nose, in which he stuck a piece of bone as thick as my finger. Seeing this, we examined all their noses, and found that they had all holes for the same purpose; they had likewise holes in their ears, but no ornaments hanging to them; they had bracelets on their arms made of hair, and like hoops of small cord. They sometimes may wear a kind of fillet about their heads, for one of them had applied some part of an old shirt which I had given them to this use.

Thursday, [July] 12. Winds and weather as yesterday, and the employment of the people the same. At 2 A.M., the yawl came on board, and brought three turtle and a large skate, and as there was a probability of succeeding in this kind of fishery, I sent her out again after breakfast. About this time five of the natives came over and stayed with us all the forenoon. There were seven in all—five men, one woman, and a boy; these two last stayed on the point of land on the other side of the river about 200 yards from us. We could very clearly see with our glasses that the woman was as naked as ever she was born; even those parts which I always before now thought nature would have taught a woman to conceal were uncovered. . . .

Saturday, [July] 14. . . . Mr. Gore, being in the country, shot one of the animals before spoke of; it was a small one of the sort, weighing only 28 pound clear of the entrails. . . . The head, neck, and shoulders very small in proportion to the other parts. It was hare-lipped, and the head and ears were most like a hare's of any animal I know; the tail was nearly as long as the body, thick next the rump, and tapering toward the end; the forelegs were 8 inches long, and the hind, 22. Its progression is by hopping or jumping 7 or 8 feet at each hop upon its hind legs only, for in this it makes no use of the fore, which seem to be only designed for scratching in the ground, etc. The skin is covered with a short, hairy fur of a dark mouse or gray color. It bears no resemblance to any European animal I ever saw. . . .

Wednesday, [July] 18. . . . About eight we were visited by several of the natives, who now became more familiar than ever. Soon after this Mr. Banks and I . . . traveled 6 or 8 miles alongshore to the northward, where we ascended a high hill, from whence I had an extensive view of the seacoast. It afforded us a melancholy prospect of the difficulties we are to encounter, for in whatever direction we looked it was covered with shoals as far as the eye could see. After this we returned to the ship without meeting with anything remarkable, and found several of the natives on board. At this time we had twelve tortoise or turtle upon our decks, which they took more notice of than anything else in the ship. . . .

Thursday, [July] 19. Gentle breezes and fair weather. Employed getting everything in readiness for sea. A.M., we were visited by ten or eleven of the natives; the most of them came from the other side of the harbor, where we saw six or seven more, the most of them women and, like the men, quite naked. Those that came on board were very desirous of having some of our turtles, and took the liberty to haul two of them to the gangway to put over the side. Being disappointed in this, they grew a little troublesome, and were for throwing everything overboard they could lay their hands upon. As we had no victuals dressed at this time, I offered them some bread to eat, which they rejected with scorn, as I believe they would have done anything else excepting turtle. Soon after this they all went ashore, Mr. Banks, myself, and five or six of our people being there at the same time.

Immediately upon their landing, one of them took a handful of dry grass and lighted it at a fire we had ashore, and before we well knew what he was going about he made a large circuit roundabout us, and set fire to the grass in his way, and in an instant the whole place was in flames. Luckily at this time we had hardly anything ashore besides the forge and a sow with a litter of young pigs, one of which was scorched to death in the fire.

As soon as they had done this they all went to a place where some of our people were washing, and where all our nets and a good deal of linen were laid out to dry. Here with the greatest obstinacy they again set fire to the grass, which I and some others who were present could not prevent, until I was obliged to fire a musket loaded with small shot at one of the ringleaders, which sent them off. As we were apprised of this last attempt of theirs, we got the fire out before it got head, but the first spread like wildfire in the woods and grass. . . .

Saturday, August 4. In the P.M., having pretty moderate weather, I ordered the coasting anchor and cable to be laid without the bar, to be ready to warp out by, that we might not lose the least opportunity that might offer; for laying in port spends time to no purpose, consumes our provisions, of which we are very short in many articles, and we have yet a long passage to make to the East Indies through an unknown and perhaps dangerous sea. . . .

The yawl I sent to the turtle bank, to take up the net that was left there; but as the wind freshened, we got out before her, and a little after noon anchored in 15 fathoms water, sandy bottom; for I did not think it safe to run in among the shoals until I had well viewed them at low water from the masthead, that I might be better able to judge which way to steer. . . .

The harbor, or river, we have been in . . . I named after the ship, Endeavour River. . . . The refreshments we got there were chiefly turtle, but as we had to go 5 leagues out to sea for them, and had much blowing weather, we were not overstocked with this article. However, what with these and the fish we caught with the seine we had not much reason to complain, considering the country we were in. Whatever refreshment we got that would bear a division I caused to be equally divided among the whole company, generally by weight; the meanest person in the ship had an equal share with myself or anyone on board, and this method every commander of a ship on such a voyage as this ought ever to observe. . . .

[Plagued by reefs and shoals, the Endeavour groped her way slowly northward until she was finally able, on August 14, to pass outside the Great Barrier Reef through the channel now known as Cook's Passage.]

Tuesday, [August] 14. . . . The moment we were without the breakers we had no ground with 100 fathoms of line, and found a large sea rolling in from the southeast. By this I was well assured we were got without all the shoals, which gave us no small joy, after having been entangled among islands and shoals, more or less, ever since the twenty-sixth of May, in which time we have sailed above 360 leagues by the lead without ever having a leadsman out of the chains when the ship was under sail—a circumstance that perhaps never happened to any ship before, and yet it was here absolutely necessary.

I should have been very happy to have had it in my power to have kept in with the land, in order to have explored the coast to the northern extremity of the country, which I think we were not far off, for I firmly believe this land doth not join to New Guinea. But this I hope soon either to prove or disprove, and the reasons I have before assigned will, I presume, be thought sufficient for my leaving the coast at this time; not but what I intend to get in with it again as soon as I can do it with safety. . . .

[Relief at getting outside the Great Barrier was short-lived, for on August 16 they found themselves in greater peril than ever, with the vessel drifting rapidly toward the reef.]

Thursday, [August] 16. . . . A little after four o'clock the roaring of the surf was plainly heard, and at daybreak the vast foaming breakers were too plainly to be seen not a mile from us, toward which we found the ship was carried by the waves surprisingly fast. We had at this time not an air of wind, and the depth of water was unfathomable, so that there was not a possibility of anchoring. In this distressed situation we had nothing but Providence and the small assistance the boats could give us to trust to. . . . The yawl was put in the water and the longboat hoisted out, and both sent ahead to tow, which, together with the help of our sweeps abaft, got the ship's head round to the northward, which seemed to be the best way to keep her off the reef, or at least to delay time. Before this was effected it was six o'clock, and we were not above 80 or 100 yards from the breakers. The same sea that washed the side of the ship rose in a breaker prodigiously high the very next time it did rise, so that between us and destruction was only a dismal valley the breadth of one wave, and even now no ground could be felt with 120 fathom. The pinnace was by this time patched up, and hoisted out and sent ahead to tow.

Still, we had hardly any hopes of saving the ship, and full as little our lives, as we were full 10 leagues from the nearest land, and the boats not sufficient to carry the whole of us. Yet in this truly terrible situation not one man ceased to do his utmost, and that with as much calmness as if no danger had been near. All the dangers we had escaped were little in comparison of being thrown upon this reef, where the ship must be dashed to pieces in a moment.

A reef such as one speaks of is scarcely known in Europe. It is a wall of coral rock rising perpendicular out of the unfathomable ocean, always overflown at high water, generally 7 or 8 feet, and dry in places at low water. The large waves of the vast ocean meeting with so sudden a resistance makes a most terrible surf, breaking mountains-high, especially, as in our case, when the general trade wind blows directly upon it.

At this critical juncture, when all our endeavors seemed too little, a small air of wind sprung up, but so small that at any other time in a calm we should not have observed it. With this, and the assistance of our boats, we could observe the ship to move off from the reef in a slanting direction; but in less than ten minutes we had as flat a calm as ever, when our fears were again renewed, for as yet we were not above 200 yards from the breakers.

Soon after, our friendly breeze visited us again, and lasted about as long as before. A small opening was now seen in the reef about a ¼ mile from us, which I sent one of the mates to examine. Its breadth was not more than the length of the ship, but within was smooth water. Into the place it was resolved to push her if possible, having no other probable views to save her, for we were still in the very jaws of destruction, and it was a doubt whether or not we could reach this opening. However, we soon got off it, when to our surprise we found the tide of ebb gushing out like a millstream, so that it was impossible to get in. We however took all the advantage possible of it, and it carried us about ¼ mile from the breakers. . . .

The ebb had been in our favor, and we had reason to suppose the flood which was now made would be against us. The only hopes we had was another opening we saw about a mile to the westward of us, which I sent Lieutenant Hicks in the small boat to examine. . . .

Friday, [August] 17. While Mr. Hicks was examining the

opening, we struggled hard with the flood, sometimes gaining a little and at other times losing. At two o'clock Mr. Hicks returned with a favorable account of the opening. Narrow and dangerous as it was, it seemed to be the only means we had of saving her [the ship], as well as ourselves. A light breeze soon after sprung up at east-northeast with which, the help of our boats, and a flood tide, we soon entered the opening, and was hurried thro' in a short time by a rapid tide like a millrace, which kept us from driving against either side, though the channel was not more than ¼ mile broad. . . . The channel we came in by . . . I have named Providential Channel. . . .

It is but a few days ago that I rejoiced at having got without the reef; but that joy was nothing when compared to what I now felt at being safe at an anchor within it. Such are the vicissitudes attending this kind of service, and must always attend an unknown navigation where one steers wholly in the dark without any manner of guide whatever. Was it not from the pleasure which naturally results to a man from his being the first discoverer, even was it nothing more than land or shoals, this kind of service would be insupportable, especially in far-distant parts like this, short of provisions and almost every other necessary. People will hardly admit of an excuse for a man leaving a coast unexplored he has once discovered. If dangers are his excuse, he is then charged with timorousness and want of perseverance, and at once pronounced to be the most unfit man in the world to be employed as a discoverer. If, on the other hand, he boldly encounters all the dangers and obstacles he meets with and is unfortunate enough not to succeed, he is then charged with temerity, and perhaps want of conduct. . . .

[From Providential Channel it is difficult to follow Cook's course through the confusion of islands and shoals until he found himself off the entrance to Torres Strait.]

Tuesday, [August] 21. . . . Seeing no danger in our way, we took the yawl in tow, and made all the sail we could until eight o'clock, at which time we discovered shoals ahead and on our larboard bow, and saw that the northernmost land, which we had taken to be a part of the main, was an island, or islands, between which and the main there appeared to be a good passage thro' which we might pass. . . .

The point of the main, which forms one side of the passage before mentioned, and which is the northern promontory of this country, I have named York Cape, in honor of his late Royal Highness, the Duke of York. . . .

[Cook describes the maze of islands that were encountered upon entering the passage. Landing upon one of these, later named Possession Island, he climbed the highest hill, from which he could see islands extending far to the north and west but as there was no land to the southwest, he had no doubt that he had at last found a passage into the Indian seas.]

Wednesday, [August] 22. Having satisfied myself of the great probability of a passage, thro' which I intend going with the ship, and therefore may land no more upon this eastern coast of New Holland, and on the western side I can make no new discovery, the honor of which belongs to the Dutch navigators. But the eastern coast from the latitude of 38 degrees south down to this place, I am confident was never seen or visited by any European before us; and notwithstanding I had in the name of His Majesty taken possession of several places upon this coast, I now once more hoisted English colors, and in the name of His Majesty King George the Third took possession of the whole eastern coast from the above latitude down to this place by the name of New Wales,[9] together with all the bays, harbors, rivers, and islands situated upon the said coast. After which we fired three volleys of small arms, which were answered by the like number from the ship.

[Threading his way westward, Cook successfully crossed a shallow bank which lay across the western end of the passage, and landed briefly on Booby Island, now a landmark for ships making Torres Strait from the westward.]

---

[9] In other manuscript copies of Cook's journal the name is given as New South Wales.

Thursday, [August 23]. . . . I made but a very short stay at this [Booby] Island before I returned to the ship: In the meantime the wind had got to the southwest and although it blowed but very faint, yet it was accompanied with a swell from the same quarter. This, together with other concurring circumstances, left me no room to doubt but we had got to the westward of Carpentaria, or the northern extremity of New Holland, and had now an open sea to the westward; which gave me no small satisfaction, not only because the danger and fatigues of the voyage was drawing near to an end, but by being able to prove that Australia and New Guinea are two separate lands or islands, which until this day hath been a doubtful point with geographers.

[Following the entry for August 23, when he was about to leave Australia behind, Cook interpolates some general remarks in his journal under the heading, "Some Account of New [South] Wales." In this he gives a detailed description of the "Appearance or aspect of the face of the country, the nature of the soil, its produce, etc." He describes the animals, birds, and fishes, and then tells all that he has been able to learn of the aborigines. Here the account of the discovery of Australia ends with Cook's own concluding remarks about the people and the country, remarks which show the sympathetic nature and breadth of vision of this great navigator.]

From what I have said of the natives of Australia they may appear to some to be the most wretched people upon earth; but in reality they are far more happier than we Europeans, being wholly unacquainted not only with the superfluous but with the necessary conveniences so much sought after in Europe; they are happy in not knowing the use of them. They live in a tranquillity which is not disturbed by the inequality of condition. The earth and sea of their own accord furnishes them with all things necessary for life. They covet not magnificent houses, household stuff, etc. They live in a warm and fine climate, and enjoy every wholesome air, so that they have very little need of clothing; and this they seem to be fully sensible of, for many to whom we gave cloth, etc. left it carelessly upon the sea beach and in the woods, as a thing they had no manner of use for. In short, they seemed to set no value upon anything we gave them, nor would they ever part with anything of their own for any one article we could offer them. This, in my opinion, argues that they think themselves provided with all the necessaries of life, and that they have no superfluities.[10]

The country itself, so far as we know, doth not produce any one thing that can become an article in trade to invite Europeans to fix a settlement upon it. However, this eastern side is not that barren and miserable country that Dampier and others have described the western side to be. We are to consider that we see this country in the pure state of nature; the industry of man has had nothing to do with any part of it, and yet we find all such things as nature hath bestowed upon it in a flourishing state.

In this extensive country it can never be doubted but what most sorts of grain, fruit, roots, etc. of every kind would flourish here were they once brought hither, planted, and cultivated by the hands of industry; and here are provender for more cattle, at all seasons of the year, than ever can be brought into the country.

---

[10] Wharton disagrees with Cook's conclusions, calling attention to the cannibalistic practices of some of the Australian natives, and to the internecine warfare that has existed between some of the tribes. He bolsters this opinion with a remark that shows the typical attitude of Europeans toward the native races they have dispossessed: "Their treachery, which is unsurpassed, is simply an outcome of their savage ideas, and in their eyes is a form of independence which resents any intrusion on *their* land, *their* wild animals, and *their* rights generally. In their untutored state they therefore consider that any method of getting rid of the invader is proper."

Chapter 17

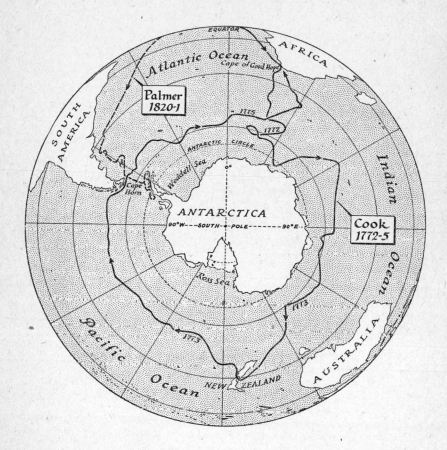

The Great Southland

THE GREAT SOUTHLAND

THE last region on earth to change from theory to fact lies in the "farthest South." Once upon a time we "knew" it was solid land, the greatest of continents. A hundred and fifty years ago we were beginning to think that there was no continent at all; twenty years ago we felt sure of the main outlines of the continent; now the solid land is beginning to break up into archipelagoes, although it still seems as if there might be enough left to form a decent continent after all.

The earth was spherical to the Mediterranean cosmographers of two thousand years ago, and remained so to the learned throughout the Middle Ages. Europe's geographers of every century believed the time would come when someone would sail around the earth east and west, or would sail to Asia and walk thence overland to Europe. But it was long believed that no one could ever go around the world from north to south, for about the earth's middle was the uncrossable burning girdle of the Torrid Zone and around either Pole were the snow caps, permanently frozen and everlastingly dead. The northern snow cap was supposed to begin not far beyond the north tip of Scotland; its fringes a traveler might approach, no doubt, and send back descriptions. There would be in the South a similar ice cap, but this could be known only by theory and by analogy from the North.

The public of 1946 still believes in a northern icecap, or at least the newspapers still use the term, although it is a hundred years and more since the geographers knew that there was no northern icecap and could not be.

True, snow does cap Greenland. But this does not correspond to the Greek-model icecap of theory; for the philosophers believed that the center of the ice would be at the Pole, whereas the center of the Greenland icecap is more than 1000 miles from the Pole. Even its northern tip is more than 400 miles from the Pole. Thus the only sizable northern icecap is eccentric from rather than central to the Arctic. Indeed, a part of it lies in the Temperate Zone. Surely one cannot with reason discuss as polar an icecap which does not include the Pole.

As has been sketched already, the burning tropics were conquered during the fifteenth century by a group of Portuguese sailors and by a man of genius who directed them, Prince Henry the Navigator. That was the closing of one task, the proving that Europeans were not prisoners in the North Temperate Zone. It was the beginning of another task, the search for the great southern continent, Terra Australis.

The Austral continent, although it seems to us now like pure theory, was very real to the Middle Ages. Africa was considered a part of it. The first of many destructive blows was dealt by the Portuguese, under Diaz, when in 1487 or 1488 he rounded the southern tip of Africa, amputating a whole continent bigger than North America from the vast theoretical Land of the South.

The second piece of major surgery was performed by Spain. When South America was discovered, it was reasonably mistaken for a peninsula running north from Terra Australis. Then came Magellan, Portuguese in blood but Spanish because of his flag, who sailed in 1520 through the strait that bears his name and cut off from the imaginary Southland another continent.

Even so, Terra Australis remained colossal. New Guinea was discovered and was thought to be a northward peninsula of the continent. Next the land we now call Australia took up a similar role. In fact, so sure were Europeans that now at last had their eyes rested upon the Terra Australis of theory that when the Hollander Tasman in 1642 finally sailed past the southern side of his Van Diemen's Land, he not only cut off a land mass of continental proportions but also deprived the hypothetical continent of its ancient name, which hereafter clung to the great island which, in addition to Tasmania, he had lopped off from the theoretical mass—Australia.

With three continents already severed from it—Africa, South America, and Australia—the Southland continued to shrink until finally James Cook, the great navigator of England, sailed around it in a much restricted and nearly circular curve during the years 1772-75. What the problems were he was then trying to solve, and what men believed around 1770 concerning the southern continent, we learn from Cook's own verbatim journal of the first voyage (of 1768-71), as published by Captain W. J. S. Wharton, London, 1893:

Cook's Speculations on a Southern Continent

As to a southern continent, I do not believe any such thing exists, unless in a high latitude. But as the contrary opinion hath for many years prevailed, and may yet prevail, it is necessary I should say something in support of mine more than what will be directly pointed out by the track of this ship in those seas; for from that alone it will evidently appear that there is a large space extending quite to the tropic in which we were not, or any other before us that we can ever learn for certain. . . .

Here is now room enough for the north cape of the southern continent to extend to the northward, even to a pretty low latitude. But what foundation have we for such a supposition? None that I know of but this, that it must either be here or nowhere.

Geographers have indeed laid down part of Quiros's discoveries in this longitude, and have told us that he had these signs of a continent, a part of which they have actually laid down in the maps, but by what authority I know not.

Quiros, in the latitude of 25 degrees or 26 degrees south discovered two islands, which I suppose may lay between the longitude of 130 degrees and 140 degrees west. Dalrymple lays them down in 140 degrees west, and says that Quiros saw to the southward very large hanging clouds and a very thick horizon, with other known signs of a continent.

Other accounts of their voyage says not a word about this; but supposing this to be true, hanging clouds and a thick horizon are certainly no signs of a continent.[1] . . .

---

[1] What Quiros saw is now supposed to have been Tahiti.

[Cook goes on to examine many alleged proofs and probabilities favoring the northward extension of the hypothetical southern continent to 40 degrees south, and to other South Temperate Zone and even subtropical latitudes. He considers most of the arguments to be of small weight, but admits they bear looking into—thinks they should be disposed of by actual searching voyages. He concludes:]

But to return to our own voyage, which must be allowed to have set aside the most, if not all, the arguments and proofs that have been advanced by different authors to prove that there must be a southern continent—I mean to the northward of 40 degrees South, for what may lie to the southward of that latitude I know not. Certain it is that we saw no visible signs of land, according to my opinion, neither in our route to the northward, southward, or westward, until a few days before we made the coast of New Zealand. . . .

Thus I have given my opinion freely and without prejudice, not with any view to discourage any future attempts being made toward discovering the southern continent; on the contrary, as I think this voyage will evidently make it appear that there is left but a small space to the northward of 40 degrees where the grand object can lay.

I think it would be a great pity that this thing, which at times has been the object of many ages and nations, should not now be wholly cleared up; which might very easily be done in one voyage without either much trouble or danger or fear of miscarrying, as the navigator would know where to go to look for it; but if, after all, no continent was to be found, then he might turn his thoughts toward the discovery of those multitude of islands which we are told [by native informants] lay within the tropical regions to the south of the line, and this we have from very good [native] authority, as I have before hinted. ▄

During his second voyage Cook was able to try his hand at solving the main problem of the Antarctic Sea, as to whether it was all water or contained a nucleus of land, some remnant of the formerly great Terra Australis. He had authority from the British Admiralty, which gave him two ships, the *Resolute* and the *Adventure.* The vessels kept getting separated during the next three years; the account here follows only the *Resolute,* with Cook aboard.

The expedition sailed from Plymouth on July 13, 1772, passed south through the Atlantic, and turned east around the Cape of Good Hope. They kept as far south as the drifting ice permitted.

The first crossing of the Antarctic Circle came on January 16, 1773.

Cook's entry into the southern polar zone is one of only a few genuine firsts in modern exploration, for most of our famous "discoverers" were in truth late-comers. Stone Age man, of our race or some other, had usually been far in advance of historical expeditions, and in a position to organize reception committees when our great pathfinders arrived. The Scots were seemingly able to tell Pytheas about Iceland in 330 B.C.; the Eskimos were in Greenland ahead of Erik the Red in A.D. 982; Eskimos or some forest Indians drove out the Europeans when they tried to plant a colony on the North American mainland in 1003; their cousins of the West Indies received Columbus in 1492.

Men of the Stone Age received the first Europeans that ever landed on what is nearly or quite the most isolated island of any ocean when the Dutch reached Easter Island in 1722. They must have crossed the Arctic Circle many thousands of years ago both in the Old World and in the New, and they reached the most northerly land on earth, the north tip of Greenland, surely a thousand years ahead of Peary. But we have no reason to think that any man of any race crossed the Antarctic Circle ahead of Cook's expedition.

Here the story is told of how, by crossing its boundary, man first entered the fifth and last zone of the earth, in James Cook's own account as found in the first volume of the two-volume quarto edition of his *Voyage towards the South Pole and around the World,* London, 1777.

Cook's Circumnavigation of the Southern Continent

We continued to steer to the east-southeast, with a fresh gale at northwest, attended with snow and sleet, till the eighth [of January, 1773], when we were in the latitude of 61 degrees 12 minutes south, longitude 31 degrees 47 minutes east. In the afternoon we passed more ice islands than we had seen for several days. Indeed they were now so familiar to us that they were often passed unnoticed, but more generally unseen on account of the thick weather. At nine o'clock in the evening, we came to one which had a quantity of loose ice about it.

As the wind was moderate and the weather tolerably fair, we shortened sail, and stood on and off, with a view of taking some on board on the return of light. But at four o'clock in the morning, finding ourselves to leeward of this ice, we bore down to an island to leeward of us, there being about it some loose ice, part of which we saw break off. There we brought to, hoisted out three boats, and in about five or six hours took up as much ice as yielded 15 tons of good fresh water. The pieces we took up were hard and solid as a rock; some of them were so large that we were obliged to break them with pick-axes before they could be taken into the boats.

The salt water which adhered to the ice was so trifling as not to be tasted, and after it had lain on deck a short time, entirely drained off; and the water which the ice yielded was perfectly sweet and well-tasted. Part of the ice we broke in pieces, and put into casks; some we melted in the copper, and filled up the casks with the water; and some we kept on deck for present use. The melting and stowing away the ice is a little tedious, and takes up some time; otherwise this is the most expeditious way of watering I ever met with.

Having got on board this supply of water, and the *Adventure* about two-thirds as much (of which we stood in great need), as we had once broke the ice, I did not doubt of getting more whenever we were in want. I therefore, without hesitation, directed our course more to the south, with a gentle gale at northwest, attended, as usual, with snow showers.

In the morning of the eleventh . . . we saw some penguins; and being near an island of ice from which several pieces had broken, we hoisted out two boats, and took on board as much as filled all our empty casks; and the *Adventure* did the same. While this was doing, Mr. Forster shot an albatross, whose plumage was of a color between brown and dark gray, the head and upper side of the wings rather inclining to black, and it had white eyebrows. We began to see these birds about the time of our first falling in with the ice islands, and some have accompanied us ever since. These, and the dark-brown sort with a yellow bill, were the only albatrosses that had not now forsaken us.

At 4 P.M., we hoisted in the boats and made sail to the southeast, with a gentle breeze at south by west, attended with showers of snow.

On the thirteenth, at 2 A.M. it fell calm. Of this we took the opportunity to hoist out a boat, to try the current, which we found to set northwest near ⅓ mile an hour. At the time of trying the current, a Fahrenheit's thermometer was immersed in the sea 100 fathoms below its surface, where it remained twenty minutes. When it came up, the mercury stood at 32°, which is the freezing point. Some little time after, being exposed to the surface of the sea, it rose to 33.5°; and in the open air to 36°. The calm continued till five o'clock in the evening, when it was succeeded by a light breeze from the south and southeast, with which we stood to the northeast with all our sails set.

Though the weather continued fair, the sky, as usual, was clouded. However, at nine o'clock the next morning it was clear, and we were enabled to observe several distances between the sun and moon. The mean result of which gave 39 degrees 30 minutes 30 seconds east longitude. . . . Our latitude at this time was 63 degrees 57 minutes, longitude 39 degrees 38.5 minutes east. . . .

Five tolerably fine days had now succeeded one another [by January 15]. This, besides giving us an opportunity to make the preceding observations, was very serviceable to us on many other accounts, and came at a very seasonable time. For, having on board a good quantity of fresh water—or ice, which was the same thing—the people were enabled to wash and dry their clothes and linen, a care that can never be enough attended to in all long voyages. The winds during this time blew in gentle gales, and the weather was mild. Yet the mercury in the thermometer never rose above 36°, and was frequently as low as the freezing point.

In the afternoon, having but little wind, I brought to under an island of ice, and sent a boat to take up some. In the evening the wind freshened at east, and was attended with snow showers and thick hazy weather, which continued great part of the sixteenth. As we met with little ice, I stood to the south, close-hauled; and at six o'clock in the evening, being in the latitude of 64 degrees 56 minutes south, longitude 39 degrees 35 minutes east, I found the variation by Gregory's compass to be 26 degrees 41 minutes west. At this time, the motion of the ship was so great that I could by no means observe with any of Dr. Knight's compasses.

As the wind remained invariably fixed at east and east by south, I continued to stand to the south, and on the seventeenth, between eleven and twelve o'clock, we crossed the Antarctic Circle in the longitude of 66 degrees 36 minutes 30 seconds south. The weather was now become tolerably clear, so that we could see several leagues around us; and yet we had only seen one island of ice since the morning. But about 4 P.M., as we were steering to the south, we observed the whole sea in a manner covered with ice, from the direction of southeast, round by the south to west.

In this space, thirty-eight ice islands, great and small, were seen, besides loose ice in abundance, so that we were obliged to luff for one piece and bear up for another; and as we continued to advance to the south, it increased in such a manner that at a quarter past six o'clock, being then in the latitude of 67 degrees 15 minutes south, we could proceed no farther, the ice being entirely closed to the south in the whole extent from east to west-southwest, without the least appearance of any opening.

This immense field was composed of different kinds of ice, such as high hills, loose or broken pieces packed together, and what I think Greenlandmen call field ice. A float of this kind of ice lay to the southeast of us, of such extent that I could see no end to it from the masthead. It was 16 or 18 feet high at least, and appeared of a pretty equal height and surface.

Here we saw many whales playing about the ice, and for

two days before had seen several flocks of the brown and white pintados, which we named Antarctic petrels because they seem to be natives of that region. They are undoubtedly of the petrel tribe; are, in every respect, shaped like the pintados, differing only from them in color. The head and forepart of the body of these are brown; and the hind part of the body, tail, and ends of the wings are white. The white petrel also appeared in greater numbers than before, some few dark gray albatrosses, and our constant companion the blue petrel. But the common pintados had quite disappeared, as well as many other sorts which are common in lower latitudes.

After meeting with this ice, I did not thnk it was at all prudent to persevere in getting farther to the south, especially as the summer was already half-spent, and it would have taken up some time to have got round the ice, even supposing it to have been practicable—which, however, is doubtful. I therefore came to a resolution to proceed directly in search of the land lately discovered by the French [Kerguelen Island, south of the Indian Ocean].

And as the winds still continued at east by south, I was obliged to return to the north, over some part of the sea I had already made myself acquainted with, and for that reason wished to have avoided. But this was not to be done, as our course made good was little better than north. In the night the wind increased to a strong gale, attended with sleet and snow, and obliged us to double-reef our topsails. About noon the next day, the gale abated, so that we could bear all our reefs out; but the wind still remained in its old quarter. ✓

By evening of January 19, the ships were in south latitude 64 degrees 12 minutes and thus well back in the South Temperate Zone.

On this voyage, which was both around the southern (unseen and as yet debatable) continent and around the world, Cook was steering east and thus reversing the direction of previous circumnavigations, which had imitated Magellan in sailing west. He was already more than 20 degrees of longitude east of the Cape of Good Hope when he crossed the Antarctic Circle. Impeded by floes of sea ice and bergs of land ice, and by the fog which these created when they got into warmer water, the ships struggled eastward. After 4000 leagues without seeing land, and after getting separated from the *Adventure* in one of the fogs, Cook reached New Zealand on March 25, having made good speed before generally favoring winds.

After resting in Dusky Bay, New Zealand, Cook moved north into the tropics and visited Tahiti and a number of other islands, rectifying their positions on the chart and carrying forward his usual program of scientific observations.

By October the *Resolute* was back in New Zealand; November 26 she started thence, heading south in quest of land. They found no sign of any. The narrative, begins again with December 12, 1773:

Cook's Story Continued

At four o'clock the next morning, being in the latitude of 62 degrees 10 minutes south, longitude 172 degrees west, we saw the first ice island, 11.5 degrees farther south than the first ice we saw the preceding year after leaving the Cape of Good Hope. At the time we saw this ice we also saw an Antarctic petrel, some gray albatrosses, and our old companions pintados and blue petrels.

The wind kept veering from southwest by the northwest to north-northeast, for the most part a fresh gale, attended with a thick haze and snow; on which account we steered to the southeast and east, keeping the wind always on the beam, that it might be in our power to return back nearly on the same track should our course have been interrupted by any danger whatever. For some days we had a great sea from the northwest and southwest, so that it is not probable there can be any land near between these two points.

We fell in with several large islands on the fourteenth, and about noon, with a quantity of loose ice, through which we sailed. Latitude 64 degrees 55 minutes south, longitude 163 degrees 20 minutes west. Gray albatrosses, blue petrels, pintados, and fulmars were seen. As we advanced to the southeast by east with a fresh gale at west, we found the number of ice islands increase fast upon us. Between noon and eight in the evening we saw but two; but before four o'clock in the morning of the fifteenth we had passed seventeen, besides a quantity of loose ice, which we ran through.

At six o'clock, we were obliged to haul to the northeast in order to clear an immense field which lay to the south and southeast. The ice, in most part of it, lay close packed together; in other places, there appeared partitions in the field, and a clear sea beyond it. However, I did not think it safe to venture through, as the wind would not permit us to return the same way that we must go in.

Besides, as it blew strong, and the weather at times was exceedingly foggy, it was the more necessary for us to get clear of this loose ice, which is rather more dangerous than the great islands. It was not such ice as is usually found in bays or rivers, and near shore, but such as breaks off from the islands, and may not improperly be called parings of the large pieces, or the rubbish or fragments which fall off when the great islands break loose from the place where they are formed.

We had not stood long to the northeast before we found ourselves embayed by the ice, and were obliged to tack and stretch to the southwest, having the field or loose ice to the south, and many huge islands to the north. After standing two hours on this tack, the wind very luckily veering to the westward, we tacked, stretched to the north, and soon got clear of all the loose ice; but not before we had received several hard knocks from the larger pieces, which, with all our care, we could not avoid.

After clearing one danger, we still had another to encounter: the weather remained foggy, and many large islands lay in our way, so that we had to luff for one and bear up for another. One we were very near falling aboard of, and if it had happened, this circumstance would never have been related.

These difficulties, together with the improbability of finding land farther south, and the impossibility of exploring it on account of the ice if we should find any, determined me to get more to the north. At the time we last tacked, we were in the longitude of 159 degrees 20 minutes west and in the latitude of 66 degrees south.

Several penguins were seen on some of the ice islands, and a few Antarctic petrels on the wing.

We continued to stand to the north, with a fresh gale at west, attended with thick snow showers, till eight o'clock in the evening, when the wind abated, the sky began to clear up, and at six o'clock in the morning of the sixteenth it fell calm. Four hours after, it was succeeded by a breeze at northeast with which we stretched to the southeast, having thick hazy weather, with snow showers, and all our rigging coated with ice. In the evening we attempted to take some up out of the sea, but were obliged to desist, the sea running too high, and the pieces being so large that it was dangerous for the boat to come near them.

The next morning, being the seventeenth, we succeeded better; for, falling in with a quantity of loose ice, we hoisted out two boats, and by noon got on board as much as we could manage. We then made sail for the east, with a gentle breeze northerly, attended with snow and sleet, which froze to the rigging as it fell. At this time we were in the latitude of 64 degrees 41 minutes south, longitude 155 degrees 44 minutes west.

The ice we took up proved to be none of the best, being chiefly composed of frozen snow, on which account it was porous, and had imbibed a good deal of salt water. But this drained off after lying awhile on deck, and the water then yielded was fresh.

We continued to stretch to the east, with a piercing cold northerly wind, attended with a thick fog, snow, and sleet that decorated all our rigging with icicles. We were hourly meeting with some of the large ice islands, which in these high latitudes render navigation so very dangerous. At seven in the evening, falling in with a cluster of them, we narrowly escaped running aboard of one and with difficulty wore clear of the others. . . .

The clear weather, and the wind, veering to northwest, tempted me to steer south; which course we continued till seven in the morning of the twentieth, when, the wind changing to northeast and the sky becoming clouded, we hauled up southeast. In the afternoon, the wind increased to a strong gale, attended with a thick fog, snow, sleet, and rain, which constitutes the very worst of weather. Our rigging at this time was so loaded with ice that we had enough to do to get our top-sails down, to double the reef.

At seven o'clock in the evening [of December 20, 1773], in the longitude of 147 degrees 46 minutes, we came, the second time, within the Antarctic or Polar Circle, continuing our course to the southeast till six o'clock the next morning.

At that time, being in the latitude of 67 degrees 5 minutes south, all at once we got in among a cluster of very large ice islands and a vast quantity of loose pieces; and as the fog was exceedingly thick, it was with the utmost difficulty we wore clear of them. This done, we stood to the northwest till noon, when, the fog being somewhat dissipated, we resumed our course again to the southeast.

The ice islands we met with in the morning were very high and rugged, forming at their tops many peaks; whereas the most of those we had seen before were flat at top, and not so high, though many of them were between 200 and 300 feet in height, and between 2 and 3 miles in circuit, with perpendicular cliffs or sides astonishing to behold. Most of our winged com-panions had now left us. The gray albatrosses only remained, and instead of the other birds, we were visited by a few Antarctic petrels.

The twenty-second we steered east-southeast, with a fresh gale at north, blowing in squalls, one of which took hold of the mizzen topsail, tore it all to rags, and rendered it forever after useless. At six o'clock in the morning, the wind veering toward the west, our course was east, northerly. At this time we were in the latitude of 67 degrees 31 minutes, the highest we had yet been in, longitude 142 degrees 54 minutes west.

We continued our course to the east by north till noon the twenty-third, when, being in the latitude of 67 degrees 12 minutes, longitude 138 degrees, we steered southeast, having then twenty-three ice islands in sight from off the deck and twice that number from the masthead; and yet we could not see above 2 or 3 miles round us.

At four o'clock in the afternoon, in the latitude of 67 degrees 20 minutes, longitude 137 degrees 12 minutes, we fell in with such a quantity of field or loose ice as covered the sea in the whole extent from south to east, and was so thick and close as wholly to obstruct our passage. At this time, the wind being pretty moderate and the sea smooth, we brought to at the outer edge of the ice, hoisted out two boats, and sent them to take some up. In the meantime, we laid hold of several large pieces alongside, and got them on board with our tackle.

The taking up ice proved such cold work that it was eight o'clock by the time the boats had made two trips, when we hoisted them in and made sail to the west, under double-reefed topsails and courses, with a strong gale at north, attended with snow and sleet which froze to the rigging as it fell, making the ropes like wires and the sails like boards or plates of metal. The shivers also were frozen so fast in the blocks that it required our utmost efforts to get a topsail down and up, the cold so intense as hardly to be endured, the whole sea, in a manner, covered with ice; a hard gale, and a thick fog.

Under all these unfavorable circumstances, it was natural for me to think of returning more to the north, seeing no probability of finding any land here, nor a possibility of getting farther south. And to have proceeded to the east in this latitude must have been wrong, not only on account of the ice, but because we must have left a vast space of sea to the north unexplored, a space of 24 degrees of latitude, in which a large tract of land might have lain. Whether such a supposition was well grounded could only be determined by visiting those parts.

While we were taking up ice, we got two of the Antarctic petrels so often mentioned, by which our conjectures were confirmed of their being of the petrel tribe. They were about the size of a large pigeon; the feathers of the head, back, and part of the upper side of the wings are of a light brown; the belly and underside of the wings, white; the tail feathers are also white, but tipped with brown. At the same time, we got another new petrel, smaller than the former, and all of a dark-gray plumage. We remarked that these birds were fuller of feathers than any we had hitherto seen, such care has nature taken to clothe them suitably to the climate in which they live.

At the same time we saw a few chocolate-colored albatrosses. These, as well as the petrels above mentioned, we nowhere saw among the ice; hence one may with reason conjecture that there is land to the south. If not, I must ask where these birds breed? A question which perhaps will never be determined; for hitherto we have found these lands, if any, quite inaccessible.

Besides these birds, we saw a very large seal, which kept playing about us some time. One of our people who had been at Greenland called it a sea horse, but everyone else who saw it took it for what I have said. Since our first falling in with the ice, the mercury in the thermometer had been from 33° to 31° at noonday.

On the twenty-fourth, the wind abated, veered to the northwest, and the sky cleared up, in the latitude of 67 degrees, longitude 138 degrees 15 minutes. As we advanced to the northeast with a gentle gale at northwest, the ice islands increased so fast upon us that this day at noon we could see near one hundred round us, besides an immense number of small pieces.

Perceiving that it was likely to be calm, I got the ship into as clear a berth as I could, where she drifted along with the ice, and by taking the advantage of every light air of wind, was kept from falling aboard any of these floating isles. Here it was we spent Christmas Day, much in the manner as we did the preceding one. We were fortunate in having continual daylight, and clear weather; for had it been as foggy as on some of the preceding days, nothing less than a miracle could have saved us from being dashed to pieces.

In the morning of the twenty-sixth, the whole sea was in a manner covered with ice, two hundred large islands and upward being seen within the compass of 4 or 5 miles—which was the limits of our horizon—besides smaller pieces innumerable. Our latitude at noon was 66 degrees 15 minutes, longitude 134 degrees 22 minutes.

[The Antarctic Circle being reckoned at 66 degrees 30 minutes, or 66 degrees 32 minutes, the *Resolute* was again back within the Temperate Zone, there to remain for a long stretch east. On January 9, for instance, they were at 48 degrees 17 minutes south, about as far south of the equator as the northern boundary of the United States is north of it. At that time they were near 127 degrees west, nearly straight south of San Francisco.

After the middle of January 1774, the *Resolute* once more strove for a high southing and the possibility of sighting land. Cook wrote concerning this attempt:]

On the twenty-third at noon, we were in the latitude of 62 degrees 22 minutes south, longitude 110 degrees 24 minutes. In the afternoon, we passed an ice island. The wind, which blew fresh, continued to veer to the west; and at eight o'clock the next morning it was to the north of west, when I steered south by west and south-southwest. At this time we were in the latitude of 63 degrees 20 minutes south, longitude 108 degrees 7 minutes west, and had a great sea from southwest.

We continued this course till noon the next day, the twenty-fifth, when we steered due south. Our latitude at this time was 65 degrees 24 minutes, longitude 109 degrees 31 minutes west. The wind was at north, the weather mild and not unpleasant, and not a bit of ice in view. This we thought a little extraordinary, as it was but a month before, and not quite 200 leagues to the east, that we were in a manner blocked up with large islands of ice in this very latitude. Saw a single pintado petrel, some blue petrels, and a few brown albatrosses.

In the evening, being under the same meridian and in the latitude of 65 degrees 44 minutes south, the variation was 19 degrees 27 minutes east; but the next morning, in the latitude of 66 degrees 20 minutes south, longitude the same as before, it was only 18 degrees 20 minutes east. Probably the mean between the two is the nearest the truth. At this time we had nine small islands in sight, and soon after we came, the third time, within the Antarctic Polar Circle, in the longitude of 109 degrees 31 minutes west.

About noon, seeing the appearance of land to the southeast, we immediately trimmed our sails and stood toward it. Soon after, it disappeared, but we did not give it up till eight o'clock the next morning, when we were well assured that it was nothing but clouds, or a fog bank; and then we resumed our course to the south, with a gentle breeze at northeast, attended with a thick fog, snow, and sleet.

We now began to meet with ice islands more frequently than before, and in the latitude of 69 degrees 38 minutes south, longitude 108 degrees 12 minutes west, we fell in with a field of loose ice. As we began to be in want of water, I hoisted out two boats and took up as much as yielded about 10 tons. This was cold work, but it was now familiar to us.

As soon as we had done, we hoisted in the boats, and afterward made short boards over that part of the sea we had, in some measure, made ourselves acquainted with. For we had now so thick a fog that we could not see 200 yards round us; and as we knew not the extent of the loose ice, I durst not steer to the south until we had clear weather. Thus we spent the night, or rather that part of the twenty-four hours which answered to night, for we had no darkness but what was occasioned by fogs.

At four o'clock in the morning of the twenty-ninth, the fog began to clear away, and the day becoming clear and serene, we again steered to the south with a gentle gale at northeast and north-northeast. The variation was found to be 22 degrees 41 minutes east. This was in the latitude of 69 degrees 45 minutes south, longitude 108 degrees 5 minutes west; and in the afternoon, being in the same longitude, and in the latitude of 70 degrees 23 minutes south, it was 24 degrees 31 minutes east.

Soon after, the sky became clouded and the air very cold. We continued our course to the south, and passed a piece of weed covered with barnacles which a brown albatross was picking off. At ten o'clock, we passed a very large ice island; it was not less than 3 or 4 miles in circuit. Several more being seen ahead, and the weather becoming foggy, we hauled the wind to the northward; but in less than two hours the weather cleared up, and we again stood south.

On the thirtieth, at four o'clock in the morning we perceived the clouds over the horizon to the south to be of an unusual snow-white brightness, which we knew denounced our approached to field ice. Soon after, it was seen from the topmast head, and at eight o'clock we were close to its edge. It extended east and west, far beyond the reach of our sight.

In the situation we were in, just the southern half of our horizon was illuminated, by the rays of light reflected from the ice, to a considerable height. Ninety-seven ice hills were distinctly seen within the field, besides those on the outside, many of them very large, and looking like a ridge of mountains, rising one above another till they were lost in the clouds.

The outer or northern edge of this immense field was composed of loose or broken ice close packed together, so that it was not possible for anything to enter it. This was about a mile broad, within which was solid ice in one continued compact body. It was rather low and flat (except the hills), but seemed to increase in height as you traced it to the south, in which direction it extended beyond our sight.

Such mountains of ice as these were, I believe, never seen in the Greenland seas—at least, not that I ever heard or read of—so that we cannot draw a comparison between the ice here and there. It must be allowed that these prodigious ice mountains must add such additional weight to the ice fields which enclose them as cannot but make a great difference between the navigating this icy sea and that of Greenland.

I will not say it was impossible anywhere to get farther to the south; but the attempting it would have been a dangerous and rash enterprise, and what I believe no man in my situation would have thought of. It was, indeed, *my* opinion, as well as the opinion of most on board, that this ice extended quite to the Pole, or perhaps joined to some land to which it had been fixed from the earliest time; and that it is here—that is, to the south of this parallel—where all the ice we find scattered up and down to the north is first formed, and afterward broken off by gales of wind, or other causes, and brought to the north by the currents, which we always found to set in that direction in the high latitudes.

As we drew near this ice some penguins were heard, but none seen, and but few other birds, or any other thing that could induce us to think any land was near. And yet I think there must be some to the south behind this ice; but if there is, it can afford no better retreat for birds, or any other animals, than the ice itself, with which it must be wholly covered.

I, who had ambition not only to go farther than anyone had been before but as far as it was possible for man to go, was not sorry at meeting with this interruption, as it, in some measure, relieved us—at least, shortened the dangers and hardships inseparable from the navigation of the southern polar regions.

Since therefore we could not proceed one inch farther to the south, no other reason need be assigned for my tacking and standing back to the north, being at this time in the latitude of 71 degrees 10 minutes south, longitude 106 degrees 54 minutes west.

[By early February the *Resolute* was near 100 degrees west longitude, which is about straight south from the middle of the United States, but a long way west from South America. Cook says:]

I now came to a resolution to proceed to the north, and to spend the ensuing winter within the tropic if I met with no employment before I came there. I was now well satisfied no continent was to be found in this ocean but what must lie so far to the south as to be wholly inaccessible on account of ice; and that if one should be found in the southern Atlantic Ocean, it would be necessary to have the whole summer before us to explore it. On the other hand, upon a supposition that there is no land there, we undoubtedly might have reached the Cape of Good Hope by April, and so have put an end to the expedition, so far as it related to the finding a continent—which indeed was the first object of the voyage.

But for me, at this time, to have quitted this southern Pacific Ocean, with a good ship expressly sent out on discoveries, a healthy crew, and not in want either of stores or of provisions, would have been betraying not only a want of perseverance, but of judgment, in supposing the South Pacific Ocean to have been so well explored that nothing remained to be done in it.

This, however, was not my opinion; for although I had proved there was no continent but what must lie far to the south, there remained, nevertheless, room for very large islands in places wholly unexamined; and many of those which were formerly discovered are but imperfectly explored, and their situations as imperfectly known. I was besides of opinion that my remaining in this sea some time longer would be productive of improvements in navigation and geography, as well as other sciences. . . .

Since now nothing had happened to prevent me from carrying these views into execution, my intention was first to go in search of the land said to have been discovered by Juan Fernandez, above a century ago, in about the latitude of 38 degrees. If I should fail in finding this land, then to go in search of Easter Island or Davis's Land, whose situation was known with so little certainty that the attempts lately made to find it had miscarried. I next intended to get within the tropic, and then proceed to the west, touching at and settling the situations of such islands as we might meet with till we arrived at Otaheite [Tahiti], where it was necessary I should stop to look for the *Adventure*.

I had also thoughts of running as far west as the Tierra Austral del Espíritu Santo, discovered by Quiros, and which M. de Bougainville calls the Great Cyclades. Quiros speaks of this land as being large, or lying in the neighborhood of large lands; and as this was a point which Bougainville had neither confirmed nor refuted, I thought it was worth clearing up.

From this land my design was to steer to the south, and so back to the east between the latitudes of 50 degrees and 60 degrees, intending, if possible, to be the length of Cape Horn in November next, when we should have the best part of the summer before us to explore the southern part of the Atlantic Ocean. Great as this design appeared to be, I however thought it possible to be executed; and when I came to communicate it to the officers, I had the satisfaction to find that they all heartily concurred in it. ✠

The plans so outlined were in substance carried out by the *Resolute*, including the discovery of several islands, chief of them New Caledonia.

By October 1774, Cook was again in New Zealand. Thence the *Resolute* sailed to try reaching the Great Southland somewhere to the southwest, south, or southeast of South America. January 14, 1775, he either discovered or rediscovered the island of South Georgia, destined to become important as a base for sealers, whalers, and Antarctic explorers. He was now well to the east of South America, and continued working easterly. He succeeded in finding no continental land, so he turned north for Africa, reaching Table Bay on March 21, and Plymouth on July 29.

Cook had disproved the existence of any supercontinent such as the Great Southland, Terra Australis, and had confined the possibilities to such reasonable proportions as were eventually demonstrated—an Antarctica somewhat larger than Europe or Australia.

The Yankees Discover a Southern Continent

Cook reported seals and whales in the berg-filled ocean the margins of which he skirted. These "great fish" were in the eighteenth century the suppliers of the oil that filled the lamps of Europe and of other commercial nations. Those were, too, days of Yankee maritime enterprise. New England led in building up the oil industry and therefore in prospecting for new sealing and whaling grounds. A natural by-product of these commercial operations was geographic discovery. Several captains found islands; Captain Palmer found a mainland.

In the first decades of the nineteenth century one of the chief centers of the fish-oil trade was Stonington, Connecticut. Thence sailed in 1820 as skipper of the sloop *Hero* a Yankee of twenty-one years, Nathaniel Brown Palmer, who had gone in for sealing at fourteen and who had been the year previous second mate of the brig *Hersilia*. He kept a log in the briefest of sailor terms, and although we have from his own pen the record of the discovery of the world's last continent, we can hardly say that he tells us the story.

In 1820 the *Hero* was at Deception Island, one of the group of South Shetland Islands which lie southeast of South America and which were then frequented by Yankee sealing fleets. For the sixteenth of November Palmer's log reads:[2]

---

[2] The following extracts from Palmer's log are taken from Lawrence Martin's "Antarctica Discovered by a Connecticut Yankee, Captain Nathaniel Brown Palmer," *Geographical Review*, October 1940, pp. 529-52. Dr. Martin's statement is based mainly on manuscript materials in the Library of Congress; facsimiles of Palmer's entries for November 16 and 17, 1820, are shown on p. 536 of his article.

"Got under weigh; at ten we were clear from the harbor [Port Williams], stood over for the land, course south by east ½ east. Ends with fresh breezes from southwest and pleasant."

Evidently Palmer had seen the extensive land, which proved to be the long-sought continent, before he left the harbor and thus probably from the slopes of Deception Island, where he had been gathering eggs, or else from his own masthead. He probably saw both Trinity Island, about 40 sea miles away, and the mainland 10 miles beyond it, but at that distance the island probably looked like a promontory from the main.

The entry for November 17 reads (this time exactly as he wrote it):

"These 24 hours commences with fresh Breeses from SWest and Pleasant   at 8 P.M. got over under the Land [Trinity Island]. found the sea filled with imense Ice Bergs   at 12 hove too under the Jib   Laid off & on until morning—at 4 A M made sail in shore and Discovered—a strait—Trending SSW & NNE—it was Literally filled with Ice and the [mainland] shore inaccessible   we thought it not Prudent to Venture in ice   Bore away to the Northerd & saw 2 small islands and the [mainland] shore every where Perpendicular we stood across towards frieseland [Friesland or Smith's or Livingston Island] Course NNW—the Latitude of the mouth of the strait was 63-45 S   Ends with fine weather wind at SSW."

The one narrative statement which we possess on the discovery of the Antarctic Continent is by a fellow Stoningtonian, Captain Edmund Fanning (1769-1841), navigator in Antarctic and tropic waters, discoverer of Fanning Island in the South Pacific, successful both as navigator and as promoter. The selection is from his *Voyages around the World*, New York, 1833:

Fanning's Account of Palmer's Discovery

The next season after the *Hersilia's* return from the South Shetlands [1820], a fleet of vessels—consisting of the brig *Frederick*, Captain Benjamin Pendleton the senior commander, the brig *Hersilia*, Captain James P. Sheffield, schooners

Express, Captain E. Williams, *Free Gift*, Captain F. Dunbar, and sloop *Hero*, Captain N. B. Palmer—was fitted out at Stonington, Connecticut, on a voyage to the South Shetlands.

From Captain Pendleton's report, as rendered on their return, it appeared that while the fleet lay at anchor in Yankee Harbor, Deception Island, during the season of 1820-21, being on the lookout from an elevated station on the mountain of the island during a very clear day, he had discovered mountains (one a volcano in operation) in the south. This was what is now known by the name of Palmer's Land. From the statement it will be perceived how this name came deservedly to be given it, and by which it is now current in the modern charts.

To examine this newly discovered land, Captain N. B. Palmer, in the sloop *Hero*, a vessel but little rising 40 tons, was dispatched. He found it to be an extensive mountainous country, more sterile and dismal if possible, and more heavily loaded with ice and snow, than the South Shetlands. There were sea leopards on its shore, but no fur seals. The main part of its coast was icebound, although it was in the midsummer of this hemisphere, and a landing consequently difficult.

On the *Hero's* return passage to Yankee Harbor she got becalmed in a thick fog between the South Shetlands and the newly discovered continent, but nearest the former. When this began to clear away, Captain Palmer was surprised to find his little bark between a frigate and sloop of war, and instantly run up the United States flag; the frigate and sloop of war then set the Russian colors.

Soon after this a boat was seen pulling from the commodore's ship for the *Hero*, and when alongside, the lieutenant presented an invitation from his commodore for Captain P. to go on board; this of course was accepted. These ships he then found were the two discovery ships sent out by the Emperor Alexander of Russia, on a voyage round the world [under command of Captain—later Admiral—Fabian Gottlieb von Bellingshausen].

To the commodore's interrogatory if he had any knowledge of those islands then in sight, and what they were, Captain P. replied he was well acquainted with them, and that they were the South Shetlands, at the same time making a tender of his services to pilot the ships into a good harbor at Deception Island, the nearest by, where water and refreshments such as the island afforded could be obtained, he also informing the Russian officer that his vessel belonged to a fleet of five sail, out of Stonington, under command of Captain B. Pendleton, and then at anchor in Yankee Harbor, who would most cheerfully render any assistance in his power.

The commodore thanked him kindly, "but previous to our being enveloped in the fog," said he, "we had sight of those islands, and concluded we had made a discovery, but behold, when the fog lifts, to my great surprise, here is an American vessel apparently in as fine order as if it were but yesterday she had left the United States; not only this, but her master is ready to pilot my vessels into port. We must surrender the palm to you Americans," continued he, very flatteringly.

His astonishment was yet more increased when Captain Palmer informed him of the existence of an immense extent of land to the south, whose mountains might be seen from the masthead when the fog should clear away entirely. Captain Palmer, while on board the frigate, was entertained in the most friendly manner, and the commodore was so forcibly struck with the circumstances of the case that he named the coast then to the south, Palmer Land; by this name it is recorded on the recent Russian and English charts and maps which have been published since the return of these ships.

The situation of the different vessels may be seen by the plate [reproduced by Fanning]. They were, at the time of the lifting of the fog and its going off to the eastward, to the south and in sight of the Shetland Islands, but nearest to Deception Island. In their immediate neighborhood were many ice islands, some of greater and some of less dimensions, while far off to the south the icy tops of some two or three of the mountains on Palmer Land could be faintly seen. The wind at the time was moderate, and both the ships and the little sloop were moving along under full sail.

The following season, in 1821-22, Captain Pendleton was again at Yankee Harbor, with the Stonington fleet. He then once more dispatched Captain Palmer in the sloop *James Mon-*

roe, an excellent vessel of upward of 80 tons, well calculated for such duties and by her great strength well able to venture in the midst of and wrestle with the ice.

Captain Palmer reported on his return that after proceeding to the southward, he met ice fast and firmly attached to the shore of Palmer Land. He then traced the coast to the east-ward, keeping as near the shore as the ice would suffer. At times he was able to come alongshore, at other points he could not approach within from 1 to several miles, owing to the firm ices, although it was in December and January, the middle summer months in this hemisphere. In this way he coasted along this continent upward of 15 degrees; viz., from 64 degrees and odd, down below the 49th of west longitude.

The coast as he proceeded to the eastward became more clear of ice, so that he was able to trace the shore better; in 61 degrees 41 minutes south latitude, a strait was discovered which he named Washington Strait. This he entered, and about a league within came to a fine bay which he named Monroe Bay. At the head of this was a good harbor; here they anchored, calling it Palmer's Harbor.

The Captain landed on the beach [of an island] among a number of those beautiful amphibious animals, the spotted glossy-looking sea leopard, and that rich golden-colored noble bird, the king penguin. Making their way through these, the Captain and party traversed the coast and country for some distance around without discovering the least appearance of vegetation excepting the winter moss.

The sea leopards were the only animals found. There were, however, vast numbers of birds, several different species of the penguin, Port Egmont hens, white pigeons, a variety of gulls, and many kinds of oceanic birds. The valleys and gulleys were mainly filled with those never-dissolved icebergs, their square and perpendicular fronts, several hundred feet in height, glistening most splendidly in a variety of colors as the sun shone upon them.

The mountains on the coast, as well as those to all appearance in the interior, were generally covered with snow, except when their black peaks were seen here and there peeping out.

In the period immediately following the discovery of the continent by Palmer, there was a deal of activity in far southern waters, with portions of the coast line revealed to one explorer or another. Most notable were the circumnavigations of the Russian Bellingshausen and the American Wilkes.

The end of this period of growing knowledge is marked by the 1841 discovery by Admiral Sir James Clark Ross of the deep embayment in the Antarctic continent, now called Ross Sea, which offers ships a favorable and comparatively near approach to the South Pole. He discovered, too, the marvelous Ross Shelf, the precipitous and magnificent cliffs of the glacier ice that floats on and fills the inner part of the sea, as well as two great volcanoes, Erebus and Terror, named after the ships of the expedition.

After the return of Ross to Britain there followed a half-century of what Hugh Robert Mill, historian of geographic discovery, has called "averted interest" with regard to the Far South. Then in the nineties of the nineteenth century came a revival of southern whaling. The "fish oil" was no longer required for light, but it was wanted for commercial uses nevertheless, chiefly for soap and for butter substitutes—margarine. In this revived fishery the British were at first the leaders, but they were overtaken and finally outdistanced by the Norwegians.

In 1897 came at last a revival of formal exploration, led by the Belgian Adrian de Gerlache in the *Belgica*. (Incidentally, two of his lieutenants eventually became well known in connection with polar matters, Dr. Frederick A. Cook and Captain Roald Amundsen.)

Meantime, the first landing on the shore of the Antarctic continent had been made from a whaler.

A young Norwegian, H. J. Bull, felt it logical that Australians should develop and finance an Antarctic whaling industry. So he went down there, campaigned around, and failed. He then realized that mental nearness can be more significant than geographical contiguity, returned to sea-minded Norway, and was promptly financed by a successful whaler of eighty, Svend Foyn. The ship was the *Antarctic*, the skipper was Leonard Kristensen, the inspirer of the voyage and the narrator of her story was a passenger. Of that story there is given here only Bull's acount of the first placing of a human foot upon the last continent, taken from his *The Cruise of the "Antarctic,"* London, 1896.

In January 1895, the *Antarctic* found herself in the Victoria Land sector:

Man Steps Ashore on a New Continent

[January 22, 1895] Still no whales. It appeared, therefore, commercially useless to continue our voyage south, however interesting a sight would have been of Mount Erebus in possible eruption, of Mount Terror, and the great ice barrier, hundreds of miles in length, described by Sir James Ross. I sometimes feel that we ought to have sacrificed a few more days and explored the Great Bay to the very end, to have dispelled the last chance of illusion as regards the existence of right whales; but at the time it appeared to us that the interests of our owners demanded an immediate return in order to give us a chance of obtaining a cargo in other latitudes.

We went about at 8 A.M., reeling off 12 to 13 miles before noon, when our observation gave us 73 degrees 49 minutes. At the time of turning northward, our position was therefore 74 degrees south within a mile either way.

The further we penetrated into the bay, the more free, strange to say, it proved itself to be as regards ice. On several occasions today we could not observe even the smallest particle from the crow's-nest. This fact, however, rather diminished any chance of meeting whales, as the small crustaceans and mollusks which these animals chiefly pursue during their polar holiday are most abundant under and between the floes.

[January 23] Coasting northward again as fast as the fresh breeze will carry us, the idea being to explore the western shore of the mainland and the sea toward Balleny Islands, as a last chance of finding the lost tribe of whales. Our second mate also thinks that our chance of finding seals in this direction is a better one, as his Arctic experience is unfavorable as regards the occurrence of seals off the entrance to extensive bays. Later on we hope to explore the still more westerly regions, where Lieutenant Wilkes fell in with "many" sea elephants, should the brief Antarctic summer allow it.

We arrived off Possession Island at 3 P.M., but the new projected landing had to be abandoned on account of the strong northerly current, which would have made it difficult to heave to in the fresh southerly breeze.

[January 24] Cape Adare was made at midnight. The weather was now favorable for a landing, and at 1 A.M. a party, including the Captain, second mate, Mr. Borchgrevink, and the writer, set off, landing on a pebbly beach of easy access, after an hour's rowing through loose ice, negotiated without difficulty. In the calm weather little or no swell was observable against the shore. Jellyfish of a considerable size were noticed in the sea, an extraordinary high latitude for this class of invertebrate.

The sensation of being the first men who had set foot on the real Antarctic mainland was both strange and pleasurable, although Mr. Boyn would no doubt have preferred to exchange this pleasing sensation on our part for a right whale, even of small dimensions.

The tide current had been setting north with a great speed, estimated at about 4 to 5 knots an hour, but it had now turned, its velocity in the opposite direction being much less.

Our surroundings and our hosts were as strange and unique as our feelings. The latter—myriads of penguins—fairly covered the flat promontory, many acres in extent, jutting out into the bay between Cape Adare and a more westerly headland; they further lined all accessible projections of the rocks to an altitude of 800 or 900 feet.

The youngsters were now almost full-grown. In their thick, woolly, and gray down they exhibited a most remarkable and comical appearance. At a distance the confused din and screaming emanating from parents and children resembled the uproar of an excited human assembly thousands in number.

Our presence was not much appreciated, considering the millions of years which must have elapsed since the last visit by prehistoric man or monkey—before the glacial period. Our sea boots were bravely attacked as we passed along their ranks. The space covered by the colony was practically free from snow; but the layer of guano was too thin, and mixed with too many pebbles, to be of commercial value in these days of cheap phosphates.

Unless the guano had been carried out to sea from time to time by rains and melting snow, the thinness of the layers compared with the massiveness of similar deposits in other climes would indicate that South Victoria Land has only during comparatively recent ages been made use of by the penguins during their breeding season. From this (assumed) fact interesting inferences may again be drawn regarding changes in the climate of Antarctica during recent times, but men of science must weigh the pros and cons of this theory, and the most permissible deductions to be made.

The mortality in the colony must be frightful, judging by the number of skeletons and dead birds lying about in all directions. A raptorial (skua) gull was present here, as everywhere in the neighborhood of penguin nurseries, and was busily occupied with its mission in life—viz., prevention of overpopulation in the colony.

The patience and endurance of the penguins are beyond praise when it is considered that thousands of them have to scale ridges hundreds of feet in height to reach their nests, although their mode of locomotion ashore is painfully awkward and slow.

Like so many other polar animals, the full-grown bird is able to subsist on its own fat for long periods; but the young birds require frequent and regular feeding, as in all other cases of animal life.

The capacity of most polar inhabitants for stowing away incredible quantities of food at one meal, and bringing it up again at will, explains no doubt how the young can be fed with fair regularity, although the parents may go for days without an opportunity of eating.

To commemorate our landing a pole was erected, carrying a box on which was painted the Norwegian colors, the date, and the vessel's name.

Before leaving we made a collection of penguins, stones, etc. Someone had the good sense to bring a sledge hammer, with which pieces of the original rock were detached and carried on board.

In searching the more sheltered clefts of the rock, Mr. Borchgrevink discovered further patches of the lichen already met with on Possession Island. The seaweed found on the shore was more doubtful evidence of vegetable life, as it may have drifted there from warmer latitudes, although no current going south is known to me, and no other evidence of such a current—as, for instance, driftwood, etc.—was met with.

On the shore were observed two dead seals, in a perfectly mummified state. I am unable to say whether they had retired there simply to die from wounds or disease, or had been cut off from the open water by the ice of an early winter, and so perished. The hairs had all come away, but the skins were smooth and hard, and the bodies had kept their original form so perfectly that they looked as if artificially preserved.

A single sea leopard was found basking on the shore, and killed by the Captain. It showed no more signs of "uneasiness and anxiety to regain the water" than the two mummies.

That Antarctica can support no land mammal, "huge" or small, is, to my mind, proved by the existence of these undisturbed remains. Even frozen seal flesh must be a titbit about midwinter in a climate so rigorous that only the lowest forms of vegetable life can survive from season to season. The unbroken ice must in wintertime extend an enormous distance from the shores, driving all higher forms of animal life up to, or beyond, the edge of the open water.

No land animal like the Arctic bear has ever been observed by any Antarctic traveler—the "mysterious tracks in the snow," etc. mentioned by one of our number were not observed by anyone else at the time—and certainly the possibility of finding Antarctic nations, etc. is too imbecile to require serious discussion.

We bade farewell about 3 A.M. to those of our hosts which we did not take away with us for a trip to natural history museums, and passed two very anxious and troublesome hours before regaining the vessel, as they had omitted to keep a lookout for us on board. We thus had the pleasure of seeing the ship working in toward the land in one direction whilst we were compelled by the ice to take an opposite one. By shouting in chorus we at last attracted attention, and saw the course altered toward us.

The mate's excuse was the report by the man aloft that he had just observed three of us on shore going down to the boat, and so thought it best to stand in as close as possible. As we had at that time been afloat for a considerable time, this proves that penguins on the march can be easily mistaken through a telescope for human beings—at least, when Mr. M. H. is at the other end of it.

During our exploration ashore we got a strong impression that the bay at Cape Adare inside the low promontory would provide many advantages as a landing-place and station for a new expedition. It is probable, at least, that a vessel moored inside this promontory would lie protected against the outer floes as well as the ice forming in the bay itself; the tide is no doubt very powerful along the whole shore, but presumably less so in this partly closed bay.

Among the rocks of Cape Adare, a shelter could be found for the house, and the low promontory would furnish plenty of space for moving about, for observatory, etc., as it occupies a space of about 1 mile in length by ¼ mile in width.

The nests along the ledges prove that no avalanches have to be feared; and if by ill luck the relief party did not succeed in fetching away the explorers during the second season, the penguin colony would afford an inexhaustible larder and stock of fuel. The bodies of the birds could be stored under the snow; their flesh is very nourishing, if not very palatable, and their blubber yields a fuel of the highest calorific value. ✠

The first wintering in the Antarctic neighborhood was on a ship drifting in the pack. This was the *Belgica* in 1898. The first wintering on land was by Carstens Egeberg Borchgrevink, a surveyor who had been a before-the-mast volunteer on the *Antarctic*. Although he was Norwegian, the expedition, in the ship *Southern Cross*, is rated as British, for it was financed and equipped in England and most of the staff and crew were British.

"On February 17 [1899] the first anchor ever dropped within

the Antarctic Circle struck ground in Robertson Bay off the low peninsula where Kristensen had landed from the whaler *Antarctic* in 1894 [1895] at the foot of Cape Adare," says the historian Hugh Robert Mill. By March 2 all stores and equipment were ashore. The steamer headed north to winter in New Zealand while ten men of the expedition settled down to spend the first winter that human beings ever spent on the seventh continent.

The winter and the following summer were passed without hardship or remarkable incident, but also without achievement. The party do not seem to have been fitted by temperament or training for other than sedentary studies. They had dogs, and even two Lapps to care for them, but they made no journey. Mill sums it up in his *The Siege of the South Pole* (Stokes, 1905): "A few excursions along the shores of Robertson Bay or across its ice, climbing the cliff of Cape Adare to a height somewhat exceeding 3000 feet, and looking at the coast to the south, summed up the exploits."

One notable achievement of the expedition was to keep in perfect health and in resulting good spirits. Mill brings out that although they had the best of foods that could be brought in from Europe they also "made a point of eating seal and penguin flesh and penguin eggs at every opportunity." As on all other expeditions which used a good deal of fresh meat, they completely avoided scurvy.[3]

While the Borchgrevink expedition proved that wintering on the new continent was feasible, they implied by their failure to penetrate the land that the blizzards, which had indeed been numerous and violent at Cape Adare, would forbid long overland journeys. It remained for the British under Scott to make the first overland exploration of the new continent.

Scott Makes the First Antarctic Sledge Journeys

Robert Falcon Scott, then a Commander in the Royal Navy, a man of great native ability but of no particular cold-weather

---

[3] While the health of the party, as a whole, was excellent in the sense of avoiding such usual troubles as scurvy, there was one death on the expedition, from occlusion of the intestines by some growth, perhaps cancer.

experience, was made the leader of what came to be known as the Discovery Expedition, from the name of their ship.

The *Discovery* left Britain August 6, 1901, and met the first Antarctic pack on January 1, 1902. After some coasting in which new land was discovered, she anchored in McMurdo Sound, a few miles southwest of Mount Erebus, on February 10, preparing herself there for the first wintering of a vessel on the Antarctic shore. This wintering-place was in the Ross Sea region, some 500 miles more southerly than that of the Southern Cross expedition, in latitude 77 degrees 49 minutes, thus 731 geographical or 843 statute miles from the South Pole.

The winter was passed in comfort but, as it proved, with too much dependence on the accustomed and tasty foods which had been brought along from Europe and New Zealand. For scurvy developed to handicap the expedition.

Spring sledge journeys had been made to establish advance depots and to get the men in training. On November 2, 1902, a three-man team started for the main journey—Scott, Ernest Henry Shackleton, and Dr. Edward A. Wilson, surgeon of the expedition. They had three sledges and nineteen dogs. This first exploratory journey to be made on the new continent is described by Scott in his *Voyage of the "Discovery,"* London, 1905. It is the plan here to recount chiefly land journeys in the Antarctic, and so the full narrative of this sledge trip is not used, for its fifty-nine days out and thirty-four back were on the floating barrier ice of the Ross Sea—they had gone 380 miles southerly from their base and still had not reached the land at the head of this great bight.

But one series of quotations is used because of their importance in the general history of geographic discovery—the passages relating to scurvy.

The enervation produced by scurvy and the fear it caused, apart from the toll of lives, was for centuries among the chief handicaps of the explorer. The Portuguese-Spanish Magellan expedition had suffered from it, as has been told in that section of this anthology; Anson's British expedition had lost 300 out of 500 men on a circumnavigation of the globe; many ships of various nations had suffered correspondingly. But Cook and others had proved that replenishing a ship frequently with large quantities of fruits and vegetables could and did prevent scurvy.

However, the medical profession had drawn the wrong conclusions from experiences like those of Cook—had concluded
that fruits and vegetables only, and not meats, were preventive
and curative. As sovereign cures they had settled upon the
juices from fruits, particularly acid juices, and most particularly
those of limes and lemons. Lime juice was considered a sure
cure, a specific. So definite were the medical men in this conviction that they secured the passage of laws in many countries
which made it a statutory requirement that ships should carry
lime juice on long voyages; hence the term "lime-juicer" as
applied to slow ships on long cruises.

Lime juice possessed around 1900 the rare distinction of
having been proclaimed by legislative bodies to be both a sure
preventative and a sure cure of a disease.

However, lime juice in practice never prevented scurvy on
long voyages. Seamen were impressed by this, the doctors un-
impressed. So there arose a feud between the laymen and the
doctors. The medical brotherhood usually if not always contended that lime juice was a specific, and explained away its
failures along the line that not enough had been administered,
that precautionary use had not started early enough, that the
juice used was not of good quality (the usual charge, a too-low
acid content), or that conditions of general hygiene had been
such as not to give the marvelous juice a fair chance. Against
this the laymen contended that wholesome, fresh foods were the
dependable preventives; that bottled or canned fruit juices
or fruits could not be relied upon. They said that fresh meats
would serve when fresh vegetables and fruits were unobtainable. (On polar voyages, fresh fruits are locally unobtainable,
fresh meats usually abundant.)

The advocates of meat as preventive and cure have cited the
absence of scurvy among the hunters and trappers of the Plains
region of North America, whereas soldiers wintering on the
Plains with Army rations sickened and died—for instance, those
under De Trobriand in Dakota following the War between the
States. They cited among polar explorers the numerous well-
known cases where standard British and other naval rations
had produced scurvy even when lime juice was administered

by the expedition doctors, and balanced these instances with equally well-known cases where there had been complete absence of scurvy through equally long periods on expeditions that used no lime juice or other vegetable preventive but instead depended on meat for the fresh element in their rations.

Of these antagonistic case histories two must have been particularly vivid in the mind of Scott. The British North Pole expedition of 1875-76 under Sir George Nares had carried lime juice, had spent only one winter away from home, and had failed in its exploratory objectives largely through the development of scurvy. Scott knew several who were connected with that expedition, among them Admiral Sir Francis Leopold McClintock, who had denounced as nonsense the current reliance on lime juice while pointing out that his own journeys of the 1840's and 1850's, far longer than those of Nares, had relied on pemmican supplemented with game, and without ever a sign of scurvy on the longest sledge journey.

Still more impressive to Scott must have been the testimony of his friend the great Norwegian explorer Fridtjof Nansen, who had spent a winter on one of the Franz Josef Islands, with his one companion Frederik Hjalmar Johansen. They had no lime juice or other so-called scurvy preventives and no food except walrus meat and water. They lived in a hut of stones and skin that had no window, and without baths or exercise. They broke practically all the standard hygienic rules, and were in perfect health and full strength when the time came to resume their traveling in the spring.

Scurvy had been through the ages a greater enemy to the explorer than wind and weather. The relation of the scourge to the successes and failures of the first four overland journeys that attempted the South Pole is crucial, Scott's experience of his first expedition particularly so.

The expedition was perhaps up to that date the most carefully outfitted in history so far as taking precautions for health is concerned; everything in the way of food, housing, cleanliness, ventilation, and diet had been planned by the foremost authorities and had been well carried out. Yet scurvy came to handicap them and, as some think, to forecast the tragedy of Scott's later expedition.

December 21, 1902, the sledging party was more than 300 miles from the home base and advancing, the men pulling hard on the sledges. The surface of the barrier ice was growing more and more difficult, upon which Scott's diary has morose comment, and then goes on:[4]

Scott's First Journey

🏴 Misfortunes never come singly. Since starting we have always had a regular examination of gums and legs on Sunday morning, and at first it seemed to show us to be in a very satisfactory condition of health, but tonight Wilson told me that Shackleton had decidedly angry-looking gums, and that for some time they have been slowly but surely getting worse. He says there is nothing yet to be alarmed at, but he now thought it serious enough to tell me in view of our future plans.

We have decided not to tell Shackleton for the present. It is a matter which must be thought out. Certainly this is a black night, but things must look blacker yet before we decide to turn.

[December 22] . . . We have decided to cease using our bacon and to increase the seal allowance, as the former seems the most likely cause of the scurvy symptoms. To Shackleton it was represented as a preventive measure, but I am not sure that he does not smell a rat. . . .

[December 24] . . . Wilson examined us again this morning. I asked him quietly the result, and he said, "A little more." It is trying, but we both agree that it is not time yet to say "Turn!"

[A week after the seal meat had been substituted for the bacon things had improved somewhat. Scott writes for December 28: "Our slight change in diet is already giving beneficial results. Late tonight we had another examination of our scurvy symptoms, and there is now no doubt they are lessening."

December 30, after sledging 380 miles over the Ross Sea ice, they decided to turn back toward the ship. By January 14, 1903, they had made good progress homeward, for they were now

---

[4] From *The Voyage of Discovery*, by Robert Falcon Scott, New York, 1905. Published by Charles Scribner's Sons.

traveling light, picking up food they had left by the trail on their forward march. The disease, after the brief recovery, was advancing. Scott writes:]

This morning we had a thorough medical examination, and the result was distinctly unsatisfactory. Shackleton has very angry-looking gums—swollen and dark. He is also suffering greatly from shortness of breath; his throat seems to be congested, and he gets fits of coughing, when he is obliged to spit, and once or twice today he has spat blood.

I myself have distinctly red gums, and a very slight swelling in the ankles. Wilson's gums are affected in one spot, where there is a large plum-colored lump; otherwise he seems free from symptoms. Both he and I feel quite fit and well, and as far as we are concerned I think a breakdown is very far removed. . . .

Soon after coming to camp I went to the sledges to feed the dogs and, looking round, found that Wilson had followed me. His face was very serious, and his news still more so. He told me that he was distinctly alarmed about Shackleton's condition; he did not know that the breakdown would come at once, but he felt sure that it was not far removed.

The conversation could only be conducted in the most fragmentary fashion for fear it should be overheard, but it was sufficiently impressive to make our supper a very thoughtful meal. It's a bad case, but we must make the best of it and trust to its not getting worse; now that human life is at stake all other objects must be sacrificed. It is plain that we must make a beeline for the next depot regardless of the northern coast; it is plain also that we must travel as lightly as possible. . . .

One of the difficulties we foresee with Shackleton, with his restless, energetic temperament, is to keep him idle in camp, so tonight I have talked seriously to him. He is not to do any camping work, but to allow everything to be done for him; he is not to pull on the march, but to walk as easily as possible, and he is to let us know directly he feels tired. I have tried to impress on him the folly of pretending to be stronger than he is, and have pointed out how likely he is to aggravate the evil if he does not consent to nurse himself.

We have decided to increase our seal-meat allowance in another effort to drive back the scurvy.

More than this I do not see that we can do at present. Every effort must be devoted to keeping Shackleton on his legs, and we must trust to luck to bring him through. In case he should break down soon and be unable to walk, I can think of absolutely no workable scheme; we could only carry him by doing relay work, and I doubt if Wilson or I am up to covering the distance in that fashion. It is a knotty problem which is best left till the contingency arises.

It looks as though life for the next week or two is not going to be pleasant for any of us, and it is rather curious, because we have always looked forward to this part of the journey as promising an easier time.

[January 15] . . . Shackleton's state last night was highly alarming; he scarcely slept at all and had violent paroxysms of coughing, between which he was forced to gasp for breath. This morning to our relief he was better, and this evening he is rather better than last, though very fagged with the day's work. We try to make him do as little pulling as possible until the pace is settled and he can lean steadily forward in his harness.

It is early to judge, but the double ration of seal meat seems already to have a good effect—gums seem a trifle better. On the other hand, I have some stiffness in the right foot, which I suppose is caused by the taint, but at present I have not mentioned it, as my gums look so well that I am in hopes it will pass away.

[January 16] The sledges have been running easily, and we have made a good march, but the surface is getting more uneven, and under the dark, gloomy sky we could not see the inequalities and stumbled frequently.

This sort of thing is very bad for Shackleton. Twice he slipped his leg down a deep crack and fell heavily, and on each occasion we had to stop several minutes for him to recover. He has been coughing and spitting up blood again, and at lunchtime was very "groggy." With his excitable temperament it is especially difficult for him to take things quietly, and at the end of each march he is panting, dizzy, and exhausted.

It is all very dreadful to watch, knowing that we can do

nothing to relieve him. If at the ship, he would be sent straight to bed, but here every effort must be made to keep him on his feet during the marches. There is now no doubt that the scorbutic symptoms are diminishing; both Wilson and I have much cleaner gums, and my leg is vastly improved.

Our seal meat at the present rate will last another fifteen days, by which time we ought to be within reach of safety.

Six weeks ago we were very much inclined to swear at the cook, who had been careless enough to leave a good deal of blubber in our seal meat, but now we bless his carelessness, and are only too eager to discover that our "whack" has a streak of yellow running through the dark flesh. I could not have believed it possible that I should ever have enjoyed blubber. . . .

[January 18] . . . All was going well with our march this afternoon, when Shackleton gave out. He had a bad attack of breathlessness, and we were forced to camp in a hurry; tonight matters are serious with him again. He is very plucky about it, for he does not complain, though there is no doubt he is suffering badly.

[January 19] Another long "blind" march. It is very distressing work, and the gloom does not tend to enliven our spirits; but Shackleton was better this morning and is still better tonight. . . .

[January 21] . . . Shackleton is improving, but takes his breakdown much to heart.

[January 23] . . . ever since the warmer weather set in we have had to be very careful to keep our provisions out of the sun's rays. After supper every night the ready provision bag is buried under the snow. In spite of such precautions we are afraid that our seal meat has suffered from the heat, and that it is not so antiscorbutic as it was. Our scurvy symptoms have remained about the same, no better and no worse.[5]

[Present knowledge of the antiscorbutic qualities of meat would indicate that the sun's shining on the blubber attached

---

[5] For a comprehensive discussion of the relation of meat, in its various forms as to preservation and cooking, to the group of deficiency diseases, especially scurvy, see "Scurvy" index entries in *Not by Bread Alone* by Vilhjalmur Stefansson, Macmillan, 1946.

to the meat, and melting it so that it leaked away through the canvas (as Scott elsewhere describes) would have lessened the caloric rather than the antiscorbutic values of this food. Scott's trouble was, first, that the seal meat was not a large enough percentage of the diet, and then that they may have cooked it too much—for there seems to be nothing in the Scott record to indicate his having known that a rare piece of meat is more curative than a well-done piece.]

[January 24] . . . Shackleton remains about the same; he is having a cruel time, but each march brings us nearer safety. . . .

[January 25] . . . The surface is bad and the work increasingly heavy, but Wilson and I are determined to leave as little as possible to chance and to get our invalid along as quickly as his state will allow. We start him off directly our breakfast is over, and whilst we are packing up camp he gets well ahead, so that he is able to take things easy; we follow on [pulling the sledges] and gradually catch him up, and after lunch the same procedure is adopted. At the night halt he sits quietly while the tent is pitched, and only goes into it when all is prepared. He feels his inactivity very keenly, poor chap, and longs to do his share of the work, but luckily he has sense enough to see the necessity of such precaution. . . .

[January 28] . . . Shackleton had a bad return of his cough, but said he thought he could manage to get along, so we spread our sail and proceeded. . . .

We hoped to reach the depot by lunch, but it was an hour after that meal before Shackleton, who was ahead, spotted the flag and we turned our course to make for it. As can be imagined, the last of the march was as near a rush as our tired legs could command. At length and at last we have reached the land of plenty; the one great and pressing evil will grip us no more.

Directly our tent was up we started our search amongst the snow heaps with childish glee. One after another our treasures were brought forth: oil enough for the most lavish expenditure, biscuit that might have lasted us for a month, and finally, a large brown provision bag which we knew would contain more than food alone.

We have just opened this provision bag and feasted our eyes

on the contents. There are two tins of sardines, a large tin of marmalade, soup squares, pea soup, and many another delight that already make our mouths water. For each one of us there is some special trifle which the forethought of our kind people has provided, mine being an extra packet of tobacco. . . .

[There was plenty of delicious European food, but no seal meat, no antiscorbutic. The three ate more than was good for them, as Scott and Wilson discovered in an hour or two. Shackleton had eaten less and was less affected in this direct way. With reference to himself and Wilson, Scott writes:]

[January 29] . . . A few hours of fitful sleep follows this uncomfortable experience, and we awoke to find a heavy blizzard and the usual obscurity without. The first thought of pushing onward was speedily abandoned when we found that Shackleton had relapsed into the worst condition. To the reaction from the excitement of last night is added the most trying condition of weather. The result is very dreadful. Our poor patient is again shaken with violent fits of coughing and is gasping for breath; it looks very serious.

Later. There is no doubt Shackleton is extremely ill; his breathing has become more stertorous and labored, his face looks pinched and worn, his strength is very much reduced, and for the first time he has lost his spirit and grown despondent.[6] It is terrible to have to remain idle knowing that we can do nothing to help.

I have talked to Wilson tonight, who thinks matters are very critical, and advises pushing on to the ship at all hazards. The only chance of improvement lies in a change of weather, and if this blizzard continues, the worst consequences may ensue.

We have enough food now to carry him on the sledge, but tonight one may well doubt whether he will be well enough for that. It is a great disappointment. Last night we thought ourselves out of the wood with all our troubles behind us, and tonight matters seem worse than ever. Luckily Wilson and I are pretty fit, and we have lots of food.

[January 30] Shackleton scarcely slept at all last night; his

---

[6] Gloom is recognized as developing inevitably as scurvy advances.

paroxysms of coughing grew less only from his increasing weakness. This morning he was livid and speechless, and his spirits were very low. He revived a little after breakfast, and we felt that our only chance was to get him going again. It took him nearly twenty minutes to get out of the tent and onto his skis; everything was done in the most labored fashion, painful to watch.

Luckily the weather had cleared, and though there was a stiff southwesterly breeze and some drift, the sun was shining brightly. At last he was got away, and we watched him almost tottering along with frequent painful halts.

Re-sorting our provisions, in half an hour we had packed our camp, set our sail, and started with the sledges. It was not long before we caught our invalid, who was so exhausted that we thought it wiser he should sit on the sledges, where for the remainder of the forenoon, with the help of our sail, we carried him. After lunch he was better, and in one way and another we have brought off a very long march. If he can only sleep tonight, there is a chance of further improvement; much depends on this.

It is all very anxious work; if there is no improvement I half-think of pushing on to the ship for assistance. Wilson thinks that the relapse is mainly due to the blizzard, and doubts if he can stand another; one would give much to ensure three or four fine days. Nothing could be better than the weather tonight, and the surface is excellent. Just here it is swept hard by the wind, and the relief of treading on something solid and firm is enormous. I did not fully realize what terribly bad surfaces we have been struggling with until we got back on this hard one.

[February 1] For two days the weather has been glorious, and has had a wonderful effect on our invalid, who certainly has great recuperative powers. He managed to sleep a little last night, and today has kept going on his skis. After the last halt he had an attack of vertigo and fell outside the tent, which alarmed us greatly; but after about ten minutes it passed off, and tonight he is better again. . . .

[February 2] Awaking to another fine day, we saw at last the prospect of an end to our troubles, and since that we have got off a long march and cannot now be more than 10 or 12 miles from home. It was not till the afternoon that we surmounted a slight rise and altered our course in passing around the corner of the White Island. As we did so the old familiar outline of our friendly peninsula burst on our view; there stood Castle Rock like some great boulder dropped from the skies, and there to the left the sharp cone of Observation Hill. Almost one could imagine the figures on it looking eagerly out in our direction. Away to the west were all the well-known landmarks which led back to the vast western range, and tonight, therefore, on every side we have suggestions of home.

That it is none too soon is evident. We are as near spent as three persons can well be. If Shackleton has shown a temporary improvement, we know by experience how little confidence we can place in it, and how near he has been and still is to a total collapse.

As for Wilson and myself, we have scarcely liked to own how "done" we are, and how greatly the last week or two has tried us. We have known that our scurvy has been advancing again with rapid strides, but as we could do nothing more to prevent it, we have not looked beyond the signs that have made themselves obvious.

Wilson has suffered from lameness for many a day; the cause was plain, and we knew it must increase. Each morning he has vainly attempted to disguise a limp, and his set face has shown me that there is much to be gone through before the first stiffness wears off.

As for myself, for some time I have hurried through the task of changing my footgear in an attempt to forget that my ankles are considerably swollen. One and all, we want rest and peace, and, all being well, tomorrow, thank Heaven, we shall get them.

At this point my sledge diary comes to an end, for on the following day I had neither time nor inclination to write, but the incidents of such a day leave too deep an impression to need the aid of any note to recall them.

Nature wore its brightest aspect to welcome us home, and early in the brilliant, cloudless morning we packed up our camp for the last time, and set our faces toward Observation

Hill. We had plodded on for some hours when two specks appeared ahead, which at first we took to be penguins, but soon made out were persons hurrying toward us. They proved to be Skelton and Bernacchi.

We had been reported early by watchers on the hills. These two had hastened out to meet us, and soon we were gathered in our small tent whilst cocoa was made, and we listened to a ceaseless stream of news, for now not only had all our other travelers returned safe and sound with many a tale to tell, but our relief ship, the *Morning*, had arrived, bringing a whole year's news of the civilized world.

And so at our last sledging lunch, and during the easy march which followed, we gradually gathered those doings of the great world which had happened between December 1901 and December 1902, and, as can be imagined, these kept our thoughts full until we rounded the cape to see once more our beloved ship.

[As usual with scurvy patients, the Scott party relished their food when they got to the base and ate a lot of it.]

But although we found our appetites very difficult to appease, for a fortnight after our return from the south our party were in a very sorry condition.

Shackleton at once took to his bed, and although he soon made an effort to be out and about again, he found that the least exertion caused a return of his breathlessness, and more than once on entering or leaving the living-quarters he had a return of those violent fits of coughing which had given him so much trouble on the journey; now, however, after such attacks he could creep into his cabin and there rest until the strain had worn off and some measure of his strength returned.

With Wilson, who at one time had shown the least signs of scurvy, the disease had increased very rapidly toward the end. He had slightly strained his leg early in the journey, and here the symptoms were most evident, causing swelling and discoloration behind the knee; his gums also had dropped into a bad state, so he wisely decided to take to his bed, where he remained perfectly quiet for ten days. This final collapse showed the grim determination which alone must have upheld him during the last marches.

If I was the least affected of the party, I was by no means fit and well. Although I was able to struggle about during the daytime, I had both legs much swollen and very uncomfortable gums. But the worst result of the tremendous reaction which overcame us I found to be the extraordinary feeling of lassitude which it produced; it was an effort to move, and during the shortest walks abroad I had an almost unconquerable inclination to sit down wherever a seat could be found.

And this lassitude was not physical only; to write, or even to think, had become wholly distasteful, and sometimes quite impossible. At this time I seemed to be incapable of all but eating or sleeping or lounging in the depths of an armchair whilst I lazily scanned the files of the newspapers which had grown so unfamiliar. Many days passed before I could rouse myself from this slothful humor, and it was many weeks before I had returned to a normally vigorous condition.

It was probably this exceptionally relaxed state of health that made me so slow to realize that the ice conditions were very different from what they had been in the previous season. I was vaguely surprised to learn that the *Morning* had experienced so much obstruction in the Ross Sea, and I was astonished to hear that the pack was still hanging in the entrance of the sound, and as yet showed no sign of clearing away to the north; but it was long before I connected these facts with circumstances likely to have an adverse bearing on our position, and the prospect of the ice about us remaining fast throughout the season never once entered my head.

My diary for this month shows a gradual awakening to the true state of affairs.

It seems curious that, although the party while on the march had realized the antiscorbutic values of seal meat, there is no mention in Scott's book that they ate much of it after they got home. Clearly they did not, for there is available now ample evidence to show that had they eaten mainly fresh meat, medium-cooked or underdone, the mental and other symptoms which Scott described in himself and Shackleton would have disappeared in about four days, certainly in less than a week.

Since there is no indication that fresh meat was used for the treatment of the scurvy patients after return to the base camp, the assumption would be that the standard methods of the time were used—the administration of fruit juices, especially lime or lemon juice. However, the fresh-meat lesson was taken seriously for the provisioning of the next year. In his historical summary Dr. Mill says:

"Great stores of seal meat and of skua gulls were laid in for the winter, and the ship's company were thus able to live almost entirely on fresh provisions. . . . The winter passed happily and surprisingly quickly, and there was not a single case of illness."

Scott himself sums it up in his diary entry for September 6, 1903, at the end of the Southern Hemisphere winter: "The word 'scurvy' has not been heard this year, and the doctor tells me there is not a sign of it in the ship. Truly our prospects look bright for the sledge work of the future."

Shackleton had been invalided home by the supply steamer *Morning* which brought them stores the previous summer. The dogs had all died on last year's sledge expedition, so the men needed their full strength; they were now the only draft animals. With them pulling in harness, Scott, who had traveled 380 miles toward the South Pole last season, now traveled 300 miles to the southwest. The first journey had been exclusively on glacier ice floating on an ocean; now they traveled on the same kind of ice that rested on land. From near the ship they commenced an ascent of 9000 feet and then found themselves on a plain more level than the Ross Sea ice had been.

The climb and the high altitude of the plateau made the physical work of this sledging expedition perhaps the most grueling, for its mileage, that ever has been carried out. In that connection Scott emphasizes the perfect health of the sledgers. September 22 he is summarizing the results of a hard preliminary trip from which they had returned to the base camp:

"It is pleasant to be back in the ship again after our hard spring journeys. They have awakened us all and given us plenty of fresh matter to talk about, so that there is a running fire of chaff and chatter all day. Everything looks very bright and hopeful: the journeys have accomplished all that was expected of them, and there is not a sign of our old enemy the scurvy, and this in spite of the fact that our travelers have endured the hardest conditions on record."

The big journey of 1903 began October 12, the men pulling the sledges up and up toward the 9000-foot plateau and then across it under high-mountain conditions of deficient oxygen. They were working, if anything, harder than the year before and still, without the help of dogs, they were making almost as many miles per day, in spite of the upgrade and thin air. They feared a breakdown in health similar to that of last season, but none came. November 29 Scott wrote: "We are all in excellent condition and health; not a sign of the scurvy fiend has appeared, though I watch narrowly for it."

No sign of the scurvy ever appeared during this journey, one of the most arduous in the records of polar exploration.

Shackleton Near the Pole

However, the records of Scott's journey, and of all sledge journeys made up to that time in the direction of either pole, were broken five years later by Ernest Henry Shackleton, the man whose weakness from scurvy had made him a handicap to Scott.

It has been conjectured reasonably, if not proved, that Shackleton's illness on the first Scott expedition, and the blame which fell on him as the weakling of that party, was the moving cause for the organization of the Shackleton expedition of 1907-09.

When in normal health Shackleton was a man of great physical strength and exuberant spirits for whom it was trying beyond the ordinary to have to appear in narratives of wide circulation, such as Scott's *Voyage of the Discovery*, as one who had proved a burden to his companions. Besides, there is in English a slur in the very name of the disease scurvy, which shows up in such expressions as "a scurvy fellow," "a scurvy trick." Shackleton was determined that in so far as possible the world should be made to forget the weakness which Scott had described, and the scurvy association.

At any rate, this rankling in the heart of Shackleton has been given as one of the reasons, or excuses, for what some then considered unsportsmanlike if not unethical—his rushing forward to organize an expedition which seemed obviously an attempt to eclipse the record of his former commander.

However, so far as the scurvy was concerned, it appears to have been chance rather than planning which enabled Shackleton to surpass the record not merely of Scott but of all other contenders for a near approach to a pole of the earth. For although Scott's narrative makes it clear that he personally understood the antiscorbutic value of fresh meat, and although Shackleton no doubt agreed with him, he was nevertheless under the thumb of the medical profession in the planning of the diet for the expedition, and the doctors at that time still clung to the old idea that they understood the true nature of scurvy and had for it a sure cure, a specific, in lime juice or in the bottled juices of other fruits, and in canned vegetables.

The medical profession advised Shackleton along the standard lines. The three doctors who accompanied him seem to have had the routine medical approach of the day to the scurvy problem.

But fortunately, as it proved, there was misplanning or miscarriage of plans such that when the expedition landed in the Antarctic they did not have nearly enough food to see them through. So they stocked up with seal and other fresh meat, the proportion of which in their diet was quite as high as Scott's had been his second winter, with equally good results. There was no sign of scurvy in winter quarters, nor yet on the sledge journey toward the Pole.

Shackleton agreed with Scott's conclusion of the previous expedition that dogs were unsuited for Antarctic sledging, a mistake due in the main to the fact that these British sailors did not know how to harness, hitch, and drive dogs, nor did they understand—which is even more important—how to feed them so as to keep them in health and strength. The seventeen dogs of the first Scott journey had lost their pulling strength quickly, so that they became useless and had to be killed.

Wrongly blaming this on the dogs, or on the local conditions, Shackleton decided to use ponies. This did not work out well in the hauling sense; but the flesh of the ponies gave the men fresh meat on the trail, which was, of course, a scurvy preventive. This food agreed with the stomachs of the hard-working sledgers, except in the case of some ponies that were not killed till they were on the verge of dying from hunger and weariness.

In the first volume of his narrative *The Heart of the Antarctic,* (Lippincott, 1909) Shackleton has discussed provisioning under "sledging foods," where he says that "one of the main items of our food supply was pemmican, which consisted of the finest beef powdered with 60 per cent [by weight] of fat added," but explains that there were a number of subsidiary items, chief among them biscuit, sugar, cheese, and chocolate In the first chapter of the second volume we are told of how they used the pony beef and with what result:

Shackleton Uses Pony Meat

. . . the [pony] meat and blood, when boiled up, made a delightful broth, while the fragments of meat sunk to the bottom of the pot. The liquor was much the better part of the dish, and no one had much relish for the little dice of tough and stringy meat, so the cook had to be very careful indeed. Poor old Chinaman was a particularly tough and stringy horse.

We found that the meat from the neck and rump was the best, the most stringy portions coming from the ribs and legs. We took all the meat we could, tough or tender, and as we went south in the days when horse meat was fairly plentiful, we used to suck frozen, raw fragments as we marched along. Later we could not afford to use the meat except on a definite allowance.

The meat to be used during the day was generally cut up when we took a spell in the morning, and the bag containing the fragments was hung on the back of the sledge in order that the meat might be softened by the sun. It cut more easily when frozen than when partially thawed, but our knives gradually got blunt, and on the glacier we secured a rock on which to sharpen them. During the journey back, when every ounce of weight was of great importance, we used one of our geological specimens, a piece of sandstone, as a knife-sharpener. The meat used to bulk large in the pot, but as fresh meat contains about 60 per cent of moisture, it used to shrink considerably in the process of cooking, and we did not have to use very much snow in the pot.

We used the meat immediately we had started to kill the [three] ponies in order to save the other food, for we knew that the meat contained a very large percentage of water, so that we would be carrying useless weight with it. The pemmican and biscuits, on the other hand, contained very little moisture, and it was more profitable to keep them for the march further south, when we were likely to want to reduce the loads as far as possible. We left meat at each depot, to provide for the march back to the coast, but always took on as much as possible of the prepared foods.

The reader will understand that the loss of Socks, which represented so many pounds of meat, was a very severe blow to us, for we had after that to use sledging stores at the depots to make up for the lost meat.[7] If we had been able to use Socks for food, I have no doubt that we would have been able to get further south, perhaps even to the Pole itself, though in that case we could hardly have got back in time to catch the ship before she was forced to leave by the approach of winter. . . .

During the last weeks of the journey outward, and the long march back, when our allowance of food had been reduced to 20 ounces per man a day, we really thought of little but food. The glory of the great mountains that towered high on either side, the majesty of the enormous glacier up which we traveled so painfully, did not appeal to our emotions to any great extent. Man becomes very primitive when he is hungry and short of food, and we learned to know what it is to be desperately hungry.

I used to wonder sometimes whether the people who suffer from hunger in the big cities of civilization felt as we were feeling, and I arrived at the conclusion that they did not, for no barrier of law and order would have been allowed to stand between us and any food that had been available. The man who starves in a city is weakened, hopeless, spiritless, and we were vigorous and keen. Until January 9 the desire for food was

[7] This pony fell into a crevasse and was lost.

made the more intense by our knowledge of the fact that we were steadily marching away from the stores of plenty.

We could not joke about food in the way that is possible for the man who is hungry in the ordinary sense. We thought about it most of the time, and on the way back we used to talk about it, but always in the most serious manner possible. We used to plan out the enormous meals that we proposed to have when we got back to the ship and, later, to civilization.

On the outward march we did not experience really severe hunger until we got on the great glacier, and then we were too much occupied with the heavy and dangerous climbing over the rough ice and crevasses to be able to talk much. We had to keep some distance apart in case one man fell into a crevasse. Then on the plateau our faces were generally coated with ice, and the blizzard wind blowing from the south made unnecessary conversation out of the question. Those were silent days, and our remarks to one another were brief and infrequent.

It was on the march back that we talked freely of food, after we had got down the glacier and were marching over the barrier surface. The wind was behind us, so that the pulling was not very heavy, and as there were no crevasses to fear we were able to keep close together. We would get up at 5 A.M. in order to make a start at 7 A.M., and after we had eaten our scanty breakfast, that seemed only to accentuate hunger, and had begun the day's march, we could take turns in describing the things we would eat in the good days to come. We were each going to give a dinner to the others in turn, and there was to be an anniversary dinner every year, at which we would be able to eat and eat and eat. . . .

The dysentery from which we suffered during the latter part of the journey back to the coast was certainly due to the meat from the pony Grisi. This animal was shot one night when in a greatly exhausted condition, and I believe that his flesh was made poisonous by the presence of the toxin of exhaustion, as is the case with animals that have been hunted. Wild was the first to suffer at the time when we started to use Grisi meat with the other meat, and he must have been unfortunate enough to get the greater part of the bad meat on that occasion. The other meat we were using then came from Chinaman, and seemed to be quite wholesome. A few days later we were all eating Grisi meat, and we all got dysentery.

The meat could not have become affected in any way after the death of the pony, because it froze hard within a very short time. The manner in which we managed to keep on marching when suffering, and the speed with which we recovered when we got proper food, were rather remarkable, and the reason, no doubt, was that the dysentery was simply the result of the poison, and was not produced by organic trouble of any sort. ✍

The last week of October 1908, Shackleton and three of his best men—Naval Lieutenant J. B. Adams, Dr. Eric Marshall (surgeon), and Frank Wild, merchant sailor—started south, each leading one of the expedition's four ponies with its sledge. The season corresponds to late April in the Northern Hemisphere and there was daylight the whole time, but with temperatures still running down into the thirties and forties below zero.

They were hoping to reach the South Pole in ninety-two days, averaging 19 miles per day, thus nearly three times the 6½ miles a day that had been the average rate when Shackleton was a handicap to Scott six years before. Shackleton's biographer, Hugh Robert Mill, thinks they would have made the Pole if they could have had their main base where Scott's had been, but ice conditions had prevented them from getting that far; Shackleton thought they would have made it if one of the ponies, on which they relied both for hauling power and for beef, had not fallen in a crevasse too deep for them to salvage the meat. Either may be right; it seems reasonably certain that if Shackleton had had both the favorable Scott base and the beef of the extra pony, the Pole would have been his.

By November 19, 1908, Shackleton was farther south than he had been with Scott on December 16, 1902; but then the first pony was outworn and had to be sacrificed, his beef partly used on the southward march and partly stored for the return journey. (In the Arctic you cannot do that sort of thing; for your depot would likely be smelled out by the keen-scented prowlers, fox, wolf, or bear. In the Antarctic there are no land animals, not even a rat or a hare.)

November 26 Shackleton passed Scott's farthest, which had

been made on December 29, so that now they were, relatively, five weeks to the good. Two days later the second horse was sacrificed, its beef used in part and partly cached for the return. The third pony went on December 1. By then temperatures in the shade were rising almost to the freezing point, which meant uncomfortable warmth in the sun, particularly for men who were now their own draft animals.

In connection with the diary entry for November 26, when they had reached a new farthest south, we have a "note" from Shackleton which he evidently wrote at a later time:

Man in Antarctica

Note. It falls to the lot of few men to view land not previously seen by human eyes, and it was with feelings of keen curiosity, not unmingled with awe, that we watched the new mountains rise from the great unknown that lay ahead of us. Mighty peaks they were, the eternal snows at their bases, and their roughhewn forms rising high toward the sky. No man of us could tell what we would discover in our march south, what wonders might not be revealed to us, and our imaginations would take wings until a stumble in the snow, the sharp pangs of hunger, or the dull ache of physical weariness brought back our attention to the needs of the immediate present.

As the days wore on, and mountain after mountain came into view, grimly majestic, the consciousness of our insignificance seemed to grow upon us. We were but tiny black specks crawling slowly and painfully across the white plain, and bending our puny strength to the task of wresting from nature secrets preserved inviolate through all the ages. Our anxiety to learn what lay beyond was none the less keen, however, and the long days of marching over the Barrier surface were saved from monotony by the continued appearance of new land to the southeast.

By early December the party were convinced they must not follow the Ross Sea ice farther, for the shore line trended too much east of south and they wanted southing, to the Pole. So on December 4 they turned off to the right, ascended a 2000-

foot ridge, and descended from it to a glacier which, a great river of slow-flowing ice, wound down from the south between two ranges of mountains. This was their road toward the Pole; though superficially level, it was crevassed and therefore dangerous.

On the third day one of the crevasses swallowed the last pony. What saved the lives of the men was that the swiveltree broke so that the weight of the horse did not pull the sledge in after it; for it is doubtful that with half the equipment gone the party could have regained the home camp.

During the middle weeks of December the ascent became so steep and rough that progress should have been measured rather in rise above sea level than in advance south. December 11 they were at 3300 feet up and 340 miles short of the Pole; three days later they were 5600 feet up but only 15 miles ahead.

On December 17 they discovered bands of coal in the slopes of the mountains, showing that once upon a time the land had been both low and warm.

By Christmas Day 1908, the party were nearly or quite through with their climbing. They were 280 miles from the Pole, 9500 feet above sea level, and, by all the signs, nearly up to the edge of a plateau within which lay their goal. Since there was no appreciable slope, there would be few or no crevasses. Here we take up Shackleton's own story.[8]

Shackleton's Journey to the Polar Plateau

[December 26] Got away at 7 A.M. sharp, after dumping a lot of gear. We marched steadily all day except for lunch, and we have done 14 miles 480 yards on an uphill march, with soft snow at times and a bad wind. Ridge after ridge we met, and though the surface is better and harder in places, we feel very tired at the end of ten hours' pulling. Our height tonight is 9590 feet above sea level according to the hypsometer.

The ridges we meet with are almost similar in appearance. We see the sun shining on them in the distance, and then the rise begins very gradually. The snow gets soft, and the weight

---

[8] From *The Heart of the Antarctic*, by Ernest Henry Shackleton, copyright 1909, published by J. B. Lippincott Company.

of the sledge becomes more marked. As we near the top the soft snow gives place to a hard surface, and on the summit of the ridge we find small crevasses. Every time we reach the top of a ridge we say to ourselves, "Perhaps this is the last"; but it never is the last, always there appears away ahead of us another ridge.

I do not think that the land lies very far below the ice sheet, for the crevasses on the summits of the ridges suggest that the sheet is moving over land at no great depth. It would seem that the descent toward the glacier proper from the plateau is by a series of terraces. We lost sight of the land today, having left it all behind us, and now we have the waste of snow all around.

Two more days and our maize [left over from the pony feed] will be finished. Then our hooshes [stews] will be more woefully thin than ever. This shortness of food is unpleasant, but if we allow ourselves what under ordinary circumstances would be a reasonable amount, we would have to abandon all idea of getting far south.

[December 27] If a great snow plain, rising every 7 miles in a steep ridge, can be called a plateau, then we are on it at last, with an altitude above the sea of 9820 feet. We started at 7 A.M. and marched till noon, encountering at 11 A.M. a steep snow ridge which pretty well cooked us, but we got the sledge up by noon and camped. We are pulling 150 pounds per man.

In the afternoon we had good going till 5 P.M., and then another ridge as difficult as the previous one, so that our backs and legs were in a bad way when we reached the top at 6 P.M., having done 14 miles 930 yards for the day. Thank heaven it has been a fine day, with little wind. The temperature is minus 9° Fahrenheit. This surface is most peculiar, showing layers of snow with little sastrugi [wavelike hard ridges] all pointing south-southeast.

Short food makes us think of plum puddings, and hard half-cooked maize gives us indigestion, but we are getting south. The latitude is 86 degrees 19 minutes south tonight. Our thoughts are with the people at home a great deal.

[December 28] If the Barrier is a changing sea, the plateau is a changing sky. During the morning march we continued to go uphill steadily, but the surface was constantly changing. First there was soft snow in layers, then soft snow so deep that we were well over our ankles, and the temperature being well below zero, our feet were cold through sinking in. No one can say what we are going to find next, but we can go steadily ahead.

We started at 6:55 A.M., and had done 7 miles 200 yards by noon, the pulling being very hard. Some of the snow is blown into hard sastrugi; some that looks perfectly smooth and hard has only a thin crust through which we break when pulling; all of it is a trouble. Yesterday we passed our last crevasse, though there are a few cracks or ridges fringed with shining crystals like diamonds, warning us that the cracks are open.

We are now 10,199 feet above sea level, and the plateau is gradually flattening out, but it was heavy work pulling this afternoon. The high altitude, and a temperature of 48° of frost [16° below zero] made breathing and work difficult. We are getting south—latitude 86 degrees 31 minutes south tonight.

The last 60 miles we hope to rush, leaving everything possible, taking one tent only and using the poles of the other as marks every 10 miles, for we will leave all our food 60 miles off the Pole except enough to carry us there and back. I hope with good weather to reach the Pole on January 12, and then we will try and rush it to get to Hut Point by February 28.

We are so tired after each hour's pulling that we throw ourselves on our backs for a three minutes' spell. It took us over ten hours to do 14 miles 450 yards today, but we did it all right. It is a wonderful thing to be over 10,000 feet up at the end of the world almost.

The short food is trying, but when we have done the work we will be happy. Adams had a bad headache all yesterday, and today I had the same trouble, but it is better now. Otherwise we are all fit and well. I think the country is flattening out more and more, and hope tomorrow to make 15 miles, at least.

[December 29] Yesterday I wrote that we hoped to do 15 miles today, but such is the variable character of this surface that one cannot prophesy with any certainty an hour ahead. A strong southerly wind, with from 44° to 49° of frost, combined with the effect of short rations, made our distance 12 miles 600 yards instead. We have reached an altitude of 10,310 feet, and an uphill gradient gave us one of the most severe pulls for ten hours that would be possible.

It looks serious, for we must increase the food if we are to get on at all, and we must risk a depot at 70 miles off the Pole and dash for it then. Our sledge is badly strained, and on the abominably bad surface of soft snow is dreadfully hard to move. I have been suffering from a bad headache all day, and Adams also was worried by the cold.

I think that these headaches are a form of mountain sickness, due to our high altitude. The others have bled from the nose, and that must relieve them. Physical effort is always trying at a high altitude, and we are straining at the harness all day, sometimes slipping in the soft snow that overlies the hard sastrugi. My head is very bad. The sensation is as though the nerves were being twisted up with a corkscrew and then pulled out.[9]

Marshall took our temperatures tonight, and we are all at about 94°, but in spite of this we are getting south. We are only 198 miles off our goal now. If the rise would stop, the cold would not matter, but it is hard to know what is man's limit. We have only 150 pounds per man to pull, but it is more severe work than the 250 pounds per man up the glacier was. The Pole is hard to get.

[December 30] We only did 4 miles 100 yards today. We started at 7 A.M., but had to camp at 11 A.M., a blizzard springing up from the south. It is more than annoying. I cannot express my feelings. We were pulling at last on a level surface, but very soft snow, when at about 10 A.M. the south wind and drift commenced to increase, and at 11 A.M. it was so bad that we had to camp.

And here all day we have been lying in our sleeping-bags trying to keep warm and listening to the threshing drift on the tentside. I am in the cooking tent, and the wind comes through, it is so thin. Our precious food is going, and the time also, and it is so important to us to get on. We lie here and think of how to make things better, but we cannot reduce food now, and the

---

[9] A contributing cause may have been a too-high percentage of protein in the diet, due to the lean pony beef. At any rate it was the experience of the third Stefansson expedition that when living exclusively by hunting, they developed headaches whenever they had to live on the flesh of skinny animals.

only thing will be to rush all possible at the end. We will do, and are doing, all humanly possible. It is with Providence to help us.

[December 31] The last day of the old year, and the hardest day we have had almost, pushing through soft snow uphill with a strong head wind and drift all day. The temperature is minus 7° Fahrenheit, and our altitude is 10,477 feet above sea level. The altitude is trying. My head has been very bad all day, and we are all feeling the short food, but still we are getting south.

We are in latitude 86 degrees 54 minutes south tonight, but we have only three weeks' food and two weeks' biscuit to do nearly 500 geographical miles. We can only do our best. Too tired to write more tonight. We all get iced-up about our faces, and are on the verge of frostbite all the time.

Please God the weather will be fine during the next fourteen days. Then all will be well. The distance today was 11 miles.

[January 1, 1908] Head too bad to write much. We did 11 miles 900 yards (statute) today, and the latitude at 6 P.M. was 87 degrees, 6.5 minutes south, so we have beaten North and South records.[10] Struggling uphill all day in very soft snow. Everyone done up and weak from want of food. When we camped at 6 P.M., fine weather, thank God.

Only 172½ miles from the Pole. The height above sea level, now 10,755 feet, makes all work difficult. Surface seems to be better ahead. I do trust it will be so tomorrow.

[January 2] Terribly hard work today. We started at 6:45 A.M. with a fairly good surface, which soon became very soft. We were sinking in over our ankles, and our broken sledge, by running sideways, added to the drag. We have been going uphill all day, and tonight are 11,034 feet above sea level. It has taken us all day to do 10 miles 450 yards, though the weights are fairly light. A cold wind, with a temperature of minus 14° Fahrenheit, goes right through us now, as we are weakening from want of food, and the high altitude makes every movement an effort, especially if we stumble on the march.

---

[10] At this time the farthest-north record was 87 degrees 6 minutes north, held by Peary and made by sledging north from Ellesmere Island over the drifting sea ice.

My head is giving me trouble all the time. Wild seems the most fit of us. God knows we are doing all we can, but the outlook is serious if this surface continues and the plateau gets higher, for we are not traveling fast enough to make our food spin out and get back to our depot in time. I cannot think of failure yet. I must look at the matter sensibly and consider the lives of those who are with me. I feel that if we go on too far it will be impossible to get back over this surface, and then all the results will be lost to the world.

We can now definitely locate the South Pole on the highest plateau in the world, and our geological work and meteorology will be of the greatest use to science; but all this is not the Pole. Man can only do his best, and we have arrayed against us the strongest forces of nature. This cutting south wind with drift plays the mischief with us, and after ten hours of struggling against it one pannikin of food with two biscuits and a cup of cocoa does not warm one up much. I must think over the situation carefully tomorrow, for time is going on and food is going also.

[January 3] Started at 6:55 A.M., cloudy but fairly warm. The temperature was minus 8° Fahrenheit at noon. We had a terrible surface all the morning, and did only 5 miles 100 yards. A meridian altitude gave us latitude 87 degrees 22 minutes south at noon. The surface was better in the afternoon, and we did 6 geographical miles. The temperature at 6 P.M. was minus 11° Fahrenheit.

It was an uphill pull toward the evening, and we camped at 6:20 P.M., the altitude being 11,220 feet above the sea. Tomorrow must risk making a depot on the plateau, and make a dash for it, but even then, if this surface continues, we will be two weeks in carrying it through.

[January 4] The end is in sight. We can only go for three more days at the most, for we are weakening rapidly. Short food and a blizzard wind from the south, with driving drift at a temperature of 47° of frost, have plainly told us today that we are reaching our limit, for we were so done up at noon with cold that the clinical thermometer failed to register the temperature of three of us at 94°.

We started at 7:40 A.M., leaving a depot on this great wide

plateau, a risk that only this case justified, and one that my comrades agreed to, as they have to every one so far, with the same cheerfulness and regardlessness of self that have been the means of our getting as far as we have done so far. Pathetically small looked the bamboo, one of the tent poles, with a bit of bag sewn on as a flag, to mark our stock of provisions which has to take us back to our depot, 150 miles north. We lost sight of it in half an hour, and are now trusting to our footprints in the snow to guide us back to each bamboo until we pick up the depot again. I trust that the weather will keep clear.

Today we have done 12½ geographical miles, and with only 70 pounds per man to pull it is as hard, even harder, work than the 100-odd pounds was yesterday, and far harder than the 250 pounds were three weeks ago, when we were climbing the glacier. This, I consider, is a clear indication of our failing strength. The main thing against us is the altitude of 11,200 feet and the biting wind.

Our faces are cut, and our feet and hands are always on the verge of frostbite. Our fingers, indeed, often go, but we get them round more or less. I have great trouble with two fingers on my left hand. They have been badly jammed when we were getting the motor up over the ice face at winter quarters, and the circulation is not good. Our boots now are pretty well worn out, and we have to halt at times to pick the snow out of the soles. Our stock of sennegrass [dried grass from northern Norway] is nearly exhausted, so we have to use the same frozen stuff day after day. Another trouble is that the lampwick with which we tie the *finnesko* [Lapp-type shoes] is chafed through, and we have to tie knots in it. These knots catch the snow under our feet, making a lump that has to be cleared every now and then.

I am of the opinion that to sledge even in the height of summer on this plateau, we should have at least 40 ounces of food a day per man, and we are on short rations of the ordinary allowance of 32 ounces. We depoted our extra underclothing, to save weight, about three weeks ago, and are now in the same clothes night and day. One suit of underclothing, shirt and guernsey, and our thin Burberries, now all patched. When we get up in the morning out of the wet bag, our Burberries become like a coat of mail at once, and our heads and beards get iced-up with the moisture when breathing on the march.

There is half a gale blowing dead in our teeth all the time. We hope to reach within 100 geographical miles of the Pole; under the circumstances we can expect to do very little more. I am confident that the Pole lies on the great plateau we have discovered, miles and miles from any outstanding land. The temperature tonight is minus 24° Fahrenheit.

[January 5] Today head wind and drift again, with 50° of frost, and a terrible surface. We have been marching through 8 inches of snow, covering sharp sastrugi, which plays hell with our feet, but we have done 13⅓ geographical miles, for we increased our food, seeing that it was absolutely necessary to do this to enable us to accomplish anything. I realize that the food we have been having has not been sufficient to keep up our strength, let alone supply the wastage caused by exertion, and now we must try to keep warmth in us, though our strength is being used up. Our temperatures at 5 A.M. were 94° Fahrenheit.

We got away at 7 A.M. sharp and marched till noon, then from 1 P.M. sharp till 6 P.M. All being in one tent makes our campwork slower, for we are so cramped for room, and we get up at 4:40 A.M. so as to get away by 7 A.M. Two of us have to stand outside the tent at night until things are squared up inside, and we find it cold work. Hunger grips us hard, and the food supply is very small.

My head still gives me great trouble. I began by wishing that my worst enemy had it instead of myself, but now I don't wish even my worst enemy to have such a headache. Still, it is no use talking about it. Self is a subject that most of us are fluent on. We find the utmost difficulty in carrying through the day, and we can only go for two or three more days. Never once has the temperature been above zero since we got onto the plateau, though this is the height of summer. We have done our best, and we thank God for having allowed us to get so far.

[January 6] This must be our last outward march with the sledge and camp equipment. Tomorrow we must leave camp with some food, and push as far south as possible, and then plant the flag. Today's story is 57° of frost [25° below zero], with a strong blizzard and high drift; yet we marched 13¼ geographical miles through soft snow, being helped by extra food. This does not mean full rations, but a bigger ration than we have been having lately. The pony maize is all finished.

The most trying day we have yet spent, our fingers and faces being frostbitten continually. Tomorrow we will rush south with the flag. We are 88 degrees 7 minutes south tonight. It is our last outward march. Blowing hard tonight. I would fail to explain my feelings if I tried to write them down, now that the end has come. There is only one thing that lightens the disappointment, and that is the feeling that we have done all we could. It is the forces of nature that have prevented us from going right through. I cannot write more.

[January 7] A blinding, shrieking blizzard all day, with the temperature ranging from 60° to 70° of frost. It has been impossible to leave the tent, which is snowed up on the lee side. We have been lying in our bags all day, only warm at food time, with fine snow making through the walls of the worn tent and covering our bags. We are greatly cramped. Adams is suffering from cramp every now and then. We are eating our valuable food without marching.

The wind has been blowing 80 to 90 miles an hour. We can hardly sleep. Tomorrow I trust this will be over. Directly the wind drops, we march as far south as possible, then plant the flag, and turn homeward. Our chief anxiety is lest our tracks may drift up, for to them we must trust mainly to find our depot; we have no land bearings in this great plain of snow. It is a serious risk that we have taken, but we had to play the game to the utmost, and Providence will look after us.

[January 8] Again all day in our bags, suffering considerably physically from cold hands and feet, and from hunger, but more mentally, for we cannot get on south, and we simply lie here shivering. Every now and then one of our party's feet go, and the unfortunate beggar has to take his leg out of the sleeping-bag and have his frozen foot nursed into life again by placing it inside the shirt against the skin of his almost equally unfortunate neighbor.

We must do something more to the south, even though the food is going, and we weaken lying in the cold, for with 72° of frost, the wind cuts through our thin tent, and even the drift is finding its way in and onto our bags, which are wet enough as it is. Cramp is not uncommon every now and then, and the drift all round the tent has made it so small that there is hardly room for us at all.

The wind has been blowing hard all day; some of the gusts must be over 70 or 80 miles an hour. This evening it seems as though it were going to ease down, and directly it does we shall be up and away south for a rush. I feel that this march must be our limit. We are so short of food, and at this high altitude, 11,600 feet, it is hard to keep any warmth in our bodies between the scanty meals. We have nothing to read now, having depoted our little books to save weight, and it is dreary work lying in the tent with nothing to read, and too cold to write much in the diary.

[January 9] Our last day outward. We have shot our bolt, and the tale is latitude 88 degrees 23 minutes south, longitude 162 degrees east.

The wind eased down at 1 A.M. and at 2 A.M. were up and had breakfast. At 4 A.M. started south, with the Queen's Union Jack, a brass cylinder containing stamps and documents to place at the furthest south point, camera, glasses, and compass. At 9 A.M. we were in 88 degrees 23 minutes south, half running and half walking over a surface much hardened by the recent blizzard. It was strange for us to go along without the nightmare of a sledge dragging behind us. We hoisted Her Majesty's flag, and the other Union Jack afterward, and took possession of the plateau in the name of His Majesty.

While the Union Jack blew out stiffly in the icy gale that cut us to the bone, we looked south with our powerful glasses, but could see nothing but the dead-white snow plain. There was no break in the plateau as it extended toward the Pole, and we feel sure that the goal we have failed to reach lies on this plain. We stayed only a few minutes, and then, taking the Queen's flag and eating our scanty meal as we went, we hurried back and reached our camp about 3 P.M. 🞖

The return journey was difficult in that the sledgers were hunger-weakened, disappointed, and wearied; but their sledges were lighter, the grade was downhill, and the wind was often at their backs, helping them always and sometimes carrying the sledge along at a good clip under the mere pull of the sail. They picked up food depots as they went; but at one of them they were sickened by the flesh of a poor and exhausted pony (on which Shackleton has been quoted above).

After a round-trip journey of one hundred and seventeen days, Shackleton and his companions reached the base camp on February 28, 1909.

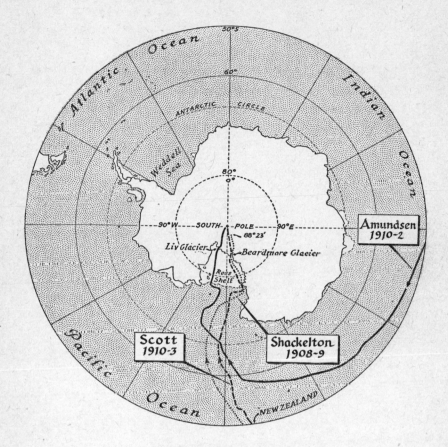

The Attainment of the South Pole

THE ATTAINMENT OF THE SOUTH POLE

CHAPTER 18

Thus far all sledge journeys in the Antarctic had been made by inexperienced men who needed to make up in courage, hardihood, and determination what they lacked in skill and a grasp of local conditions and needs.

Among others, Admiral Peary had been saying that if ever men of northern experience went south they would find easy to do in the Antarctic summer, with its perpetual daylight, what the Arctic men had to do in winter, particularly as the southern travel would be on nearly level and very stable land, while travelers like himself had been forced to contend with drifting and sometimes tumbling floes of the Arctic Sea. Peary did not want to go himself; for after reaching the North Pole he considered he already had won the chief prize of the game and that a South Pole journey would be an anticlimax. So he tried to get an expedition started from the United States, preferably with his comrade Robert A. Bartlett in command, but was not successful.

Another northerner was successful, the Norwegian Roald Engelbregt Gravning Amundsen. He did not have much experience with Arctic sledging, but he had at least made one short journey in the vicinity of King William Island on sea ice and prairie land, and one sled trip of several weeks through the forest of Alaska, from Herschel Island to the Yukon River and back, as well as several trips by sledge, of one or two days each, between King Point and Herschel Island on the north coast of Canada.

That was not much of this type of experience compared with Peary's nine Arctic sledging winters, with an aggregate of thousands of miles of the most difficult work both on sea ice and on glaciers, but it was a great deal compared with no previous experience at all in the cases of both Scott and Shackleton. At any rate, Amundsen knew how to feed, harness, and drive dogs, precious learning not possessed by either Scott or Shackleton.

In 1909 Scott was preparing in Britain a second expedition for research in the Antarctic and for closing the hundred-mile gap between Shackleton's farthest and the South Pole. Amundsen was preparing at the same time in Norway an expedition which would attempt to forestall Peary at the North Pole. It was being said constantly in both countries that neither of these expeditions, Scott's and Amundsen's, would interfere with the other, since they were poles apart in their objectives; so there were many British contributions of both financial and moral support to Amundsen.

When the news of Peary's success came over the telegraph wires Amundsen privately (as he later said) decided to shift his objective and try to forestall Scott at the South Pole. Amundsen continued saying through the press that he was going north by way of Bering Strait for another Arctic venture —a "strictly scientific" expedition, now that the North Pole was attained. That he was going to try for the South Pole was not announced until his ship touched in South America on its way to the Antarctic.

Two things that proved very helpful to Amundsen in the attainment of the South Pole were his favorable base and his excellent dogs. His ship reached her port easily and lay at the Bay of Whales, across the Ross Sea from where the British had been wintering, a more favorable location, in view of what Amundsen knew from reading Scott's and Shackleton's books. The dogs were a hundred of Greenland's best that had come through to the Antarctic in as good condition as they were in when they left home. The Amundsen party knew where to buy dogs and how to select the best, how to keep them in health and strength, how to use them in sledging. True, they were not really expert in dog-driving—we see that from Amundsen's stories and complaints about all the trouble they had with them. But they and their management were good enough

to reach the Pole as easily as Peary had forecast in case a northerner were ever to go south.

Amundsen's greatest advantage of all was that he knew how
to dress himself and his men so that they would be as lightly
as they were warmly clad—able to run easily, without having
legs bounds by stiff clothing, and to work with free play of all
muscles; and yet so as to be warmly dressed for comfort in
garments easy to keep dry and thus of constant warmth. Wet
clothes, which are never comfortable, are doubly bad in cold
weather, for they stiffen with frost and increase steadily in
weight as they accumulate more ice, while they are at the same
time losing their insulating qualities, their power to keep you
warm.

It had been Amundsen's great good fortune that when he
wintered in the Arctic at King William Island, the seasons of
1903-05, he was among Eskimos who had not as yet adopted
any white men's fashions and who thus had still in full play
that unequaled technique of their which enables them to
be warmer in a ten-pound suit as flexible as velvet than white
men are when dressed, like Scott and Shackleton, in stiff garments of double the weight—clumsy garments that will not
stay dry and which therefore get steadily heavier, stiffer, less
warm to a point where the wearer has to eat a lot more food
than otherwise to fight the increasing chill by generating
warmth through the metabolic process.

The fundamental difficulty about the Antarctic clothing of
the British expeditions (and this has applied to later Antarctic
workers scarcely less) is that they have been of wool or a combination of wool and fur. Amundsen states the correct principle
on pages 149-50, Volume I, of his *The Northwest Passage*
(Dutton, 1908). He is describing a journey he made in King
William Island in 1904:

"On March 1 we were ready to start. The thermometer
stood at 63½° below zero (Fahr.). But in the course of the
month of February we had become so used to cold that it
really did not make any great impression on us. We were, indeed, extremely well clad, some of us in complete Eskimo
costume, others in a partly civilized style.

"My experience is that the Eskimo dress in winter in these

regions is far superior to our European clothes. But one must either wear it all or not at all; any mixture is bad. Woolen underclothing absorbs all the perspiration and soon becomes wet through and through.

"Dressed in nothing but reindeer skin, like the Eskimo, and with garments so loose and roomy on the body that the air can circulate between them, one can generally keep his things dry. Even if you are working so hard that you can't help getting wet, the skin dries again much easier than wool. Besides, woolen things soon become dirty and then they do not impart much warmth. Skin clothing keeps nearly as well without washing.

"A further great advantage of skin is that you feel warm and comfortable the moment you put it on. In woolen things you have to jump and dance about like a madman before you can get warm. Finally, skins are absolutely windproof, which, of course, is a very important point."

Dressed Eskimo-style for their Antarctic journey, Amundsen and his men would be comfortably warm if they sat on their sledges, pulled along by the dogs; they would be lightly clad for easy running if that were required, or for pulling on the sledges to help along in heavy going.

The South Pole party left the Bay of Whales October 19, 1911, with four sledges drawn by thirteen dogs each. An advance depot had been made at 80 degrees south latitude, so the fresh dogs and light sleds moved with speed, the five men running along or riding on the loads—all very different from the slow and sturdy march of the Britishers from their more remote base on the first Scott expedition, the Shackleton expedition (and now on the second Scott expedition that would start in two weeks for the same destination). Amundsen's four companions were Olav Bjaaland, Helmer Hanssen, Sverre Hassel, and Oscar Wisting.

The frisky dogs and light sledges made 90 miles the first four days, with some danger, but only slight delay from crevasses. The dogs did not properly need a rest when they reached the advance depot, but they got one anyhow, two days of feasting on seal meat, which was there in superabundance.

On leaving this base, Amundsen planned to walk ahead of the teams; but he could not keep ahead, and the dogs kept stepping on his skis, so he fixed a rope to a sledge and ski-drove along behind. "And there I stood," says Amundsen, "until we reached 85 degrees 5 minutes south—340 miles. Yes, that was a pleasant surprise. We had never dreamed of driving on skis to the Pole! Thanks to Hanssen's brilliant talents as a dog-driver we could easily do this."

It was not, of course, literally true that Amundsen ski-drove these whole 340 miles; for part of the distance was overland and up fairly steep slopes where none of the five men rode or got pulled along. There were even some places where they assisted the dogs with the loads. There were spells of soft snow and slow progress.

At this stage a balanced picture of the good and the bad is given by Charles Turley in his *Roald Amundsen, Explorer* (London, 1935):

"Climbing on and on, Bjaaland, who led the way, performing miracles of skill on his skis, they reached a height of 4550 feet. From this point Amundsen says: 'The mighty glacier opened out before us, stretching, as we could now see, right up from the Barrier between the lofty mountains running east and west. It was by this glacier that we should have to advance to the plateau; we could see that.'

"He, however, underestimated both the difficulties and the distances of their journey before the great plateau was reached, the snow being so deep and loose that the dogs could not get a firm hold. But progress, though slow, was made, and on the next day the surface was so favorable that Bjaaland had to go all out to keep ahead of the sledge teams.

"It is curious to note that at this height and in this latitude the atmosphere was far too warm to be pleasant. Wearing only the lightest clothes they 'sweated as if running races in the tropics.' Under such conditions one imagines that Bjaaland would, if possible, have preferred to travel a shade less rapidly, but with the dogs determined to go at full speed there was no respite for him."

In one respect the Amundsen party had more difficulty than Scott or Shackleton—while climbing from 5500 to 8000 feet they had steeper slopes and seemingly more crevasses than are found anywhere on the British route to the Pole, which lies considerably to the right, or west, of Amundsen's. There were stretches when two dog teams had to be hitched to one sledge. Because of the steep grade, there were avalanches in their neighborhood at times.

There came a grade so steep that they went up 1 mile in 20 miles of advance. The power of doubled teams had managed this; the final plateau, discovered by Shackleton two years before, had been reached, and the strength of all the dogs was required no longer.

Amundsen was using a method which may have been introduced into polar work by his countryman Fridtjof Nansen, but which a good many of the explorers have never had the heart to adopt—to plan a journey so as to kill a certain number of dogs at certain stages and feed them to the other dogs, the men finally eating the last dog or two. Amundsen now gave the order for the killing of forty. He explains that he did not like hearing the shots and was hoping that the primus stove, on which he was doing the cooking, would make a noise that would deaden the reports.

The margin of safety which Amundsen had is brought out in connection with the gruesome tale of slaughter. In describing their arrival upon the plateau, he writes that "one would have thought the dogs would have had enough work that day to tire them, but this ridge, with its unpleasant snow waves, did not seem to trouble them in the least. We all drove up gaily, towed by the sledges, onto what looked to us like the final plateau." So the teams were not weak with hunger or even tired. But forty were nevertheless to be killed, for that was the plan. Amundsen sat there in the tent, hunched over the stove:

Amundsen and Dog Meat

🐾 The pemmican was cooked remarkably quickly that evening, and I believe I was unusually industrious in stirring it. There went the first shot—I am not a nervous man, but I must admit that I gave a start.

Shot now followed upon shot—they had an uncanny sound over the great plain. A trusty servant lost his life each time. It was long before the first man reported that he had finished. . . .

The holiday humor that ought to have prevailed in the tent that evening—our first on the plateau—did not make its appearance; there was depression and sadness in the air—we had grown so fond of our dogs. The place was named the Butcher's Shop. It had been arranged that we should stop here two days to rest and eat dog.

There was more than one among us who at first would not hear of taking any part in this feast; but as time went by, and appetites became sharper, this view underwent a change, until during the last few days before reaching the Butcher's Shop [on the return journey] we all thought and talked of nothing but dog cutlets, dog steaks, and the like. But on this first evening we put a restraint on ourselves; we thought we could not fall upon our four-footed friends and devour them before they had had time to grow cold. . . .

The effect of the great and sudden change of altitude made itself felt at once. When I wanted to turn round in my bag, I had to do it a bit at a time, so as not to get out of breath. That my comrades were affected in the same way, I knew without asking them; my ears told me enough.

It was calm when we turned out, but the weather did not look altogether promising; it was overcast and threatening. We occupied the forenoon in flaying a number of dogs.

As I have said, all the survivors were not yet in a mood for dog's flesh, and it therefore had to be served in the most enticing form. When flayed and cut up, it went down readily all along the line; even the most fastidious then overcame their scruples. But with the skin on we should not have been able to persuade them all to eat that morning. Probably this distaste was due to the smell clinging to the skins, and I must admit that it was not appetizing.

The meat itself, as it lay there cut up, looked well enough, in all conscience; no butcher's shop could have exhibited a finer sight than we showed after flaying and cutting up ten dogs. Great masses of beautiful fresh, red meat, with quantities of the most tempting fat, lay spread over the snow.

The dogs went round and sniffed at it. Some helped themselves to a piece; others were digesting. We men had picked out what we thought was the youngest and tenderest one for ourselves. The whole arrangement was left to Wisting, both the selection and the preparation of the cutlets. His choice fell upon Rex, a beautiful little animal—one of his own dogs, by the way. With the skill of an expert, he hacked and cut away what he considered would be sufficient for a meal.

I could not take my eyes off his work; the delicate little cutlets had an absolutely hypnotizing effect as they were spread out one by one over the snow. They recalled memories of old days, when no doubt a dog cutlet would have been less tempting than now—memories of dishes on which the cutlets were elegantly arranged side by side, with paper frills on the bones, and a neat pile of petits pois in the middle.

Ah, my thoughts wandered still farther afield—but that does not concern us now, nor has it anything to do with the South Pole. . . .

Inside the tent Wisting was getting on well when we came in after making these observations [for latitude]. The pot was on, and, to judge by the savory smell, the preparations were already far advanced. The cutlets were not fried; we had neither frying pan nor butter. We could, no doubt, have got some lard out of the pemmican, and we might have contrived some sort of a pan, so that we could have fried them if it had been necessary; but we found it far easier and quicker to boil them, and in this way we got excellent soup into the bargain. . . .

The meat was excellent, quite excellent, and one cutlet after another disappeared with lightninglike rapidity. I must admit that they would have lost nothing by being a little more tender, but one must not expect too much of a dog. At this first meal I finished five cutlets myself, and looked in vain in the pot for more. Wisting appeared not to have reckoned on such a brisk demand. 📓

Apart from the flesh of each other, the dogs were living on pemmican, the men on pemmican and biscuit as the main items, with a little chocolate and milk powder. Dog meat apart, it was much the same as the ration which had taken Peary to the North Pole.

At the Butcher's Shop camp the party were detained five

days, which they could well afford, for the dog beef was enough for a much longer wait; but the men were in full strength, the dogs eager, and so they began traveling into the gale on the sixth day.

For several days the party advanced in thick weather. Their last sufficient view of the sun had given them south latitude 86 degrees 47 minutes. By December 7 they should be near Shackleton's farthest, by their dead reckoning. From that day and vicinity the story is told in Amundsen's own words from his two-volume book *The South Pole* (London, 1913):

The South Pole Attained

We had a great piece of work before us that day [December 7, 1911]: nothing less than carrying our flag farther south than the foot of man had trod. We had our silk flag ready; it was made fast to two ski sticks and laid on Hanssen's sledge. I had given him orders that as soon as we had covered the distance to 88 degrees 23 minutes south, which was Shackleton's farthest south, the flag was to be hoisted on his sledge.

It was my turn as forerunner, and I pushed on. There was no longer any difficulty in holding one's course; I had the grandest cloud formations to steer by, and everything now went like a machine. First came the forerunner for the time being, then Hanssen, then Wisting, and finally Bjaaland. The forerunner who was not on duty went where he liked; as a rule he accompanied one or other of the sledges.

I had long ago fallen into a reverie—far removed from the scene in which I was moving. What I thought about I do not remember now, but I was so preoccupied that I had entirely forgotten my surroundings. Then suddenly I was roused from my dreaming by a jubilant shout, followed by ringing cheers. I turned round quickly to discover the reason of this unwonted occurrence, and stood speechless and overcome.

I find it impossible to express the feelings that possessed me at this moment. All the sledges had stopped, and from the foremost of them the Norwegian flag was flying. It shook itself out, waved and flapped so that the silk rustled; it looked wonderfully well in the pure, clear air and the shining white surround-

ings. 88 degrees 23 minutes was past; we were farther south
than any human being had been.

No other moment of the whole trip affected me like this. The
tears forced their way to my eyes; by no effort of will could I
keep them back. It was the flag yonder that conquered me and
my will. Luckily I was some way in advance of the others, so
that I had time to pull myself together and master my feelings
before reaching my comrades. We all shook hands, with mutual
congratulations. We had won our way far by holding together,
and we would go farther yet—to the end.

We did not pass that spot without according our highest
tribute of admiration to the man who—together with his gallant
companions—had planted his country's flag so infinitely nearer
to the goal than any of his precursors. Sir Ernest Shackleton's
name will always be written in the annals of Antarctic exploration in letters of fire. Pluck and grit can work wonders, and I
know of no better example of this than what that man has
accomplished.

The cameras of course had to come out, and we got an
excellent photograph of the scene which none of us will ever
forget. We went on a couple of miles more, to 88 degrees 25
minutes, and then camped. The weather had improved, and
kept on improving all the time. It was now almost perfectly
calm, radiantly clear, and, under the circumstances, quite
summerlike: −0.4° Fahrenheit. Inside the tent it was quite
sultry. This was more than we had expected.

After much consideration and discussion we had come to the
conclusion that we ought to lay down a depot—the last one—at
this spot. The advantages of lightening our sledges were so
great that we should have to risk it. Nor would there be any
great risk attached to it, after all, since we should adopt a
system of marks that would lead even a blind man back to the
place. We had determined to mark it not only at right angles to
our course—that is, from east to west—but by snow beacons at
every 2 geographical miles to the south.

We stayed here on the following day [December 8] to
arrange this depot. Hanssen's dogs were real marvels, all of
them; nothing seemed to have any effect on them. They had
grown rather thinner, of course, but they were still as strong as

THE ATTAINMENT OF THE SOUTH POLE

ever. It was therefore decided not to lighten Hanssen's sledge, but only the two others; both Wisting's and Bjaaland's teams had suffered, especially the latter's.

The reduction in weight that was effected was considerable —nearly 110 pounds on each of the two sledges; there was thus about 220 pounds in the depot. The snow here was ill-adapted for building, but we got up quite a respectable monument all the same. It was dogs' pemmican and biscuits that were left behind; we carried with us on the sledges provisions for about a month. If, therefore, contrary to expectation, we should be so unlucky as to miss this depot, we should nevertheless be fairly sure of reaching our depot in 86 degrees 21 minutes before supplies ran short.

The cross-marking of the depot was done with sixty splinters of black packing case on each side, with 100 paces between each. Every other one had a shred of black cloth on the top. The splinters on the east side were all marked, so that on seeing them we should know instantly that we were to the east of the depot. Those on the west had no marks.

The warmth of the past few days seemed to have matured our frost sores, and we presented an awful appearance. It was Wisting, Hanssen, and I who had suffered the worst damage in the last southeast blizzard; the left side of our faces was one mass of sores, bathed in matter and serum. We looked like the worst type of tramps and ruffians, and would probably not have been recognized by our nearest relations.

These sores were a great trouble to us during the latter part of the journey. The slightest gust of wind produced a sensation as if one's face were being cut backward and forward with a blunt knife. They lasted a long time, too; I can remember Hanssen removing the last scab when we were coming into Hobart—three months later. We were very lucky in the weather during this depot work; the sun came out all at once, and we had an excellent opportunity of taking some good azimuth observations, the last of any use that we got on the journey.

December 9 arrived with the same fine weather and sunshine. True, we felt our frost sores rather sharply that day, with −18.4° Fahrenheit and a little breeze dead against us, but that could not be helped. We at once began to put up beacons

—a work which was continued with great regularity right up to the Pole.

These beacons were not so big as those we had built down on the Barrier; we could see that they would be quite large enough with a height of about 3 feet, as it was very easy to see the slightest irregularity on this perfectly flat surface.

While thus engaged we had an opportunity of becoming thoroughly acquainted with the nature of the snow. Often— very often indeed—on this part of the plateau, to the south of 88 degrees 25 minutes, we had difficulty in getting snow good enough—that is, solid enough—for cutting blocks. The snow up here seemed to have fallen very quietly, in light breezes or calms. We could thrust the tent pole, which was 6 feet long, right down without meeting resistance, which showed that there was no hard layer of snow. The surface was also perfectly level; there was not a sign of sastrugi in any direction.

Every step we now took in advance brought us rapidly nearer the goal; we could feel fairly certain of reaching it on the afternoon of the fourteenth. It was very natural that our con- versation should be chiefly concerned with the time of arrival. None of us would admit that he was nervous, but I am inclined to think that we all had a little touch of that malady.

What should we see when we got there? A vast, endless plain that no eye had yet seen and no foot yet trodden, or—— No, it was an impossibility; with the speed at which we had traveled, we must reach the goal first, there could be no doubt about that. And yet—and yet—— Wherever there is the small- est loophole, doubt creeps in and gnaws and gnaws and never leaves a poor wretch in peace. "What on earth is Uroa scent- ing?" It was Bjaaland who made this remark, on one of these last days, when I was going by the side of his sledge and talking to him. "And the strange thing is that he's scenting to the south. It can never be——"

Mylius, Ring, and Suggen showed the same interest in the southerly direction; it was quite extraordinary to see how they raised their heads, with every sign of curiosity, put their noses in the air, and sniffed due south. One would really have thought there was something remarkable to be found there.

From 88 degrees 25 minutes south, the barometer and hyp-

someter indicated slowly but surely that the plateau was beginning to descend toward the other side. This was a pleasant
surprise to us; we had thus not only found the very summit of
the plateau, but also the slope down on the far side. This would
have a very important bearing for obtaining an idea of the
construction of the whole plateau.

On December 9 observations and dead reckoning agreed
within a mile. The same result again on the tenth: observation
2 kilometers behind reckoning. The weather and going remained
about the same as on the preceding days: light southeasterly
breeze, temperature −18.4° Fahrenheit. The snow surface was
loose, but ski and sledges glided over it well.

On the eleventh, the same weather conditions. Temperature
−13° Fahrenheit. Observation and reckoning again agreed
exactly. Our latitude was 89 degrees 15 minutes south. On the
twelfth we reached 89 degrees 30 minutes, reckoning 1 kilometer
behind observation. Going and surface as good as ever. Weather
splendid—calm with sunshine. The noon observation on the
thirteenth gave 89 degrees 37 minutes south. Reckoning 89
degrees 38.5 minutes south. We halted in the afternoon, after
going 8 geographical miles, and camped in 89 degrees 45
minutes, according to reckoning.

The weather during the forenoon had been just as fine as
before; in the afternoon we had some snow showers from the
southeast.

It was like the eve of some great festival that night in the
tent. One could feel that a great event was at hand. Our flag
was taken out again and lashed to the same two ski sticks as
before. Then it was rolled up and laid aside, to be ready when
the time came. I was awake several times during the night,
and had the same feeling that I can remember as a little boy
on the night before Christmas Eve—an intense expectation of
what was going to happen. Otherwise I think we slept just
as well that night as any other.

On the morning of December 14 the weather was of the
finest, just as if it had been made for arriving at the Pole. I
am not quite sure, but I believe we dispatched our breakfast
rather more quickly than usual and were out of the tent sooner,
though I must admit that we always accomplished this with all

reasonable haste. We went in the usual order—the forerunner, Hanssen, Wisting, Bjaaland, and the reserve forerunner.

By noon we had reached 89 degrees 55 minutes by dead reckoning, and made ready to take the rest in one stage. At 10 A.M., a light breeze had sprung up from the southeast, and it had clouded over, so that we got no noon altitude; but the clouds were not thick, and from time to time we had a glimpse of the sun through them. The going on that day was rather different from what it had been. Sometimes the ski went over it well, but at others it was pretty bad.

We had advanced that day in the same mechanical way as before; not much was said, but eyes were used all the more. Hanssen's neck grew twice as long as before in his endeavor to see a few inches farther. I had asked him before we started to spy out ahead for all he was worth, and he did so with a vengeance. But however keenly he stared, he could not descry anything but the endless flat plain ahead of us. The dogs had dropped their scenting, and appeared to have lost their interest in the regions about the earth's axis.

At three in the afternoon a simultaneous "Halt!" rang out from the drivers. They had carefully examined their sledge meters, and they all showed the full distance—our Pole by reckoning. The goal was reached, the journey ended.

I cannot say—though I know it would sound much more effective—that the object of my life was attained. That would be romancing rather too barefacedly. I had better be honest and admit straight out that I have never known any man to be placed in such a diametrically opposite position to the goal of his desires as I was at that moment. The regions around the North Pole—well, yes, the North Pole itself—had attracted me from childhood, and here I was at the South Pole. Can anything more topsy-turvy be imagined?

We reckoned now that we were at the Pole. Of course, every one of us knew that we were not standing on the absolute spot; it would be an impossibility with the time and the instruments at our disposal to ascertain that exact spot. But we were so near it that the few miles which possibly separated us from it could not be of the slightest importance. It was our intention to make a circle round this camp, with a radius of 12½ miles (20 kilometers), and to be satisfied with that.

After we had halted, we collected and congratulated each other. We had good grounds for mutual respect in what had been achieved, and I think that was just the feeling that was expressed in the firm and powerful grasps of the fist that were exchanged. After this we proceeded to the greatest and most solemn act of the whole journey—the planting of our flag.

Pride and affection shone in the five pairs of eyes that gazed upon the flag as it unfurled itself with a sharp crack, and waved over the Pole. I had determined that the act of planting it— the historic event—should be equally divided among us all. It was not for one man to do this; it was for *all* who had staked their lives in the struggle and held together through thick and thin. This was the only way in which I could show my grati- tude to my comrades in this desolate spot. I could see that they understood and accepted it in the spirit in which it was offered.

Five weather-beaten, frostbitten fists they were that grasped the pole, raised the waving flag in the air, and planted it as the first at the geographical South Pole. "Thus we plant thee, beloved flag, at the South Pole, and give to the plain on which it lies the name of King Haakon VII's Plateau." That moment will certainly be remembered by all of us who stood there.

One gets out of the way of protracted ceremonies in those regions—the shorter they are, the better. Everyday life began at once. When we had got the tent up, Hanssen set about slaughtering Helge, and it was hard for him to have to part from his best friend.

Helge had been an uncommonly useful and good-natured dog; without making any fuss he had pulled from morning to night, and had been a shining example to the team. But during the last week he had quite fallen away, and on our arrival at the Pole there was only a shadow of the old Helge left. He was only a drag on the others, and did absolutely no work. One blow on the skull, and Helge had ceased to live.

"What is death to one is food to another" is a saying that can scarcely find a better application than these dog meals. Helge was portioned out on the spot, and within a couple of hours there was nothing left of him but his teeth and the tuft at the end of his tail.

This was the second of our eighteen dogs that we had lost. The Major, one of Wisting's fine dogs, left us in 88 degrees 25 minutes south, and never returned. He was fearfully worn out, and must have gone away to die. We now had sixteen dogs left, and these we intended to divide into two equal teams, leaving Bjaaland's sledge behind.

Of course there was a festivity in the tent that evening— not that champagne corks were popping and wine flowing— no, we contented ourselves with a little piece of seal meat each, and it tasted well and did us good.

There was no other sign of festival indoors. Outside we heard the flag flapping in the breeze. Conversation was lively in the tent that evening, and we talked of many things. Perhaps, too, our thoughts sent messages home of what we had done.

[They camped at the Pole from December 14 to 17, 1911, during which time they circled the spot at a distance of several miles to make sure that the actual Pole had been circumvented. They marked and dated things they had brought along as souvenirs for themselves and as gifts to friends, and they had special dinners. The narrative begins again on December 17:]

When this festival dinner at the Pole was ended, we began our preparations for departure.

First we set up the little tent we had brought with us in case we should be compelled to divide into two parties. It had been made by our able sailmaker, Rönne, and was of very thin windproof gabardine. Its drab color made it easily visible against the white surface.

Another pole was lashed to the tent pole, making its total height about 13 feet. On the top of this a little Norwegian flag was lashed fast, and underneath it a pennant, on which "Fram" was painted. The tent was well secured with guy ropes on all sides.

Inside the tent, in a little bag, I left a letter, addressed to H.M. the King, giving information of what we had accomplished. The way home was a long one, and so many things might happen to make it impossible for us to give an account of our expedition.

Besides this letter, I wrote a short epistle to Captain Scott, who I assumed would be the first to find the tent. Other things we left there were a sextant with a glass horizon, a hypsometer case, three reindeer-skin foot bags, some kamiks [Eskimo-type boots] and mitts.

When everything had been laid inside, we went into the tent, one by one, to write our names on a tablet we had fastened to the tent pole. On this occasion we received the congratulations of our companions on the successful result, for the following messages were written on a couple of strips of leather sewed to the tent: "Good luck," and "Welcome to 90°." These good wishes, which we suddenly discovered, put us in very good spirits. They were signed by Beck and Rönne. They had good faith in us. When we had finished this we came out, and the tent door was securely laced together, so that there was no danger of the wind getting a hold on that side.

And so good-bye to Polheim. It was a solemn moment when we bared our heads and bade farewell to our home and our flag. And then the traveling tent was taken down and the sledges packed. Now the homeward journey was to begin—homeward, step by step, mile after mile, until the whole distance was accomplished.

We drove at once into our old tracks and followed them. Many were the times we turned to send a last look to Polheim. The vaporous, white air set in again, and it was not long before the last of Polheim, our little flag, disappeared from view.

The going was splendid and all were in good spirits, so we went along at a great pace. One would almost have thought the dogs knew they were homeward bound. A mild, summer-like wind, with a temperature of −2.2° Fahrenheit, was our last greeting from the Pole.

[As on the southward march, the average daily stint on the return journey was to be 17 miles, which was considered best for the dogs and fast enough for the season and distance. As on the poleward journey, the men occasionally rode or ski-drove. The trail had been marked clearly with snow beacons so that they not merely knew the way but could be reasonably sure to avoid any but a newly developed crevasse.

There were only two sleds left now, and thus only two men to drive them; the other three walked along on their skis. Part of Amundsen's comment upon the third day of the return journey is quoted, for it contains general reflections as well:]

Our appetite had increased alarmingly during the last few days. It appeared that we ski-runners evinced a far greater voracity than the drivers. There were days—only a few days, be it said—when I believe any of us three—Bjaaland, Hassel, and myself—would have swallowed pebbles without winking.

The drivers never showed such signs of starvation. It has occurred to me that this may possibly have been due to their being able to lean on the sledges as they went along, and thus have a rest and support which we had to do without. It seems little enough simply to rest one's hand on a sledge on the march, but in the long run, day after day, it may perhaps make itself felt.

Fortunately we were so well supplied that when this sensation of hunger came over us, we could increase our daily rations. On leaving the Pole we added to our pemmican ration, with the result that our wild-beast appetites soon gave way and shrank to an ordinary good, everyday twist.

Our daily program on entering upon the return journey was so arranged that we began to get breakfast ready at 6 P.M., and by 8 P.M. we were usually quite ready to start the day's march. An hour or so after midnight the 15 geographical miles were accomplished, and we could once more put up our tent, cook our food, and seek our rest. But this rest soon became so insufferably long. And then there was the fearful heat—considering the circumstances—which often made us get out of our sleeping-bags and lie with nothing over us.

These rests of twelve, fourteen, and sometimes as much as sixteen hours were what most tried our patience during the early part of the return journey. We could see so well that all this rest was unnecessary, but still we kept it up as long as we were on the high ground. Our conversation at this time used to turn very often on the best way of filling up these long, unnecessary waits.

That day, December 20, Per—good, faithful, conscientious Per—broke down utterly and had to be taken on the sledge the last part of the way. On arrival at the camping-ground he had his reward. A little blow of the back of the ax was enough for him; without making a sound the worn-out animal collapsed.

[There were on the march back some narrow escapes from crevasses and other dangers and some difficulties, but hardly more than to keep a narrative of the trip from being dull. They had a superfluity of food in the various depots, to which they were guided by the monuments erected on the way south, and their health was the best. Amundsen says for January 8, 1912:]

That was not bad steering in the dark. At 9 P.M. we reached the depot in 85 degrees south. Now we could begin to be liberal with the dogs' food, too; they had double pemmican rations, besides as many oatmeal biscuits as they would eat. We had such masses of biscuits now that we could positively throw them about.

Of course we might have left a large part of these provisions behind; but there was a great satisfaction in being so well supplied with food, and the dogs did not seem to mind the little extra weight in the least. As long as things went so capitally as they were going—that is, with men and dogs exactly keeping pace with one another—we could ask for nothing better. . . .

On our way southward we had taken a good deal of seal meat and had divided it among the depots we built on the Barrier in such a way that we were now able to eat fresh meat every day. This had not been done without an object; if we should be visited with scurvy, this fresh meat would be invaluable. As we were—sound and healthy as we had never been before—the seal beef was a pleasant distraction in our menu, nothing more.

The temperature had risen greatly since we came down on to the Barrier, and kept steady at about 14° Fahrenheit. We were so warm in our sleeping-bags that we had to turn them with the hair out. That was better; we breathed more freely and felt happier. "Just like going into an ice cellar," somebody remarked. The same feeling as when on a really warm summer day one comes out of the hot sun into cool shade.

[Pleasantly uneventful days of steady progress, long rests in camp, men and dogs on the verge of overeating, food left behind or thrown away—such was the story of the return to Framheim. Says Amundsen:]

On January 25, at 4 A.M., we reached our good little house again, with two sledges and eleven dogs; men and animals all hale and hearty. . . . We agreed that it was good outside, but still better at home. Ninety-nine days the trip had taken. Distance about 1860 miles. 🖋

Through a technique borrowed in the main from the Smith Sound Eskimos by Peary, and from those of King William Island by Amundsen, the two poles had been attained less than three years apart—just two years, eight months, and eight days.

Peary started for the North Pole shortly after the middle of the Arctic winter, traveled toward it at the coldest season over drifting floes, now and then handicapped by unsafe young ice and open water; he reached the Pole on April 6, 1909, before the end of the northern winter. Amundsen started for the South Pole shortly after the beginning of the Antarctic summer, traveled toward it at the warmest season over stationary and comparatively level ice, now and then handicapped by steep slopes and crevasses. He reached his Pole on December 14, 1911, a week before the middle of the southern summer. The use of Eskimo clothes and methods had made the trip relatively easy.

So through the use of northern technique two groups of men had at last been able to stand "far as the Poles apart"; it was no longer possible that anyone could go farther away from the equator, north or south. But in exploration much still remained to be done, even in such crude things as the discovery of new islands, new ranges of mountains; an infinity remained to be done in accumulating and studying facts about the earth.

Acknowledgments

I<small>T</small> <small>WOULD</small> be difficult to make sufficient acknowledgment to all the authors, ancient and modern, whose works have served as source material in the preparation of *Great Adventures and Explorations*. An attempt at this has, however, been made by introducing each selection that has been included in this volume so that its source, and therefore our indebtedness, may be entirely clear. Similarly, where the ideas of certain authors are discussed without introducing passages from their writings, we have endeavored to cite their works fully enough so that the interested reader may, if he desires, read them at first hand.

Specifically, grateful appreciation is due to the following for their kind permission to include certain copyrighted selections:

American Geographical Society, for *The Discovery of the Amazon, According to the Account of Friar Gaspar de Carvajal and Other Documents*, by José Toribio Medina; Translated from the Spanish by Bertram T. Lee, Edited by H. C. Heaton, New York, 1934

D. Appleton-Century Company, Inc., for selections from Robert E. Peary's *Secrets of Polar Travel*, New York, 1917, used by permission from the publishers and Mrs. Edward Stafford, daughter of Admiral Peary.

Argonaut Press of London, for permission to use selections from *The Three Voyages of Martin Frobisher*, edited by Vilhjalmur Stefansson, London, 1938.

Doubleday and Company, Inc., for permission to use extracts from *Greenland*, by Vilhjalmur Stefansson, New York, 1942.

Hakluyt Society, of London, England, for permission granted by the Society's President, Edward Lynam, to reprint selections from the publications of the Hakluyt Society. Specific credit is given in our text to the Society and to the editors and translators of the extracts which have been used from narratives contained in several of the volumes published by the Hakluyt Society.

Halldor Hermannsson (editor and translator) for permission to use selections from *The Book of the Icelanders* (Islendingabok), by Ari Thorgilsson, published by the Cornell University Library in *Islandica*, Vol. XX, Ithaca, New York, 1930.

Hudson's Bay Company and Clifford Wilson, editor, for permission to use extracts from "Arctic Odyssey," published in the magazine *The Beaver*, March, 1945.

J. B. Lippincott Company and Peter H. Buck for permission to reprint the Maori sea poem from Dr. Buck's *Vikings of the Sunrise*, New York, 1938.

J. B. Lippincott Company, for passages from Robert E. Peary's *The North Pole*, New York, 1910, used by permission from the publishers and Mrs. Edward Stafford, daughter of Admiral Peary.

J. B. Lippincott Company, for permission to use extracts from Ernest Henry Shackleton's *The Heart of the Antarctic*, Philadelphia, 1909.

Lawrence Martin and the American Geographical Society for permission to use extracts from "Antarctica Discovered by a Connecticut Yankee, Captain Nathaniel Brown Palmer," *The Geographical Review*, October, 1940.

The Macmillan Company, for permission to use selections from Richard Hakluyt's *The Principall Navigations Voiages Traffiques & Discoveries of the English Nation, Made by Sea or Over-land to the Remote and Farthest Distant Quarters of the Earth at any time within the compasse of these 1600 Yeeres*. Reprinted in 12 vols. by James MacLehose and Sons, Glasgow, 1903-05.

The Macmillan Company, for permission to use selections from *Hakluytus Posthumus or Purchas His Pilgrimes*, by Samuel Purchas. Reprinted in 20 vols. by James MacLehose and Sons, Glasgow, 1905-07.

The Macmillan Company, for permission to use extracts from Vilhjalmur Stefansson's *The Friendly Arctic*, New York, 1921.

The Royal Geographical Society, London, for permission to use extracts from "Pytheas, The Discoverer of Britain," by Clements R. Markham, *The Geographical Journal*, June, 1893.

Charles Scribner's Sons, for passages from Robert Falcon Scott's *The Voyage of the "Discovery,"* New York, 1905, used with the permission of the publishers and of the Scott family.

Index

Abruzzi, Duke of the, 594
Adam of Bremen, quoted, 120
Adams, Clement, 407-418
Africa, circumnavigation of, by Phoenicians, 5; discovery of, ix; da Gama voyage to, 163-188; Portuguese voyages to, 161-162
African natives, 163-168, 169, 171-173
Aleutian Islands, 109, 111
Alexander VI, Pope, 52, 239-240, 257
Alfred, King of England, 23; quoted, 23-26
Althing, 43, 44-45
Amazon River, 269; Indians seen by Orellana, 279-283, 285-313; Pinzon on, 269
"Amazons" reported by Orellana, 304, 305, 308-310, 311
American expeditions. See United States expeditions.
Amundsen, Roald Engelbregt Gravning, 718; Northwest Passage expedition, 536-537; South Pole expedition, 620, 760-778, dogs as transportation on, 760-777, dogs as food on, 764-767, 773-774, use of Eskimo clothing on, 761-762
Anian, Strait of, 443
Animal life, 49-50, 167, 168-169, 424, 433, 461, 478, 481, 487-488, 493-494, 508-509, 519, 521, 526-527, 528-529, 531, 532, 550, 553, 554, 555, 561, 570, 582, 583, 586, 587, 590, 592, 619, 657, 669, 672, 675-676, 679-680, 682, 684, 698-699, 700, 701, 702, 704, 706-707, 708, 710, 717, 720-722, 723
Antarctic Circle, 705, 707; first crossing of, 697, 700
Antarctica, animal life in, 717, 720-722; discovery of, ix-x, 713-717; first wintering in, 723-724
Arctic, extremes of heat and cold in, 476-477; Mediterranean discovers the, 3-26
Arthur, "King," conquests of, 36-37
Arzina River, 389, 406
Asher, G. M., quoted, 548-561
Asia, discovery of, ix
Athabaska Lake, 329, 383
Australia, discovery of, xi, 625-690, 694; by Dutch, 626-630, 632-658; by English, 659-690; by Indonesians, ix; by Portuguese, 626
Australian natives, 634-636, 638-640, 641, 647, 665, 666, 667-668, 689-690
Austrian voyages, Payer and Weyprecht, 442
Avienus, Rufius Festus, quoted, 5-6; on Thule, 20

Back, George, 529, 530, 534
Baffin Island, animal life in, 478; Frobisher at, 480-482
Balboa, Vasco Núñez de, 225-233; discovers Pacific, 227, 230-231; in Hispaniola, 225-226; Indians seen by, 229-230, 231, 232
Banks, Joseph, 660, 661, 666, 670, 672, 675, 682
Banks Island, McClure leaves document on, 535
Bardarson, Ivar, sailing directions of, 83, 562
Barents, Willem, death of, 439-440; discovery of Bear Island and Spitsbergen, 433-434; monoxide poisoning, 437-438; polar bear encounters, 429; scurvy, 436, 437, 438, 439-440; voyages of, 428-440, 628
Barros, João de, 162
Barrow, John, quoted, 442
Bartlett, Robert Abram, 620, 759; with Peary expedition, 597, 601-603, 605, 614
Bass Strait, 658
Bastidas, Rodrigo de, 225
Bear Island, 433-434, 436
Beaufort Sea, ice in, 538
Beazley, Charles Raymond, on China, 110, 111; on Columbus, 85, 203; quoted, 110
Beechey Island, 533
Beerenberg Mountain, 35
Behaim, Martin, 252
Behrens, Carl Friedrich, quoted, 95-105
Beke, Charles T., quoted, 428-440
Belcher, Edward, expedition, 536
Belgian voyages, Gerlache, 718
Bellingshausen, Fabian Gottlieb von, 715, 718
Bering, Vitus, voyage of, 443-444

Bering Strait, 443, 462, 466
Best, George, 53, 475-577; quoted, 477-484
Biggar, H. P., quoted, 143-145, 145-148, 151-153
Bjaaland, Olav, 762, 763, 767, 769, 770, 772, 774, 776
Bjarni, 121
Blosseville Coast, 548
Boats, Eskimo, 65, 68, 77, 455; Irish curraghs, 6, 30, 31; native Australian, 667
Borchgrevink, Carsten Egeberg, 720, 722, 723-724
Botany Bay, 666, 672
Brainard, David L., 593
Brazil, Magellan at, 244
Brazil, Isle of, 149; as Markland, 149
Brendan, Saint, voyage of, 31-36; legends, 35-36, 113; O'Donoughue on, 32-35
Bristol, 193; voyages from 149-150, 561
British Isles, discovery of, 17
British expeditions, Belcher, 536; Borchgrevink, 723-724; Collinson, 534, 536, 537; Cook, 659-690; Franklin, xi, 468, 516, 517, 518, 533-534; McClure, 534-536; Mackenzie, 323-384; Parry, 486-514, 567-593, 618; Scott, 724-725, 727-739; Shackleton, 739-756; Simpson, 515-533. See English expeditions.
Bronze Age voyages, 6, 29
Brunel, Oliver, 428, 430
Buchan, David, expedition, 563, 567
Buck, Peter H., on Easter Island, 90; on Polynesians, 90-91; Maori sea chantey translated by, 93-94
Burrough, Stephen, 400, 419; on Nentsi, 424-425; voyage to Novaya Zemlya, 420-426

Cabot, John, 26, 148-155, 475
Cabot, Sebastian, 155-156, 388, 399, 418, 420; instructions to Willoughby-Chancellor expedition, 389-399
Cadiz, see Gades.
Cagni, Umberto, 594
Calicut, 188
Canadian expeditions, Larsen, 538-543
Canary Islands, 160, 195, 202, 205, 206, 241
Cannibalism, 200, 212, 312; among Australian natives, 690; on Franklin expedition, 534
Cantino, Alberto, 145-148
Cape Chelyuskin, 455, 459, 470
Cape of Good Hope, 161, 165-166, 240, 241, 254, 628, 642, 663, 701, 702, 711
Cape Horn, 663, 712
Cape Jesup, 617, 618
Cape North, see Cape Schmidt
Cape Schmidt, 459, 463; natives, 460
Carbon monoxide poisoning on Barents expedition, 437-438
Carstensz (Carstenszoon), Jan, 633-641

Carvajal, Gaspar de, 275-320; quoted, 276-320; on Orellana's "treason," 275-276
Cassiterides (islands), 7
Chancellor, Richard, 26, 389-419; reaches Muscovy, 389; death, 419
Chinese, character of ancient, Beazley on, 110; Leland on, 109-110
Chinese discovery of North America, 109-115
Chinese expeditions, Hoei-sin, 109-115
Chukchis, 455-458, 460, 463, 464-465, 466
Church of Rome, x, 135, 191; in Greenland, 51-52, 137-138; in Iceland, 44-45; in Latin America, 202, 217, 218, 231; in Philippines, 261
Clavus, Claudius, 85
Cleomedes, on Thule, 18
Coelho, Nicolau, 163, 169, 174, 176-177, 178, 186
Collinson, Richard, 534, 536, 537; quoted, 477-484
Columbia River, 382
Columbus, Christopher, 192, 195-221, 547; natives seen by, 197-199, 200-201, 207-208, 210-211; voyage to Iceland, 192-193
Columbus, Ferdinand, 192
Company for Remote Countries, 628
Cook, Frederick A., 718
Cook, James, xi, 330, 459, 516, 659, 690, 695, 696-713; death of, 659; natives seen by, 665, 666, 667-668, 670, 671, 673, 680-683; scurvy, 679; speculations on "Southern Continent," 695-696
Coppermine River, 516, 517, 532
Cornelis, Jerom, 648-652
Coronation Gulf, 515, 516, 517
Cortereal, Gaspar, Miguel and Vasqueanes, voyages of, 143-148
Cretans, 3-4
Crozier, Francis Rawdon Moira, 533, 534, 569, 593
Cuba, 195
Curraghs. See Boats.

da Gama, Paolo, 163, 176, 179
da Gama, Vasco, 162, 163-188; African natives seen by, 163-168, 169, 171, 173
Dalrymple, Alexander, 631, 695
Dampier, William, 94-95, 97
Dano-Portuguese voyages, 83-84, 143, 148
Darien, 225, 226, 227, 228, 230, 232
Davis, John, 55-63, 80
Dease, Peter Warren, 516, 527, 529, 531, 532
Deception Island, 713, 714, 715, 716
Dezhnev, Cape, 462, 467
Dezhnev, Simon, 443, 467, 516
Diaz, Bartholomeu, 161, 166, 170, 694
Dickson Island, 445
Dickson, Oscar, 445, 446

Dickson, Port, 445, 447, 463
Dicuil, quoted on Iceland, 37-39
Dionysius Periegetes on Thule, 19
Disko Island, 127
Dudley, Ambrose, 479-480, 484
Dutch East India Company, 427, 441, 626, 629-630, 633, 642, 654, 655
Dutch secrecy policy, 653-655
Dutch voyages, Barents, 428-440; Brunel, 428, 430; Carstensz, 633, 641; Houtman, 440, 626, 628-629; Janszoon, 632; Nai & Tetgales, 429-430; Pelsart, 642-655; Roggeveen, 95-105; Tasman, 632, 655-658

Earth, circumference of, Eratosthenes on, 238; Ptolemy on, 238-239
Earth, sphericity of, 237-239; Magellan proves, 239-265; Pythagorean school on, 237
East India Company, see Dutch East India Company
Easter (Paäsch) Island, 89-90, 94, 712; Buck on, 90; Dampier voyage to, 94-95; discovery of, 95-105; religion, 102
Egede, Hans, on Greenlanders, 78-80
Ellesmere Island, 593, 597, 601
Ellis, John, 661
Elson, Thomas, 516, 517
Emanuel, see Manuel
Enciso, Martin Fernández de, 225-226, 228
English expeditions, Burrough, 420-426; Cabot, 148-155; Chancellor, 309-419; Davis, 55-63; Frobisher, 53-55, 475-485; Hudson, 547-562; Pet and Jackman, 427; Willoughby, 388-412; Wood & Flawes, 427, 441-442. See British expeditions.
Eratosthenes, 12, 238
Erik the Red, x, 46, 119; colonizes Greenland, 48; Saga of, 119, 121-135
Eskimo kayaks, Tunes on, 65-68, See Boats.
Eskimo techniques adopted by white men, 595-596
Eskimo umiaks, 68
Eskimos, Alaska, 111; Baffin Island, 481-483; "Blond," 64; Labrador, Cortereal on, 144, 147; Vinland, 130-133
Eskimos, Greenland, 48; Davis on, 56-64; Frobisher on, 54, 55; Sundt on, 78-80; Tunes on, 64-78. See Greenlanders.
Eskimos with Peary, 601-618
Estridsson, Svein, see Svein Estridsson
Europe, discovery of, ix

Fanning, Edmund, quoted, 714-717
Faeroe Islands, 30, 83, 561
Fernandez, Juan, 712
Fiji Islands, discovery of, 655, 658
Finmark, 402-403
"Fisheries" around Spitsbergen, 433, 562; Best on northern, 477; in Antarctic, 713

Flawes, William, 427, 441-442
Floki (Raven-Floki), colonizes Iceland, 42-43
Fort Chipewyan, 383
Fort Ross, 537
Foxes, 436-437
Franklin, John, xi, 468, 516, 517, 518, 533-534; cannibalism on third expedition, 534; death of, 533
Franz Josef Land, 594, 727; discovery of, 442
Fraser River, Mackenzie mistakes for Columbia, 331, 382-383
Freeselande, 480
Freydis, 132
Frieseland, 714
Frobisher Strait (Bay), 481, 484, 485
Frobisher, Martin, 53-55, 475-485; Eskimos seen by, 54, 55, 80, 481-483; "gold" discovered by, 483-484, 484-485; relics of, found by Hall, 485-486
Frostbite, 464, 769
Fusang, discovery of, 109, 110-115

Gades (Cadiz, Gadeira), 4, 13
Gardar, 40-41
Gardiner, Charles L. W., 438
Geoffrey of Monmouth, 36
Gerlache, Adrian de, 718
Gisli Oddson, 137-138
Gjerset, Knut, quoted, 40
Gonneville, Binot de (Paulmier), 626
Great Bear Lake, 515, 532
Great Circle voyages, in Bronze Age, 6
Greely, A. W., on Simpson, 516; U. S. Army expedition of, 593
Greenland, Brendan voyage to, 31-35; Church of Rome in, 48-49, 51-52, 124-125, 137-138, 139, colonization by Icelanders, 48; colony, disappearance of, 79-81; "conquered" by Arthur, 36; Cortereal voyages to, 143-148; discovery of, 31, 46-48; English trade with, 52; English voyages to, 52-53; Frobisher, 53-55; Davis, 55-63; Cabot, 148-155; Hudson, 547-549, 560; ice cap, 693-694; Peary on, 607; -Iceland trade relations, 136-137; insularity determined, 594; Knutson expedition to, 138-142; Magnus Eriksson expeditions to, 138-142; Medieval European knowledge of, 81-82, 85; Nordenskiöld in, 444-445; Peary in, 594, 597, 607; republic, union with Norway, 50-51; republic, population of, 48; resources of, 49-50
Greenlanders, Davis on, 55-64; Egede on, 78-80; Frobisher on, 54, 55; Sundt on, 78-80; Tunes on, 65-77
Guignes, Joseph de, 110
Gunnbjörn, 45-46, 121
Gunnbjörn Islands, 45-46

Hall, Charles Francis, 596; Franklin Search expedition, 485; Frobisher relics found by, 485-486
Hamilcar, 5

Hanno, 5
Hansen, Godfred, 536
Hanssen, Helmer, 762, 767, 768, 769, 772
Hassel, Sverre, 762, 776
Hartog, Dirck, 641
Hawaiian Islands, 90; see Sandwich Islands
Hawkesworth, John, 662
Hay, Denys, on Cabot, 154
Hearne, Samuel, 515
Heberstein, Sigismund von, quoted, 388
Heemskerck, Jacob van, 430, 432, 438, 440, 628
Heeres, Jan Ernst, quoted, 633-641
Helluland, 121, 127
Hencken, H. O'Neill, on Bronze Age voyages, 6
Henry the Navigator, x, 159, 161, 694
Henson, Matthew A., on Peary North Pole expedition, 601, 603-605, 615, 617, 618; Peary on, 604-605
Hermannsson, Halldor, 43, 47
Herschel Island, 541, 542
Herodotus, 159; Phoenician tales of, 5
Himilco voyage, 5-6, 7-8
Hispaniola, Balboa in, 225-226; Columbus on, 196, 199-201; natives of, 197-199, 200-201
Hoei-sin, voyage of, 110-115
Holand, Hjalmar R., 139-142
Hold with Hope, 547, 549
Holtved, Erik, 81
Houtman, Cornelis, 440, 626, 628-629, 642
Hudson, Henry, 83-84, 547, 562
Hudson Strait, 484
Hudson's Bay Company, 323-324, 329, 595; Arctic outposts, 537, 541, 542; Northwest Passage Search, 514-533; relations with Indians, 324-325, 515

Ice forecasting, 470-471
Ice, Peary on differences between land and sea, 607
Iceland, ancient knowledge of, 29-31; Brendan voyage to, 32-34; colonization of, x, 42-43; Columbus visits, 192-193; "conquered" by Arthur, 36; Dicuil on, 37-39; discovery of, 30, 31, by Gardar, 40-41, by Naddodd, 40-41; religion in, 43-45; slavery in, 43; sunlight in, 19-20, 38-39; as Thule, 17-20. See Thule.
Icelandic voyages, Erik the Red to Greenland, 48; Thorfinn Karlsefni to North America, 126-134
Indians, enslavement of, by Columbus, 203, 220; seen by Balboa, 229-230, 231, 232; seen by Columbus, 197-199, 200-201, 207-208, 210-212; seen by Mackenzie, 331, 334-337, 361-369; seen by Magellan, 241, 245-250; on Pizarro expedition, 271-272
"Indies," Columbus' first voyage to, 195-202

Indies, Portuguese find a way to, 159-188
Innocent III, Pope, 51
Irish influence in Iceland, 44
Irish voyages, 31-36
Isabella, 203
Isadore, quoted, 38
Istoma, Gregory, 388
Ivory, Nordenskiöld on mammoth, 450, 451

Jackman, Charles, 427
Jameson Land, 548
Jan Mayen Island, Irish voyage to, 32, 35
Jane, Cecil, quoted, 194-202, 206
Janszoon, Willem, 632
Johansen, Frederik Hjalmar, 594, 727
Jonsson, Björn, 45
Joy, A. H., 539

Kara Sea, Pet and Jackman voyage to, 427; Barents expedition to, 430, 431; Nordenskiöld in, 445
Kellett, Henry, 536
Kensington rune stone, 140-142
King Arthur, see Arthur
King William Island, 536; Amundsen at, 759, 761
King's Mirror (Speculum Regale, Konungs Skuggsja), 81-82
Knutsson, Powell (Paul), 138-142
Kola, Barents expedition at, 440
Kola River, Burrough at, 421
Kolyuchin Bay, 461-462, 463

Labrador, 659; Cortereal voyage to, 144, 145, 146. See Markland
Labrador natives, 144, 145, 147
Lancaster Sound, 537, 542; Parry expedition in, 487-497
Lao-tse, 109
Lapland, Willoughby expedition in, 406
Larsen, Henry A., 538-543; on navigability of Northwest Passage, 542-543
Leif Eriksson, 121-122; discovery of North American mainland by, 119, 121, 122
Las Casas, Bartolomé de, 198, 203
Leland, Charles G. on Chinese people, 109-110; quoted, 109, 111-115
Lena River, 449-450, 452, 469, 470
Ligurians, 7
Linschoten, Jan Huyghen van, 430
Little Table Island, 570, 574, 578, 588, 592
Lockwood, J. B., 593

Mackenzie, Alexander, 323-384; Indians seen by, 331, 334-337, 361-369; mistakes Fraser for Columbia River, 382-383; on pemmican, 328, 361, 363, 383; quoted, 331-382.
Mackenzie River, 329-330, 516, 537
MacRitchie, David, 64
McCaskill, Eloise, 37
McClintock, Francis Leopold, 596, 727

McClure, Robert, 534-536; record found by Stefansson, 535; receives Northwest Passage award, 536
Madariaga, Salvador de, on Columbus, 192
Magellan, Ferdinand, 239, 265, 694; death of, 261-262, 263-264, discovery of Philippines, 258; mutiny on expedition, 250-251, 253-254; natives seen by, 241, 245-250, 258, 259-264
Magellan, Strait of, 255
Magellanic Clouds, 257
Magnetic Pole, 496-497, 522
Magnus Eriksson, 137-139
Malindi, da Gama expedition at, 184-187
Mammoth, Nordenskiöld on, 450-451
Manuel (Emanuel, Manoel) of Portugal, 162, 163
Maori sea chantey, 93-94
Maoris, 657
Marco Polo, 191, 625
Mariana Islanders, 258
Markham, Albert Hastings, 56; on medieval European graves in Greenland, 61
Markham, Clements, on Pytheas, 10-11; quoted, 11-17
Markland, 121, 127, 134, 135, 136
Markland, Brazil as, 149
Marquesas Islands, 90
Martin, Lawrence, quoted, 713-714
Massilia (Massalia, Marseille), 11
Matochkin Shar, 429
Maxwell Bay, 493, 496, 498
Means, Philip Ainsworth, quoted, 142-143
Medina, Jose Toribio, quoted, 273-320
Mediterranean discovers the Arctic, 3-26
Mediterranean Sea, 3
Mela on Thule, 19
Melville Island, 538; Larsen at, 539; McClure at, 535, 536; Parry at, 506-513, 595
Melville Sound, 539, 540, 542
Merchant Adventurers, 388, 390, 399, 418, 421
Merk, Frederick, on pemmican, 326
Mill, Hugh Robert, 718, 724, 744; quoted, 724, 738
Mombasa, da Gama expedition at, 183
Morison, Samuel Eliot, quoted, 204
Mozambique, 177
Muscovy, see Russia
Muscovy Company, 418-419, 426, 427

Naddodd, 40-41
Nai, Cornelis Corneliszoon, 429, 430
Nansen, Fridtjof, 49, 80, 594, 727, 764; on Oestrimnides, 7-8; on Pytheas, 10, 17, 21-22
Narborough, John, quoted, 656

Nares, George, 593; North Pole expedition, 727, scurvy on, 727
Natives, attitude of Dutch toward, 98, 99-100, 103, 431, 634-636, 638-640, 641; of English, 482-483, 667-668, 680-683, 689-690; of fur traders, 324-325; of Norse, 130-133; of Portuguese, 144, 147, 165, 183; of Spanish, 197-198, 203, 207-208, 210-211, 229-230, 231, 248-249, 258, 261, 271-272, 280, 282, 286-287, 291-292, 300, 301, 303-304; of Swedish, 458, 460, 464-466. See African natives, Chukchis, Eskimos, Indians, Maoris, Nentsi, Patagonians, etc.
Navigation, Bronze Age, 6, 29, 204; Hispaniola native, 199; Norse, 91-92; river, 331-384; Stone Age, 89-93, 106
Navy Board Inlet, 490
Nentsi (Samoyeds), 419, 431; Burrough on, 424-425
Ncumann, Karl Friedrich, 111-112, 113
New Caledonia, discovery of, 712
New Guinea, 625, 630, 632, 633, 654, 655, 658, 659, 689, 694
New Holland, 626, 654, 658, 659, 660, 663, 688, 689
New Siberian Islands, 448, 450, 452, 463
New South Wales, 662, 688
New Zealand, 655, 657, 661, 696, 702, 712
Newfoundland, 659
Newland, see Spitsbergen
Newport Tower, 142-143
Nicholas II, Pope, 51
Nootka Sound, 330
Nordenskiöld, (Nils) Adolf Erik, 388, 444, 446-468, 470; on Barents, 431; on Burrough, 419; on mammoths, 450-452; natives seen by, 455-458, 460-463, 464-465, 466; on Northeast Passage, 441, on Wood expedition, 442
Norse voyages, 39. See Icelandic, Norwegian, Swedish voyages
North America, first crossing of, 323-384
North American mainland, discovery of, x; by Chinese, 109-115; Leif Eriksson's discovery of, 119; pre-Columbian colonization of, 126-134, 138-142
North Pole, attainment of, 567-622; Nordenskiöld attempt, 444; Parry, 567-593; Peary, 600-620
North and South Poles compared by Peary, 620-622
North West Company, 323-324; competition with Hudson's Bay Company, 324-325; relations with Indians, 325-326; use of pemmican by, 324
Northeast Land, 444
Northeast Passage, 387-471; compared with Northwest, 543-544

Northern Sea Route, 445, 470. See Northeast Passage

Northwest Passage, Cabot and, 155-156; compared with Northeast, 543-544; discovery of, 475-544; Frobisher and, 53-55; variants of, 538

Norway, Ottar's voyage round, 23-26; Ottar on, 25-26

Norwegian colonization of Iceland, 40-43; voyages, Amundsen, 536-537, 760-778; Bull, 718-723; Floki, 42; Gunnbjörn, 45-46; Knutsson, 138-142; Naddodd, 40-41; Ottar, 23-26, 387

Novaya Zemlya, 387, 428; Barents voyage to, 428, 429; Barents winters at, 434-440; Burrough voyage to, 423-424; English voyages to, 420; Portuguese voyage to, 388; Wood expedition at, 442

Ob River, 420, 425, 428, 469

O'Donoughue, Denis, quoted, 32-33, 34-35

Oestrimnian Bay, 6

Oestrimnides Islands, 6, 7

Ojeda, Alonso de, 225, 226

Orinoco River, 209

Orkney Islands, 16-17, 30

Orellana, Francisco de, 269-320; Indians seen by, 279-283, 285-313; Pizarro's charges against, 273-275

Ottar (Othere, Octher), voyage of, 23-26, 387

Ovalle, Alonso de, quoted, 227-233

Paäsch Island, see Easter Island

Pacific Ocean, Balboa discovers, 227, 230-231; named by Magellan expedition, 252, 255

Palmer Land, 715, 716, 717; animal life in, 715, 717

Palmer, Nathaniel Brown, 713, discovery of Antarctica by, 713-717

Papanin, Ivan, North Pole expedition, 619

Parry, Edward, 618; quoted, 486-514, 567-593

Patagonians, 241, 245-250

Payer and Weyprecht, 442

Peace River, Mackenzie on, 330, 331-372

Peary, Robert Edwin, xi, 594-595, 759; attainment of North Pole by, 594, 600-620; develops new polar travel technique, 596-597; on pemmican, 327-328, 596, 597-600; North and South Poles compared by, 620-622; quoted, 327-328; 597-599; 601-620

Pechora River, Burrough expedition at, 422, 424

Pelsart (Pelsaert), Francis, Australian voyage of, 642-655

Pemmican on Amundsen expedition, 764, 766, 769, 776; Mackenzie on, 328, 361, 363, 383; Merk on, 326; North West Company use of, 324; on Parry expedition, 573-574, 582, 584, 587; Peary on, 327-328, 597-599; on Peary expedition, 327, 596; Priestley on, 329; role of, in fur trade, 326; on Shackleton expedition 741, 742; on Simpson expedition, 517, 528, 529

Pemmican War, 323

Pendleton, Benjamin, 714, 715, 716

Penguins in Antarctica, 717, 720-721, 723; on da Gama expedition, 168-169; on Magellan expedition, 245. See animal life

Pet, Arthur, 427

Peter the Great, Great Northern Expeditions of, 443

Phillip, William, 435

Philippine Islands, death of Magellan in, 261-262, 263-264; discovery of, 258; natives, 259-264; Torres and Prado voyage to, 630-631

Phipps, C. J., 562

Phoenicians, circumnavigation of Africa by, 5; Gades expeditions of, 4; found colony of Utica, 4; secrecy and terror policy of, 4-5, 7-8

Pigafetta, Antonio, quoted, 241, 242-265

Pining, Dietrich, 83-84, 143, 148

Pink snow, 584

Pinzon, Vincente Yanez, 269

Pizarro, Francisco, 226, 269, 270

Pizarro, Gonzalo, 270-275, 284; his charges against Orellana, 273-275

Playse, John, 548

Pliny, 5; on Thule, 18, 19, 20, 38

Point Turnagain, 517, 529

Polar bear liver, "poisonous" qualities of, 436, 553

Polar bears on Barents expedition, 429, 436; on Burrough expedition, 424; in Greenland, 50; at North Pole, 619; on Parry expedition, 590, 593

Polar sea, Parry on weather of, 586; Peary on ice in, 607, 609, 610, 611, 613; rain on, 585-586

Polo, Marco, 625

Polybius, 11, 21

Polynesian voyages, 89-94

Ponies, use of, for transportation and food, 740-745

Portuguese conquest of "Burning Tropics," 160-161; discovery of Australia, 626; secrecy policy, 204, 388, 628; voyage to Novaya Zemlya, 388; voyages, 204; voyages, Cortereals, 143-148; voyages, da Gama, 162, 163-188; see Dano-Portuguese voyages

Pothorst, Hans, 83-84

Prado y Tovar, Diego de, 630-632

Prehistoric man, discoveries of, 29
Prester John, 162, 175
Priestley, Raymond, quoted, on pem-
   mican, 329
Prince Leopold's Isles, 493, 495-496,
   497
Prince Regent Inlet, 497
Prince of Wales Strait, Larsen in, 540
Priscian on Thule, 38
Ptolemy and Columbus, 239; on earth
   circumference, 238-239
Pythagoreans on sphericity of earth,
   237
Pytheas, x, 8-17, 29; as astronomer and
   mathematician, 11-13, 237-238; books
   of, 9; Markham on, 10-17; Nansen
   on, 10; route of, 13-17; Strabo on,
   20-21; and Thule, 10, 17

Quaris Island, natives of, 200-201
Quiros, Pedro Fernandez de, 630-631,
   663, 676, 695, 712

Rae, John, 574, 595-596
Ravenstein, E. G., quoted, 162-188
Reindeer, 457, 465
Reindeer Chukchis, 465
Religion, see Church of Rome; Easter
   Island; Iceland
Rijp, Jan Corneliszoon, 430, 432, 434,
   440
Richardson, John, 516
Robertson Bay, 724
Rochefort, Charles de, quoted, 65-77
Roggeveen, Jacob, on Easter Islanders,
   95-105
Ross, James Clark, 568, 569, 570, 579,
   580, 582, 590; discoveries in Ant-
   arctica, 718, 719
Ross, John, 486, 533; northern magnetic
   pole discovered by, 497
Ross's Pillar, 522
Royal Canadian Mounted Police, in
   Arctic, 537; Northwest passage
   voyages of, 538-543
Russia, Burrough expedition to, 420-
   426; Chancellor establishes commer-
   cial relations with, 389, 418; Chan-
   cellor expedition in, 415-418
Russian voyages, 163; Bellingshausen,
   715, 718; Dezhnev, 443, 467, 516;
   Great Northern Expeditions, 443

Samoa, 90
Samoyeds, see Nentsi
Sandia man, ix
Sandwich (Hawaiian) Islands, 563
Sarton, George, 82
Schwatka, Frederick, 596
Scoresby, William, 562
Scott, Robert Falcon, xi, 724-725, 727-
   739, 740, 760, 775; quoted, 728-737;
   scurvy, 725, 727-739

Scurvy, absence of, on Amundsen expedition, 778; on Borchgrevink expedition, 724; on Nansen expedition,
   727; on Nordenskiöld expedition, 464
Scurvy during Yukon Gold Rush, 330;
   in polar exploration, 726-727; Mc-
   Clintock on, 727; on Anson expedition, 725; on Barents expedition,
   436, 437, 438, 439-440; on Cook
   expedition, 679; on Franklin expedition, 533; on da Gama expedition,
   173; on Magellan expedition, 256;
   on Scott expedition, 725, 727-739;
   on Willoughby expedition, 389
Sea ice, freshening of, 591
Sealing, Antarctic, 719; Yankee, 713
Sellman, Edward, 45
Serdze Kamen, 466, 467
Servius on Thule, 18
Shackleton, Ernest Henry, 725, 738,
   739-756, 764, 768; absence of scurvy
   on expedition, 740-741; ponies used
   for food and transportation, 740-
   745; quoted, 741-755; suffers from
   scurvy on Scott expedition, 728-736,
   737
Shetland Islands, 30, 80, 401
Siberia, northern coast of, 387-471
Sibiriakov, A., 446
Sidney, Henry, on Cabot, 409-410
Simpson, Alexander, quoted, 517-533
Simpson, George, 326, 515-516, 520
Simpson, Thomas, 515-533; animal life
   seen by, 519, 521, 526-527, 528-529,
   531, 532; pemmican used by, 517,
   528, 529
Skraelings, see Eskimos
Sky map, 494-495, 609
Slave Lake, 329, 372, 517
Slavery, x, 156, 221; Dutch attempts
   at (Australian), 633-636, 638-640; in
   Iceland, 43; Portuguese, 144-145;
   Spanish, of New World Indians, 203,
   220
Snorri, 134, 135
Snow. See pink snow
Society Islands, 90, 661
Solander, Daniel Charles, 660-661, 666,
   669, 670, 672
Solinus, G. Julius, on Thule, 18, 19, 20,
   38
Solomon Islands, 657
Soncino, Raimondi de, on Cabot, 151-
   153
South America, discovery of, ix, 204;
   first crossing of, 269-320
South Georgia Island, 712
South Pole, attainment of, 759-779;
   Amundsen discovery of, 760-778;
   Peary on, 620-622; Shackleton ex-
   pedition toward, 739-756
South Shetland Islands, 713, 715, 716
Southern Continent, Cook's circum-
   navigation of, 697; Cook's specula-

tions on, 695-696; see Terra Australis
Spanish secrecy policy, 631-632
Spanish voyages, Balboa, 225-233; Columbus, 192-219; Magellan, 239-265; Prado and Torres, 630-632; Quiros, 630-631
Spitsbergen, discovery of, 433-434; Buchan voyage to, 563; Hudson voyage to, 547-562; Nordenskiöld voyage to, 444; Parry North Pole expedition at, 567-571, 593
Stefansson, Vilhjalmur, 17, 37, 80, 121, 516, 538, 540, 731, 749; finds McClure note, 535
Stone Age voyages, 89-93, 106, 697
Strabo, quoted, 9; on Pytheas, 9-10, 20-21, 22; on Thule, 18, 19, 20
Sundt, Eilert, quoted, 78-80
Svein Estridsson, 120
Swedish voyages, Gardar, 40-41; Nordenskiöld, 444-468

Tahiti, 90
Tasman, Abel Janszoon, 632, 655-658, 694
Tasmania, 655, 664; Tasman's description of, 656-657
Terra Australis, 693-713; see Southern Continent
Testu, Guillaume Le, 626
Tetgales, Brant (Ysbrandtszoon), 429, 430
Thjodhild, builder of first church in Greenland, 121, 123
Thordarson, Sturla, quoted, 40
Thorfinn Karlsefni, 125, 126; attempts colonization of North American mainland, 126-134
Thorgilsson, Ari, quoted, 47
Thorhall the Hunter, 126-127, 128-129, 133
Thorne, Robert, 547
Thorstein Eriksson, 122, 123-124
Thule, Avienus on, 20; Cleomedes on, 18; Dicuil on, 37-39; Dionysius Periegetes on, 19; Iceland as, 17-20; location of, 17-20; Mela on, 19; Pliny on, 18, 19, 20, 38; Pytheas on, 10, 17; Servius on, 18; Solinus on, 18, 19, 20, 38; Strabo on, 18, 19, 20. See Iceland
Torres, Luis Vaez de, 630-632
Torres Strait, 630-632, 633, 658, 661
Torrid Zone, 159-160, 693; crossing of, by Diaz, 161
Tryggvason, Olaf, 44-45, 119, 121-122, 137
Tropics, conquest of "burning," by Portuguese, 160-161
Tunes, Nicolas, quoted on Greenland Eskimos, 64-78
Turley, Charles, quoted, 763

Ulloa, Luis de, on Columbus, 192
USSR opens Northeast Passage as alternate transportation route, 468-471
U.S. expeditions, Greely, 593; Hall, 485-486, 596; Palmer, 713-717; Peary, 600-620; Wilkes, 718, 720
Uniped, 133
Utica, founded by Phoenicians, 4

Vaigach Island, 447; Barents at, 429, 430, 431; Burrough at, 419, 424, 426; Pet and Jackman at, 427
Vaigach Strait. See Yugorski Shar
Van Diemen, Anton, 655, 658
Van Diemen's Land, see Tasmania
Vardö (Wardhouse island), 403, 414, 421, 438, 477
Veer, Gerrit de, 428, 429, 432, 435, 436, 437-440; on discovery of Spitsbergen, 433-434
Victoria Island, 535, 536, 537
Vining, Edward P., quoted, 111
Vinland (Wineland), 119, 120, 126, 135; Church in, 135; discovery of, 120-121; colonization of, 126; Eskimos in, 130-133

Wafer, Lionel, 94-95, 97
Walrus "fisheries," 433
Wardhouse (island), see Vardö
Water sky, see sky map
West India Company, 94, 95
Whaling, Antarctic, 713, 718-719. See "Fisheries"
Wharton, W. J. L., quoted, 662, 695
Wilkes, Charles, 718, 720
Williamson, J. A., quoted, on Cabot, 150, 154-155; on decades following 1492, 220-221
Willoughby, Hugh, 26, 388-413, 432, 467; expedition perishes in Lapland, 399, 406; scurvy on expedition, 389; "true copie of a note," etc., 399-406
Wilson, Clifford, quoted, 539-542
Wilson, Edward A., 725, 728-737
Wineland, see Vinland
Wisting, Oscar, 762, 766, 767, 769, 772, 774
Wood, John, 427, 441-442; Nordenskiöld on, 442
Wytfliet, map of 1597, 625

Yenisei River, 431, 442, 445, 447, 450, 469, 470
Yugorski Shar (Vaigach Strait, Yugor Strait), 419, 427, 428, 430, 433, 447

Zeno brothers, 547
Zones, theory of five, 9, 159; Best on, 476-477, 478; Columbus on, 205

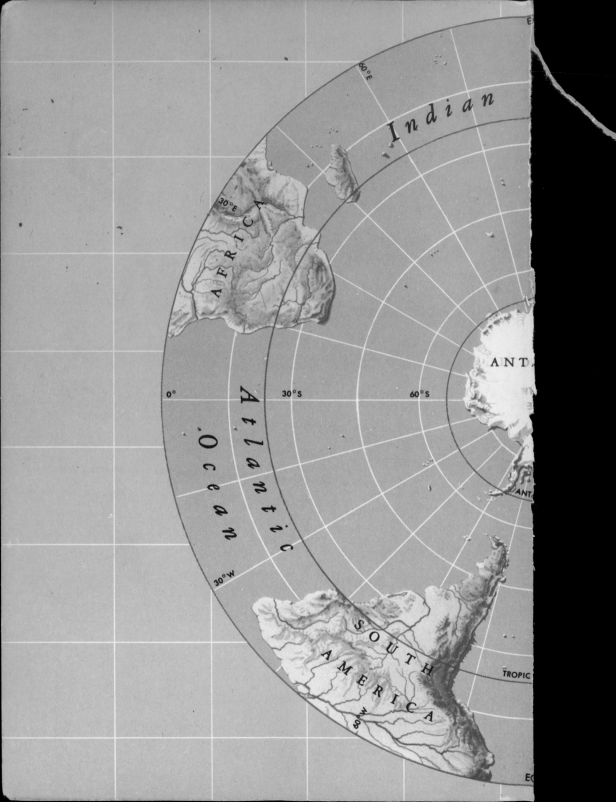